Machine Learning Methods for Commonsense Reasoning Processes:
Interactive Models

Xenia Naidenova
Military Medical Academy, Russia

INFORMATION SCIENCE REFERENCE

Hershey · New York

Director of Editorial Content: Kristin Klinger
Senior Managing Editor: Jamie Snavely
Assistant Managing Editor: Michael Brehm
Publishing Assistant: Sean Woznicki
Typesetter: Kurt Smith
Cover Design: Lisa Tosheff
Printed at: Yurchak Printing Inc.

Published in the United States of America by
    Information Science Reference (an imprint of IGI Global)
    701 E. Chocolate Avenue
    Hershey PA 17033
    Tel: 717-533-8845
    Fax: 717-533-8661
    E-mail: cust@igi-global.com
    Web site: http://www.igi-global.com/reference

Library of Congress Cataloging-in-Publication Data

Naidenova, Xenia, 1940-
  Machine learning methods for commonsense reasoning processes : interactive
models / by Xenia Naidenova.
     p. cm.
  Summary: "The main purpose of this book is to demonstrate the possibility of
transforming a large class of machine learning algorithms into integrated
commonsense reasoning processes in which inductive and deductive inferences
are not separated one from another but moreover they are correlated and
support one another"--Provided by publisher.
  Includes bibliographical references and index.
  ISBN 978-1-60566-810-9 (hardcover) -- ISBN 978-1-60566-811-6 (ebook) 1.
Machine learning. 2. Correlation (Statistics) 3. Recursive partitioning. I.
Title.
  Q325.5.N35 2010
  006.3'1--dc22
              2009021595

British Cataloguing in Publication Data
A Cataloguing in Publication record for this book is available from the British Library.

Table of Contents

Chapter 9

Chapter 10

Chapter 11

Preface

This book is an attempt to build the theory of classification both as a cognitive process and as its result. Until now, the theory of logical inference did not include classification reasoning as its inalienable component, although precisely the classification reasoning constitutes an integral part of any mode of reasoning. Furthermore, the current models of commonsense reasoning also do not include classification. However, the role of classification in inferences is enormous. Classification as a process of thinking performs the following operations: 1) forming knowledge and data contexts adequate to a current situation of reasoning; 2) reducing the domain of the search for a solution of some problem; 3) generalizing or specifying object descriptions; 4) interpreting logical expressions on a set of all thinkable objects; 5) revealing essential elements of reasoning (objects, attributes, values of attributes, etc); 6) revealing the links of object sets and their descriptions with external contexts interrelated with them. This list can be continued.

In this book, commonsense reasoning is understood as a process of thinking, on the basis of which the causal connections between objects, their properties and classes of objects are revealed. In fact, commonsense reasoning is critical for the formation of conceptual knowledge or ontology in the contemporary terminology.

Studying the processes of classification within the framework of machine learning and knowledge discovery led to the necessity of reformulating the entire class of symbolic machine learning problems as the problems of finding the approximations for the given classifications of objects.

The approach to machine learning problems we propose is based on the concept of a good diagnostic test for the given classification of objects. The problem of inferring good diagnostic tests is formulated as searching for the best approximations of the given classification (partition) on the given set of object examples. The good classification test has a dual nature: on the one hand, it is a logical expression in the form of implication or functional dependency (strict or approximate one), on the other hand, it generates the partition of the training set of objects equivalent to the given classification of this set or the partition that is nearest to the given classification with respect to the inclusion relation.

The concept of good diagnostic test (GDT) has been initially formed within the framework of searching for functional and implicative dependencies in relational databases. But later, the fact has been revealed that the task of inferring all good diagnostic tests for a given object classification is this task that some well-known machine-learning problems can be reduced to: finding keys and functional dependencies in database relations, finding association rules, finding implicative dependencies, inferring logical rules (if-then rules, rough sets, "ripple down" rules), decision tree construction, learning by discovering concept hierarchies, eliminating irrelevant features from the set of exhaustively generated features.

Since the tasks of classification can be reduced to deductive-inductive commonsense reasoning, the same reduction proves to be possible and for the tasks of machine learning.

We consider the theory of algebraic lattices as a mathematical language for constructing algorithms of inferring good classification tests. The advantage of the algebraic lattice approach is based on the fact that an algebraic lattice can be described both as an algebraic structure that is declarative, and as a system of dual operations with the use of which the elements of this lattice and the links between them can be generated.

The problem of constructing good diagnostic tests is formulated in algebraic terms as constructing the chains of elements of dual lattice or Galois lattice ordered by the inclusion relation.

The analysis of the algorithms of searching for all GDTs for a given object classification in terms of constructing Galois lattice allowed us not only to determine the structure of inferences but also to decompose the algorithms into sub-problems and operations that represent known deductive and inductive modes (modus operandi) of commonsense reasoning. Each step of constructing a classification lattice is interpreted as a mental act. These are mental acts that can be found in any reasoning: stating new propositions, choosing the relevant part of knowledge and/or data for further steps of reasoning, involving a new rule of reasoning (deductive, abductive, inductive, traductive, etc.).

The concept acts as the principal "atom" in commonsense reasoning. This reasoning is based on the knowledge system, with objects, properties (values of attributes) and classifications (attributes) being its elements. If we take into account that implications express relations between concepts (the object $\leftrightarrow$ the class, the object $\leftrightarrow$ the property, the property $\leftrightarrow$ the class), we can assume that schemes of inferring and applying implications (rules of the "if–then" type) form the core of classification processes, which, in turn, form the basis of commonsense reasoning. Deductive steps of commonsense reasoning imply using known facts and statements of the "if–then" type to infer consequences from them. To do it, we apply deductive rules of reasoning, the main forms of which are modus ponens, modus tollens, modus ponendo tollens and modus tollendo ponens. Inductive steps imply applying known facts and existing knowledge to infer new implicative assertions and correct those that turned out to be in contradiction with the existing knowledge. These steps rely on inductive rules of reasoning represented by inductive canons stated by British logician John Stuart Mill. These canons are known as five inductive methods, viz. the Methods of Agreement, the Method of Difference, the Joint Method of Agreement and Difference, the Method of Concomitant Variations and the Method of Residues.

The analysis of inferences for lattice construction allows demonstrating that these inferences engage both inductive and deductive reasoning rules. The implicative dependencies (implications, interdictions, rules of compatibility) generated in a process of good tests construction are used immediately in this process with the aid of deduction for pruning the space of search for new tests.

The theory of classification, stated in the book, proves to be somewhat more general with respect to the formal conceptual analysis (FCA) since this theory allows constructing concepts that are not closed on the lattice operations. In particular, such concepts are good irredundant classification tests.

Thus we come to a new view on modeling commonsense reasoning and machine learning algorithms.

In the book, some methodological approaches to the organization of data and knowledge in intelligent computer systems are discussed. We give some examples of expert system construction based on the integration of data and knowledge via machine learning mechanism. One of the chapters is dedicated to the development of a CASE-technology of automated programming of psycho-diagnostic expert systems. This technology combines two interconnected processes: knowledge specification and knowledge interpretation. A generator of knowledge is capable of using inductive inference for constructing some incompletely specified constituent elements of expert systems and an interpreter uses deductive inference for interpreting knowledge. The ideas placed in the realization of this technology can be developed and personified in a new programming language with the built-in mechanism of commonsense reasoning.

In the book, the basic difficulties of realizing commonsense reasoning in computers are formulated. The solution of these difficulties is the matter of future studies and setting of new problems in the computer sciences. To similar problems the author relates the integrating of conceptual clustering and supervised machine learning in such a way that an intelligent system would be capable of finding the best interpretations of the results of clustering by using its internal knowledge rather than some external instructions of the supervisor.

To the problems requiring future studies, we also relate the representation of data and knowledge as algebraic lattice structures. Some steps in this direction have been already done within the framework of OLAP and OLAM technologies.

The crucial problem of commonsense reasoning implementation in computers is also connected with the need for the pre-processes of analyzing and synthesizing objects of different nature—image, words and proposals of natural languages, speech, music and other objects of the external world.

It is the author's hope that this book will be interesting for the specialists of different fields, first of all for the specialists in artificial intelligence. The problems touched upon in the book will draw the attention of the developers of machine learning algorithms, knowledge engineers, programmers who create intelligent computer systems, and also psychologists and philosophers who are interested in questions of the psychology of thinking.

The book can draw the attention of logicians and mathematicians who will develop the theory of classification at the higher professional level and advance new models of logical inference, which will include, finally, the theory of classification expanding logical inference by commonsense reasoning. Moreover, the book can contribute to stimulate new ideas, new collaborations and new research activity in this research area.

The arrangement of the chapters follows a natural exposition of the main subjects in classification theory and practice.

Chapter 1 gives a view of historical development of the concepts of knowledge and human reasoning both in mathematics and psychology. Mathematicians create the formal theory of correct inferences; psychologists study cognitive mechanisms that underpin knowledge construction and thinking as the most important functions of human existence. They study how the human mind works. The progress in understanding human knowledge and thinking will be undoubtedly related to combining the efforts of scientists in these different disciplines. Considering the problems of knowledge and human reasoning unable to be treated separately, we strive to cover in this chapter the key ideas of knowledge and logical inference that have been manifested in the works of outstanding thinkers and scientists of past time. These ideas reveal all the difficulties and obstacles on the way to comprehending the human mental processes.

In **Chapter 2**, we focus on the tasks of knowledge engineering related mainly to knowledge acquisition and modeling integrated logic-based inference. We have reviewed the principal and more important directions of research that pave the ways to understanding and modeling human plausible (commonsense) reasoning in computers.

Chapter 3 develops a conception of commonsense reasoning based on mutually coordinated classification operations on objects, classes of objects, and properties of objects. This conception goes back to the model of classification processes given by J. Piaget, the outstanding psychologist of the 20th century.

The operations of classification are an integral part of any reasoning about time, space, things, events, motions and so on. They consolidate all the forms of reasoning and make it possible to present knowledge as the system of interconnected relations. We analyze the logical semantics of classification connections between objects, classes of objects, properties of objects and the role of commonsense reasoning operations in creating classification structures.

In **Chapter 4**, we describe a model of commonsense reasoning that has been acquired from our numerous investigations on the human reasoning modes used by experts for solving diagnostic problems in diverse areas such as pattern recognition of natural objects (rocks, ore deposits, types of trees, types of clouds etc.), analysis of multi-spectral information, image processing, interpretation of psychological testing data, medicine diagnosis and so on. The principal aspects of this model coincide with the rule-based inference mechanism that has been embodied in many expert systems.

We can assume that schemes of inferring and applying implications (rules of the "if–then" type) form the core of classification processes, which, in turn, form the basis of commonsense (plausible) reasoning. Deductive steps of commonsense reasoning imply using known facts and statements of the "if–then" type to infer consequences from them. To do it, we apply deductive rules of inference, the main forms of which are modus ponens, modus tollens, modus ponendo tollens and modus tollendo ponens. Inductive steps imply applying known facts and existing knowledge to infer new implicational statements and correct those that turned out to be in contradiction with the existing knowledge. These steps rely on inductive rules of reasoning represented by inductive canons known as five inductive methods formulated by English logician Mill, viz. the Methods of Agreement, the Method of Difference, the Joint Method of Agreement and Difference, the Method of Concomitant Variations and the Method of Residues.

Chapter 5 contains some examples of natural human commonsense reasoning related to both scientific pattern recognition problems and logical games. An analysis of inference structure shows that inductive and deductive rules communicate in reasoning. An automated model for detecting the types of woodland from the incomplete descriptions of some evidences is also given in this chapter. An interesting part of this model is a small knowledge base containing the representation of experts' knowledge about natural woodlands as biological formations.

Chapters 6 and 7 give the main ideas of the classification theory and its connections with machine learning problems.

Chapter 6 discusses a revised definition of a classification (diagnostic) test advanced earlier within the framework of information theory. This revised definition allows considering the problem of inferring classification tests as a problem of searching for the best approximations of a given classification on a given set of training data.

In this quality, the concept of a classification (diagnostic) test became a key concept of machine learning problems dealing with inferring conceptual knowledge of the following types: conceptual descriptions of object classifications and logical links (expressed in the form of logical rules) between these classifications.

We demonstrate that a class of well-known machine learning problems related to inferring logical dependencies (implicative, functional, and associative), decision trees from examples, discovering concept hierarchies (ontology), eliminating irrelevant features from the set of exhaustively generated features and some others can be reduced to the task of inferring diagnostic (classification) tests. In fact, the diagnostic task covers all the tasks of symbolic supervised machine learning.

An algebraic model of diagnostic task (algebra of classifications) is brought forward on the foundation of the partition lattice in which object, class, attribute, and value of attributes take their interpretations. This model possesses both declarative and procedural properties.

In **Chapter 7**, the definition of good diagnostic test and the characterization of good tests are introduced and the concepts of good maximally redundant test (GMRT) and good irredundant test (GIRT) are given.

The definition of good test is based on the partition model of classifications that has been given in the previous chapter. Some characteristics of good tests allow choosing a strategy for inferring all kinds of good diagnostic tests. We describe an algorithm called Background Algorithm based on the method of mathematical induction. This algorithm is applicable to inferring all kinds of good classification tests and, consequently, for inferring functional, implicative dependencies and association rules from a given data set. We discuss also, in this chapter, the possible ways of constructing an efficient algorithm for inferring good tests of any kind.

The concept of good classification test is redefined in **Chapter 8** as an element of the dual lattice or Galois lattice. Inferring the chains of Galois lattice elements ordered by the inclusion relation lies in the foundation of generating all types of diagnostic tests. The concept of an inductive transition from one element of a chain to its nearest element in the lattice is determined. The following special rules are introduced for realizing the inductive transitions: generalization rule, specification rule, dual generalization rule, and dual specification rule.

Note that reasoning begins with using a mechanism for restricting the space of searching for tests: for each collection of attributes' values and objects, to avoid constructing all its subsets. For this goal, the concepts of admissible and essential values (objects) are introduced. Searching for admissible or essential values (objects) is based on inductive diagnostic rules. During the lattice construction, the implicative assertions are generated and used immediately. It means that the knowledge acquired during the process of generalization (specification) is used for pruning the search in the search space. All the operations of lattice generation take their interpretations in human mental acts.

In this chapter, we propose a non-incremental learning algorithm NIAGaRa based on a reasoning process realizing one of the ways of Galois lattice generation. Next we discuss the relations between the good test construction and the Formal Concept Analysis (FCA).

The methodology presented in this chapter provides a framework for solving diverse and very important problems of constructing machine learning algorithms based on a unified logical model in which it is possible to interpret any elementary step of logical inferring as a human mental operation. This methodology is more general than the FCA because it deals with some objects that are not formal concepts in terms of the FCA (for example, good irredundant tests, contained in a good maximally redundant test).

The important steps in the direction to an integrative model of deductive-inductive commonsense reasoning are made in **Chapter 9**. The incremental approach to developing machine learning algorithms is one of the most promising directions in creating intelligent computer systems. The decomposition of inferring good classification tests is advanced into two kinds of subtasks that are in accordance with human mental acts.

This decomposition involves searching for essential values and objects, eliminating values, cutting off objects, choosing values or objects for subtasks, extending or narrowing collections of values, extending or narrowing collections of objects, using forbidden rules, forming subtasks and some others actions. This decomposition allows, in principle, to transform the process of inferring good tests into a "step by step" reasoning process.

We give two basic recursive procedures based on two kinds of subtasks for inferring all good maximally redundant classification tests (GMRTs): ASTRA and DIAGaRa. An incremental algorithm INGOMAR for inferring all GMRTs is presented too. The problems of creating an integrative inductive-deductive model of commonsense reasoning are discussed in the last section of this chapter.

Chapter 10 presents some fast heuristics for inferring approximately minimal diagnostic tests based on which a model of commonsense reasoning by analogy is constructed. This model has been implemented in the system called DEFINE. The results of this system's application for recognizing the type of tree species with the use of aerial photographs is described.

Next, we discussed the different approach to mining approximate rules. Mining approximate functional, implicative dependencies and approximate association rules is based on the same criteria and on the application of one and the same algorithm of machine learning realized in the Diagnostic Test Machine described shortly in this chapter. The Diagnostic Test Machine is destined for inferring the broad class of logical dependencies from raw data: functional dependencies (strict and fuzzy), implicative dependencies (strict and fuzzy), decision trees based on obtained dependencies, logical rules based on obtained dependencies (implicative ones), association rules.

A technology for rapid prototyping and developing expert systems or intelligent systems as a whole is proposed in **Chapter 11**. The main parts of the technology are the object-oriented model for data and knowledge representation and the mechanism for data-knowledge transformation on the basis of an effective algorithm of inferring all good classification tests. An approach to expert system development by means of the technology proposed is analyzed. The toolkits for expert system generation are described and the application of these tools is demonstrated for the development of a small geological expert system.

Chapter 12 proposes an automated technology for creating the applied psycho-diagnostic expert systems (APDS) the main peculiarity of which consists in using machine learning to choose, validate, define and redefine the main constituent elements of testing and decision making procedures utilized in the developed psycho-diagnostic systems.

Machine learning and knowledge acquisition from experts have distinct capabilities that appear to complement one another. The integration of these approaches to knowledge discovering can both improve the accuracy of system knowledge bases and reduce the time of APDS development. The expert systems created by means of the integrated approach possess higher accuracy than those created only by knowledge elicitation from experts without using machine learning methods. We describe a software, called GENINTES (GENERATOR + INTERPRETER of EXPERT SYSTEMS) realizing the integrated CASE – technology for expert system rapidly prototyping, creating, and evolution.

We consider both statistical and logical (symbolic) methods of machine learning, so our approach encompasses the automated knowledge acquisition methods for a wide range of knowledge types.

The CASE-technology is based on two models of knowledge: the model of knowledge embodied in APDS (M1) and the model of knowledge of the designing of APDS (M2). Both models are object-oriented. M1 is a meta-structure describing the concepts, connections between them and processes of knowledge and data transformation used in any APDS. M1 includes the following main concepts: psychological characteristic (Ch) (measured and inferred), computational scheme (CS), computational expression (CE), operation (Op), scale (Sc), logical rule (LR), inference model (IM), and conclusion or diagnosis (C-D).

The process of constructing APDS is a sequence of transforming incomplete specification of a projected PDS from one state to another until its final state will be obtained under which the union of the specification with the program of an INTERPRETER gives the ready APDS.

Models M1 and M2 are object-oriented and operational: the relationships between concepts can be viewed as both the schemes of inference and the procedures of concepts transformation when the operations are added to the schemes of relationships.

The process of APDS specification is analogous to the process of specifying computations with the use of any programming language. The peculiarity of our programming language consists in the fact that the forward deductive and inductive engines are incorporated in it.

Chapter 13 deals with the description of possible mechanisms for data-knowledge organization and management in intelligent computer systems. Challenges and future trends are discussed in the last section of this chapter, followed by the concluding remarks.

The term "intelligent system" means that the system is capable of performing commonsense reasoning operations at any stage of its functioning (i.e., under performing query answering and updating data and knowledge). More exactly, the functioning of intelligent system as a whole is a commonsense reasoning process. The incorporation of commonsense reasoning mechanisms into data-knowledge processing is becoming an urgent task in intelligent computer system and conceptual data-knowledge design. There is not a methodology supporting the solution of this task. We tried briefly to describe the problems awaiting a solution. We began with the consideration that data-knowledge communication at all stages of functioning an intelligent computer system is central for realizing commonsense reasoning. We believe that a new methodology for data-knowledge communication has to be created by the use of a systemic approach to modeling the cognitive activity.

All the above chapters contain a number of examples explaining the ideas of the author and the proposed algorithms.

Acknowledgment

I would like first of all to thank the IGI Global staff, mainly Julia Mosemann, Development Editor, for their professional guidance and continuous support. I also want to thank the Acquisitions Editors, especially Lindsay Johnston and Kristin M. Klinger for their attention to my modest previous contribution and for the opportunity to initiate this project.

I would like to thank each of my reviewers for their significant job providing constructive and comprehensive comments, for invaluable critical remarks.

The author is very grateful to Professor Evangelos Triantaphyllou (Louisiana State University), who inspired and supporting my first publication on this subject.

Many thank to my family, colleagues, and friends for the encouragement and company received during my work. The monograph would have never been prepared without their patience, and unique inspiration.

Chapter 1
Knowledge in the Psychology of Thinking and Mathematics

ABSTRACT

This chapter offers a view on the history of developing the concepts of knowledge and human reasoning both in mathematics and psychology. Mathematicians create the formal theories of correct thinking; psychologists study the cognitive mechanisms that underpin knowledge construction and thinking as the most important functions of human existence. They study how the human mind works. The progress in understanding human knowledge and thinking will be undoubtedly related to combining the efforts of scientists in these different disciplines. Believing that it is impossible to study independently the problems of knowledge and human reasoning we strive to cover in this chapter the central ideas of knowledge and logical inference that have been manifested in the works of outstanding thinkers and scientists of past time. These ideas reveal all the difficulties and obstacles on the way to comprehending the human mental processes.

INTRODUCTION

This chapter acquaints the reader with the circle of ideas about the human thinking and its laws. If we know something in general about the world, then this is due to the fact that we know how to reason. While the logic or science about how to think correctly and how to come to true conclusions was developed in the course of millenniums, the science of knowledge as the result of reasoning arose in our time within the framework of a scientific direction called 'artificial intelligence'. The use of computers in all spheres of our life requires studying and a fundamental understanding of how men extract knowledge from observations. Plausible reasoning, «fuzzy» reasoning reflecting the properties of human thinking

DOI: 10.4018/978-1-60566-810-9.ch001

in everyday life, became the subject of study in computer sciences, cognitive psychology, logic, and mathematics. The problem of the synthesis of knowledge and reasoning is not yet solved, but it is the forward edge of studies, and the experience of past times is extremely valuable for these studies.

THE PROBLEM OF KNOWLEDGE

The main problems that have disturbed humanity at all times are the problems of origin and accuracy of knowledge. The philosopher Berkeley, for example, discussed as follows (Mill, 1900): «Yesterday I thought about a certain thing, and then I ceased to think about it. Today I again think about it. Thus, I yesterday had in my mind an idea of object. Today I again have an idea about it: it is obvious that this idea not another, but the same, meanwhile some time passed between its two appearances when I did not have it. But where was the idea in the flow of this time? Somewhere it had to be… But an idea can be conceived existing only in the spirit, consequently, there must exist a certain Universal Spirit, in which constantly are all ideas in the period of time between their appearance in the consciousness of a person». When it became clear that the brain creates ideas, scientists were faced with the problem what processes generate knowledge. The opinions of the scientists were different. Many of them considered the brain to produce not more than what already exists in the sensations. Other scientists came to the conclusion that knowledge does not result from a mere recording of observations without a structuring activity on perceived patterns and no do any a priori or innate cognitive structures. However, the development of sciences required answering the question of true and false knowledge. Later the idea of probability appeared. Already Leibniz wanted to create logic of probable knowledge. All these problems have agitated scientists till our time. As examples, we can note the works of Tarski (1947) about the semantic conception of truth and Black (1954) about the semantic definition of truth.

Duns Scotus (1270-1308), the scientist of the Middle Ages, classified the forms of inference of consequences (conclusions) and subdivided them into correct and the incorrect ones. His disciple, William Ockhamm (1300-1347) dealt with the concept of logical deduction, which is very close to the contemporary concept of material implication. He developed the rules of deduction, among which we find the following ones: 1. from impossible judgment follows everything; 2. necessary judgment follows from everything; 3. a true judgment never implies a false one; 4. a possible judgment never implies an impossible one.

Ralph Strode (1350-1400), the follower of Duns Scotus, has developed the theory of formal implication for which he has introduced 24 rules. Along with concepts (modi operandi) of «truth» and «falsity», he has introduced the concept "doubtful assertion" or "uncertainty". Elements of propositional logic and first-order logic appeared already in the works of Ramon Lull (1234 – 1315). In his work "Introduction into the Dialectics" he divides judgments into true and the false ones, furthermore, he analyzes the inter-relations between the constants "and" and "or". He knew already the rules for expressing conjunction via disjunction and negation and vice versa.

The problem of insolvency (Insolubilia) was studied very extensively during the 15th and 16th centuries. For example, Iogan Buridan (died in 1358) considered such a paradoxical judgment: "Everything, which is written in this volume, is false" (Prantl, 1855), (Stjajkin, 1959). We find the methods of deductive proof in the tractates of Pascal (1623-1662), he considered axiomatic definitions too.

Formal languages for knowledge representation were considered only in the framework of deductive sciences. The requirement of the uniqueness of concepts in these languages led to the complete detachment from real thinking, closely related to natural languages and the human existence in the real world.

The laws of knowledge discovering were investigated (for example, by Bacon) separately from the formal deductive reasoning. Induction was separated from deduction on the grounds that inductive reasoning does not lead to knowledge of the truth, but only to probabilistic knowledge. The science of knowledge – "knowledge engineering" - was born only in the second-half of the past century within the framework of the scientific branch called "artificial intelligence". The ideas which appeared were about declarative and procedural knowledge, about knowledge explicit and hidden, intuitive and realistic, fuzzy and exact, axiomatic and uncertain.

However, artificial intelligence as science inherited the same problems and went in the same way as the thinkers of the past centuries. The basis of computer thinking in the form of the theory of deduction or the theory of proof has developed and was enriched by the theorists of our time. Induction was considered without its connections with deduction and the problem arose how these two modes of reasoning can be combined. Declarative and procedural knowledge are considered separately. An attempt to combine these models of knowledge exists only in the object-oriented approach to developing data and knowledge bases.

The term "knowledge discovering" was born from the completely specific tasks of mining knowledge from various sources - specialists (experts), documents, texts, "damp" or experimental data, and data, which are contained in different computer depositories - databases and data banks. In connection with the complexity of knowledge mining, the researchers turn themselves to study natural human reasoning. It is not precise and not always demonstrative, but it makes it possible for man to live in the complex real world, to come to the understanding of the laws of the world and to create newer concepts, enlarging the boundaries of acquired knowledge.

Step by step, scientists come to the belief that knowledge cannot be separated from the processes of its creation; thinking cannot be limited by the narrow purpose of proof of the knowledge of the truth. The intellect ensures the very existence of man in his environment. Without interaction with the environment there is no thinking: it loses any support, any sense. It is possible that humanity learns too slowly what thinking is and what its highest purposes are. The problems of modeling cognitive processes become crucial in the application of computers in the life of human beings.

Logic and Knowledge. The Problem of the Knowledge of Truth

Most clearly and uncompromisingly the tasks of demonstrative knowledge have been expressed by Ernst Schröder, the most important logician of the end of 19th century. He asserted that thinking is directed to cognition (knowledge) of the truth and he opposed logical-cognitive thinking to art creativity, thinking by fantastic images, simple narration and description. By Schröder, the process of thinking can be reduced (at least partially) to logic. The part of lingual-cognitive processes is excluded previously from the sphere of logical thinking.

From the time of F. Bacon, inductive logic has been considered as an instrument for investigating only how experimental data are used for enlarging knowledge. Since the results of inductive reasoning are not absolutely true and reliable, inductive logic has been separated from deductive logic the goal of which is the true knowledge achievement. By Schröder, deductive and consecutive reasoning excludes turning to experience for checking its correctness. Logic is independent from philosophy and the theory of knowledge. Only its independence can grant logic the possibility to be developed. The views of Schröder have a clearly expressed anti-psychological tension.

In the second-half of 19th century, experimental psychology arose. This evoked the conception of "psychologism" in logical science. The psychological approach to the theory of knowledge has been developed especially in Germany in the works of such scientists as Siegwart, Ch., Wundt, Brentano and some others.

These scientists considered logic as part of the psychology. They were occupied by the physics of thought, by its real functioning. For example, the representative of "psychologism", Siegwart, Ch. did not deny that the task of logic is the management of thinking in the search for truth (Siegwart, 1908.). He noted also that logic constructs artificial languages and logical schemes of true inferences, but he believed that logic is an empirical science in the sense that the construction of these diagrams and their interpretation rest on the specific properties of thinking discovered by experimental psychology. (Siegwart, 1909).

The position against "psychologism" was defended by Frege, G. and Husserl, E. The enemy of "psychologism" in logic was Bolzano. He demarcated the logical as the cognitive content, from the psychological one as a cognitive process.

Birukov and Turovtzeva (1978) noted that the simulation of cognitive processes requires the synthesis of logical and psychological positions in the study of thinking.

Returning to the object of formal logic, it is important to note Schröder's views according to which logic deals with analyzing the methods of obtaining the truth. Schröder has formulated the concept of logical inference according to which the scheme of reasoning is correct if it allows for getting the true conclusion from the true assumptions with any interpretation of non-logical expression entering it.

All expressions that are not true and not false are excluded from the field of logic, but as a result, it turns out that logic cannot substantiate standards, plans, purposes, lingual-cognitive formations connected with the expressions not having truth values.

The significance of symbols in logic is one of very interesting parts of Schröder's views. He wrote that with the aid of symbol it is possible to divide the merging with each other's ideas, to associate them with unique names and, due to this action, to fix the difference between these ideas. It is also possible to form a new unity from the received separate ideas. Sign is the means, with the aid of which we form abstract ideas. The unity of thoughts and purposes of many people is possible only because of using signs. Symbols (signs) are necessary for the formation of thoughts. An unsuccessful sign can bring even a simple problem to a blind alley. An adequate sign can solve half of the problem.

Schröder investigates also the content of the term "concept" as a cognitive form on which any logical calculus can be constructed.

Commonsense Reasoning as an Instrument for Constructing Knowledge

The role of commonsense reasoning in constructing knowledge remains unstudied. Only a deductive component of commonsense reasoning is investigated extensively in many issues on artificial intelligence. Researches can be clustered into a few areas, which have remained relatively stable lately. These areas include default or non-monotonic reasoning, temporal as well as spatial reasoning, and the theories of belief, desire, and intention (Davis, & Morgenstern, 2004). It is necessary to add to this list the formalisms for modeling actions, situations, and events (McCarthy, & Hayes, 1969; Kowalski, & Sergot, 1986; Shanahan, 1997; McCaine, 1997). The theory of causation is also developed separately from the other directions in modeling commonsense reasoning (Sandewall, 1991).

It is indicative that the integration of different fields of commonsense reasoning, the development of unified, expressive theories is very slow. Moreover, many researchers develop their own theories to solve a particular reasoning problem. This entails the result that a large number of theories are incomparable. There have been some efforts to formalize the notion of causation with solving several temporal reasoning problems (Sandewall, 1991): 1) determining which time-varying properties do not change as the result of an action without having to explicitly list all such properties (the frame problem); 2) determining the indirect effects of an action without having to explicitly list all such effects (the ramification problem), and 3) representing the conditions necessary for the successful performance of an action (the qualification problem) (Davis, & Morgenstem, 2004). The need to integrate different formal reasoning algorithms is one of the driving forces in implementing a robot that senses and acts in the real world. An example of integrative reasoning model is the system implemented on a Nomad 200 Robot. This Robot can travel to different rooms in a multi-story building. This system is mentioned in (Davis, & Morgenstem, 2004).

But the main difficulties in modeling commonsense reasoning are connected with adding new facts to knowledge, new details to a problem statement without having to rework large parts of used commonsense reasoning theory. This problem is tightly interconnected with the problems of both learning new knowledge from facts or by a dialog with experts and improving current knowledge of a thinking system. However, the theories of learning and commonsense reasoning are developed in parallel. We can note only one work of Khardon and Roth (1999) in which learning and reasoning are studied as a single task. In this work it is shown that in some cases the learning and reasoning problems that are intractable when studied separately become tractable when performed as a "learning to reasoning" task. In contrast to the paradigm of "learning to classify", the paradigm "learning to reason" aims at reasoning about the environment. The interaction of a learner with his\its environment follows standard models of learning (Angluin, 1988). In this work, the problem of the treatment of partially specified queries is also discussed. The "learning to reason" approach has also been extended to consider the tasks including some forms of default reasoning, learning in order to act in the world, and learning of active classifiers.

With our point of view, commonsense reasoning is an instrument not only for thinking based on knowledge but for acquiring new knowledge about the environment or the world. It is a function of intelligent systems. So, it is interesting to turn to a historical survey of the ideas about knowledge and reasoning proposed by different scientists in the past.

A HISTORICAL SURVEY OF THE IDEAS ABOUT KNOWLEDGE AND REASONING

The Significance of Aristotle's Works for Modeling Commonsense Reasoning

As it's known, Aristotle had an enormous effect on the evolution of logical thought. Its logic, until now, continues to preserve its scientific value. However, from the entire heritage of Aristotle, only his study of the syllogisms is mostly separated, analyzed, and cited in computer sciences. Meanwhile such parts of his work as "Categories", "About the interpretation", "Topics" (Aristotle, 1978) actually describe the ontology of knowledge and the models of plausible reasoning, directed toward the construction of knowledge and its use. Such expressions of Aristotle, in these works, as "it is shown of", "it is spoken of" can be treated operationally as the description of mental actions with the help of which concepts are formed and used. First of all, Aristotle gives the classification of names covering general names, derivatives names (and rules of forming terms). He considers also the use of one and the same word for different objects (for example, a person and his portrait). Then Aristotle gives the concept of predication and analyzes the binding of words as a cognitive operation.

Aristotle considers 10 categories: essence, quantity, quality (also relation), place, time, state, possession, action, to be the object of action. He describes all relationships between objects, their properties, and classes of objects. He also describes the hierarchical relations between classes. He investigates not only the form and content of these relations, but also the mental operations on which the construction and the use of classification structures are based. For example, determining an object, one always calls its nearest class - one will say that "a fir tree is a tree", but not that "a fir tree is a plant". Aristotle describes the phenomenon of inheritance in classifications.

By Aristotle, the properties of essences can be developed in course of time. Assertions about truth and falsity depend on circumstances. There are essences, which are neither true nor false.

Aristotle investigates the concepts of discretion and continuity. He also speaks about the relativity of estimations "large" and "small". One and the same thing simultaneously can be great and small (in comparison with the different objects). Examining the different forms of relationships, Aristotle analyzes in detail the concepts of similarity and degree of similarity. Then he examines all forms of qualities, dividing them into the groups of relatively steady qualities and of variable ones. Properties are connected by him with the states and the actions.

One of the chapters of "Topica" is devoted to the ontological relationships between the names or the terms of natural languages. In the chapter "About the Interpretation", Aristotle deals with the problem of using symbols as a tool of human thinking. Finally, "Topica" is dedicated to the plausible reasoning, with the aid of which it is possible to make conclusions about any proposed problem from a plausible assumption and not to fall into the contradiction.

Aristotle introduces the concept of dialectical conclusion, which is built on the basis of plausible assumptions. In contrast to heuristics, Aristotle calls an assumption a plausible one, if it seems correct to all or the majority of people or only to wisest people.

It would be desirable to dedicate a separate work to the interpretation of Aristotle's ideas from the point of view of modeling plausible reasoning and constructing an ontological base for extracting knowledge from data.

The Method of Deduction. The R. Descartes' Theory of Reasoning

R. Descartes (1596-1650) has given the main characteristics of scientific language. He believes that our thoughts have a natural order similar to the order of numbers. Hence, Descartes assumed that there is nothing impossible in the fact that, in the course of time, there will be created a universal language covering not only numbers but also any object that is the subject for investigating. This language will allow for describing any idea by the use of symbols and dividing any thought into its elementary constituents.

On June 8, 1637 in the Dutch city Leyden was published the book of René Descartes "*Discourse on Method in order to direct well own reason and to find the truth in the sciences, furthermore "Dioptrics", "Meteors" and "Geometry", which are the application of this method*" (Descartes, 1897; 1960). The following questions disturbed Descartes: What is reason? How to distinguish the truth from the errors? "What is true knowledge in the sciences and the personal life? According to Descartes, to think correctly means to act correctly. Virtue rests on the real knowledge of things that are in conformity with our position and abilities, i.e., on the authentic knowledge of nature of man and society.

The logic of his time did not answer Descartes' demands and then he decided to search for a new method of reasoning combining the merit of mathematical reasoning in algebra and geometry with the natural rules of reasoning, on which he leaned as scientist himself.

Descartes builds the new science of the method of reasoning, which he "opens in himself and the great book of life". He much traveled, and his life gave to him the possibility to manifest courage not only in his scientific researches. Once traveling at sea, he fell on a pirate vessel. Knowing Dutch, he understood that the command planned to rob him and throw him outside. Managing one sword alone, Descartes forced the pirates to moor to the coast and to let him go.

The following quote from *Discourse on Method* presents four general rules about how to think correctly and clearly:

- "The first was never to accept anything for true which I did not clearly know to be such; that is to say, carefully to avoid precipitancy and prejudice, and to comprise nothing more in my judgment than what was presented to my mind so clearly and distinctly as to exclude all ground of doubt.
- The second, to divide each of the difficulties under examination into as many parts as possible, and as might be necessary for their adequate solution.
- The third, to conduct my thoughts in such order that, by commencing with objects the simplest and easiest to know, I might ascend by little and little, and, as it were, step by step, to the knowledge of the more complex; assigning in thought a certain order even to those objects which in their own nature do not stand in a relation of antecedence and sequence.
- And the last, in every case to make enumerations so complete, and reviews so general that I might be assured that nothing was omitted".

Descartes assumed that nature is regulated, and everything occurring in it is regular and necessary. The most fundamental properties of material - form, extent and motion - are subordinated to constant mathematical laws. Mathematics is sufficient to describe the physical world. "It can not be that the truths are neither so removed that they would be unattainable, or so secret that it was not possible to discover them" - so he wrote in his book. As far as premises for deduction, it is necessary to rest on intuition for their understanding. And although Descartes himself in his studies leans on the experience and the experiment, he believes that the principles are perceived by intuition and God input them into our reason.

Descartes separates the thinking substance from the corporal substance. Fundamentally new is the fact that Descartes identifies the material with the space (according to Aristotle, the body and place are different). According to Descartes, each body is a mathematical object, and geometry is the science of the physical world. Material is divided "ad infinitum". There is neither void space nor indivisible atoms.

Understanding the physical world mechanically as a system of designed machines leads to disappearance, in the theory of Descartes, the difference between the natural and the artificial (created by man). But Descartes believed that the skill of the infinite creator, i.e., God, must exceed the skill of the finite creator, i.e., man. If the world is a mechanism, and the science of it is mechanics, then knowledge is the constructing of the machine of the world from the simplest beginnings, which we find in the human reason. Descartes considered algebra as universal mathematics and he attempted to give the algebraic description of geometry and arithmetic.

Descartes identifies soul and mind, calling imagination and feeling the 'modi operandi' of mind. Specifically, after Descartes arose the problem of the connection of soul and body. He considered passions and affections as the consequences of influence of body motions on the reasonable soul, and if they are not explained by the light of reason, then they generate the errors of mind, which cause evil behavior. Errors are sin, and only reason saves us from the sin. The source of errors - free will, since it impels the voice of reason and act when reason does not have clear and distinct knowledge.

Descartes' influence on the development of scientific knowledge was many-sided. His rationalism contributed to the improvement of deductive thinking. His reduction of nature to mechanical device exists, until now, in the ideas of some scientists, convinced of the possibility of recreating human intelligence in computers. The convincing criticism of mechanical view on nature can be found in (Capra, 1983).

Reasoning as a Calculus. The G. Leibniz's Theory of Reasoning

Leibniz did not create the developed system of logic, but in his letters and sketches during his life he voiced the thoughts, which became within the course of time the starting point of the contemporary concept of logic. Already at the age of 15 years, he promoted the idea of converting the entire human knowledge with the aid of some logical-combinatorial means. This project became the program of a universal characteristic, i.e., of a logical calculus, in which it would be possible to present objects and relations between them as numbers and the relations between them are represented in mathematics. Leibniz wanted to reduce reasoning to a calculus (calculus racionator). In these calculations, it would be possible to ignore the content of expressions represented by signs. The logical views of Leibniz are illuminated in many works in the Russian language (Bogomolov, 1913; Kotarbiński, 1963; Getmanova, 1959; Tanhilevitch, 1961; Birjukov, & Trostnikov, 1977).

Schröder attempted to carry out the ideas of Leibniz (Schröder, 1898; 1899). According to Schröder, calculation does not contradict understanding. It is, on the contrary, the precondition of understanding. Calculation entails understanding. The program of Schröder was the following: the isolation of simple elements of thought – concepts and methods of their connection, but each sign must have the single-valued content (Schröder, 1890; 1891; 1895).

Further Schröder has proposed to operate not with the content of concepts, but with the volume of concepts. He noted that there are concepts the content of which does not exist, but they have clearly outlined volume, for example, the concept "not a human being".

Logic must include three parts: 1. calculation of classes 2. calculation of propositions and 3. calculation of relationships. Schröder gives an idea of pasigraphical language as a universal language of things (Schröder, 1898). This language, capable of expressing completely and exactly all concepts of any science, strongly agrees with the contemporary studies on ontology.

In order to express adequately and compactly the minimal set of principal initial concepts and categories it is necessary to rest on purely logical operations possessing the property of total applicability.

Schröder has formulated five categories of total logic (Birukov, & Turovtzeva, 1978): equality, intersection, negation, conversion, and relation. For these categories, he has introduced special signs (operations):

1. The sign of equality indicates the identity;
2. An additional sign is introduced for relative equality denoting the class of things that are equal;

3.   The sign of multiplication expresses the category of intersection: "*ab*" means the thing which is simultaneously *a* and *b*;
4.   The sign of negation: "not *a*" means the thing that is not *a*;
5.   The sign of conversion of binary relations (conversion of "a child of some parents" is "the parents of a child");
6.   The sign of relation expressed in English by the preposition "of". This operation is the composition of relations or relative product: "loved by whom and benefactor of whom = loved benefactor".

Schröder believed that these categories are sufficient for expressing all the concepts which are essential for logic and arithmetic. However, he introduces still 11 derived symbols for the following operations:

- "nothing": simultaneously *a* and not *a*;
- "something" designated by1, it means everything about which it is possible to speak
- the universe of reasoning
- "other than", "different from", "not being identical with";
- $a + в$ means "*a* or *в* or both together";
- relative addition – this operation is dual to multiplication of binary relations;
- inference or inclusion relation (implication): "*a* is contained in *b*" or "*a* is a part of *b*";
- negation of inclusion;
- "*a* is a proper part of *b*";
- "not equal to";
- "*a* is not a proper part of *b*".

There exist similar operations in the works of G. Peano (1894) and Ch. Peirce (1883), but Peano did not introduce the category of relation.

Schröder also defined the following relations: "*a* is a class", "*a* is an individual thing/person", "*a* is equivalent to *b* in volume/power", "*a* is a finite set", "*a* is actually infinite set". The concept of function was also defined by him.

The most known result of Schröder is the improvement of Boolean algebra (Boole, 1854). However, it is practically little known that the works of Schröder were first, in which was systematically investigated a very important class of the algebraic systems such that the structures or the lattices (Schröder, 1877).

Schröder anticipated the development of artificial intelligence (Birukov, & Turovtzeva, 1978), when the thinking machine would perform a great part of tiresome mental work as steam engine successfully performs physical work. However, Schröder did not consider thinking to be completely substituted by mechanically figurative calculations.

The Method of Induction. The F. Bacon's Theory of Reasoning

Francis Bacon (1561–1626) was one of the leading figures in natural philosophy and in the field of scientific methodology in the period of transition from the Renaissance to the early modern era.

As a lawyer, Member of Parliament, and Queen's Counsel, Bacon wrote on questions of law, state and religion, as well as on contemporary politics; but he also published works in which he speculated on possible conceptions of society. He pondered questions of ethics (*Essays*) even in his works on natural philosophy (for example in *The Advancement of Learning*, (Bacon, 1962)).

To the present day, Bacon is well known for his treatises on empiricist natural philosophy (*The Advancement of Learning, Novum Organum Scientiarum*) and for his doctrine of the idols, which he put forward in his early writings, as well as for the idea of a modern research institute, which he described in *Nova Atlantis* (Bacon, 1982).

Bacon criticized scholasticism, mysticism of Pythagoreans, idealism of Platoneans, agnosticism of skeptics. Ancient Creek philosophers attracted him because they understood material as an active principle. He gives preference to Democritus' natural philosophy in contrast to the scholastic – and thus Aristotelian focus on deductive logic and belief in authorities. The attitude of Bacon toward the Ancient Philosophy is expressed in his works "*About the beginnings and sources*" written in 1653 year and "*On the wisdom of ancient*" written in 1609 year.

Bacon has developed the new "natural philosophy", based on experimental knowledge. It foresaw the enormous role of science in human life. He dedicated his unfinished work "*Instauratio Magna Scientiarum*" to the description of some effective methods of scientific research and to the prospects of the development of science. This work included the following parts (treatises): "*De Dignitate et Augmentis of Scientiarum* - On Dignity and Augmentation of Sciences" (appeared in 1623), "*Novum Organum or True Instructions for interpretations of nature*" (appeared in 1620) (Bacon, 1962) and a number of works on natural history and description of separate phenomena and natural processes, in particular, "*Historia de ventis*" (appeared in 1622), "*Historia vitae et mortis*" (appeared in 1623), and many others.

Bacon developed the detailed classification of sciences, including such disciplines as ones only had to be developed in the future. It also gave the typology of the fallacies of human mind, which he called the Idols. He discusses the idols together with the problem of information gained through the senses, which must be corrected by the use of experiments. These Idols are described as follows:

1. Idols of the Tribe

    The Idols of the Tribe have their origin in the production of false concepts due to human nature, because the structure of human understanding is like a crooked mirror, which causes distorted reflections (of things in the external world).

2. Idols of the Cave

    The Idols of the Cave consist of conceptions or doctrines which are dear to the individuals who cherish them, without possessing any evidence of their truth. These idols are due to the preconditioned system of every individual, comprising education, custom, or accidental or contingent experiences.

3. Idols of the Marketplace

    These idols are based on false conceptions which are derived from public human communication. They enter our minds quietly by a combination of words and names, so that not only does reason govern words, but words react on our understanding.

4. Idols of the Theatre

    According to the insight that the world is a stage, the Idols of the Theatre are prejudices stemming from received or traditional philosophical systems. These systems resemble plays in so far as they render fictional worlds, which were never exposed to an experimental check or to a test by experience. The idols of the theatre thus have their origin in dogmatic philosophy or in wrong laws of demonstration.

Bacon substantiated different methods of experimental knowledge, different ways and modifications of experiment, formulated induction as the method of discovering the laws (forms) of natural phenomena. He developed this method in detail, namely in his *Novum Organum*, a part of *Instauratio Magna Scientiarum*.

Bacon came to the fundamental insight that *facts* cannot be collected from nature, but must be constituted by methodical procedures, which have to be put into practice by scientists in order to ascertain the empirical basis for inductive generalizations. His induction, founded on collection, comparison, and exclusion of factual qualities in things and their interior structure, proved to be a revolutionary achievement within natural philosophy. The movements of thoughts have two contrary directions "upwards" and "downwards": from *axioms (general assertions) to experiments and actions and backwards from experiments to generalizations*. Bacon's induction was conceived as an instrument or method of discovery. The very important element of Bacon's method was his emphasis on involving negative instances in the procedure of inductive inference. It has been an innovation for the time of Bacon. Bacon's methodology of induction includes aspects of deduction and abstraction on the basis of negation and exclusion.

Experiment is the main category in Bacon's philosophy, since knowledge begins with experiment and knowledge leads to it. The faithfulness of knowledge is checked by experiment, experiment gives food for reasoning. According to Bacon, experiments can be fruit-bearing and light-bearing, the former bring new knowledge useful for man, this is the lowest form of experiences; and the latter reveal the truth.

Induction can be complete and incomplete. Complete induction is the ideal of knowledge; it means that absolutely all facts, which relate to the region of the studied phenomenon, are assembled. Generally incomplete induction is used; as a result acquired knowledge is hypothetical.

In order to reach the truth, it is necessary to accumulate a fair amount of fruit-bearing experiences, similar to an ant, which on the grit assembles its anthill, in contrast to the spider that creates the intricate pattern of its cobweb. Bacon compared scientist-naturalists with ants, and scientist-scholastics with spiders. If the former make many useful discoveries, then the latter detain the development of knowledge. However, the best type of scientist, by Bacon, is the scientist who as a bee, on the grain, gathers the nectar of experience in order to obtain from it new, valuable and useful product - useful knowledge, capable of changing the world for the good of man.

Bacon demarcated the regions of scientific knowledge and religious faith, but he assumed Christianity to be one of the forces, which unite people into the society. He has also written the utopian narrative «*New Atlantic*» (appeared 1627) (Bacon, 1982), in which he has presented the project of the state organization of science - «*House of Solomon*». It is the scientific and technical center of a utopian society in which the scientists are occupied by managing and planning scientific studies and technical inventions and they also govern natural resources and production. House of Solomon has served as the prototype of scientific societies and academies. English scientists of the Boyle's circle (*Invisible College*) took up the idea of a cooperative research institution in their plans and preparations for establishing the Royal Society.

The main works of F. Bacon are contained in the multivolume publication "*The Oxford Francis Bacon*" (Bacon, 2000b) and in "The Works" edited by J. Spedding et al. during 1889-1892 (Bacon, 1889). Some additional reading about Francis Bacon can be found in (Farrington, 1949), (Anderson, 1962), (Bacon 2000a), and (Spedding, 1861-74).

On the general problem of induction, it is possible to address C. G. Hempel (1966), R. Swinburne (1974), *and* K. Lambert & G. G. Brittan (1987).

The Role of Classification and Learning in Commonsense Reasoning. The Works of H. Spencer, and I. Sechenov

We combined in this chapter the description of the treatises of two outstanding scientists – Herbert Spencer (1898), and Ivan Sechenov (2001) not only because of the generality of their ideas, but also because of the explanation of the mental acts of living organisms on the basis of their physiological structure and the interaction with the environment. The strong side of these scientists consists in the fact that they do not detach thinking from learning. They also consider classification and recognition as the basic connecting links between different spheres of the cognitive processes application. Really Spencer's and Sechenov's works encompass the following: 1) the explanation how the mental operations arise as a product of learning, 2) the investigation of the elements of thought in the order of their development from simple to complex ones, 3) the interconnections of the elements of thoughts with the relationships discovered by their use in objects and phenomena both of external and internal order, 4) the consideration of the cognitive processes and their products in their unity. The unity of three relations is examined - co-existence, time sequence, three-dimensional relations in space.

Considering the existence of many relations between objects, these scientists show the existence of basic cognitive operations, critical for discovering the knowledge of all forms. These basic operations are: aggregation, splitting to the part or the disintegration, the establishment of similarity and difference. In the works of Sechenov, the physiological mechanism of the development of these operations is described especially clearly. Later J. Piaget (1969) and also together with Inhelder, B (1964) investigated psychologically and experimentally the process of developing the logical thinking in children from early childhood and up to 10-11 years. He also showed the integrative role of classification in the formation of cognitive abilities.

Mental activity appears only in connection with complicated interaction of organisms with the environment. The complication of this process leads to the appearance of nervous system and mental reactions to the actions of the environment. Spencer also describes the phenomenon of consciousness. The mental motions are tightly connected with the physical life. And each cognitive act is explained on the basis of corresponding processes that proceed in the nervous system. The genesis of cognitive activity can be traced in the child. But if this idea is described by Spencer and Sechenov only qualitatively, then Jean Piaget investigated the development of logical abilities in children via direct observation and the ingenious planning of experiment. Studies show that the formation of mental reports is connected with gaining of experience and the aggregation of ever more complex and more different impressions in the coordinated systems. Some impressions generate the mental conditions aggregated with them earlier but at the given moment not perceived, the latest are appearing in the form of conclusion.

Spencer (1898) examines all forms of reasoning from the simple to the synthetic and the complex. In contrast to Aristotle, Mill and many of his predecessors on the way of studying the structure of thoughts and reasoning, Spencer does not investigate only the tip of the iceberg - syllogisms and the laws of obtaining true conclusions. He opens "the anatomy of reasoning". He shows that any act of thinking consists of the comparison of the internal nervous patterns formed under the effect of environment. As a result of the comparison, there occur both the isolation of the general, repetitive parts of patterns and the determination of their differences. The meaning of equality is really the impossibility to differentiate patterns. Both in the temporary and in the three-dimensional reasoning, it is necessary to compare, to find the equality or inequality, similarity or difference in two relations.

Figure 1. Scheme of syllogism

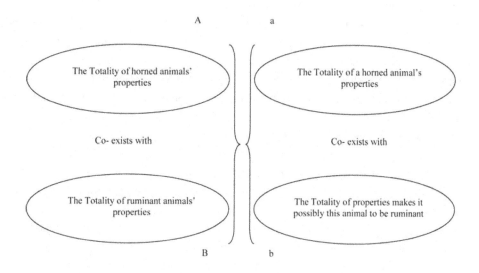

Spencer examines simple and complex, quantitative and qualitative reasoning. The perfect qualitative reasoning is the establishment of necessary relations, which exist between objects, individuals, and phenomena. For example, the triangle, whose all angles are equal, must have equal sides. Seeing one side of an object, we conclude the existence of its other side. With the aid of this reasoning we establish relations such as "simultaneously", "earlier", and "afterwards" for events. For example, two people know that they left the house at the moment of the explosion, they conclude from this fact that they left the house simultaneously. In the perfect qualitative reasoning the negations are unthinkable.

To the imperfect qualitative, i.e., approximate reasoning, Spencer relates syllogism. Syllogism includes the result of accumulated experience in its general premise; conclusion is done at a current time. Hence it follows that syllogism connects some present moment with the passed time. Syllogism is plausible reasoning. The conclusions of the imperfect qualitative reasoning are easy to be negated.

Spencer criticizes the determination of syllogism, given by J. S. Mill (1900), and refines its determination. Syllogism includes the following assertions (Figure 1):

1. The assertion of premise relates to each member of a certain class;
2. A certain particular property always accompanies the totality of the properties, inherent in each member of the class;
3. Certain individual or phenomenon possesses the totality of the properties similar (but not the same!) with the properties of premise. It follows from the similarity of these properties that
4. A particular property accompanies the totality of properties of the individual or the phenomenon in question.

If syllogism is reasoning from the general to the particular, then inductive reasoning goes from the particular to the general, i.e. it converts deduction. Induction also, according to Spencer, is the imperfect qualitative reasoning. But all forms of reasoning are based on the operations of comparison and isolation of similarity - difference. Spencer says that reasoning assumes classification, and simultaneously classification assumes reasoning. They supplement each other.

Sechenov gives the psycho-physiological theory of knowledge. He analyzes the wide spectrum of phenomena from unconscious reactions to the highest forms of perception and thinking. The thought of the child from the beginning to the end revolves in the region accessible to the feeling. The mind of the adult, moving by means of abstractions, almost always goes in the so-called extra-sensual region. Thus, people consider material with its invisible atoms, explain the phenomena of the external world by the game of invisible forces, and discover dependencies, reasons, consequences, order, law and so forth.

Being personified into the word, any thought in the child and in the adult always takes one and the same form - trinomial proposition. Because of the invariability of this form in people of different ages, different epochs and degrees of development we can understand the reflections of savage and child, thought of contemporaries and ancestors. Thus there is a succession of thought, which passes through centuries in the life of people.

At the basis of thought, the specific organization lies. This organization does not depend on the content of thoughts. Thought can be considered as the comparison of the conceivable objects with respect to different relations. From the side of objects, the thought can be extremely diverse, but it is not characterized by the same variety from the side of the relations, in which objects are compared with each other. If we compare thoughts from the region of object with thoughts from the sphere of purely mental and moral relations, then it occurs that in all these higher spheres of thoughts there is not any relation that would not be encountered in the object thinking. As if man transfers the connections, dependencies, and relations of studied object to the new objects.

Objects appear in the thought in three main forms of the comparison: as the members of groups or classes, as the members of three-dimensional combinations and as the members of successive lines in the time.

Another way of the development of thoughts - splitting objects into parts, the mental isolation of parts from the whole. Once more method in developing thought is determined by the reunification of the disconnected parts into the groups in view of their coexistence and consequence.

The sum of all transformations of thoughts composes the process that can be considered as generally processing initial sensual and mental material in the ideological direction. Here Sechenov anticipates future concepts of information processing and control in animals and machines (cybernetics).

The concrete features of cognitive acts are discovered by Sechenov via the analysis of the verbal forms of thought.

Sechenov investigates by what properties of neural-psychic organization and by what sides of influence from the side of environment it is possible to explain 1) the distinctiveness of objects, 2) the comparisons of objects, and 3) the general direction of these comparisons. He reveals the important role of motor reactions of organism in cognitive processes. Adaptive motor reactions lead to the maximization of impression and they also transform impressions to the sequence of the bright samples. Motor reactions serve as the connective links between the adjacent impressions.

Shechenov investigates the phenomenon of memory, describes the processes of "keeping in mind" and "reproduction" of impressions, patterns, images, and thoughts. He believes that memory is not separated from memorized materials. The patterns memorized in mind are transformed in time. The memory has a lot of relations (rubrics or directions), for example, the relations "a part – the whole", "similarity". Each object is memorized with all its relations to other objects.

The J. Piaget's Theory of Intelligence: Operational Aspect

The Piaget's theory of intelligence is considered from the point of view of genesis and gradual development of human thinking operations. Attention is given to operational aspects of cognitive structures and knowledge. The significance of Piaget's theory of intelligence is revealed for modeling conceptual reasoning in the framework of artificial intelligence. The key problem of intelligence (both natural and artificial) is knowledge constructing and reasoning. The traditional methodology of artificial intelligence does not consider computer as an active source of knowledge. Cognitive structures are installed in the computer by copying directly the experts' knowledge. The concept of "scheme" in artificial intelligence means a graphical image reflecting some known relationships between the units of knowledge. Computer cognitive structures are declarative, mechanisms of their using are separated from them and these mechanisms are often fixed. In this sense, one can say that an "apriorism" reigns over artificial intelligence. The "apriorism" of cognitive structures ignores their active nature, namely, the mechanisms of their constructions. However it is clear intuitively that reasoning must include not only cognitive structures themselves but also the methods of their creating and recreating. In the process of reasoning there could arise the necessity to correct knowledge due to the impossibility to explain new facts via known ones or to reduce a new task to some already familiar subtasks. Hence it becomes clear that the process of using knowledge and the process of its creating can not be anything but two different aspects of a single process: only what is constructed is recognized.

Partly the "apriorism" in artificial intelligence is a consequence of those psychological theories that consider judgment as a received or rejected relationship or a state of thought (the works of Buhler, K. and Selz, O. criticized by Piaget (1969)). In these theories, thought appears in the form of the consciousness of a relationship (for example, A < B) or in the form of the consciousness of rules "if-then" or in the form of clear formal intention. The psychology of artificial intelligence goes along the way of analyzing the final stages or states of cognitive structures. Operations of thinking as a result of which there appear objects, properties, classes, relations remain to be unused, unclaimed, not called for. In the 70s-80s, the foundation of knowledge engineering was being created, that is why the attention of the investigators was given firstly to the question how human knowledge could be organized and used in computer systems. However it is clear that to know what is the structure of knowledge is insufficient. It is not less important to understand the operational aspect of knowledge, i.e., the mechanisms by the use of which knowledge is generated. We consider it to be very interesting to turn to the operational theory of intelligence which assumes the thought as an interiorized mental action and does not separate thinking from acts in the real world. This theory was created by J. Piaget and his disciples on the base of the long-term experimental investigations of the genesis of intellectual operations in the child's mind from the moment of birth until the period when thought takes its perfect form of logical formal operations and cognitive structures take the form of "grouping" (Piaget, 1969).

Our primary goal for addressing ourselves to the works of Piaget was to find a foundation for our computer model of conceptual reasoning based on the theory of lattices. But we believe that Piaget's theory of intelligence has the enormous methodological significance for solving many key problems of artificial intelligence. It can be noted that nowadays we can surely say that the theory of Piaget has stood the test on "solidity", and for the proof of it we refer to the fact that the main assertions of Piaget are recognized by the psychologists engaged in cross-cultural investigation (Cole, 1997).

Piaget believed the intelligence to be a mechanism (both on biological and on cognitive level) by the use of which an organism adapts to the environment, i.e., creates the schemata of his activity or behavior that allow him to be in an equilibrium with his environment. This equilibrium is a dynamic one; it is achieved by means of two global processes appearing in the different forms depending on the sphere of intellectual activity: assimilation and accommodation.

Assimilation consists in treating output stimuli by the use of already created schemes of behavior without their changing (because stimuli are familiar to or recognizable by an organism). But when the process of recognizing stimuli fails due to the insolvency of available schemata, then the accommodation process appears on the stage. Accommodation consists in changing schemata or inventing new ones to assimilate new stimuli.

Scheme is one of the main concepts of Piaget - it is a cognitive structure by which the individual intellectually adapts to and organizes his environment. The organization of behavior (sensory-motor, speech, cognitive and so forth) consists in constructing schemata of behavior. Scheme, according to Piaget, is absolutely not identical to the scheme of relation. Scheme is a dynamical union of a relation and operations by means of which this relation is constructed. Scheme determines the possibility of combining operations thus permitting to construct and reconstruct the typical sequences of operations in typical situations.

Scheme, in any sphere of behavior, tends to conserve the organism's identity and thereby to conserve the organism's representation of the environment. For example, the sensory-motor intelligence constructs the schemata of real world objects: the individual can do many different operations with objects - one can hide, throw, and turn over an object. But with all these manipulations, an object remains identical to itself conserving its color, shape, size and so on. The sensory-motor operations provide the flexibility for the motor behavior, for example, one can get an object in different ways, can come to it from different places in space. The sensory-motor operations constitute a group which is invariant with respect to the set of all real objects, but any object is also invariant with respect to the group of sensory-motor operations. Piaget believed the mind constructs structures much in the same way that the body does. Thus concepts as cognitive structures are invariant with respect to reasoning operations: the different expressions of natural language can correspond to the same concept; at the same time, the operations of reasoning are invariant with respect to all concepts a person operates on.

In the sense of the adaptive nature of intelligence we can give the following definition of reasoning: it is a mental activity which is expressed by means of language and tends to form in mind cognitive structures and to maintain (to conform) them in the equilibrium during the constant interaction with people and objects in reality.

Piaget asserted the existence of balance between the processes of assimilation and accommodation. Probably there is a criterion that does not allow one of these two processes to prevail over the other.

In summary, intelligence, according to Piaget, is not ability. It is a form of adaptation, leading to an equilibrium to which tend all the interactions between the organism and its environment beginning with the set of biological, physiological, sensory-motor adaptations and ending with the highest form of adaptation - thinking. This continuous row of adaptations must be viewed to be constructed during the evolution process and by means of the laws of the evolution. Figure 2 shows this evolutionary row.. Each form of adaptation provides a more stable and widely spreading equilibrium. In Piaget's theory, the major source of motivation for intellectual development is disequilibrium which can be thought of as a "cognitive conflict" when expectations or predictions are not confirmed by experience.

There exists the problem of determining the lowest boundary of intelligence. The numerous investigations move this boundary further and further away from humans to animals. For example, it is known

Figure 2. Evolutionary row of adaptations

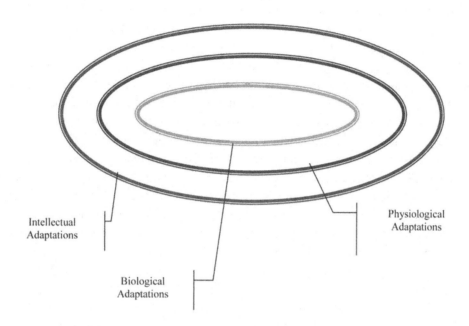

nowadays that some birds and primates possess a rudimentary understanding of numbers. Chimpanzee Sara, known due to the works of David Primack (Cole, 1997), was able to numbering objects from one to four and to show an object with the correct number. She has learned to establish a one-to-one correspondence between two different sets of objects. However, she failed to solve an analogous task but formulated with new stimuli, hence her ability was firmly incorporated in the context.

Sara Boise, S.T. has shown (Cole, 1997) that when training the actions with numbers is incorporated in life rich with interpersonal patterns of interactions and when training arises from prior established relations based on games, then the chimpanzee is found to be able not only to understand a one-to-one correspondence but she can also learn to add numbers and even to solve the arithmetical tasks with which children of 3 years old have success.

The question arises of determining the peculiarity of the highest form of intelligence - human intelligence (maybe, a particular case of intelligence or intermediate stage of it). Each new form of behavior is connected with the new forms of assimilation and accommodation. People change objects in reality and create new material and mental objects (artifacts (Cole, 1997)), using them as a tool for regulating their interactions with the world. Broadly speaking, the artifacts are not only instruments of work but they are also representations, concepts, operational schemata, i.e., all mental constructions invented and created by people and, without which it would be impossible to create new objects in reality. Conversely, mental activity would be impossible without practical actions.

Creating artifacts is the manifestation of the activity of knowledge, the activity of intelligence. It is important that the development of intelligence proceeds in the social environment, i.e., through the interaction between people. Due to cultural interactions, the artifacts can be improved and assimilated by the individuals. What is invented by one person is not viable until the innovation will be communicated to, mastered and assimilated by others.

Individuals, like societies and cultures, are active subjects of their development, although their behavior is not fully determined by their own choice in their environment. However, people have one principal characteristic distinguishing them from animals - they conceive their mental operations and they are able actively to use, control and improve them (operations) making them more and more perfect. Thereby an individual (like a society) can change himself; he is able to learn and to invent new mental functions using mental operations that have been already assimilated by him. In summary, we can conclude that the highest form of intelligence demonstrates ever more and more increasing changes of the environment in the enormous and more and more increasing scope in time and in space. The communicative structures in the human society develop continuously in their intensity and in their content; they develop in time as well as in space. The possibilities to move and memorize increase too; the capability of thinking can be improved and increased to a large extent by means of computers (Papert, 1980). But at the same time, the highest forms of intelligence are provided with (supported by) all the lowest forms of intelligence.

Piaget defined four main stages of intellectual development: 1) sensory-motor stage, i. e., direct action upon environment, 2) preoperational/pre-logical period during which cognitive behavior is still influenced by perceptional activity. Actions are internalized via representations but thought is still tied to perception; during this stage there proceeds the development of speech and of the ability to operate symbols and signs), 3) the stage of operations (logical thought), i.e., in this stage the child is capable to reason in a way that is not dependent on immediate perceptual and motor actions (the stage of concrete operations), 4) the stage of logical formal operations (complete logical thought independent on context). During this stage operational grouping becomes invariant with respect to concrete objects of reasoning and they can be transferred into a new context (in which monkeys fail). We call the last capability unification. The fourth stage appears due to the awareness, of the individual, of his (or her) mental operations which he (or she) used during the prior stage of concrete mental operations. Once realizing the fact that an operation executed on a pair of objects can be transferred on any pair of analogous objects or on any subset of objects with the same properties an individual can be ready to release operations from a context, to control them and to consider them as subjects of mathematical, philosophical, aesthetic reflections.

The stages of intellectual development (it is better to say the spheres) are closely tight. All intellectual capabilities develop consecutively and in parallel with one another, although some of them can dominate the others at a certain stage. During the sensory-motor stage when the cognitive structures of object, time and space are formed, in parallel with them, the concepts of causality and of goal appear too. Child begins to understand the causal links between an object and its properties as well as between the properties of object and the action he (or she) can make with it.

Children begin to understand that people, unlike things (inanimate objects), act deliberately. According to Tomasello M. (Cole, 1997), the appearance of the ability to think of other people as acting deliberately plays an important role in the development of imitative forms of behavior.

Communicative function becomes more complicated as well. For example, if a toy-car unexpectedly has gone upon the floor, then a child aged one year, as a rule, shows the toy-car and after that he will inspect whether the mother sees the toy-car too. At about 18-months, a child, as a rule, firstly looks at the mother in order to be sure that she sees the toy and after that he shows the toy-car. If a child of this age is alone in the room then he does not point at the car until somebody of the adults enters the room.

The achievement of the higher level of intellectual development does not mean stopping the development of the abilities that appeared at the prior stages. On the contrary, these abilities continue to develop. For example, the motor activity becomes more sophisticated. The complex movement such as slalom, juggling, acrobatics, windsurfing could not occur at the early stage of intellectual development since they request more developed logical operations. Complex movements are learnable and in the learning process, there must be engaged memory, speech, feelings, muscles, and visual images coordinated with one another (Gatev, 1973). For example, Efimov, L.F. (Lomov, & Surkov, 1980) investigating the self-reportage of slalom racers in the periods they analyze a new route before the competition informs us: slalom racer goes several times along the route by foot, explores the state of snow, steepness of slope, the distance between the obstacles; he determines the speed he can (or need to) achieve at each part of the route, he tries to keep in mind the route in detail to be able to recreate mentally his future movement along the route as a whole. The analogous examples one can find in (Kritchevsky, 1968). Deliberate behavior at the sensory-motor stage is connected with the development of anticipation mechanisms. Anticipation permits to coordinate the actions of an individual with those of other people. In all complex actions, it is necessary to involve the mechanisms of anticipation. Figure 3 shows the levels and the forms of anticipation.

The parallelism, the development "stage by stage" and the coordination of intellectual actions can partly account for the fact that some relationships and operations formed at the preliminary stages turn out later to be not discerned. For example, adults are not aware of the links between object (class) and its properties as the causal relationships.

Modeling cognitive structures in artificial intelligence presupposes that all their necessary elements (images, representations of objects, concepts, relationships of time and space and so forth) are already available in their final forms ready to use. But we believe modeling intellectual structures to be impossible without taking into account not only the mechanisms of their forming and functioning but also the mechanisms of their gradual development (genetic mechanisms) from their simplest forms up to the more complicated ones.

Figure 3. Levels and forms of anticipations

Levels:
1. *Sensory-motor anticipation*
2. *Perceptive anticipation*
3. *Anticipation on the level of representations*
4. *Anticipation in reasoning (hypotheses)*

Forms:
1. *Reflex and habit*
2. *Program of coordinated actions*
3. *Predictions of a class by properties, a totality by its part*
4. *Prediction of next member in the succession*

Knowing the genetic mechanisms allows us to understand the relations of the succession between intellectual structures (or/and operations) at the different stages of their development. For example, pattern recognition surely passes the way from the very simple assimilating forms of "grasping" the similarity between objects or stimuli up to the more complicated forms such as determining the logical identity of concepts or the unification of complex cognitive constructions. We have to answer the questions how the more complicated cognitive structures interact with the less complicated but more ancient ones. Any relation has two aspects: declarative and productive. How could one assert that $7 > 2$? For this goal we need an operation that removes two units from the set of seven units and discovers that the number of units remaining after deleting two units is not equal to zero. When we prove that "class A is a subset of class B" (A is a B or $A \leq B$), where A, B are the names of some classes (concepts), it is necessary to check the following relation: "A is a B" is satisfied if and only if the set of all conceivable objects of class A is included in the set of all conceivable objects of class B.

The declarative part of "is a" relation is an expression constructed from the names of concepts by means of the signs of operations or relationships (maybe, syntactic rules). Expressions consist of words, for example, "mammal is an animal" The productive part of this relation is a mental action performed with conceivable sets of objects. This action is acquired from experience, firstly by manipulating with real objects, and later with their representations.

Piaget introduced the concept of grouping in order to determine reasoning operations. Grouping, according to Piaget, corresponds to algebraic structure in mathematics. The laws of grouping are defined as follows:

$A + B = C$, $B + A = C$ – commutative law,
$A = C - B$, $B = C - A$ - reversibility,
$(A + B) + C = A + (B + C)$ – associative law,
$A - A = 0$ - identity,
$A + A = A$ - tautology.

An example of additive grouping is: the set of classes with addition operation. Let A, B, C be classes (concepts) and a, b, c - be the properties of classes. A logical class is the union of objects having the same common property. So, class A, for example, is the set of beads, defined by their brown color "a", class B is the set of beads "not a", namely the set of beads defined by their white color "b". To add classes $A + B = C$ means to define the least class of beads including the two classes A and B where C is defined by the common property of classes A and B, i.e., in a given example, by the property "c" - wooden beads.

The reversibility of operations, according to Piaget, occurs when a person becomes aware of his own mental operations. Piaget called social interaction one of the variables that facilitates cognitive development and leads to the appearance of logical reversible operations. Coming to look at something from another's point of view, questioning one's reasoning and seeking validations from others are all essential acts of accommodation, which imply the transition from concrete nonreversible mental operations to mobile and reversible ones.

All intellectual operations are coordinated with one another. This coordination ensures the integrity of an organism. We will give some examples of coordinated intellectual operations. The description of visual-motor coordinated operations is given in (Rokotova et al., 1971). Children at the age of 3-5 years have been asked to draw a direct line on a paper and to stop drawing at the moment when a certain vertical line can be achieved. Young children (of 3 years old) fail to do this: vision and hand's movement have been not coordinated in this age. Children of 5-6 years old can do the task and also demonstrate the anticipating behavior. Wadsworth (2004) have shown that if one's hand is moving, then one's eyes always repeat the same way the hand passes but the vision passes ahead the hand in order to inform it about the location of the goal of the hand's movement. The eyes and the hand cooperate as "the agents" coordinating their actions.

The coordination of classifying operations means that the operations on class's names, the operations on conceivable objects and the operations on object's descriptions are performed simultaneously and they are in agreement with one another (Piaget, & Inhelder, 1959). The coordinated classifying operations generate some set of logical assertions which can be understood if the classification is performed as the system of coordinated operations. First of all the classification is connected with understanding the operations of quantification: "not all C is A", "all B are some C", "all A are some C", "some C are B" and so on (in the case $C = A + B$). The violation of the coordination of classifying operations implies the violation of reasoning. Piaget has shown that 1) operational reasoning is a result of gradual development of a person; 2) the appearance of formal operations is connected with the spontaneous appearance of the ability to coordinate mental operations; 3) a key problem of the development of operational classification in the mind is the problem of understanding the inclusion relation. If understanding the inclusion relation is not achieved by a person, then it is impossible for him to understand either classifying or quantifying operations.

Piaget and Inhelder (1959) have created special tests in order to study the development of classifying operations for young children of different ages. The results of their investigations are informed in (Piaget, & Inhelder, 1964). For example, a child is presented with the collection of three red squares, two blue squares and three blue circles. A typical example of the answers of a young child to the questions of an experimenter is the following (see also, please, Figure 4):

Q.: Are all the red ones squares?
A.: No, because some are blue too.

Figure 4. A test for controlling the understanding of inclusion relation

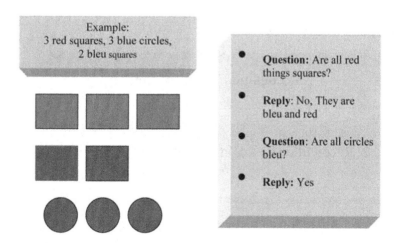

Q.: Are all the blue ones circles?
A.: Yes.
Q.: Are all the circles blue?
A.: Yes.
Q.: Are all the squares red?
A.: Yes.

The young children frequently were referring to the entire collection as "all", in an absolute sense, instead of focusing on the sub-collections.

Any grouping is a system of coordinated operations, but in the case of classification we deal with three such groupings. The understanding can not be partial. It is a difficulty. But if a child realizes the mental coordinated operations then a vast leap occurs in his thinking.

Many activities must be learned together. It is argued in (Wadsworth, 2004) that "reading, writing and spelling to be isolated from one another in a curriculum, as they typically are, makes no sense at all. The three need to occur together, not as separate subjects".

The mechanisms of recognition go much in the same way as all intelligent capabilities do. The simplest form of recognition is based on the similarity of objects. The following and more complicated form of recognition is based on the logical identity or the equivalence of concepts. And the most perfect and complex form of recognition is the process of unification, i.e., the recognition of complex cognitive structures, for example, grouping or even the system of coordinated grouping (Figure 5).

Each previous scheme of recognition is assimilated by the following one. We assume that the results of all earlier proceeded acts of establishing the similarity between objects or the identity between concepts are conserved (maybe in the form of links or rules) and thereby facilitate passing more complex acts of recognition. If we assume continuity between perceived stimuli, images, representations and concepts, then we must conclude that once established relations of similarity or identity at the level of perception will form the analogous relations between corresponding images, representations, concepts at the other intellectual levels. Thus, we must consider the coordinated multi-level relations of similarity (distinction) which underlie the complex unification schemata.

We believe that any act of recognition begins with acquiring the similarity of various entities. The operation establishing the similarity on a set of entities of the same nature forms a grouping, the prop-

Figure 5. The forms of pattern recognition

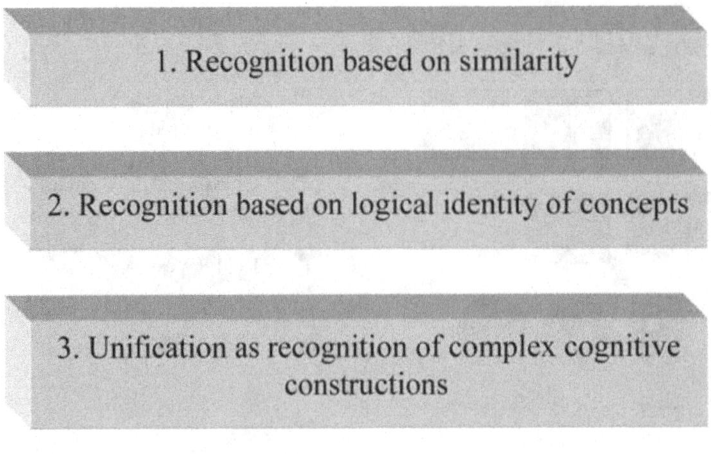

1. Recognition based on similarity

2. Recognition based on logical identity of concepts

3. Unification as recognition of complex cognitive constructions

erties of which are defined by the properties of the operation itself: it is symmetrical but not transitive operation. The similarity is measurable; we say that entities are "not familiar at all,""much familiar", "identical". On the one hand, we can construct the set of all entities in pairs familiar to one another (the transitive closure).

On the other hand, we can order entities in accordance with the degree of their similarity. Hence the relationship of similarity generates two groupings: the first one with the operation establishing similarity of entities, and the second, in the form of the ordered set of entities.

Logical identity of concepts requires the mastered processes of classification. Already the act itself of forming a class is an act of establishing the equivalence between the objects of this class and, at the same time, it is an act of establishing the identity between the class and the common property of objects of this class.

One of the fundamental capabilities of intelligence consists in using the same cognitive scheme for solving the different problems as well as obtaining the same result by means of different operational schemata. This phenomenon we connect with transferring (tuning) the complex operational schemata from one domain of intellectual activity to another. For example, mechanisms of assimilation and accommodation at the biological level and at the cognitive level are familiar. The syntactic structure of arithmetical expressions is analogous to that of logical expressions as well as to the syntactic structure of natural language's expressions. For example, to find x, y such that $x + y = 32$ means to find one of the decompositions of the number 32. Just the same, to find a, b such that "a + blue * b = good weather" means to find one of the descriptions (decompositions) of the concept "good weather": the sun + blue * sky = good weather. We consider unification to be the process of transferring the complex operational schemata from one context to another in order to solve new tasks in a new domain of thinking. The unification is the most perfect and creative ability of human reasoning.

Piaget's theory of intelligence had an enormous influence on educational philosophy and methods of teaching children. Seymour Papert, who had worked with Piaget in Geneva, used his ideas for creating the LOGO Programming Language designed as a tool for learning (Papert, 1993). Thousands of teachers throughout the world became excited by the intellectual and creative potential of LOGO. The kind of learning that children do with computers is called "learning by doing". Using a computer the child is able to build a model and learn from seeing a complete system in action as opposed to learning by rote, or in fragment. We believe that knowing the Piaget's theory of intelligence is important for the specialists on artificial intelligence too.

The G. Gentzen's Natural Calculus

The main goal of Gentzen's natural calculus (Gentzen, 1969) was to set up a formal system that reflects as accurately as possible the actual logical reasoning involved in mathematical proof. The result was a 'calculus of natural deduction' ('NJ' for intuitionist, 'NK' - for classical logic). In order to show what form the natural deductions have in practice, Gentzen gives the examples of deriving the truth of three formulas. These examples are the following (Gentzen, 1969).

First Example (Gentzen, 1969, p. 74). The formula

$$(X \vee (Y \& Z)) \supset ((X \vee Y) \& (X \vee Z))$$

is known to be true. To prove this fact we shall reason as follows. Suppose that either X or Y & Z hold. We have the two cases. 1. X holds. 2. Y & Z holds.

In the first case, it follows that $X \vee Y$ holds and also $X \vee Z$ holds. Hence $(X \vee Y)$ & $(X \vee Z)$ also holds.

In the second case Y & Z holds; it means that both Y and Z hold. From Y follows $X \vee Y$; from Z follows $X \vee Z$. Thus the formula $(X \vee Y)$ & $(X \vee Z)$ again holds. But this formula has been derived from $X \vee (Y$ & $Z)$, i.e., we have that the formula $(X \vee (Y$ & $Z)) \supset ((X \vee Y)$ & $(X \vee Z))$ is true.

Second Example (Gentzen, 1969, p. 74) for proving the formula

$$(\exists x \forall y \mathbf{F}xy) \supset (\forall y \, \exists x \mathbf{F}xy).$$

The proof runs as follows. Suppose that there is an x such that for all $y \mathbf{F}xy$ holds. Let a be such an x. Then for all $y \mathbf{F}ay$ holds. Let b be an arbitrary object. Then $\mathbf{F}ab$ holds. Thus there is an x, say a, such that $\mathbf{F}xb$ holds. Since b is arbitrary, our result holds for all objects, i.e., for all y there is an x such that $\mathbf{F}xy$ holds.

Third example (Gentzen, 1969, p.75) for proving the formula

$$(\neg \exists x \mathbf{F}x) \supset (\forall y \, \neg \mathbf{F}y),$$ where the symbol $\neg$ is used for the negation.

This formula is intuitionistically true. In order to prove it, we shall reason as follows. Assume that there is no x for which $\mathbf{F}x$ holds. From this we have to infer that for all $y \, \neg \mathbf{F}y$ holds. Suppose that a is some object for which $\mathbf{F}a$ holds. It then follows that there is an x for which $\mathbf{F}x$ holds; assume that a is such an object. But this contradicts the hypothesis that $\neg \exists x \mathbf{F}x$. Therefore $\mathbf{F}a$ cannot hold. Since a was completely arbitrary, it follows that for all $y \, \neg \mathbf{F}y$ holds.

The essential difference between natural deduction (NJ- derivation) and logistic calculus (as in the systems of Russel, Hilbert and, Heyting) consists in the following: in the latter systems true formulas are derived from a set of 'basic logical formulas' (axioms) by means of a few rules of inference. Natural deduction does not use logical axioms but it starts from assumptions (as we have seen in the examples above) to which logical deductions are applied. Then, by means of some later inferences, the result is made independent of the assumptions.

Now we have to describe the terminology and notations used in the text below.

Two groups of symbols are distinguished: constant symbols and variables.

Constant symbols
Symbols for definite objects: 1, 2, 3,..
Symbols for definite functions: +, -, ..
Symbols for definite propositions: "True" (the true proposition),"False" (the false proposition).
Symbols for definite predicates: =, <, ...
Logical symbols: &, and, $\vee$, or, $\supset$, 'if .... then', $\equiv$ (is equivalent), $\neg$ (not), $\forall$ (for all), $\exists$ (there is).
Variables
Object variables: these are of two kinds – free object variables $a, b, c, \ldots, m$, and bound object variables n, $\ldots v, y, z$.
Propositional variables: $A, B, C, \ldots$

Expressions

The concept of propositional expression, called a 'formula', is defined inductively:

- a symbol for a definite proposition (i.e., the symbols "True" and "False") is a formula;
- a propositional variable followed by a number of free object variables is a formula, e.g. *Abab*;
- if **U** is a formula, then ¬**U** is also a formula;
- if **U** and **B** are formulas, then **U** & **B**, **U** ∨ **B**, **U** ⊃ **B**, and **U** ≡ **B** are also formulas;
- a formula not containing the bound object variables forms another formula, if we prefix either ∀r or ∃r. We may substitute r in a number of places for a free object variable occurring in the formula.

Figures

Two kinds of figures are introduced: inference figures and proof figures. The figures consist of formulas.

An inference figure may be written as follows:

$$\frac{U_1, \ldots, U_k}{B}, \text{ where } k \geq 1.$$

Here $U_1, \ldots, U_k$, **B** – formulas, $U_1, \ldots, U_k$, - are called the upper formulas, and **B** is called the lower formula of the inference figure.

A proof figure, called a derivation, consists of a number of formulas (at least one) forming inference figures in the following way:

1. Each formula is a lower formula of at most one inference figure;
2. Each formula (with the exception of exactly one, namely the endformula) is an upper formula of at least one inference figure;
3. The system of inference figures is noncircular, i. e., there is no cycle in the derivation.

The formulas of a derivation that are not lower formulas of an inference figure are called initial formulas of the derivation. Thus, a derivation is in 'tree form' if each one of its formulas is an upper formula of at most one inference figure. It is convenient because of the tree form permits only a single use of a derived formula in an inference process.

The formulas composing a derivation are called D-formulas or derivation formulas. Analogously, the inference figures of the derivation are called D-inference figures or derivation inference figures.

Now we are ready to describe the NJ calculus for natural derivations of true formulas.

An inference figure is formed according to particular schemes. The schemes reflect the mental acts of introducing (I) or eliminating (E) the logical symbols. Thus, there are the following schemes: &-I (the introduction of conjunction), &-E (the elimination of conjunction), ∨-I (the introduction of disjunction), ∨-E (the elimination of disjunction), ∀-I (the introduction of the universal quantifier), ∀-E (the elimination of the universal quantifier, ∃-I (the introduction of existential quantifier), ∃-E (the eliminating of existential quantifier), ⊃-I (the introduction of the implication), ⊃-E (the elimination of the implication), ¬-I (the introduction of the negation), and ¬-E (the elimination of the negation).

These schemes are depicted as follows:

&-I:

$$\frac{U \quad B}{U \,\&\, B}$$

&-E:

$$\frac{U \,\&\, B}{U} \qquad \frac{U \,\&\, B}{B}$$

∨-I:

$$\frac{U}{U \vee B} \qquad \frac{B}{U \vee B}$$

∨-E:

$$\frac{U \vee B \quad \overset{[U]}{G} \quad \overset{[B]}{G}}{G}$$

This figure (distinction of cases): if **U** ∨ **B** (**U** or **B**) has been proved, then that it is possible to conduct the proof by distinguishing two cases. Let us assume that **U** holds and from it we have derived, let us say, **G**. If it is possible to derive **G** also by assuming that **B** holds, then **G** holds generally, i. e., it is now independent of both assumptions.

Symbols written in square brackets have the following meaning. An arbitrary number (possible zero) of formulas of this form may be adjoined to the inference figure as assumption formulas. They must be initial formulas of derivation and occur, moreover, in those paths of the proof to which the particular upper formula of the inference figure belongs. This formula may itself be an assumption formula.

∀-I:

$$\frac{Fa}{\forall r Fr}$$

The figure ∀-I is explained as follows. If **F**a has been proved 'for an arbitrary *a*, then the formula ∀*r***F***r* holds. The assumption that *a* is 'completely arbitrary' can be expressed more accurately as follows: the formula **F**a must not depend on any assumption in which the object variable *a* occurs.

This assertion together with obvious requirement that every occurrence of *a* in **F**a must be replaced by an *r* in **F***r* constitutes exactly that part of the restrictions on variables which applies to the scheme of the figure ∀-I.

∀-E:

$$\frac{\forall r F r}{F a}$$

∃-I:

$$\frac{F a}{\exists r F r}$$

∃-E:

$$\frac{\exists r F r \quad \overset{\left[F a\right]}{G}}{G}$$

This figure has the following meaning. We have ∃*r***F***r*. Then we reason as follows: let *a* be precisely such an object for which **F** holds, i.e. we assume that **F***a* holds. (Naturally, for *a*, it is necessary to take an object variable, which does not yet occur in the formula ∃*r***F***r*). If, by this assumption, we prove a proposition **G** which no longer contains *a* and does not depend on any other assumption containing *a*, then **G** has been proved independently on the assumption **F***a*.

There is an analogy between figures ∃-E and ∨-E; this is explained by the fact that the sign ∃ is the generalization of the sign ∨ (or), and that the sign ∀ is the generalization of the sign &.

⊃-I:

$$\frac{\overset{\left[U\right]}{B}}{U \supset B}$$

The figure ⊃-I has the following meaning. If formula **B** has been proved with the use of an assumption **U**, then **B** follows from **U** already without this assumption. (Naturally, the other admissions may have been made, and the result still continues to depend on them).

⊃-E:

$$\frac{U \quad U \supset B}{B}$$

¬-I:

$$\begin{array}{c} \left[U\right] \\ \textit{False} \\ \hline \neg U \end{array}$$

The figure ¬-I (reduction ad absurdum). If from the assumptions **U** follows something false, then **U** is not true and ¬**U** holds.

¬-E:

$$\begin{array}{c} U \quad \neg U \\ \hline \textit{False} \end{array}$$

This figure is explained as follows. **U** and ¬**U** signifies a contradiction, and it cannot correspond with reality. It is expressed formally by the figure ¬-E, where the symbol "False" designates the contradiction (the false).

Now we shall write the second Example (Gentzen, 1969, p. 74) for proving the formula $(\exists x \forall y \mathbf{F} xy) \supset (\forall y \, \exists x \mathbf{F} xy)$ in the form of NJ inference:

$$\begin{array}{c} \cfrac{ \begin{array}{c} \cfrac{1}{\forall y F a y} \, \forall - E \\ \cfrac{F a b}{\exists x F x b} \, \exists - I \\ \cfrac{}{\forall y \exists x F x y} \, \forall - I \end{array} }{ \begin{array}{c} 2 \\ \exists x \forall y F x y \end{array} \qquad \cfrac{\forall y \exists x F x y}{ } \, \exists - E \, 1 } \\[2ex] \cfrac{\forall y \exists x F x y}{(\exists x \forall y F x y) \supset (\forall y \exists x F x y)} \, \supset - I \, 2 \end{array}$$

The calculus NJ has the following advantages:
It lends itself to the formalization of mathematical proofs:

- In most cases the natural calculus derivations for true formulas are shorter than those in logistic derivations in which the same formula appears, as a rule, several times (as a part of other formulas), whereas this situation occurs very rarely in the case of NJ-derivations.
- To every logical symbol belongs exactly one inference figure introducing the symbol and one eliminating it.

The natural deduction calculi open the way for applying this technique as an automatic reasoning tool in a decision making framework for various tasks of artificial intelligence.

Kolmogorov (1932) was the first who has proposed an explicit and systematic account of all the intuitionistic logical operations. He has given an interpretation of intuitionistic logic based on the notion of 'problem' and 'solution to a problem' instead of the notion of 'truth'. Kolmogorov's interpretation of the intuitionistic connectives is the following one:

A & B is "the problem of solving both A and B";
A ∨ B is "the problem of solving at least one of A and B";

A $\supset$ B is "the problem of solving B supposing that the solution to A is given";

$\neg$A is "the problem of obtaining a contradiction supposing that the solution to A is given".

After explaining the meaning of the logical connectives, Kolmogorov has given his interpretation, also in terms of problems, of the universal quantifiers. If x is a variable and $P(x)$ is a problem, whose meaning depends on the variable x, then $\forall x P(x)$ is the problem of indicating a general method for the solution of $P(x)$ for each particular value of x. The solution to $\exists x P(x)$ is the indication of a particular object a and a solution to $P(a)$.

Recently, natural deduction (ND) systems have been studied in many directions. The ND technique initially defined for the classical propositional logic has been extended to the first-order logic. It has also been extended to the non-classical propositional intuitionistic logic, where the proof-searching strategies are based on a propositional ND calculus.

The proof theory and semantics of intuitionistic modal logic have been developed by Simpson (1994). Fisher et al. (2001) have advanced a kind of clausal temporal resolution. We can also note a model of intuitionistic linear logic advanced in (Polakow, & Pfenning, 1999). This model serves as a basis to define an ND proof system for propositional linear-time temporal logic (PLTL) (Marchignoli, 2002).

Bolotov et al. (2004, 2005) have described a particular approach to build an ND-calculus. It is a modification of Quine's (1950) representation of subordinate proof developed for the classical propositional and first-order logic. In (Pfenning, 2001), the notion of hypothetical derivation, i. e., reasoning from hypothesis, has been given in the framework of ND. The ND has the broad possibility for various applications in artificial intelligence areas, most notably, in agent engineering (Wooldridge, 2000).

CONCLUSION

We tried, in this chapter, to give an overview of the ideas about human knowledge and thinking in the works of philosophers, mathematicians and psychologists from the antique times up to now. The history of the development of these ideas is reflected in the development of the theory of logical inference and knowledge in the framework of contemporary approaches to modeling human reasoning with the aid of computers.

REFERENCES

Anderson, F. H. (1962). *Francis Bacon. His career and his thought*. Los Angeles.

Angluin, D. (1988). Queries and concept learning. *Machine Learning, 3*(4), 319–342.

Aristotle. (1978). *Selected Works in the 4th Volumes* (Vol. 2). Moscow: the Academy of Sciences of the USSR.

Bacon, F. (1889). *The works* (J. Spedding, R. L. Ellis, & D.D. Heath, Eds.).

Bacon, F. (1962). *The advancement of learning* (G. W. Kitchin, Ed.). New York.

Bacon, F. (1982). *Neu Atlantis* (G. Bugge, Trans., J. Klein, Ed.). Stuttgart, Germany.

Bacon, F. (2000a). *A critical edition of the major works*. (B.Vickers, Ed.). New York: Oxford.

Bacon, F. (2000b). *The Oxford Francis Bacon* (G. Rees & L. Jardine, Eds.).

Birjukov, B. V., & Trostnikov, V. N. (1977). *Heat of the cold numbers and the enthusiasm of impassive logic. Formalization of thinking from the antique times to the epoch of cybernetics*. Moscow: Nauka.

Birukov, B.V. (1973). Problems of the abstraction and faultlessness in logic (on one aspect of the influence of scientific and technical revolution on a study of the logical thinking). *Questions of philosophy*, 11, 95-106.

Birukov, B. V., & Turovtzeva, A. J. (1978). Logical – Gnosiological Views of Schröder. In B.V. Birukov, & A. G. Spirkin (Eds), *Cybernetic and logic* (pp. 153-252). Moscow, Russia: Nauka.

Black, M. (1954). The semantic definition of truth. In M. McDonald (Ed), *Philosophy and analysis*. Oxford.

Bogomolov, S. (1913). *The questions of geometry's foundation, part 1. Intuition, mathematical logic, idea of order in geometry*. Saint-Petersburg-Moscow, Russia.

Bolotov, A., Bocharov, V., Gorchakov, A., Makarov, V., & Shangin, V. (2004). *Logic and computer, Issue 5: Let computer prove it*. Moscow, Russia: Nauka.

Bolotov, A., Bocharov, V., Gorchakov, A., & Shangin, V. (2005). Automated first-order natural deduction. In B. Prasad (Ed), *Proceedings of 2nd International Conference on Artificial Intelligence* (IICAI'05) (pp. 1292-1311). Puna, India: IICAI.

Boole, G. (1854). *Investigation of the laws of thought, on which are founded the mathematical theories of logic and probabilities*. London: Cambridge.

Capra, F. (1983). *The turning point*. Flamingo.

Cole, M. (1997). *Cultural psychology: A once and future discipline*. Moscow: "Cogito - Center" (in Russian).

Davis, E., & Morgenstern, L. (2004). Introduction: Progress in Formal Commonsense Reasoning. *Artificial Intelligence, 153*, 1–12. doi:10.1016/j.artint.2003.09.001

Descartes, R. (1960). *Discourse on method and meditations* (L. J. Lafleur, Trans.). New York: The Liberal Arts Press.

Descartes, R. *Oeuvres*. (1897-1913). Publiées par Ch. Adam et P. Tannery, t. 1-12; and suppl, Paris. 1897-1913; *Correspondence*, v. 1-6, Paris, 1936-1956.

Farrington, B. (1949). *Bacon: Philosopher of industrial science*. New York.

Fisher, M., Dixon, C., & Peim, M. (2001). Clausal temporal resolution. [TOCL]. *ACM Transactions on Computational Logic, 1*(2), 12–56. doi:10.1145/371282.371311

Gatev, B. A. (1973). *The development of child's visual-motor reactions*. Sofia, Bulgaria: Academy of Science (in Russian).

Gentzen, G. (1969). *The collected papers of Gerhard Gentzen* (M. E. Szabo, Ed.). Amsterdam & London: North-Holland Publ. Co.

Getmanova, A. D. (1959). About Leibniz's views on relationships between mathematics and logic. In K. A. Ribnikov, Ch. M. Fataliev, & M. I. Shaparonov (Eds), *Philosophical questions of natural science*, (178-212). Moscow: USSR: Moscow University Press.

Hempel, C. G. (1966). *Philosophy of natural science*. Englewood Cliffs, NJ: Prentice Hall.

Khardon, R., & Ross, D. (1999). Learning to reason with a restricted view. *Machine Learning, 3*(5), 96–116.

Kolmogorov, A. N. (1932). Zur Deutung der Intuitionistischen Logik. *Mathematische Zeitschrift, 35*, 58–65. doi:10.1007/BF01186549

Kotarbiński, T. (1963). Lections on the history of logic. In T. Kotarbiński *Selected Works*(I. S. Narskij, Ed.; M. M. Gurenko, Trans.). Moscow, USSR: Foreign Literature.

Kowalski, R. A., & Sergot, M. J. (1986). A logic based calculus of events. *New Generation Comput., 4*(1), 67–95. doi:10.1007/BF03037383

Kritchevsky, R. L. (1968). Experimental studies of tactical thinking in sport. [in Russian]. *The Theory and Practice of Physical Culture, 8*, 13–15.

Lambert, K., & Brittan, G. G. (1987). *An introduction to the philosophy of science* (3rd ed). Atascadero, California: Ridgeview.

Lomov, B. F., & Surkov, E. N. (1980). *Anticipation in the structure of activity*. Moscow, USSR: Nauka.

Marchignoli, D. (2002). *Natural Deduction systems for temporal logic*. Unpublished doctoral dissertation, Department of Informatics, University of Pisa.

McCain, N. (1997). *Causality in commonsense reasoning about actions*. Unpublished doctoral dissertation dissertation, University of Texas at Austin.

McCarthy, J., & Hayes, P. (1969). Some philosophical problems from the standpoint of artificial intelligence. In B. Meltzer, & D. Michie (Eds), *Machine Intelligence* (Vol. 4, pp. 463-502). Edinburgh: University Press.

Mill, J. S. (1900). *The system of logic*. Moscow, Russia: Book Affair.

Papert, S. (1993). *Mindstorms: Children, computers and powerful ideas*. Basic Books.

Peano, G. (1894). *Introduction an formulaire de mathematique*. Turin.

Peirce, Ch. S. (1883). The logic of relatives. In *Studies in Logic by Members of the Johns Hopkins University*. Boston.

Pfenning, E. (2001). Logical frameworks. In J. A. Robinson, & A. Voronkov (Eds), *Handbook of automated reasoning* (pp. 1063-1147). Elsevier.

Piaget, J. (1969). The psychology of intelligence. In V.A.Lekarskij et al (Eds.), *Selected psychological works by Piaget, J.* Moscow, USSR: Prosvetchenie.

Piaget, J., & Inhelder, B. (1959). *La genèse des Structures Logiques Elementaires. Classifications et Sériations*. Neuchâtel: Delachaux & Niestlé.

Piaget, J., & Inhelder, B. (1964). *The early growth of logic in the child*. London: Routledge and Kegan Paul.

Polakow, J., & Pfenning, F. (1999). Natural deduction for intuitionistic non-commutative linear logic. In J.-Y. Girard (Ed), *Proceedings of the 4th International Conference on Typed Lambda Calculi and Applications* (TLCA'99), L'Aquila (LNCS 1581, pp. 295-309). Springer-Verlag, Prantl, K. (1855-1870). *Geschichte der Logic in Abendlande*. Bd. 1-4, Leipzig.

Quine, W. (1950). On natural deduction. *Journal of Symbolic Logic, 15*, 93–102. doi:10.2307/2266969

Rokotova, N. A. Beregenaja, E. K., Gorbunova, I. M., & Rogovenko, E.S. (1971). *Motor tasks and performing*. Moscow, Russia: Nauka.

Sandewall, E. (1991). *Features and Fuentes: The representation of knowledge about dynamical systems* (Vol. 1). Oxford: University Press.

Schröder, E. (1877). *Der Operationskreis des Logikkalkuls*. Leipzig.

Schröder, E. (1890). *Vorlesungen über die Algebra der Logik (exacte Logik)*. Bd. I. Leipzig.

Schröder, E. (1890). *Über das Zeichen*. Festrede bei dem Direktoratswechsel an der Technischen Hochschule zu Karlsruhe am 22. Karlsruhe.

Schröder, E. (1891). *Vorlesungen über die Algebra der Logik (exacte Logik)*. Bd. II, Abt. 1, Leipzig.

Schröder, E. (1895). *Vorlesungen über die Algebra der Logik (exacte Logik)*. Bd. III, Abt. 1, Leipzig.

Schröder, E. (1898). Über Pasigraphie, Ihren Gegenwärtigen Stand und die Pasigraphische Bewegung in Italien. In Hrsg. Von F. Rudio (Ed), *Verhandlungen des Ersten Internationalen Mathematiker-Kongresses in Zurich*, vom 9. bis 11. August 1897. Leipzig.

Schröder, E. (1899). On Pasigraphy, its present state and the Pasigraphic Movement in Italy. *The Monist, 1*, 1898–1899.

Sechenov, I. M. (2001). *Elements of thoughts*. Saint-Petersburg, Russia: Piter.

Shanahan, M. (1997). *Solving the frame problem*. Cambridge, MA: MIT Press.

Siegwart, Ch. (1908). *Logic: The judgment, concept and inference* (Vol. 1) (translated from German in Russian). St. Petersburg, Russia.

Siegwart, Ch. (1909). *Logic: Logical Methods* (Vol. 2) (translated from German in Russian). St. Petersburg, Russia.

Simpson, A. (1994). *The proof theory and semantics of intuitionistic modal logic*. Unpublished doctoral dissertation, College of Science and Engineering, School of Informatics, University of Edinburgh.

Spedding, J. (Ed.). (1861-74), *The Letters and the Life of Francis Bacon* (7 volumes). London.

Spencer, H. (1898). *Principles of psychology*. Vol. I, II. Moscow, Russia: I.I. Bilibin.

Stjajkin, N. I. (1959). The elements of Algebraic Logic and the Theory of Semantic Antinomies in the Last Middle Age Logic. In E. Kolman, G.N. Povarov, P.V. Povanetz, & C.A. Janovskaja (Eds.), *Logical investigations*, (pp 20-32). Moscow, USSR: Academy of Sciences Press.

Swinburne, R. (Ed.). (1974). *The justification of induction*. Oxford.

Tanhilevitch, O. M. (1961). Leibniz's conception of symbolic science. *Philosophy of Science*, 2.

Tarski, A. (1947). The semantic conception of truth. In H. Feigl & W. Sellars. (Eds.), *Reading in philosophical analysis*.

Wadsworth, B. J. (2004). *Piaget's theory of cognitive and affective development*. Boston: Pearson Education, Inc.

Wooldridge, M. (2000). *Reasoning about rational agents*. MIT Press.

Chapter 2
Logic–Based Reasoning in the Framework of Artificial Intelligence

ABSTRACT

This chapter focuses on the tasks of knowledge engineering related mainly to knowledge acquisition and modeling integrated logic-based inference. We have overlooked the principal and more important directions of researches that pave the ways to understanding and modeling human plausible (common-sense) reasoning in computers.

INTRODUCTION

Man invented computer, and the computer became his inevitable assistant with complex calculations. Then the computer became an irreplaceable memory unit of gigantic volume, it stores not only data, but also knowledge. We address the computers as a source of data and knowledge. But in order to convert the computer into the valuable assistant, we must teach it to reason, to acquire knowledge from its own memory as well as input signals, and to transfer knowledge to us.

Within the framework of a scientific direction, called artificial intelligence, the simulation of human reasoning was always the main task of both theoretical and applied researches. The theory of reasoning includes the notion of logical ability. Traditionally this notion has been confined to algorithmic (deductive) inference. A critical examination of the presuppositions underlying this tradition exhibited the insufficiency of any theory of rationality that limits itself to classical deductive logic. As a result, inductive reasoning has been formalized and implemented in many intelligent computer systems with the goal to teach computer to mine knowledge from databases. The theory of reasoning is constantly enlarged by new models of logical inference reflecting the different aspects of natural human reasoning, for example,

DOI: 10.4018/978-1-60566-810-9.ch002

abduction, non-monotonic property, and different modes of negations. In this chapter, we focus on the logic-based models of human reasoning developed in the framework of artificial intelligence.

THE TASKS OF KNOWLEDGE ENGINEERING

Knowledge engineering is the most ancient human activity. Knowledge is necessary for solving even the simplest tasks and for the very life of man. Knowledge is extracted practically from everywhere and by a lot of different methods. Transferring and accumulating knowledge are not possible without the means of natural languages. Furthermore, knowledge is specialized, i.e. it is task-dependent. Inasmuch as the quantity of tasks solved by man is multiplied and knowledge is multiplied. Knowledge engineering covers extracting, collecting, analyzing, modeling, representing, validating, and using knowledge, in general, acquiring and managing knowledge. In our knowledge-driven society, the knowledge engineering systems have their place as an important mainstream technology. Figure 1 illustrates the main components of knowledge engineering.

An important part of knowledge engineering is the knowledge acquisition the task of which is to extract knowledge from data into the forms that can be used by computers. Knowledge is obtained directly from domain's specialists (experts) or from the other sources, in which knowledge is potentially contained (texts in natural languages, data banks, images, the Internet and so on).

The stages of knowledge acquisition are actually the stages of intellectual activity on processing the data. The purpose of this work is to understand, what useful information exists in or can be extracted from the data, such as facts, events, situations, and links between them. This process is tightly connected with learning. Figure 2 illustrates the idea that learning is a binding link in knowledge acquisition.

We note the following characteristics of knowledge acquisition:

1. multi-level
2. multi-systemic
3. interactive
4. learning-based
5. purpose-dependent

Figure 1. Constitutive elements of knowledge engineering

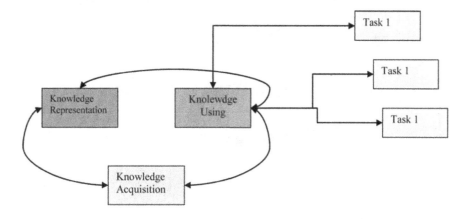

Figure 2. Learning as a binding unit in knowledge acquisition

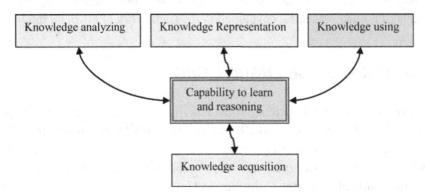

6. task dependent
7. continuous
8. cyclic (back forward links).

METHODS OF KNOWLEDGE ACQUISITION

The methods of knowledge acquisition is divided into two classes: 1) acquiring knowledge directly from the domain's specialists (experts) and 2) using machine learning methods for obtaining knowledge from different sources (information bearers), which explicitly or implicitly contain knowledge, useful for solving applied problems.

The methods of machine learning are used for extracting knowledge from observations and experimental data. The application of these methods, as a rule, requires the participation of domain's specialists or experts.

It has a sense to integrate both classes of knowledge acquisition methods (as it is shown in Figure 3) in order that the experts could use their knowledge for directing the process of machine learning.

Figure 3. Integration data mining (machine learning with knowledge of experts)

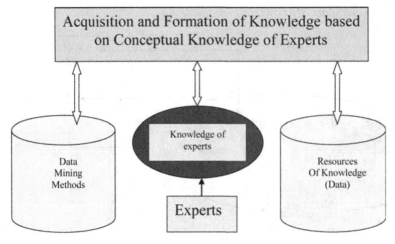

Knowledge acquisition is a multi-stage activity, at each step of which the conversion of concepts of lower level to concepts of higher level of knowledge occurs; this conversion can be performed on the basis of one and the same principles independent of the level of data generalization.

There are principally two ways of constructing the concepts or patterns of higher level from a lower one: to use program modules realizing elaborated in advance mathematical methods of concept construction, and to apply machine learning methods for inferring concepts via expert's examples. The methods of machine learning are applicable when the concepts of lower levels are described with the aid of some attributes.

Besides being grouped into the direct and indirect categories, knowledge acquisition methods can also be grouped (to some extent) with respect to the type of knowledge. For example, many of the indirect knowledge acquisition methods are best at obtaining conceptual (classification) knowledge while the direct methods are more adequate for obtaining procedural knowledge.

Mining Expert's Knowledge

The methods of knowledge acquisitions from experts are developed in many directions. Their variety is determined by learning methods and context or situation in which knowledge acquisition proceeds. An incomplete list of these methods includes the following ones: Interviewing, Case Study, Protocols, Criticizing, Role Playing, Simulation, Prototyping, Teach-back, Observation, Goal Related, List Related, Construct Elicitation, Sorting, Laddering, 20 Questions, and some others (Burge, 1998).

In Simulation method, a task is simulated with the use of a computer system or other means. This is applicable when it is not possible to actually perform the task. In Prototyping, the expert is asked to evaluate a prototype of the system to be developed. The system is refined iteratively. In Teach-back method, the knowledge engineer attempts to give the information back to the expert, who then provides corrections and fills in gaps. In Goal Related method, the discussion techniques are used to elicit information about goals and sub-goals of considered problem. Construct Elicitation method is used to obtain information about how the expert discriminates between entities in the problem domain. The most commonly used Construct Elicitation method is Repertory Grid Analysis (Kelly, 1955). For this method, the domain expert is presented with a list of entities, and then he is asked to describe the similarities and differences between them. The similarities and differences are used to determine informative attributes of the entities. In Sorting, the domain entities are sorted to determine how the expert classifies his knowledge. In Laddering, a hierarchical structure of the domain is formed by asking the questions in order to move up, down, and across the hierarchy (Diaper, 1989), (Hudlicka, 1997), (McNeese, & Zaff, 1991).

However, the methods of knowledge acquisition from experts turn out without success. This can be explained mainly by psychological reasons. In (Kobrinskiy, 2004), the problem of extracting knowledge from expert by the traditional methods via dialogue with him is analyzed. The field of clinical medical diagnostics is examined in this work. It is noted that on this traditional way, knowledge engineer is faced with serious difficulties, especially interacting with highly skilled experts. Direct methods involve questioning domain experts on how they do their job. One danger consists in the involuntary distortion and depletion of real reflections of experts with an attempt at their recreation and formulation in the verbal form. Another danger lies in the fact that intuitively figurative thinking of experts is substituted by pseudo-reasoning in a traditional manner.

There is a problem of discovering "hidden" knowledge of experts. The purpose of interacting between the knowledge engineer and the expert is to describe maximally fully and without contradiction problematic region and mechanism of decision making. Kobrinskiy (2004) proposes a new method of interaction with the group of physicians (Group Method). The essence of this method can be described as follows. In the work with the group of experts, knowledge engineer does not so much raise the question as he refines the divergences in opinions and the differences of descriptions. He forms questions for obtaining the coordinated solution and directs, as far as possible, the discussion of experts. In any case, the process of disease identification is a differential diagnosis. It is necessary to estimate each separate symptom with respect to its authenticity and significance, to conclude about its primary or secondary appearance, to analyze its differentiating role in combination with other symptoms. The medical field of clinical knowledge includes the variety of symptoms, syndromes, mechanisms of their transitions and diagnoses with their changes with time.

Knowledge engineer must be a good translator from one language to another and (from language of the specialist to a formal language of knowledge representation) and, simultaneously, he must well know the corresponding problem area.

A new method of modeling human communication, called Sketching, is described for knowledge acquisition in (Forbus, & Usher, 2002). Sketches provide a shared interaction medium where participants achieve a mutual understanding by creating, modifying, and agreeing upon the meaning of sketches. By the opinion of the authors, Sketching can be a powerful tool for human-computer interaction in knowledge acquisition and joint problem solving. An application of this method of knowledge elicitation is discussed in (Forbus et al., 2003).

Machine Learning and Knowledge Discovery

The methods of machine learning are the methods of learning classifications of objects, represented by their descriptions in a feature space. The goal of learning is to obtain necessary and sufficient rules or 'concept descriptions' with the use of which it can be performed the classification of new objects familiar with those belonging to a training set of object instances. In this case, we deal with learning from examples or **supervised learning**. Each instance (object description) in a training set has a pointer (label) to the class which it belongs to. It is possible to say that a classifier is built for predicting the class of new coming unknown object by analogy with a "teacher". Figure 4 describes generally the function of classifier. If features are continuous, then classification is called regression.

The methods of supervised learning include also the artificial neural networks (Scarcelli, & Tsoi, 1998), (Bodyanskij,& Rudenko 2004), (Judd, 1990), (Hush, & Horne, 1993). Neural network consists of layers of connected artificial neurons. Neurons have inputs from other neurons, some weighting functions which weight the input of each of these neurons, and an aggregation function combining all the

Figure 4. The description of classifier

Classifier:

- It is given a set of categories $\Omega = \{K1\ K2, ..., Kn\}$.
- It is given a set of objects $\Sigma = \{O1, O2, ..., Om\}$.
- It is given a goal function $F : \Omega \times \Sigma \to \{0, 1\}$.
- It is necessary to build a classifier F^*, which is the best approximation of F.

weighted inputs. If a result of this combination is over a certain threshold, the neuron is activated and propagates the signal to some other neurons. The weights of connections during the learning process change in such a way that the output element (elements) of network would give correct classification answer to the input signal (Fahlman, 1998), (Ahlawat, & Pandey 2007). The basis of learning is the approximation of discriminating nonlinear functions in feature space, which gives a good accuracy of prediction, but the obtained solution has not an explanation via values of features. The paper (Diaz et al. 2007) has introduced the computational model for Networks of Evolutionary Processors (NEPs). NEPs can be easily applied to knowledge-driven Decision Support Systems due to their inherent rule-based behavior. JAVA implementation of this model works as defined by the theoretical background of NEPs: massive parallelization and non-deterministic behavior.

An analytical review of supervised machine learning classification techniques is contained in (Kotsianti, 2007). This excellent overview paper covers the major theoretical ideas on which these techniques are based.

Learning without a teacher (**unsupervised learning**) solves the task of grouping objects into disjoint blocks based on a given measure of their similarity-distinction. This task is usually called clustering or taxonomy of objects (Zagorujko et al., 1999). After clustering, the induced function for discriminating objects of different clusters in a feature space is used for decision making to what group a new object belongs.

The most distributed method of constructing clusters is the method of k- the nearest neighbor (Duda, et al. 2001; Zagorujko, 1999). This algorithm classifies object according to the majority "of the voices" of its adjacent objects in the multidimensional space of features. Object is related to the class, to which the greatest number of its k-the closest neighbors belongs, where k is a certain integer. With two classes, the number k is selected odd. "Neighbors" are selected from the set of correctly recognized objects.

Unsupervised learning is usually used for analyzing data structures, but also for forming a training set of examples for the following application of supervised learning in order to find a logical rule (in terms of attributes values) approximating the obtained partition of objects into clusters and to construct conceptual description of these clusters in the feature space. Ciaramata et al. (2005), for example, use unsupervised learning for extracting semantic relations between concepts in molecular biology. Designing clustering methods for ontology building is considered in (Bisson et al., 2000).

The following are the key aspects of machine learning:

- Choice and formation of feature space;
- Checking hypotheses related to the similarity-distinction of objects and their classes; defining the binary operations for determining the similarity-distinction relationships between objects and between classes of objects;
- Forming a training set of object examples;
- Forming a control set of object examples;
- Choice of an adequate learning algorithm.

The choice of feature space determines a learning task with respect to its content and the type of learning algorithm. The formation of training and control sets of object examples in the case of supervised learning determines the accuracy, rapidity and effectiveness of learning. Correctly selected examples can direct the learning process. An incremental procedure and a certain sequence of examples (from simple examples to more complex ones) allow minimizing the number of examples necessary for learning.

The control set of examples is necessary for checking the correctness of classifier's work, improving its work, and for goal-directed learning of classifier or giving to it required properties.

We give some examples of choosing objects and features in the tasks of natural language text processing.

Example 1 (Lodhi et al., 2002).
Objects: text documents D_j, $j = 1, ..., n$;
Task: to learn the rules for classifying texts (supervised learning);
Features: key words T_i, $i = 1, ..., t$;
VectorD_j of features describing j-th document: a) value $d_{ji} \in \{1,0\}$ of vector, where 1 means the presence of i-th key word in text, 0 – its absence; for $D_j = [011110]$, key words T_1, T_6 – are absent in D_j, T_2, T_3, T_4, T_5 are present in it; б) value $w_{ij} \in [0,00; 1,00]$ of vector $W_j = [0,00\ 1,00\ 0,10\ 0,75\ 0,90\ 1,00]$ shows the frequency of occurrence of i-th key word in j-th document.

Example 2.

This example is taken from (Cimiano et al., 2005) and it relates to one of the methods of ontology acquisition from text. Objects in this example are the nouns playing the role of actor (subject) or direct object of verbs in the sentence. Verbs associated with nouns serve as the features of these nouns. Table 1 presents the relations extracted from the publicity text of a tourist agency. In this table, the lines correspondent with objects, the columns – with features.

The following classification (ontology) has been constructed based on the obtained object (terms) descriptions (Figure 5).

Under mining semantic relations from texts, syntactic dependencies, in particular, between verb and its arguments are used rather frequently as a special kind of features. This idea is developed in (Gamallo et al 2002; Buitelaar et al, 2004; Kavalec and Svatek, 2005; Ciaramita et al, 2005; Schutz and Buitelaar, 2005). It is very important to find an adequate level of generalizing verbal arguments with respect to a given conceptual hierarchy. Much attention is devoted to this problem in computer linguistics in the context of so called selective restrictions (Melamed, &Resnik, 200; Clark and Weir, 2002). Another problem consists in extracting verbs having one and the same ontological content. It requires semantic clustering of verbs (Schulte & Walde, 2000).

Latent semantic analysis (LSA) (Landauer et al., 1998) is based on the statistical estimation of the similarity of words with respect to their meaning. Words are similar by their meaning if they are used in familiar contexts. Context becomes a feature of words. Semantic similarity of contexts is also estimated

Table 1. Knowledge about the services of tourist agency

	To book (bookable)	To rent (rentable)	To drive (driveable)	To ride (rideable)	To join (joinable)
Hotel	x				
Apartment	x	x			
Car	x	x	x		
Bike	x	x	x	x	
Excursion	x				x
Trip	x				x

Figure 5. Ontology of tourist agency services

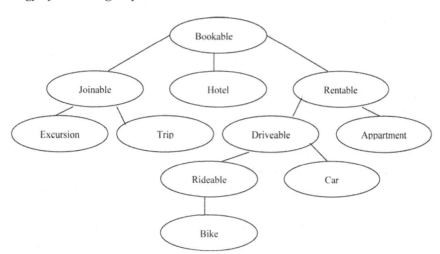

in LSA. In the system iSTART (McNamara et al., 2004), for example, the semantic similarity between sentences from different texts and between any fragments of texts are also calculated with the use of LSA.

Mining semantic relations between words is usually performed based on discovering some patterns (templates) of the type: «P1 interacts with P2», «P1 is activated via P2». The features can be: 1) sets of words – Σ_1, 2) set of tags (labels identifying parts of speech) - Σ_2, words located before P1 and P2 – Σ_3 and so on. Then each position of sentence is associated with a vector of features from the set $\Sigma = \Sigma_1 \times \Sigma_2 \times \ldots \times \Sigma_k$, where $\times$ means the direct product of sets.

Theoretically, any definable relation can serve as a feature. Thus extracted patterns can characterize texts, and the pattern themselves can be reduced to some specific idiomatic, syntactic or semantic relationships. Table 2 presents the patterns of semantic relationships extracted during the automatic annotation of English texts with the use of Web (Maedche et al., 2002).

These relations are considered as ontology, because of proper names are associated with classes and concepts (Cimiano et al., 2004; Hearst, 1992; Hahn and Schnattinger, 1998; Maedche, & Staab, 2003).

Table 2. Examples of the patterns under annotating texts with the use of WEB

Pattern	Example of pattern
<CONCEPT>s such as <INSTANCE>	Hotels such as Ritz
Such <CONCEPT>s as <INSTANCE>	Such hotels as Hilton
<INSTANCE> (and |or) other<CONCEPT>	The Eiffel Tower and other sights in Paris
<CONCEPT>s, (especially | including) <INSTANCE>	Presidents, especially George Washington
The <INSTANCE> <CONCEPT>	The Hilton hotel
The <CONCEPT> <INSTANCE>	The hotel Hilton
<INSTANCE>, a <CONCEPT>	Excelsior, a hotel in the center of Nancy
<INSTANCE> is a <CONCEPT>	The Excelsior is a hotel in the center of Nancy

The machine learning methods (both supervised and unsupervised) are partitioned into statistical and logical ones (symbolic classification methods) depending on the nature of object features and the kind of decision rules or functions with the use of which a given classification is approximated. The formers deal with objects with numerical descriptions, the latter ones deal with object described by the use of symbolic attributes.

One of the founders of **statistical learning** theory is Vladimir N. Vapnik. The second edition of his book (Vapnik, 2000) is completely devoted to the theoretical problems of practically all substantive statistical learning methods.

This book acquaints the readers with the fundamental ideas which lie behind the statistical theory of learning and generalization. The author considers learning as a general problem of function estimation based on empirical data. He generalizes the main results of statistical learning theory covering:

- The setting of the learning problems including the Function Estimation Model, the Empirical Risk Minimization (ERM) Inductive Principle, Regression Estimation, Density Estimation (Fisher-Wald setting), Maximum Likelihood Method, and Discrimination Analysis in pattern recognition;
- The investigation of nonparametric methods in statistics and their application for the learning problems;
- The Principle for solving problems using a restricted amount of information;
- Stochastic approximation inference.

The book covers the mathematical theory of induction in the framework of which the author considers such the methods as the Minimum Description Length (MDL) principle, neural networks, and the Bayesian approach in learning theory.

The problem of constructing optimal separating hyper plane is also discussed in the book. This problem is connected with the development of Support Vector Machines techniques.

The second edition of the book contains some new chapters devoted to the theory of direct method of learning based on solving multidimensional integral equations for density, conditional probability, and conditional density estimation.

The Bayes's method determines the probability of appearing an event from a given class of events under the condition when only partial information about the events is available. The interested reader can address to (Mitchell, 1997), (Witten and Frank 1999), and (Perez et al., 2009).

Bayesian networks are the most known representation of statistical learning algorithms. A comprehensive book on Bayesian network is by Jensen (1996). Cestnik (1987, 1990) was the first who used the Naïve Bayes classifier in machine learning. Cheng et al. (2001, 2002) have proposed an information-theory based approach to learning Bayesian networks from data.

The Method of Support Vector Machine (Cristianini, & Shawe-Taylor, 2000), (Lovell & Walder, 2005) relates to the linear discrimination methods. Each vector of features (object) is represented by point in the multidimensional space. Giving a classification of objects, two parallel hyper planes (boundaries) are constructed. The objects are divided into groups in such a way that the distance between these hyper planes is maximized. The examples, located along the hyper planes, are called supporting vectors. Values of features are real numbers. An excellent survey of SVMs techniques can be found in (Burges,1998).

The probabilistic models of learning include the hidden Markov model (hidden Markov chains) (Rabiner, 1989). This is the statistical model, which imitates a certain sequential process, in which the latent states have effects on the observed variables. Passage from one state to another occurs with some probability. Investigating the sequence of observations, it is possible to obtain information about the sequence of the states. The description of this method and its application for the recognition of phonemes can be found in (Zagorujko, 1999). One way or another, the probabilistic methods of learning realize the diverse variants of probabilistic reasoning.

The logical or symbolic methods of machine learning encompass both supervised and unsupervised learning. The supervised symbolic learning covers mining logical rules and dependencies from data: "if-then" rules, decision trees (Quinlan, 1986, 1993), functional and association dependencies. The supervised symbolic learning also includes learning concept from data, constructing rough sets, constructing hierarchical classification of objects (Basili et al., P. 1993), mining ontology from data (Cimiano, 2006; Maedche et al., 2002), generating hypotheses, and some others. The unsupervised symbolic learning covers conceptual clustering.

The symbolic methods of machine learning work on objects with symbolic, Boolean, integer, and categorical attributes. With this point of view, these methods can be considered as the methods of mining conceptual knowledge or the methods of conceptual learning.

Conceptual learning is a special class of methods based on mining and using conceptual knowledge the elements of which are objects, attributes (values of attributes), classifications (partitions of objects into classes), and links between them. These links are expressed by the use of implications: "object ↔ class", "object ↔ property", "values of attributes ↔ class", and "subclass ↔ class".

Statistical clustering deals with datasets described by continuous features. Hence, this method is difficult to apply to tasks involving symbolic features. In addition, this method does not help the user in interpreting results of clustering. In contrast to statistical clustering, conceptual clustering is oriented to symbolic data representation. Talevera, & Béjar (2001) have proposed a method of conceptual clustering with probabilistic concepts. Their method associates a probability or weight with each property of the concept definition. The model obtained of hierarchical clustering allows users to specify both the number of levels and the degree of generality of each level.

Formal Conceptual Analysis (FCA) (Ganter & Wille, 1999) is sometimes referred to as conceptual clustering. An example of the FCA application for modeling lexical data base is given in (Priss and Old, 2004).

Incremental clustering allows enhancing crucially inference ability of constructing clusters. The article of Douglas (1987) presents COBWEB, a conceptual incremental clustering system.

Fanizzi et al. (2008) present a method based on clustering techniques to detect concept drift or novelty in a knowledge based expressed in Description Logics. The method uses an effective and language-independent semi-distance measure defined for the space of individuals (object to be clustered). This measure is based on a finite number of dimensions corresponding to a set of discriminating features (represented by concept descriptions). A maximally discriminating group of features can be obtained with the randomized optimization methods described in the paper.

The most interesting idea advanced in this paper is about integrating conceptual clustering, as an unsupervised learning, with supervised learning. With a supervised learning phase, each cluster can be assigned with a refined or newly constructed intensional definition expressed in the adopted language. A method for exploiting the clustering results for concept drift and novelty detection is also proposed in this paper.

In our book, we concentrate on the supervised conceptual learning methods. Our approach to machine learning problems is based on the concept of a good diagnostic (classification) test. We have chosen the lattice theory as a model for inferring good diagnostic tests from examples from the very beginning of our work in this direction. This concept has been advanced firstly in the framework of inferring functional and implicative dependencies from relations (Naidenova & Polegaeva, 1986). But later the fact has been revealed that the task of inferring all good diagnostic tests for a given set of positive and negative examples can be formulated as the search for the best approximation of a given classification on a given set of examples and that it is this task that some well known machine learning problems can be reduced to (Naidenova, 1996): finding keys and functional dependencies in data base relations, finding association rules, finding implicative dependencies, inferring logical rules (if-then rules, rough sets, "ripple down" rules), decision tree construction, learning by discovering concept hierarchies, eliminating irrelevant features from the set of exhaustively generated features.

In this book, we would like to demonstrate the possibility of transforming a large class of supervised machine learning algorithms for inferring good classification tests into the commonsense reasoning processes based on using well-known logical reasoning rules.

All enumerated problems similar in using the inclusion relation on the set of all subsets of a set of given objects and are solved with the use of one and the same data and knowledge structure and by the use of one and the same class of machine learning algorithms (Naidenova et al., 1995; Naidenova, 2006).

Figure 6 illustrates that required configuration of a learning algorithm can be generated by giving the parameters determining representation form, the number and some properties of the outcome and some properties of inference mechanism.

Figure 6. Tuning the configuration of learning methods

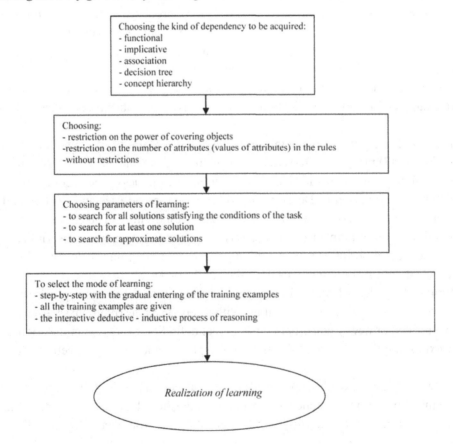

The Works of R. S. Michalski on Machine Learning

R. Michalski is one of the founders of the theory of symbolic classification methods in machine learning. His works on machine learning did not lose value up to now, since the processes of natural human inductive and classification reasoning are investigated and simulated in them. As an example can serve the conceptual clustering procedure implemented into a lot of algorithms and well known programs. An idea of conceptual clustering has been advanced in (Michalski, 1980), (Michalski & Stepp, 1981; 1983), (Stepp & Michalski, 1985), and (Rendell, 1983). The language for cluster descriptions is the APC – Annotated Predicate Calculus, a typical predicate calculus with additional operators. Concept descriptions of higher levels are inferred from concepts descriptions of lower levels. The process of relevant object descriptions is controlled by the Goal Dependency Network advanced by Michalski and his assistants.

The algorithm of conceptual clustering lies in the foundations of many algorithms, namely, the Cluster3 – the system for goal-oriented conceptual clustering (Michalski, et al., 2006), (Seeman, & Michalski, 2006), the Natural Induction System AQ21 (Wojtusiak et al., 2006), (Wojtisuak, 2005), and many other algorithms for inferring decision tree and implicative rules from examples.

The Machine Learning and Inference Laboratory at George Mason University conducts fundamental and experimental research on the development of intelligent systems. The systems are experimentally applied to a wide spectrum of practical problems. Their application areas include engineering design and optimization, medicine, bioinformatics, earth sciences, sociology, biochemistry, communication networks, geographic information systems, world economy, computer vision, education and software engineering. The following descriptions of the scientific programs of Machine Learning and Inference Laboratory at George Mason University have been drawn from the Internet site of this laboratory.

Intelligent Agents with Learning Capabilities (Michalski, & Watanabe, 1988), (Ko, & Michalski, 1988).

This project is concerned with the development of a PC-based expert system shell with learning capabilities. The system incorporates a knowledge base for storing rules and data base for storing facts and examples. It has a learning program for rule acquisition with a powerful inference mechanism. The project is based on the experience with ADVISE and AURORA systems. ADVISE is a large-scale inference system with rule learning capabilities and multiple control mechanisms. The system served as a tool for experimenting with methods of knowledge discovery, multiple knowledge representation and machine learning. AURORA is a PC-based inference system, and an expert system shell that incorporates a program for incremental rule learning.

Cognitive Models of Plausible Reasoning

Plausible reasoning is one of the modes of human natural reasoning. In plausible reasoning, the premises may be incomplete, uncertain, imprecise or only partially relevant to the task. But people can make useful conclusions from such premises. The initial core theory of plausible reasoning was developed by Collins and Michalski (1989). The goal of this project is to develop a computational theory and models of plausible reasoning.

Inferential Theory of Learning (ITL)

This project aimed at the development of "the theory of learning that considers learning as a goal-oriented process of improving the learner's knowledge "by basing on the learner's experience". This theory is intended to understanding the competence aspects of learning processes, in contrast to their computational aspects. ITL raises such questions as what types of inference and knowledge transformations underlie learning processes and strategies; what types of knowledge the learner is able to learn from a given input and a prior knowledge; what logical relationships exist among the learned knowledge, possible inputs and prior knowledge, and so on.

The theory analyzes the following high level inference processes: generalization, abstraction, generation, insertion, and replication. Then the following formula has been advance in the framework of ITL: "Learning = "Inferencing" + Memorizing" (Michalski, 1993), (Michalski, 1994).

The ITL postulates that a complete learning theory has to encompass all major type of inference: conclusive deduction, contingent deduction, analogical inference, conclusive induction, and abduction.

The proposed classification of inferences divides them into deductive and inductive ones, and into conclusive (strong) and contingent (weak) ones. Conclusive inference involves domain-independent inference rules, while contingent inference involves domain-dependent inference rules. Contingent deduction produces plausible consequences of given causes, and contingent induction produces plausible causes of given consequences. Analogy can be considered as induction and deduction combined. Using this approach, several basic reasoning operations have been analyzed and clarified: inductive and deductive generalization, inductive and deductive specialization, and abstraction. The ITL and its application for creating database models are described in (Michalski, 2003).

Multi-Strategy Task-Adaptive Learning (MTL) based on ITL

A methodology for multi-strategy learning based on the ITL has been advanced in (Alkharouf, & Michalski, 1996). This methodology integrates two basic learning paradigms: empirical learning and analytical learning. Empirical learning is based on inductive inference from facts, while analytical learning is based on deductive inference from prior knowledge. It includes also constructive induction, analogical learning, and abstraction. Constructive induction generates problem-relevant concepts and via them derives the most plausible inductive hypotheses. Analogical learning transfers knowledge from one problem domain to another by the use of similarity between concepts or problem solving methods. Abstraction transfers a description from high-detail level to a low detail but more goal-oriented level. The goal of learning is viewed as a central factor in controlling learning processes. This research provides the foundation for such tasks as knowledge discovery, planning, problem solving, intelligent robot construction and many others. Some works devoted to this methodology have appeared recently (Kaufman et al., 2007).

Learning Problem-Oriented Decision Structures from Decision Rules

This project is concerned with learning problem-optimized decision trees from rules. It has been inspired by the observation of a disadvantage of the standard approach to learning decision trees from examples. This disadvantage is that once a decision tree is learned, it is difficult to modify it to fit different decision making situations. Such problems arise, for example, when an attribute assigned to some node can not be measured, or there is a significant change in the costs of measuring attributes or in the frequency distribution of events from different decision classes.

Imam and Michalski (1993) have advanced to generate new knowledge from already inferred and memorized decision rules. An advantage of such an approach is that it facilitates building compact and simple decision trees, which can be much simpler than the logically equivalent conventional decision trees. A compact tree is the decision tree that may contain branches assigned to a set of values, and nodes assigned to attributes that are logical or mathematical functions of the original ones. The project describes an efficient methods, AQDT-1, that takes decision rules generated by an AQ-type learning system (AQ15-AQ17), and builds from them a decision tree optimizing a given criterion (Michalski, & Imam, 1997).

The preliminary experiments with AQDT-1 have shown that the decision trees generated by it from decision rules (conventional and compact) have outperformed those generated from examples by the well-known C4.5 program both in terms of their simplicity and their predictive accuracy. Some recent investigation of constructing decision trees from a set of logical rules can be found in (Pietrzykowski, & Wojtusiak, 2008), (Michalski, & Pietrzykowski, 2007), and (Michalski, & Wojtusiak, 2007).

Data-Driven Constructive Induction: AQ17-DCI (Bloedom, & Michalski, 1996).

In this project, a method has been developed for automatically answering the questions about the best representation language (in a class of languages describing objects and knowledge in terms of attributes values) for a given learning task. The data-driven approach can perform both the expansions of representation space through attribute construction, and the reductions of it through attribute removal and abstraction. The approach is interactive and a certain form of constraints provided by the expert is used (Wojtusiak, 2008).

Environments for Natural Induction: STAR-AQ19/A20

This project deals with the developing of an integrated program system conducting experiments and applications in the areas of machine learning and data mining (Michalki, & Kaufman, 1998; 1999; 2001).

The JSM Method of Hypotheses' Generation

In terms of synthesizing plausible reasoning, the JSM-method of automated hypothesis generation seems to be the most interesting (Zabezjailo et al., 1987), (Finn, 1984), (Finn, 1991), (Finn, 1988), and (Finn, 1999). Theoretically, this method synthesizes several cognitive procedures: empirical induction based on simulating the John Stuart Mill's joint rule of agreement and difference, with initials forming the name of the method (Mill, 1872), causal analogy and abduction Charles S. Peirce (1995).

Similarity in the JSM-method is both a relation and an operation, that is idempotent, commutative and associative (i.e. it induces a semi-lattice on objects' descriptions and their generalizations). Being described in algebraic terms, the JSM-method can be implemented in the procedural programming languages.

Inductive generalizations in the JSM method are performed via inferences of logical formula with generality quantifier from the set of examples that can be represented in terms of some extension of multivalued logic of first-order predicates (Anchakov et al., 1987). Rules of plausible inference are stated in terms of the same language while procedures of inductive inference are given as those that calculate the range of truth of the corresponding predicates.

The way of implementing the JSM method is described in (Vinogradov, 1999), (Galitsky at al., 2005), and (Anchakov et al., 1989). In (Galitsky et al., 2005), the system JASMINE based on the JSM-method is presented. The system extends this methodology by implementing (i) a combination of abductive, inductive and analogical reasoning for hypotheses generation, and (ii) multivalued logic-based deductive reasoning for verification of their consistency. Formally, all the above components can be represented as deductive inference via logic programming (Anshakov et al., 1989), (Finn, 1999). In fact, JASMINE is based on the logic programming implementation (Vinogradov, 1999).

The Formal Concept Analysis (FCA)

The Formal Concept Analysis (FCA) has been advanced by Wille, R. (1992).

By using terminology and notation from (Ganter & Wille, 1999), the formal context K is a triple (G, M, I), where G is a set of objects, M is a set of attributes, and $I \subseteq G \times M$ is an incidence relation. Given a subset of object $O \subseteq G$ and a subset of attribute $A \subseteq M$, two mappings are defined as follows:

$$O^I = \{m \in M: g \, I \, m \text{ for all } g \in O\},$$

$$A^I = \{g \in G: g \, I \, m \text{ for all } m \in A\}.$$

For singleton sets, the following abbreviations are used $g^I = \{g\}^I = I(\{g\}) =$ and $m^I = \{m\}^I = I(\{m\})$.

The *formal concept* is a pair (O, A) of (G, I, I) if and only if $O^I = A$ and $A^I = O$. In other words, (O, A) is a formal concept if the set of all attributes shared by the objects of O is identical with A, and, simultaneously, O is also the set of all objects that have all attributes of A. O is then called the **extend** and A the **intent** of the formal concept K = (O, A).

The ordering of formal concepts is defined as follows:

$$(O_1, A_1) \leq (O_2, A_2) \Leftrightarrow O_1 \subseteq O_2 \; (\Leftrightarrow A_2 \subseteq A_1).$$

Thus formal concepts are partially ordered with regard to inclusion relation of their extents or – which is equivalent – to inverse inclusion of their intents. It is shown (Ganter, & Wille, 1999) that the order relation on formal concepts forms a complete lattice (concept lattice and Galois's lattice are synonyms) which is denoted by $(B(G, M, I), \leq)$.

Table 3 shows an example of formal context, where "x" means that the connection exists between corresponding object and attribute. The following formal concepts can be constructed for the context presented in Table 3:

C1 = ({1,2,3,4,6}, {g, l}),
C2 = ({1,2,3,6}, {e, g, k, l}),
C3 = ({1,2,4}, {d, g, j, l}),
C4 = ({1,2}, {b, d, e, g, h, j, k, l}),
C5 = ({1,3}, {c, e, g, i, k, l}).

Table 3. An example of a small context

	a	b	c	d	e	f	g	h	i	j	k	L
1	x	x	x	x	x	x	x	x	x	x	x	x
2		x		x	x		x	x		x	x	x
3			x		x				x		x	x
4				x			x			x		
6					x		x				x	x

The diagram or the concept structure ordered by ≤ relation is shown in Figure 7.

The FCA is a method mainly used for the analysis of data and knowledge representation. In particular, FCA finds closed sets on the basis of a formal context, thus leading to obtaining coherent groups or formal concepts with the structure of their ordering. The FCA can be seen as a conceptual clustering method. It is extensively used for learning ontology from texts, namely, for forming concepts and their hierarchical organizations (Cimiano, 2006), (Kalfoglou, & Schorlemmer, 2005), and (Ferre et al., 2005).

A survey of FCA applications in linguistics is given in (Priss, 2000a; 2000b; 2005). These applications involve the identification of features such as phonemes, syntactical or grammatical markers. Modeling and storage of lexical information is very important for natural language processing. Priss and Old (2007) use the FCA to model and construct lexical databases from corps of texts in a semi-automated manner.

The problems of the FCA have been extensively studied by Stumme (2002), Dowling (1993), and Salzberg (1991). Building concept lattices are considered in (Nourine & Raynaud, 1999), (Ganter, 1984), (Kuznetsov, 1993), (Stumme et al., 2000), and (Kuznetsov & Obiedkov, 2001). Kuznetsov, S. (2007) investigates the stability of formal concepts. He introduces a stability index of concept in the foundation of which an idea lies that dependency in a data set can be reconstructed from different parts of this set. Combinatorial properties of the advanced stability index are also analyzed with estimating algorithmic complexity of its computation as well as its dynamics with arrival of new examples. The books (Kuznetsov, & Schmidt, 2007), (Madina, & Obiedkov, 2008), and (Ferré, & Rudolph, 2009) comprise state of the art research and present new results in FCA and related fields. These results encompass both the theoretical novelties with respect to algorithmic issues and application domains of FCA including data visualization, information retrieval, machine learning, data analysis and knowledge engineering.

Figure 7. The structure of formal concepts C1, C2, C3, C4, C5

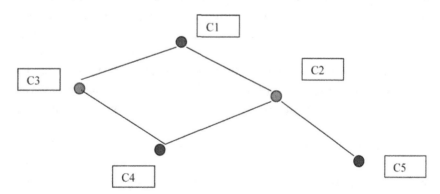

On-Line Analytical Mining of Data Warehouse

Great efforts have been paid to constructing on-line analytical data mining systems. These efforts have been focused on the integration of data mining methods and on-line analytical processing (OLAP) techniques (Han, 1998). OLAP conducts its beginning from the system DBMiner. DBMiner has been developed for interactive mining of multiple-level knowledge in large relational databases and data warehouses. It also covers the knowledge discovery in different kinds of databases (Lu et al., 1993), (Han et al., 1994b), including object-oriented (Han et al., 1998), deductive, spatial, and active databases, global information systems, and the application of knowledge discovery for intelligent query answering (Han et al., 1996), multiple-layered database construction (Han et al., 1994a), etc.

Combining OLAP and data mining generates OLAM technology, a powerful tool for multiple functional, on-line analytical processing and analytical mining in large databases and data warehouses. The OLAM systems implement a lot of data mining functions including characterization, comparison, association, classification, prediction, and clustering. They also build up a user-friendly interactive data mining environment and a set of knowledge visualization tools. Mining can be performed interactively, i.e. by mouse clicking and with quick response. Data mining techniques has been extended to spatial data mining, multimedia data mining, text mining, and Web mining. As the examples of OLAP systems, we can point the systems GeoMiner, MultiMediumMiner, and WeblogMiner (Zaiane et al., 1998).

The most essential part of OLAM is the Data Cube Technology connecting the data bases and the user. Effective data mining needs flexible traversing through a database, selecting any portions of relevant data, analyzing data at different granularities, and presenting knowledge in different forms. Data Cube construction provides facilities for data mining on different subsets of data and at different levels of abstraction, by drilling, pivoting, filtering, dicing, and slicing on a data cube and on some intermediate data mining results. This, together with data/knowledge visualization tools, enhances greatly the power and flexibility of data mining task exploration.

The methods of efficient data cube computation have been developed by integration of MOLAP (where views are represented as multi-dimensional arrays) and ROLAP (where views are represented as relational tables) data representation techniques (Gray et al., 1997), (Yu, & Lu, 2001). The pre-computation of the different views (group-bys) of data cube is important for improving the response time of OLAP queries. For a given raw data set R with n records and d attributes (dimensions), a view is constructed by an aggregation of R along a subset of attributes. This results in 2^d different possible views. The set of all possible views ordered by inclusion relation is the lattice; hence the data cube methods are realized by the use of lattice construction algorithms.

The pre-computation of the entire data cube allows for fast execution of subsequent OLAP queries. Many methods have been proposed for generating the data cube on sequential and parallel systems a survey of which can be found in (Chen et al., 2004). The parallel solution for generating data cubes is increasingly important. The parallel approach is grouped into two classes: work partitioning and data partitioning. In (Chen et al., 2004), the data partitioning methods for ROLAP are studied. In this case, the raw data set is given as a d-dimensional relation (table of d-tuples) and all views are to be created as relational tables as well. The advantage of this method is that it allows for tight integration with relational database technology.

Integrating Boolean predicates with ranked queries was recently studied by Zhang et al. (2006). In this work, searches for the results are achieved by merging multiple indices. In this work, the Boolean predicates are treated as a part of the ranking function. An improved version of index merging was studied by Xin et al. (2007), where the authors proposed progressive and selective merging strategy.

Li et al. (2008) has proposed a *Sampling Cube* framework, which efficiently calculates confidence intervals for any multidimensional query and uses the OLAP structure to group similar segments to increase sampling size when needed. Also a *Sampling Cube Shell* method is proposed to handle high dimensional data, to effectively reduce the storage requirement while still preserving query result quality.

Supporting ranking queries in database systems has been a popular research topic recently. However there is a lack of study on supporting ranking queries in data warehouses where ranking is based on multidimensional aggregates instead of on measures of base facts. To address this problem, Tianyi Wu et al. (2008) propose a query execution model to answer different types of ranking to aggregate queries based on a unified, partial cube structure, ARCube.

In the paper (Lin et al., 2008), a novel cube model is proposed, which called *text cube* with OLAP operations in *dimension hierarchy* and *term hierarchy* to analyze multi-dimensional text data. It supports two important measures, term frequency vector TF and inverted index IV. Algorithms are designed to process OLAP queries with the optimal processing cost, and to partially materialize the text cube provided that the optimal processing cost of any query is bounded. Experimental results on a real dataset show the efficiency and effectiveness of this text cube model.

Some kinds of OLAP subsystems are described in (Han, 2008) for spatial OLAP, in (Lo et al., 2008) for OLAP on sequence data, and in (Tian et al., 2008) for aggregation of graphs.

LOGIC-BASED REASONING

Inductive Logic Programming (ILP)

The results of modeling deductive reasoning in artificial intelligence have been implemented firstly in creating Deductive Data Based Systems based on the Logical Programming (Das, 1992). The logical programming language Datalog has been developed and described in detail in (Ceri, et al., 1990). It is a function-free Horn-clausal language with well-understood model and proof-theories. The deductive database is defined to be a set of Datalog clauses partitioned into intensional part (intensional database) denoted by IDB, and extensional part (extensional database) denoted by EDB. The IDB consists of rules in which every variable occurring in the head occurs in at least one literal in the body. EDB consists of ground facts. In deductive databases, the predicate symbols occurring in the head of clauses in IDB are not allowed to occur in the head of clauses in EDB. Queries can only involve predicate symbols in IDB.

The query evaluation process over deductive databases has been extensively studied in both a bottom-up and a top-down direction (Das, 1992), (Minker, 1996). A query evaluation algorithm over deductive databases is realized as deductive inference.

Knowledge engineering has concentrated on the problems of knowledge representation. Inference on knowledge has been considered as procedural knowledge. Data Management Systems and Knowledge Management Systems have been constructed with the use of different theoretical considerations and different programming tools. The necessity to induce knowledge from data has given birth to Inductive Logic Programming (Muggleton and Raedt, 1994).

ILP is a discipline that investigates the inductive construction of first-order clausal theories from examples and background knowledge. ILP has the same goal as machine learning, namely, to develop tools and techniques to induce hypotheses from examples and to obtain new knowledge from experience. But the traditional theoretical basis of ILP is in the framework of first-order predicate calculus. Inductive inference in ILP is based on inverting deductive inference rules; for example, inverting resolution (rules of absorption, identification, intraconstruction, and interconstruction), inverting implication (inductive inference under θ-subsumption).

Integration Deductive and Inductive Reasoning

The development of a full on-line computer model for integrating deductive and inductive reasoning is one of vital tasks in computer sciences. The main tendency of integration is to combine into a whole system some already well-known models of learning (inductive reasoning) and deductive reasoning. For instance, the idea of combining inductive learning from examples with prior knowledge and default reasoning has been advanced in (Giraud-Carrier & Martinez, 1994). Obviously, this way leads to a lot of difficulties in knowledge representation because deductive reasoning tasks are often expressed in the classical first-order logic language but machine learning tasks use a variant of symbolic-valued attribute language.

There is a distinction between concept learning and program synthesis. Concept learning and classification problems, in general, are inherently object-oriented. It is difficult to interpret concepts as subsets of domain examples in the frameworks of ILP. One of the ways to overcome this difficulty has been realized in a transformation approach: an ILP task is transformed into an equivalent learning task in different representation formalism. This approach is implemented in LINUS (Lavraĉ & Džeroski, 1994), (Lavraĉ et al, 1999) which is an ILP learner inducing hypotheses in the form of constrained deductive hierarchical database (DHDB) clauses. The main idea of LINUS is to transform the problem of learning relational DHDB descriptions into the attribute-value learning task. This is achieved by the so-called DHDB interface. The interface transforms the training examples from the DHDB form into the form of attribute-value tuples. Some well known attribute-value learners can then be used to induce "if-then" rules. Finally, the induced rules are transformed back into the form of DHDB clauses. The LINUS uses already known algorithms, for example, the decision tree induction system ASSISTANT, and two rule induction systems: an ancestor of AQ15, named NEWGEM, and CN2.

A simple form of predicate invention through first-order feature construction is proposed by Lavraĉ and Flash (2000). The constructed features are used then for propositional learning.

Another way for combining ILP with an attribute-value learner has been developed in (Lisi & Malerba, 2004). In this work, a novel ILP setting is proposed. This setting adopts AL-log as a knowledge representation language. It allows a unified treatment of both the relational and structural features of data. This setting has been implemented in SPADA, an ILP system developed for mining multi-level association rules in spatial databases and applied to geographic data mining.

AL-log is a hybrid knowledge representation system that integrates the description logic ALC (Schmidt-Schauss & Smolka, 1991) and the deductive database language DATALOG (Ceri et al, 1990). Therefore it embodies two subsystems, called structural and relational, respectively.

The description logic ALC allows for the specification of structural knowledge in terms of concepts, roles, and individuals. Individuals represent objects in the domain of interest. Concepts represent classes of these objects, while roles represent binary relations between concepts. Complex concepts can be defined from primitive concepts and roles by applying constructors such as ∩ (conjunction), ∪ (disjunction), and ¬ (negation).

ALC knowledge bases have an intensional part and an extensional part. In the intensional part, relation between concepts are syntactically expressed as inclusion statements of the form $C \subseteq D$ where C

Figure 8. The role of machine learning in data-knowledge transformation

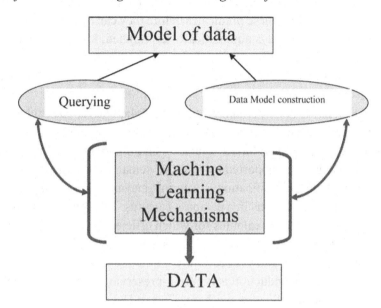

and D are two arbitrary concepts. As for the extensional part, it is possible to specify instances of relations between individuals and concepts. Relations are expressed as membership assertions or concept assertions of the form *a*: C ("*a* belongs to C").

A logic based approach to integrating knowledge discovery and deductive query answering has been proposed by Marcelo A. T. Aragão and Alvaro A. A. Fernandes (2002). Their idea is excellent: to combine management and exploitation of data and knowledge stocks. The role of machine learning in combining data and knowledge is shown in Figure 8. It means that query answering will be performed with the use of on-line inductive processes over data in the framework of the uniformity of data-knowledge representation. This paper presents one of the inductive-deductive database models (IDDBs models).

The representation language of this model is DATALOG in which the set of deducible and inducible predicate symbols are considered. A query evaluation algorithm over deductive database is assumed and referred to as **deduce**. An expression such as A:: = **deduce**(Q, (IDB, EDB)) assigns to A the answer to a query Q over a deductive database IDB $\cup$ EDB, where IDB and EDB are the intensional and extensional parts of database, respectively.

The inductive inference is based on ILP. Thus, given a set B of clauses, taken to be background knowledge, and sets E+, E- of positive and negative examples, respectively, the goal of inductive inference is to find a set H of clauses (the hypothesis), such that all elements in E+ would be true in $LHM^{B \cup H}$ and all elements in E- would be false in $LHM^{B \cup H}$, where LHM is Least Herbrand Model (Muggleton, & Raedt, 1994).

A concept learning algorithm is referred to as **induce**. Any learning algorithm described in the literature, for example, (Lavrac, and Dzeroski, 1994), (Muggleton, 1995) may be applied for **induce**. An expression such as H:: = **induce**(L, (B, E+, E-)) assigns to H a hypothesis conforming to the language bias L that, given background knowledge B, covers all positive examples in E+ and none of the negative ones in E-.

If clauses in the intensional database are allowed to refer in their bodies to predicates that need to be learned, then it is necessary to induce these predicates before they can be used in answering a query. The results of inductive inference are always automatically assimilated, i. e. the target concept is replaced in expressions by the new definition of it.

A prototype of IDDB has been implemented in Prolog and the analysis of this database is given in (Fernandes, 2000).

Marcelo A. T. Aragão, Alvaro A.A. Fernandes, (2003; 2004a, 2004b, 2004c) have developed a new model of Combined Inference Databases (CID). The paper of Alvaro, & Fernandes (2004a) has described a concrete proposal for a class of logic-based databases that integrate querying data and discovering knowledge (CIDs). This database is supported by a unified semantics of both deductive (query answering) and inductive tasks including classification, clustering, and association rules inference. The results of inductive inference are the expressions in a database calculus. The calculus builds upon Fegaras and Maier's (2000) monoid comprehension calculus for which efficient physical algebras exist.

The logic language used in CID is p-Datalog (Lakshmanan, & Shiri-Varnaamkhaasti, 2001). P-Datalog extends classical Datalog by allowing certainty annotations that are asserted of (and derived for) clauses. This is essential insofar as induction is not truth-preserving; therefore inductive consequences have to be annotated with some justification measure. Thus, p-Datalog is a language for reasoning with uncertainty.

A p-Datalog clause is the Datalog clause annotated with a validity assessment C and with a triple of validity constructors $f^\wedge$; f^-; $f^\vee$ (called the conjunctive, propagator and disjunctive constructors, respectively). The validity assessment can be interpreted as the degree of certainty associated with the clause (Lakshmanan, & Shiri-Varnaamkhaasti, 2001)). The validity constructors determine, respectively, a) how the validity of the literals in the body are to be combined, b) how the validity of the body is assigned to the clause as a whole, and c) how the different validities associated with the different clauses that share the same predicate name are to be combined into a single validity assessment. A p-Datalog program is a set of p-Datalog clauses.

In (Aragão, & Fernandes, 2004b), an overview of CIDs is given, and two applications are considered. In this paper, it is shown that CIDs meets some challenging application needs in contrast with other attempts at integrating knowledge discovery and databases technology. The paper (Aragão, & Fernandes, 2004c), the work of CID is investigated in the context of a case study where the specific characteristics of this system turned out to be greatly relevant and nontrivial.

The other proposals of combining inductive and deductive inference cover different special applications. In the paper (Greco et al., 2001), the combined use of inductive and deductive techniques to improve the data analysis process is proposed. This approach uses several inductive techniques such as clustering, decision trees induction, classification, and features selection. All techniques are supported by a lot of visualization tools helping to manipulate data sets easily.

David Vaz and Michel Ferreira (2007) describe the extension of the Yap Prolog compiler, a free, open-source logic programming system, in order to handle spatial data, providing a state-of-the-art solution for modeling, querying and mining data. A proposal of extending Datalog to Spatial Datalog has been advanced in the framework of Constraint Databases. Spatial-Yap system (Vaz et al., 2007) can build spatial logic terms from vector data in spatial relations. Spatial Datalog provides a highly declarative programming environment. For instance, the natural specification of recursions, which are very important for topological relationships, is realized by means of this language.

The deductive-inductive databases and the possibilities of their application are currently very interesting for domain specialists and the development of these databases are enriched by a lot of works related to modeling special modes of reasoning in different problem domains. In (Foneska et al., 2006) is presented a new system of Inductive Logic Programming. Michel Ferreira et al. (2006) investigate efficient and scalable Induction of Logic Programs using a Deductive Database System. An efficient Support for Incomplete and Complete Tables in the YapTab Tabling System is considered by Rocha (2006). A new relation storage model DBTAB for YapTab Tabling System is presented in (Costa et al., 2006). Parallelism in Deductive and Inductive Database Systems is investigated theoretically in (Fonseca, 2006) and an implementation of using database in parallel is presented by Soares (2006).

Default Reasoning

Natural human reasoning in every day life is differed from logical demonstrative conclusions. Demonstrative reasoning is, of course, inherent in people, but it serves in order to conclude from the premises, which are absolutely clear and assumed to be true during the process of reasoning. However, the initial positions, on which rest demonstrative reasoning, are discovered out of any system of demonstrative reasoning. Moreover, in the real world, the initial positions of any reasoning can change in the course of time, since the world, which surrounds people, is developed. Initial positions are rejected or refined, depending on circumstances and purposes of reasoning. With the aid of natural reasoning we actually acquire knowledge about the world, we control continuously the truthfulness and reliability of knowledge, and we consider possible changes in the future. Some fundamental characteristics of natural reasoning are the following ones:

a)   The openness with respect to new facts or factors that change the context of reasoning (hypothesis of the closed constant world is not accurate);
b)   A system of structured knowledge reflecting the environment is built gradually;
c)   Knowledge is very easy to use, i.e. a unique access to the depository of knowledge and facts is realized;
d)   Knowledge changes dynamically in the course of time;
e)   Any contradiction (disagreement) of real facts with knowledge leads to refining knowledge, but not to the failure of reasoning;
f)   The incompleteness and inaccuracy initial premises and/or drawn conclusions are always evaluated and taken into consideration;
g)   The time factor is always present in the natural reasoning and what is more it makes it possible to predict future events.

It is natural that the inference, based on the logical programming, does not satisfy the enumerated requirements and it can not to be considered as a model of plausible or natural reasoning. Non-monotonic logics have been devised in order to create a model of reasoning capturing one of the characteristics of human thinking or commonsense reasoning. Several models of non-monotonic reasoning have been proposed, but two logics have been studied more extensively: circumscription and default logic. An overview of non-monotonic reasoning and Logic Programming the reader can find in (Minker, 1996). McCarthy (1977) first has introduced his theory of circumscription, and he has formalized it in (McCarthy, 1980). Doyle (1979) developed his truth maintenance system. Reiter gave preliminary ideas of default reasoning in 1978 (Reiter, 1978) and he has developed this theory in (Reiter, 1980). McCarthy, (1986) describes the applications of circumscription to formalizing commonsense knowledge.

Circumscription is based on the closed-world assumption. The idea of this kind of reasoning is to introduce particular predicates that are assumed to be 'as false as possible' – that is false for every object except those for which they are known to be true. In artificial intelligence, the following example is frequently given: "Suppose we want to assert the default rule that birds fly. We would introduce a predicate, say Abnormal(x), and write:

Bird(x) & ¬ *Abnormal*(x) ⇒ *Flies*(x).

If we say, that Abnormal is to be circumscribed, a circumscriptive reasoning is entitled to assume ¬Abnormal(x) unless Abnormal(x) is known to be true. This allows the conclusion Flies(Tweety) to be drawn from the premise Bird(Tweety), but the conclusion no longer holds if Abnormal(Tweety) is asserted" (Russel, & Norvic, 2003: p.358). Another example from (Russel, & Norvic, 2003): for most people, the possibility that car is not having four wheels does not arise unless some new evidence presents itself. Thus, it seems that the "four-wheels" conclusion is reached by default, in the absence of anything to doubt it. If evidence arrives, then conclusion can be retracted.

Default logic is a formalism in which **default rules** can be written to generate contingent, non-monotonic conclusions. A default rule looks like this:

Bird (x): *Flies* (x)/*Flies*(x).

This rule means that if *Bird* (x) is true and if *Flies* (x) is consistent with the knowledge base, then *Flies(x)* may be concluded by default. In general, a default rule has the form

$P: J_1, \ldots, J_n/C,$

where P is called the prerequisite, C is the conclusion, and $J_i, \ldots J_n$ are the justifications - if any one of them can be proven false, then the conclusion cannot be drawn. Any variable that appears in J_i or C must also appear in P.

To interpret what the default rules mean, the notion of an **extension** of a default theory is defined as a maximal set of consequences of the theory. That is, an extension S consists of the original known facts and a set of conclusions from the default rules, such that no additional conclusions can be drawn from S and the justifications of every default conclusion in S are consistent with S.

From the time, when non-monotonic logics were first proposed, a great deal of progress has been made in understanding their mathematical properties.

Knowledge is represented in default logic by default theories (D, W), where W is a set of formulas and D is a set of default rules. A default rule

α: β

γ

has two types of antecedents: a prerequisite α which is established if α can be derived and a justification β which is established if β can not be refuted. If both conditions hold, the consequent γ holds too. In this way, a default theory may induce zero, one or multiple *extensions* of the facts in *W*.

The justifications are context-sensitive. A default rule's justification could be refutable only just when all default conclusions contributing to an extension are known. Traditionally the non-refutability, or *consistency*, of a justification is verified with respect to the final extension. In such an approach, one is obliged to obtain the entire set of default rules in order to decide whether a particular default rule applies. The goal of the paper (Linke, 2000) is to give a technique allowing replacing such exhaustive process by more effective one. This approach is based on the observation that the refutation of a justification is necessarily based on the existence of a proof for its negation. A criterion has also been obtained for guaranteeing the existence and non-existence of extensions.

A new concept for default reasoning in the context of query-answering in regular default logic has been advanced in (Linke, & Schaub, 1998). In this work, the authors have developed a proof-oriented approach for deciding whether a default theory has an extension containing a given query. The other works of Linke and Schaub (1999) perfect their model of default reasoning.

Default Logic is recognized as a power framework for knowledge representation and incomplete information management. Its expressive power is suitable for non monotonic reasoning. But the difficulty of default logic application links with its very high level of computational complexity. In the paper (Nicolas et al., 2001) some heuristic such as Genetic Algorithms, Ant Colony Optimization, and Local Search have been proposed to elaborate an efficient non monotonic system of reasoning.

Genetic Algorithms are based on the principles of natural selection. Population of possible solutions evolves through a process of mutation and crossover in order to generate a better configuration. Ant Colony Optimization is inspired by the observation of the collective behavior of ants when they are seeking food. Local Search is based on incremental improvement of a potential solution on a given problem by local moves from a configuration to its neighbors.

New investigations continue to appear on the relationships of default logic to classical logic. In his very interesting article, Delgrande, J. P. (2007) gives a new view on default logic as a conditional reasoning, which has been described earlier in (Delgrande, 1987). He reviews previous works in conditional approaches to non-monotonic reasoning, describes a family of weak conditional logics, and considers the incorporation of a non-monotonic extension into a conditional knowledge base. In this article, two components of default reasoning are considered. First, there is a standard, monotonic logic of conditionals to express relations among defaults that are considered to always hold. Second, there is a non-monotonic mechanism for obtaining defaults (and default consequences). Given a default conditional $α \rightarrow β$ the underlying intuition is that, in the context of α, the proposition expressed by $α \land β$ is more "normal" than that expressed by $α \land \neg β$.

Non-monotonic inference is then defined in the standard way: given a default theory *T* and a classical (i.e. non-default) formula α, formula β is a default inference from α with respect to *T*, just if $α \rightarrow β$ is true in each of the non-monotonic "extensions" of *T*.

The default theory simulates only one characteristic of natural human thinking – the non-monotonic one. It is not correct really to consider this theory as a model of commonsense reasoning. The default theory can be viewed as a set of propositional models of inference. There does not exist, in this theory, inductive reasoning directed to knowledge acquisition and modification - default knowledge is not structured. The operations of classification, generalization, refinement are impossible in reasoning by defaults. Consider usually demonstrated example with the assertions that "all birds have wings" and "all birds fly". If a bird is observed having the wings but not flying, then, in natural reasoning, one will have the possibility to reason as follows: 1) to partition the class of birds into two subclasses "birds flying" and "birds not flying"; 2) to find a reason explaining the fact that birds with wings do not fly, i.e. to find the property implying this fact; 3) to conclude that the property "flying" is not the common one for birds.

It is naturally that the absence of inductive component in default logic inspires the appearance of a new branch in logic programming called Non Monotonic Inductive Logic Programming (NMILP).

Non-Monotonic Inductive Logic Programming

C. Sakama (2002) has presented a technique for combining non-monotonic logic programming (NMLP) and ILP in non-monotonic ILP (NMILP). Such combination extends the representation language on the ILP side and enriches default reasoning by a mechanism of learning.

NMLP represents logic based reasoning over incomplete knowledge. This reasoning is referred to as commonsense reasoning (Sacama, 2002). Discovering human knowledge is iterative and inherently non-monotonic. Combining non-monotonic reasoning with inductive reasoning is very important because it is a way toward modeling more realistic commonsense reasoning. The questions related to the techniques for combining non-monotonic and inductive reasoning can be found in the following publications: (Sacama, 2002; 2005), (Sacama, & Inoue, 2001).

Deductive and Inductive Inference in the BOOLEAN Space of Attributes

A common logic approach to data mining and pattern recognition has been developed by A. Zakrevskij (1982, 2005, 2006). This approach is based on using finite spaces of Boolean or multi-valued attributes for modeling natural subject areas. It combines inductive inference used for extracting knowledge from data with deductive inference solving pattern recognition problems.

This logical approach seems to be the most general and promising. Its efficiency depends substantially on the choice of proper representation of real world objects. Suppose that W is a set of objects which can differ in values of attributes composing a set $X = \{x_1, x_2, x_n\}$. Each x_i takes its values in a corresponding finite set V_i of alternative values, and the Cartesian product of these sets $V_1 \times V_2 \times \ldots \times V_n$ constitutes a space M of multi-valued attributes. Objects are identified with some elements of M.

Hence a world of objects is represented by a relation $W \subseteq M = V_1 \times V_2 \times \ldots \times V_n$ or by a corresponding finite predicate $\varphi(x_1, x_2, x_n)$ taking value 1 on the elements of W. In case of two-valued attributes, this predicate degenerates into a Boolean function $f(x_1, x_2, x_n)$. The world is trivial when $W = M$. But in the majority of practical applications, the number of objects is essentially less than the whole number of elements in M.

Zakrevskij (1982) has advanced an idea that the type of regularities is the non-existence of objects with some definite combinations of properties. So, the inductive inference consists in looking for empty (not containing examples of objects from a training set) intervals of M, putting forward corresponding hypotheses (suggesting prohibited or empty intervals in the whole subject area), evaluating the plausibility of these hypotheses and accepting the more plausible of them as regularities.

The main recognition problem relates to the situation when an object is observed with known values of some attributes and unknown values of some others, including goal attributes. The values of goal attributes must be determined via deductive inference based on known regularities.

Data and Knowledge Representation

- The case of two-valued attributes: an object is represented by a point in the Boolean space or by a corresponding Boolean vector having 1s in some components if the properties associated with these components belong to the object; for example, if $X = \{x_1, x_2, x_3, x_4\}$, then vector 1001 means that the described object possesses properties x_1 and x_4 but not x_2 or x_3. When the information about the object is incomplete, a ternary vector is used for its representation; for example, vector '1 0 - 1' means that it is not known whether the object has property x_3 or not. A set of objects is represented by a Boolean matrix.

- The case of multi-valued attributes: an object is represented by the use of sectional Boolean vector. A section of vector corresponds to an attribute, and each section has several binary digits corresponding to the attribute values. Suppose $X = \{x, y, z\}$, $V_1 = \{a, b, c\}$, $V_2 = \{a, e, f, g\}$, and $V_3 = \{h, i\}$. Then vector 010.1000.01 describes an object with value b of attribute x, value a of attribute y and value i of attribute z.

Representation of Regularity

Any regularity defines a logical connection between some attributes: it means that some combinations of their values are declared impossible (prohibited); this regularity is expressed by logical expression $k_i = 0$ or $d_i = 1$, where k_i is a conjunct formed of some attributes (in direct or inverse mode) of X and d_i is a disjunct, and $d_i = \neg k_i$. Such regularity is called implicative (Zakrevskij, 1982); Consider some examples of this regularity given in (Zakrevskij, 2001).

The case of binary attributes: $X = \{a, b, c, d, e, f\}$, $k_i = ab'e$ and $d_i = a' \vee b \vee e'$ (here a' means the negation of variable a); equations $k_i = 0$ and $d_i = 1$ are equivalent, forbidding combinations 101 of values of attributes a, b, e, accordingly. The corresponding empty interval of space M contains eight (2^3) elements 100010, 100011, 100110, 101010, 100111, 101110, 101011, and 101111.

The case of multi-valued attributes: any interval in the space of multi-valued attributes is defined as a direct product of non-empty subsets α_i taking by one from V_i. Its characteristic function is defined as a conjunct; and the negation of it is a disjunct.

Consider a previous example of multi-valued attributes: $X = \{x, y, z\}$, $V_1 = \{a, b, c\}$, $V_2 = \{a, e, f, g\}$, and $V_3 = \{h, i\}$. Suppose $\alpha_1 = \{a\}$, $\alpha_2 = \{a, e, g\}$, and $\alpha_3 = \{h, i\}$. The interval $I = \alpha_1 \times \alpha_2 \times \alpha_3$ has the following characteristic function (conjunct) $k = (x = a) \wedge ((y = a) \vee (y = e) \vee (y = g))$ presented by vector 100.1101.11. If this product enters equation $k = 0$ representing a regular connection between x and y, then interval I turns out to be empty $I \cap W = \varnothing$.

One can avoid the complexity of using the two-stage form of the type "$\wedge \vee$". For this goal, one can change equation $k = 0$ for equivalent equation $\neg k = 1$ and transform $\neg k$ into one-stage disjunctive term d. Such transformation is based on de-Morgan rule and changing expressions $\neg(x_{i+} \in \alpha_i)$ for equivalent expressions $(x_i \in V_i \setminus \alpha)$. We assume that all sets V are finite. For the considered examples, we have $d = \neg k = (x \neq a) \vee ((y \neq a) \wedge (y \neq e) \wedge (y \neq g)) = (x = b) \vee (x = c) \vee (y = f)$.

Traditionally, similar expressions are referred to as disjuncts. Suppose that the knowledge of the world is represented by a set of disjuncts $d_1, d_2, ..., d_m$. Equations $d_i = 1$ are interpreted as conditions which should be satisfied for any object of the world, and it is possible to reduce them to one equation $\mathbf{D} = 1$ the left part of which is presented in the conjunctive normal form – CNF: $\mathbf{D} = d_1 \wedge d_2 \wedge \wedge d_m$.

Table 4. Example of knowledge matrix

a	b	c	d	e	f	g	h
1	-	-	0	-	-	0	-
-	-	-	1	-	1	-	-
0	1	-	-	-	-	-	-

A set of regularities is represented by a sectional Boolean matrix **D** that could be called a disjunctive matrix, or knowledge matrix. The knowledge matrix in Table 4 affirms that every object of the considered area must satisfy the equations: $a \vee d' \vee g' = 1$, $d \vee f = 1$ and $a' \vee b = 1$. In other words, in the considered Boolean space it is impossible the existence of objects having the following attribute values' combinations: $(a = 0, d = 1, g = 1)$, $(d = 0, f = 0)$, and $(a = 1, b = 0)$.

Inferring Knowledge from Data

The data are given by a training set F – a set of some randomly selected objects from the world W. The search for implicative regularities is performed by observing a Boolean data matrix **K** and looking for the combinations of attribute values not occurring in the matrix.

The number of attributes coming into an implicative regularity is called its rank. It coincides with the rank of the corresponding interval. The less attributes are connected by a regularity, the stronger it is. For example, consider the following data matrix (Table 5):

There are no empty intervals of rank 1, because each column contains 1s and 0s. So we look further for empty intervals of rank 2 and find five of them, corresponding to the following combinations: $(a = 0, f = 1)$, $(b = 1, d = 0)$, $(b = 0, e = 0)$, $(c = 1, f = 1)$, and $(d = 0, e = 0)$. In a more compact form these intervals may be represented by conjuncts $a'f$, bd', $b'e'$, cf, and $d'e'$. The question arises whether we can consider that these empty intervals reflect real regularities inherent in the world from which the data were extracted. Consider the general case of n binary attributes and m elements in training set F. Suppose we have found an empty interval of rank r (comprising 2^{n-r} elements of Boolean space M) and put forward the corresponding hypothesis. The hypothesis can be accepted and used further in procedures of deductive inference only if its probability is small enough. It was proposed in (Zakrevskij, 1982) to

Table 5. Example of selected objects

a	b	c	d	e	f
1	0	0	1	1	0
0	1	1	1	0	0
1	1	0	1	0	1
0	0	0	1	1	0
0	1	0	1	1	0
0	0	1	0	1	0
1	1	1	1	0	0
1	0	0	0	1	1

evaluate the plausibility of hypotheses by the mathematical expectation $W(n, m, r)$ of the number of empty intervals of the rank r. It can be calculated as follows:

$$W(n, m, r) = C_n^r \, 2^r \, (1 - 2^{-r})^m,$$

where C_n^r – is the number of r- element subsets of an n- element set, $C_n^r \, 2^r$ – is the number of interval of rank r in the space M, and $(1 - 2^{-r})^m$ is the probability of some definite interval of rank r being empty, i. e. not containing any elements from F.

It turns out that the value of this function grows very rapidly with rising r. It is shown in (Zakrevskij, 1982) that searching for empty intervals can be reasonably restricted by the relation $r < 4$.

Extracting knowledge from the space on n multi-valued attributes is considered in (Zakrevskij, 1994).

Deductive Inference

The classical problem of deductive inference is described as follows: there are given a disjunctive matrix **D** and a vector **d** defined on the same patterns as **D**; it is necessary to find out if **d** is a logical consequence of **D**.

There are known two ways for solving this problem: the direct inference and the back one. When the direct inference is used, the initial set of disjuncts is expanded consecutively by including new disjuncts (resolvents) following from some pairs of disjuncts existing already in the set. The procedure continues until disjunct **d** is obtained or the expansion is exhausted without obtaining **d** – the last case proves that **d** does not follow from **D**.

The back inference begins with including **d** into the initial system of disjuncts. After that the latter is transformed into such a system which is consistent if and only if **d** does not follow from **D**. So, this problem is reduced to the problem of checking some disjunctive matrix for consistency. A matrix **D** is consistent if the corresponding conjunctive normal form (CNF) **D** is satisfiable, i.e. if there exists at least one solution of the equation **D** = 1. Checking **D** for consistency is a hard combinatorial problem. The methods of reducing the complexity of this procedure are considered in (Zhang, 1997).

Pattern Recognition as a Logical Inference (Zakrevskij, 1988, 2006)

Assume that the empty intervals of the rank no more than 3 were found and presented in the following Table 6.

The matrix of Table 6 serves as the model of a given class of object. For example, line 1 of the matrix asserts that the class does not contain any object possessing the properties a, c and not possessing in the same time the property f. This model can be given by means of the following DNF:

$$\varphi = acf' \vee be'f \vee a'd'e \vee b'df \vee b'c'd'.$$

Assume that an observable object possesses the property a, but does not possess the property f. Our task consists in deriving the values of remaining properties based on the matrix of Table 6.

Table 6. Example of selected intervals

a	b	c	d	e	f
1	-	1	-	-	0
-	1	-	-	0	1
0	-	-	0	1	-
-	0	-	1	-	1
-	0	0	0	-	-

For this goal, it is sufficient to put the values $a = 1$ and $f = 0$ into the function φ and to transform it as follows:

$$\varphi(a = 1, f = 0) = 1cf' \vee be'0 \vee 0'd'e \vee b'd0 \vee b'c'd' = c \vee b'c'd' = c \vee b'd'.$$

The same result can be received from the matrix of Table 6 via a correspondent transformation.

The range of possible values for the properties b, c, d, and e are described by the inversion of the function φ:

$$\neg (c \vee b'd') = c'(b \vee d).$$

Classical pattern recognition task is formulated by the following way: given the values of all properties of an observable object to define the value of a given goal property, say, as in our example, the property f.

The decision rule for this task is also based on the matrix of Table 6. We consider the two regions in Boolean space of properties a, b, c, d, e: $M1$ – the region in which the value $f = 0$ is not allowed and $M0$ – the region in which the value $f = 1$ is not allowed. If the observable object by the values of properties a, b, c, d, e belongs to the region $M1$, then the goal property f can be equal only to 1. If the observable object by the values of properties a, b, c, d, e belongs to the region $M0$, then the goal property f can be equal only to 0. However the object can belong to the region $M1 \cap M0$. This case corresponds with the contradiction: the observable values of properties contradict with the known implicative forbidding rules. The object can also belong to the region $M \backslash (M1 \cup M0)$. Then we deal with the case of uncertainty when the knowledge of objects is insufficient for decision making.

The mode of dynamic (incremental) pattern recognition has been also developed by Zakrevskij (1988). The various procedures of pattern recognition are given in (Zakrevskij, 2001; 2005).

CONCLUSION

This chapter examined the problems of knowledge engineering and logic-based inference as they are considered and solved in the framework of artificial intelligence. These problems are fundamental in modeling human thinking and creating both intelligent computer systems and data-knowledge bases. It may be hard to determine the best way to develop the systems capable to integrated deductive – inductive reasoning. Currently there is not any theory of logical inference including the theory of classification without which modeling commonsense reasoning is impossible. But all approaches to logic inference do much effort to extend the existing theories of reasoning by including in it some modes of reasoning possessing characteristics of real human thinking.

REFERENCES

Ahlawat, A., & Pandey, S. (2007). A Variant of Back – Propagation Algorithm for multilayer feed-forward network. In Kr. Markov, & Kr. Ivanova (Eds.), *Proceeding of the Fifth International Conference on Information Research and Application* (iTECH'2007) (pp. 238-246). Sofia, Bolgaria: iTECH.

Alkharouf, N. W., & Michalsi, R. (1996). Multi-strategy task-adaptive learning using dynamic interlaced hierarchies: A methodology and initial implementation of INTERLACE. In *Proceedings of the Third International Workshop on Multi-strategy Learning* (MSL-96), (pp.117-124). Harpers Ferry, WV.

Anchakov, O. M., Skvortzov, D. P., & Finn, V. K. (1987). Logical environment of JSM-method of automated hypotheses generation: A system of rules and its imitation. *Scientific-Technical Information, Series 2*, *11*, 21–30.

Anshakov, O. M., Finn, V. K., & Skvortsov, D. P. (1989). On axiomatization of many-valued logics associated with formalization of plausible reasoning. *Studia Logica*, *42*(4), 423–447. doi:10.1007/BF00370198

Aragão, M. A. T., & Fernandes, A. A. A. (2002). Inductive-deductive databases for knowledge management. In . *Proceedings of the ECAI KM&OM*, *02*, 11–19.

Aragão, M. A. T., & Fernandes, A. A. A. (2004 a). *Combined inference databases* (Retrieved version 1.0.0, 2004 from http://www.cs.man.ac.uk/~alvaro/publications/aragao-fernandes-CID-tech-report.pdf).

Aragão, M. A. T., & Fernandes, A. A. A. (2004b). Logic-based integration of query answering and knowledge discovery. In H. Christiansen, M.-S. Hacid, T. Andreasen, & H. Larsen (Eds.), *Proceedings of the 6th International Conference on Flexible Query Answering Systems* (FQAS'2004) (LNCS 3055, pp. 68-83). Springer.

Aragão, M. A. T., & Fernandes, A. A. A. (2004c). seamlessly supporting combined knowledge discovery and query answering: A case study. *Discovery Science* (LNCS 3245, pp.403-411). Berlin-Heidelberg: Springer.

Basili, R., Pazienza, M. T., & Velardi, P. (1993). Hierarchical clustering of verbs. In B. Boguraev, & J. Pustejousky (Eds), *Proceedings of the Workshop on Acquisition of Lexical Knowledge from Text.* (pp. 70-81). Columbus, Ohio: Association for Computational Linguistics.

Bisson, G., Nedellec, C., & Canamero, L. (2000). Designing clustering methods for ontology building – The Mo'K Workbench. In S.Staab, A. Maedche, C. Nedellic, & P. Wiemer-Hastings (Eds.), *Ontology Learning, Proceedings of the ECAI First Ontology Learning Workshop*. Berlin, Germany: CEUR – WS.

Bloedom, E., & Michalski, R. S. (1996). The AQ17 – DCI system for data-driven constructive induction and its application to the analysis of world economics. In Z. W. Ras, & M. Michalewicz (Eds), *Foundation of Intelligent System, Proceedings of the Ninth International Symposium on Methodologies for Intelligent Systems* (ISMIS-96) (LNCS/LNAI 1952, pp. 108-117). Zakopane, Poland: Springer.

Bodyanskij E., Rudenko O. (2004). *Artificial neural networks: Architecture, training, implementation.* Kharkov: Teletex.

Buitelaar, P., Olejnik, D., & Sintek, M. (2004). A protégé plug-in for ontology extraction from text based on linguistic analysis. In C. Bussler, J. Davies, D. Fensel, & R. Studer (Eds.), *The Semantic Web: Research and applications, Proceedings of the 1st European Semantic Web Symposium* (ESWS) (LNCS 3053, pp. 31-44). Springer.

Burge, J. (1998). *Knowledge elicitation for design task sequencing knowledge.* Unpublished Thesis submitted for the Degree of Master of Science in Computer Science, Worcester Polytechnic Institute.

Burges, C. (1998). A tutorial on support vector machines for pattern recognition. *Data Mining and Knowledge Discovery, 2*(2), 1–47. doi:10.1023/A:1009715923555

Ceri, S., Gottlob, G., & Tanca, L. (1990). Logic programming and databases. *Surveys in Computer Science.* Heidelberg: Springer-Verlag.

Cestnik, B. (1990). Estimating probabilities: A crucial task in machine learning. In *Proceedings of the 9th European Conference on Artificial Intelligence* (ECAI'90) (pp. 147-149). Stockholm, Sweden.

Cestnik, B., Kononenko, I., & Bratko, I. (1987). Assistant 86: A knowledge elicitation tool for sophisticated users. In: I. Bratko, & Lavrač, N. (Eds), *Proceedings of the Second European Working Session on Learning* (pp. 31-45). Bled, Yugoslavia.

Chen, Y., Dehne, F., & Rau-Chaplin, T. E. A. (2004). Parallel ROLAP data cube construction on shared-nothing multiprocessors. *Distributed and Parallel Databases, 15*, 219–236. doi:10.1023/B:DAPD.0000018572.20283.e0

Cheng, J., & Greiner, R. (2001). Learning Bayesian belief network classifiers: Algorithms and system. In E. Stroulia, & S. Matwin (Eds.), *Advanced in AI*, AI 2001 (LNAI 2056, pp. 141-151). Springer-Verlag.

Cheng, J., Greiner, R., Kelly, J., Bell, D., & Liu, W. (2002). Learning Bayesian networks from data: An information-theory based approach. *Artificial Intelligence, 137*, 43–90. doi:10.1016/S0004-3702(02)00191-1

Ciaramita, M., Gangemi, A., Ratsch, E., Šarić, J., & Rojas, I. (2005). Unsupervised learning of semantic relation between concepts of molecular biology ontology. In L.P. Kaelbling, & A. Saffotti (Eds), *Proceedings of the 19th International Joint Conference on AI* (IJCAI) (pp. 659-664). Edinburg, Scotland, UK: Professional Book Center.

Cimiano, P. (2006). *Ontology learning and population from text. Algorithms, evaluation and applications.* Springer Science + Business Media, LLC.

Cimiano, P., Handschuh, S., & Staab, S. (2004). Towards the self-annotating Web. In S. Feldman, M. Uretski, M. Najork, & C. Wills (Eds.), *Proceedings of the 13th World Wide Web Conference* (pp. 462-471). ACM.

Cimiano, P., Hotho, A., & Staab, S. (2005). Learning concept hierarchies from text corpora using formal concept analysis. *Journal of Artificial Intelligence Research*, *24*, 305–339.

Clark, S., & Weir, D. (2002). Class-based probability estimation using a semantic hierarchy. *Computational Linguistics*, *28*(2), 187–206. doi:10.1162/089120102760173643

Collins, A., & Michalsi, R. (1989). The logic of plausible reasoning: A core theory. *Cognitive Science*, *13*, 1–49.

Costa, P., Rocha, R., & Ferreira, M. (2006). *DBTAB: A relational storage model for the YapTab Tabling System*. Paper presented at the 6th Colloquium on Implementation of Constraint and Logic Programming Systems (CICLOPS 2006). New Mexico State University Documents, (pp. 95-109). Seattle, Washington, USA.

Cristianini, N., & Shawe-Taylor, J. (2000). *An introduction to support vector machines and other kernel-based learning methods.*, Cambridge: Cambridge University Press.

Das, S. K. (1992). *Deductive databases and logic programming*. Addison Wesley.

Delgrande, J. P. (1987). A first-order conditional logic for prototypical properties. *Artificial Intelligence*, *33*(1), 105–130. doi:10.1016/0004-3702(87)90053-1

Delgrande, J. P. (2007). On a rule-based interpretation of default conditionals. *Annals of Mathematics and Artificial Intelligence*, *48*, 135–167. doi:10.1007/s10472-007-9044-7

Diaper, D. (Ed.). (1989). *Knowledge elicitation: Principles, techniques and applications*. Chichester, England: Ellis Horwood Ltd.

Díaz, M. A., Blas, N. G., Menéndez, E. S., Gonzalo, R., & Gisbert, F. (2007). Networks of evolutionary processors (NEP) as decision support systems. In Kr. Markov, & Kr. Ivanova (Eds), *Proceedings of the Fifth International Conference on Information Research and Application* (iTECH'2007), (pp.197-203). Sofia, Bulgaria: iTECH.

Douglas, F. H. (1987). Knowledge acquisition via incremental conceptual clustering. *Machine Learning*, *2*(2), 139–172.

Dowling, C. E. (1993). On the irredundant generation of knowledge spaces. *Journal of Mathematical Psychology*, *37*(1), 49–62. doi:10.1006/jmps.1993.1003

Doyle, J. (1979). A truth maintenance system. *Artificial Intelligence*, *12*, 231–272. doi:10.1016/0004-3702(79)90008-0

Duda, R. O., Hart, P. E., & Stork, D. G. (2001). *Pattern classification*. John Wiley & Sons, Inc.

Fahlman, E. (1998). Faster-learning variations on back propagation: An Empirical Study. In D. Touretzky, G. Hinton, & T. Sejnowski (Eds.), *Proceedings of the 1988 Connectionist Models Summer School* (pp. 38-51). Morgan Kaufmann.

Fanizzi, N., Claudia d'Amato, C., & Esposito, F. (2008). *Conceptual clustering and its application to concept drift and novelty detection*. Presented at 5th European Semantic Web Conference (ESWC2008).

Fegaras, L., & Maier, D. (2000). Optimizing object queries using an effective calculus. *ACM Transactions on Database Systems, 25*(4), 457–516. doi:10.1145/377674.377676

Fernandes, A. A. A. (2000). Combining inductive and deductive inference in knowledge management tasks. In *Proceedings of 11th Intern Workshop on Data Base and Expert System Application* (the 1st Workshop on the Theory and Application of Knowledge Management – TAKAMA'2000) (pp.1109-1114). London: IEEE Press.

Ferré, S., Ridoux, O., & Sigonneau, B. (2005). Arbitrary relations in formal concept analysis and logical information systems. In F. Dau, M.-L. Mugnier, & G. Stumme (Eds.), *Conceptual structures: Common semantics for sharing knowledge* (pp. 166-180), Berlin-Heidelberg: Springer Verlag.

Ferré, S., & Rudolph, S. (Eds.). (2009). Formal concept analysis. 7th International Conference ICFCA'09, Darmstadt, Germany, May 21-24 - Proceedings, LNAI 5548. Springer.

Ferreira, M., Fonseca, N. A., Rocha, R., & Soares, T. (2007). Efficient and scalable induction of logic programs using a deductive database system. In S. Muggleton, R. Otero, & A. Tammaddoni-Nezhad (Eds), *Logical Programming, The Proceedings of 16th International Conference on Inductive Logic Programming* (ILP'2006) (LNAI 4455, pp. 184-198). Berlin/Heidelberg: Springer-Verlag.

Finn, V. K. (1984). Inductive models of knowledge representation in man-machine and robotics systems. *The transactions of VINITI*, Vol. A, 58-76.

Finn, V. K. (1988). Commonsense inference and commonsense reasoning. *Review of Science and Technique (Itogi Nauki i Tekhniki), Series "The Theory of Probability. Mathematical Statistics. Technical Cybernetics, 28*, 3–84.

Finn, V. K. (1991). Plausible reasoning in systems of JSM type. *Review of Science and Technique (Itogi Nauki i Tekhniki), Series " . Informatika, 15*, 54–101.

Finn, V. K. (1999). The synthesis of cognitive procedures and the problem of induction. *NTI* [Moscow, Russia: VINITI.]. *Series, 2*(1-2), 8–44.

Fonseca, N. A. (2006). *Parallelism in inductive logic programming systems*. Unpublished doctoral dissertation. University of Porto.

Fonseca, N. A., Silva, F., & Camacho, R. (2006). April - An Inductive Logic Programming System. In M. Fisher, W. van der Hock, B. Konev, & A. Lisitsa, A. (Eds.), *Logic in Artificial Intelligence, Proceedings of the 10th European Conference on Logics in Artificial Intelligence* (JELIA06) (LNAI 4160, pp. 481-484). Springer-Verlag.

Forbus, K., & Usher, J. (2002). Sketching for knowledge capture: A progress report. In *Proceedings of Intelligent User Interfaces International Conference* (pp. 71-77). San Francisco, CA: ACM.

Forbus, K., Usher, J., & Chapman, V. (2003). Sketching for military courses of action diagrams. In *Proceedings of Intelligent User Interfaces International Conference* (pp. 61-68). Miami, FL: ACM.

Galitsky, B. A., Kuznetsov, S. O., & Vinogradov, D. V. (2007). Applying hybrid reasoning to mine for associative features in biological data. *Journal of Biomedical Informatics*, *40*(3), 203–220. doi:10.1016/j.jbi.2006.07.002

Gamallo, P., Gonzalez, M., Agustini, A., Lopes, G., & de Lima, V. S. (2002). Mapping syntactic dependencies onto semantic relations. In N. Aussenac-Gilles, & A. Maedche (Eds.), *Proceedings of the ECAI Workshop on Machine Learning and NLP for Ontology Engineering* (pp. 15-22). Kluwer Academic Publisher.

Ganter, B. (1984). Two basic algorithms in concepts analysis. *FB4-Preprint*, No. 831. Technische Hochschule, Darmstadt.

Ganter, B., & Wille, R. (1999). *Formal concept analysis, mathematical foundations*. Berlin/Heidelberg: Springer Verlag.

Giraud-Carrier, C., & Martinez, T. (1994). An incremental learning model for commonsense reasoning. In *Proceedings of the Seventh International Symposium on Artificial Intelligence (ISAI'94)*, (pp. 134-141). ITESM.

Gray, J., Chaudhuri, S., Bosworth, A., Layman, A., Reichart, D., & Venkatrao, M. (1997). Data cube: A relational aggregation operator generalizing group-by, cross-tab, and sub-totals. *J. Data Mining and Knowledge Discovery*, *1*(1), 29–53. doi:10.1023/A:1009726021843

Greco, S., Masciari, E., & Pontieri, L. (2001). Combining inductive and deductive tools for data analysis. *AI Communications*, *14*(2), 69–82.

Hahn, U., & Schnattinger, K. (1998). Towards text knowledge engineering. In AAAI'98/IAAI'98 *Proceedings of the 15th National Conference on Artificial Intelligence and the 10th Conference on Innovative Applications of Artificial Intelligence*. (pp. 524-531). Madison, WI: AAAI Press.

Han, J. (1998). Towards on-line analytical mining in large databases. *SIGMOD Record*, *27*(1), 97–107. doi:10.1145/273244.273273

Han, J. (2008). Olap spatial. In S. Shekhar & H. Xiong (Eds.), *Encyclopedia of GIS*, (pp. 809-812). Springer.

Han, J., Fu, Y., & Ng, R. (1994a). Cooperative query answering using multiple-layered databases. In M.L. Brodie, M. Jarke, & M.P. Papasoglou (Eds.), *Proc. 2nd Int. Conf. Cooperative Information Systems*, (pp. 47-58). Toronto, Canada: Univ. Toronto Press.

Han, J., Ng, R. T., & Fu, Y. (1996). Intelligent query answering by knowledge discovery techniques. *IEEE Transactions on Knowledge and Data Engineering*, *8*, 373–390. doi:10.1109/69.506706

Han, J., Nishiro, S., & Kawano, H. (1994b). Knowledge discovery in object-oriented and active databases. In F. Fuchi & T. Yokoi (Eds.), *Knowledge building and knowledge sharing*, (pp. 221-230). Ohmsha, Ltd. and IOS Press.

Han, J., Nishiro, S., Kawano, H., & Wang, W. (1998). Generalization-based data mining in object-oriented databases using an object cube model. *Data & Knowledge Engineering*, *25*(1-2), 55–97. doi:10.1016/S0169-023X(97)00051-7

Hearst, M. A. (1992). Automatic acquisition of hyponyms from large text corpora. In *Proceedings of the 14th International Conference on Computational Linguistics* (COLING-92) (pp. 539-545).

Hudlicka, E. (1997). *Summary of knowledge elicitation techniques for requirements analysis, course material for human computer interaction*. Worcester Polytechnic Institute.

Hush, D. R., & Horne, B. G. (1993). Progress in supervised neural networks. *IEEE Signal Processing Magazine, 10*(1), 8–39. doi:10.1109/79.180705

Imam, I. F., & Michalski, R. S. (1993). Learning decision trees from decision rules: A method and initial results from a comparative study. [JIIS]. *Journal of Intelligent Information Systems, 2*(3), 279–304. doi:10.1007/BF00962072

Jensen, F. (1996). *An introduction to Bayesian networks*. Springer.

Judd, J. S. (1990). *Neural network design and the complexity of learning*. Cambridge, MA: MIT Press.

Kalfoglou, Y., & Schorlemmer, M. (2005). Using formal concept analysis and information flow for modeling and sharing common semantics: Lessons learnt and emergent issues. In F. Dau, M.-L. Mugnier, & G. Stumme (Eds.), *Conceptual structures: Common semantics for sharing knowledge* (pp. 107-118) Berlin/Heidelberg: Springer Verlag.

Kaufman, K., Michalski, R. S., Pietrzykowski, J., & Wojtusiak, J. (2007). An integrated multi-task inductive database VINLEN: Initial implementation and early results. In *Knowledge discovery in inductive databases*: *The 5th International Workshop on KDID, Revised Selected and Invited Papers* (LNCS 4747, pp. 116-133) Berlin/Heidelberg: Springer.

Kavalec, M., & Svátek, V. (2005). A study on automated relation labeling in ontology learning. In P. Buitelaar, P. Cimiano, B. Magnini, B. (Eds.), *Ontology learning from text: Methods, evaluation and applications, number 123 in Frontier sin AI and Applications* (pp. 44-58). IOS Press.

Kelly, G. A. (1955). *The psychology of personal constructs*: *A theory of personality*. New York: Norton.

Ko, H., & Michalski, R. S. (1988). Types of explanation and their role in constructive closed-loop learning. *Report of the Machine Learning and Inference Laboratory, MLI88-2*. School of Information Technology and Engineering, George Mason University, Faifax, VA.

Kobrinskiy, B. (2004). Expert knowledge extraction: Group variant. *News of Artificial Intelligence, 3*, 58–66.

Kotsianti, S. B. (2007). Supervised machine learning: A review of classification technique. *Informatica, 31*, 249–268.

Kuznetsov, S. (2007). On stability of a formal concept. *Annals of Mathematics and Artificial Intelligence, 49*, 101–115. doi:10.1007/s10472-007-9053-6

Kuznetsov, S. O. (1993). Fast algorithm of constructing all the intersections of finite semi-lattice objects. *NTI* [Moscow, Russia: VINITI.]. *Series, 2*(1), 17–20.

Kuznetsov, S. O., & Obiedkov, S. A. (2001). Comparing performance of algorithms for generating concept lattices. *Journal of Experimental & Theoretical Artificial Intelligence, 14*(2-3), 183–216.

Kuznetsov, S. O., & Schmidt, S. (Eds.). (2007). *Formal Concept Analysis: 5th International Conference ICFCA'07*. Clermont-Ferrand, France, February 12-16 (LNAI 4390).

Lakshmanan, L. V. S., & Shiri-Varnaamkhaasti, N. (2001). A Parametric approach to deductive databases with uncertainty. *IEEE Transactions on Knowledge and Data Engineering, 13*(4), 554–570. doi:10.1109/69.940732

Landauer, T. K., Foltz, P. W., & Laham, D. (1998). Introduction to latent semantic analysis. *Discourse Processes, 25*, 259–284.

Lavrac, N., & Dzeroski, S. (1994). *Inductive logic programming: Techniques and applications*. Chichester, UK: Ellis Horwood.

Lavraĉ, N., & Flash, P. (2000, March). An extended transformation approach to inductive logic programming. *CSTR – 00 -002* (pp. 1-42).University of Bristol, Department of Computer Science.

Lavraĉ, N., Gamberger, D., & Jovanoski, V. (1999). A study of relevance for learning in deductive databases. *The Journal of Logic Programming, 40*(2/3), 215–249. doi:10.1016/S0743-1066(99)00019-9

Ledley, R. S., & Lusted, L. B. (1959). Reasoning foundations of medical diagnosis. *Science, 130*(3366), 9–21. doi:10.1126/science.130.3366.9

Li, X. Han, J., Yin, Z., Lee, J.-G., & Sun, Y. (2008). Sampling cube: A framework for statistical OLAP over sampling data. In: J. Tsong-Li Wang (Ed,), *Proceedings of SIGMOD'08* (pp. 778-790). Vancouver, BC, Canada: ACM.

Lin, C. X., Bolin Ding, B., Han, J., Zhu, F., & Zhao, B. (2008). Text cube: Computing IR measures for multidimensional text database analysis. In *Proceedings of Int. Conf. on Data Mining* (ICDM'08), (pp. 905-910). Pisa, Italy: IEEE Computer Society.

Linke, T. (2000). *New foundations for automation of default reasoning*. Akad. Verl.- Ges. Berlin.

Linke, T., & Schaub, T. (1998). An approach to query-answering in Reiter's default logic and the underlying existence of extensions problem. In J. Dix, L. Farïnas del Cerro, & U. Furbach (Eds.), *Proceedings of the Sixth European Workshop on Logics in Artificial Intelligence* (pp. 233-247). Springer Verlag.

Linke, T., & Schaub, T. (1999). Default reasoning via blocking sets. In M. Gelfond, N. Leone, & Pfeifer (Eds), *Proceedings of the Fifth International Conference on Logic Programming and Nonmonotonic Reasoning (LPNMR'99)* (pp. 247-261). Springer-Verlag.

Lisi, F., & Malerba, D. (2004). Inducing multi-level association rules from multiple relations. *Machine Learning, 55*, 175–210. doi:10.1023/B:MACH.0000023151.65011.a3

Lo, E., Kao, B., Ho, W.-S., & Lee, S. D. Chui, Kit, C., & Cheung, D. W. (2008). Olap on Sequence Data. In J. Tsong-Li Wang (Ed.), *Proceedings* of *SIGMOD Conference* (pp. 649-660). ASM.

Lodhi, H., Saunders, C., Shawe-Taylor, J., Cristianini, N., & Watkins, C. (2002). Text classification using string kernels. *Journal of Machine Learning Research, 2*, 419–444. doi:10.1162/153244302760200687

Lovell, B. C., & Walder, C. J. (2005). Support vector machines for business applications. In G. Felici & C. Vercellis (Eds.), *Mathematical methods for knowledge discovery and data mining* (pp. 82-100). Hershey, PA: IGI Global.

Lu, W., Han, J., & Ooi, B. C. (1993). Knowledge discovery in large spatial databases. In H-J. Lu, & Beng Chin Ooi (Eds.) *GIS Technology and Application, Proceeding of the Far East Workshop on Geographic Information Systems* (pp. 275-289). World Scientific Publishing Co Pte Ltd.

Mäedche, A., Pekar, V., & Staab, S. (2002). Ontology Learning Part One - On discovering taxonomic relations from the Web. In N. Zhong, et al. (Eds.), *Web intelligence.* (pp. 1-19). Springer-Verlag.

Mäedche, A., & Staab, S. (2003). KAON: The Karlsruche ontology and Semantic Web meta project. *Künstliche Intelligenz, 3,* 27–30.

McCarthy, J. (1977). Epistemological problems of artificial intelligence. In *Proceedings of the Int. Joint. Conf. on Art. Intell.* (pp. 223-227).

McCarthy, J. (1980). Circumscription - A form of non-monotonic reasoning. *Artificial Intelligence, 13,* 27–39. doi:10.1016/0004-3702(80)90011-9

McCarthy, J. (1986). Applications of circumscription to formalizing commonsense knowledge. *Artificial Intelligence, 28,* 89–116. doi:10.1016/0004-3702(86)90032-9

McNamara, D. C., Levinstein, I. B., & Boonthum, C. (2004). iSTART: Interactive strategy training for active reading and thinking. *Behavior Research Methods, Instruments, & Computers, 36,* 222–233.

McNeese, M. D., & Zaff, B. S. (1991). Knowledge as design: A methodology for overcoming knowledge acquisition bottlenecks in intelligent interface design. In *Proceedings of the HumanFactors Society 35th Annual Meeting* (pp. 1181-1185). Santa Monica, CA: Human Factors & Ergonomics Society.

Medina, R., & Obiedkov, S. (Eds.). (2008). *Formal Concept Analysis: 6th International Conference, ICFCA 2008.* Montreal, Canada, February 25-28 (LNCS 4933).

Melamed, I. D., & Resnik, P. (2000). Tagger evaluation given hierarchical tag sets. *Computers and the Humanities, 34*(1-2), 79–84. doi:10.1023/A:1002402902356

Michalski, R. (1993). Learning = Inferencing + Memorizing: Basic concepts of inferential theory of learning and their use for classifying learning processes. In S. Chipman & A. Meyrowitz (Eds.), *Foundation of Knowledge Acquisition (Vol. 2): Machine Learning* (pp. 1- 42). Boston/Dordrecht/London: Kluwer Academic Publishers.

Michalski, R. (1994). Inferential theory of learning: Developing foundations for multi-strategy learning. In R. Michalski & G. Tecuci (Eds.), *Machine learning: A multi-strategy approach,* vol. IV. (pp. 3 - 61). San Mateo, CA: Morgan Kaufmann Publishers.

Michalski, R., & Kaufman, K. (1998). Data mining and knowledge discovery: A review of issues and a multi-strategy approach. In R.S. Michalski, I. Bratko, & M. Kubat (Eds.), *Machine learning and data Mining: Methods and applications* (pp. 71-112). London: John Wiley & Sons.

Michalski, R., & Kaufman, K. (2001). The AQ19- System for machine learning and pattern discovery: A general description and user's guide. *Reports of Machine Learning and Inference Laboratory*, MLI01-2, George Mason University, Fairfax, VA.

Michalski, R., & Stepp, R. (1981). Revealing conceptual structure in data by inductive inference. In J. Hayes, D. Michie, & Y-H Pao (Eds.), *Machine Intelligence* (Vol. 10). Chichester: Ellis Horwood, N.Y. Halsted.

Michalski, R., & Stepp, R. (1983). Automated construction of classification: Conceptual clustering versus numerical taxonomy. *IEEE Transaction PAMI*, *5*(4), 396–410.

Michalski, R. S. (1980). Knowledge acquisition through conceptual clustering: A theoretical framework and an algorithm for partitioning data into cognitive concepts. *Int. J. Policy Anal. Inform. Syst.*, *4*(3), 219–244.

Michalski, R. S. (1983). A theory and methodology of inductive learning. *Artificial Intelligence*, *20*, 111–161. doi:10.1016/0004-3702(83)90016-4

Michalski, R. S., (2003). *The inferential theory of learning and inductive databases.* Invited paper at the UQAM Summer Institute in Cognitive Sciences, Montreal, Canada, June 30-July 11.

Michalski, R.S., & Imam, I.F. (1997). On learning decision structures. *Fundamenta Matematicae*, (dedicated to the memory of Dr. Cecylia Raucher, Polish Academy of Sciences), *31*(1), 49-64.

Michalski, R. S., Kaufman, K., Pietrzykowski, J., Wojtusiak, J., Mitchell, S., & Seeman, W. D. (2006). Natural induction and conceptual clustering: A review of applications. *Reports of the Machine Learning and Inference Laboratory*, MLI 06-3, George Mason University, Fairfax, VA.

Michalski, R. S., & Pietrzykowski, J. (2007). iAQ: A Program that Discovers Rules. *AAAI-07 AI Video Competition, Twenty-Second Conference on Artificial Intelligence (AAAI-07)*. Vancouver, British Columbia, July 22-26.

Michalski, R. S., & Watanabe, L. (1988). Constructive closed-loop learning: Fundamental ideas and examples. *Report of the Machine Learning and Inference Laboratory*, MLI88-1, School of Information Technology and Engineering, George Mason University, Fairfax, VA.

Michalski, R. S., & Wojtusiak, J. (2007). Semantic and syntactic attribute types in AQ learning. *Reports of the Machine Learning and Inference Laboratory*, MLI 07-1, George Mason University, Fairfax, VA.

Mill, J. S. (1872). *The system of logic ratiocinative and inductive being a connected view of the principles of evidence, and the methods of scientific investigation* (Vol.1). London, West Strand.

Minker, J. (1996). Logic and databases. A 20 Year retrospective. In P. Dini, & Z. Carlo (Eds.), *Logic in databases* - Proceedings of the International Workshop LID'96 (LNCS 1154, pp. 3-57). San Miniato, Italy: Springer-Verlag.

Mitchell, T. (1997). *Machine learning.* New York: McGraw-Hill.

Muggleton, S., & Luc de Raedt (1994). Inductive logic programming. Theory and Methods. *JLP, 19*(20), 629-679.

Muggleton, S. (1995). Inverse entailment and Progol. *New Generation Computing, 13,* 245–286. doi:10.1007/BF03037227

Naidenova, X. A. (1996). Reducing machine learning tasks to the approximation of a given classification on a given set of examples. In *Proceedings of the 5-th National Conference at Artificial Intelligence* (Vol. 1., pp. 275-279). Kazan, Tatarstan.

Naidenova, X. A. (2006). An incremental learning algorithm for inferring implicative rules from examples. In E. Triantaphillou, & G. Felici (Eds.), *Data Mining and knowledge discovery approaches based on rule induction techniques* (pp. 90-146). New York: Springer-Verlag.

Naidenova, X. A., & Polegaeva, J. G. (1986). An algorithm of finding the best diagnostic tests. In G. E. Mintz, & P. P. Lorents (Eds.), *The application of mathematical logic methods* (pp. 63-67). Tallinn, Estonia: Institute of Cybernetics, National Acad. of Sciences of Estonia.

Naidenova, X. A., Polegaeva, J. G., & Iserlis, J. E. (1995). The system of knowledge acquisition based on constructing the best diagnostic classification tests. In J. Valkman (Ed), *Knowledge-dialog-solution, Proceedings of International Conference in two volumes* (Vol. 1, pp. 85-95). Kiev, Ukraine: Institute of Applied Informatics.

Nicolas, P., Saubion, F., & Stéphan, I. (2001). New generation systems for non monotonic reasoning. In T. Elter, W. Faber, & M. Truszczynski (Eds.), *Logic programming and non-monotonic reasoning* (LNCS 2173, pp. 309-321). New York: Springer-Verlag.

Nourine, L., & Raynaud, O. (1999). A fast algorithm for building lattices. *Information Processing Letters, 71,* 199–204. doi:10.1016/S0020-0190(99)00108-8

Peirce, C. S. (1995). Abduction and induction. In L. Buchler. (Ed.), *Philosophical writings of Peirce, 4,* (pp. 150-156). New York: Dover Publications.

Perez, A., Larraoaga, P., & Inza, I. (2009). Bayesian classifiers based on kernel density estimation: Flexible classifiers. *International Journal of Approximate Reasoning, 50*(2), 341–362. doi:10.1016/j.ijar.2008.08.008

Pietrzykowski, J., & Wojtusiak, J. (2008). *Learning attributional rule trees.* Paper presented at the 16th International Conference on Intelligent Information Systems, Zakopane, Poland.

Priss, U. (2000a). Lattice-based information retrieval. *Knowledge Organization, 27*(3), 132–142.

Priss, U. (2000b). Knowledge discovery in databases using formal concept analysis. *Bulletin of the American Society for Information Science, 27*(1), 18–20. doi:10.1002/bult.186

Priss, U. (2005). Linguistic applications of formal concept analysis. In B. Ganter, G. Stumme, & R. Wille (Eds.), *Formal concept analysis: Foundation and applications* (LNAI 3626, pp. 149-160). Springer-Verlag.

Priss, U., & Old, L. J. (2004). Modeling lexical databases with formal concept analysis. *Journal of Universal Computer Science, 10*(8), 967–984.

Priss, U., & Old, L. J. (2007). Bilingual word association networks. In Priss, Polovina, & Hill (Eds.), *Proceedings of the 15th International Conference on Conceptual Structures, ICCS'07* (LNAI 4604, pp. 310-320). Springer-Verlag

Quinlan, J. R. (1986). Induction of decision trees'. *Machine Learning, 1*, 81–106.

Quinlan, J. R. (1993). *C4.5: Programs for machine learning*. San Mateo, CA: Morgan Kaufmann.

Rabiner, L. R. (1989). A tutorial on hidden Markov models and selected application in speech recognition. *Proceedings of the IEEE, 77*(2), 257–286. doi:10.1109/5.18626

Reiter, R. (1978). On reasoning by default. In *TINLAP-2. Theoretical Issues in Natural Language Processing-2*, (pp. 210-218). University of Illinois at Urbana-Champaign: ACM.

Reiter, R. (1980). A logic for default reasoning. *Artificial Intelligence, 13*(1 & 2), 81–132. doi:10.1016/0004-3702(80)90014-4

Rendell, L. (1983). Toward a unified approach for conceptual knowledge acquisition. *AI Magazine, 4*(4), 19–27.

Rocha, R. (2006). Handling incomplete and complete tables in tabled logic programs. In S. Etallo, & M. Truszczynski (Eds.), *Logic Programming – The Proceedings of 22nd ICLP* (LNCS 4079, pp. 427-428). Seattle, WA: Springer-Verlag.

Russel, S. J., & Norvig, P. (2003). *Artificial intelligence: A modern approach* (2nd ed.). Prentice Hall.

Sakama, C. (2002). Towards the integration of inductive and non-monotonic logic programming. In Arikawa & A. Shinohara (Eds.), *Progress in Discovery Science 2001* (LNAI 2281, pp.178-188). Berlin/Heidelberg: Springer-Verlag.

Sakama, C. (2005). Induction from answer sets in non-monotonic logic programs. *ACM Transactions on Computational Logic, 6*(2), 203–231. doi:10.1145/1055686.1055687

Sakama, C., & Inoue, K. (2000). Abductive logic programming and disjunctive logic programming: Their relationship and transferability. *The Journal of Logic Programming, 44*(1-3), 75–100. doi:10.1016/S0743-1066(99)00073-4

Salzberg, S. (1991). A nearest hyper rectangle learning method. *Machine Learning, 6*, 277–309.

Scarcelli, F., & Tsoi, A. S. (1998). Universal approximation using feed-forward neural networks: A survey of some existing methods and some new results. *Neural Networks, 11*, 15–37. doi:10.1016/S0893-6080(97)00097-X

Schmidt-Schauss, M., & Smolka, G. (1991). Attributive concept descriptions with complements. *Artificial Intelligence, 48*(1), 1–26. doi:10.1016/0004-3702(91)90078-X

Schulte im Walde. S. (2000). Clustering verbs semantically according to their alternation behavior. In *Proceedings of the 18th International Conference on Computational Linguistics (COLING - 00)* (Vol. 2, pp.747-753). Universität Des Saarlandes Saarbrucken, Germany: Morgan Kaufman.

Seeman, W. D., & Michalski, R. S. (2006). The CLUSTER3 system for goal-oriented conceptual clustering: Method and preliminary results. In A. Zanasi, S.A.Temis, C.A. Brebbia, & N.F.F. Ebecken (Eds), *Data mining VII: Data, text and web mining business application and management* (pp. 81-92). Boston: WIT Press.

Shutz, A., & Buitelaar, P. (2005). RelExt: A tool for relation extraction from text in ontology extension. In Y. Gil, E. Motta, V. R. Benjamins, & M. Musen (Eds.), *The Semantic Web – The Proceedings of 4th ISWC* (LNCS 3729, pp. 593-606). Galway, Ireland: Springer-Verlag.

Soares, T. (2006). Deductive Databases: Implementation, Parallelism and Applications. In S. Etallo, & M. Truszczynski (Eds.), *Logic programming: The Proceedings of the 22nd ICLP* (LNCS 4079, pp. 467-468). Seattle, WA: Springer-Verlag.

Stepp, R., & Michalski, R. (1985). Conceptual clustering of structured objects: A goal-oriented approach. *Artificial Intelligence, 28*, 1.

Stumme, G. (2002). Efficient data mining based on FCA. In A. Hameurlain, R. Cicchetti, & R. Traunmüller (Eds.), *Database & expert system applications, Proceedings DEXA'09* (LNCS 2453, pp. 534-546). Springer.

Stumme, G., Taouil, R., Bastide, Y., Pasquier, N., & Lakhal, L. (2000). Fast computation of concept lattices using data mining techniques. In M. Bouzeghoub, M. Klusch, W. Nutt, & U. Sattler (Eds.), *Proceeding of the 7th International Workshop on Knowledge Representation Meets Databases* (KRDB 2000) (Vol. 29, pp. 129-139). Berlin, Germany: CEUR-WS.org.

Talevera, L., & Béjar, J. (2001). Generality-based conceptual clustering with probabilistic concepts. *IEEE Transactions on Pattern Analysis and Machine Intelligence, 23*(2), 196–206. doi:10.1109/34.908969

Tian, Y., Hankins, R. A., & Patel, J. M. (2008). Efficient aggregation for graph summarization. In J. Tsong-Li Wang (Ed.), *Proceedings of SIGMOD Conference* (pp. 567-580). ACM.

Vapnik, V. (2000). *The nature of statistical learning theory*. Springer-Verlag.

Vaz, D. Ferreira, M., & Lopes, R. (2007). Spatial-Yap: A logic based geographic information system. In V. Dahl, & I. Niemal (Eds.), *Logic Programming*: *Proceedings of the 23rd ICLP* (LNCS 4670, pp.195-208). Porto, Portugal: Springer-Verlag.

Vaz, D., & Ferreira, M. (2007). Spatial deductive database system. *OSGeo Journal, 3*, 44–47.

Vinogradov, D. V. (1999). Logic programs for quasi-axiomatic theories. *NTI* [Moscow, Russia: VINITI.]. *Series, 2*(1-2), 61–64.

Wille, R. (1992). Concept lattices and conceptual knowledge system. *Computers & Mathematics with Applications (Oxford, England), 23*(6-9), 493–515. doi:10.1016/0898-1221(92)90120-7

Witten, I., & Frank, E. (1999). *Data mining practical machine learning tools and techniques with Java implementation*. Morgan Kaufmann.

Wojtusiak, J. (2005). AQ21 User's Guide. *Reports of the Machine Learning and Inference Laboratory, MLI 04-3*, George Mason University, Fairfax, VA, September, 2004 (updated in September, 2005).

Wojtusiak, J. (2008, June). *Data-driven constructive induction in the learnable evolution model*. Paper presented at the 16th International Conference on Intelligent Information Systems, Zakopane, Poland.

Wojtusiak, J., Michalski, R. S., Kaufman, K., & Pietrzykowski, J. (2006). The AQ21 Natural induction program for pattern discovery: Initial version and its novel features. In *Proceedings of The 18th IEEE International Conference on Tools with Artificial Intelligence* (pp. 523-526). Washington, D.C.: IEEE Computer Society.

Wu, T., Xiny, D., & Han, J. (2008). ARCube: Supporting ranking aggregate queries in partially materialized data cubes. In J. Tsong-Li Wang (Ed.), *Proceedings of IGMOD'08,* (pp. 79-92). ACM.

Xin, D., Han, J., & Chang, K. C.-C. (2007). Progressive and selective merge: Computing Top-k with ad-hoc ranking functions. In S. Chaudhuri, V. Hristidis, & N. Polyzotis (Eds.), *SIGMOD Conference* (pp. 103-114). ACM.

Yu, I., & Lu, H. (2001). Multi-cube computation. In *Proceedings of 7th International Symposium on Database Systems for Advanced Application* (pp. 126-133). IEEE Computer Society.

Zabezjalo, M. I., Ivashko, V. G., & Kuznetsov, S. O. (1987). Algorithmic and programming means of JSM-method of automated hypotheses generation. *NTI, Series 2, 10,* 1–14.

Zagorujko, N. G. (1999). *Applied methods of analyzing data analysis and knowledge*. Novosibirsk: Publishing House of the Institute of Mathematics.

Zaiane, O. R., Xin, M., & Han, J. (1998). Discovering Web Access patterns and trends by applying OLAP and data mining technology on Web logs. In *Proceedings of the IEEE Forum on Research and Technology Advances in Digital Libraries* (IEEE ADL'98) (pp. 19-29). IEEE Computer Society.

Zakrevskij, A. D. (1982). Revealing implicative regularities in the Boolean space of attributes and pattern recognition. *Kibernetika, 1,* 1–6.

Zakrevskij, A. D. (1988). *Logic of pattern recognition*. Minsk, Belorussia: "Nauka and Tecnika

Zakrevskij, A. D. (1994). Logical recognition in the space of multi-valued attributes. *Computer Science Journal of Moldova, 2*(2), 169–184.

Zakrevskij, A. D. (2001). A logical approach to the pattern recognition problem. In *Proceedings of the International Conference "Knowledge-Dialog-Solution"* (KDS'2001) (Vol. 2, pp. 238-245). Saint-Petersburg, Russia: State North-West Technical University, Publishing House "Lan".

Zakrevskij, A. D. (2006). A common logic approach to data mining and pattern recognition problem. In E. Triantaphyllou, & G. Felici (Eds.), *Data mining and knowledge discovery approaches based on rule induction techniques* (pp. 1- 42). New York: Springer.

Zhang, Z., Hwang, S.-W., Chang, K. C.-C., Wang, M., Lang, C. A., & Chang, Y.-C. (2006). Boolean + ranking: Querying a database by k-constrained optimization. In S. Chaudhuri, V. Hristidis, & N. Polyzotis (Eds.), *SIGMOD International Conference,*(pp. 359-370). ACM.

Chapter 3
The Coordination of Commonsense Reasoning Operations

ABSTRACT

In this chapter, a conception of commonsense reasoning is developed based on mutually coordinated operations on objects, classes of objects, and properties of objects. This conception goes back to the model of classification processes advanced and described in (Piaget, & Inhelder, 1959). The classification operations are the integral part of any reasoning about time, space, things, events, motions, etc. They consolidate all the forms of reasoning and make it possible to present knowledge as a system of interconnected relations.

INTRODUCTION

Classifications are usually considered in the literature on artificial intelligence as the diagrams of relations between classes of objects. These diagrams have declarative character. They constitute knowledge called the upper ontology. Being a declarative structure, classification loses its connection with the data and the operations with the use of which this classification has been revealed. In order to dynamically adapt classification schemes to newly entering data we need in reasoning operations. In this chapter, we analyze the logical semantics of classification connections between objects, classes of objects, properties of objects and the role of commonsense reasoning operations in creating classification structures.

DOI: 10.4018/978-1-60566-810-9.ch003

THREE INTERRELATED ALGEBRAIC LATTICES OF CLASSES, OBJECTS, AND PROPERTIES

The principle "atom" of commonsense human reasoning is concept. The concepts are represented by the use of names. We shall consider the following roles of names in reasonings: a name can be the name of an object, the name of a class of objects and the name of a classification or collection of classes. With respect to the role of name in knowledge representation schemes, it can be the name of attribute and the name of attribute's value. A class of objects may contain only one object, hence the name of object is a particular case of the name of class. For example, fir-tree can serve as the name of a tree or as the name of a class of trees. Each attribute genarates a classification of a given set of objects, hence the names of attributes can be considered as the names of classifications and the attribute values can be considered as the names of classes.. In the knowledge bases, the sets of names for objects, classes and classifications must not intersect.

Let k be the name of an objects' class, let c be the name of a property of objects (the value of an attribute), and let o be the name of an object. Each class or property has only one maximal set of objects as its interpretation that is the set of objects belonging to this class or possessing this property: $k \rightarrow I(k)$ = { $o: o \leq k$}, $c \rightarrow I(c)$ = { $o: o \leq c$}, where the relation '$\leq$' denotes 'is a' relation and has causal nature (the dress is red, an apple is a fruit). Each object has only one corresponding set of all its properties: $C(o)$ = { $c: o \leq c$}. We shall say that $C(o)$ is the description of object o. The link o $\rightarrow C(o)$ is also of causal nature. We shall say that $C(k)$ = { $\cap C(o): o \leq k$} is the description of class k, where $C(k)$ is a collection of properties associated with each object of class k. The link $k \rightarrow C(k)$ is also of causal nature. Figure 1 illustrates the causal links between classes of objects, properties of objects, and objects.

It is clear that each description (a set of properties) has one and only one interpretation (the set of objects possessing this set of properties). But the same set of objects can be the interpretation of different descriptions (equivalent with respect to their interpretations). The equivalent descriptions of the same class are to be said the different names of this class. The task of inferring the equivalence relations between names of classes and properties underlies the processes of commonsense reasoning.

Figure 1. Links between objects, classes, and properties of objects

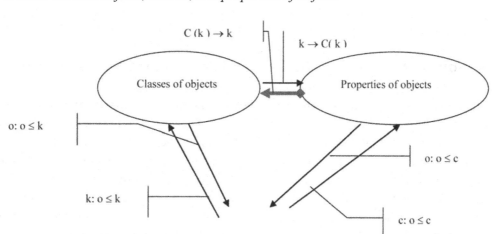

The identity has the following logical content: class A is equivalent to property a ($A \leftrightarrow a$) if and only if the interpretations $I(A)$, $I(a)$ on the set of conceivable objects are equal $I(A) = I(a)$. It is possible to define also the relationship of approximate identity between concepts: a approximates B ($a \leq B$) if and only if the relation $I(a) \subseteq I(B)$ is satisfied. We can consider instead of one property (concept) any subset of properties joined by the union $\cup$ operation: $(c_1 \cup c_2 \cup \ldots c_i \cup \ldots \cup c_n) \leq B$.

Connection directed from 'Properties of objects' to 'Classes of objects' is constructed by learning from examples of objects and their classes. This connection is also of causal nature, it is expressed via the "if – then" rule: to say that "if tiger, then mammalian" means to say that $I(tiger) \subseteq I(mammalian)$.

The Operations of Addition and Multiplication Given on the Set of Classes

Two operations are given on the set of classes' names: the addition operation + and the multiplication operation °. To add classes A and B means to define the least class D including objects of both A and B classes. Class D is determined simultaneously by the common properties of classes A and B: $d = a \cap b$, where a, b, d are the set of properties of objects of classes A, B, D, accordingly.

For example, A - the class of '*blue wooden beads*', B - the class of '*white wooden beads*', D - the class of '*wooden beads*': $I(wooden\ beads) = I(blue\ wooden\ beads) \cup I(white\ wooden\ beads)$ and at the same time $d =$ '*blue wooden beads*' $\cap$ '*white wooden beads*' = '*wooden beads*'.

It is insufficient to have only addition operation to deals with classes. How could one form the set of objects possessing at the same time the properties of different classes, for example, "water transport", "mountain landscape", throat-microphone, "snow-slip", "tragicomedy" and so forth. We need in multiplication operation.

To multiply classes A and B means to define the greatest class D, including the objects belonging to classes A and B simultaneously and having all the properties of class A and all the properties of class B, that is $d = a \cup b$. For example, A - '*a person who has a child*', B - '*a person who is a man*', D - '*father*': $I(father) = I(a\ person\ who\ has\ a\ child) \cap I(a\ person\ who\ is\ a\ man)$ and $d =$ '*has a child*' $\cup$ '*is a man*'.

For the completeness of operation's definition, we shall consider the cases of empty interpretation and empty description. It is possible that the multiplication operation has not a result because of obtaining empty interpretation. In this case, the description obtained is said to be contradictory and to be equal to the special symbol α - 'inconsistent description'.

Also, it is possible that the result of addition operation is a class with empty description. It means that the objects of the class obtained have no common property. In this case, the description of this class is said to be equal to the special symbol ω.

The Operations of Subtraction and Division Given on the Set of Classes

One of the important aspects of mental operations is their reversibility. Addition operation has subtraction as its reverse operation. ($A = D - B$). Reverse operation with respect to multiplication operation is division ($A = D : B$). If subtraction is easy to understand (it is the dissociation of classes), then for division operation it is not the case. Consider the meaning of division operation. For example, a child saw a fox at the picture but he said that it is a dog. According to a child, a dog and a fox are very similar. However an adult does not agree with a child, he begins to explain: it is not a dog, it does not bike, a fox is wild, it lives in the forest, steals hens, a dog does not do this, it lives at home with people, and it guards hens, eats meals of people and so on. Division operation is necessary for differentiating two concepts. Let's the concept Z be equal to DOG + FOX, z be the common property for dog and fox. To divide concepts is to find a property y such that the union of y and z results in the property $c = y \cup z$ corresponding only with the set of dogs and only with this set: $I(c) = I(\text{DOG})$.

The Operations of Generalization and Specification Given on the Set of Objects' Descriptions

Two operations are given on the sets of objects' descriptions: the operation *, or the generalization operation, and the operation •, or the specification or refinement operation. The first one produces for any pair of descriptions $C(o_1)$, $C(o_2)$ their maximal common part $C(o_1) \cap C(o_2)$, the second one produces the minimal description including (containing) $C(o_1)$ and $C(o_2)$, that is $C(o_1) \cup C(o_2)$.

If the result of generalization operation is equal to ω, then it means that object o_1 is unlike o_2. The specification operation is not defined in case of $C(o_1)$ and $C(o_2)$ are inconsistent ($I(C(o_1)) \cap I(C(o_2)) = empty$). Then the result of this operation will be equal a special symbol α. It means that there is no object which possesses $C(o_1)$, ($C(o_2)$ at a time.

Boldyrev, N.G. (1974) advanced a formalization of object description procedures as algebra with two binary operations of refinement and generalization defined by an axiom system including lattice axioms. This work turned to be basic for developing the classification theory in the scope of algebraic lattices.

We describe in short the formal system proposed by Boldyrev.

Let P be a set of undefined elements. P is called the complete pattern ensemble (in our terminology this is the set of properties). Two binary operations a * b and a • b are defined for any two subsets of the complete pattern ensemble P. Let's suppose the results of these operations to be either subset of the complete pattern ensemble or one of algebraic symbols ω and α indicating impracticability of these operations, In other words, the fact that the results of the operations are not defined. We call the first operation, denoted by the symbol *, a generalization operation (G - operation) and the second operation, denoted by the symbol •, a refinement operation (R - operation).

Let 2^P be the set of all subsets of P. Then these operations map each pair $a, b \subseteq P$ into the set 2^P.

If a pair (a, b) has not an image in the mapping defined by R-operation, then we suppose that the result of R-operation is equal to the symbol α. It means that there is no object which possesses the properties a and b at a time. Similarly, if a pair (a, b) has not an image in the mapping defined by G-operation, then we suppose that the result of G-operation to is equal to the symbol ω. The meaning of ω is: "a is unlike b". These operations are defined by the following systems of postulates (Boldyrev, 1974).

1. Postulate of Refinement:

if $a \bullet b \neq \alpha$, $a \bullet c \neq \alpha$, and $b \bullet c \neq \alpha$, then $(a \bullet b) \bullet c \neq \alpha$ and $a \bullet (b \bullet c) \neq \alpha$.

2. Lattices Postulates:

$(a \bullet b) \bullet c = a \bullet (b \bullet c)$; $(a * b) * c = a * (b * c)$

$a \bullet b = b \bullet a$; $a * b = b * a$

$a* \ a \cdot b = a; \ a \cdot a * b = a.$

3. Inclusion Postulates:

$a \cdot b \subseteq a; \ a \subseteq a * b$

$a \cdot b \subseteq b; \ b \subseteq a * b.$

It is not difficult to prove that the result of the generalization operation $c = a * b$ is the lattice least element satisfying the relationships $c \cdot a = a, \ b \ c \cdot b = b$. Analogously, the result of the specification operation $c = a \cdot b$ is the lattice greatest element satisfying the relationships $c * a = a, \ c * b = b$.

Boldyrev (1974) has given an interpretation of this formal system as the minimization of partial switching functions with a large number of "don't care" conditions and so the formal system was found to be helpful in computer design.

It should be noted that computer design problems related to the developing of Boolean function minimization methods are directly connected with the pattern recognition problem. The problems of this type were solved by Quine (1952) and Miller (1965). A. Zakrevskij and his assistants have paid much attention to solving this problem too (Zakrevskij, & Toropov, 1966; Toropov, 1967). Specifically, N. Toropov was the first who noted that it is possible to consider the minimization of weakly speci-fied Boolean functions as the principal interpretation of the pattern recognition formal system. In this interpretation, object is represented by the ternary code, in which the values of its elements are selected from the set {0, 1, -}. Symbol `-`indicates "unimportantly zero or one"; geometrically object is an in-terval of the Boolean space. The refining operation in this interpretation is defined as the intersection of intervals, which is feasible, if intersection is not empty. The operation of generalization is determined somewhat more complicatedly. Let a, b be two objects (intervals of Boolean space) belonging to one of two given classes. The operation of generalization builds new object c as the interval of Boolean space inside which intervals a and b lie. If interval c does not contain any point of another class (i.e. the class, to which a and b do not belong), then the operation of generalization is feasible. Otherwise this opera-tion is considered to be unsatisfiable.

The formal model of pattern recognition system makes a great number of interpretations possible. We shall consider in more details the interpretation of this model as a modular lattice on a set of relations in the many-valued feature space.

Let $A = \{a_1, a_2, ..., a_k\}$ be a finite set of integers and let $\leq$ be the relation of coincidence. This rela-tion holds for a pair of elements $a_i, a_j, i \neq j, a_i, a_j \in A$ if and only if $a_i = a_j$. This relation possesses all the properties of partial ordering. Let us supplement the set A with two elements ω and α such that $\forall \ a_i \in A, a_i < \omega, \alpha < a_i$. Then the set $A' = \{A, \omega, \alpha\}$ with the relation $\leq$ forms the complete lattice $U = (A', \leq)$. It is possible to define U by binary operations * (addition) and • (multiplication), defining $\sup(a_i, a_j)$ and $\inf(a_i, a_j)$, respectively, for all $a_i, a_j \in A$ as it is shown in Table 1, Table 2.

Let us define the lattice U^n on the set $A^n = A_1' \times A_2' \times .... \times A_n'$ as a direct product of the lattices $U^i = (A_i', \leq), i = 1, 2, ..., n$. The operations {*, •} in U^n are the component operations namely $r_1 \leq r_2, r_1, r_2 \in A^n$ holds if and only if $x_j[r_1] \leq x_j[r_2], j = 1, 2, ..., n$ holds for every pair of corresponding components.

$U^n = (A^n \leq)$ is a complete modular lattice. The unit element in this lattice is the n-component cortege whose all components are ω, and the zero element of this lattice is the n-component cortege whose all components are α.

Table 1. The addition operation on finite set of integers

*	a_1	a_2	....	a_k	ω	α
a_1	a_1	ω	ω	ω	ω	a_1
a_2		a_2	ω	ω	ω	a_2
..				ω	ω	...
a_k				a_k	ω	a_k
ω					ω	ω
α						α

Table 2. The multiplication operation on finite set of integers

•	a_1	a_2	....	a_k	ω	α
a_1	a_1	α	α	α	a_1	α
a_2		a_2	α	α	a_2	α
..				α	...	α
a_k				a_k	a_k	α
ω					ω	α
α						α

The elements of A^n may be considered as the descriptions of objects defined by means of attributes (features) $A_1, A_2, ..., A_n$. The relation $r_1 \leq r_2, r_1, r_2 \in A^n$ may be read as the expression "r_1 possesses the feature r_2", then the operation * for $r_1, r_2 \in A^n$ forms the description of its nearest general feature $r_3 \in A^n$ such that $r_1, r_2 \leq r_3$, and for any $r_4 \in A^n, r_4 \neq r_3$ and $r_1, r_2 \leq r_4$ we have $r_3 < r_4$. The operation • for $r_1, r_2 \in A^n$ forms the description of the nearest element r_5 possessing the feature r_1 as well as the feature r_2, that is $r_5 \leq r_1, r_2$ and for any $r_6, r_6 \in A^n, r_6 \neq r_5$ such that $r_6 \leq r_1, r_2$ we nave $r_6 < r_5$. The unit element of the lattice has the semantics "no feature at all" and the zero element of the lattice has the semantics "no object at all". It is naturally to map all the corteges containing at least one symbol α into the zero element $\boldsymbol{\alpha}$ of U^n (into n-component cortege all the components of which are equal to α).

Practically many others object-feature spaces are described as lattices: topological lattice, lattice of intervals, Boolean algebra, lattice of fuzzy sets (Tepavcevic, & Trajkovski, 2001). In each particular case the degree of accuracy in data description and the proper lattice are chosen.

The Set-Theoretical Operations Given on the Set of all Subsets of Objects

The set-theoretical operations of union ∪ and intersection ∩ are given on the set of all subsets of objects and, consequently, on the set of all classes of objects.

A non-empty class $L(X)$ of subsets of a space X such that the union and the intersection of two sets belonging to $L(X)$ also belong to $L(X)$ is an example of a lattice, called a *lattice of sets* or *set lattice* (Rasiova, 1974).

The coordination of classification operations means that the operations on classes' names, on conceivable objects and on objects' descriptions are performed simultaneously and they are in agreement with one another.

The coordinated classification operations generate logical implicative assertions. These assertions can be understood if classifications are performed as the system of coordinated operations. First of all, the classification operations are connected with understanding the operations of quantification: "not all *c* are *a*", "all *b* are c", "no *b* are *c*", "some *c* are *b*", "some *b* are not *a*" and so on. The violation of the coordinated classification operations implies the violation of reasoning. Piaget & Inhelder (1959). have shown that

1) Classification reasoning is a result of gradual development of a person;
2) Appearing the ability to apply formal logical operations is connected with spontaneous appearing the ability to coordinate mental operations;
3) A key problem of the development of operational classification in mind is the problem of understanding the inclusion relation. If the understanding of this relation is not achieved by a person, then it is impossible for him understanding both the classification and quantification operations.

THE CONCEPTS OF NAME AND EXPRESSION ON NAMES

The operations on concepts have a complex structure. These operations involve the expressions on properties and classes of objects as well as objects themselves. With the use of these operations, we construct the expressions which can be interpreted on the set of all conceivable objects. For example, the class of "flying frogs" is formed by generalizing the properties of two classes: the class of flying objects and the class of frogs. The word "flying" presupposes that the mental generalization had place in the past by acquiring in mind the class of all flying objects. It is important that expressions of natural language are interpreted by means of logical mental constructions which, in their turn, are interpreted by means of mental operations on conceivable (thinkable) sets of objects.

Reasoning as Searching for the Equivalence Relationships on a Set of Expressions

The equivalence relations on names serve as the foundation of commonsense reasoning. For example the expression "Whale is a mammal" is true because of the fact that the property C exists such that the following expressions occur simultaneously: "$Whale \leq C$" and "$mammal = C$", interpreted on the set of all thinkable animals. By the law of transitivity, we have "$whale \leq mammal$".

In the thinking, some concepts are determined via others with the aid of equivalence relations between their names, for example, "father is a man having a child" is the word representation of the dependency on classification names "$father = man \circ to\ have\ a\ child$", interpreted on the set of all thinkable men. The knowledge of equivalence relations on the names of classifications makes it possible to draw the conclusions, which would be impossible without this knowledge.

Assume that in one of the agencies the unemployed persons of young age and the unemployed women are registered. Can one infer that, in this agency, unemployed young women are registered too (in other words, whether the interpretation of expression "$unemployed \circ young \circ women$" is not empty set)?. No, it is impossible to achieve this conclusion. But if it is known that "$unemployed \leq young$", then it is possible to assert that there are "$unemployed\ young\ women$" in the agency (Laurent, & Spyratos, 1988).

With the use of the + and ° operations on names of classes, of the * and • operations on descriptions of objects we produce the expressions which are interpreted with the use of the set-theoretical operations on the set of all subsets of objects, but the mechanisms of generating expressions do not exhaust reasoning. The main point of reasoning is finding the equivalences between the expressions constructed over the names of classes or properties. Two expressions are equivalent if their interpretations are equal. Already the act itself of constructing a class requires establishing the identity between the name of the class and the expression on the object properties which this class is defined by.

The equivalent expressions are simply the different names of the same interpretation. For example, we can meet in the crosswords the following definitions of the concepts requested: "it is the same that destiny", "the title of prince of royal dynasty in Spain and Portugal", "a fodder or food plant with fleshy root". It had been shown that the task of defining the equivalence of words (expressions) underlies not only constructing concepts and their definitions via object properties but also updating conceptual knowledge, diagnostic reasoning, supplementing imperfect descriptions of objects (classes, situations) with new properties, inferring causal dependencies between properties, and functional dependencies between classifications.

Definition of a class of objects via the properties of objects is the traditional task of learning concepts from examples. The relationships between properties are implications in the form $a\ b\ c \rightarrow p$, where a, b, c – properties of objects or values of corresponding attributes, p – the name of class of object.

The relationships between classes are defined by the relationships between properties of object belonging to these classes. These relationships generate hierarchical structures on the names of classes coordinated with the structures of properties and the structures of appropriate sets of objects used for interpreting considered classes and properties. The inference of these relationships is also one of the machine learning problems. Moreover this inference is basic to creating the methodology of ontology construction.

The relationships between classifications are expressed formally by functional dependencies between attributes of objects. The inference of these relationships can be considered as hierarchical knowledge integration.

REASONING AS A SPECIAL KIND OF COMPUTING

Reasoning can be reduced to solving the equations of the following types:

a)   "Call things by their correct names": $y = \varphi\ (x)$, $x = a$, $y = ?$
b)   Find the interpretation x satisfying the equality of expressions $\varphi 1$, $\varphi 2$: $\varphi 1(x) = \varphi 2(x)$ or $a = \varphi 1(x)$;
c)   "Approximate $\varphi\ ()$ with the use of $\varphi 1(), \varphi 2(), \ldots, \varphi k()$ and the set of given operations.

In these equations, x is a sub-domain of reasoning and φ is an expression on the names the interpretation of which is equal to or included in x. Given y, it is necessary to find an interpretation x satisfying the equation $y = \varphi\ (x)$; Given x it is necessary to find y as an expression the interpretation of which is equal to or included in x.

Example 1. $y = $ "*an infectious children's disease * name of 5 letters * the fist letter is "m" * the last letter is "s"* (x)". To find x is to find the name of the concrete children's disease: $x = mumps$.

Example 2. $y = \varphi(voltmeter)$; voltmeter belongs to a class of electric instruments, since "*voltmeter $\leq$ electric instrument*". Furthermore, this instrument serves for measuring tension. Thus, $y = electric$ *instrument * measuring tension*".

Example 3. $y = \varphi(quilted\ jacket)$; $y =$ "*warm clothing *working clothing* wadded jacket *jacket without the collar*".

Example 4. "$y_1 + y_2$ * *blue* $= \varphi(good\ weather)$ ". Let us define this expression so that it would not contradict with the observed true situation: "*the sun + the sky * blue.*

In resolving equations, the passages from the expressions to their interpretations and from some expressions to the others through the known dependences between them are performed.

For example, assume that the expression "*birthday in the piggery*" is given. It is necessary to find another equivalent expression, which consists of one word (this example is taken from a crosswords).

The concept "*birthday*" defines the region of reasoning or the region of interpretation "*the living beings*" ("*the living beings $\leq$ birthday*"). Note that the region of interpretation is expressed by using words, i., e., by using its name. Thus, we pass from the properties to the names of their interpretations. Since the discussion deals with the piggery, then the region of reasoning is "*the living beings born in the piggery*".

The contraction of the region of reasoning occurs by means of the multiplication of properties "*the living beings * born in the piggery*".

But "*the living beings born in the piggery*" = "*piggy*", thus, we pass to the search for equivalent expression for $y =$ "*the birthday * piggy*". It is now clear that $y =$ "*farrow*".

In our next example, we consider the following geometrical figures: 1) square, 2) rhombus, 3) parallelogram, 4) quadrilateral with two right angles, 5) trapezium with the pair of equal sides, 6) trapezium with one side perpendicular to the base of it, 7) trapezium whose sides are all of different length, 8) quadrilateral whose sides are all of different length, 9) rectangle, 10) quadrilateral with one right angle (Table 3).

Consider the following set of attributes: 1) A_1 – "there is at least one right angle", 2) A_2- "there are at least two right angles", 3) A_3 – "there are at least three right angles", 4) A_4 – "there are four right angles", 5) A_5 – "at least one pair of opposite sides parallel", 6) A_6 – "two pairs of opposite sides parallel", 7) A_7 – "diagonals bisecting each other".

Table 3. The descriptions of geometrical figures (set 1)

	Object (Classes of objects)	A_1	A_2	A_3	A_4	A_5	A_6	A_7
1	Square	+	+	+	+	+	+	+
2	Rhombus	-	-	-	-	+	+	+
3	Parallelogram	-	-	-	-	+	+	+
4	Quadrilateral	+	+	-	-	+	-	-
5	Trapezium	-	-	-	-	+	-	-
6	Trapezium	+	+	-	-	+	-	-
7	Trapezium	-	-	-	-	+	-	-
8	Quadrilateral	-	-	-	-	-		-
9	Rectangle	+	+	+	+	+	+	+
10	Quadrilateral	+	-	-	-	-	-	

Table 4. The classes of geometrical figures

	Object (Class of Object)	A_1	A_2	A_3	A_4	A_5	A_6	A_7
1,9	Square and rectangle	+	+	+	+	+	+	+
2,3	Rhombus and parallelogram	-	-	-	-	+	+	+
4,6	Quadrilateral	+	+	-	-	+	-	-
5,7	Trapezium	-	-	-	-	+	-	-
8	Quadrilateral	-	-	-	-	-	-	-
10	Quadrilateral	+	-	-	-	-	-	-

To solve the equation: "two pairs of opposite sides are parallel(x) = diagonals bisecting each other(x)" means to find the domain of interpretation satisfying two conditions (properties): $x = ?$ $x = \{square, rhombus, parallelogram, rectangle\}$.

In the Table 3, "+" indicates the presence of feature, "-" indicates the absence of feature. With this collection of attributes, it is not possible to distinguish some figures, namely, square and rectangle, rhombus and parallelogram, quadrilateral with two right angles and trapezium with one side perpendicular to base, isosceles trapezium and trapezium, all whose sides have different length.

We combine equivalent figures into the classes. The result is shown in Table 4.

It is easy to see, that the collection of attributes 1, 5, 6 and 1, 5, 7 are tests in Table 4 for the partition of figures into the classes and they, therefore, generate the structure of their sub-classes.

Let us take another collection of the attribute: 1) A_1 – "the pairs of opposite sides are parallel", 2) A_2 – "all angles are right", 3) A_3 – "all sides are equal", 4) A_4 – "only one pair of the opposite sides is parallel", 5) A_5 –"only one pair of the opposite sides is equal". The descriptions of some geometrical figures with the use of these attributes are given in Table 5.

In table 5, each object possesses a unique collection of attribute's values or properties: $C(o) = \{ c: o \leq c\}$, where $C(o)$ is a description of object "o". Let * and • be binary operations such that * operation finds for a pair of object descriptions $C(o_1)$, $C(o_2)$ their maximal common part (if this part is not empty), i.e. $C(o_1) \cap C(o_2)$; • operation finds a minimal description in which the properties of both objects $C(o_1)$ and $C(o_2)$ are combined (if such combination is possible), i.e. $C(o_1) \cup C(o_2)$. If maximal common property is empty set, then it means that there is not a common property of the given pair of objects. If • operation is unsatisfiable, then it means that there is not an object in which could be combined the properties of both given objects. The inclusion relation between two collections of properties $C_1 \subseteq C_2$

Table 5. The descriptions of geometrical figures (set 2)

	Object (Class of objects)	A1	A2	A3	A4	A5
1	Square	+	+	+	-	-
2	Rhombus	+	-	+	-	-
3	Rectangle	+	+	-	-	-
4	Trapezium	-	-	-	+	-
5	Quadrilateral	-	-	-	-	-
6	Parallelogam	+	-	-	-	-

is realized if and only if $I(C_1) \supseteq I(C_2)$, where $I(C_1) = \cap\ I(c_i)$, for all $c_i \in C_1$, $C_1 = \cup\ c_i$ (it is analogous for the collection C_2).

In Table 5 $C(rhombus) \subseteq C(square)$, $C(parallelogram) \subseteq C(rhombus)$, $C(rectangle) \subseteq C(square)$, $C(parallelogram) \subseteq C(rectangle)$.

Here the names of the figures serve as the names of classes: all squares, all rhombus, etc. The inclusion relations on the properties (classes) correspond to the inclusion relations on their interpretations: "all *squares* are the *rhombuses*", "all *rhombuses* are the *parallelograms*", "all *squares* are the *rectangles*", and "all *rectangles* are the *parallelograms*"; *square* → *rhombus* (*square* is a *rhombus*), rhombus → *parallelogram*, *square* → *rectangle*, and *rectangle* → *parallelogram*.

The following dependencies are satisfied:

Pairs of opposite sides are parallel * all sides are equal(x) = rhombus (x);
Pairs of opposite sides are parallel * all sides are equal * all angles are right(x) = square(x);
Pairs of opposite sides are parallel * all angles are right(x) = rectangle(x);
Pairs of opposite sides are parallel(x) = parallelogram(x).

Note that the role of words in reasoning is dual: they can be both the names of classes or properties and the names of their interpretations.

The operations on classes, properties, interpretations are the coordinated operations, which are carried out simultaneously and in interconnection with one another.

Commonsense reasoning is based on the replacement of some expressions by the others, the explanation of some concepts through the others. "Good reasoning" makes it possible to perform the best replacements or accurate unifications, such that the interchangeable expressions have either the same interpretation in the domain of reasoning or the interpretations approximately equivalent.

Naturally, commonsense reasoning includes not only the use of equivalent expressions, but also very process of searching for equivalent descriptions of objects or classes of objects. Poets as well as scientists tend to express accurately their thoughts. As a result of reasoning, the conceptual structure of knowledge is created and renewed in the form of the connections between conceivable objects, classes of objects and their properties.

CONCLUSION

In this chapter, we examined the classification as the system of interconnected structures of objects, properties and classes together with the operations, with the aid of which these structures are built.

We showed that the structural connections between classes and properties of objects, between different classes, and between properties of objects make it possible to build logical expressions on the names of objects, classes and properties, interpreted on the set of all subsets of conceivable objects.

The tasks of machine learning deal with mining the classification connections making it possible to establish equivalence relations between the logical expressions, utilized in the processes of commonsense reasoning.

REFERENCES

Boldyrev, N. G. (1974). Minimization of boolean partial functions with a large number of "don't care" conditions and the problem of feature extraction. In *Discrete Systems, Proceedings of International Symposium* (pp.101-109). Riga, Latvia: Publishing House "Zinatne".

Laurent, D., & Spyratos, N. (1988). Partition semantics for incomplete information in relational databases. In H. Boral, & P. Larson (Eds), *The Proceedings of ACM – SIGMOD'88* (pp. 66-73). ACM Press.

Miller, R. E. (1965). *Switching theory. Combinational circuits.* New York: John Wiley and Sons.

Piaget, J., & Inhelder, B. (1959). La Genèse des Structures Logiques Elémentaires: Classifications et Sériations. Neuchâtel: Delachaux & Niestlé.

Quine, W. N. (1952). The problem of simplifying truth functions. *The American Mathematical Monthly, LIX*(8).

Rasiova, H. (1974), *An algebraic approach to non-classical logic* (Studies in Logic, Vol. 78). London: North-Holland Publishing Company.

Tepavcevic, A., & Trajkovski, G. (2001). L-fuzzy lattices: An introduction . *Fuzzy Sets and Systems, 123*(2), 209–216. doi:10.1016/S0165-0114(00)00065-8

Toropov, N. R. (1967). An algorithm of the minimization of boolean partial functions with a large number of "don't care" conditions. In *The Theory of Automates, Materials of the Seminar on the Automate Theory, issue 4*. Kiev, Ukraine: Kiev Institute of Cybernetics.

Zakrevskij, A. (1971) *Algorithms of the synthesis of discrete automata.* Moscow: Nauka.

Zakrevskij, A., & Toropov, N. R. (1966). Learning pattern recognition rules in Boolean space. In A.A Feldbaum (Ed), *Self-learning automated systems* (pp. 67-72). Moscow: Nauka.

Chapter 4
The Logical Rules of Commonsense Reasoning

ABSTRACT

In this chapter we describe a model of commonsense reasoning that has been acquired from our numerous investigations on the human reasoning modes used by experts for solving diagnostic problems in diverse areas such as pattern recognition of natural objects (rocks, ore deposits, types of trees, types of clouds etc.), analysis of multi-spectral information, image processing, interpretation of psychological testing data, medicine diagnosis and so on. The principal aspects of this model coincide with the rule-based inference mechanism that is embodied in the KADS system (Ericson, et al., 1992), (Gappa, & Poeck, 1992). More details related to our model of reasoning and its implementation can be found in (Naidenova, & Syrbu, 1984; Naidenova, & Polegaeva, 1985a; 1985b).

INTRODUCTION

An expert's rules are logical assertions that describe the knowledge of specialists about a problem domain. Our experience in knowledge elicitation from experts allows us to analyze the typical forms of assertions used by experts. As an example, we give the rules of an expert's interpretation of data obtained with the use of Pathological Character Accentuation Inventory for Adolescents. This psycho-diagnostic method elaborated by Lichko (1983) is a classical example of an expert system.

Some examples of the expert's rules are:

DOI: 10.4018/978-1-60566-810-9.ch004

1. "If $(D - F) \geq 4$, then DISSIMULATION decreases the possibility to reveal any character accentuation and completely excludes the CYCLOID and CONFORM types of character".
2. "If the index $E > 4$, then the CYCLOID and PSYCHASTENOID types are impossible".
3. "If the type of character is HYPERTHYMIA, then ACCENTUATION with psychopathies is observed in 75%, with transit disturbances – in 5%, and with stable adaptation – in 5% of all cases".
4. "If the index $A > 6$ and the index $S > 7$ and the index $Con = 0$ and the index $D > 6$, then the LABILE type is observed".
5. "If the index $E \geq 6$, then the SCHISOID and HYSTEROID types are observed frequently".
6. "If after the application of rules with the numbers x, y, z the values of at least two indices are greater than or equal to the minimal diagnostic threshold, then the mixed types are possible with the following consistent combinations of characters: Hyp - C, Hyp - N, Hyp - Hyst, C - L, L - A, L - S, and L - Hyst".

We used the following abbreviations: Hyp - hyperthymia, C - cycloid, L - labile, A – asthenia, N – neurotic, S - schizoid, Con - conformable, Hyst - hysteroid, Sens - sensitive, D - dissimulation, F - frankness, E - emancipation, and P - psychasthenia.

These rules describe the system of knowledge formed by the specialists through a long-time process of learning. One of the inevitable and important steps in learning is connected with extracting objects or concepts from the observation data. The definition of object is a very complex task. Object is a phenomenon with invariable (to some extent) form and a set of constituent parts each of which can be described by a particular collection of attributes measurable or not measurable (qualitative). Object possesses a specifical way of genesis, it also possesses age and follows a certain law of development. The examples of natural objects are: forest, mushroom, berry, plant, tree, birch, fir-tree ect. Tree has crown, trunc, branches, leaves etc.

The specialists construct boundaries between objects in space and in time. By this reason, the following assertions appear: "with height ≥ 800 meters above see-level, there does not appear the meadow type of woodland".

Object is connected with its environment. There exist, as a rule, factors determining the way of object development. The links between object and its environment factors are reflected by causal relations. For example, the forest is under the influence of landscape, climate, ground, and water conditions.

There are associative links between coexistent objects in time and space. For example, each type of woodland is associated with a certain type of predominent trees and vice versa. Predominant type of trees can have concomitant ones.

The properties of object can be independent or connected through causal (functional) links. So the age of tree determines the image and properties of crown, the age of forest determines the properties of its curtain. The images of forests on photographes are determined by the condition of aerial survey and the type of instrument.

In a forest region, the specialists study the distribution of the forest types. The boudaries between the types of forest are established and the sub-regions are generated. The number of sub-regions is generalized or harmonized. If some types of forest occur very rarely, then they are excluded from consideration, some types of forest can be joined in one type. Each type of forest (sub-region) is estimated with the use of a confidence coefficient, for example in terms of the frequency of its occurrence in the given region.

Our own study of the specialists' thinking in forestry shows that they discover the boundary values of features as the informative ones. The boundary values of features are characteristic for passing a certain phenomenon from one state to another. So, the forester will note the steepness of slope into 3 degrees, if with this steepness changes the type of forest conditions (a biological unity of different interconnected forest features). He will order features according to the degree of their manifestation and to the degree of their prevalence or domination. He keeps in mind the most difficult situations from the diagnostic point of view and he has some rules in the reserve for the diagnostics of difficult (boundary) cases.

We summarize the main stages of expert knowledge acquisition as follows.

Stages of Intellectual Data Analysis:

1. Revealing objects, their features, and classes of objects.
    This task includes
    1a) Finding the most informative intervals of observed features' values and their bounds with the point of view of discerning or identifying phenomena, objects, and/or classes of objects in question;
    1b) Conceptual clustering or natural classifying, i. e. forming groups of objects with similar features by their structure and variety of their characteristics;
    1c) Finding causal explanation or meaning of the obtained groups (classes) of objects.
2. Pure Supervised Learning or searching for the regularities in the form of implicative, associative or functional dependencies between features or values of features.
    This task includes
    2a) Coding features, forming new descriptions of objects in terms of the chosen intervals or symbols substituting these intervals;
    2b) The formation of concepts, rules, decision making procedures for the solution of tasks in various applications;
    2c) The investigation of the distributions of classes of objects and their attributes' values.
3. Forming decision making processes (algorithms) based on the object descriptions and causal relations between properties of objects and between properties of objects and their classes.

The problems listed above in the points **1b** and **1c** are dynamically interconnected. They relate to integrating Conceptual Clustering with Supervised Learning. The content of this integration can be explained as follows: it is the formation of classes of objects with the specific similarity of objects inside classes and the difference of objects from different classes, in such a way, that they could be meaningfully interpreted in terms of the concepts known to the researcher, but not participating in describing objects (any external criterion was not assigned; it is necessary to find such classification that explains causally the observed phenomenon). For example, long before the temperature of stars became measurable all stars were ordered in terms of their spectra and divided into the spectral classes along the characteristic spectral lines. Later it turned out that star's spectral classes correspond to their temperature classes.

The natural classification is the interaction of two main processes:

*   If a common property of objects is observed, to determine, whether it is possible to give a name to this totality of objects, i.e. whether it is possible to interpret meaningfully this totality; if yes, then this common property is permitted; otherwise it is simply useless;
*   If some group of objects has the name with a certain meaning, to find the general property of this group or give the description of this group in terms of assigned properties in such a way that this

description would be equivalent to the name of this group (new description must separate this and only this group from all other conceivable objects).

For example, let us give the description of a data analysis task formulated by one of the experts on the problems of soldiers' health and quality of life estimation. This expert is unfamiliar with the machine learning problem (boldface of words in the text belongs to the expert himself).

The task of Investigation:

1) Selecting adequate **criteria** and methods of diagnostics and evaluating the soldiers' mental health and quality of life;
2) To extract three groups of mental health based on clinical- psychopathological and psychological study of soldiers;
3) To build **models** for diagnostics and prognostication of the soldiers' mental health and quality of life;
4) To study **the degree of influence** of medical psychological and sociological factors, and also of physical development and functional state of cardio - respiratory system on the soldiers' mental health and quality of life;
5) To reveal **the special features of obtained groups** of mental health and quality of life according to the medical psychological, sociological, and physiological indices;
6) To develop **an algorithm of studying the influence** of different factors (for example, the application of pharmacological preparations, social programs) on the soldiers' mental health and quality of life.

Here, of course, the term "degree of influence" requires to be refined, but as a whole the content of expert's tasks is adequate to the above described knowledge acquisition problems.

One can say that the result of learning is an upper ontology. The upper ontology is based on categories and so called "the event calculus" (Russel, & Norvig, 2003). It covers structured objects, time and space, change, processes, substances, and belief. But the specialists on artificial intelligence often consider ontology separately from data and learning, in contrast to the domain specialists probably keeping in mind the ontology as a system of knowledge, together with data on the foundation of which their knowledge has been constructed.

THE RULES OF THE FIRST TYPE IN THE FORM OF "IF – THEN" ASSERTIONS

Practically without loss of knowledge, an expert's assertions can be represented with the use of only one class of logical rules, namely, the rules based on implicative dependencies between names.

We need the following three types of rules in order to realize logical inference (deductive and inductive):

INSTANCES or relationships between objects or facts really observed. Instance can be considered as a logical rule with the least degree of generalization. On the other hand, instances can serve as a source of a training set of positive and negative examples for inductive inference of generalized rules.

RULES OF THE FIRST TYPE or logical rules. These rules describe regular relationships between objects and their properties and between properties of different objects. The rules of the first type can be given explicitly by an expert or derived automatically from examples with the help of some learning process. These rules are represented in the form "if-then" assertions.

RULES OF THE SECOND TYPE or commonsense reasoning rules with the help of which rules of the first type are used, updated, and inferred from data (instances). The rules of the second type embrace both inductive and deductive reasoning rules.

The rules of the first type can be represented with the use of only one class of logical statements, namely, the statements based on implicative dependencies between names. Names are used for designating concepts, things, events, situations, or any evidences. They can be considered as attributes' values in the formal representations of logical rules. In our further consideration, the letters A, B, C, D, a, b, c, d ...will be used as attributes' values in logical rules.

We consider the following rules of the first type.

The Rules of the First Type as a Language for Knowledge Representation in the Framework of Commonsense Reasoning

The rules of the first type can be represented with the use of only one class of logical statements, namely, the statements based on implicative dependencies between names. Names are used for designating concepts, things, events, situations, or any evidences. They can be considered as attributes' values in the formal representations of logical rules. In our further consideration, the letters A, B, C, D, a, b, c, d ... will be used as attributes' values in logical rules.

We consider the following rules of the first type.

Implication

Implication: $a, b, c \rightarrow d$. This rule means that if the values standing on the left side of the rule are simultaneously true, then the value on the right side of the rule is always true.

One may find a lot of examples of using the first type rules in our every day life but these rules are revealed very distinctly in detective stories. We preferred to draw the examples from Sherlock Holmes's practice because he was "the most perfect reasoning and observing machine that the world have seen" in Doctor Watson's opinion. Here is a typical example of Sherlock Holmes's reasoning (Doyle, 1992): "As to your practice, if a gentleman walks into my rooms smelling of iodoform, with a black mark of nitrate of silver upon his right fore-finger, and a bulge on the side of top-hat to show where he has secreted his stethoscope, I must be dull indeed, if I do not pronounce him to be an active member of the medical profession."

Interdiction or Forbidden Rule

Interdiction or forbidden rule (a special case of implication): $a, b, c \rightarrow false$ (*never*). This rule interdicts a combination of values enumerated on the left side of the rule. The rule of interdiction can be transformed into several implications such as $a, b \rightarrow$ not c; $a, c \rightarrow$ not b; $b, c \rightarrow$ not a.

We can observe some interdictions among the rules obtained by the use of Pathological Character Accentuation Inventory for Adolescents – these are rules 1 and 2.

As an example of forbidden rule, we can quote the famous assertion of the Great Russian poet A. Pushkin: "Genius and violence are incompatible".

Compatibility

Compatibility: $a, b, c \rightarrow VA$ where VA is the frequency of occurrence of the rule.
   The compatibility is equivalent to the collection of implications as follows:

a, b $\rightarrow$ c rarely VA;

a, c $\rightarrow$ b rarely VA;

b, c $\rightarrow$ b rarely VA.

Experts in many research areas use this rule to show the following observation: "values in the left-hand side of the rule do not always exist simultaneously but can occur rather frequently (seldom)". Generally, the compatibility rule represents the most common combination of values which is characterized by an insignificant number of exceptions (contrary examples) from the regularity or the rule that is met always.
   An example of this rule is from Sherlock Holmes's collection of observations (Doyle, 1992): "You have heard me remark that the strangest and most unique things are *very often* connected not with the larger but with the smaller crimes". Another example from the same collection: "I'm a business man", said Straker, "and in business you make enemies. I'm also very rich, and people *sometimes* envy a rich man."
   Rules 3 and 5 among the rules obtained by the use of Pathological Character Accentuation Inventory for Adolescents serve as the examples of the compatibility ones.

Diagnostic Rule

Diagnostic rule: $x, d \rightarrow a$; $x, b \rightarrow$ not a; $d, b \rightarrow false$. For example, d and b can be two values of the same attribute. This rule works when the truth of 'x' has been proven and it is necessary to determine whether 'a' is true or not. If 'x & d' is true, then 'a' is true, but if 'x & b' is true, then 'a' is false.
   An example of this rule is in the following Sherlock Holmes's reasoning (Doyle, 1992): "This Godfry Norton was evidently an important factor in the matter. He was a lawyer. …And what the object of his repeated visits (to her)? Was she his client, his friend, or his mistress? If the former, she had probably transferred the photograph to his keeping. If the latter, it was less likely."

Rule of Alternatives

Rule of alternatives: a or $b \rightarrow true$ (*always*); $a, b \rightarrow false$. This rule says that a and b cannot be simultaneously true, either a or b can be true but not both. This rule is a variant of interdiction.
   We see the examples of using this rule in the argumentation which Sherlock Holmes (Doyl, 1992) addressed to the King of Bohemia: "If the lady loves her husband, she does not love your Majesty. If she does not love your Majesty there is no reason why she should interfere with your Majesty's plan."

THE RULES OF THE SECOND TYPE OR COMMONSENSE REASONING RULES

Deductive steps of commonsense reasoning consist of inferring consequences from some observed facts with the use of statements of the form "if-then" (i.e. knowledge). For this goal, deductive rules of reasoning are applied the main forms of which are modus ponens, modus tollens, modus ponendo tollens, and modus tollendo ponens.

Let x be a collection of true values of some attributes (or evidences) observed simultaneously.

Deductive Reasoning Rules of the Second Type

Using implication: Let r be an implication, left(r) be the left part of r and right(r) be the right part of r. If left(r) $\subseteq x$, then x can be extended by right(r): $x \leftarrow x \cup$ right(r). Using implication is based on modus ponens: if A, then B; A; hence B.

Using interdiction: Let r be an implication $y \rightarrow$ not k. If left(r) $\subseteq x$, then k is the forbidden value for all extensions of x. Using interdiction is based on modus ponendo tollens: either A or B (A, B – alternatives); A; hence not B; either A or B; B; hence not A.

Using compatibility: Let $r =$ '$a, b, c \rightarrow k, VA$', where VA is the value of the special attribute that characterizes the frequency of occurrence of the rule. If left(r) $\subseteq x$, then k can be used to extend x along with the calculated value VA for this extension. Calculating the estimate VA requires special consideration. In any case, we need the function which would be monotonous, continuous and bounded above. The compatibility rule is used on the basis of modus ponens.

Using diagnostic rules: Let r be a diagnostic rule such as '$x, d \rightarrow a$; $x, b \rightarrow$ not a', where 'x' is true, and 'a', 'not a' are hypotheses or possible values of some attribute. Using the diagnostic rule is based on modus ponens and modus ponendo tollens.

There are several ways for refuting one of the hypotheses:

- To infer either d or b using existing knowledge;
- To involve new known facts and/or propositions for inferring (with the use of inductive reasoning rules of the second type) new rules of the first type for distinguishing between the hypotheses 'a' and 'not a'; to apply the newly obtained rules;
- To get the direct answer on whether d or b is true; in this case, involving an external source of knowledge is required.

Using rule of alternatives: Let 'a' and 'b' be two alternative (mutually exclusive) hypotheses about the value of some attribute, and the truth of one of hypotheses has been established by the second-type rule of inference, then the second hypothesis is rejected. Using the rule of alternatives is based on modus tollendo ponens: either A or B (A, B – alternatives); not A; hence B; either A or B; not B; hence A.

We can call the rules listed above the rules of "forward inference". Another way to include implicational patterns (first-type rules) in natural reasoning is commonly used, which can be called "backward inference" and implemented by a number of rules.

Generating hypothesis or abduction rule. Let r be an implication $y \rightarrow k$. Then the following hypothesis is generated "if k is true, then y may be true".

Using modus tollens. Let r be an implication $y \rightarrow k$. If 'not k' is inferred, then 'not y' is also inferred.

When applied, the above given rules generate the reasoning, which is not demonstrative. The purpose of the reasoning is to infer all possible hypotheses on the value of some objective attribute. It is essential that hypotheses do not contradict with knowledge (first-type rules) and the observable real situation, where the reasoning takes place. Inference of hypothesis is reduced to constructing all intrinsically consistent extensions of the set of values x, in which the number of involved attributes is maximum possible (there are no prohibited pairs of values in such extensions). Each extension corresponds to one hypothesis only. All hypotheses have different admissibility, which is determined by the quantity and "quality" of rules of compatibility involved in the inference of each of them.

Inductive Reasoning Rules of the Second Type

Performing inductive steps of commonsense reasoning, we operate with known facts and propositions, observations and experimental results to obtain or correct first-type rules. A British logician, John Stuart Mill (1872), stated main forms of induction as canons that combine method of agreement, method of difference, the joint method of agreement and difference, the method of concomitant variations and the method of residues.

Two first Methods are most natural modes of human thinking. The Method of Agreement is the comparing of the different instances in which some phenomenon occurs. The method of Difference is the comparing of the instances, in which some phenomenon does occur, with the instances in other respects similar in which the phenomenon does not occur. Both Methods are destined for inquiring about the cause of a given effect, or about effects or properties of a given cause. We shall denote antecedents by the large letters, and the consequents corresponding to them by the small ones.

The Method of Agreement

The Method of Agreement is determined by Mill (1872/1959) as follows:

The Method of Agreement: "If two or more instances of the phenomenon under investigation have only one circumstance in common, the circumstance in which alone all the instances agree is the cause (or effect) of the given phenomenon" (Mill, 1872/1959, p. 450).

This rule means that if the previous events (values) A, B, C lead to the events (values) a, b, c and the events (values) A, D, E lead to the events (values) a, d, e, then A is a plausible reason of a.

However, Mill (1872) has considered the following Method to be "a still more potent instrument of the investigation of nature".

The Method of Difference

The method of Difference: *"If an instance in which the phenomenon under investigation occurs, and an instance in which it does not occur, have every circumstance save one in common, that one occurring only in the former; the circumstance in which alone the two instances differ, is the effect, or the cause, or a necessary part of the cause, of the phenomenon"* (Mill, 1872, p. 454).

This rule means that if the previous events (values) A, B, C lead to (or give rise to) the events (values) a, b, c and the events (values) B, C lead to the events (values) b, c, then A is a plausible reason of a.

Instead of comparing different instances of a phenomenon in order to discover in what they agree, this method compares an instance of its occurrence with an instance of its non-occurrence in order to discover in what they differ.

if we begin, at the other end, and desire to investigate the cause of an effect *a*, we select an instance, as *abc*, in which the effect occurs, and in which the antecedents were *ABC*, and we must look out for another instance in which the remaining circumstances *bc* occur without *a*. If the antecedents, in that instance, are *BC*, it means that the cause of *a* may be *A*: either it alone, or *A* in conjunction with some of the other circumstances present.

The Method of Agreement stands on the ground that whatever can be eliminated is not connected with the phenomenon by any law. The Method of Difference has for its foundation, that whatever can not be eliminated is connected with the phenomenon by a law.

The method of Difference is more particularly a method of artificial experiment; while that of Agreement is more convenient for using in case of experimentation is impossible.

Mill, in his treatise, has given simple examples of a logical process to which we owe almost all the inductive conclusions we draw in daily life.

One of Mill's examples is the following. If a number of people who are suffering from a certain disease and have all gone for a considerable time without fresh fruits or vegetables, but, in other respects, have had quite different diets, have lived in different conditions, belong to different races, and so on, so that the lack of fresh fruits and vegetables is the only feature common to all of them, then we can conclude that the lack of fresh fruits and vegetables is the cause of this particular disease.

Another example of Mill is the following. If two exactly similar pieces of iron are heated in a charcoal-burning furnace and hammered into shape in exactly similar ways, except that the first is dipped into water after the final heating while the second is not, and the first is found to be harder than the second, then the dipping of iron into water while it is hot is the cause of such extra hardness—or at least an essential part of the cause, for the hammering, the charcoal fire, and so on may also be needed.

Both previous methods are intended to be methods of implicative induction, that is, methods by which we can reason from a limited number of observed instances to a general causal relationship.

The Joint Method of Agreement and Difference

The Joint Method of Agreement and Difference or the Indirect Method of Difference: *"If two or more instances in which the phenomenon occurs have only one circumstance in common, while two or more instances in which it does not occur have nothing in common save the absence of that circumstance; the circumstance in which alone the two sets of instances differ, is the effect, or cause, or a necessary part of the cause, of the phenomenon"* (Mill, 1872, p. 460).

This rule means that if the previous events (values), *A* and *a* are connected and events *A*, *B*, *C* are observed together with event *a*, and events *B*, *C* without *A* lead to (or give rise to) the absence of event *a*, then *A* is a plausible reason of *a*.

The method combines the first two methods to make strong assertions of causality. There are many cases in which the Method of Difference either cannot be made available at all, or not without a previous employment of the Method of Agreement. This occurs when the phenomenon has not only one single antecedent, but a combination of antecedents, which we have no possibility to separate from each other.

An example has been given by Mill (1872): "Suppose the subject of inquiry to be the cause of the double refraction of light. We can produce this phenomenon by employing any one of the many substances which are known to refract light in that peculiar manner. But if, taking one of those substances, as Iceland spar for example, we wish to determine on which of the properties of Iceland spar this remarkable phenomenon depends, we can no use, for that purpose, of the Method of Difference; for we cannot find another substance precisely resembling Iceland spar except in some one property. (p. 460)". But we can use the Method of Agreement in order to compare all the known substances which had the property of doubly refracting light and such that they agreed in the single property being crystalline substances. We can conclude that there is a connection between two properties and we can also apply the method of Difference to check this conclusion.

Suppose that as we previously examined a variety of instances in which *a* occurred, and found them to agree in containing *A*, so we now observe a variety of instances in which *a* does not occur and find them agree in not contained *A*. Then we conclude that (by the Method of Agreement) the connection between the absence of *A* and the absence of *a* is the same which was before established between their presence.

Now *A B C*, *a b c* and *B C*, *b c* the positive and negative instances which the Method of Difference requires. Thus, if it is true that all animals which have a well-developed respiratory system, and therefore aerate the blood perfectly, agree in being warm-blooded, while those whose respiratory system is imperfect do not maintain a temperature much exceeding that of the surrounding medium, we may argue from this, that the change which taken place in the blood by respiration is the cause of animal heat.

The Method of Residues

The Method of Residuum is formulated as follows: *Subduct from any phenomenon such part as is known by previous inductions to be the effect of certain antecedents, and the residue of the phenomenon is the effect of the remaining antecedents* (*Mill, 1872* p. 464).

Let *U* be a complex phenomenon *abcd* and we know that *A* is the reason of *a*, *B* is the reason of *b*, and *C* is the reason of *c*. Then it is possible to suppose that there is an event *D* that is a reason of *d*.

If all the alternative pathways to a variable can be eliminated as causes on the basis of other proof, the remaining path suspected as causal is the cause.

This Method is a modification of the Method of Difference.

J. S. Mill has shown that the Method of Residues in not independent of deduction, however it is included among inductive methods of direct observation and experiment.

The Method of Concomitant Variations

The Method of Concomitant Variations is formulated as follows: "*Whatever phenomenon varies in any manner whenever another phenomenon varies in some particular manner, is either a cause or an effect of that phenomenon, or is connected with it through some fact of causation*" (Mill, 1872, p. 466).

This rule means that if the change of a previous event (value) *A* is accompanied by the change of an event (value) *a*, and all the other previous events (values) do not change, then *A* is a plausible reason of *a*.

It is often usefully to apply this method after the Method of Difference. When, by the Method of Difference, it has been established that a certain object produces a certain effect, the Method of Concomitant Variations may used to determine according to what law the different relations of the effect follow those of the cause.

Though these canons are very helpful, there are some difficulties connected with this form (and any form) of inductive reasoning. Inductive reasoning can only lead to conclusions that have a high probability of being true. Furthermore, these methods work best when careful control is practiced and when all the possible antecedent circumstances are controlled or taken carefully into account. In essence, the cause cannot be identified until the researcher already knows all of the possible causes.

The validity of the inductive generalization was grounded in the invariance of the natural laws. This is a point of disagreement between Mill and Pierce.

The Methods of Mill are applicable to objects and their properties: object can be considered as the cause of its properties, some properties can be considered as a cause of a class of objects, i. e. the membership of an object to a certain class is considered as the consequence of its properties (or a part of its properties).

For example, the Method of Agreement will be applicable as follows. Let c be the intersection of the descriptions of a set of observed objects O of class C: $c = \cap \{ T_i \}$, where T_i is the description of i-th object. Let the property p be the pointer to the membership of objects to class C. If c exists (the intersection is not empty), then *c is a plausible reason of property p.*

We give several examples of using the inductive canons in a logical game "The letter's Lotto" described in (Bizam, & Herczeg, 1975).

A person thinks of a word with the fixed number of letters. A guesser names the words with the same number of letters. Each time he is informed how many letters in his word have been guessed correctly (a letter is guessed correctly if it is equal to the letter taking up the same position in the thought word).

A set of logical rules are considered for guessing letters. Some rules are the relations which extract true and false letters in compared words. Some rules are the relations subdividing the set of letters into the blocks containing and not containing true letters. But these rules seem to be the Inductive Methods of J. S. Mill.

Rule 1. If the change of letters in a certain number of positions in a word is accompanied by the decrease of the same number of true letters, then the letters in these positions were correct before the change of this word.

For example, the word BACK has 3 letters correctly guessed; the word BOOK has 1 letter correctly guessed. We can conclude that the letters A and C in the second and the third positions of the word BACK are correct.

This rule implements the Method of Concomitant Variations or the Method of Difference.

Rule 2. If the change of letter in only one position of a word does not change the number of correctly guessed letters, then the letters in this position in both words are false.

For example, the word LEAST has 3 letters correctly guessed and the word LEASE has also 3 letters correctly guessed. We can conclude that the letters T and E in the last position are both false.

This rule implements the Joint Method of Agreement and Difference.

Rule 3. If two words include the same number N_{true} of true letters and this number is more than N/2, where N is the length of words, then the intersection of these words must include at least $(2N_{true} - N)$ true letters. If the intersection is void, then the task's condition is inconsistent. If the intersection includes the number of letters exceeding $(2N_{true} - N)$, then some letters in it may be false. This rule has been obtained on the basis of deductive reasoning.

This rule is based on The Method of Agreement.

Rule 4. Let the letter s be correct in a given position k. This relation subdivides the set of letters for this position into two blocks of true and false letters.

Rule 4 is based on the deductive rule of alternatives.

For example, let "PAT (2), MAT (2), COD (1)" be the sequence of words named by a guesser (in brackets, we have the estimation of the number of correct letters). Compare the words PAT and MAT. By rule 2, the letters *P* and *M* in the first position are not correct and the letters *A* and *T* are correct Then in the word COD (1) the letters *O* and *D* are not correct and the first letter C must be correct.

The idea to model one of J.S.Mill's inductive canons, namely, the Method of Agreement, has been realized in the JSM-reasoning method (Finn, 1988; 1991).

This method is a formal construction combining induction, analogy, and abduction. The JSM – reasoning realizes an argumentation based on generating hypotheses of the following kind: "*B* is a cause of the presence (the absence) of a set *A* of objects' properties". The method is based on the following rules: the first canon of induction, the rules for predicting the presence or the absence of some properties, and the rules for checking an axiom of causal completeness (Finn, 1999).

RELATED WORKS

Larichev (2002, 2000, and 1994) has investigated the structure of expert's knowledge in medicine pattern recognition tasks. His analysis has given the following results:

- The experienced doctors use for diagnostics a small number of generalized diagnostic features; this number is substantially smaller than that the beginning doctors use (Larichev, 2000).
- The experienced doctors make diagnosis rapidly and almost without errors with the use of a straight, but not reverse inference.
- The number of decision rules used for solving one medicine diagnostic task is usually not greater than 7 - 9 rules but the dimensionality of task can be from 64 to 32300, where the dimensionality of task is the product of the numbers of values for all features used in this task (according to Larichev, (2002)).
- For continuous values of features (for example, arterial pressure), the doctors reveal informative interval of values or ranges of features (for example, increased, normal, lowed arterial pressure). Usually, the doctors deal with 2 – 4 diapasons of values on a scale.

Larichev (1994) has advanced the hypothesis that generally decision rule can be represented in the form of functional operator (assertion) as follows:

$$f(X_1 \& X_2 \& X_3 \& \& X_n) + C^k_{N-n},$$

where *N* – the quantity of diagnostic features; $f(X_1 \& X_2 \& X_3 \& \& X_n)$ – conjunction of particular and most important values of *n* diagnostic features; C^k_{N-n}, - combinations of *k* from *N-n* values of remained features characteristic for disease in consideration. There is an example of such rule:

There is a suspicion for the acute poisoning by barbiturates in the cases when motor excitation and aggression were observed before the coma and some values of not less than three of five remained features characteristic for poisoning are observed.

Elliott Sober (2003) defends the theses about probabilistic reasoning. He concludes that *modus ponens* has a probabilistic analog, but *modus tollens* does not.

CONCLUSION

In this chapter, we concentrated our attention on the rules that are connected with knowledge representation, generation, modification, and using in commonsense reasoning. We classified the rules into two main groups: the rules of the first and second types. The first type rules are assertions with the help of which knowledge is represented. The second type rules are commonsense reasoning rules with the help of which knowledge is generated and renovated. We joined deductive and inductive rules in one group because these rules interact in human reasoning interlacing deduction and induction in a single process of reasoning.

REFERENCES

Bizam, G., & Herczeg, J. (1978). *Many-colored lLogic*. Moscow: Mir.

Doyle, A. C. (1992). *The adventures of Sherlock Holmes*. UK: Wordsworth Editions Limited.

Ericson, H., Puerta, A. R., & Musen, M. A. (1992). Generation of knowledge acquisition tools from domain ontologies. *International Journal of Human-Computer Studies, 41*, 425–453. doi:10.1006/ijhc.1994.1067

Finn, V. K. (1988). Commonsense inference and commonsense reasoning. *Review of Science and Technique (Itogi Nauki i Tekhniki), Series "The Theory of Probability. Mathematical Statistics. Technical Cybernetics, 28*, 3–84.

Finn, V. K. (1991). Plausible reasoning in systems of JSM type. *Review of Science and Technique (Itogi Nauki i Tekhniki), Series " . Informatika, 15*, 54–101.

Finn, V. K. (1999). The synthesis of cognitive procedures and the problem of induction. *NTI* [Moscow, Russia: VINITI.]. *Series, 2*(1-2), 8–44.

Gappa, U., & Poeck, K. (1992). Common ground and differences of the KADS and strong problem solving shell approach, In Th. Wetter, K.-D. Althoff, J. Boose, M. Linster, & F. Schmalhofer (Eds), *Current development in knowledge acquisition* (EKAW – 92), LNAI 599 (pp. 52-73).Springer Verlag.

Larichev, O. I. (1994). The structure of expert's knowledge in pattern recognition tasks. *Reports of Russian Academy of Sciences, 6*, 750–752.

Larichev, O. I. (2000). Theory of the subconscious decisive rules and its application in the diagnostic tasks. *Psychological Journal, 24*(1), 56–72.

Larichev, O. I. (2002). Close imitation of expert knowledge: The problem and methods. *International J. of Information Technology & Decision Making, 1*, 27–42. doi:10.1142/S021962200200004X

Lichko, E. (1983). *Psychopathies and accentuations of character of teenagers* (2nd ed). Leningrad, USSR: Medicine.

Mill, J. S. (1872). *The system of logic ratiocinative and inductive being a connected view of the principles of evidence, and the methods of scientific investigation* (Vol. 1). London, West Strand.

Naidenova, X. A., & Polegaeva, J. G. (1985a). Model of human reasoning for deciphering forest's images and its implementation on computer. In *Semiotic aspects of the intellectual activity formalization, Theses of Papers and Reports of School-Seminar* (pp. 49-52). Kutaisy, Georgia Soviet Socialist Republic.

Naidenova, X. A., & Polegaeva, J. G. (1985b). The project of expert system GID KLARA. Geological interpretation of data based on classification and pattern recognition. *Report I-A VIII.2 10-3/35, "Testing and Mastering Experimental Patterns of Flying (Aircraft) and Surface Spectrometry Apparatus, Working out Methods of Automated Processing Multi-Spectral Information for Geological Goals."* Saint-Petersburg All Union Scientific Research Institute of Remote Sensing Methods for Geology.

Naidenova, X. A., & Syrbu, V. N. (1984). Classification and pattern recognition logic in connection with the problem of forming and using knowledge in expert systems. In Y. Pecherskij (Ed.), *Interactive systems and their practical application, Theses of Papers of Republican Scientific-Technical Conference* (pp.10-13). Kishinev, the Moldavian Soviet Socialist Republic: Mathematical Institute with Computer Center.

Russel, J. S., & Norvig, P. (2003). *Artificial Intelligence. A modern approach* (2nd ed.). Upper Saddle River, NJ: Prentice Hall.

Sober, E. (2003). The design argument. In W. Mann (Ed.), *Blackwell companion to the philosophy of religion*. Oxford: Blackwell.

Chapter 5
The Examples of Human Commonsense Reasoning Processes

ABSTRACT

In this chapter, we concentrate our attention on analyzing and modeling natural human reasoning in solving different tasks: pattern recognition in scientific investigations, logical games, and investigation of crimes.

INTRODUCTION

This chapter contains some examples of natural human commonsense reasoning related to both scientific pattern recognition problems and logical games. An analysis of inference structure shows that inductive and deductive rules communicate in reasoning. An automated model for detecting the types of woodland from the incomplete descriptions of some evidences is also given in this chapter. An interesting part of this model is a small knowledge base using the representation of experts' knowledge of natural woodlands as biological formations.

AN EXAMPLE OF REASONING PROCESS IN PATTERN RECOGNITION WITH THE USE OF KNOWLEDGE BASE

The investigation of human reasoning process in different real situations is the inevitable step foregoing any work on creating automated algorithms modeling this process. For studying, we have taken the process of visual deciphering forest photographic images. In this case, the features of forest regions

DOI: 10.4018/978-1-60566-810-9.ch005

are investigated under stereoscope by a decipherer (operator or executer), registered on blanks, and analyzed by the use of the decision rules created in advance by the specialists on the basis of previous explorations and experiences.

The attempt of automation of the process of deciphering forest images leads, first of all, to investigating the algorithms used by experts for this goal. We have analyzed, the dichotomous diagram (scheme) elaborated by an expert for Lena - Angara forest region under deciphering the types of forest plant conditions. The scheme is a decision tree the nodes of which are associated with some factors or attributes' values to be checked. The sequence of checking the factors associated with the nodes of scheme is rigidly determined. It is optimum with respect to the length of branches coming to each of the nodes.

Our studies show that a strict collection of attributes and a strict sequence of their use in all situations do not reflect adequately the processes of specialists' reasoning during deciphering forest photographs. Decision trees help greatly to increase the productivity of the work of decipherers, but they decrease the number of correctly recognized objects. The strict order of the use of attributes is easier for inexperienced decipherers and more difficult psychologically for experienced ones.

We have compared the two forms of experts' knowledge representations: 1) the dichotomous scheme familiar to a decision tree, 2) the table of rules reflecting the links between the factors (attributes) and the types of forest plant conditions with the indication of the factor occurrence frequency.

Two decipherers worked: one having experience of work more than 10 years (Executor 1) and the second, which did not have an experience of forest deciphering, but he knew how to carry out the preliminary processing photographs and how to work with the simplest stereo - instruments (Executor 2).

Two regions have been chosen: the basin of rivers Lena - Angara (Region 1) and Khentey - Chikoy region (Zabaykalie and Mongolia) (Region 2). The results of deciphering are represented in Table 1 and Table 2. The data of the ground-based assessment have been taken as true. The trustworthiness of recognition was estimated for 214 parts of Region 1 and for 192 parts of Region 2.

For experienced Executor 1, in familiar Region 1, the percent of correct answers with the use of the strict algorithm falls. Although the percent of correct answers grows in unknown Region 2 but it grows insignificantly.

Table 1. The results of deciphering the types of woodland

Executer	Region 1		Region 2	
	By rules	By decision tree	By rules	By decision tree
	% correct results	% correct results	% correct results	% correct results
1	88	79	66	69
2	43	62	49	64

Table 2. The productivity of Executor 1 and 2

Executer	Region 1		Region 2	
	By rules	By decision tree	By rules	By decision tree
	The number of parts	The number of parts	The number of parts	The number of parts
1	100	326	92	289
2	65	209	70	238

For inexperienced Executer 2, the use of strict algorithm both in the familiar and in the unknown region leads to an increase % of the correct answers, but the level of correct recognition remains still very low: 62-64%. Thus, in the absence of experience and knowledge, it is unimportant for him what to use – table of rules or strict algorithm, the application of strict algorithm leads only to an increase in the productivity of operator's labor.

But if the executor possesses the experience and knowledge of region (Executor 1 and Region 1), then he recognizes worse with the use of strict algorithm than without it, he psychologically rejects the rigid diagram. The tabular form of rule representation is proved to be for him nearer to the natural procedure of deciphering. But in the unknown region, the behavior of Executer 1 is the same as the behavior of inexperienced one, but also, in this case, the strict algorithm does not lead to the significant improvement in the results - they are located approximately at the same level as for the inexperienced decipherer.

The experienced specialist deteriorates his result in unknown regions. As far as the inexperienced specialist it is unimportant for him, in what region to work.

If we remember that, from the point of view of information quantity, the set of rules is equivalent to the form of dichotomous scheme, it will become clear that only additional knowledge of regions helps to increase the percent of correct recognitions and that the rules contribute to more complete utilization of knowledge than the rigid dichotomous diagrams.

The more detail analysis of the examples of solving pattern recognition tasks by the specialists (experts) makes it possible to formulate several properties of their natural modes of reasoning:

1. It is difficult for them to describe the sequence of their considerations (reasoning). Sometimes an expert can not describe it at all. The experienced specialist realizes that the sequence of his argumentations depends on the concrete situation in which the deciphering occurs.
2. The same results can be established by using different collections of factors or attributes. For example, the degree of forest health can be refined, in some cases, according to the closeness of forest canopy and the sizes of the projections of crowns, and, in other cases, with the use of height above sea level, steepness of slopes and admixture of the deciduous species to the conifers.
3. Any factor, whose value is recognized (determined) in the course of reasoning, is involved, in turn, in the process of deciphering and used as a new factor for supporting or rejecting hypotheses. For example, after establishing the type of forest by the use of landscape features, the specialist can use it for evaluating the degree of forest health and the composition of forest (forest structure).
4. The priority of recognizing the characteristics of forest cannot be established previously First of all, there are examined the features having the greatest degree of manifestation on aero-cosmos-photographs. The greatest priority belongs to forbidding features, since they exclude impossible solutions. Diagnostic features play the important role - they make it possible to divide the hypotheses appearing in reasoning process.
5. The cause-effect relations are used in reasoning not only in the direction "from the reason to the consequence", but also in the direction "from the consequence to the reason". This reasoning generates the statements of the form: "if A is true, then at least B may be true". Let us consider this statement to be hypothetical.

Any process of reasoning covers, in general, introducing or deleting assumptions (values of attributes or factors), hypotheses (values of goal (sub-goal) attributes), factors, objects (class of objects), measured or observed values of attributes or factors (they are considered to be established correctly). The assumptions, hypotheses and recognized values of forest features are ranged by their degree of possibility. As a whole, the process of deciphering can be presented as follows. By known (or recognized) features and known causal relations, hypotheses are generated of values of unknown features of the forest plant conditions. The hypotheses, by means of known causal relations, generate assumptions of values of new involved features. The assumptions are checked against an observed situation on photographs. The assumptions can be supported or rejected. The hypotheses associated with rejected values of attributes or factors are deleted from consideration. A hypothesis is admissible if its description is consistent. So the reasoning process is continued until the values of all necessary characteristics of forest plant conditions and the totality of features connected with them are obtained. In particular case, the decision set is empty or it contains a certain set of decisions not contradicting an observed situation, but having the different degree of confidence.

Let us consider an example of reasoning for Lena - Angara Region with the use of Table 3 (this example has only illustrative character).

Table 3. The rules for Lena-Angare Forest Region

Experts Rules Describing Lena-Angara Forest Region
Connection between the type of woodland and predominant type of trees
1. (*pine-tree, spruce, cypress, cedars, birch, larch, asp, fir-tree*) → *dominating kinds of trees*;
2. (*meadow, bilberry wood, red bilberry wood ....*) → *types of woodland*;
Meadow, birch → very frequently
Meadow, pine-tree → false
Meadow, fir-tree → rarely
Meadow, cedar → very frequently
Meadow, larch → very frequently
Meadow, aspen → very frequently
Ledum, marsh tea-wood
Ledum, marsh tea-wood, birch → rarely
Ledum, marsh tea, fir-tree → false
Ledum, marsh tea-wood, cedar → very frequently
Ledum, marsh tea-wood, larch → very frequently
Bilberry-wood, birch of 40-50 years → very frequently
Bilberry-wood, pine-tree, ripe, overmature → very frequently
Bilberry-wood, fir-tree → rarely
Bilberry-wood, cedar → very frequently
Bilberry-wood, larch → rarely
Red bilberry-wood, pine-tree → very frequently
Red bilberry-wood, larch → rarely
Red bilberry-wood, fir-tree → false
Red bilberry-wood, cedar → false
Badan, pine-tree → rarely
Badan, larch → very frequently
Badan, fir-tree → false
Badan, cedar → very frequently
Connection between features of landscape and predominant (prevailing) type of trees
Slope, (*south, east*), *pine-tree* → frequently
Slope, (north, west), cedar → frequently
Slope, steepness < 10°, cedar → frequently
Slop, larch → frequently
Watercourse, head of watercourse, fir-tree →frequently
Glade, site after fire, birch, asp → frequently
Connection between feature of landscape and the type of woodland
Slope, without watercourse, steepness 4°-10°, north/west, bilberry → frequently;
Slope, in valley along with watercourse, steepness 7°-10°, east exposition, meadow → frequently;
Slope, in valley along with watercourse, steepness < 10°, south, meadow → rarely

Assume that two features are recognized correctly with the use of photographs: the presence of slope and the steepness of slope equal to 7°. Then two hypotheses are generated: the type of forest can be "meadow" or "bilberry". These hypotheses do not contradict with the following rules of Table 3:

Slope, without watercourse, Steepness 4°-10°, north/west → bilberry, frequently;
Slope, in valley along with watercourse, steepness 7°-10°, east exposition. → meadow, frequently;
Slope, in valley along with watercourse, steepness 10°, south → meadow, rarely.

In order to select one of the hypotheses we check two new features: the presence of watercourse and the exposition of slope. Assume that a watercourse is observed on the photograph. Then we select two hypotheses of meadow with the following assumptions:

Slope, in valley along with watercourse, east exposition;
Slope, in valley along with watercourse, south exposition.

Assume that both expositions are interesting.
Hypothesis "meadow" excludes the presence of pine-tree in this place and introduces some assumptions of predominant species of trees:

Meadow → very frequently, birch after fire
Meadow → rarely, fir tree
Meadow → very frequently, cedar
Meadow → very frequently, aspen after fire
Meadow → very frequently, larch.

These assumptions of predominant species of trees generate new assumptions of some landscape features. '*Birch*' and '*aspen*' speak about the possibility of cutting down and cinder. Assume that it is not the case (the assumptions of '*birch*' and '*aspen*' can be disproved with the aid of observing both the morphological features of forest curtain and the absence of cutting down or cinder on the images). Three assumptions remain: '*fir tree*', '*cedar*', and '*larch*'. Let the assumption of '*larch*' be rejected by the tone of image. The presence of water flow confirms the assumption of '*fir tree*'.

Furthermore, for the fir tree, the upper flow of watercourse is most likely. Assume that in the image the water course is in the average flow. The hypothesis of cedar forest remains.

It remains to answer the question of the quality class of forest.

Let the closeness of cultivation be small. The decipherer can consider that the cultivation is clean. The quality class is the third one.

Consider the situation with the north-west exposition of slope. Then we must accept the hypothesis of bilberry type of forest.

If there is not a watercourse on this part of slope, then the type of forest is '*cedar-bilberry*'.

If the hypotheses of bilberry and meadow types of forest were both rejected, it would be possible to begin to investigate other morphological or landscape signs, for example, the height above sea level, first of all, and after that to form the hypotheses of predominant species.

If all hypotheses were rejected, then the causal relations do not fully characterize the region and the classification carried out in the stage of studying this region is not successful.

A situation can occur when it is not possible to recognize necessary features on the photograph. In this case, it is possible to select the hypotheses coinciding with the concrete situation in maximum quantity of features. Clearly that several hypotheses can be obtained each of which has the certain degree of probability.

It is important that the process of natural reasoning makes it possible to estimate not only the authenticity of a conclusion, but also to explain meaningfully how this conclusion was obtained.

Of course, the Table 3 does not describe Lena - Angara region comprehensively, but it makes it possible to investigate the characteristics of experts' reasoning.

The Structure of a Small Knowledge Base for Inferring the Type of Woodland via an Analysis of Forest's Aerial Photographs

Structure of the Knowledge Base

We describe a very simple structure of a knowledge base that is sufficient for our illustrative goal. The knowledge base (KB) consists of two parts: the Attribute Base (*AtB*), containing the relations between problem domain concepts, and the Assertion Base (*AsB*), containing the expert's assertions formulated in terms of the concepts.

The domain concepts are represented by the use of names. With respect to its role in the KB, a name can be one of two kinds: name of attribute and name of attribute value. However, with respect to its role in the problem domain, a name can be the name of an object, the name of a class of objects and the name of a classification or collection of classes. A class of objects can contain only one object hence the name of an object is a particular case of the name of a class. In the KB, names of objects and of classes of objects become names of attribute values, and names of classifications become names of attributes.

For example, let objects be a collection of trees such as asp, oak, fir-tree, cedar, pine-tree, and birch. Each name calls the class or the kind of trees (in a particular case, only one tree). Any set of trees can be partitioned into the separate groups depending on their properties. '*Kind of trees*' will be the name of a classification, in which '*asp*', '*oak*', '*fir-tree*', '*cedar*', '*pine-tree*', and '*birch*' are the names of classes. Then, in the KB, '*kind of trees*' will be used as the name of an attribute the values of which are '*asp*', '*oak*', '*fir-tree*', '*cedar*', '*pine-tree*', and '*birch*'. The link between the name of an attribute and the names of its values is implicative. It can be expressed by the following way:

$$(\text{<name of value}_1\text{>}, \text{<name of value}_2\text{>}, ..., \text{<name of value}_k\text{>}) \rightarrow \text{<name of attribute>},$$

where the sign "$\rightarrow$" denotes the relation "is a".

In our example (*asp, oak, fir-tree, cedar, pine-tree, birch*) $\rightarrow$ *kind of trees*, and, for each value of '*kind of trees*', the assertion of the following type can be created: "*asp* is a *kind of trees*".

The set of all attributes' names and the set of all values' names must not intersect. This means that the name of a classification cannot simultaneously be the name of a class. However, this is not the case in natural languages: the name of a class can be used for some classification and vice versa. For example, one can say that '*pine-tree*', '*fir-tree*', '*cedar*' are '*conifers*'. But one may also say that '*conifers*', '*leaf-bearing*' are '*kinds of trees*'. Here the word '*conifers*' serves both as the name of a classification and as the name of a class. In this setting, class is a particular case of classification like object is a particular case of class.

By using names in the way we do in real life we permit the introduction of auxiliary names for the subsets of the set of an attribute's values. Let A be an attribute. The name of a subset of values of A will be used as the name of a new attribute which, in its turn, will serve as the name of a value with respect to A.

The *AsB* (Assertion Base) contains the expert's assertions. Each assertion links a collection of values of different attributes with a certain value of a special attribute (*SA*) that evaluates how often this collection of values appears in practice. The values of a special attribute are: *always*, *never*, *rarely*, and *frequently*. Assertions have the following form:

(<name of value>, <name of value>, ..., <value of *SA*>) = *true*.

For simplicity, we omit the word '*true*', because it appears in any assertion. For example, the assertion "pine-tree and cedar can be found frequently in the meadow type of forest" will be expressed in the following way: (*meadow, pine-tree, cedar, frequently*). We also omit the sign of conjunction between values of different attributes and the sign of disjunction (separating disjunction) between values of the same attribute. For example, the assertion in the form (*meadow, pine-tree, cedar, often*) is equivalent to the following expression of formal logic: P((type of forest = *meadow*) & ((kind of trees = *pine-tree*) ∨ (kind of trees = *cedar*)) & (*SA = frequently*)) = *true*.

Only one kind of requests to the KB is used: SEARCHING VALUE OF <name of attribute> [, <name of attribute>,...] IF (<name of value>, <name of value>, ...), where "name of value" is the known value of an attribute, "name of attribute" means that the value of this attribute is unknown. For example, the request "to find the type of forest for a region with plateau, without watercourse, with the prevalence of pine-tree" will be represented as follows: SEARCHING VALUE OF the type of forest IF (*plateau, without watercourse, pine-tree*).

Inferring All Possible Hypotheses about the Type of Woodland from an Incomplete Description of Some Evidences

Let x be a request to the KB equal to:

SEARCHING VALUE OF type of woodland IF (*plateau, without watercourse, pine-tree*). Let the content of the Knowledge Base be the following collection of assertions:

AtB:
1.   (meadow, bilberry wood, red bilberry wood ....) → types of woodland;
2.   (pine-tree, spruce, cypress, cedars, birch, larch, asp, fir-tree) → dominating kinds of trees;
3.   (plateau, without plateau) → presence of plateau;
4.   (top of slope, middle part of slope, ...) → parts of slope;
5.   (peak of hill, foot of hill) → parts of hill;
6.   (height on plateau, without height on plateau) → presence of a height on plateau;
7.   (head of watercourse, low part of watercourse, ...) → parts of water course;
8.   (steepness ≥ 4°, steepness ≤ 3°, steepness < 3°, ...) → features of slope;
9.   (north, south, west, east) → the four cardinal points;
10.   (watercourse, without watercourse) → presence of a watercourse.

AsB:
1. (meadow, pine-tree, larch, frequently);
2. (meadow, pine-tree, steepness ≤ 4°, never);
3. (meadow, larch, steepness ≥ 4°, never);
4. (meadow, north, west, south, frequently);
5. (meadow, east, rarely);
6. (meadow, fir-tree, birch, asp, rarely);
7. (meadow, plateau, middle part of slope, frequently);
8. (meadow, peak of hill, watercourse heads, rarely);
9. (plateau, steepness ≤ 3°, always);
10. (plateau, watercourse, rarely);
11. (red bilberry wood, pine-tree, frequently);
12. (red bilberry wood, larch, rarely);
13. (red bilberry wood, peak of hill, frequently);
14. (red bilberry wood, height on plateau, rarely);
15. (meadow, steepness < 3°, frequently).

The process of reasoning evolves according to the following sequence of steps:

Step 1. Take out all the assertions t in AsB containing at least one value from the request, i.e., $t \in$ AsB and $t \cap x \neq \emptyset$, where x is the request. These are assertions 1, 2, 7, 9, 10, 11, and 14.

Step 2. Delete (from the set of selected assertions) all the assertions that contradict with the request. Assertion 10 contradicts with the request because it contains the value of attribute 'presence of water course' which is different from the value of this attribute in the request. The remaining assertions are 1, 2, 7, 9, 11, and 14.

Step 3. Take out the values of attribute '*type of woodland*' appearing in assertions 1, 2, 7, 9, 11, and 14. We have two hypotheses: '*meadow*' and '*red bilberry*'.

Step 4. An attempt is made to refute one of the hypotheses. For this goal, it is necessary to find an assertion that has the value of *SA* equal to '*never*' and contains one of the hypotheses, some subset of values from the request and does not contain any other value. There is only one assertion with the value of *SA* equal to '*never*'. This is assertion 2: (*meadow, pine-tree, steepness ≤ 4°, never*). However, we cannot use this assertion because it contains the value '*steepness ≤ 4°*' which is not in the request.

Step 5. An attempt is made to find a value of some attribute that is not in the request (in order to extend the request). For this goal, it is necessary to find an assertion with the value of *SA* equal to '*always*' that contains a subset of values from the request and one and only one value of some new attribute the values of which are not in the request. Only one assertion satisfies this condition. This is assertion 9: (*plateau, steepness ≤ 3°, always*).

Step 6. Forming the extended request:

SEARCHING VALUE OF *the type of woodland* IF (*plateau, without watercourse, pine-tree, steepness ≤ 3°*).

Steps 1, 2, and 3 are repeated. Assertion 15 is involved in the reasoning.

Step 4 is repeated. Now assertion 2 can be used because the value '*steepness* $\leq 4°$' is in accordance with the values of '*feature of slope*' in the request. We conclude now that the type of woodland cannot be '*meadow*'. The non-refuted hypothesis is "*the type of woodland = red bilberry*".

The process of pattern recognition can require inferring new rules of the first type from data when it is impossible to distinguish inferred hypotheses. In general, there exist two main situations to learn rules of the first type from examples in the process of pattern recognition: i) the result of reasoning contains several hypotheses and it is impossible to choose one and only one of them (uncertainty), and ii) there does not exist any hypothesis.

Analysis of Inference Structure. The Interaction of Deductive and Inductive Reasoning Rules in Solving Pattern Recognition Problems

It is not difficult to see that the steps of reasoning described in the previous section realize some deductive reasoning rules of the second types.

Step 1 performs **Introducing Assertions** into the reasoning process. This step is an element of commonsense reasoning the task of which is the drawing of knowledge into reasoning process. The selected assertions form (constitute) the meaningful context of reasoning or the field of reasoning.

Step 2 performs **Deleting Assertions** from the reasoning process. This step uses **Rule of Alternative**. If an assertion contains a value of attribute not equal to the value of this attribute in the request, then, by Rule of Alternative, this assertion must be deleted from consideration. Consequently, step 2 narrows the context of reasoning.

Step 3 performs **Introducing Hypotheses** of the goal attribute values. These hypotheses are the values of goal attribute appearing in the selected assertions. Hence the source of hypotheses is the context of reasoning.

Step 4 performs **Deleting Hypotheses** by means of using **Interdiction (Forbidden) Rules**. Let H be a hypothesis and FR be a forbidden rule '$H,\{Y\} \rightarrow never$', and X be a request, where X, Y – the collections of attributes values. If $Y \subseteq X$, then hypothesis H is disproved.

Step 5 performs **Introducing Assumptions** of values of attributes. Let A be the value of an attribute not contained in the request, IR be the rule '$A, Y \rightarrow always$', and X be a request, where X, Y – the collections of attributes values. If $Y \subseteq X$, then the request can be extended as follows: $X' = X \cup A$.

For extending the request, it is possible to use Compatibility Rules and Diagnostic Rules.

The assumptions, introduced by a Compatibility Rule, or Diagnostic Rule can be checked against the evidence by means of the photographs. The assumptions contradicting with visible image of forest are deleted from consideration.

Step 6 performs **Forming the Extended Request** in accordance with each not disproved hypothesis.

With the extended requests for each hypothesis, the steps 1 – 6 are performed untill only one hypothesis remains.

The compatibility rule can be used for extending the request also as an implication, but the request extended by a compatibility rule acquires the estimation VA associated with this rule. The attribute VA must have the ordering scale and the procedure for calculating the values '*rarely*', '*more rarely*', '*very rarely*' or '*frequently*', '*less frequently*', '*very frequently*' must be elaborated.

We introduce some limitations on using the compatibility rules: value $v(A)$ of an attribute A can be determined by a compatibility rule R with VA equal to Z, if value $v(A)$ has been inferred independently with the same or higher value of *VA* and by means of the rules containing a combination of attributes not intersecting with the combination of attributes associated with compatibility rule *R*. Really, the scheme of knowledge base usually permits to do so. In our example, the following knowledge base scheme is created by the specialists:

Landscape features $\Rightarrow$ Type of woodland (forest plant conditions);
Morphological features of forest $\Rightarrow$ Type of woodland (forest plant conditions);
Landscape features $\Rightarrow$ Predominant type (species) of trees;
Morphological features of forest $\Rightarrow$ Predominant type (species) of trees;
Landscape features $\Rightarrow$ Productivity of forest (the class of quality);
Morphological features of forest $\Rightarrow$ Productivity of forest (the class of quality);
Type of woodland (forest plant conditions) $\Leftrightarrow$ Predominant type (species) of trees;
Type of woodland (forest plant conditions) $\Leftrightarrow$ Predominant type (species) of trees; Productivity of forest
     (the class of quality).

This scheme corresponds with the ideas of forest as a biological unity, in which climate, soil, moisture, watercourses, relief, trees, and associated plants are consistent. The sign $\Rightarrow$ means that the attributes in the left part of scheme determine functionally the attribute in the right part of scheme. The sign $\Leftrightarrow$ means that the attributes in the left and right parts of scheme are strongly interconnected. So, if the type of woodland was determined by the landscape features and the predominant type of trees has been inferred based on the type of woodland with certain value *Z* of *VA*, then this type of trees must be supported, for example, by the morphological features of forest with value of *VA* not less than *Z*.

If the number of hypotheses is more than 1 and no one of them can be disproved, then we deal with a difficult situation and it is necessary to resort to the aid of diagnostic rules.

Let *r* be a diagnostic rule such as '*X*, *d* $\rightarrow$ *a*; *X*, *b* $\rightarrow$ *z*', where '*X*' is true, and '*a*', '*z*' are hypotheses or possible values of some attribute, say *A*. In this rule, *X* is the combination of attribute values not distinguishing hypotheses '*a*' and '*z*' ($z \neq a$); *d*, *b* are the values of an attribute distinguishing these hypotheses under condition that '*X*' is true. If '*X*' is included in the request and the pair of considered hypotheses coincide with the hypotheses in *r*, then this rule is applicable to the situation in question. If value of attribute *A* is not yet determined, then *d* and *b* become the assumptions to be inferred or checked against the evidence. Examples 1 and 2 present some diagnostic rules.

Example 1:

"With other equal landscape features, if there are two hypotheses '*bilberry*' and '*red bilberry*' of the type of woodland, then, with the highest possibility, if the predominant type of trees is *cedar*, then the type of woodland is *red bilberry*, and if the predominant type of trees is *pine-tree*, then the type of woodland is *bilberry*".

Example 2. (for aero - photographs produced by the survey of the small scale):

"With other equal morphological features, if it is observed the flat structure of forest curtains, uniform granularity and equal height of trees, then the species of trees is *pine tree*; if it is observed the uneven structure of forest curtains, uneven granularity, and different height of trees, then the species of trees is *larch*".

However if the inferring or observing of indispensable values of diagnostic attributes was without success, then it is necessary to draw into reasoning the inductive inference of a new portion of rules of the first type for extending the Knowledge Base.

If the initial context of reasoning does not contain any hypothesis about the value of goal attribute, it is natural to extend the request by the use of Introducing Assumptions (step 5) taking as a goal any attribute with unknown value from the reasoning context. Of course, the equality to 0 of the hypotheses' number can indicate the need of expanding the very base of knowledge.

The result of reasoning is considered to be satisfactory if the number of hypotheses of the woodland type is equal to 1 and this type is consistent with the predominant type of trees and the class of forest quality. If the inference terminates with several hypotheses or the number of hypotheses is equal to 0, then the Knowledge Base is incomplete and it is necessary to expand it. For this goal, the inductive rules of the second type are used.

Inductive Extension of Incomplete Knowledge with the Use of Rules of the Second Type

The deductive reasoning rules act by means of extending the incomplete descriptions of some evidences with disproving the impossible extensions. The extension is based on good knowledge of the forest regions and interconnections between the main forest characteristics and the natural factors such as climate, soil, relief, watercourses and so on.

But the deductive inference depends on the quality of forest images, the type of instruments used for aero-cosmos-survey of earth surface, the accuracy of knowledge, and many other different factors. This dependency introduces a lot of uncertainties in the inference process. That's why it is indispensable to draw into reasoning the steps of inductive inference. The inductive inference involves in reasoning new rules of the first type, new attributes (context of reasoning), and new observations obtained by the use of both direct surveys on earth surface and by the use of instrument surveys of forest regions.

Two variant of drawing inductive inference in reasoning are thinkable: 1) using a part of existing Knowledge Base not included in the context of reasoning if this part contains a set of observations potentially applicable as the source of new implicative assertions related to the difficult situations of the previous reasoning process; 2) to initiate a new investigation of the forest region for collecting observations to enrich the Knowledge Base. In the first variant, we do the purpose-directed steps of inductive reasoning, in the second variant; we have to interrupt the reasoning process.

Let A, B be the hypotheses or phenomena under investigations. The purpose-directed steps of inductive reasoning means that we must choose in KB the instances containing a set of attributes' values of the request, say X, then, among these instances, we must select the instances in which phenomenon A occurs but phenomenon B does not occur and the instances in which phenomenon B occurs but phenomenon A does not occur. These two sets of instances must be compared. The attributes' values in which the instances of these sets are different are diagnostic ones; they can be included in some new diagnostic rules for distinguishing hypotheses A and B.

We can find a lot of good examples of natural human deductive and inductive reasoning in the novels of a famous English writer Conan Doyle, who is the real begetter of the detective-fiction genre as we know it. In the novel "The Adventure of the Second Stain", Sherlock Holmes knows several international spies who could possess the documents stolen from the Foreign Ministry (Office). But "It is a capital mistake to theorize in advance of the facts" – said he, -"I will begin my research by going round and finding if each of them is at his post. If one is missing - especially if he has disappeared since last night — we will have some indication as to where the document has gone". There were several men under suspicion with equal possibility to steal the documents: Oberstein, La Rothiere, and Eduardo Lucas.

But one of these men differed from all the others by the fact that he lived near the Foreign Ministry (Office). Finally, the following reasoning helps Sherlock Holmes to discover the thief. Holmes said: 'There is one obvious point which would, in any case, have turned my suspicions against Lucas. Godolphin Street, Westminster, is only a few minutes' walk from Whitehall Terrace. The other secret agents whom I have named live in the extreme West End. It was easier, therefore, for Lucas than for the others to establish a connection or receive a message from the European Secretary's household - a small thing, and yet where events are compressed into a few hours it may prove essential".

In the novel "Murder into Abby-Grange", there are three glasses, from which, supposedly, men drunk vine. In one of the glasses there was sediment, in two others sediment absents. Holmes searches for the explanation, which would satisfy this difference in the glasses. The following explanations were possible: 1) In two glasses, they shook vine before using, while, in the third glass, they did not shake up vine; 2) They drunk only from two glasses, they poured off the remainders in the third glass.

In the novel "The Adventure of the Yellow Face" (Doyle, 1992), there are two hypotheses and the second one is supported by an assumption, that the inmates were warned of Grant Munro's coming. With the second assumption, the way of Holmes' reasoning can be described as follows:

Facts (Evidences):

The inmates of the cottage do not want to meet Grant Munro;

Grant Munro returned at home and spoke with the maid;

Grant Munro saw the maid with whom he had been speaking running across the field in the direction of the cottage;

Grant Munro meets his wife and the maid hurrying back together from the cottage;

Grant Munro entered the cottage;

The cottage was absolutely empty.

Assertions:

If one does not want to meet a person and he is warned that this person is going to visit him, then he conceals himself or goes away;

If one only conceals himself, then he must return;

If one goes away, then his house will be permanently deserted;

If one knows something, then he can say it somebody.

Reasoning:

The maid knows that Grant Munro returned at home, then, knowing this, she visited the cottage, hence she warned the inmates and the wife of Grant Munro that he returned at home.

The inmates do not want to meet Grant Munro, hence they concealed themselves or went away.

Holmes says to Grant Munro: "If the cottage is permanently deserted we may have some difficulty, if on the other hand, as I fancy is more likely, the inmates were warned of your coming, and left before you entered yesterday, then they may be back now, and we should clear it all up easily".

A dialog between Holmes and Watson is very remarkable with respect to what must be a good reasoning:

Holmes: - What do you think of my theory?

Watson: - It is all surmise.

Holmes: - But at least it covers all the facts. When new facts come to our knowledge, which cannot be covered by it, it will be time enough to reconsider it.

This strategy is supported by the novel "Murder into Abby-Grange". Sherlock Holmes begins his investigation from studying the facts. There is an initial hypothesis, but some facts are not coordinated with this hypothesis and the story of witnesses. The story contradicts with the usual and most probable ideas (rules) about the behavior of robbers. The facts attest to the idea that the robber had to know house and its inhabitants.

Holmes returns to the place of crime and inspects it more thoroughly. Thus he obtains some newly facts. These facts make it possible to advance some new hypotheses of the nature and the physical force of robber and to support the assumption that he acted alone. But this makes possible for Holmes to conclude that the lady speaks untruth.

AN EXAMPLE OF REASONING IN THE GAME "THE LETTERS' LOTO"

In logical game "The letters' Loto" (Bizam, 1978), the oracle (one of the players) thinks of a word with the fixed number of letters in it. A guesser names a word with the same number of letters. Then the oracle says how many letters in this word are correct. A letter is guessed correctly if it is equal to the letter taking up the same position in the thought word.

Example 1.

The oracle thought a word of 3 letters and the guesser said the following words in sequence: LAP, HAP, HAM, HAT, RAT, and CUR (Table 4). Numbers in the last line of Table 4 are the estimations of the oracle.

A set of reasoning rules for guessing letters is in Table 5. Each rule is based on comparing words and differentiating situations of the game. These rules localize the positions with correctly and not correctly guessed letters using the oracle's estimations.

Since there can be only one correct letter in each position of word the correctly guessed letters are used in the same positions in the following trials (words) of the guesser, and the incorrect letters are replaced by new ones.

These steps are reduced to the classification of letters in each word and in each position of word into two classes "correct letters" and "incorrect letters".

Return to Example 1 (Table 4).

Since only one letter is changed in words LAP and HAP and the estimation of the oracle is not changed letters L and H in the first position are not correct (Rule 1).

Table 4. Example 1, the initial state of the task

L	H	H	H	R	C	
A	A	A	A	A	U	
P	P	M	T	T	B	
1	1	1	2	2	1	

Table.5. The reasoning rules

№	Reasoning rule	The meaning of rule
1	If changing the letter only in one position does not lead to changing the estimation of the oracle, then in this position both letters are incorrect (before and after changing)	Diagnostic rule
2	If two words are different in letters only in one position and the estimations of the oracle of these words are different by 1, then the letter in this position is correct in the word with greater estimation of the oracle and it is incorrect in the word with smaller estimation of the oracle	Diagnostic rule
3	If, in a position of word, the letter is identified as correct, then all other letters in this position are incorrect	Letters' classification in a position of words
4	If, in a position of word, the letter is identified as incorrect, then it is incorrect in any word in this positiono	Letters' classification in a position of words
5	If, in a word, the estimation of the oracle is equal to the number of letters remaining after deleting all incorrect letters, then these letters are correct in this word	Localization of correct letters in words
6	If the number of correct letters in a word is equal to the estimation of the oracle, then all other letters in this word are incorrect	Localization of incorrect letters in words
7	Let W1 and W2 be two words of lengths H with estimations H1 and H2 of the oracle respectively. If the sum C = H1 + H2 is greater than H, then there exist at least C-H positions with coinciding letters and these coinciding letters are correct	Localization of correct letters in words
8	If, for two words, the estimations of the oracle are different by K and there are T positions with coinciding letters in these words, then the change of the estimation of the oracle is associated with H – T remaining positions of words	Localization of correct (incorrect) letters in words
9	If, in two words, the letters in all positions are different, then the sets of positions with correct letters in these words do not intersect	Localization of correct (incorrect) letters in words
10	If changing the estimation of the oracle by K is followed by changing K letters in a word, then, in the word with greater estimation, these K letters are correct	Generalization of rule 2
11	If, in some positions, the letters are identified as correct, then a subtask can be considered with the length of words less by the number of positions with correct letters. The estimations of oracles must be recalculated	Reducing a task to the subtask of smaller dimension
12	The previous rules are applicable for subsets of letters of words with recalculating the estimations of oracle	Reducing a task to the subtask of smaller dimension

One of letters A or P must be correct (appearing the hypotheses).

The result is shown in Table 6.

Compare words HAM and HAP. Since only one letter is changed in these words but the estimation of the oracle is not changed letters M and P in the last position are not correct (Rule 1).

We know that H in the first position is not correct. Hence letter A in the second position is correct (Rule 5).

Table 6. Example 1, deleting the incorrect letters

L	H	H	H	R	C		
A	A	A	A	A	U	A	
P	P	M	T	T	B		P
1	1	1	2	2	1		

The result is in Table 7 (one letter correctly guessed).

Compare words HAM and HAT. Since we have change the last letter and the estimation of the oracle is change to 2, letter T in the last position is correct (Rule 2). Result is in Table 8.

The comparing of words HAT and RAT and the fact that the estimation of the oracle is not changed imply that letter R in the first position is not correct (Rule 1).

Consider word CUB. We know that letters U and B in this word are incorrect, but the estimation of the oracle is equal to 1. Hence letter C in the first position is correct and the word thought by the oracle is CAT (Rule 5).

The result is in Table 9.

Example 2.

Let the guesser says word PAN and the estimation of the oracle is equal to 1. It is possible to change any letter of this word. Let the next word be PAP with the estimation of the oracle equal to 1. Since the estimation of the oracle is not changed both letters N, P in the last position are incorrect and one of letters - P in the first position or A in the second position is correct. Suppose that letter A is correct and change the letter in the first position (introducing a hypothesis). Let the next word be CAP (Table 10).

Since the estimation of the oracle is not changed letter A in the second position is correct. Now we will keep letter A in the second position but change letter in the first or last positions. Let the next word be RAP. The estimation of the oracle is 2. We conclude that R in the first position is correct.

The result is in Table 11.

Table 7. Example 1, one letter is correctly guessed

L	H	H	H	R	C	
A	A	A	A	A	U	A
P	P	M	T	T	B	
1	1	1	2	2	1	

Table 8. Example 1, two letters are correctly guessed .

L	H	H	H	R	C	
A	A	A	A	A	U	A
			T	T	B	T
1	1	1	2	2	1	

Table 9. Example 1, all the letters are correctly guessed

L	H	H	H	R	C	C
A	A	A	A	A	U	A
			T	T	B	T
1	1	1	2	2	1	

Now we shall choose the words changing only letter in the last position. Finally, we guess the word RAT. The result is in Table 12.

Example 3

Consider the sequence of words: OAF (2), OAT (2), TOR (1).

We conclude that letters O and A in the first and second positions are correct. We may choose any of the words with different letters in the last position. Consider word TOR. We know that T and O in two first positions are incorrect, but the estimation of oracle is equal to 1. Hence letter R in the last position is correct and the word OAR is one that the oracle thought.

Example 4

The initial state of the task is GIG (2), GUN (2), PIN (2).

Table 10. Example 2, one letter in the second position is correct

P	P	C	
A	A	A	A
N	P	P	
1	1	1	

Table 11. Example 2, two letters are correct

P	P	C	R	R
A	A	A	A	A
N	P	P	P	
1	1	1	2	

Table 12. Example 2, all letters are guessed

P	P	C	R	R
A	A	A	A	A
N	P	P	P	T
1	1	1	2	3

Compare words GIG and GUN. By rule 7, we conclude that there exists correct letter in one position; since correct letter in this position must be the same in both words we conclude that letter G in the first position is correct. Analogously, by comparing words GUN and PIN, we conclude that letter N in the last position is correct; then we conclude that letter I in the second position is correct. Consequently, the word GIN is correct.

Example 5.

The initial state of the task is FAN(2), GUN(1), LAD(1). Consider several ways of reasoning in this example.

1. Words GUN и LAD have not a coincident letter, however, there is one correct letter in each of these words. Hence correct letters are in two different positions in the thought word. Word FAN contains exactly two positions with correct letters. Then the correct letters in words GUN and LAD must coincide with the letters in correspondent positions of correct letters in word FAN. We conclude that letter A and N in two last positions are correct.

2. Since changing two letters in word FAN with obtaining word GUN decreases the estimation of the oracle by 1 the remaining correct letter (by rule 8) can be in those positions where the letters were not changed. But there is only one position in which the letter was not changed – the last position of words. Consequently, letter N in the last position is correct. Analogously, comparing words FAN and LAD leads to the conclusion that letter A in the second position is correct.

3. Suppose that letter N in word FAN is incorrect. Then letters F and A in two first positions must be correct. But then, in word GUN, there is not any correct letter. It is in contradiction with the estimation of the oracle for word GUN. So, letter N in the last position is correct. Analogously, comparing words FAN and LAD, we conclude that letter A in the second position is correct.

In all three ways of reasoning, we conclude that the letters in the first position of words are not correct.

Example 6

Table 13 contains the initial state of the task.

Comparing words PIE and PIG, we conclude that letters E and G in the last position are incorrect.

Only two variants are possible for two first positions of the correct word: PO or RI (Table 14). Consequently, letter A in the second position and letter B in the first position are incorrect.

We can conclude that letter T in the last position is correct.

Table 13. Example 6, the initial state of the task

P	P	R	R	B
I	I	O	A	A
E	G	E	T	T
1	1	1	1	1

Table 14. Example 6, two possible variants for two first positions of the correct word

P	P	R	R	B	P	R
I	I	O	A	A	O	I
E			T	T		
1	1	1	1	1		

Table 15. Example 6, the last state of the task

P	P	R	R		P	R
I	I	O			O	I
E	G	E	T	T	T	T
1	1	1	1	1		

Table 16. Example 7, the initial state of the task

R	P	R
O	L	O
C	O	U
K	T	T
2	2	3

The thought word can be only POT or RIT (suppose that meaningless combinations of letters may be assumed). However, word RIT contradicts the estimation of the oracle for word RAT.

The thought word is POT (Table 15).

Example 7.

The initial state of the task is presented in Table 16. Analyzing words PLOT and ROUT with the estimation of the oracle, we conclude that letter T in the last position is correct.

Then we consider only three first positions and form the subtask shown in Table 17.

Now it is easy to see that letters R and O in two first positions are correct (Table 18).

Then in sub-word PLO there is only one correct letter in the third position – letter O – and the thought word is ROOT (Table 19).

Table 17. Example 7, one letter is correct

R	P	R	
O	L	O	
C	O	U	
			T
2	1	2	

Table 18. Example 7, two letters are correct

R	P	R	R
O	L	O	O
C	O	U	
			T
2	1	2	

Table 19. Example 7, all the letters are correct

R	P	R	R
O	L	O	O
C	O	U	O
			T
2	1	2	

The Analysis of Inference Structure. The Interaction of Deductive and Inductive Reasoning Rules in Solving Logical Problems

Besides the rules, given in the table 5, the process of reasoning contains such logical rules and component of thinking as the introduction of assumptions, the selection of versions, and the deductive mode of proving. The quantitative assessments such that the word length, the number of positions with accurate or incorrect letters, the difference between the number of accurate positions and the estimation of the oracle are very important.

There is a certain freedom in selecting position for testing new letters in it and in selecting rule for using it in the appropriate situation. This fact implies the necessity to recognize the applicability of rules. It means that the descriptions of situations must be well structured, sufficiently complete, and reflecting all their intrinsic properties. Thus, the deduction is not separated from the inductive steps of reasoning.

The induction is used for the generalization of rules to adjust them for playing with words of any length or decomposing a task into subtasks. As a whole, it is possible to say that the reasoning is well organized, when there is a good decomposition of task into the sub-tasks and when the good interrelation between these sub-tasks is systematically performed.

CONCLUSION

This chapter examined the problem of human natural reasoning in some real world situations. One of the fundamental questions of natural reasoning is the interaction of deductive and inductive reasoning rules. The analysis of several examples selected from different fields of thinking shows that the natural reasoning is based on both deductive and inductive rules of the first and second kinds. Inductive reasoning supports deductive one and vice versa.

REFERENCES

Bizam, G., & Herczeg, J. (1978). *Many-colored logic*. Moscow: Mir.

Doyle, A. C. (1992). *The adventures of Sherlock Holmes*. UK: Wordsworth Editions Limited.

Chapter 6
Machine Learning (ML) as a Diagnostic Task

ABSTRACT

This chapter discusses a revised definition of classification (diagnostic) test. This definition allows considering the problem of inferring classification tests as the task of searching for the best approximations of a given classification on a given set of data. Machine learning methods are reduced to this task. An algebraic model of diagnostic task is brought forward founded upon the partition lattice in which object, class, attribute, value of attribute take their interpretations.

INTRODUCTION

Classification as a logical meta-procedure plays an important part in thinking processes. The efficiency of using knowledge depends on what classifications will be formed and what relations will be considered. Classification (as a procedure) lies in the foundation of our knowledge. With the use of it, knowledge is obtained, ordered, transformed in a systematic construction. Every science begins with the classification, because it permits not only systematizing facts but explaining them through establishing the causal relationships between classes of objects and their properties. We believe that non-interrelated classifications do not exist.

One can find the examples of interconnected classifications in the functioning of both living organisms and technical devices, say, automata or robots capable to adaptive behavior. In principle the adaptation

DOI: 10.4018/978-1-60566-810-9.ch006

of an organism or an automaton to some environment is a classification of its reactions into groups in accordance with the environment influences. Also comprehending the sense of phrases (sayings) is based on the classification of interconnected relations between such parts of phrases as words, word combinations and phrases themselves.

The history of creating the Law of Periodicity of chemical elements, of course, is an excellent illustration of classification process. It is known that much time was required for realizing the fact that the elements can be classified in accordance with the Law of Periodicity.

The first steps in grouping elements were made in 1817, when German chemist Döbereiner showed that the atomic weight of strontium has the average value between the atomic weights of other two elements - calcium and barium. He established other triads of similar elements - (chlorine, bromine, and iodine), (lithium, sodium, and potassium). Then other chemists showed that the elements can be united into the groups, which include more than three elements. Fluorine was added to the triad of chlorine, bromine, and iodine, and magnesium to the triad of calcium, strontium, and barium. Then, oxygen, sulfur, selenium, and tellurium were in 1854 united into one group. Into another group entered nitrogen, phosphorus, arsenic, antimony, and bismuth. In 1862, French chemist Emile de Shankurtua arranged elements in ascending order of their atomic weight and assumed that the properties of elements are functionally determined by their positions in this ordering.

In 1863 English chemist Reina Newlands proposed the classification of elements in ascending order of their atomic weights; moreover, he divided elements into seven groups of seven elements in each. He named his classification "the law of octaves" by analogy with intervals of musical range.

Finally very major step was made in 1869 by Russian chemist Mendeleyev, who thoroughly studied the relationship between the atomic weights of elements and their physical and chemical properties, focusing specially on valence.

Thus, the Law of Periodicity is the result of analyzing the interrelations between atomic weights of elements, their properties and valence. This system considers the coordination of these characteristics.

Considering classification as a process, we reveal two interacting tasks:

A)   If a general feature of some collection of objects has been established, then it is necessary to decide whether it is possible to name this collection of objects, i.e. to explain it in terms of some phenomena or reasons, in other words, via other classifications. If the reply is positive, then the feature and the name are associated with the group of phenomena, explaining it. If the reply is negative, the feature has to be considered as useless;

Б)   If for some collection of objects, its name and meaning are known, then it is necessary to find a general feature equivalent to the meaning of this object collection.

An interesting fragment related to the properties of classifications has been revealed by us in a report of Patrick Geddesm to The Edinburgh Royal Scientific Society (1881) dealing with the systematization of statistical data: "Our classification must be natural, not artificial; must be capable of complete specialization, so as to include the minutest details, and capable, too, of the widest generalization; it must be universal in application, and it must be, as far as possible, simple understanding, and convenient in use" (Geddes, 1881).

FUNDAMENTAL DIAGNOSTIC (CLASSIFICATION) TASK

The classical determination of diagnostic (classification) test has been advanced within the framework of information theory (see, please, the works of (Cheguis, & Jablonsky, 1958). This determination is based on the discrimination of objects to be recognized. For example, in (Juravlev, 1958), (Soloviev, 1978), the following definition of diagnostic test is given: let T be an arbitrary table of n–dimensional pair-wise different vectors partitioned into blocks $k_1, k_2, ...k_n, n > 2$. A collection of coordinates $x_{i1}, ...,$ $x_{im}, 1 \leq m \leq n$ is called diagnostic test with respect to a given partitioning into blocks if the projections of vectors from different blocks defined by $x_{i1}, ..., x_{im}, 1 \leq m \leq n$ are also pair-wise different. Otherwise $x_{i1}, ..., x_{im}, 1 \leq m \leq n$ are to be said non-admissible collection of coordinates.

In the beginning of the 70's, the connection of the search for diagnostic tests has been revealed not only in the framework of the information theory and synthesis of discrete devices but also in the framework of pattern recognition problems (Boldyrev, 1974), (Juravlev, 1978), (Parkhomenko, 1970), and (Zakrevskij, 1971). A new logical-combinatorial approach began to be developed in different applications related to the search for tests. In contrast to the probabilistic methods of pattern recognition, this approach does not require strong assumptions about the properties of objects such as the subordination to the probabilistic laws or to a certain measure system (the measurability). Furthermore, this approach makes it possible to solve the problems of pattern recognition with sufficiently small training samples (Dukova, 1982).

However, the application of diagnostic tests for the tasks of pattern recognition in no way was reflected in the determination of diagnostic test - as before the attention was paid only to the discernability relation given on identified objects. Let us refer, for example, to the definition of diagnostic test given in (Dukova, 1982, p. 167): "Diagnostic test of a table T is a subset of its columns such that any two lines formed by these columns are different if they belong to the different classes of a given partition of table rows".

The application of diagnostic tests for the solution of pattern recognition problems was actually limited to two purposes: extracting informative features or minimizing the number of features and constructing decision classification trees for identifying new objects, which were not contained in the training material. The last direction goes back to the theory of questionnaires (Parkhomenko, 1970). By the way, precisely, the theory of questionnaires is one of the sources for the task of constructing decision trees by examples, which became central in the machine learning applications for knowledge discovering. The connection of diagnostic task with the conceptual reasoning remained out of the framework of current studies.

Together with diagnostic tasks, in pattern recognition was also developed still one independent direction connected with learning a concept from a given set of examples of this concept. Learning concepts was not connected with the search for diagnostic tests. The formalization of this task as minimization of Boolean function has been proposed by several authors (Toropov, 1967), (Hunt et al., 1965), (Banerji, 1969). The task of describing concepts, in the setting proposed, can be considered in logical sense as the approximation of partially assigned Boolean functions. It is possible that the task of concept formation has served as the prototype of second fundamental problem of machine learning, namely, learning concepts or logical rules from examples. It is interesting that, in contrast to diagnostic task, learning concepts from examples is understood very clearly as a model of human cognitive ability to generalize patterns, to reason by induction, to hypothesize (Finn, 1983), (Hunt et al., 1965), (Banerji, 1969), (Gladun, & Vaschenko, 1975; 1978), (Vaschenko, 1976; 1983). Figure 1 illustrates three main problems related to both technical diagnostics and pattern recognition.

Figure 1. The key problems of technical diagnostics and pattern recognition

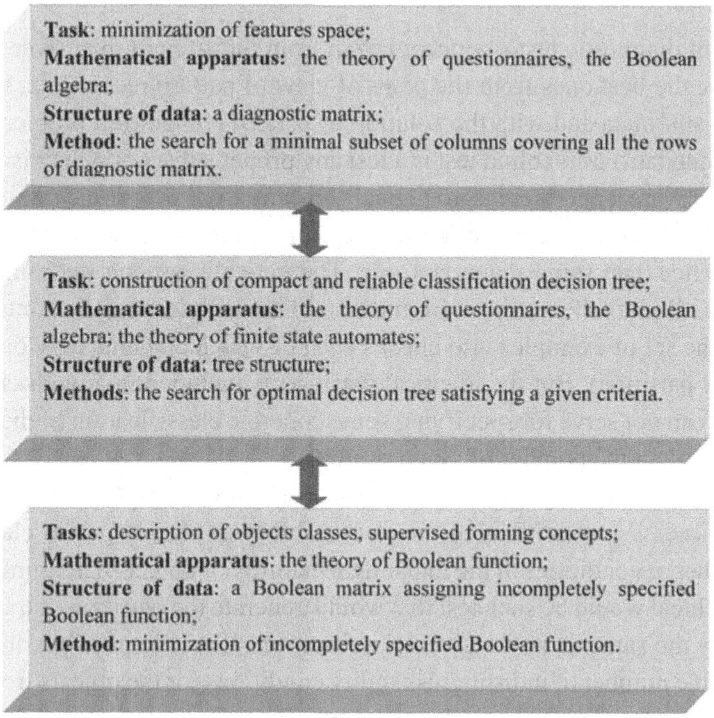

Task: minimization of features space;
Mathematical apparatus: the theory of questionnaires, the Boolean algebra;
Structure of data: a diagnostic matrix;
Method: the search for a minimal subset of columns covering all the rows of diagnostic matrix.

Task: construction of compact and reliable classification decision tree;
Mathematical apparatus: the theory of questionnaires, the Boolean algebra; the theory of finite state automates;
Structure of data: tree structure;
Methods: the search for optimal decision tree satisfying a given criteria.

Tasks: description of objects classes, supervised forming concepts;
Mathematical apparatus: the theory of Boolean function;
Structure of data: a Boolean matrix assigning incompletely specified Boolean function;
Method: minimization of incompletely specified Boolean function.

However, into the 70s years, in the framework of discrete automata synthesis, a new view on the diagnostic task was formed. At the same time, a new definition of diagnostic test was formulated by Zakrevskij (1982). Two sets, for certainty, the set of events and the set of their features, $A = \{a_1, a_2, ..., a_n\}$ and $B = \{b_1, b_2, ..., b_m\}$, respectively, are given, they are connected by the causal relations, i. e. an event a_i implies feature b_j ($a_i \rightarrow b_j$) or from a_i it follows inevitably b_j. A - reasons, B – consequencies or concomitant reasons. Pattern recognition problem is formulated as follows: observing features from B, one constructs hypotheses about events from A. To determine diagnostic test, the following relations are considered for distinguishing events: 1) feature b_k discerns events a_i, a_j, if $a_i \rightarrow b_k$, $a_j \rightarrow$ not b_k or $a_i \rightarrow$ not b_k, $a_j \rightarrow b_k$; 2) a collection of features $B_p \subseteq B$ discerns a collection of events $A_q \subseteq A$ if for any pairs a_i, $a_j \in A_q$ there exists $b_k \in B_p$ which discerns this pair of events; collection $B_p \subseteq B$ is called unconditional diagnostic test for $A_q \subseteq A$. Events from the set A can be interpreted both as objects (patterns) and as classes of objects. Features from the set B can be interpreted as properties of objects or classes of objects. It is important that diagnostic test is determined as a collection of implicative dependencies between objects (classes) and their features.

Basic construct for the search for diagnostic test in the approach stated is a diagnostic matrix or matrix of the discernability C, $C = \{C_{ij} = 1$, if $a_i \rightarrow$ not b_j and $C_{ij} = 0$ otherwise$\}$. Constructing diagnostic tests is reduced to the solution of minimal column covering problem for a diagnostic matrix (Yankovskya, & Gedike, 1999). Test generates a decision tree (perhaps, not only one) with the use of which a process of pattern recognition is performed.

The Necessity of a New Definition of Diagnostic Test

The reconsideration of diagnostic test's concept began from the attempt to answer the question, which of diagnostic tests are the best ones from the point of view of pattern recognition tasks. Both with the synthesis of discrete automata and with the solution of pattern recognition problems, it has a sense to search for blind (irredundant) tests (blind test is a test any proper subset of which is not a test). But their number is exponentially great and there is no logical substantiation why some minimal test is better for pattern recognition than another minimal one with the same number of attributes; or why some minimal irredundant test is better than some redundant one. Theoretically among the minimal blind tests the tests, that distinguish all pairs of examples from the training samples, can be contained. It means that these tests partition the set of examples into classes each of which contains only one example (it is the complete or identical partition). But the identical partition is included in any classification of a given training samples and can not serve for specifying some concrete classification of these samples with the number of classes less than the number of given examples.

Obviously, all blind tests for a given classification of training examples are equivalent in the sense that they satisfy all necessary conditions of the discernability of classes in this classification but they satisfy different number of conditions of the indistinguishability of objects belonging to the same classes in this classification. Ideal would be such test that would generate the partition of training examples into the classes accurately the same as in the given classification. If it is impossible, then the test carrying out the greatest possible number of indistinguishability conditions for the objects from one and the same classes of the classification considered, will be the best. Thus the best diagnostic test must be the best approximation of the given classification on the given set of examples.

The question arises, whether is it possible to build an algorithm of finding diagnostic tests for a given classification *K* of examples, which 1) would exclude the formation of identical partitions and thus was reduced the complexity of the search for tests, 2) would make it possible to find the best tests satisfying the greatest number of indistinguishability conditions required by classification *K*? This consideration leads to taking into account the set of partitions generated by all possible sub-collections of a given set of attributes together with the ordering of partitions by set-theoretical inclusion relation. Since the system of all partitions (all equivalence relations) of finite set of objects forms the complete algebraic lattice (Ore, 1942), we arrived at the fundamentally new algebraic model of diagnostic task. For the first time, the model of diagnostic task on the basis of the partition lattice with two operations of addition and multiplication on partitions was proposed in (Naidenova, 1979). The development of this model results in a new concept of good diagnostic test for a given classification on a given set of training examples (Polegaeva, 1985; Naidenova, & Polejaeva, 1986).

Partition semantics for diagnostic task made it possible to prove the equivalence of the task of search for diagnostic tests for classifications and the task of inferring functional dependences between collections of attributes considered as the names of classifications generated by them. The proof is based on the demonstration of the equivalence between functional dependency and partition dependency generated by attributes whose names enter into this functional dependency. This proof was given for the first time into (Naidenova, 1982) and later into (Cosmadakis et al., 1986). Since the inferring implicative dependences between values of attributes is a special case of inferring functional dependences, it is natural that the diagnostic task is equivalent to the task of search for implicative dependences in data (it is already reflected in the definition of diagnostic test given by Zakrevskij (1971).

The methodological value of this, being, at first glance, an insignificant discovery of particular equivalences proved to be very essential for the problems of constructing database and knowledgebase systems.

The algebraic lattice of partitions was that mathematical model, within the framework of which it proved to be possible to reveal that the tasks, which were considered to be different (and they were solved by different methods), in reality not only are algorithmically equivalent, but they represent with respect to their content one and the same task. The task of inferring good diagnostic tests is formulated as the search for the best approximations of a given classification (a partitioning) on a given set of objects' examples. It is this task that some well known machine learning problems can be reduced to (Naidenova, 1996): finding keys and functional dependencies in database relations, finding implicative dependencies and association rules, inferring logical rules (if-then rules, rough sets, and "ripple down" rules) and decision tree from examples, learning by discovering concept hierarchies, and some others.

The partition semantics for implicative and functional dependencies yielded a plethora of new researches on deductive database models (Spyratos, 1987), incorporating functional dependencies in deductive query answering (Spyratos, & Lecluse, 1987), universal scheme interfaces (Laurent, & Spyratos, 1994). However, the problem of inferring functional dependencies from data did not arise in these works.

The application of partition model to the search for functional dependences made it possible to build a new deductive model of database systems in which the concepts of attribute, value of attribute, functional dependence, relation, scheme of relation, scheme of database received the natural object-oriented interpretation (Spiratos, 1991), (Lécluse, &. Spyratos, 1986a; 1986b; 1987), (Laurent et al., 2003).

Partition semantics revealed the algebraic nature of the most common database dependency - functional dependency. Using partition semantic, it was shown in (Cosmadakis et al., 1986) that the implication problem for functional dependencies, i. e. the problem of answer to a question whether a certain functional dependency is inferred from a given set of functional dependencies, is reduced to a problem of inferring an equation between algebraic expressions from other such equations. In more mathematical terms, this problem is equivalent to the uniform word problem for idempotent commutative semi-groups (Cosmadakis et al., 1986). This is a restricted form of the uniform word problem for lattices (Crawley and Dilworth, 1973). Moreover, a new polynomial time inference algorithm for the uniform word problem for lattices has been given in (Cosmadakis et al., 1986). It would not be possible without using partition semantics for functional dependencies.

The process of constructing the schemes of databases began to be considered as one of the stages of the process of transforming data into knowledge. The result of this process is no longer the database scheme, but an object-oriented model of data and knowledge obtained in the course of inductive analysis of initial datasets. The mechanism of inferring good diagnostic tests for classifications is the key-stone of data processing into knowledge.

Figure 2 illustrates the role Good Tests in designing data and knowledge systems.

MACHINE LEARNING PROBLEMS AS THE SEARCH FOR GOOD CLASSIFICATION TESTS

We consider two main machine learning problems:

- Learning concepts or conceptual descriptions of a given training set of examples;
- Learning decision trees from examples.

Figure 2. The role of good tests in creating and functioning data and knowledge bases

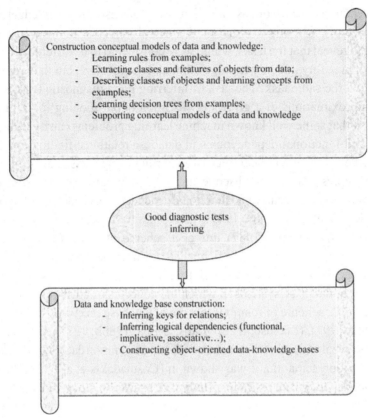

The first problem is based on generalization of given examples. The second one is based on specification (specialization) of given examples (Ganascia, 1989).

Machine Learning Methods Based on Generalization

These methods of machine learning use a way of reasoning "from the specific to the general". The most typical task of this type can be schematically expressed as follows (Ganascia, 1989):

Given:

- A concept C (class C);
- A set of positive examples $E_1, ..., E_n$ of C;
- A set of counter-examples or negative examples $CE_1, ..., CE_p$.

Step 1: Construction of generalized description (call it E_g) of $E_1, ..., E_n$ such that it holds for $E_1, ..., E_n$ and does not hold for any $CE_1, ..., CE_p$.

Step 2: Construction of the rule $E_g \rightarrow C$.

This schematically description of generalization does not depend on the language for representation of examples and on the generality relations used for this task. For instance, the following relations can be considered as the generality ones (Ganascia, 1989).

Replacing constant by variable: if x is a variable, A is a constant, P is a predicate and $P(t_1, t_2, .., t_n)$ is an atomic expression, then $P(x, t_2, ..., t_n)$ is more general than $P(A, t_2, ..., t_n)$.

Use of eliminating rule: if P_1 and P_2 are two propositions, then P_1 is more general than $P_1 \& P_2$.

Climbing in a conceptual hierarchy: given a conceptual hierarchy of plane figures, one concludes that polygon more general than square and, consequently, the proposition (shape = polygon) & (color = red) is more general than the proposition (shape = square) & (color = red).

Extension of boundaries: (in the case of attributes' domains of values are ordered sets): (size > 7) is more general than (size > 30), (size belongs to [- 7, 7]) is more general than (size belongs to [-5, 5]).

Machine Learning methods "from the specific to the general" cover such learning tasks as learning concepts descriptions, logical rules (if-then rules, rough sets, "ripple down" rules), implicative dependencies, and association rules from examples.

Machine Learning Methods Based on Specification

These methods of Machine Learning use a way of reasoning "from the general to the specific". The most typical task of this kind can be schematically expressed as follows (Ganascia, 1989).

Given:

- A set of disjoint classes $C_1, ...,C_k$;
- A set of examples E_i, $i = 1, ..., k$ for each class C_i.

Step 1: Construction of a logical rule in the form of decision tree classifying all the examples E_i, $i = 1, ..., k$ in accordance with a given classification into classes $C_1, ...,C_k$.

Learning algorithm builds a decision tree for a set S of examples by generating their partitions with the use of attributes' values describing examples of S:

```
IF all examples of S belongs to the same class C,

THEN - label the corresponding node with C;

ELSE - select most informative attribute A the values of which are,
say, v1, ..., vn;

   - partition S into classes S1,   ..., Sn by values v1,   ..., vn;

-    construct sub-tree for S1, ..., Sn.
```

J. R. Quinlan (1987) views the decision tree construction as a classification procedure. The nodes of tree are associated with diagnostic questions that can be asked about attributes' values in object descriptions. The answers are the labels of the arcs leaving the decision nodes. Decision tree defines a classification or diagnostic procedure in a natural manner. Any object (even one not in the original set of examples) is associated with a unique leaf of the tree obtained as a result of decision tree construction.

A decision tree generates a classification of objects or partition of objects into disjoint classes.

It is natural to think of constructing the best decision tree. What is "best" depends on using trees for solving practical problems.

For example, one might consider the decision tree to be "best" if:

1. It gives the smallest possible error rate when classifying previously unseen objects (pattern recognition problems);
2. It is the most adequate ontology for the given domain of objects.

In (Quinlan, & Rivest, 1989), the Minimum Description Length Principle is used for constructing an optimal size decision tree. This principle allows constructing decision trees with the smallest length of their encoding (in bits).

As a result of decision tree construction, a collection of attributes X generating this tree gives the partition, say $P(X)$, of examples into classes each of which is contained in one and only one class C_i, $C_i \in \{C_1, ...,C_k\}$. On the other hand, decision tree is a form of representation of the functional dependency $X \rightarrow C$ between the collection X of attributes and the given classification of examples into classes C_1, ...,C_k. Indeed, $P(X) = \{p_1, p_2, ..., p_m\}$, where $p_j, j = 1, 2,..., m, m \geq k$, are classes of partition $P(X)$, each of which is associated with one and only one collection of values of attributes of X and each such collection of values of X corresponds with one and only one class C_i, $C_i \in \{C_1, ...,C_k\}$.

Return to the task "from the specific to the general". Let $E+$ and $E-$ be the set positive and negative examples, respectively. The result of learning is the generalized description E_g of set $E+$ such that implicative rule $E_g \rightarrow C$, where C is a constant (a symbol) denoting class to which positive examples belong to, holds for any example from E+ and does not hold for any example from $E-$. Clearly, E_g is an expression generating the partition of given examples equivalent to the given partition into two classes $E+$ and $E-$.

A hypothesis arises that these tasks of machine learning consist in searching for the approximations of the given classifications on the given set of examples and hence these tasks are equivalent, by their goal, to the task of searching for good diagnostic tests. In every such task we have a goal (target) classification of examples. This classification is given by two ways as it is shown in Figure 3: 1) by a target attribute K or 2) by a value k of target attribute K. The target attribute partitions the given set of example

Figure 3. Two modes of giving the goal classification

	A	B	C	K
1				1
2				0
3				1
4				0
5				0

	A	B	C	D
1				h
2				v
3				v
4				f
5				f0

K – the goal attribute;   v – the goal value of attribute

into disjoint classes the number of which is equal to the number of values of this attribute. The target value of an attribute partitions the given set of examples into two disjoint classes: 1) the examples in the description of which the target value appears and 2) all the other examples.

Given value *k* of attribute *K*, the logical rule is in the following form:

```
if ((value of attribute A = "a" ) &

     (value of attribute B = "в") &

...........................................),

     then (value of attribute K = "k" ).
```

Given attribute K, the following logical rules are formed:

```
A B C → K or

     D S → K or

                         or

A S Q V → K
```

where A, B, C, D, Q, S, V – the names of attributes.

The expressions of the left parts of rules can be considered as the descriptions of given classifications.

ALGEBRAIC MODEL OF DIAGNOSTIC TASK

Basic Concepts

Lattices (Rasiowa, 1974)

An abstract algebra $(A, \cap, \cap)$ with two binary operations is said to be a lattice provided the following equations are satisfied for all $a, b, c \in A$:

(el) commutativity $a \cup b = b \cup a, a \cap b = a \cap b,$

(e2) associativity $a \cup (b \cup c) = (a \cup b) \cup c, a \cap (b \cap c) = (a \cap b) \cap c,$

(e3) absorption $(a \cap b) \cup b = b, a \cap (a \cup b) = a.$

For all $a, b, c, a \cup b$ is called the join of a and b, and $a \cap b$ the meet of a and b.

We give without proof the following theorem:

Theorem 6.1 If $(A, \cup, \cap)$ is a lattice, then for all $a, b \in A$

(1) $a \cup b = b$ if and only if $a \cap b = a$.

The relation $\leq$ on A, is defined as follows:

(2) $a \leq b$ if and only if one of the equations (1) holds (this relation is an ordering on A, called the lattice ordering on A). Moreover,

(3) $a \cup b = \text{l.u.b.}\{a, b\}, a \cap b = \text{g.l.b.}\{a, b\}$,

where l.u.b. $\{a, b\}$ and g.l.b. $\{a, b\}$ are, respectively, the least upper bound of $\{a, b\}$ and the greatest low bound of $\{a, b\}$ in the ordered set $(A, \leq)$.

The following properties of join and meet operations $\cup$, $\cap$ follow directly from Theorem 6.1:

(4) $a \cup a = a; a \cap a = a$

(5) $a \leq a \cup b; a \cap b \leq a$

(6) $b \leq a \cup b; a \cap b \leq b$

(7) $a \leq c$ and $b \leq c$ imply $a \cup b \leq c$,

    c $\leq a$ and $c \leq b$ imply $c \leq a \cap b$

(8) $a \leq c$ and $b \leq d$ imply $a \cup b \leq c \cup d$

    a $\leq c$ and $b \leq d$ imply $a \cap b \leq c \cap d$.

We also give without proof the following theorem:

Theorem 6.2 If in an ordered set $(A, \leq)$ for all $a, b \in A$ there exist l.u.b. $\{a, b\}$ and g.l.b. $\{a, b\}$, then the abstract algebra $(A, \cup, \cap)$, where $\cup$ and $\cap$ are binary operations defined by equations (3), is a lattice, i.e., the equations (e1), (e2), (e3) hold for all $a, b, c \in A$. The relation $\leq$ is the lattice ordering in this lattice.

Let $L = (A, \cup, \cap)$ be a lattice. If in the ordered set $(A, \leq)$, where $\leq$ is the lattice ordering on A, there exists a greatest (a least) element, it is called the unit element (the zero element) and is denoted by $V(\Lambda)$.

In any lattice, the notions of a maximal element and of the greatest element coincide. The same is true for the notions of a minimal element and of the least element in any lattice.

By definition $\forall x, x \in A$:

9) $x \leq V, \Lambda \leq x$

10) $x \cup V = V, x \cap V = x$

11) $x \cup \Lambda = x, x \cap \Lambda = \Lambda$.

If we add to a lattice $L = (A, \cup, \cap)$ the elements V, Λ and extend the operations $\cup, \cap$ on V, Λ by means of (10), (11), respectively, where $x \in A \cup \{V\} \cup \{\Lambda\}$, then we obtain the lattice $LL = (B, \cup, \cap)$ where $B = A \cup \{V\} \cup \{\Lambda\}$ and V, Λ are the unit element and the zero element of LL, respectively.

Subsequently the following definitions will be necessary.

Definition 6.1. Non-empty subset ∇ of the set A of all elements of a lattice $(A, \cup, \cap)$ is said to be a *filter*, if for all elements $a, b \in A$

(a) $a \cap b \in \nabla$ if and only if $a \in \nabla$ and $b \in \nabla$.

The condition (a) is equivalent to the following two conditions:

(b)   if $a \in \nabla$ and $b \in \nabla$, then $a \cap b \in \nabla$,
(c)   if $a \in \nabla$ and $a \leq b$, then $b \in \nabla$.

The condition (c) can be replaced by the following condition:

(d) $a \in \nabla$, then for all $b \in A$, $a \cup b \in \nabla$.

Definition 6.2. Non-empty subset Δ of the set A of all elements of a lattice $(A, \cup, \cap)$ is said to be an *ideal*, if for all $a, b \in A$

(a) $a \cup b \in \Delta$, if and only if $a \in \Delta$ and $b \in \Delta$.

The condition (a) is equivalent to the following two conditions:

(b)   if $a \in \Delta$ and $b \in \Delta$, then $a \cup b \in \Delta$,
(c)   if $a \in \Delta$ and $b \leq a$, then $b \in \Delta$.

The condition (c) can be replaced by the following condition:

(d) $a \in \Delta$, then for all $b \in A$, $a \cap b \in \Delta$.

The whole lattice A is a filter (an ideal). If a lattice has a unit element $\vee$ (a zero element$\wedge$), then $\{\vee\}$ ($\{\wedge\}$) is a filter (an ideal), called the unit filter (the zero ideal).

Definition 6.3. For every fixed element $a \in A$ the set $\nabla(a) = \{x \in A: a \leq x\}$ (the set $\Delta(a) = \{x \in A: x \leq a\}$) is the least filter (ideal) containing a and is called the **principal filter (principal ideal)** generated by a.

If a lattice contains the unit element (the zero element), then each filter in this lattice contains the unit element (each ideal in this lattice contains the zero element).

The filter (ideal) generated by a non-empty set A_0 of elements of a lattice L (i. e. the least filter (ideal) in L containing A_0) is the set of all elements a in L such that there exist $a_1, ..., a_n$ in A_0 for which $a_1 \cap ... \cap a_n \leq a$ (for which $a \leq a_1 \cup ... \cup a_n$).

The filter (ideal) generated by a fixed element a^* and a filter ∇ (an ideal Δ) in a lattice L is the set of all elements a in this lattice such that $a^* \cap c \leq a$ (such that $a \leq a^* \cup c$) for some element $c \in \nabla$ (for some element $c \in \Delta$).

A filter (an ideal) in a lattice L is said to be proper provided there exists an element a in L such that a does not belong to this filter (this ideal). In particular, if L has the zero element $\wedge$ (the unit element $\vee$), then a filter ∇ (an ideal Δ) is proper if and only if $\wedge \notin \nabla$ ($\vee \notin \Delta$).

A filter ∇ (an ideal Δ) in a lattice *L* is said to be maximal provided it is proper and it is not a proper subset of any proper filter (ideal) in *L*.

A filter ∇ (an ideal Δ) in a lattice *L* is said to be irreducible provided it is proper and for any two proper filters ∇_1, ∇_2 (two proper ideals Δ_1, Δ_2) the condition $\nabla = \nabla_1 \cap \nabla_2$ (the condition $\Delta = \Delta_1 \cap \Delta_2$) implies either $\nabla = \nabla_1$ or $\nabla = \nabla_2$ (implies either $\Delta = \Delta_1$ or $\Delta = \Delta_2$). In other words, a filter (an ideal) is irreducible provided it is proper and it is not the intersection of two proper filters (of two proper ideals) different from it.

A filter ∇ (an ideal Δ) in a lattice *L* is said to be prime provided it is proper and $a \cup b \in \nabla$ ($a \cap b \in \Delta$) implies that either $a \in \nabla$ or $b \in \nabla$ (implies that either $a \in \Delta$ or $b \in \Delta$).

The following assertions are valid.

Every maximal filter (maximal ideal) in a lattice is irreducible.
Every prime filter (prime ideal) in a lattice is irreducible.

The union of any chain of filters (ideals) in a lattice *L* is a filter (an ideal) in *L*.

The union of any chain of proper filters (proper ideals) in a lattice *L* which contains the zero element (the unit element) is a proper filter (proper ideal).

If a lattice *L* has a zero element (a unit element), then every proper filter (ideal) in *L* is contained in a maximal filter (ideal).

If a lattice *L* contains the zero element Λ (the unit element V), then for every element $a \neq \Lambda$ ($a \neq V$) there exists a maximal filter ∇ (a maximal ideal Δ) such that $a \in \nabla$ ($a \in \Delta$).

If ∇_0 (Δ_0) is a filter (an ideal) in a lattice *L* and $a \notin \nabla_0$ ($a \notin \Delta_0$), then there exists an irreducible filter ∇ (an irreducible ideal Δ) in *L* such that $\nabla_0 \subset \nabla$ ($\Delta_0 \subset \Delta$) and $a \notin \nabla$ ($a \notin \Delta$).

If ∇ and Δ are two disjoint subsets of the set *A* of all elements of a lattice $(A, \cup, \cap)$ and the union of ∇ and Δ is equal to *A*, then the set Δ is a prime ideal if and only if the set ∇ is a prime filter.

For a detailed exposition of lattice theory see, please, (Birkhoff, 1948) and (Rasiowa, 1974).

Partitions and Equivalence Relations

In the following, we shall denote by *S* some fixed set of elements. An equivalence relation *E* in *S* is a binary relation *a E b* between two elements *a* and *b* in *S*, defined by the four properties (Ore, 1942):

(1) Determination: for any pair of elements *a* and *b* the relation *a E b* either holds or does not hold.
(2) Reflexivity: for any *a* one has *a E a*.
(3) Symmetry: if *a E b*, then *b E a*.
(4) Transitivity: if *a E b* and *b E c*, then *a E c*.

The special equivalence relation *a* U *b* which is defined to hold for any pair *a*, *b* of elements will be called the universal relation. Similarly the equivalence relation *a* I *b* which holds only when *a = b* will be called the identity or unit relation.

A partition *P(S)* of the set *S* is decomposition of *S* into subsets C_a such that every element in S belongs to one and only one set C_a. We shall call the sets C_a the blocks of the partition *P(S)* and write $P(S) = P(C_a)$.

The connection between partitions and equivalence relations is expressed in the following Theorem 6.3.

Theorem 6.3 (Ore, 1942). Any partition $P(S)$ defines an equivalence relation E in the set S when one puts a E b whenever a and b belong to the same block C_a of $P(S)$. Conversely, any equivalence relation E defines a partition $P(C_a)$ where the blocks C_a consist of all elements equivalent to any given element a.

Proof of Theorem 6.3.

The correctness of the first part of the theorem is seen immediately, and to prove the converse one need only observe that every element in S belongs to some set C_a and that two such sets C_a must be either identical or disjoint according to the axioms for an equivalence relation.

Among the special partitions of S we note the universal partition P_u in which S is the only block and the complete or identical partition P_i in which every block is a single element.

When the set S is a finite set with n elements, the number N_p of partitions or equivalence relations over S is also finite. The number N_p has been studied extensively by many investigators. For a more complete set of references the reader may be address (Epstein, 1939). The number N_p may be determined successively through the recursion formula (Ore, 1942):

$$p_{n+1} = \sum_{i=0}^{n} \binom{n}{i} p_i$$

Definition 6.4. A partition $P(S)$ of a set S is the set $\{S_a\}$ of non-intersecting subsets of S such that their union is equal S. The subsets of the partition $P(S)$ of S are called the classes (blocks) of this partition.

All the elements of S contained in one class of a partition $P(S)$ of S are said to be equivalent in the partition $P(S)$. Every partition $P(S)$ of S generates on S an equivalence relation $E(p)$. The reverse assertion is correct too (Ore, 1942; Theorem 1).

Let **PS** be the set of all the partitions of the set S and **ES** be the set of all the equivalence relations corresponding to the partitions in **PS**.

Definition 6.5. A pair of partitions P_1 and P_2 are said to be in inclusion relation $P_1 \subseteq P_2$ if and only if every class of P_1 is contained in one and only one class of P_2. The relation $\subseteq$ means that P_1 is a sub-partition of P_2.

Definition 6.6. A pair of partitions P_1 и P_2 are said to be equal or equivalent if and only if the conditions $P_1 \subseteq P_2$ and $P_2 \subseteq P_1$ holds simultaneously.

Thus equivalent partitions possess the same number of classes and every class of one of these partitions coincides with one and only one class of another of these partitions.

Definition 6.7. Let $P_1 \subseteq P_2$. Then the according equivalence relations $E(p_1)$, $E(p_2)$ generated on S by P_1 and P_2 satisfy the following inclusion relation $E(p_1) \subseteq E(p_2)$ meaning that $aE(p_1)b$ implies $aE(p_2)b$, for all a, b в S.

The system of all partitions of a set S forms a partially ordered set when one writes $P_1 \subseteq P_2$ whenever the blocks in P_2 are obtained by subdivisions of the blocks in P_1. The zero element of S is the partition contained in all others (the complete partition), the unit element of S is the all-element containing all others (the universal partition consisting only of the block S). In term of equivalence relations, one writes

$E_1 \supset E_2$ when aE_2b always implies aE_1b. The following Theorem 6.4 has been proved by G. Birkhoff (1935).

Theorem 6.4. The system of all partitions or all equivalence relations of a set S forms a complete algebraic lattice (see the proof in (Ore, 1942; theorem 5).

The unit element of this lattice is the partition Pe containing only one class – the set S, the zero element of this lattice is the partition Pi in which every class is a single element of S.

Algebraic lattice of partitions (partition lattice) can be defined (and generated) by means of two binary operations $\{+,*\}$ – addition (generalization) and multiplication (refinement). The first of these forms a partition $P_3 = P_1 + P_2$ such that $P_1 \subseteq P_3, P_2 \subseteq P_3$, and if there exists a partition P in **PS** for which $P_1 \subseteq P$ and $P_2 \subseteq P$, then it implies that $P_3 \subseteq P$. Partition P_3 is the least upper bound of partitions P_1 и P_2. The second operation forms a partition $P_4 = P_1 * P_2$ such that $P_4 \subseteq P_1, P_4 \subseteq P_2$, and if there exists a partition P in **PS** for which $P \subseteq P_1$ and $P \subseteq P_2$, then it implies that $P \subseteq P_4$. Partition P_4 is the greatest lower bound of partitions P_1 и P_2.

For any $x, y, z \in$ **PS**, the following equations are satisfied:

(1) associativity: $(x*y)*z = x(y*z)$, $(x+y)+z = x+(y+z)$,
(2) commutativity: $x*y = y*x$, $x+y = y+x$,
(3) absorption: $x+(x*y) = x$, $x*(x+y) = x$.

Given a partitions P_1, P_2 of S their product $*$ is defined as $P_1 * P_2 = \{x: x = y \cap z, y$ belongs to P_1, z belongs to $P_2\}$.

Their sum is defined as $P_1 + P_2 = \{x:$ two elements h, g in S are in set x if and only if there is a chain of sets $x_1, x_2, ..., x_q$ from $(P_1 \cup P_2)$ such that h belongs to x_1, g belongs to x_q, and $(x_i \cap x_{i+1} \neq \emptyset$ for all i, $1 \leq i \leq q - 1\}$.

For definition of addition operation on partitions, it is necessary to introduce the concept of a chain connected by a family of subsets of some set.

Definition 6.8. Two sets A, B of a family M of sets will be said connected and we shall write $A \# B$ when their intersection is not empty.

Definition 6.9. Let A, C be some sets of a family M of sets; A and C shall be said to be chain connected in M when there exists a series $A = A_1, A_2, ..., A_n = C$, of sets in M such that A_i is connected with A_{i+1}, $i = 1, ..., n-1$.

Let P_1 and P_2 be partitions of S. By the definition of addition operation on partition, every class C_2 of P_2 having nonempty intersection with class C_1 of P_1 must belong to the same class C' of partition $P_1 + P_2$ to which class C_1 must belong in $P_1 + P_2$. By repeating this way of reasoning, it is easy to show that class C' must contain all classes C_1', C_2' of P_1 and P_2, respectively, connected by a chain with class C_1 in the family M formed by all classes of partitions P_1 and P_2.

In other words, the operation $*$ produces the coarset common refinement of P_1 and P_2. The operation $+$ produces their finest common generalization.

In (Ore, 1942; Birkhoff, 1948), it has been proven that the maximal chains of chain connected subsets of family M generate a partition of S and this partition is the least upper bound of P_1 and P_2 in **PS**.

The addition operation on partitions can be defined in terms of equivalence relations. Let $E(p_1)$ and $E(p_2)$ be the equivalence relations in **ES** corresponding to partition P_1, P_2 respectively. The equivalence relation $a(E(p_1) + E(p_2))b$ is satisfied if and only if there exists the following chain of connected equivalence relations $aE(p_1)a_1, a_1E(p_2)a_2, a_2E(p_1)a_3, ..., a_nE(p_2)b$.

It has been shown that relation $E(p_1) + E(p_2)$ is transitive closure of the relation $E(p_1) \cup E(p_2)$ which is the union of relations $E(p_1)$ and $E(p_2)$. Relation $a(E(p_1) \cup E(p_2))b$, in general case, is not an equivalence relation (Hartmanis, 1960; Shreider, 1971).

Partition Interpretation of Object, Class (Classification), Attribute, and Value of Attribute

The principle concept of data-knowledge transformation is a concept of classification. Let Q be a universal set of objects and KL be a classification of objects with respect to some property. Let V be any subset of Q. The classification induces on V the partition $P(V)$ into disjoint blocks (no object can have two different properties from the same domain). For example, let Q be the set of all trees, KL be the classification of trees with respect to their type, $KL = \{spruce, birch, oak ...\}$. Let $N = \{1, 2,...,7\}$ be the set of integers where each integer denotes a different tree in V. Then $P(V)$ can be represented by equivalent partition $P(N)$. We assume that in our example: $spruce \Leftrightarrow \{1, 2, 3\}$, $birch \Leftrightarrow \{4, 7\}$, $oak \Leftrightarrow \{5, 6\}$, then $P(V) = P(N) = \{\{1, 2, 3\}, \{4, 7\}, \{5, 6\}\}$.

For objects description, we begin with a finite, nonempty set $U = \{A_1, ..., A_n\}$. The set U is called the universe and A_i's are called the attributes. The attributes describe objects in terms of their properties. Let $dom(A_i) = \{a_{i1}, a_{i2}, ... \}$ be a finite set of symbols (values) called the domain of A_i. We assume that $dom(A_i)$ doesn't intersect with U for all $i \in \{1, ..., n\}$ and that the intersection of $dom(A_i)$ and $dom(A_j)$ is empty for all $i, j, i \neq j, i, j \in \{1, ..., n\}$ We denote the union of $dom(A_1),..., dom(A_n)$ by D.

Assume that objects are identified by positive integers and $S = \{1, 2, ..., m\}$ is the set of object indices. Each j in S is associated with the description of jth object, i. e. with a tuple $t_j = x_{j1} ... x_{jn}$ such that $t_j[A_i] = x_{ji}$ is in $dom(A_i)$ for all A_i in U.

Let T over U be a collection T of object descriptions. The example of T is given in Table 1 with $S = \{1, 2, 3, 4, 5, 6\}$, $U = \{A, B, C, D, E, F, G\}$, $T = \{t_1, t_2, t_3, t_4, t_5, t_6\}$, where K is a special attribute giving a classification of objects.

By $I(a)$, $a \in D$, we denote the subset $I(a) = \{i \in S: a$ appears in $t_i, t_i \in T\}$. Following (Casmodakis et al., 1986), we call $I(a)$ the interpretation of a in S.

Let $D_a \subseteq dom(A_i)$ be the set of all values of A_i appearing in object descriptions of T. Construct the interpretation $I(A_i)$ of A_i in S as the union of $I(a)$ for all $a \in D_a$. Since for all a, b in $dom(A_i)$ if $a \neq b$, then $I(a) \cap I(b)$ is empty, we have that the interpretation of any attribute is a partition of S into a family of mutually disjoint blocks. This partition will be denoted by $P(A)$ and called "atomic partition".

Table 1. An example of object descriptions

T	A	B	C	D	E	F	G	K
t_1	a_1	b_1	c_1	d_1	e_1	f_1	g_1	k_1
t_2	a_2	b_1	c_2	d_2	e_2	f_2	g_1	k_1
t_3	a_1	b_1	c_2	d_1	e_1	f_3	g_2	k_1
t_4	a_1	b_2	c_3	d_2	e_1	f_1	g_1	k_1
t_5	a_2	b_2	c_3	d_2	e_1	f_1	g_2	k_2
t_6	a_3	b_3	c_3	d_3	e_3	f_1	g_3	k_2

In our example (Table 1), we have for the attribute A: $I(a_1) = \{1,3,4\}$, $I(a_2) = \{2,5\}$, $I(a_3) = \{6\}$, and $I(A) = P(A) = \{\{1,3,4,\}, \{2,5\}, \{6\}\}$. We can extend the interpretation I to tuples as follows: for any tuple t, $t = x_1 \dots x_n I(t) = I(x_1) \cap I(x_2) \cap \dots \cap I(x_n) = \{i \in S: t$ is included in $t_i \in T\}$.

Table 2 contains the interpretations of main classification concepts.

Interpretation $I(x)$ for any value x in D is the mapping $f(x)$ from D into the set 2^S of all subsets of S, i. e. for any $x \in D$, $I(x) = \{i: t_i$ contains $x\}$.

Naturally, given T, the interpretation is determined for any collection d of values from D and for any collection Y of attributes from U: $I(d) = \{\cap I(x), x \in d\}$, $I(Y) = \{\cap I(A), A \in Y\}$.

It is not difficult to see that the mapping $I(Y)$ induces a partition of the set S into disjoint classes and this partition is the product of atomic partitions induced on S by attributes of the collection Y.

Following by (Cosmadakis et al., 1986), we define a partition interpretation $I(T)$ over U as the set of triples $\{(S(A), P(A), I_A(x) \mid$ for all A from U$\}$, where for each attribute A:

1. $S(A)$ is a nonempty set of indices of object descriptions in which the values of A appear;
2. $P(A)$ is a partition of $S(A)$, the atomic partition of A;
3. $I_A(x)$ is a function from dom(A) to $P(A)$ or $\{\emptyset\}$, such that $P(A) = \{I_A(x): x \in$ dom(A), $I(x) \neq \emptyset\}$ and if $x \neq y$, then $I(x) \cap I(y) = \emptyset$.

When all $S(A) = S$, the partition interpretation can be redefined as $\{S, I_A(x), P(A)\}$, where $I_A(x) = \{\cup I(x): x \in$ dom(A)$\}$.

Partition Dependencies and Algebra of Classifications

Consider the set $L(I(T))$ of partitions produced by closing atomic partitions of $I(T)$ with the use of operations addition + and multiplication * on partitions. In (Cosmadakis et al., 1986), it is shown that

Table 2. Interpretation of classification concepts

Concept	Interpretation
Classification	Attribute
Name of classification	Name of attribute
Value of property	Value of attribute
Example of an object	Collection of mapping from an object to the values of its properties (object description)
A collection of object examples	Table of object descriptions
Index of object example	Identifier of object example
Class	Value of classification (attribute)
The domain of vision of objects	The set S of indices of object examples
The domain of interpretation of classes	The set 2^S, i. e. the set of all subsets of S
Interpretation of class (value of attribute)	A subset of S
The domain of vision of classifications (attributes)	The set U of names of classifications (attributes)
The domain of interpretation of classifications (attributes)	The set of all partitions of S
Interpretation of classification (attribute)	A partition of S

Figure 4. Example of the partition lattice

	A₁	A₂	A₃	A₄
t₁	a₁	b₂	a₃	a₄
t₂	a₁	a₂	b₃	a₄
t₃	a₁	c₂	a₃	B₄

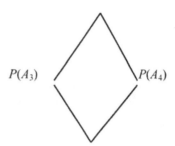

$L(I(T))$ is the algebraic lattice with constants over U. We can use the attributes and the symbols of these operations to construct finite expressions. The expressions are built by the following way: A, $A \in U$ is an expression, a collection of attributes connected by * operation is an expression; also an expression is a collection of attributes connected by + operation. We shall denote an expression by e. If e and e' are expressions, then $e+e'$, $e*e$ are expressions too.

Each expression has one only one interpretation in $L(I(T))$ called the meaning of it.

The meaning of attribute A is partition $P(A)$.

The meaning of $(e * e')$ is partition $P(e) * P(e')$.

The meaning of $(e + e')$ is partition $P(e) + P(e')$.

Let $W(U)$ be the set of finite expressions generated by attributes of U as generators with the use of +, * (, and) as operators. Each expression in $W(U)$ can be considered as the name of exactly one element in $L(I(T))$. However each element P in $L(I(T))$ can serve as the meaning of several expressions in $W(U)$ considered as different names of this partition. An illustrative example of the lattice $L(I(T))$ is given in Figure 4.

Any equation $e = e'$, where e, e' are different expressions, is a partition dependency.

Definition 6.10. A partition interpretation $I(T)$ of T on partitions over U satisfies partition dependency $e = e'$ (notation $I(T) |- e = e'$) if and only if $P = P'$ and $S = S'$, where partitions P, P' of sets S, S' are the respective meanings of e, e' in $I(T)$.

The following theorem is important.

Theorem 6.5 (Cosmadakis et al., 1986). Let $I(T)$ be a partition interpretation of T over U, $e = e'$ be a partition dependency, and $L(I(T))$ be the lattice with constants over U. Then $I(T) |- e = e'$ if and only if $L(I(T)) |- e = e'$

Let X, Y be nonempty sets of attributes. Consider a special type of partition, namely, a functional partition dependency, defined by the equality $X = X*Y$. The Theorem 6.6 follows from theorem 6.5 and the properties of partition lattice operations.

Theorem 6.6 (Cosmadakis et al., 1986). Let $I(T)$ be a partition interpretation of T on partitions over U, $X = X*Y$ be a partition dependency, and partitions $P(X)$, $P(Y)$ of S be the meanings of expressions X, Y in $I(T)$. Then $I(T) |- X = X*Y$ if and only if $P(X) \subseteq P(Y)$, i. e. for all $x \in P(X)$ there exists $y \in P(Y)$ such that $x \subseteq y$.

$S = \{1, 2, 3\};$

$D = \{a_1, a_2, a_3, a_4, b_2, b_3, b_4, c_2\}$;

$I(a_1)$: $a_1 \rightarrow \{1,2,3\}$;

$I(a_2)$: $a_2 \rightarrow \{2\}$, $b_2 \rightarrow \{1\}$, $c_2 \rightarrow \{3\}$;

$I(a_3)$: $a_3 \rightarrow \{1,3\}$, $b_3 \rightarrow \{2\}$;

$I(a_4)$: $a_4 \rightarrow \{1,2\}$, $b_4 \rightarrow \{3\}$;

$P(A_1) = \{\{1, 2, 3\}\}$; $P(A_2) = \{\{1\}, \{2\}, \{3\}\}$;

$P(A_3) = \{\{1, 3\}, \{2\}\}$; $P(A_4) = \{\{1, 2\}, \{3\}\}$.

The meaning of $A_1 * A_3$ is partition $P(A_3)$ because $P(A_1) * P(A_3) = P(A_3)$,

The meaning of $A_2 * A_3$ is partition $P(A_2)$ because $P(A_2) * P(A_3) = P(A_2)$,

The meaning of $A_1 * A_4$ is partition $P(A_4)$ because $P(A_1) * P(A_4) = P(A_4)$.

The duality of lattice operations $+$, $*$ implies that the partition dependency $X * Y = X$ is equivalent to the partition dependency $Y + X = Y$. This dependency can be written as $X \leq Y$, where $\leq$ is used to denote the natural partial order in the lattice $L(I(T))$. Thus, for non-empty subsets X, Y of attributes in U, there are three equivalent ways to express partition dependency: $X * Y = X$, $Y + X = Y$, and $X \leq Y$.

Expressive Power of Partition Dependencies

In (Cosmadakis et al., 1986), the following important results are obtained related to the expressive power of partition dependencies. The first result is formulated and proven by the following theorem.

Theorem 6.7 (Cosmadakis et al., 1986). Let $U = \{A, B, C\}$; the partition dependency $C = A + B$ cannot be expressed by any set of first-order sentences, with a single ternary relation symbol R as the only non-logical symbol.

The second result concerns multi-valued dependencies (MVDs) in database relations and it is formulated and proven by the following theorem.

Theorem 6.8 (Cosmadakis et al., 1986). Let $U = \{A, B, C\}$; the MVD φ cannot be expressed by any set of partition dependencies.

Functional and Implicative Dependencies as Partition Dependencies

Equivalence of Functional and Partition Dependencies

The traditional definition of functional dependency goes back to the theory of relational databases, it can be found, for example, in (Tzalenko, 1977; Maier, 1983).

Definition 6.11. A collection of attribute X depends functionally on a collection of attributes Y in $T(U)$ if $t_i[X] = t_j[X]$ implies $t_i[Y] = t_j[Y]$, $i,j \in S$, $i \neq j$. This dependency is denoted by $X \rightarrow Y$.

Note that any collection of attributes $X = A_1 A_2 \ldots A_m$ is considered as an expression $A_1 * A_2 * \ldots * A_m$, the value of which in the lattice $L(I(T))$ is the partition $P(X)$. Really, X induces the partition of the set S into disjoint blocks (classes) and this partition is the product of atomic partitions generated by the attributes of collection X.

Prove the following theorem.

Theorem 6.9. (Cosmadakis et al., 1986). Let $T(U)$ be a table of examples and $I(T)$ be its interpretation on partitions over U. Let also X, Y be two collections of attributes contained in U and generating the partitions $P(X)$, $P(Y)$ of the set S, respectively. Then $T(U) \,|{-}\, X \rightarrow Y$ if and only if $I(T) \,|{-}\, P(X) \subseteq P(Y)$.

Proof of the part "if". Let $i, j \in S$ such that $t_i[X] = t_j[X]$. But it means that $t_i[A] = t_j[A]$ for all A, $A \in X$. Thus i, j belongs to some class $a \in P(A)$ for all A, $A \in X$. But $P(X) \subseteq P(Y)$, consequently, for each $B \in Y$, i, j belongs to some class $b \in P(B)$. But it means that $t_i[B] = t_j[B]$ for all B, $B \in Y$, i. e. $t_i[Y] = t_j[Y]$. This means that $T(U) \,|{-}\, X \rightarrow Y$.

Proof of the part "only if". Let X, Y be a pairs of attributes' collections of U such that the functional dependency $X \rightarrow Y$ is satisfied in $T(U)$. Consider a pair t_i, t_j, $i, j \in S$, $i \neq j$. By the assumption that $X \rightarrow Y$, the following condition is satisfied: for every A of X, i, j belong to the same class a in the partition $P(A)$. It implies that $t_i[X] = t_j[X]$ and, since $X \rightarrow Y$, $t_i[B] = t_j[B]$ for all B, $B \in Y$. And we have for every B in Y that there exists a class $b \in P(B)$ such that $i, j \in b$. Hence $I(T) \,|{-}\, P(X) \subseteq P(Y)$.

Equivalence of Implicative and Partition Dependencies

The definition of implicative dependency between values of attributes is given as follows.

Definition 6.12. A collection $t = a_1, a_2, \ldots, a_m$ of values of attributes of a subset of $X = A_1 A_2 \ldots A_m$, $X \subseteq U$ implies a value k of attribute K in $T(U)$ (what is denoted by $t \rightarrow k$) if and only if the following condition is satisfied: for all t_i, $t \subseteq t_i$, $t_i[K] = k$. In other words, if $t_i[X] = t$, then always $t_i[K] = k$ in $T(U)$.

Note that any collection $t = a_1, a_2, \ldots, a_m$ of values of a subset of attributes $X = A_1 A_2 \ldots A_m$ is considered as an expression $a_1 * a_2 * \ldots * a_m$, the interpretation of which is the subset of indices of examples t_i such that this collection of values appears in them, i. e. $I(t) = \{ \cap I(a_j), a_j \in t \}$.

It is clear that implicative dependency holds if and only if $I(t)$ is included in $I(k)$.

Theorem 6.10. Let $T(U)$ be a table of examples and $I(T)$ be its interpretation on partitions over U. Let also t, k be two collections of attributes' values contained in D with partition interpretations $I(t)$, $I(k)$ respectively. Then $T(U) \,|{-}\, t \rightarrow k$ if and only if $I(T) \,|{-}\, I(t) \subseteq I(k)$.

Definition of Diagnostic (Classification) Test

As earlier, U is a set of attributes $U = \{A_1, A_2, \ldots, A_m\}$, X, Y, Z – the subsets of U, and T is a table of examples $T = \{t_1, t_2, \ldots, t_n\}$ with interpretation $I(T)$ over U. Let K be a goal attribute generating a classification of examples of T. The values of attribute K can be considered as the names of classes to which belong the examples under this classification.

The traditional definition of diagnostic test takes into account only the distinguishing relations between objects from different classes of a given classification. Hence we have the following definition of diagnostic test for a given classification K of a given set of examples $T(U)$.

Definition 6.13. A collection of attributes X of U is a diagnostic test for a given classification K of the examples given by table $T(U)$ if the following condition is satisfied:

$\forall (i,j), i,j \in S, i \neq j,$

$$t_i[K] \neq t_j[K] \rightarrow t_i[X] \neq t_j[X], \tag{1}$$

where S is the set of indices of examples of $T(U)$.

Condition (1) of definition 6.13 is the condition of distinguishing examples belonging to different classes in classification K. However in order to define a given classifications of examples more completely we have to consider the equivalence relations between objects inside of each block of this classification too.

The Equivalence of Functional Dependency and Diagnostic Test

Let K be a given classification of examples of $T(U)$ and $X \subseteq U$ such that X is a diagnostic test for K in $T(U)$. Now we show that if X is a test for K then the following condition is satisfied:

$\forall (i,j), i,j \in S, i \neq j,$

$$t_i[X] = t_j[X] \rightarrow t_i[K] = t_j[K], \tag{2}$$

where S - the set of indices of examples of $T(U)$.

Condition (2) is the condition of non-distinguishing examples belonging to the same classes in classification K.

In order to demonstrate the equivalence of conditions (1) and (2), we prove the following proposition.

Proposition 6.1. Let $T(U)$ be a table of examples and $I(T)$ be its interpretation on the partitions over U. Let X, Y be a pair of collections of attributes of U generating the partitions $P(X), P(Y)$ of examples of $T(U)$ (they are the interpretations of X, Y in $I(T)$, respectively). The following condition $T(U) \mid\!- t_i[Y] \neq t_j[Y] \rightarrow t_i[X] \neq t_j[X]$ is satisfied for all $i,j \in S, i \neq j$ **(1)** if and only if the condition $T(U) \mid\!- t_i[X] = t_j[X] \rightarrow t_i[Y] = t_j[Y]$ is satisfied for all $i,j \in S, i \neq j$ **(2)**.

a) Assume that condition **(2)** in $T(U)$ is true for a pair of attributes' collections X and Y. Assume also that condition **(1)** is not satisfied. Then there exists in T a pair of examples t_d, t_q belonging to different classes in partition $P(Y)$ such that these examples agree on the values of attributes of X: $t_d[X] = t_q[X]$. Hence these examples belong to the same class in partition $P(X)$. Then, by condition **(2)**, the equality $t_d[Y] = t_q[Y]$ must be satisfied. This contradicts with our assumption that condition **(1)** is not satisfied.

b) Assume that condition **(1)** in $T(U)$ is true for a pair of attributes' collections X and Y but condition **(2)** is not satisfied. Then there exists in T a pair of examples t_d, t_q belonging to the same class in partition $P(X)$ such that these examples do not agree on the values of attributes of Y: $t_d[Y] \neq t_q[Y]$. Hence these examples belong to the different classes of partition $P(Y)$. Then, by condition **(1)**, examples t_d, t_q must be distinguished by the values of attributes of X and, consequently, they must belong to different classes in the partition $P(X)$, and $t_d[X] \neq t_q[X]$. This contradicts with our assumption that condition **(2)** is not satisfied.

In other words, both conditions **(1)** and **(2)** of proposition 6.1 are equivalent and each of these conditions determines the partition dependency $P(X) \subseteq P(Y)$. Really, if condition **(1)** holds, then collection X of attributes distinguishes any pair of examples from different classes of partition $\boldsymbol{P(Y)}$. It means that each class of partition $P(X)$ is contained in one and only one class of partition $P(Y)$ because, in the opposite case, some examples belonging to different classes of partition $P(Y)$ could be in one and the same class of partition $P(X)$ and, consequently, not distinguished in $P(X)$. Thus we have $P(X) \subseteq P(Y)$. But it implies $X \rightarrow Y$ and then condition **(2)** holds.

Assume that condition **(2)** is satisfied, i. e. that $X \rightarrow Y$. Then $P(X) \subseteq P(Y)$ and each class of partition $P(X)$ is contained in one and only one class of partition $P(Y)$. It means that if examples belong to different classes of partition $P(Y)$, then they must belong also to different classes of partition $P(X)$ and, consequently, condition **(1)** holds.

By proposition 6.1, the assertion that a collection X of attributes is a diagnostic test for a given classification K of examples of table $T(U)$ is equivalent to the existence of functional dependency $X \rightarrow K$.

By theorem 6.9, the assertion that a collection X of attributes is a diagnostic test for a given classification K of examples of table $T(U)$ is equivalent to the existence of partition dependency $P(X) \subseteq P(Y)$. Consequently, we have three equivalent definitions of diagnostic test.

Definition 6.14. A collection of attributes X in U is a test for a given classification in table $T(U)$ of examples, if and only if one of the following equivalent conditions are satisfied:

(e₁) $\forall (i, j), i, j \in S, i \neq j$

$t_i[K] \neq t_j[K] \rightarrow t_i[X] \neq t_j[X]$ $(t_i[X] = t_j[X] \rightarrow t_i[K] = t_j[K])$;

(e₂) $X \rightarrow K$;

(e₃) $P(X) \subseteq P(K)$ $(X \rightarrow K \equiv X*K = X \equiv X + K = K)$.

The following consideration demonstrates also the equivalence of **(e₁)**, **(e₂)**, **(e₃)**. Let $P(X)$, $P(K)$ be the partitions of examples generated by a collection of attributes X and a goal attribute K, respectively. Assume that $P(X) \leq P(K)$. The partition $P(X)$ $(P(K))$ unites examples which agree by the values of attributes' collection X (by the values of attribute K). Thus we have, for all pairs of examples in $T(U)$, that the following relationships hold:

$t_i E(P(X)) \, t_j \Leftrightarrow t_i[X] = t_j[X]$,

$t_i E(P(K)) \, t_j \Leftrightarrow t_i[K] = t_j[K\}$ $(1*)$

$\forall i, j = 1, 2, ..., n, i \neq j$.

The relationship $P(X) \leq P(K)$ implies that $t_i E(P(X)) \, t_j \Rightarrow t_i E(P(K)) \, t_j$ and, simultaneously,

$t_i \sim E(P(K)) \, t_j \Rightarrow t_i \sim E(P(X)) \, t_j$ (2*)

$\forall \, i, j = 1, 2, ..., n, \, i \neq j.$

Consequently, (1*), (2*) can be rewritten as follows:

$t_i[X] = t_j[X] \rightarrow t_i[K] = t_j[K],$

$t_i[K] \neq t_j[K] \rightarrow t_i[X] \neq t_j[X]$ (3*)

$\forall \, i, j = 1, 2, ..., n, \, i \neq j.$

But conditions (3*) coincide with conditions (e_2), (e_1) of definition 6.14. Analogously, having conditions (e_2), (e_1) of definition 6.14 being satisfied, we can, using the relationship (1*), transform these conditions into the form (2*) implying that $P(X) \leq P(K)$.

The following theorem about the equivalence of inferring diagnostic tests and functional dependencies has been proven in (Naidenova, 1982).

Theorem 6.11. Let $T(U)$ be a table of examples and $I(T)$ be its interpretation on partitions over U. Let $X \subseteq U$ and $P(X) \in I(T)$. The following tasks are equivalent:

(i)   to find a minimal collection Y of attributes $Y \subseteq U$, $Y \neq X$, $Y \not\subseteq X$ such that the functional dependency

$Y \rightarrow X$ holds in $T(U)$;

(ii)   to find a minimal collection Y, $Y \subseteq U$, $Y \neq X$, $Y \not\subseteq X$ such that it does not agree on all the pairs of examples belonging to different classes in the partition $P(X)$.

It has been proven in (Naidenova, 1982), that any minimal collection of attributes obtained as a result of solving the tasks of theorem 6.11 is a collection of mutually functionally independent attributes.

The Equivalence Implicative Dependency and Diagnostic Test

Implicative dependency relates to diagnostic test distinguishing a class of examples in a given classification from all the other classes of this classification. We use, in this case, the following definition of diagnostic test.

Definition 6.15. A collection of values $t = a_1, a_2, ..., a_m$ of a subset of attributes $X = A_1 A_2 ... A_m$ of U is a diagnostic test for a class k of a given classification K in a table $T(U)$ of examples if and only if the following conditions are satisfied in $T(U)$:

(1)   if $t[X] = t$ then $t[K] = k$,
(2)   if $t[K] \neq k$ then $t[X] \neq t$.

Table 3. The equivalence between diagnostic tests and functional and implicative dependencies

Attribute A	Values of A in dom(A)
$X = <A_1 A_2 \dots A_n>$	$x = t[X] = <a_1 a_2 \dots a_n>$
Interpretation of X: $P(X) = \{$intersection of $I(A_i), A_i$ belongs to $X\}$	Interpretation of a_i, $a_i \in \text{dom}(A_i)$: $I(a_i), I(a_i) \in P(a_i)$
$X \to A$: for $\forall t_i[X]$ in $T(U) \ \exists \ b, b \in \text{dom}(A) \ (I(t_i[X]) \subseteq I(b))$	$x \to b$: $t[X] = x \in T(U), b \in \text{dom}(A)$ $I(x) \subseteq I(b)$
X is a diagnostic test for $P(A)$	x is a diagnostic test for class b in $P(A)$

It is clear that (1) and (2) are the conditions of implicative dependency between values of attributes and class k of a given classification K.

Moreover, functional dependency can be expressed through several implicative dependencies: it is illustrated in Table 3.

The following definitions of diagnostic test are equivalent to definition 6.15.

Definition 6.16. A tuple x over a subset of attributes X of U is a diagnostic test for a class k of a given classification K in a table $T(U)$ of examples if and only if the following implicative dependency (refinement dependency or causal dependency) $x \to k$ is satisfied.

Definition 6.17. A tuple x over a subset of attributes X of U is a diagnostic test for a class k of a given classification K in a table $T(U)$ of examples if and only if the following condition is satisfied in $T(U)$: $I(x) \subseteq I(k)$ or $I(x) \cap I(k) = I(x)$.

Note that every value of attribute divides the examples into two blocks: block of examples possessing this value (positive examples) and block of examples not possessing this value (negative examples). Hence we can associate with each value a new attribute giving the partition of examples into two blocks (classes).

The initial Table 4 of examples can be transformed into a new one as follows: the value of example t_i in a column y (column corresponding to value y) must be equal to 1 if value y appears in t_i and it must be equal to 0 if value y does not appear in t_i. Table 5 shows the transformed table of examples.

Now implicative dependencies are inferred in the Boolean space of features. Table 6 contains the set of implicative dependencies satisfied in Tables 4 and 5.

Table 4. Table of examples for demonstrating implicative dependencies

	A	B	C	P_1	P_2	P_3	E
1	a_1	b_1	c_1	p_{11}	p_{21}	p_{31}	+
2	a_1	b_2	c_2	p_{11}	p_{21}	p_{31}	+
3	a_2	b_1	c_2	p_{12}	p_{22}	p_{31}	+
4	a_1	b_1	c_2	p_{12}	p_{21}	p_{32}	-
5	a_1	b_2	c_1	p_{12}	p_{21}	p_{31}	-
6	a_2	b_1	c_1	p_{11}	p_{22}	p_{32}	-
7	a_2	b_2	c_1	p_{12}	p_{21}	p_{32}	-
8	a_2	b_2	c_2	$_{11}$	p_{21}	$_{31}$	-

Table 5. The new form of descriptions of examples given in table 4

t	a_1	a_2	b_1	b_2	c_1	c_2	p_{11}	p_{12}	p_{21}	p_{22}	p_{31}	p_{32}	$E+$	$E-$
1	1	0	1	0	1	0	1	0	1	0	1	0	1	0
2	1	0	0	1	0	1	1	0	1	0	1	0	1	0
3	0	1	1	0	0	1	0	1	0	1	1	0	1	0
4	1	0	1	0	1	0	1	0	0	1	0	1	0	1
5	1	0	0	1	1	0	0	1	1	0	1	0	0	1
6	0	1	1	0	1	0	1	0	0	1	0	1	0	1
7	0	1	0	1	1	0	0	1	1	0	0	1	0	1
8	0	1	0	1	0	1	1	0	1	0	1	0	0	1

Table 6. Diagnostic tests for classes E+ and E- in tables 4, 5

Class	Tuples	Tests
$E+$	1,2	$\{a_1 p_{11} p_{21} p_{31}\}$
	1,3	$\{b_1 p_{31}\}$
$E-$	4,6,7	$\{a_2 c_1 p_{32}\}$
	4,6,8	$\{a_2 p_{11}\}$
	5,7	$\{bc_1 p_{12} p_{21}\}$
	7,8	$\{a_2 b_2 p_{21}\}$

DECISION TREES: DIAGNOSTIC APPROACH

In our approach, decision trees play the role of structures for packing classification tests:

Find test ⇒ Pack it in tree-like structure ⇒ Use this structure for pattern recognition.

Next, decision trees play the role of classification procedures. We propose to construct decision trees based on the attributes' collections obtained as a result of inferring tests for a given classification:

Find test for classification K ⇒ Construct a decision tree possessing the best constructive properties.

Thus, we propose to build decision trees as a sort of decision making procedures.

Let *T* be a collection of training examples presenting some models of correct expert reasoning in the assigned situations. Usually, the training examples are the combinations of attribute values describing the situations in question, and each such combination is accompanied by the description of action or report of the expert.

Table 7 contains the training examples determining the Probability of Corona Discharge (PCD) in the system TOGA (Transformer Oil Gas Analysis) (Riese, & Stuart, 1988; p. 37). The solution about the probability of corona discharge (PCD) starts in terms of the values of four attributes: **H2** - the concentration of hydrogen, **Termal** - the presence of gaseous hydrocarbons, which were being formed under the

Table 7. The collection of training examples

N	H2	Termal	H2/C2H2	Temperature	PCD
1	High	-	High	Low	High
2	Average	No	High	Low	High
3	High	-	High	Moderate	Possible
4	Average	No	High	Moderate	Possible
5	High	-	High	High	Unlikely
6	Average	No	High	High	Unlikely
7	Average	Yes	-	Moderate	Unlikely
8	Average	Little	-	Moderate	Unlikely
9	Low	-	-	-	Unlikely
10	-	-	ow	-	Unlikely

action of high temperature, **H2/C2H2** – the relation of the concentrations of hydrogen and acetylene, **Temperature** - the temperature, at which gaseous hydrocarbon is formed.

The expert, in terms of the values of these four attributes, determines the value of PCD by evaluating it with the aid of three values - *High* (high probability), *Possible* (average probability), and *Unlikely* (very low probability).

For further discussing, let us rename the attributes of Table 7 as A_1, A_2, A_3, and A_4. Let us rename also the values of attributes as follows: *High - H, Average - A, Low - L, Moderate – M, Little - Li, Possible - P,* and *Unlikely – Un*. After the appropriate substitutions we shall obtain Table 8.

It is necessary also to determine, what indicates symbol "-" as the value of attribute. It is reasonable to think that any value of attribute is possible in appropriate position. Let us express formally the property of a collection X of attributes to determine the values of *PCD*. A subset X determines uniquely the values of *PCD*, if the following condition is satisfied:

$$\forall t_i, t_j, i \neq j, i, j = 1, 2, \ldots, 10$$

Table 8. The transformed collection of training examples

N	A_1	A_2	A_3	A_4	PCD
1	H	-	H	L	H
2	A	No	H	L	H
3	B	-	H	M	P
4	A	No	H	M	P
5	H	-	H	H	Un
6	A	No	H	H	Un
7	A	Ye	-	M	Un
8		Li	-		Un
9	L	-	-	-	Un
10	-	-	L	-	Un

$$(t_i[PCD] \neq t_j[PCD] \rightarrow t_i[X] \neq t_j[X]). \tag{1}$$

This is the condition of discerning the values of *PCD* by the values of attributes of *X*. The same condition can be written down in the following equivalent form:

$$\forall t_i, t_j, i \neq j, i, j = 1,2,...,10$$

$$(t_i[X] = t_j[X] \rightarrow t_i[PCD] = t_j[PCD]). \tag{2}$$

Initial set *U* of attributes satisfies conditions (1), (2). This is naturally; otherwise Table 7 (Table 8) would not be the table of training examples.

We shall verify whether condition (1) or the property "to be diagnostic test for *PCD*" is satisfied by attributes or by their collections in Table 8. Let us begin from checking this condition separately for each attribute.

Let us examine A_4. It does not determine the values of *PCD*, since there is a pair of examples t_3, t_8, for which $A_4 = M$, but PCD has two different values *P* and *Un*, respectively. We observe that no one attribute determines unambiguously the values of *PCD*.

We reveal that the necessary condition is satisfied at least for some pairs of lines, i.e. although an attribute is not diagnostic test, it satisfies certain quantity of necessary diagnostic conditions for *PCD*.

Let us return to the attribute A_4. We find that the following relation is satisfied for examples t_5, t_6:

if $t_5[A_4] = t_6[A_4] = H$, then $t_5[PCD] = t_6[PCD] = Un$.

This is very similar to implicative dependence, but so that it would occur, it is necessary that in all the lines (including those, where the value of $A_4 = $ "-"), for which the value of *PCD* is different from *Un*, the attribute A_4 had a value, different from *H*. This means that for all *i*, except *i* = 5 and *i* = 6 the following condition must be satisfied:

$$(t_i[PCD] \neq Un \rightarrow t_i[A_4] \neq H). \tag{3}$$

Since condition (3) is satisfied, then we formulate the inductive hypothesis:

H1:
{Whatever the value of attributes A_1, A_2, A_3, if the value of $A_4 = H$, then the value of $PCD = Un$}.

Since the value of *PCD* for examples t_5, t_6 is defined by the hypothesis H1, and no example from Table 8 contradicts with this hypothesis, we can move away from further consideration examples t_5, t_6, just as all other examples, for which the value of $A_4 = H$ (except those examples, in which the value of $A_4 = $ "-").

Next we examine examples t_1, t_2, for which the value of $A_4 = L$ and the value of $PCD = P$. It corresponds to the hypothesis

H2:
"whatever value of A_1, A_2, A_3, if $t[A_4] = L$, then $t[PCD] = P$".

But this hypothesis is refuted by examples t_9, t_{10}, for which the value of PCD is not equal to P, but the set of possible values of A_4 includes value L. It is erroneous assumption that PCD is independent on the values of other attributes, except A_4. Obviously, we formulate the condition (let us name this condition "the condition of branching reasoning process"): if the value of $A_4 = L$, then investigate the values of attributes from $U\backslash A_4$.

Now we examine examples t_9, t_{10}, which refute the previous hypothesis, and we attempt to find the values of A_1, A_2, A_3 determining unambiguously the values of PCD if the value of $A_4 = L$.

Next we select the examples forming hypothesis H2 i.e. all those examples for which the value of A_4 is equal to or can be equal to L. We select also all the attributes except A_4. Thus, we obtain Table 9:

Analogously, for the value of attribute A_4 equal to M, we obtain the following condition of branching "if the value of $A_4 = M$, then investigate the values of attributes from $U\backslash A_4$" and we form Table 10.

Let us return to Table 9 for selecting new hypotheses determining the values of PCD. The number of hypotheses for each attribute depends on the number of its values, and each hypothesis can be either consistent or meet a certain number of counterexamples. Let us give some definitions, useful for refining the concepts of discrepancy and consistency of a hypothesis.

Definition 6.18. A hypothesis h is an expression in the form: "if the value of attribute $A = a$, then the value of goal attribute $K = k$", where $a \in$ dom (A) and $k \in$ dom (K).

Definition 6.19. A hypothesis h in the form defined above is refuted if there exists at least one example t, for which the value of $A = a$, but the value of $K \neq k$. Example t is called a counterexample.

Definition of 6.20. A hypothesis h is consistent on a given set of examples, if, in this set, there does not exist any example refuting this hypothesis.

Definition 6.21. Let h_1, h_2 be two different hypotheses on a given set of examples. Hypothesis h_1 is stronger than hypothesis h_2, if the number of refuting examples for it is less than the number of refuting examples for h_2.

Table 9. Branching with $A_4 = L$

N	A_1	A_2	A_3	PCD
1	H	-	H	P
2	A	No	H	P
9	L	-	-	Un
10	-	-	L	Un

Table 10. Branching with $A_4 = M$

N	A_1	A_2	A_3	PCD
3	H	-	H	P
4	A	No	H	P
7	A	Yes	-	Un
8	A	Li	-	Un
9	L	-	-	Un
10	-	-	L	Un

Definition 6.22. Let h_1, h_2 be two different hypotheses on a given set of examples. Hypothesis h_1 is more productive than hypothesis h_2, if the number of examples carrying out this hypothesis is more than the number of ones carrying out hypothesis h_2. (Example t carries out hypothesis h if for this example the values of attributes A and K coincide with the values of these attributes in this hypothesis).

It is naturally to select stronger hypotheses and, at the same time, more productive ones.

As an estimation of attribute, it can be taken the relation of the number of counterexamples for all its hypotheses to the total productivity of this attribute. The total productivity of attribute is equal to the sum of productivities of all its hypotheses.

The best attribute is one with minimal value of this estimation. With equal estimations, an attribute with smaller number of hypotheses will be better one.

The criteria of force and productivity of hypotheses guarantee that generated decision tree will possess the best design properties - smaller number of nodes and branches in the nodes, since the appearance of a new node is necessitated by introducing in the process a new attribute, and the number of branches in the nodes is determined by the number of hypotheses of this attribute.

Return to Table 9. For each attribute, let us estimate its hypotheses with respect to the productivity and the force (Table 11):

For our example, we have the following values of estimation: 0,66 for A_1, 1 for A_2, 0,6 for A_3, and best proves to be the attribute A_3.

Choose attribute A_3 and form hypothesis H21:

H21:: =

{whatever the value of attributes A_1 and A_2, if the value of

attribute $A_4 = L$, then investigate the value of attribute A_3;

Table 11. Estimation of hypotheses for table 9

A	H	Refuting examples	Productivity
A_1	h_1: if the value of A_1 = H, then the value of PCD = H	t_{10}	1
	h_2: if the value of A_1 = A, then the value of PCD = H	t_{10}	1
	h_3: if the value of A_1 = L, then the value of PCD = Un	No	2
	h_4: if the value of A_1 = H, then the value of PCD= Un	t_1	1
	h_5: if the value of A_1 = A, then the value of PCD = Un	t_1	1
A_2	h_1: if the value of A_2 = No, then the value of PCD = H	t_9,t_{10}	2
	h_2: if the value of A_2 = Yes, then the value of PCD = H	t_9,t_{10}	1
	h_3: if the value of A_2 = Li, then the value of PCD = H	t_9,t_{10}	1
	h_4: if the value of A_2 = No, then the value of PCD = Un	t_1,t_2	2
	h_5: if the value of A_2 = Yes, then the value of PCD = Un	t_1	2
	h_6: if the value of A_2 = Yes, then the value of PCD = Un	t_1	2
A_3	h_1: if the value of A_3 = H, then the value of PCD = H	t_9	2
	h2: if the value of A_3 = L then the value of PCD = Un	No	2
	h_3: if the value of A_3 = H, then the value of PCD = Un	t_1,t_2	1

Table 12. Branching with $A_4 = L$ and $A_3 = H$

N	A_1	A_2	PCD
1	H	-	H
2	A	Yes	H
9	L	-	Un

if the value of attribute $A_3 = L$, then the value of $PCD = Un$;

else if the value of $A_3 = H$, then investigate the values of attributes from $U\backslash\{A_4, A_3\}$.

And, with the use of the new branching situation, we obtain the following hypothesis H211 (see, please, Table 12):

H211::=

{whatever the value of attribute A_2, if the value of

attribute $A_4 = L$, then investigate the value of attribute A_3;

if the value of attribute $A_3 = L$, then the value of $PCD = Un$;

else if the value of $A_3 = H$, then investigate

the value of attribute A_1; if the value of attribute $A_1 = L$,

then the value of $PCD = Un$; else the value of $PCD = H$}.

Analogously, we continue to build the decision tree according to Table 10:

H22::=

{whatever the value of attributes A_1 and A_2, if the value of

attribute $A_4 = M$, then investigate the value of attribute A_3;

if the value of attribute $A_3 = L$, then the value of $PCD = Un$;

else if the value of $A_3 = H$, then investigate the value of attributes $U\backslash\{A_4, A_3\}\}$.

Table 13 is formed for continuing the process.
In Table 13, we select attribute A_1 and form the hypothesis:

H221::=

Table 13. Branching with $A_4 = M$ and $A_3 = H$

N	A_1	A_2	PCD
3	H	-	P
4	A	No	P
7	A	Yes	Un
8	A	Li	Un
9	L	-	Un

{If the value of attribute $A_4 = M$, then investigate the value of

attribute A_3; if the value of $A_3 = L$, then the value of $PCD = Un$;

else, if the value of $A_3 = H$, then investigate the value of attribute A_1;

if the value of $A_1 = H$, then the value of $PCD = P$;

else, if the value of $A_1 = L$, then the value of $PCD = Un$;

else investigate the value of attribute A_2;

if the value of $A_2 = No$, then the value of $PCD = P$;

else the value of $PCD = Un$}.

Constructing decision tree can be based on the search for an appropriate value from the total set of all attributes' values.

We convert Table 8 into Table 14 as follows: the columns of Table 14 correspond to the values of attributes of Table 8. For each example t in Table 14: in the column, which corresponds to the value x of a certain attribute A, we shall place 1, if in the Table 8 $t[A] = x$; and we will place 0, if $t[A] \neq x$.

If an example has value "-" at least for one attribute, then, in Table 14, this example is substituted by the lines, which correspond to all possible combinations of attributes' values.

Following the previous procedure of decision tree construction, we reveal that there are the following consistent hypotheses:

h_1: if the value of $A_4 = H$, then the value of $PCD = Un$;
h_2: if the value of $A_3 = L$, then the value of $PCD = Un$;
h_3: if the value of $A_1 = L$, then the value of $PCD = Un$.

The examples satisfying the first hypothesis are t_5, t_6, t_9, t_{10}, the examples satisfying the second hypothesis are t_{10}, t_7, t_8, t_9, and the examples satisfying the third hypothesis are t_{10}, t_9. It is possible to exclude these examples and to correct Table 14 with obtaining Table 15.

Table 14. Converted training examples

	A₁			A₂			A₃		A₄			PCD		
N	H	A	L	No	Yes	Li	H	L	L	M	H	H	P	Un
1	1			1			1		1			1		
	1				1		1		1			1		
	1					1	1		1			1		
2		1		1			1		1			1		
3	1			1			1			1			1	
	1				1		1			1			1	
	1					1	1			1			1	
4		1		1			1			1			1	
5	1			1			1				1			1
	1				1		1				1			1
	1					1	1				1			1
6		1		1			1				1			1
7		1			1		1			1				1
		1			1			1		1				1
8		1				1	1			1				1
		1				1		1		1				1
9			1	1			1		1					1
			1		1		1		1					1
			1			1	1		1					1
			1	1			1			1				1
			1		1		1			1				1
			1			1	1			1				1
			1	1			1				1			1
			1		1		1				1			1
			1			1	1				1			1
			1	1				1	1					1
			1		1			1	1					1
			1			1		1	1					1
			1	1				1		1				1
			1		1			1		1				1
			1			1		1		1				1
			1	1				1			1			1
			1		1			1			1			1
			1			1		1			1			1
10	1			1			1	1						1
	1				1		1	1						1
	1					1	1	1						1
	1			1			1				1			1
	1				1		1		1				1	
	1					1	1		1				1	

Table 14. continued

1			1			1			1		1
1				1		1			1		1
1					1	1			1		1
	1		1			1	1				1
	1			1		1	1				1
	1				1	1	1				1
	1		1			1		1			1
	1			1		1		1			1
	1				1	1		1			1
	1		1			1			1		1
	1			1		1			1		1
	1				1	1			1		1
		1	1			1	1				1
		1		1		1	1				1
		1			1	1	1				1
		1	1			1		1			1
		1		1		1		1			1
		1			1	1		1			1
		1	1			1			1		1
		1		1		1			1		1
		1			1	1			1		1

The condition for continuing the process is described by the expression: $\sim [A_4 = H$ or $A_3 = L$ or $A_1 = L]$.

We find in Table 15 a new consistent hypothesis:

h_4: if the value of $A_4 = L$, then the value of $PCD = H$.

This hypothesis is satisfied by the examples t_1, t_2. After deleting these examples and modifying Table 15 (with obtaining Table 16), we find the following consistent hypotheses:

h_5: if the value of $A_1 = H$, then the value of $PCD = P$;
h_6: if the value of $A_2 = No$, then the value of $PCD = P$.

These hypotheses are satisfied by examples t_3, t_4. For the rest examples, all the hypotheses are consistent. Constructing the decision tree is terminated by the rule:

else if $[A_1 = A$ and $A_2 = (Yes$ or $Li)]$, then the value of $PCD = Un$.

The following algorithm (Naidenova et al., 1995a) constructs a decision tree based on choosing hypotheses associated with attribute values. In this algorithm, $T(N, M)$ is the table of training examples,

Table 15. The training examples after deleting examples satisfying hypotheses h_1, h_2 and h_3

N	A₁			A₂			A₃		A₄			PCD		
	H	A	L	No	Yes	Li	H	L	L	M	H	H	P	Un
1	1			1			1		1			1		
	1				1		1		1			1		
	1					1	1		1			1		
2		1		1			1		1			1		
3	1			1			1			1			1	
	1				1		1			1			1	
	1					1	1			1			1	
4		1		1			1			1			1	
7		1			1		1			1				1
8		1				1	1			1				1

Table 16. The training examples after deleting examples satisfying hypotheses h_4

N	A₁			A₂			A₃		A₄			PCD		
	H	A	L	No	Yes	Li	H	L	L	M	H	H	P	Un
3	1			1			1			1			1	
	1				1		1			1			1	
	1					1	1			1			1	
4		1		1			1			1			1	
7		1			1		1			1				1
8		1				1	1			1				1

where N is the number of examples and M is the number of attributes. By A_i, $i = 1,...M$, we denote i-th attribute. The j-th value of i-th attribute is denoted by l_{ij}, $i = 1,..., M$, $j = 1,..., r_i$, where r_i – the number of values of attribute A_i. We denote by $L = \{l_{ij}\}$ the set of values of all considered attributes. Attribute K gives the goal classification of examples.

Two functions D and S are defined on L: $D(l_{ij})$ computes the number of classes in K with which l_{ij} appears, $S(l_{ij})$ computes the number of examples in which l_{ij} appears. The values of functions D and S for Table 17 are given in Table 18.

The structure of decision tree is described as follows:

<node>::= <leaf>/<rule>;

<leaf>::="$K = k_r$", where k_r is the name of a class;

<rule>::= if <condition>, then <node>; else <node>.

The algorithm uses the following procedures: Analysis(T), Decreasing(T), Partitioning(T).

Table 17. Training examples (algorithm of Polegaeva J.G.)

N	A_1	A_2	A_3	A_4	K
1	1	1	1	1	1
2	2	1	1	1	1
3	1	2	1	1	1
4	1	1	1	2	2
5	1	2	1	2	2
6	2	1	1	2	2
7	3	2	1	1	2
8	1	1	2	3	3
9	2	1	1	3	3
10	2	2	1	2	3
11	3	2	1	2	3
12		2	2		3

Table 18. The values of functions D and S

A_i	L_{ij}	D	S	A_i	L_{ij}	D	S
A_1	1	3	6	A_3	1	3	10
	2	3	4		2	1	2
	3	2	2	A_4	1	3	5
	1	3	6		2	2	5
A_2	2	3	6		3	1	2

Procedure Analysis(T):

1) computing $D(l_{ij})$, $S(l_{ij})$, $l_{ij} \in L$;
2) if the minimum of $D(l_{ij}) = 1$, then Decreasing(T); else Partitioning(T).

Procedure Decreasing(T):
For all l_{ij}, $D(l_{ij}) = 1$, the following rule is formed:*

1) "Rule x: if $A_i = l_{ij}$, then $K = k_r$ else Rule y".
The rules with one and the same class can be combined into one rule;
2) Table T^* is formed by deleting from T all lines satisfying the conditions of constructed rules;
3) If Table T'^* contains the examples from several classes, then Analysis(T'^*); else to replace the last rule by the following one: "Rule x: if <condition>, then $K = k_r$ else $K = k_p$".

Procedure Partitioning(T):

Table 19. Result of decreasing (T) after construction rule 1

N	A_1	A_2	A_3	A_4	K
1	1	1	1	1	1
2	2	1	1	1	1
3	1	2	1	1	1
4	1	1	1	2	2
5	1	2	1	2	2
6	2	1	1	2	
7	3		1	1	
10	2	2	1	2	3
11	3	2	1	2	3

1) For all l_{ij}, $D(l_{ij})$ is maximal, select l_{pq} with minimal value of S, and for these values the rules are formed of the following kind:

"Rule x: if $A_p = l_{pq}$, then Rule y; else Rule z";

2) It is formed sub-table T^* of T containing those and only those examples in which $A_p = l_{pq}$, and also all the columns, except A_p;

3) Analysis(T^*);

4) It is formed sub-table T^{**} of T containing those and only those examples in which $A_p \neq l_{pq}$;

5) Analysis(T^{**});

In Tables 18, we have that $D = 1$ for the values $A_3 = 2$, $A_4 = 3$, and $K = 3$. Consequently, the following rule is formed:

Rule 1: if $A_3 = 2$ or $A_4 = 3$, then $K = 3$; else Rule 2.

As a result of the Procedure Decreasing, we obtain table T^* (Table 19), for which the analysis gives the results demonstrated in Table 20.

Next Procedure Partitioning(T^*) selects $A_1 = 3$ and forms two sub-tables T^{**} (Tables 21) and T^{***} (Table 22), and the following rule:

Rule 2: if $A_1 = 3$, then Rule 3; else Rule 4.

Table 20. Result of the analysis after decreasing(T)

A_1	L_{ij}	D	S
A_1	1	2	4
	2	3	3
	3	2	2
A_2	1	2	4
	2	3	5
A_3	1	3	9
A_4	1	2	4
	2	2	5

Table 21. Sub-table T**

N	A_2	A_3	A_4	K
7	2	1	1	2
11	2	1	2	3

Procedure Decreasing(T^{**}) based on analyzing functions D and S for Table T^{**} (see, please, Table 23) gives

Rule 3: if $A_4 = 1$, then $K = 2$ else $K = 3$.

Analysis(T^{***}) gives the following values of D and S (Table 24):
Procedure Decreasing(T^{***}) forms Rule 4:

Rule 4: if $A_4 = 1$, then $K = 1$ else Rule 5.

After Decreasing (T^{***}), we have table T^{****} (Table 25). Next, Table 25 is analyzed with obtaining functions D and S showed in Table 26 and the following rule:

Rule 5: if $A_1 = 1$ or $A_2 = 1$, then $K = 2$ else $K = 3$.

The work of algorithm is over.

RELATED WORKS

The approach to pattern recognition using traditional determination of diagnostic test is developed up to now. With the greatest completeness this approach is personified in the works of the group of researchers under Yankovskaya, A. E. The approach is based on the matrix model of data and knowledge representation. In this model, two matrices traditionally are used: matrix of object descriptions and matrix of object discernability, which gives the classifications of objects (Yankovskaya, 1996a; Yankovskaya, 1966б). The

Table 22. Sub-table T***

N	A_1	A_2	A_3	A_4	K
1	1	1	1	1	1
2	2	1	1	1	1
3	1	2	1	1	1
4	1	1	1	2	2
5	1	2	1	2	2
6	2	1	1	2	2
10	2	2	1	2	3

Table 23. Result of the analysis of sub-table T**

A_i	L_{ij}	S	D
A_2	2	2	2
A_3	1	2	2
A_4	1	1	1
	2	1	1

search for diagnostic tests is based on minimization of Boolean Functions (Matrosova, & Yankovskaya, 1992; Yankovskaya, 1996a; Yankovskaya, 2001). Many applied pattern recognition systems have been created with the use of test model of knowledge in different fields such as medicine, geology, sociology, prediction of catastrophes and some others. Several examples of test recognition systems can be found in (Yankovskaya, & Gedike, 1995; Yankovskaya et al., 2001; Kolesnikova, & Yankovskaya, 2006). In the framework of this works, genetic algorithms for inferring diagnostic tests have been advanced (Yankovskaya, 1999). The conditional nondeterministic diagnostic tests are considered in (Matrosova, & Jankovskaya, 1992) as fuzzy recognition rules.

CONCLUSION

In this chapter we refined the concept of diagnostic test advanced in the theory of finite automates. We determined diagnostic test as an approximation of a given object classification. In this quality, diagnostic test became a key concept of machine learning problems dealing with constructing conceptual knowledge

Table 24. Result of the analysis of sub-table T***

A_i	L_{ij}	D	S
A_1	1	2	4
	2	3	3
A_2	1	2	4
	2	3	3
A_3	1	3	7
A_4	1	1	3
	2	2	4

Table 25. Sub-Table T****

N	A_1	A_2	A_3	A_4	K
4	1	1	1	2	2
5	1	2	1	2	2
6	2	1	1	2	2
10	2	2	1	2	3

Table 26. Functions D and S for Table 25

A_i	L_{ij}	D	S
A_1	1	1	2
	2	2	2
A_2	1	1	2
	2	2	2
A_3	1	2	4
A_4	2	2	4

of the following kinds: conceptual descriptions of object classifications and logical links (expressed in the form of logical rules) between these classifications. We also propose an algebraic model of classification (algebra of classifications) based on the partition lattice. As the mathematical model, the partition model possesses both declarative and procedural properties. Our next goal to which we proceed in next Chapter 7 is to find the best ways for inferring classification tests from a given set of examples.

REFERENCES

Banerji, R. (1969). *Theory of problem solving: An approach to artificial intelligence*. New York: Elsevier.

Birkhoff, G. (1935). On the structure of abstract algebras. *Proceedings of the Cambridge Philosophical Society*, *31*, 433–454. doi:10.1017/S0305004100013463

Birkhoff, G. (1948). *Lattice theory* (2nd ed.). Providence, RI: Amer. Math. Soc. (Russian edition: Moscow, "Foreign Literature", 1952).

Boldyrev, N. G. (1974). Minimization of Boolean partial functions with a large number of "don't care" conditions and the problem of feature extraction. In *"Discrete Systems,"* *Proceedings of International Symposium* (pp.101-109). Riga, Latvia: Zinatne.

Cheguis, I. A., & Jablonskij, S. V. (1958). Logical methods for electrical schemes control. *Transactions of Steklov, V. A.* [Moscow: Nauka.]. *Mathematical Institute of USSR Academy of Sciences*, *51*, 269–360.

Cosmadakis, S., Kanellakis, P. C., & Spyratos, N. (1986). Partition semantics for relations. *Journal of Computer and System Sciences*, *33*(2), 203–233. doi:10.1016/0022-0000(86)90019-X

Crawley, P., & Dilworth, R. (1973). *Algebraic theory of lattices*. Englewood Cliffs, NJ: Prentice-Hall.

Dukova, E. V. (1982). *Asymptotically optimal test algorithms in the pattern recognition tasks*. In S. V. Jablonskij (Ed.), *The problem of cybernetics*, 39 (pp. 166-199). Moscow: Nauka.

Epstein, L. F. (1939). A function related to the series for exp (exp x). *Journal of Mathematics and Physics*, *18*, 153–173.

Finn, V. K. (1983). On machine-oriented formalization of plausible reasoning in the style of F. Backon – J.S. Mill. In A. I. Michailov (Ed.), *Semiotika and informatika*, 20 (pp. 35-101). Moscow, USSR: VINITI.

Ganascia, J. - Gabriel. (1989). EKAW - 89 tutorial notes: Machine learning. In J. Boose, B. Gaines, & J.G. Ganascia (Eds.), *EKAW'89: Third European Workshop on Knowledge Acquisition for Knowledge-Based Systems* (pp. 287-296). Paris, France.

Geddes, P. (1881). On the classification of statistics and its results. *Proceedings of the Royal Society of Edinburgh*, *11*(109), 295–322.

Gladun, V. P., & Vaschenko, N. D. (1975). Methods of concepts formation on computers. *Kibernetika*, *2*, 107–112.

Gladun, V. P., & Vaschenko, N. D. (1978). Automation of concept extraction in scientific investigations. In M.B. Shtark, & V.N. Burakovskij (Eds.), *Automation of medico-biological investigations on the basis of computers* (pp. 7-10). Novosibirsk, USSR: The Siberian branch of Academy of Medical Sciences (AMS).

Hartmanis, J. (1960). Symbolic analysis of decomposition of information processing machines. *Information and Control*, *3*, 154–178. doi:10.1016/S0019-9958(60)90744-0

Hunt, E., Marin, J., & Stone, P. (1965). *Experiments in induction*. New York: Academic Press.

Juravlev, J. N. (1958). About of separability of subsets of vertices of N-dimensional unite cube. In *Proceeding of Steklov, V.A. Mathematical Institute*, vol. LI, (pp. 143-157).

Juravlev, J. N. (1978). About algebraic approach to solving the pattern recognition and classification tasks. In S. V. Jablonskij (Ed.), *The problems of cybernetics*, 33 (pp. 5-68). Moscow: Nauka.

Kolesnikova, S. I., & Yankovskaya, A. E. (2006). To the calculating of feature weight coefficients in intellectual dynamic systems. In *Proceedings of 10-th National Conference on Artificial Intelligent with International Participation* (pp.783-791). Moscow, Russia: Publishing House of Literature on Physics and Mathematics.

Laurent, D., & Luong, V. Phan, & Spyratos, N. (2003). Querying weak instances under extension chase semantics: A complete solution. *International Journal of Computer Mathematics*, *80*(5), 591–613. doi:10.1080/0020716031000079509

Laurent, D., & Spyratos, N. (1994). A partition model approach to updating universal scheme interfaces. *IEEE Transactions on Knowledge and Data Engineering*, *6*(2), 316–330. doi:10.1109/69.277774

Lécluse, C., & Spyratos, N. (1986a). The semantics of queries and updates in relational databases. *LRI Technical Research Report*, 291. Orsay, Paris, France: Univ. of Paris – Sud.

Lécluse, C., & Spyratos, N. (1986b). A logic for data and knowledge bases. *LRI Technical Research Report*, 311. Orsay, Paris, France: Univ. of Paris – Sud.

Lécluse, C., & Spyratos, N. (1987). Updating weak instances using partition semantics. *LRI Technical Research Report*, 364. Orsay, Paris, France: Univ. of Paris – Sud.

Maier, D. (1983). *The theory of relational databases*. Computer Science Press.

Matrosova, A. Yu., & Yankovskaya, A.E. (1992). Use of conditional nondeterministic diagnostics tests in pattern recognition problems. *Pattern recognition and Image Analysis, 2*(2), 164-168.

Naidenova, X. A. (1979). *Automation of experimental data classification processes based on the algebraic lattice theory.* Unpublished doctoral dissertation, Saint-Petersburg Electro-Technical University.

Naidenova, X. A. (1982). Relational model for analyzing experimental data. *The Transaction of Acad. Sci. of USSR*, Series . *Technical Cybernetics, 4*, 103–119.

Naidenova, X. A. (1996). Reducing machine learning tasks to the approximation of a given classification on a given set of examples. In *Proceedings of the 5-th National Conference on Artificial Intelligence* (Vol. 1, pp. 275-279). Kazan, Tatarstan.

Naidenova, X. A., & Polegaeva, J. G. (1986). An algorithm of finding the best diagnostic tests. In G. E. Mintz, & P. P. Lorents (Eds.), *The application of mathematical logic methods* (pp. 63-67). Tallinn, Estonia: Institute of Cybernetics, National Acad. of Sciences of Estonia.

Naidenova, X. A., Polegaeva, J. G., & Iserlis, J. E. (1995a). The system of knowledge acquisition based on constructing the best diagnostic classification tests. In J. Valkman. (Ed.), *"Knowledge-Dialog-Solution", Proceedings of International Conference in two volumes* (Vol. 1, pp. 85-95). Kiev, Ukraine: Kiev Institute of Applied Informatics.

Ore, O. (1942). Theory of equivalence relation. *Duke Mathematical Journal, 9*(4), 573–627. doi:10.1215/S0012-7094-42-00942-6

Parkhomenko, P. P. (1970). The theory of questionnaires (a Survey). [Automation and Telemechanics]. *Avtomatika and Telemechanika, 4*, 140–159.

Polegaeva, J. G. (1985). The choice of best tests in pattern recognition tasks. In Y. Pecherskij (Ed), *"Logic-combinatorial Methods in Artificial Intelligence and Pattern Recognition", Theses of Lectures of Republican School-Seminar* (pp. 46-47). Kishinev, the Moldavian Soviet Socialist Republic: The Institute of Mathematics with computer centre of Moldavian Academy of Sciences.

Quinlan, J. R. (1987). Induction of decision trees. *Machine Learning, 1*, 81–106.

Quinlan, J. R., & Rivest, R. L. (1989). Inferring decision trees using the minimum description length principle. *Information and Computation, 80*, 227–248. doi:10.1016/0890-5401(89)90010-2

Rasiowa, H. (1974). *An algebraic approach to non-classical logics.* Warsaw & Amsterdam: PWN – Polish Scientific Publishers & North-Holland Publishing Company.

Riese, C. E., & Stuart, J. D. C. E. (1988). RuleMaster: A knowledge engineering facility for building scientific expert systems. In T.H. Pierce, & B.A. Hohne (Eds.), *Artificial intelligence applications in chemistry, ACS Symposium*, series 306 (pp. 33-48). Translated from English. Moscow, Russia: Mir.

Shreider, J. A. (1971). *Equality, similarity, order.* Moscow, USSR: Nauka.

Soloviev, N. A. (1978). *Tests (theory, construction, application).* Novosibirsk: Nauka.

Spyratos, N. (1987). The partition model: A deductive database model. *ACM Transactions on Database Systems*, *12*(1), 1–37. doi:10.1145/12047.22718

Spyratos, N. (1991). Data modeling in a type system. In J. L. Alty, L. I. Mikulich (Eds.), *Industrial applications of artificial intelligence, Proceedings of the IFIP TC5/WG5.3 International Conference in CIM, Leningrad, USSR, 1990* (pp.152-161). New York: Elsevier.

Spyratos, N., & Lécluse, C. (1987). Incorporating functional dependencies in deductive query answering. In *Proceedings of the Third International Conference on Data Engineering, Los Angeles, California, USA (ICDE)* (pp. 658-664). IEEE.

Toropov, N. R. (1967). An algorithm of the minimization of boolean partial functions with a large number of "don't care" conditions. In *The Theory of Automates, Materials of the Seminar on the Automate Theory, issue 4*. Kiev, Ukraine: Kiev Institute of Cybernetics.

Tzalenko, M. S. (1977). Database relational methods (a survey). In V. Savinkov (Ed.), *Algorithms and organization of solving economic tasks, issue 10* (pp. 16-28). Moscow, USSR: Statistika.

Vaschenko, N. D. (1976). Automation of concept formation processes in scientific investigations. In Ribak (Ed.), *The questions of the robot theory and artificial intelligence* (pp. 45-51). Kiev, Ukraine: The Institute of Cybernetics.

Vaschenko, N. D. (1983). Concept formation in semantic networks. *Kibernetika*, *2*, 101–107.

Yankovskaya, A. E. (1996a). Minimization of orthogonal disjunctive normal forms of Boolean function to be used as a basis for similarity and difference coefficients in pattern recognition problems. *Pattern Recognition and Image Analysis*, *6*(1), 60–61.

Yankovskaya, A. E. (1996b). Design of optimal mixed diagnostic test with reference to the problems of evolutionary computation. In *Proceedings of the First International Conference on Evolutionary Computation and Its Applications - EVCA'96* (pp. 292-297). Moscow, Russia: Russian Academy of Science.

Yankovskaya, A. E. (1999). Test pattern recognition with the use of genetic algorithms. *Pattern Recognition and Image Analysis*, *9*(1), 127–130.

Yankovskaya, A. E. (2001). Logical test in knowledge-based recognizing system. *Pattern Recognition and Image Analysis*, *11*(1), 121–123.

Yankovskaya, A. E., & Gedike, A. I. (1995). Integrated intelligence system EXAPRAS and its application. *Journal of Intelligent Control* [Nova Science Publishers, Inc.]. *Neurocomputing and Fuzzy Logic*, *1*, 243–269.

Yankovskaya, A. E., & Gedike, A. I. (1999). Finding all shortest column coverings of large dimension boolean matrices. In *Proceedings of the First International Workshop on Multi-Architecture Low Power Design* (MALOPD) (pp. 52 -56). Moscow, Russia.

Yankovskaya, A. E., Gedike, A. I., & Ametov, R. V. (2001). Intellectual dynamic system. In *"Knowledge – Dialog – Solution, [KDS]. Proceedings of International Conference*, *2*, 645–652.

Zakrevskij, A. D. (1971). *Algorithms of discrete automates' synthesis*. Moscow: "Nauka

Zakrevskij, A. D. (1982). Revealing implicative regularities in the Boolean space of attributes and pattern recognition. *Kibernetika, 1,* 1–6.

Zakrevskij, A. D. (1988). *Pattern recognition logic.* Minsk, Belorussija: "Nauka and Technika

Chapter 7
The Concept of Good Classification (Diagnostic) Test

ABSTRACT

In this chapter, the definition of good diagnostic test and the characterization of good tests are introduced and the concepts of good maximally redundant and good irredundant tests are given. The algorithms for inferring all kinds of good diagnostic tests are described in detail.

INTRODUCTION

The definition of the good test is based on the partition model of classifications that is discussed in the previous chapter. Some characteristics of good tests allow proposing a strategy for inferring all kinds of these tests. We describe an algorithm called Background Algorithm based on the method of mathematical induction. This algorithm is applicable to inferring all kinds of good classification tests and, consequently, for inferring functional, implicative dependencies and association rules from a given data set. We discuss also, in this chapter, the possible ways of constructing an efficient algorithm for inferring good tests of any kind.

DEFINITION OF GOOD DIAGNOSTIC TEST

In chapter 6, we considered the set $L(I(T))$ of partitions produced by closing atomic partitions of $I(T)$ with the use of operations $+$ and $*$ on partitions. This set is the algebraic lattice with constants over U. Now we consider the table of examples $T(U \cup K)$ with partition interpretation $I(T \cup K)$ over $U' = U \cup K$ and the algebraic lattice $L(I(U'))$ with constants over U', where K is a given goal attribute.

DOI: 10.4018/978-1-60566-810-9.ch007

Let $X \subseteq U$ is a test for a goal attribute K, and partitions $P(X)$, $P(K)$ are the interpretations of X and K, respectively.

Denote by $Q(K)$ the set of all diagnostic tests for K: $Q(K) = \{X: X \subseteq U: P(X) \le P(K))\}$.

Sub-lattice $LK(I(U'))$ of $L(I(U'))$: $LK(I(U')) = \{P: P \le P(K)\}$ is the principal ideal generated by $P(K)$ in $L(I(U'))$ (see, please, definition 6.3 of principal ideal in Chapter 6).

For definition of good test, we use partition dependency: $P(X) \subseteq P(K)$ ($X \le K \equiv X*K = X \equiv X + K = K$).

If $P(X) = P(K)$, then X is the ideal approximation of classification K.

Of all tests X, $X \subseteq U$, $P(X) \subset P(K)$, the good test will be X such that $P(X)$ is the closest to $P(K)$ element of $LK(I(U'))$, i. e., for all $P(Y)$, $Y \subseteq U$ condition $(P(X) \subseteq P(Y) \subseteq P(K))$ implies $P(X) = P(Y)$. Thus, we come to the following definition of a good diagnostic test.

Definition 7.1. A collection $X \subseteq U$ is a good test or a good approximation of K of T if the following conditions are satisfied

a) $X \in Q(K)$;

b) there does not exist a collection of attributes Z, $Z \subseteq U$, $X \ne Z$ such that $Z \in Q(K)$ and $P(X) < P(Z) \le P(K)$.

We introduce the concept of the best diagnostic test as follows.

Definition 7.2. A good test X, $X \subseteq U$ is the best one for a given classification K of T if the number of classes in partition $P(X)$ is the smallest for all tests of $Q(K)$.

Let us illustrate definitions of 7.1 and 7.2 based on the following example (see, please, Table 1).

In this table, $P(K) = \{\{t_1, t_2, t_3, t_4\}, \{t_5, t_6\}\}$.

We consider the set Q of tests containing not more than 2 attributes:

$Q = \{AB, AC, AF, AG, FG, AE, BG, DG\}$.

But we have only three good tests in Q:

$P(AE) = \{\{t_1, t_3, t_4\}, \{t_2\}, \{t_5\}, \{t_6\}\}$ contains 4 classes;

$P(BG) = \{\{t_1, t_2\}, \{t_3\}, \{t_4\}, \{t_5\}, \{t_6\}\}$ contains 5 classes;

$P(DG) = \{\{t_1\}, \{t_2, t_4\}, \{t_3\}, \{t_5\}, \{t_6\}\}$ contains 5 classes

Table 1. The table of example for illustration good test definition

T	A	B	C	D	E	F	G	K
t_1	a_1	b_1	c_1	d_1	e_1	f_1	g_1	k_1
t_2	a_2	b_1	c_2	d_2	e_2	f_2	g_1	k_1
t_3	a_1	b_1	c_2	d_1	e_1	f_3	g_2	k_1
t_4	a_1	b_2	c_3	d_2	e_1	f_1	g_1	k_1
t_5	a_2	b_2	c_3	d_2	e_1	f_1	g_2	k_2
t_6	a_3	b_3	c_3	d_3	e_3	f_1	g_3	k_2

because of

$$P(AB) = \{\{t_1,t_3\}, \{t_4\}, \{t_2\}, \{t_5\}, \{t_6\}\} \subseteq P(AE);$$

$$P(AC) = \{\{t_1\},\{t_3\}, \{t_4\}, \{t_2\}, \{t_5\}, \{t_6\}\} \subseteq P(AF), \subseteq P(AB), \subseteq P(BG), \subseteq P(DG), \subseteq P(AE);$$

$$P(AF) = P(AG) = P(AF) = \{\{t_1,t_4\}, \{t_3\}, \{t_2\}, \{t_5\}, \{t_6\}\} \subseteq P(AE).$$

It is easy to see that the number of classes in the partition of T (Table 1), formed by any test for classification K, cannot be less than 4 and, consequently, test AE is the best one. Really, each attribute divides classes k_1, k_2 of $P(K)$ into some number of subclasses. In table 1, the number of such subclasses produced by each of attributes A, B, C, D, E, F, G is equal to 4. Then partitions produced by any pair of attributes can have the number of classes equal to or greater than 4. The fact that AE, BG, DG are good tests for K requires to be proven. Further we shall give a constructive determination of a good test and a procedure for generating all good tests for a given classification on a given set of examples.

THE CHARACTERIZATION OF GOOD DIAGNOSTIC (CLASSIFICATION) TESTS

Let $G = 2^U$ be the set of all subsets of U. Each element of G is mapped to exactly one element of the set $L(I(U))$. However several elements of G can be mapped to one and the same element of $L(I(U))$. Let us determine on the set G the relation Θ as follows:

$X\Theta Y$ if and only if $P(X) = P(Y)$ $(P(X) \subseteq P(Y), P(Y) \subseteq P(X))$. Then the following partition dependencies are satisfied $X*Y = X$ and $X*Y = Y$.

Denote by $I = <G, \cup>$ the upper semi-lattice on G with the union operation.

Theorem 7.1 The relation Θ on the upper semi-lattice I is the congruence.

In order to proof Theorem **7**.1, we need the following definition.

Definition 7.3 Relation Θ on the upper semi-lattice I is a congruence on I if $X0 \equiv Y0$ $[\Theta]$ and $X1 \equiv Y1$ $[\Theta]$ implies simultaneously $X0 \cup X1 \equiv Y0 \cup Y1$ $[\Theta]$ (Skornjakov, 1982).

Proof of Theorem 7.1

Suppose that for any $X0, X1, Y0, Y1 \in I$ the following condition holds:

$X0 \equiv Y0$ $[\Theta]$ and $X1 \equiv Y1$ $[\Theta]$. We shall show that $X0 \cup X1 \equiv Y0 \cup Y1$ $[\Theta]$.

Let $Z1, Z0 \in I$ such that $Z0 = X0 \cup X1$, $Z1 = Y0 \cup Y1$ and the equalities $P(Z0) = P(X0) * P(X1)$, $P(Z1) = P(Y0) * P(Y1)$ hold. It follows from $X0 \equiv Y0$ $[\Theta]$ and $X1 \equiv Y1$ $[\Theta]$ that $P(X0) = P(Y0)$ and $P(X1) = P(Y1)$ are satisfied.

We get $P(X0) * P(X1) = P(Y0) * P(Y1)$ as a consequence of the uniqueness of the least upper bound in the lattice. Consequently, $(X0 \cup X1) \equiv (Y0 \cup Y1)$ $[\Theta]$.♠

Table 2.An example for demonstrating the congruence relation

N	A_1	A_2	A_3	A_4
r_1	1	1	1	1
r_2	1	2	2	1
r_3	1	3	1	2

Theorem 7.2. Two collections of attributes X and Y belong to one and the same class of congruence Θ if and only if the union of these collections also belongs to the same class, i. e. $X \equiv Y(\Theta)$ if and only if $X \equiv X \cup Y(\Theta)$ & $Y \equiv X \cup Y(\Theta)$.

The Proof of Theorem 7. 2

a) Let $X \equiv X \cup Y(\Theta)$ & $Y \equiv X \cup Y(\Theta)$, but $X \equiv Y(\Theta)$ does not hold. Then $P(X \cup Y) = P(X)*P(Y) = P(X)$, consequently $P(X) \subseteq P(Y)$. Simultaneously, $P(X \cup Y) = P(X)*P(Y) = P(Y)$, consequently $P(Y) < P(X)$. But then $P(Y) = P(X)$ and $X \equiv Y(\Theta)$ holds. We get the contradiction.

b) Let $X \equiv Y(\Theta)$, but $X \equiv X \cup Y(\Theta)$ & $Y \equiv X \cup Y(\Theta)$ does not hold. Then $P(X \cup Y) = P(X)*P(Y)$ and we have $P(X \cup Y) \subseteq P(X)$ and $P(X \cup Y) \subseteq P(Y)$. But then $P(X)$ and $P(Y)$ are incomparable, i.e. $P(X) \neq P(Y)$. Hence, it is not true that $X \equiv Y(\Theta)$, and we get the contradiction.♠

By $[a]\Theta$, where $a \in G$, we shall denote the equivalence class of congruence Θ containing a as $[a]\Theta = \{X: X \subseteq U, X \equiv a(\Theta)\}$.

Figure 1 demonstrates the diagram of all possible partitions of examples of Table 2 and Figure 2 demonstrates the upper semi-lattice on the set G with the congruence classes for a small example of Table 2.

In this table:

$G = \{\{A_1\}, \{A_2\}, \{A_3\}, \{A_4\}, \{A_1A_2\}, \{A_1A_3\}, \{A_1A_4\}, \{A_2A_3\}, \{A_2A_4\}, \{A_3A_4\}, \{A_1A_2A_3\}, \{A_1A_2A_4\}, \{A_1A_3A_4\}, \{A_2A_3A_4\}, \{A_1A_2A_3A_4\}\}$;

$P(A_1) = \{r_1, r_2, r_3\}, P(A_2) = \{\{r_1\}, \{r_2\}, \{r_3\}\}, P(A_3) = \{\{r_1, r_3\}, \{r_2\}\}, P(A_4) = \{\{r_1, r_2\}, \{r_3\}\}$.

Figure 1. The diagram of all possible partitions of the set {r_1, r_2, r_3}

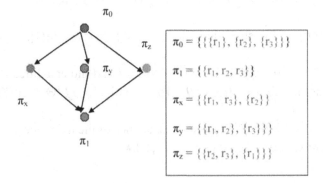

$\pi_0 = \{\{\{r_1\}, \{r_2\}, \{r_3\}\}\}$

$\pi_1 = \{\{r_1, r_2, r_3\}\}$

$\pi_x = \{\{r_1, r_3\}, \{r_2\}\}$

$\pi_y = \{\{r_1, r_2\}, \{r_3\}\}$

$\pi_z = \{\{r_2, r_3\}, \{r_1\}\}$

Figure 2. The upper semi-lattice on the set G with the congruence classes for example in Table 1

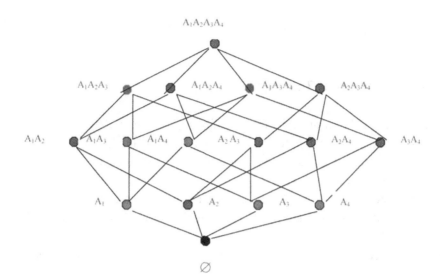

Any equivalence class of congruence relation Θ contains the greatest element, being the union of all elements of this class. This follows from Theorem 7.1.

The following is a direct consequence of the definition of congruence relation.

Proposition 7.1. If two collections of attributes X, Y are connected by partition dependency $X*Y = X$ $(X \leq Y)$, then $X \cup Y$ and X belong to one and the same equivalence class of congruence relation (Θ): $[X \cup Y](\Theta) = [X](\Theta)$.

For the brevity, we will omit the sign $\cup$ an, therefore, $X \cup Y$ will be simply designated as XY.

Proposition 7.2. If for attributes' collections X, $Y \subseteq U$ the partition dependency $X*Y = X$ holds, then attributes' collection XY is a subset of maximal collection of attributes belonging to the equivalence class $[X]\Theta$ of congruence relation Θ.

The number of maximally redundant collections is equal to the number of classes of congruence Θ defined on the set G.

In Figure 2, we have the following irredundant collections of attributes A_1, A_2, A_3, A_4, and A_3A_4 and the following equivalence classes $[A_1]\Theta$, $[A_2]\Theta = [A_3A_4]\Theta$, $[A_3]\Theta$, $[A_4]\Theta$ of the congruence relation Θ.

The set of partition dependencies in this example is:

$$\{A_1A_4 = A_4; \ A_1A_3 = A_3; \ A_1A_2 = A_2; \ A_2A_3 = A_2; \ A_2A_4 = A_2; \ A_2A_3A_4 = A_2; \ A_2A_3A_4 = A_3A_4\}.$$

These dependencies can be represented in another form: $A_4 \rightarrow A_1; \ A_3 \rightarrow A_1; \ A_2 \rightarrow A_3; \ A_2 \rightarrow A_4; \ A_3A_4 \leftrightarrow A_2; \ A_3A_4 \rightarrow A_3; \ A_3A_4 \rightarrow A_4.$

We have also four maximally redundant attribute collections including all corresponding irredundant collections of the each equivalence class of congruence Θ:

$clo(A_2) = clo(A_3A_4) = [A_1A_2A_3A_4] \ \Theta$

$clo(A_1) = [A_1] \ \Theta$

$clo(A_3) = [A_1A_3] \Theta$

$clo(A_4) = [A_1A_4] \Theta$

Good Maximally Redundant Test (GMRT)

The following definitions will play an important part for inferring good diagnostic tests.

Definition 7.4. A collection of attribute $X \subseteq U$ is said to be maximally redundant one if for any attribute $A \nsubseteq X$, $A \in U$, collections AX and X belong to different equivalence classes of the congruence relation, i.e. $[XA] \Theta \neq [X]\Theta$ for all $A \nsubseteq X$, $A \in U$.

This means that if a collection X of attribute is maximally redundant, then the addition to X any attribute, not belonging to it, leads to changing the equivalence class of congruence relation for obtained collection XA.

A diagnostic test X is said to be maximally redundant one if it is maximally redundant collection of attributes.

Definition 7.5. A collection X of attributes is a good maximally redundant test for a given classification K if it is a good test for K and, simultaneously, it is a maximally redundant collection of attributes.

If X is a good maximally redundant test for K, then after the adding to it any attribute $A \nsubseteq X$, $A \in U$ it will be a test for K but not good one.

Good Irredundant Test (GIRT)

Definition 7.6. A collection of attribute X is said to be irredundant one, if for all Z, $Z \subset X$, Z does not belong to the equivalence class of congruence Θ to which X belongs, i.e. $[X]\Theta \neq [Z]\Theta$ (for any Z, $Z \subset X$ partition dependency $X*Z = X$ is satisfied).

This means that if a collection of attribute X is irredundant, then deleting any attribute A, $A \in X$ from it leads to changing the equivalence class of congruence relation for obtained collection $X\backslash A$.

A diagnostic test X is said to be irredundant one if it is irredundant collection of attributes.

Definition 7.7. A collection X of attributes is a good irredundant test for a given classification K if it is a good test for K and, simultaneously, it is irredundant collection of attributes.

If X is irredundant test for K, then deleting any attribute A, $A \in X$ from it leads to the fact that obtained collection $X\backslash A$ is not a test for K.

The Best Maximally Redundant (BMR) and Irredundant (BIR) Tests

By definition 7.2, the best test X for a given classification K of T is a good test for K such that the number of classes of partition $P(X)$ is the smallest one for all tests approximating this classification.

For example, the best test for classification K in Table 1 is equal AE because it generates 4 classes in the partition of examples, but at that time all the other good tests generate the partitions into 5 classes.

The best test as well as every collection of attributes can be maximally redundant, redundant or irredundant one.

The Role of Good Diagnostic Tests in Human Thinking

Symbols designating attributes can be thought of as names of classifications generated by these attributes. Symbols designating values of attributes can be thought of as names of classes in corresponding classifications. Class is a special kind of classification separating a group of objects from all the other objects. One and the same classification can have several different names or descriptions (expressions). For example, we say that Saint Petersburg is a town founded by Peter the Great or a town where the Hermitage is located. On the set of classification names, the operations of multiplication * and addition + are defined and interpreted on the set of objects partitions generated by corresponding classifications.

Any expression formed by names of classifications connected by the use of symbols * and + is the name of a classification obtained by means of "calculating" this expression, i. e. by performing operations * and + on corresponding classifications (partitions) of objects involved in the domain of thinking. For simplicity, we shall omit the sing of multiplication in expressions on names of atom expressions (attributes).

Constructing classification tests is the process of finding expressions equivalent to a given classification of objects. Each test X for classification K is the name of a classification which is equal to or included in K. Let $X_1, X_2, ..., X_m$ be tests for K. By property (7) of operations $\cup$, $\cap$ (Theorem 6.1), tests $X_1 X_2 ... X_m$ satisfy the expression $X_1 + X_2 + ... + X_m \leq K$. So, for examples in Table 1, we have the following expressions: $AE + BG + DG = K$, $AE + BG = K$, $AE + DG = K$, $BG + DG = K$.

The equivalence relations on names serve as the foundation of commonsense reasoning as it has been shown in Chapter 3. Commonsense reasoning is based on the replacement of some expressions by others, the explanation of some concepts through the others. Good tests make it possible to produce the equivalent replacements (best replacements or unifications), such that the interchangeable expressions have either the same interpretation or very familiar interpretations in the domain of reasoning.

INFERRING ALL GOOD CLASSIFICATION TESTS

A good diagnostic test as a collection of attributes can be maximally redundant or irredundant one. It can be also not maximally redundant, but redundant collection of attributes as it is shown in Figure 3.

Since an irredundant good test (as any irredundant collection of attributes) belongs to one and only one equivalence class of the congruence relation Θ, it is contained in one and only one maximally re-

Figure 3. Classification of diagnostic tests

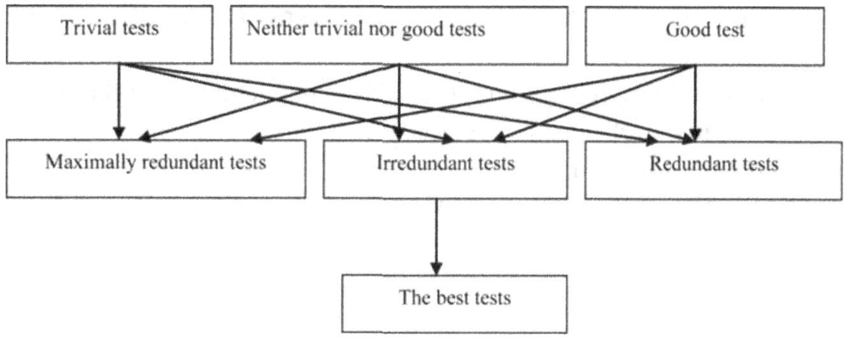

dundant good test. This implies one of the possible methods for searching for good irredundant tests for a given classification on a given set of examples:

- Find all good maximally redundant tests;
- For each good maximally redundant test, find all good irredundant tests contained in it.

This is a very convenient strategy for good tests generation.

In principle, all three equivalent determinations of diagnostic test can be placed as the basis of good test construction algorithms. It is expedient to use the indistinguishability relation (relation (e1) of definition of 6.14, Chapter 6) for generating good diagnostic tests. In this case, trivial tests are naturally excluded from the set of generated tests (we call trivial the diagnostic tests generating the partition of a given set of examples into classes each of which contains a single example). Firstly, this idea has been advanced in (Naidenova, & Polegaeva, 1986) and used for creating a first algorithm for good tests' generation. At the fist step of this algorithm, all maximally redundant attributes' collections not distinguishing at least one pair of examples are constructed. From these collections, the set Test -1 of maximally redundant tests for a given classification are selected. For this selection, the following consideration is used: a collection of attributes not distinguishing at least one pair of examples of one and the same class in a given classification is a test for this classification if and only if it is not included in an attributes' collection not distinguishing at least one pair of examples belonging to different classes of this classification. At the second step, all maximally redundant good tests for a given classification of examples are constructed. At the third step, for each good maximally redundant test, all good irredundant tests contained in it are obtained.

In (Naidenova, & Polegaeva, 1986), Step 3 is performed by deleting attributes from good maximally redundant tests with the use of a recursive procedure based on the following rule: if $zVW \rightarrow a$, where z, a – attributes, and V, W – collections of attributes, then $V \rightarrow z \Rightarrow VW \rightarrow a$. Thus, the following partition dependencies are checked: $X \backslash \{z\} \rightarrow z$, where $z \in X$.

The search for good tests can be performed with the use of condition e3 of definition 6.14 (Chapter 6). In this case, irredundant good tests are obtained directly as the elements of the partition lattice the generators of which are the atomic partitions produced by given attributes. This idea is incarnated in an algorithm described in (Megretskaya, 1989).

The algorithms mentioned above can be used for searching for good tests in the form of implicative dependencies if the set U of attributes is replaced by the set D of attributes' values.

Further we shall examine in detail the methods of constructing all good tests for a given classification on a given set of examples with the use of relations (e1) and (e3) of definition 6.14, Chapter 6.

Informal Description of an Idea for Inferring All Good Classification Tests

Let us return to the condition (e1) of definition 6.14. This definition **gives** the **relation** of discernability (distinguishing relation) **and** the relation of indiscernability (non-distinguishing or identifying relation) of examples with a given classification.

It is clear that if a collection of attributes is a good test for a given classification K, then it must satisfy the following relations:

a) the relations of discernability for all pairs of examples belonging to different classes of K;

b) the relations of indiscernability for the largest possible numbers of pairs of examples belonging to the same classes of K.

We denote by $QX(K)$ the set of tests for K, i.e. $QX(K) = \{X, X \subseteq U: P(X) \leq P(K)\}$, and, by $PQX(K)$, we denote the set of partitions generated by tests of this set, i.e. $PQX(K) = \{P(X): X \in QX(K)\}$.

Definition 7.8. An element a of an ordered set $(A, \leq)$ is said to be maximal (minimal) if there is no element b in A such that a $\leq$ b (b $\leq$ a) and a $\neq$ b.

An ordered set can have several maximal or minimal elements.

Proposition 7.3. The set $PQX(K)$ is partially ordered by $\leq$ relation on partitions.

By definition of good test and definition **7.8,** good tests are the maximal elements of the set $PQX(K)$.

The following useful properties of partitions are important.

Let $\mathrm{Pair}(T)$ be the set of all pairs of examples of T. Every partition P of examples of T generates a partition of $\mathrm{Pair}(T)$ into two disjoint classes: $\mathrm{PairIN}(P)$ and $\mathrm{PairBETWEEN}(P)$. $\mathrm{PairIN}(P)$ contains all pairs of examples belonging to the same classes of partition P (these are pairs of examples, connected with the relation of equivalence in partition P). The set $\mathrm{PairBETWEEN}(P)$ contains all the pairs of examples belonging to different classes of partition P. It follows from the definition $\leq$ relation between partitions that if $P1 \leq P2$ is true, then simultaneously $\mathrm{PairIN}(P1) \subseteq \mathrm{PairIN}(P2)$ and $\mathrm{PairBETWEEN}(P2) \subseteq \mathrm{PairBETWEEN}(P1)$ are satisfied.

We note also the very important property of partitions generated by good tests for a given classification. The fact that the good tests are maximal elements of partially ordered set $PQX(K)$ implies directly that if $X1, X2$ are good tests, then $P(X1)$ and $P(X2)$ are not compared with respect to relation $\leq$: $P(X1) \not\subseteq P(X2)$ and $P(X2) \not\subseteq P(X1)$. Consequently, $\mathrm{PairIN}(P(X1)) \not\subseteq \mathrm{PairIN}(P(X2))$ and $\mathrm{PairIN}(P(X2)) \not\subseteq \mathrm{PairIN}(P(X1))$.

The family of sets in which every two sets are incomparable is called the Sperner family (Sperner, 1928).

The family of sets $\{\mathrm{PairIN}(P(X_i)), i = 1, ..., mx: X_i$ – the good test for K, mx – the number of good tests for $K\}$ is a Sperner family.

For an illustration of inferring all good tests for a given classification, we consider the table of objects' examples with their goal classification K generated by attribute "*Class*" (Table 3). Here U = {Height, Color of hairs, Color of eyes}.

We begin with acquiring all the collections of attributes not distinguishing at lest a pairs of given examples.

Step 1.

The construction of the set E of attributes' collections:

$E = \{F_{ij}: 1 \leq i < j \leq n\}$, where $F_{ij} = \{A \in U: t_i[A] = t_j[A]\}$.

For table 3 we have the following set E (Table 4):

If a collection F_{ij} is empty, then the pair of examples with indices i, j is distinguished by any attribute from U.

Table 3. The set of object examples

T	Height	Color of hairs	Color of eyes	Class
t1	Low	Blond	Bleu	1
t2	Low	Brown	Bleu	2
t3	Tall	Brown	Hazel	2
t4	Tall	Blond	Hazel	2
t5	Tall	Brown	Bleu	2
t6	Low	Blond	Hazel	2
t7	Tall	Red	Bleu	1
t8	Tall	Blond	Bleu	1

Step 2.

We construct the partitioning of E into two disjoint parts: part IN of attributes' collections F_{ij}, such that for corresponding t_i, t_j, $t_i[K] = t_j[K]$ holds, and part BETWEEN of attributes collections F_{ij} such that for corresponding t_i, t_j, $t_i[K] \neq t_j[K]$ holds. We call BETWEEN the set of anti-tests for K.

We have for classification K generated by attribute "Class" in Table 6 the following parts IN and BETWEEN:

```
IN = {color of eyes;
      color of hairs, color of eyes;
      height, color of eyes;
      color of hairs;
      height;
   height, color of hairs },
BETWEEN = {height;
           color of hairs;
           color of eyes;
           height, color of hairs;
           height, color of eyes }.
```

Table 4. The set E for examples of Table 3

F_{12} = height, color of eyes	$F_{13} = \emptyset$	F_{14} = color of hairs	F_{15} = color of eyes
F_{16} = height, color of hairs	F_{17} = color of eyes	F_{18} = color of hairs, color of eyes	F_{23} = color of hairs
$F_{24} = \emptyset$	F_{25} = color of hairs, color of eyes	F_{26} = height	F_{27} = color of eyes
F_{28} = color of eyes	F_{34} = height, color of eyes	F_{35} = height, color of hairs	F_{36} = color of eyes
F_{37} = height	F_{38} = height	F_{45} = height	F_{46} = color of hairs, color of eyes
F_{47} = height	F_{48} = height, color of hairs	$F_{56} = \emptyset$	F_{57} = height, color of eyes
F_{58} = height, color of eyes	$F_{67} = \emptyset$	F_{68} = color of hairs	F_{78} = height, color of eyes

Every element of IN and BETWEEN is associated with a certain subsets of pairs of examples. For IN, we have the following correspondences:

```
Color of eyes → {(1,7),(3,6)}
color of hairs, color of eyes → {(1,8),(2,5),(4,6)}
height, color of eyes → {(7,8),(3,4)}
color of hairs → {(2,3)}
height → {(2,6)(4,5)}
height, color of hairs → {(3,5)}
```

We denote by PairIN(K,T) the set of all equivalent pairs of examples in classification K For every collection X of attributes, $X \subseteq U$, such that X is a test for K, the set PairIN(X,T) of equivalent pairs of examples in the partitioning $P(X)$ is included in the set PairIN(K,T).

But if X is a test for K, it must differentiate all pairs of examples from different classes of K, and consequently, X can not be included in BETWEEN. It follows from Proposition 7.4 that it can not also be included in any of anti-tests contained in BETWEEN.

Proposition 7.4. If for two collections $Y, Z \subseteq U$ of attributes, the relation $Y \subseteq Z$ is satisfied and Y is a test for a given classification K, then Z is also a test for a given classification K.

Proof Proposition 7.4.

Suppose that Z is not a test for K. Then Z is an anti-test for K or it is included in an anti-test. Consequently, Y is included at least in the same anti-test that Z is included. Hence, Y is not a test for K. This contradiction proves the proposition.♠

If X does not distinguish at least one pair of examples in K, then, by the fact that it does not belong to BETWEEN and it is not included in an anti-test of BETWEEN, there exists a collection Y of attributes in part IN such that Y is equal to X or X is included in Y.

The next step in searching for good tests is the selection tests for K in part IN.

Step 3.

We construct the set test-1(T,K) = {F_{ij}: $F_{ij} \in$ IN and $\forall F, F \in$ BETWEEN $F_{ij} \not\subseteq F'$}.

For the classification generated by attribute "*Class*", the set test-1(T,K) contains only one test "*color of hairs, color of eyes*". This test is also good for "*Class*". Table 5 is the projection of this test on the examples of Table 3. Class "1" includes individuals with blue eyes and blond or red hairs, Class "2" are individuals with brown hairs or hazel eyes.

In general case, the set test-1(T,K) contains more than one collection of attributes. We need the following definitions for analyzing the set test-1(T,K).

We introduce the concepts of minimal and maximal subsets of a fixed set of elements with respect to a given property of these elements. This permits to define maximally redundant and irredundant good tests from the point of view different from the previous one used by us earlier.

Let S be a fixed set of elements and 2^S be the set of all subsets of S. Let f be a property checked for every s, $s \in 2^S$ and s possesses or does not possess f.

The subset s is said to be maximal with respect to f if:

Table 5. *The projection of good test on the examples of Table 3*

t	Color of Hairs	Color of eyes	Class
t_1, t_8	Blond	Blue	1
t_7	Red	Blue	1
t_2, t_5	Brown	Blue	2
t_3	Browne	Hazel	2
t_4, t_6	Blond	Hazel	2

a)   It possesses f,
b)   Adding to it any element y such that $y \in S$, $y \notin s$ implies the loss of f.

The subset s is said to be minimal with respect to f if:

a)   It possesses f,
b)   Any its proper subset does not possess f, hence eliminating any element from s implies the loss of f.

Every attributes' collection of test-1(T,K) does not differentiate at least one pair of examples inside of some class in partition $P(K)$. The attributes' collection not differentiating several pairs of examples inside of some classes in $P(K)$ must be included in all those attributes' collections which correspond to these pairs of examples, hence it must be included in the intersection of these collections.

We formulate the necessary and sufficient condition for the intersection of several collections of test-1(T,K) to be a good test for a given classification.

Let $S = \{1, 2, ..., nt\}$ be the set of indices of elements of test-1(T,K). Denote by $s(X) = \{i_1, i_2, ..., i_s\}$ the set of indices of elements of test-1(T,K) the intersection of which is equal to X, $s(X) \subseteq S$. Denote by $t(s)$ the attributes' collection equal to the intersection of elements of test-1(T,K) indices of which compose s.

We shall show that if X is a good test for a given classification, then $s(X)$ is a maximal set with respect to the property "$t(s)$ is a test for a given classification".

Proposition 7.5. If X is a good test for a given classification K, then $s(X)$ is maximal subset of S in the sense that for any extension $s' = s(X) \cup i^*$, where $i^* \in S$, $i^* \notin s(X)$, $t(s')$ is not a test for a given classification.

Proof of Proposition 7.5.

Suppose that $s(X)$ is not maximal with respect to the condition of proposition 7.5. Then there is in S an index j such that $X(s) \cap Y_j$, say Z, will be a test for a given classification. Z must be included in all elements of test-1(T,K) which include X, hence $s(X) \subseteq s(Z)$. But $Z \neq X$ implies that $s(X) \subset s(Z)$. It follows from this that PairIN(X) $\subset$ PairIN(Z) and, consequently, $P(X) < P(Z)$. By our assumption, Z is a test for a given classification K, hence, $P(Z) \leq P(K)$. Then we have that $P(X) < P(Z) \leq P(K)$ and X is not a good test for a given classification K. This contradiction proof Proposition **7.5.**♠

This proposition is the basis for constructing good tests for a given classification with the use of the set test-1(T,K). Let X be equal to the intersection of a number of elements of test-1(T, K), and the set $v(X) = \{F_i\colon F_i = X \cap t_i,\ t_i \in$ test-1$(T,K),\ i \notin s(X)\}$. Then X is a good test for a given classification if for all $F_i \in v(X)$, $F_i \neq \varnothing$, one of the following conditions is satisfied:

a) F_i – is not a test for a given classification,
b) $F_i = X$.

Step 4.

For every t of test-1(T,K): the set $v(t)$ is constructed: $v(t) = \{F_i\colon F_i = t \cap t_i,\ t_i \in$ test-1$(T,K),\ i \notin s(X)\}$.
   The set $vtest(t)$ of new tests is constructed: $vtest(t) = \{F\colon F \in v(t),\ F \nsubseteq F^*$ for $\forall\ F^* \in$ BETWEEN$\}$.
   If $vtest(t)$ is:

1)   empty, then t is a good test;
2)   not empty and contains tests different from t, then t is not a good test and it is deleted from consideration. Newly obtained tests are memorized in test-2(T,K) of the next level of generalization, for which step 4 is repeated.

A newly obtained good test t is inserted in the set of good tests if the following condition $s(t) \nsubseteq s(t^*)$ holds for all t^*, t^* already obtained good tests.
   The process of good tests inferring is over when test-q(T,K) is neither empty nor has not a test.
   For collection of examples of Table 6, we have the following result: BETWEEN = $\{EF, AD, EG, BCDEF, F, CF\}$, test-1$(T, K) = \{BG, ABDE, AEFG, DG, AE\}$.
   For every test from test-1(T,K), we have:

$v(BG) = \{B, G\}$; B and G are not tests, hence BG – a good test;

$v(DG) = \{D, G\}$; D and G are not tests, hence DG – a good test;

$v(AE) = \varnothing$; AE – a good test;

$v(ABDE) = \{AE\}$; $ABDE$ is not a good test and it is deleted from consideration;

Table 6. The collection of examples for inferring the good tests

T	A	B	C	D	E	F	G	K
t_1	a_1	b_1	c_1	d_1	e_1	f_1	g_1	k_1
t_2	a_2	b_1	c_2	d_2	e_2	f_2	g_1	k_1
t_3	a_1	b_1	c_2	d_1	e_1	f_3	g_2	k_1
t_4	a_1	b_2	c_3	d_2	e_1	f_1	g_1	k_1
t_5	a_2	b_2	c_3	d_2	e_1	f_1	g_2	k_2
t_6	a_3	b_3	c_3	d_3	e_3	f_1	g_3	k_2

$v(AEFG) = \varnothing$; but $s(AEFG) \subseteq s(AE)$, hence $AEFG$ is not a good test and it is deleted from consideration.

Finally test$(T,K) = \{BG, DG, AE\}$.

Now we are interested in analyzing attributes' collections satisfying the definition of good test and obtained as the intersection of a fixed number of tests from the set test-1(T,K).

First of all, let us show that any element of test-1(T,K) is a maximally redundant collection of attributes.

In fact, if Y is an element of test-1(T,K) then, by step 1, it does not distinguish a pair of examples in the partition $P(K)$, moreover, it contains those and only those attributes which do not distinguish this pair of examples. Suppose that we compose an attributes' collection Y' by adding to Y an attribute not belonging to it but belonging to U. Clearly, Y' is a test for K. But Y' will differentiate a pair of examples not distinguished by Y. Hence $\mathrm{PairIN}(Y') \subseteq \mathrm{PairIN}(Y) \subseteq \mathrm{PairIN}(K)$ and, consequently, $P(Y') < P(Y) \leq P(K)$. As a result, Y' is not a good test and, consequently, Y satisfies the definition of good maximally redundant test for K.

Now we show that the intersection of maximally redundant collections of attributes is also a maximally redundant collection of attributes.

Lemma 1. The intersection of maximally redundant collections of attributes is also a maximally redundant collection of attributes.

Proof of Lemma 1.

Let X and Y be maximally redundant collections of attributes. We shall show that $Z = X \cap Y$ is the maximally redundant collection of attributes.

Suppose that Z is not maximally redundant. Then there exists an attribute A such that it belongs to $U \setminus Z$ and $P(AZ) = P(Z)$ (1). We have $X = Z \cup X'$ and $Y = Z \cup Y'$. Hence, $P(X) = P(ZX') = P(Z) * P(X')$ and $P(ZY') = P(Z) * P(Y')$. By (1), we get $P(Z) * P(X') = P(AZ) * P(X') = P(A) * P(ZX') = P(A) * P(X) = P(AX)$. Consequently, $P(X) = P(AX)$. We can analogously get that $P(Y) = P(AY)$. It follows that X and Y are not maximally redundant.♠

We can also prove Lemma 1 as follows. Suppose that Z is not maximally redundant. Then there exists an attribute A such that it belongs to $U \setminus Z$ and $P(AZ) = P(Z)$. Then $\mathrm{PairIN}(ZA) \subseteq \mathrm{PairIN}(Z)$. This implies that ZA must be included in Z, i. e. $Z \subset ZA$ and, simultaneously, $Z = ZA$. This contradicts with our assumption that Z is not maximally redundant and Lemma 1 is proven.

Thus good test obtained by intersection of maximally redundant collections of attributes is also maximally redundant.

Consider Y, $Y \subseteq X$, where X is maximally redundant good test for K. Obviously, $P(Y) > P(X)$ or $P(Y) = P(X)$. However, since X is a good test then $P(Y) > P(X)$ and Y is not a test for a given classification. In the case $P(Y) = P(X)$, Y is equivalent X and it does not distinguish exactly the same set of pairs of examples in K as X.

Thus, deleting attributes from a good maximally redundant test leads to finding the good tests equivalent to it.

Now we shall find all the irredundant good tests contained in a good maximally redundant test.

Let $X = A_1 A_2 \ldots A_j \ldots A_m$ be a maximally redundant good test for a given classification. Each attribute A_j is an irredundant collection of attribute. We shall compose attributes' collections containing one, two, three and more attributes from X. For each composed collection, we shall check whether it irredundant or not. If a composed attributes' collection is not irredundant, then it is eliminated. If a composed attributes' collection is irredundant and not a test for a given classification, then it can be extended. If it is a test, then it is a good irredundant one. This process continues as long as there exists the possibility to extent at least one irredundant attributes' collection. The rule for extending attributes' collections relies on the following consideration: if a collection of attributes is irredundant one, then all its proper subsets must be irredundant too. We use the function to_be_irredundant$(X) =$ if $(\forall A)$ $(A \in X)$ $P(X) \neq P(X/A)$ then *true* else *false*.

Background Algorithm of Inferring all GMRTs

Let $U = \{A_1, ..., A_m\}$, $T = \{t_1, ..., t_n\}$, $N = \{1, ..., n\}$, and K be as defined earlier. Inferring tests for classification K makes sense if the functional dependency $U \to K$ $(P(U) \leq P(K))$ is carried out. Usually U is a trivial test for K.

Background Algorithm. Inferring all the GMRTs for K

Input: U, T, N, K;

Output: test(T,K) – the set of all GMRTs for K

Part 1 Initialization process:

1. Let us construct the set $S = \{s_{12}, s_{13}, ..., s_{ij}, ..., \}$, $1 < i < j < n$ of all subsets of N containing exactly two elements and form the set first$(T, K) = \{F_{ij}, \{i, j\} \in S: \{A \in U: t_i[A] = t_j[A]\}\}$.
2. Let us break first(T,K) into two subsets:
   firstIN $(T,K) = \{F_{ij} \in$ first$(T,K): t_i[K] = t_j[K]\}$ and
   firstBETWEEN$(T,K) = \{F_{ij} \in$ first$(T,K): t_i[K] \neq t_j[K]\}$.
3. Let us construct the set FM of all maximal elements of firstBETWEEN (T,K) with respect to the inclusion relation: $FM = \{F \in$ firstBETWEEN $(T,K): (\forall G)$ $(G \in$ firstBETWEEN $(T,K))$ $(G \supset F)$ $\Rightarrow G = F\}$.
4. Let us construct the set test-1 $(T,K) = \{F \in$ firstIN $(T,K): (\forall G)$ $(G \in FM)$ $F \not\subseteq G \}$.

Let $NT = \{1,2,...,nt\}$ be the set of indices of the elements of test-1(T, K) and $NF = \{nt +1, nt +2, ...,$ $nf\}$ be the set of indices of the elements of FM.

The following theorem and corollary from it determine the properties of sets first(T,K) and test-1(T,K).

Theorem 7.3. The set first(T,K) is the set of maximally redundant subsets of attributes.

Corollary from Theorem 7.3. The set test-1 (T,K) is the set of maximally redundant tests for K, none of which is a trivial test for K.

The following theorem gives a method for inferring all good maximally redundant tests for a given classification.

Theorem 7.4. A maximally redundant good test for K either belongs to the set test-1(T,K) or there exists a number q, $2 \leq q \leq nt$, such that this test will be equal to the intersection of exactly q elements from the set test -1(T,K), where nt is the cardinality of test -1(T,K).

By $s_q = (i_1, i_2, ..., i_q)$, we denote a subset of NT, containing q indices from NT. Let S(test-q) be the set of elements $s = \{i_1, i_2, ..., i_q\}$, $q = 1, 2, ..., nt$ satisfying the condition that $t(s)$ is a maximally redundant test for K. The mapping $t(s)$ is determined as follows: $t(s)$ = the intersection of all t_j, $t_j \in$ test-1(T,K), $j \in s$.

We shall use an inductive rule for constructing $\{i_1, i_2, ..., i_{q+1}\}$ from $\{i_1, i_2, ..., i_q\}$, $q = 1, 2, ..., nt-1$. This rule relies on the following consideration: if the set $\{i_1, i_2, ..., i_{q+1}\}$ corresponds to a test for K, then all its proper subsets must correspond to tests too and, consequently, they must be in S(test-q):

$$S_q = \{s: \|s\| = q \text{ and } \forall s', s' \subset s, \|s'\| = q - 1 \text{ we have } s' \in S_{q-1}\}.$$

Thus the set $\{i_1, i_2, ..., i_{q+1}\}$ can be constructed if and only if S(test-q) contains all its proper subsets.

Having constructed the set $s_{q+1} = \{i_1, i_2, ..., i_{q+1}\}$, we have to determine whether it corresponds to a test or not. If $t(s_{q+1})$ is not a test, then s_{q+1} is deleted, otherwise s_{q+1} is inserted in S(test-$(q+1)$). The algorithm is over when it is impossible to construct any element for S(test-$(q+1)$).

Thus for the search for tests we form by induction (thus far this is possible) the sequences: $S_2, S_3, ...,$ S_q and test-2 (T,K), test-3 (T,K), ..., test-q (T,K).

The function to_be_test(s) can be defined by two ways:

to_be_test(s)::= if $(\forall F')(F' \in FM)$ $t(s) \not\subset F'$ then *true* else *false*.

to_be_test(s): if $P(t(s)) * P(K) = P(t)$, then *true* else *false*.

The algorithm is based on the following lemmas.

Lemma 2. $(\forall s)(\forall s')(s \subseteq NT)$ $(s' \subseteq NT)(s \subset s')$ $((\text{to\_be\_test } (s') = true) \Rightarrow (\text{to\_be\_test } (s) = true))$.

Lemma 3. $(\forall q)(2 \leq q \leq nt)$ $(\text{to\_be\_test } (\{i_1, ..., i_q\}) = true) \Rightarrow (\forall j)$ $(1 \leq j \leq q)$ to_be_test $(\{i_1, ..., i_{(j-1)}, i_{(j+1)}, ..., i_q\}) = true$.

Lemma 3 is a consequence of Lemma 2.

Background Algorithm. Inferring all GMRTs for a given classification K

Part 2 (The main process of inferring GMRTs).

```
1.    Input: q = 1, test-1(T,K), NT = {1,2,…, nt}, S(test-q) = {{1},
{2}, ..., {nt}}, FM.

Output: the set test(T,K) of all GMRTs for K.

2.    S_q ::= S(test-q);

3.    While ||S_q|| ≥ q + 1 do

3.1 Generating S(q + 1) =

{s ={i_1, ..., i_(q + 1)}: (∀ j) (1 ≤ j ≤ q + 1) (i_1, ..., i_(j-1), i_(j + 1),
..., i_(q + 1)} ∈ S_q};
```

3.2 Generating S(test-(q + 1)) =

{$s = \{i_1, \ldots, i_{(q + 1)}\}$: ($s \in S(q + 1)$) & (to_be_test($s$) = *true*)};

3.3 Reducing S(test-q):

S(test-q)::= {$s = \{i_1, \ldots, i_q\}$: ($s \in S$(test-q)) & (($\forall s'$)($s' \in$ S(test-(q + 1)) $s \not\subset s'$)};

3.4. q::= $q + 1$;

3.5. max::= q;

end while

4.   test(T, K)::= $\varnothing$;

5.   While $q \leq max$ do test(T, K)::= test(T, K) $\cup$ {$t(s)$: $s = \{i_1, \ldots,$ $i_s\} \in S$(test-q) };

5.1 q::= $q + 1$;

end while

end

Table 7. The set test-1(T, K)

index of example	test-1(T,K)
1	$A_1 A_2 A_5 A_6 A_{21} A_{23} A_{24} A_{26}$
2	$A_4 A_7 A_8 A_9 A_{12} A_{14} A_{15} A_{22} A_{23} A_{24} A_{26}$
3	$A_3 A_4 A_7 A_{12} A_{13} A_{14} A_{15} A_{18} A_{19} A_{24} A_{26}$
4	$A_1 A_4 A_5 A_6 A_7 A_{12} A_{14} A_{15} A_{16} A_{20} A_{21} A_{24} A_{26}$
5	$A_2 A_6 A_{23} A_{24}$
6	$A_7 A_{20} A_{21} A_{26}$
7	$A_3 A_4 A_5 A_6 A_{12} A_{14} A_{15} A_{20} A_{22} A_{24} A_{26}$
8	$A_3 A_6 A_7 A_8 A_9 A_{13} A_{14} A_{15} A_{19} A_{20} A_{21} A_{22}$
9	$A_{16} A_{18} A_{19} A_{20} A_{21} A_{22} A_{26}$
10	$A_2 A_3 A_4 A_5 A_6 A_8 A_9 A_{13} A_{18} A_{20} A_{21} A_{26}$
11	$A_1 A_2 A_3 A_7 A_{19} A_{20} A_{21} A_{22} A_{26}$
12	$A_2 A_3 A_{16} A_{20} A_{21} A_{23} A_{24} A_{26}$
13	$A_1 A_4 A_{18} A_{19} A_{23} A_{26}$
14	$A_{23} A_{24} A_{26}$

Table 8. The set of FM

Index of example	FM	Index of example	FM
15	$A_3A_8A_{16}A_{23}A_{24}$	32	$A_1A_2A_3A_7A_9A_{10}A_{11}A_{13}A_{18}$
16	$A_7A_8A_9A_{16}A_{18}$	33	$A_1A_5A_6A_8A_9A_{10}A_{19}A_{20}A_{22}$
17	$A_1A_{21}A_{22}A_{24}A_{26}$	34	$A_2A_8A_9A_{18}A_{20}A_{21}A_{22}A_{23}A_{26}$
18	$A_1A_7A_8A_9A_{13}A_{16}$	35	$A_1A_2A_4A_5A_6A_7A_9A_{13}A_{16}$
19	$A_2A_6A_7A_9A_{21}A_{23}$	36	$A_1A_2A_6A_7A_8A_{10}A_{11}A_{13}A_{16}A_{18}$
20	$A_{10}A_{19}A_{20}A_{21}A_{22}A_{24}$	37	$A_1A_2A_3A_4A_5A_6A_7A_{12}A_{14}A_{15}A_{16}$
21	$A_1A_{10}A_{20}A_{21}A_{22}A_{23}A_{24}$	38	$A_1A_2A_3A_4A_5A_6A_9A_{11}A_{12}A_{13}A_{16}$
22	$A_3A_5A_6A_7A_9A_{10}A_{16}$	39	$A_1A_2A_3A_4A_5A_6A_{14}A_{15}A_{19}A_{20}A_{23}A_{26}$
23	$A_2A_6A_8A_9A_{14}A_{15}A_{16}$	40	$A_2A_3A_4A_5A_6A_7A_{11}A_{12}A_{13}A_{14}A_{15}A_{16}$
24	$A_1A_4A_5A_6A_7A_8A_{11}A_{16}$	41	$A_2A_4A_5A_6A_7A_9A_{10}A_{11}A_{12}A_{13}A_{14}A_{15}A_{19}$
25	$A_7A_{10}A_{11}A_{13}A_{19}A_{20}A_{22}A_{26}$	42	$A_1A_2A_3A_4A_5A_6A_{12}A_{16}A_{18}A_{19}A_{20}A_{21}A_{26}$
26	$A_1A_2A_3A_5A_6A_7A_{10}A_{16}$	43	$A_4A_5A_6A_7A_8A_9A_{10}A_{11}A_{12}A_{13}A_{14}A_{15}A_{16}$
27	$A_1A_2A_3A_5A_6A_{10}A_{13}A_{16}$	44	$A_3A_4A_5A_6A_8A_9A_{10}A_{11}A_{12}A_{13}A_{14}A_{15}A_{18}A_{19}$
28	$A_1A_3A_7A_{10}A_{11}A_{13}A_{19}A_{21}$	45	$A_1A_2A_3A_4A_5A_6A_7A_8A_9A_{10}A_{11}A_{12}A_{13}A_{14}A_{15}$
29	$A_1A_4A_5A_6A_7A_8A_{13}A_{16}$	46	$A_1A_3A_4A_5A_6A_7A_{10}A_{11}A_{12}A_{13}A_{14}A_{15}A_{16}A_{23}A_{24}$
30	$A_1A_2A_3A_6A_{11}A_{12}A_{14}A_{15}A_{16}$	47	$A_1A_2A_3A_4A_5A_6A_8A_9A_{10}A_{11}A_{12}A_{14}A_{16}A_{18}A_{22}$
31	$A_1A_2A_5A_6A_{11}A_{14}A_{15}A_{16}A_{26}$	48	$A_2A_8A_9A_{10}A_{11}A_{12}A_{14}A_{15}A_{16}$

Table 9. The sets test-2 and S(test-2)

index	s	t(s)	index	S	T(s)
1	1,2	$A_{23}A_{24}A_{26}$	18	4,7	$A_4A_5A_6A_{12}A_+A_{20}A_{24}A_{26}$
2	1,4	$A_1A_5A_6A_{21}A_{24}A_{26}$	19	4,8	$A_6A_7A_+A_{20}A_{21}$
3	1,5	$A_2A_6A_{23}A_{24}$	20	4,11	$A_1A_7A_{20}A_{21}A_{26}$
4	1,7	$A_5A_6A_{24}A_{26}$	21	4,12	$A_{16}A_{20}A_{21}A_{24}A_{26}$
5	1,12	$A_2A_{21}A_{23}A_{24}A_{26}$	22	5,12	$A_2A_{23}A_{24}$
6	2,3	$A_4A_7A_{12}A_+A_{24}A_{26}$	23	6,4	$A_7A_{20}A_{21}A_{26}$
7	2,4	$A_4A_7A_{12}A_+A_{24}A_{26}$	24	6,8	$A_7A_{20}A_{21}$
8	2,7	$A_4A_{12}A_+A_{22}A_{24}A_{26}$	25	6,11	$A_7A_{20}A_{21}A_{26}$
9	2,8	$A_7A_4A_+A_{22}$	26	7,8	$A_3A_6A_+A_{20}A_{22}$
10	2,10	$A_4A_+A_{10}A_{26}$	27	7,11	$A_3A_{20}A_{22}A_{26}$
11	2,12	$A_{23}A_{24}A_{26}$	28	7,12	$A_3A_{20}A_{24}A_{26}$
12	3,4	$A_4A_7A_{12}A_+A_{24}A_{26}$	29	8,10	$A_3A_6A_+A_{13}A_{20}A_{21}$
13	3,7	$A_3A_4A_{12}A_+A_{24}A_{26}$	30	8,11	$A_3A_7A_{19}A_{20}A_{21}A_{22}$
14	3,8	$A_3A_7A_{13}A_+A_{19}$	31	9,11	$A_{19}A_{20}A_{21}A_{22}A_{26}$
15	3,10	$A_3A_4A_{11}A_{13}A_{18}A_{26}$	32	14,1	$A_{23}A_{24}A_{26}$
16	3,11	$A_3A_7A_{19}A_{26}$	33	14,2	$A_{23}A_{24}A_{26}$
17	3,12	$A_3A_{24}A_{26}$	34	14,12	$A_{23}A_{24}A_{26}$

Table 10. The set S₃

1,2,4	1,2,7	1,2,12	1,2,14	1,12,14	1,4,7
1,4,12	1,5,12	1,7,12	1,12,14	2,3,4	2,3,7
2,3,8	2,3,10	2,3,12	2,4,7	2,4,8	2,4,12
2,7,8	2,7,12	2,8,10	2,12,14	3,4,7	3,4,8
3,4,11	3,4,12	3,7,8	3,7,11	3,7,12	3,8,10
3,8,11	4,7,8	4,7,11	4,7,12	6,4,8	6,4,11
6,8,11	7,8,11				

Table 11. The set S(test-3)

1,2,12	1,2,14	1,4,7	1,5,12	1,12,14	2,3,4
2,3,7	2,4,7	2,7,8	2,12,14	3,4,7	3,7,12
4,6,8	4,6,11	4,7,12	4,8,11	6,8,11	7,8,11

Let us give an example of inferring all the GMRTs with the use of Background Algorithm, which we call "**Main Current Example**". We shall consider only Part 2 of Background Algorithm. The sets test-1(T, K) and *FM* are given in the following Table 7 and Table 8.

The set $S_1 = S(\text{test-1}) = \{\{1\}, \{2\}, ..., \{14\}\}$; the set $S_2 = \{$all pairs of elements of $S_1\}$. The sets test-2 and $S(\text{test-2})$ are given in Table 9. In Table 9, A_*, A_+ denote the collection of values $\{A_8, A_9\}$ and $\{A_{14}, A_{15}\}$, respectively.

The set $S(\text{test-1})$ after reducing: $\{13\}$.

The sets S_3 and $S(\text{test} - 3)$ are given in Table 10 and Table 11.

The set S_4 is equal $S(\text{test-4})$; Table 12 gives the set S(test-2) after reducing and Table 13 and Table 14 give the sets S(test-4) and S(test-3) after reducing, respectively. Table 15 gives the set of obtained GMRTs.

Table 12. The set S(test-2) after reducing

2,10	3,8	3,10	3,11	8,10	9,11

Table 13. The set S(test-4)

1,2,12,14	2,3,4,7	4,6,8,11

Table 14. The set S(test-3) after reducing

1,4,7	1,5,12	2,7,8	3,7,12	4,7,12	7,8,11

Table 15. The set test(T,K)

index	S	T(s)
1	(13)	$A_1A_4A_{18}A_{19}A_{23}A_{26}$
2	(2,10)	$A_4A_8A_9A_{10}A_{26}$
3	(3,10)	$A_3A_4A_{11}A_{13}A_{18}A_{26}$
4	(8,10)	$A_3A_6A_8A_9A_{13}A_{20}A_{21}$
5	(9,11)	$A_{19}A_{20}A_{21}A_{22}A_{26}$
6	(3,11)	$A_3A_7A_{19}A_{26}$
7	(3,8)	$A_3A_7A_{13}A_{14}A_{15}A_{19}$
8	(1,4,7)	$A_5A_6A_{24}A_{26}$
9	(2,7,8)	$A_{14}A_{15}A_{22}$
10	(1,5,12)	$A_2A_{23}A_{24}$
11	(4,7,12)	$A_{20}A_{24}A_{26}$
12	(3,7,12)	$A_3A_{24}A_{26}$
13	(7,8,11)	$A_3A_{20}A_{22}$
14	(2,3,4,7)	$A_4A_{12}A_{14}A_{15}A_{24}A_{26}$
15	(4,6,8,11)	$A_7A_{20}A_{21}$
16	(1,2,12,14)	$A_{23}A_{24}A_{26}$

Proof of the Formulated Lemmas and Theorems

Here we give the proof of lemmas and theorems formulated above (Naidenova, 1999).

Theorem 7.3. The set first(T,K) is a set of maximally redundant collections of attributes.

Proof of Theorem 7.3.

Let X be an element of first(T,K). Then there exists a pair of tuples t_{i*}, t_{j*} in T, $i, j \in \{1,, n\}$ such that $t_i(X) = t_j(X)$. Then the fact that $A \in U \backslash X$ implies that $t_{i*}(A) \neq t_{j*}(A)$ **(1)**.

Assume that X is not maximally redundant. Then there exists an attribute A in $U \backslash X$ such that $P(XA)$ = $P(X)$. Consequently, $P(X) * P(A) = P(X)$. Then $t_i(X) = t_j(X)$, $i, j \in \{1,2..., n\}$ implies that $t_i(A) = t_j(A)$ and we have that $t_{i*}(A) = t_{j*}(A)$. But this contradicts with condition **(1)**. This completes the proof of Theorem 7.3.♠

Corollary from Theorem 7.3. The set test-1(T,K) is a set maximally redundant tests for classification K none of which is trivial one.

Proof of Corollary from Theorem 7.3.

Observe that any $X \in$ test-1(T,K) belongs to first (T,K). For every $X, X \in$ first (T,K), there exist $i, j, \in \{1,2, ..., m\}$ such that $t_i(X) = t_j(X)$, $t_i, t_j, \in T$. By theorem 7.3, if $X \in$ first (T,K), then it is maximally redundant collection of attributes. Hence, we get immediately that test-1(T,K) is a set of nontrivial tests for K.♠

Theorem 7.4. A maximally redundant good test for K either belongs to the set test-1(T,K) or there exists a number q, $2 \le q \le nt$, such that this test will be equal to the intersection of exactly q elements from the set test -1(T,K), where nt is the cardinality of the test -1(T,K).

Let Vp (X) be a set of all pairs of examples t_i, t_j, $\in T$, i, j, $\in \{1, 2, ..., n\}$ not distinguished in the partition P(X).

We shall use the following proposition.

Proposition 7.7. For all X, $Y \subseteq U$ the following equivalence holds $P(X) \le P(Y) \Leftrightarrow Vp(X) \subseteq Vp(Y)$.

Lemma 4. Let X be a good maximally redundant test for K, $X \notin$ test-1(T,K) such that $X \subset Y$, $Y \in$ test-1(T,K). Then there is at least one collection Y^* of attributes, $Y^* \in$ test-1(T,K) such that $X \subseteq Y \cap Y^*$.

Proof of Lemma 4.

Let us consider $P(X)$ and $P(Y)$. Since $X \subset Y$ the relation $P(Y) < P(X)$ is satisfied and, consequently, $Vp(Y) \subset Vp(X)$. Hence there exists a pair of examples (t^*_1, t^*_2) in $Vp(X)$ such that $t^*_1(X) = t^*_2(X)$ and $t^*_1(Y) \ne t^*_2(Y)$. Let us consider a collection of attributes Y^*, $Y^* = \{A: t^*_1(A) = t^*_2(A)\}$. Clearly, that $Y^* \in$ test-1(T,K). Hence, X is a proper subset of Y^* or $X = Y^*$. Then we have $X \subseteq Y \cap Y^*$. ♠

Proof of Theorem 7.4.

Let X be a good maximally redundant test for a classification K. Two cases are possible.

Case 1: there exists at least one pair of examples t^*_1, t^*_2 for which $X = \{A: t^*_1(A) = t^*_2(A)\}$. Of course, X belongs to test-1(T,K).

Case 2: there is not any pair of examples in T such that X contains exactly the attributes not distinguishing this pair of examples. Then $X \notin$ test-1(T,K). But X is a test for K. This implies that there exists a pair of examples in $Vp(X)$ such that it is not distinguished by X. Let Y be the maximally redundant set of attributes not distinguishing this pair of examples. It means that $X \subset Y$, for some $Y \in$ test-1(T,K). **By Lemma 4, there exists a collection of attributes** Y' in test-1(T,K) such that $X \subseteq Y \cap Y'$, $Y \cap Y' = Z$. If $X = Z$, then $q = 2$; if $X \subset Z$, then $P(Z) < P(X) \le P(K)$ and, consequently, there exists a pair of examples not distinguished by X, but simultaneously distinguished by Z. Let Y'' be a maximally redundant collection of attributes not distinguishing this new pair of examples. Then $X \subseteq Y \cap Y' \cap Y''$, and $q = 3$.

Now we shall show that this inductive process of reasoning terminates with q not more than the number of elements in the set $Vp(X)$. Suppose that X does not equal to the intersection of some number of tests from test-1(T,K). But X must be included at least in all maximally redundant collections of attributes not distinguishing the pairs of examples belonging to $Vp(X)$. Let Y^* be the intersection of these maximally redundant collections of attributes, $X \subset Y^*$. Then $Y^* = XZ$ and $Vp(XZ) = Vp(Y^*)$. This implies that $P(XZ) = P(Y^*)$. It means that X is not maximally redundant collection of attributes, and we have a contradiction. ♠

For the proof of **Lemma 3,** we shall use the following **Lemma 5.**

Lemma 5 For Y, $Y \subseteq X$, X, $Y \subseteq U$, the functional dependency $X \to Y$ holds.

Proof of the Lemma 5.

Let Z be equal to $X \backslash Y$. Then $X = Y \cup Z$ and $P(X) = P(Y) * P(Z)$ and, by the definition of * operation, $P(X) \le P(Y)$. Then, by the equivalence of functional and partition dependencies we get $X \to Y$. ♠

Lemma 3. $(\forall s)(\forall \ s')$ $(s \subseteq NT)$ (s' $\subseteq NT$) ((s' $\subset s$) ((to_be_test (s) = $true$) $\Rightarrow$ (to_be_test (s') = $true$)).

Proof of Lemma 3.

Let $X = t(s)$ and $Y = t(s')$. Since $s' \subset s$ we have $t(s) \subset t(s')$ and, by Lemma 5, we have that $t(s') \rightarrow t(s)$. But $t(s)$ is the test for K, i.e., $t(s) \rightarrow K$. Consequently, we have $t(s') \rightarrow t(s) \rightarrow K$. This means that $t(s')$ is the test for K.♠

Using Background Algorithm for Inferring All GIRTs

Background Algorithm can be used for inferring all the GIRTs contained in a GMRT for a given classification K. The idea of this algorithm consists in enlarging collections of attributes by using the same inductive rule that has been used for enlarging collections of examples' indices.

Every collection consisting of $q+1$ attributes is generated only once and only if there have been obtained all its sub-collections containing q attributes. Enlarging a collection of attributes is admissible if it is irredundant and it is not a test for a given classification. If an obtained collection of attributes is a test, then it is irredundant one and it is a good test because it is included in a given maximally redundant good test for K. It is inserted in the set test (T, K).

Using Background Algorithm for inferring GIRTs is based on Lemma 6 and Lemma 7.

Let $X = \{A_1, A_2, \ldots, A_m\}$ be a collection of attributes such that X is a GMRT for a given classification K and s be a subset of X. The function to_be_irredundant(s) is defined as follows:

to_be_irredundant(s)::= if for $(\forall A_i)\,(A_i \in s)\,P(s) \neq P(s/A_i)$ then *true* else *false*,
where $P(s)$ and $P(s\backslash A_i)$ designate the partitions of T, generated by the collections s and $s\backslash A_i$, respectively.

Lemma 6. $(\forall s)(\forall s')(s \subseteq X)(s' \subseteq X)(s \subset s')$ ((to_be_irredundant(s') = *true*) $\Rightarrow$ (to_be_irredundant(s) = *true*)).

Lemma 7. $(\forall q)(2 \leq q \leq nt)$ (to_be_irredundant $(\{i_1, \ldots, i_q\})$ = *true*) $\Rightarrow$ $(\forall j)\,(1 \leq j \leq q)$ to_be_irredundant $(\{i_1, \ldots, i_{(j-1)}, i_{(j+1)}, \ldots, i_q\})$ = *true*.

We use the following variant of the function to_be_test(s):

to_be_test(s)::= if $P(s) * P(K) = P(s)$ then *true* else *false*.

Background Algorithm for Inferring all GIRTs Contained in a GMRT for a Given Classification K.

```
Input: q = 1, T, K, X = {A₁, A₂,…, Aₘ} - a GMRT for K, S(irredundant
- q) = {{A₁}, {A₂}, ...,{Aₘ}} - the set of irredundant collections of
attributes with the cardinality equal q, q = 1.

Output: test(T,K) - the set of all GIRTs containing in X.

Sq::= S(irredundant - q);
```

1.1 Construct $S(test-q) = \{s = \{A_{i1}, \ldots, A_{iq}\}: (s \in S_q) \;\&\; (\text{to\_be\_test}(s) = true)\}$;

1.2 Reduce S_q:

$S_q ::= S_q \setminus S(test-q)$;

While $\|S_q\| \geq q + 1$ do 2.

$S(q + 1) ::= $ 2.1.

$\{s = \{A_{i1}, \ldots, A_{i(q + 1)}\}: (\forall j)\ (1 \leq j \leq q + 1)\ (A_{i1}, \ldots, A_{i(j-1)}, A_{i(j + 1)}, \ldots, A_{i(q + 1)}\} \in S_q\}$;

Construct $S(irredundant - (q +1))$:   2.2.

$S(irredundant - (q+1)) ::= \{s \in S(q + 1): \text{to\_be\_irredundant}(s) = true\}$;

$q ::= q + 1$;   2.3.

$max ::= q$;   2.4.

end while

$test(T, K) ::= \emptyset$; 3.

4. While $q \leq max$ do

4.1. $test(T, K) ::= test(T, K) \cup \{s: s = \{A_{i1}, \ldots, A_{is}\} \in S(test-q)\}$;

4.2. $q ::= q + 1$; 4.2.

end while

end

Part 2 of Background Algorithm can be used for inferring all implicative dependencies for a given value of attribute (the name of a given class of positive example in a given classification of examples). For this goal, it is quite enough to define the set test-1(T,K) as the set of positive examples and the set *FM* as the set of negative examples in a given classification. By *t*, we shall denote a collection of attribute values and $s(t)$ will be the set of indices of examples in which *t* is included. The function to_be_test(*s*) can be defined by two methods as follows. The first method is:

to_be_test(s)::= if $(\forall F')(F' \in FM)$ $t(s) \nsubseteq F'$ then *true* else *false*.

By the second method, the function to_be_test(s) is defined as directly checking the partition dependency between the collection of values t and the given classification into positive in negative examples:

to_be_test(s)::= if $s(t) \cap s(+) = s(t)$ then *true* else *false*,

where $s(+)$ is the set of indices of positive examples. Inferring implicative dependencies from examples based on Background Algorithm is described in (Naidenova et al., 1995), (Naidenova, 2005).

The problem of discovering association rules has recently received much attention in the data mining community. The following is a formal definition of the problem (Agrawal & Srikant, 1994): let $T = \{i_1, i_2, ..., i_m\}$ be a set of literals, called items. Let D be a set of transactions, where each transaction t is a set of items such that $t \subseteq T$. A unique identifier ID is associated with each transaction. The rule $X \rightarrow Y$ holds in the transaction set D with confidence c if $c\%$ of transactions in D that contain X also contain Y. The rule $X \rightarrow Y$ has support s in the transaction set D if $s\%$ of transactions in D contain $X \cup Y$.

Given a set of transactions D, the problem of mining association rules is to generate all association rules that have support and confidence greater than given minimum support (called minsup) and minimum confidence (called minconf). In (Agrawal & Srikant, 1994), two algorithms, Apriori and AprioriTid, have been presented for finding this problem. These algorithms generate firstly the candidate itemsets based on the idea that any subset of a large itemset must be large too. Therefore, the candidate itemsets having k items can be generated by joining large itemsets having $k - 1$ items, and deleting those that contain any subset that is not large. It is clear that Background Algorithm can be used for mining all association rules from a given set D of transactions.

Using Background Algorithm for Inferring All BIRTs Based on the Multiplication Operation of Partition Lattice

An original algorithm for finding all the best diagnostic tests for a given classification has been advanced in (Megretzskaya, 1988). In this algorithm, a partition lattice is directly constructed on attributes as generators of this lattice. The idea of the best diagnostic test goes back to the search for the best approximation of a given classification K on a given set of examples. If it is impossible to obtain a test generating exactly the same partition of examples as classification K, then the best test will be one that generates a classification of examples with the minimal number of classes included in classes of classification K. Thus we define the best test as follows.

Definition 7.9. An attributes' collection X, $X \subseteq U$ is the best test for K if it is a test for K and the implication $(\forall Y)(P(Y) \subset P(K) \Rightarrow \|P(X)\| \le \|P(Y)\|$ is satisfied, where $\|P(s)\|$ is the number of classes of partition $P(s)$.

The task of inferring all best tests is formulated as follows. Let $\{A_i\}$, $i = 1,..., n$ be a set of attributes and T be a table of examples with a given classification K of examples. It is necessary to find all irredundant best tests $t = \{A_{i1}, A_{i2}, ..., A_{ip}\}$, for K satisfying the following conditions:

1) t – is one of the best tests,
2) t – is an irredundant collection of attributes, i. e. $(\forall t') (t' \subset t) \Rightarrow P(t') \ne P(t)$,

3) $2 \le p \le \text{MAXLEN}$, where p – is the number of attributes in t and MAXLEN is a given constant limited the cardinality of t.

The following characteristic of attributes' collections is introduced for controlling best tests construction: $kl(X) = \|P(XK)\|$ where $P(XK)$ is the partition induced on T by a collection of attributes $\{X \cup K\}$. We observe that any collection X of attributes can not generate partition of the set T having the number of classes less than $kl(X)$.

The following lemmas underlie the generation of attributes' collections with increasing characteristic kl.

Lemma 8. For any proper subset Y of X we have $kl(Y) \le kl(X)$.

Proof of Lemma 8. Let $Z = X \backslash Y$. $kl(Y) = \|P(YK)\| \le \|P(YKZ)\| = \|P(XK)\| = kl(X)$.♠

The next lemma follows directly from lemma 8.

Lemma 9. Let $U = \{A_1, A_2, \ldots, A_n\}$. $(\forall q)(2 \le q \le n)$ $(kl(\{A_{i1}, \ldots, A_{iq}\}) = k) \Rightarrow (\forall j)$ $(1 \le j \le q)(kl(\{A_{i1}, \ldots, A_{i(j-1)}, A_{i(j+1)}, \ldots, A_{iq}\}) \le k)$.

Lemma 10. Let $U = \{A_1, A_2, \ldots, A_n\}$, and $(A_{i1}, A_{i2}, \ldots, A_{in})$ be a permutation of $(A_1, A_2, \ldots, A_n)$ ordered by increasing the characteristic $kl(\{A_i\})$. Let $k = kl(\{A_{i2}\})$. Then there does not exist a test for K the cardinality of which not less than 2 and the number of classes in the partition generated by it on examples is less than k.

Proof of Lemma 10. Let $(\exists X)$ $X = \{A_{i1}, A_{i2}, \ldots, A_{iq}\}: (2 \le q \le n)$ & $(kl(X) = k_1)$ & $(k_1 < k)$.

Then, by lemma 8, we have $(\forall m)$ $(1 \le m \le q)$ $kl(\{A_{im}\}) \le k_1 < k$.

But there is only one attribute $A_{i1}: kl(\{A_{i1}\}) < k \Rightarrow q = 1$.

Then $q \le 2$ and, simultaneously, it ≥ 2, This contradiction proves that

$$(\forall X)\ (X = \{A_{i1}, A_{i2}, \ldots, A_{iq}\})\ (2 \le q \le n) \Rightarrow kl(X) \ge k.♠$$

The algorithm of inferring all best tests begins with the initial value $k = kl(\{A_{i2}\})$ (see, please, lemma 10) and it looks for the best tests with number of classes equal to k. Then k is increased by 1 and the same task of search for tests with number of classes equal to $k+1$ is solved. The process of increasing k by 1 and searching for test works till at least one best test will be found. The current value of k is the minimal possible number of classes generated by the good tests for K.

The algorithm consists of the following steps.

Step 1. Checking whether the necessary initial conditions are satisfied by the data (examples of T). If $(\exists i)$: $\{A_i\}$ satisfying conditions 1) and 2) or $\{A_1, A_2, \ldots, A_n\}$ is not a test for K, then the algorithm terminates its work.

Step 2. Calculating the initial value of k: $k = kl(\{A_{i2}\})$, where $(A_{i1}, \ldots, A_{in})$ is the permutation of $(A_1, \ldots, A_n)$ ordered by increasing the characteristic $kl(\{A_j\})$.

Step 3. For current q, beginning with $q = 2$, we construct all possible attributes' collections of the cardinality $(q + 1)$. Collection of the cardinality $q + 1$ can be constructed if 1) There exist all its sub-collections of the cardinality q, 2) all its sub-collections of the cardinality q generate partitions into not greater than k classes and at least one of these sub-collections generates a partition into k classes. The same process is performed for $q = 3, 4, \ldots$ and so on till this constructions are possible ($q + 1$ must not be greater than MAXLEN).

Each new collection is checked whether it is a test for K. If it is a test and it generates the partition of T into k classes then it is memorized in the set test(T, K). If it is a test but it generates a partition into the number of classes greater than k, then it is memorized in the set SAVE of tests.

Step 4. All tests with $kl(X) = k$ from SAVE are transferred into the set test(T, K).

Step 5. If the set test(T, K) is not empty then the task is over. If the set test(T, K) is empty and $q =$ MAXLEN the algorithm ends the work without receiving any best test for K. If the set test(T, K) is empty and $q <$ MAXLEN, k is increased by 1 and the algorithm repeats Step 3.

By the law of test's generation for $q = 1, 2, 3, \ldots$, and the consideration that the redundant test has a number of attributes greater than irredundant one with the same partition, the tests generated by this algorithm will obligatory be irredundant tests for K.

Background Algorithm for Inferring the BIRTs for a Given Classification K

```
Input: q = 1, U = {A₁,…, Aₙ}, S_q = {{A₁}, {A₂},...,{Aₙ }}, T.
Output: the set test(T,K) of the best tests for K.
Input: q = 1, U = {A₁,…, Aₙ}, S_q = {{A₁}, {A₂},...,{Aₙ }}, T.
Output: the set test(T,K) of the best tests for K.
1. (∀s)(s∈ S_q) do
            if to_be_test (s) = true then test(T,K)::= test(T,K)
∪ s;
1.1. if test(T,K) ≠ Ø then stop;
2. (∀s)(s∈ S_q) do
2.1. Calculating kl(s);
2.2. Ordering s ∈ S_q by increasing the value kl(s): result is a per-
mutation S_q = {{A_i1}, {A_i2},…, {A_in}};
2.3. k::= kl({A_i2});
3. While q ≤ MAXLEN and ||S_q|| ≥ q + 1 do
        3.1. Constructing S(q + 1) =
            {s ={A_i1, ..., A_i(q + 1)}: (∀j) (1 ≤ j ≤ q + 1) (A_i1, ...,
A_i(j-1), A_i(j + 1), ..., A_i(q + 1)) ∈ S_q and (∀j) (1 ≤ j ≤ q
1) kl ({A_i1, ..., A_i(j-1), A_i(j + 1), ..., A_i(q + 1)}) ≤ k, ∃ j: kl ({A_i1,
..., A_i(j-1), A_i(j + 1), ..., A_i(q + 1)}) = k};
        3.2. Constructing test(T, K) = test(T,K) ∪ {s ∈ S(q + 1): to_
be_test(s) = true and kl(s) = k};
        3.3 Constructing SAVE ::={s ∈ S(q + 1): to_be_test(s) = true
and kl(s) > k};
    3.4 Reducing S(q+1):
            S(q+1) ::= S(q +1)\{test(T, K) ∪ SAVE};
        3.5. q::= q + 1;
            end while
    4.   if q ≤ MAXLEN then k = k + 1;
            4.1. If ∃ s, s ∈ SAVE, kl(s) = k, then s is transferred
from SAVE to test(T,K);
            4.2 if test(T,K) ≠ Ø then stop;
go to 3;
end
```

Computing characteristic $kl(s)$ and the function to_be_test(s) related to calculating the product of the partitioning $P(s)$ and $P(K)$:

$kl(s) = \|P(s) * P(K)\|$;

to_be_test$(s) ::=$ if $P(s) * P(K) = P(s)$ then *true* else *false*.

Computing $P(s) * P(K)$ is based on constructing the partition $P(s \cup K)$, as like computing $P(s)$ is based on computing the partition $P(\cup \{A_j\}, j = 1, 2, \ldots i_s)$ where i_s is the cardinality of s, and $A_j, j = 1, 2, \ldots i_s$ are the constituent elements of s.

We shall consider the details of computing the product of partitions in the following part of this chapter. Now we consider an instance of BIRTs construction for the collection of examples with a given classification K, represented by Table 16.

We have in this task:

$q = 1, S_q = \{\{A_1\}, \{A_2\}, \{A_3\}, \{A_4\}\}$,

$kl(s), s \in S_q$: $kl(A_1) = 4, kl(A_2) = 3, kl(A_3) = 4, kl(A_4) =$ 6.

The permutation of $S_q = \{\{A_2\}, \{A_1\}, \{A_3\}, \{A_4\}\}, k = 4, q = 2$;

$S_q = \{\{A_1A_2\}, \{A_3A_2\}, \{A_3A_1\}\}$;

A_1A_2 is not a test for K, $kl(A_1A_2) = 5$;

A_3A_2 is not a test for K, $kl(A_3A_2) = 5$;

A_3A_1 is not a test for K, $kl(A_3A_1) =$ 6.

$q = 3, S_q = \varnothing$,

If MAXLEN $= 2$, then the algorithm terminates the work without obtaining any best test for K: there do not exist the tests with $k = 4$ and $q = 2$ (see, please, the results in Table 17).

Table 16. The examples with its classification for inferring BIRTs

T (index of examples)	A_1	A_2	A_3	A_4	K
1	4	5	3	3	1
2	5	5	2	2	1
3	5	5	2	2	1
4	4	3	4	4	2
5	2	3	2	2	2
6	4	5	3	1	2
7	4	3	2	3	2

Table 17. The result of inferring BIRTs for q = 1 and q = 2, MAXLEN = 2

$S(q=1) \cup S(q=2)$	A_2	A_1	A_3	A_1A_2	A_3A_2	A_4	A_3A_1
$kl(s)$	3	4	4	5	5	6	6
Test?	No	No	No	No	No	No	No

Table 18. The result of inferring BIRTs for MAXLEN = 4, q = 2, and k = 6

$S(q=1) \cup S(q=2)$	A_1	A_3	A_1A_2	A_3A_2	A_4	A_3A_1	A_4A_1	A_4A_3
$kl(s)$	4	4	5	5	6	6	6	6
Test?	No	No	No	No	No	No	No	No

If MAXLEN = 3, then the algorithm goes on:

$k = k+1 = 5$;

$q = 2, S_q = \varnothing$;

$q = 3, S_q = \varnothing$;

There are not tests with $k = 5$ and $q = 3$.
If MAXLEN = 4, then the algorithm goes on (the results are in Table 18):

$k = 6$;

$q = 2, S_q = \{\{A_4A_2\}, \{A_4A_1\}, \{A_4A_3\}\}$;

$kl(A_4A_2) = 6, kl(A_4A_1) = 6, kl(A_4A_3) = 6$;

A_4A_2 is a test for K, A_4A_1, A_4A_3 are not tests for K.

One test with $k = 6$ is found, but it is possible that there are the equivalent tests of greater length.

Table 19. The first method of partitions' representation

S	P	ms	mk
A	S1	1	1
B	S1	2	1
C	S2	3	3
D	S2	4	3
E	S1	5	1
F	S3	6	6

Table 20. The second methods of partitions' representation

S	P	ms	mk
A	S1	1	1
B	S1	2	1
C	S2	3	2
D	S2	4	2
E	S1	5	1
F	S3	6	3

We have, with $k = 6$, $q = 3$, $S_q = \{\{A_1A_3A_4\}, \{A_1A_2A_3\}\}$, where $\{A_1A_3A_4\}$ is a test.

Since a test with $k = 6$ is found, the algorithm is over.

The computation complexity of the algorithm is of O ($n\uparrow$MAXLEN) in the worst case, when $kl(\{A_i\})$, $1 \leq i \leq n$ are equal or in proximity to n, or the task has not a solution.

Implementation of Partition Lattice Operations

The effectiveness of multiplication and addition operations on partitions depends on the way of partition representation. Two ways of partition representation have been given in (Naidenova, 1977).

Let S be a fixed set of elements and P be a partition of S into disjoint classes S_1, S_2, S_3, ..., S_k, where k is the number of classes. Let the order of elements of S be fixed. Consider the relation $R \subseteq N \times N$, mapping the index of an element of S to the number (index) of the class in P containing this element. The request of the equality for the representations of equivalent partitions implies a special method of indexing classes in partitions. The indexing is performed as follows: same values are replaced by same integers and different values are replaced with different integers.

The first method of indexing classes: the number of class is the index of the first in the order element of S belonging to this class. This method is illustrated by Table 19.

The second method of indexing classes: classes in partition are numerated with the use of the sequence of integers 1, 2, ..., k. Class, containing the first element of S has the least integer. Every next class has the integer increased by 1. This method is illustrated by Table 20.

Partition is represented by the pairs of columns ms, mk the first of which contains the ordered sequence of indices of the elements of S, the second one contains the indices of corresponding classes of P.

Table 21. The multiplication operation for the first method of partitions' representations

S	mk1	mk2	mk3
1	1	1	1
2	2	1	2
3	3	3	3
4	3	3	3
5	2	1	2
6	6	6	6

Table 22. The multiplication operation for the second method of partitions' representations

S	mk1	mk2	mk3
1	1	1	1
2	2	1	2
3	3	2	3
4	3	2	3
5	2	1	2
6	4	3	4

If the order of elements of S is fixed, then it can use only one column mk for representation of partitions.

Computing the Product and Sum of Partitions. Operation of Multiplication

Let P_1 and P_2 be two partitions of S. We have to construct partition $P_3 = P_1 * P_2$. Let $\{mk_1 mk_2\}$ be the minor of two columns representing partitions P_1 and P_2, respectively.

It follows from the definition of multiplication operation on partitions (see, please, Chapter 6) that two different elements of S belongs to the same class in P_3, if and only if the pairs of indices corresponding to them in the representations of partitions P_1 и P_2 (indices of minor $\{mk_1 mk_2\}$) are identical. Hence, for implementing the multiplication operation, we have to ascribe same integer to the coincident lines of minor. The method of numeration of classes of P_3 must be identical to the method of numeration used for the partitions that are the arguments of operation.

The instances of multiplication operation for both methods of partitions' representations are given in Table 21 and Table 22, respectively.

The Addition Operation

Let P_1 and P_2 be two partitions of S. We have to construct partition $P_4 = P_1 + P_2$. Let $\{mk_1 mk_2\}$ be the minor of two columns representing partitions P_1 and P_2, respectively.

It is follows from the definition of addition operation on partitions (see, please, Chapter 6) that two different elements of S belongs to different classes in partition P_4 if and only if the pairs of indices corresponding to them in representations of partitions P_1 и P_2 (indices of minor $\{mk_1 mk_2\}$) are not identical in both components and there is not a series of elements of S such that the pairs of indices corresponding to them in representations of partitions P_1 и P_2 would compose a chain of pairs $\{i_{k1} j_{k1}\} \{i_{k2} j_{k1}\} \{i_{k2} j_{k3}\}$ $\{i_{k3} j_{k3}\}$ ..... $\{i_{kn} j_{km}\}$ such that $i_{k1} = i_1, j_{km} = j_2$.

Hence, for implementing the addition operation, we have to ascribe same integer to every pairs of lines of minor coincident at least in one of components.

The method of numeration of classes of P_4 must be identical to the method of numeration used for the partitions that are arguments of operation.

The instances of addition operations for both methods of partitions' representations are given in Table 23 and Table 24, respectively.

The multiplication operation constructs the groups of lines of minor such that the lines belong to the same group if they are not distinguished by all the components, but every pair of lines belonging to different groups is distinguished at least by one component.

The addition operation solves a dual task: it constructs the groups of lines of minor such that the lines belong to different groups if they are different in both components and any pairs of lines not distinguished at least by one component must belong to the same group. The addition is generalization operation joining all similar objects and separating unique objects having no resemblance to everything else.

Note, that in our algorithms, we use the second method of partition representation.

Implementation of Multiplication Operation

Let $m = \{mk_1, mk_2\}$ be a minor of two columns representing partitions P_1 and P_2 of the set S and *Index* be a column of indices of the elements of S. Let n be the number of elements of S. A line of the minor can be considered as one element by its associating with two-digit decimal number. Thus, the minor will be a vector-column of integers.

Multiplication operation is an operation of grouping the values of the vector and it will be reduced to known algorithms of sorting. In this case, it is not necessary to transpose the elements of sorted vector m, instead of this it is possible to transpose the values of the auxiliary vector *Index*.

The quickest sorting is the digital sorting (Aho et all, 1979). In the general case the elements of m are k - component corteges of integers. If the number of pair-wise different values of each component is previously known, then the method of lexicographical sorting can be used as the basis of multiplication operation on partitions. The exact algorithm of the sorting is given in (Aho et al., 1979). Note that the computational complexity of this algorithm is linear with respect to the number of components of m.

Table 23. The addition operation for the first method of partitions' representations

S	mk1	mk2	mk3
1	1	1	1
2	2	1	1
3	3	3	3
4	3	3	3
5	2	1	1
6	6	6	6

Table 24. The addition operation for the second method of partitions' representations

S	mk1	mk2	mk3
1	1	1	1
2	2	1	1
3	3	2	2
4	3	2	2
5	2	1	1
6	4	3	3

For 2–component cortege, the number of necessary comparisons will be equal $n * (q_1 + q_2)$, where q_1, q_2 are the numbers of different values of the first and the second component of m, respectively. With increasing n, the number of comparisons grows linearly and the estimation of computational complexity of lexicographical sorting is $0(n* q* k)$, where k – the number of components of sorted corteges, $q = \max\{q_i\}$, $i = 1, \ldots, k$, q_i – the number of different values of i–th component.

In some cases, the task of finding tests does not requires to obtain the product of partitions, it is sufficient to establish the fact that the partitions - operands are incomparable with respect to inclusion relation.

Inductive Rule for Extending Collections of q-Elements

Background Algorithm is an inductive algorithm based on a level wise manner of extending the collections of attributes, values of attributes or examples (indices of examples) such that collections of the size q are built from the collections of the size $q - 1$ of the previous level. Each collection can be built if only if, there are all its proper subsets at the previous level.

In different algorithms, we check the different properties of collections. These properties are "to be a test for a given classification of examples", "to be an irredundant collection of attributes (values)", "characteristic kl is satisfied by a collection of attributes". If a collection does not possess a required property, then it can be deleted from consideration. It strongly reduces the number of collections of all following levels to be built. The effectiveness of algorithms depends on the method of computing the following functions and the property (5):

(1) Function to_be_test(s)::= if $(\forall F')(F' \in FM)$ $t(s) \not\subset F'$, then *true* else *false*,
   where FM – the set of anti-tests, $t(s)$ – the intersection of all examples indices of which are in subset $s \in S$, S is the set of indices of all elements of test-$1(T,K)$ (tests of the first level);

(2) Function to_be_test(t)::= $(s(t) \subseteq S)$, then *true* else *false*,
   where $s(t) = \{i: i \in NTF, t \subseteq t_i, t_i \in \{$test-$1(T,K) \cup FM\}\}$, NTF – the set of indices of all elements belonging to the set $\{$test-$1(T,K) \cup FM\}$, S – the set of indices of the elements of test -$1(T,K)$.

(3) Function to_be_test(s) of direct checking the partition dependency between collection of attributes t and classification K: $P(t) * P(K) = P(t)$.

(4) Function to_be_irredundant(s)::= if for $(\forall A_i)$ $(A_i \in s)$ $P(s) \neq P(s \backslash A_i)$, then *true* else *false*;

(5) The property $kl(X) = \|P(X) * P(K)\|$.

In (4), (5), $P(s)$, $P(K)$ and $P(s \backslash A_i)$ denote the partitions of the set T generated by collections of attributes s, K and $s \backslash A_i$, respectively.

Function (1) has the greatest computation complexity. The effectiveness of functions (2) – (5) depends on the complexity of multiplication operation on partitions. As we see earlier, the computational complexity of this operation is linear with respect to the number of examples.

Another important factor influencing on computational complexity of Background Algorithm is the method of inductive generating of collections of attributes (values) or indices of examples in the level wise manner. Next, we shall consider the methods of realization of inductive rule for generating these collections.

The main algorithm has an essential disadvantage consisting in the necessity to generate all subsets of each element s of S_q, $q = 1, 2, \ldots, qmax$. But it is possible constructing directly an element $s \in S_q$, $s = \{i_1, i_2, \ldots, i_q\}$ without generating all of its subsets.

We consider some possible methods for forming subsets of $q + 1$ – elements from subsets of q – elements. All that is necessary is the following inductive rules where SN – the set containing all collections S_q of cardinality equal to q, $q = 1, \ldots, nt$, $S_q \subseteq S = \{1, \ldots, nt\}$ and $C_S(q)$ denotes the number of combinations of S on q.

(1) $q = 1, q + 1 = 2$;

    $s_q = \{i\}, s_{(q+1)} = \{i, j\}, (\forall j) (i \neq j, \{j\} \in SN$;

(2) $q = 2, q + 1 = 3$;

    $s_q = \{i, j\}, s_{(q+1)} = \{i, j, l\}$, where l different from i, j and such that there are in SN

       a)   two collections $s_1 = \{i, l\}, s_2 = \{j, l\}$ or

       b) $s = \{l\}$;

(3) $q = 3, q + 1 = 4$;

    $s_q = \{i, j, m\}, s_{(q+1)} = \{i, j, m, l\}$, where l different from i, j, m and such that there are in SN

       a)   three collections $s_1 = \{i, j, l\}, s_2 = \{i, m, l\}, s_3 = \{j, m, l\}$ or

       b)   three collections $s_1 = \{i, l\}, s_2 = \{j, l\}, s_3 = \{m, l\}$ or

       c) $s = \{l\}$;

    ......

(q) $q, q + 1$;

    $s_q = \{i_1, i_2, \ldots, i_q\}, s_{(q+1)} = \{i_1, i_2, \ldots, i_q, l\}$, where l different from $i_1, i_2, \ldots, i_q$ and such there are in SN

       a)   collections the number of which is equal to $C_S(q) = C_S(nt - q)$ and the cardinality of which is equal to q, such that $\{i_1, i_2, \ldots, i_{p-1}, i_{p+1}, \ldots, i_q, l\} \setminus \{i_p\}$ for all $p = 1, \ldots, q$ or

       b)   collections the number of which is equal to $C_S(q - 1) = C_S(nt - (q-1))$, the cardinality of which is equal to $q-1$, such that $\{i_1, i_2, \ldots, i_q, l\} \setminus \{i_{pi}, i_{pj}\}$ for all $\{pi, pj\} \subseteq \{1, \ldots, q\}$ or

       c)   collections the number of which is equal to $C_S(q - 2) = C_S(nt - (q-2))$, the cardinality of which is equal to $q-2$, such that $\{i_1, i_2, \ldots, i_q, l\} \setminus \{i_{pi}, i_{pj}, i_{pk}\}$ for all $\{pi, pj, pk\}, \{pi, pj, pk\} \subseteq \{1, 2, \ldots, q\}$ or

    ......

       d)   collections the number of which is equal to $C_S(1) = C_S(nt - 1)$, the cardinality of which is equal to 1, such that $\{l\}, l \notin \{i_1, i_2, \ldots, i_q\}$.

These inductive rules realize the method of mathematical (or complete) induction. The essence of this method consists in the following. Let an assertion be verified for a single special case, say, for $n = 1$. Let us suppose that we can demonstrate that from the validity of this assertion for $n = k$ the validity of it follows always for the next value of n, that is, for $n = k + 1$. Next, we reason as follows: we have verified our assertion for $n = 1$, but then, by what has been proven, it will be true for $n = 1 + 1 = 2$. Now, since it is valid for $n = 2$, it will also be valid for $n = 2 + 1 = 3$, and so forth, which means that it will be true for all values of n. It follows from this reasoning that the assertion for $n = k + 1$ can be true if and only if it is true for all previous value of n.

Our Background Algorithm, based on this method of reasoning, is not effective, but it allows demonstrating the equivalence of different tasks of mining functional, implicative, and associative dependencies. The algorithm is not changed, only the assertions are changed with the rules for checking their validity. The search for effective realization of Background Algorithm is the very important goal of our investigation. Consider several ways of generating collections of the cardinality $q+1$ from collections of the cardinality q.

SEARCHING FOR AN EFFECTIVE REALIZATION OF BACKGROUND ALGORITHM

An Algorithm of Extending Collections of q-Elements

We consider an algorithm of extending q-elements collections of indices under their lexicographical ordering. Let us introduce the following denotation.

$NT = \{1, \ldots, nt\}$;

$\|S\|$- the cardinality of S;

$S[j], j = 1, \ldots, \|S\|$- an element of S with the index j;

s_q – a collection of indices of the cardinality q;

S_q - the set of collections s_q;

$S_q(s)$ – the subset of collections of S_q with the cardinality q obtained by extending s, $s \in S_{q-1}$, $s \subseteq NT$;

$cand(s)$ – the set of indices admissible for $(+1)$ – extending s.

Prefix(s) - the set of indices differs from s by only one index and this index is the last in s.

The principal procedure of the algorithm is a procedure of generating all collections s_{q+1} from a collection s_q. When s_{q+1} is built, then it is determined whether $t(s_{q+1})$ is a test for a given classification or not. If the answer is positive, then s_{q+1} is memorized in the set $S_{q+1}(s_q)$, the index with the use of which this extension was obtained is memorized in the set $cand(s_q)$. Otherwise, s_{q+1} is deleted from consideration and the formation of sequential $(+1)$ – extension of s_q is produced. If $cand(s_q)$ is empty, then the next element from the set S_q is chosen together with the corresponding set of indices – the candidates for extending it. The process of extension continues, until the set S_q is exhausted.

Let us illustrate the described process. In our Main Current Example (see, please, Background Algorithm in this chapter) we consider the following two-component collections of indices obtained by extending the collection $s = \{2\}$:

$prefix ::= 2$; $prefix \in$ Prefix;

$S_q(\{2\}) = \{\{2,3\}, \{2,4\}, \{2,7\}, \{2,8\}, \{2,10\}, \{2,12\}, \{2,14\}\}$.

$cand(\{2\}) = \{3, 4, 7, 8, 10, 12, 14\}$.

$s_q = S_q(\{2\})[1] = \{2,3\}$;

$S_{q+1}(\{2,3\}) ::= \varnothing$;

$cand(\{2,3\}):: = \{4, 7, 10, 12, 14\};$

$s_{q+1}::= \{2,3,4\};$

Since $t(\{2,3,4\})$ is a test s_{q+1} is memorized:

$\{2,3,4\} \rightarrow S_{q+1}(\{2,3\});$

$s_{q+1}::= \{2,3,7\};$

Since $t(\{2,3,7\})$ is a test s_{q+1} is memorized:

$\{2,3,7\} \rightarrow S_{q+1}(\{2,3\});$

And so on, while the set $cand(\{2,3\})$ will be exhausted.
As a result, we obtain:

$S_{q+1}(\{2,3\}) = \{\{2,3,4\}, \{2,3,7\}\}, cand(\{2,3, 4\}) = \{ 7\}; cand(\{2,3, 7\}) = \varnothing;$

Further:

$S_{q+1}(\{2,4\}) = \{\{2,4,7\}\}, cand(\{2,4,7\}) = \varnothing;$

$S_{q+1}(2,7) = \{\{2,7,8\}\}, cand(\{2,7,8\}) = \varnothing;$

$S_{q+1}(\{2,12\}) = \{\{2,12,14\}\}, cand(\{2,12,14\}) = \varnothing;$

and

$S_{q+1}(\{2\}) = \{\{2,3,4\}, \{2,3,7\}, \{2,4,7\}, \{2,7,8\}, \{2,12,14\}\}.$

If, after obtaining all the extensions s_{q+1} of s_q, the set $cand(s_q)$ is empty or it contains only one element, then the further extension of s_{q+1} is impossible.

By the induction rules of creating collection s, we must have all its proper subsets at the current moment of the functioning of algorithm. Assume that $j \in cand(s_q)$) for some $s_q = \{i_1, i_2, ..., i_q\}$. Collection $s_{q+1} = \{i_1, i_2, ..., i_q, j\}$ can be constructed if collections $\{i_1, j\}, \{i_2, j\}, ..., \{i_{q-1}, j\}, \{i_q, j\}$ can be constructed and they correspond to the tests. Collection $\{i_k, j\}$ can be constructed if $j \in cand(i_k)$, for all $k \in \{1, 2, ..., q\}$. The sets of $cand(i)$ for all elements $i \in S$ are obtained and memorized in the beginning of test's construction. For example, we consider the situation where

$S_{q+1}(\{2,3\}) = \{\{2,3,4\}, \{2,3,7\}\}, cand(\{2,3, 4\}) = \{ 7\}; cand(\{2,3, 7\}) = \varnothing;$

For $s = \{2,3,4\}$, it is possible only one extension equal to $\{2,3,4,7\}$. Because of index 7 belongs to *cand*($\{2\}$) we have to check whether this index belongs to *cand*($\{4\}$) or not. If the reply is positive, then collection of indices $\{2,3,4,7\}$ can corresponds to a test. If the reply is negative, then this collection must not be considered.

An analogous procedure is used in the algorithm TANE for effective generating functional and approximate functional dependencies in relational databases (Huhtala et al., 1999):

Procedure GENERATE_NEXT_LEVEL (L_q)

```
1.  L_{q+1}::=∅
2.  for each K ∈ PREFIX_BLOCKS(L_q)
3.  for each {Y, Z} ⊆ K, Y ≠ Z do
4.          X::= Y ∪ Z
5.          if for all A ∈ X, X \{A} ∈ L_q, then
6.              L_{q+1}::= L_{q+1} ∪ {X}
7.  return L_{q+1}.
```

The procedure PREFIX_BLOCKS(L_q) divides the set L_q into disjoint blocks as follows. Let $X \in L_q$ be a lexicographically ordered collection of attributes. Two collections $X, Y \in L_q$ belongs to one and only one block, if they have the same prefix of the length equal to $q - 1$, i.e. they differ by only one attribute and this attribute is the last one in these collections. Elements of blocks are also lexicographically ordered. The lexicographical ordering on L_q makes it easy to construct these prefix blocks.

The ideas of this procedure of the algorithm TANE goes back to the work (Agraval, et al., 1996). Detailed explanation of the algorithm is given in the work (Mannila, & Toivonen, 1997). The computational complexity of the algorithm depends on the number of collections generated at each q – level. Denote by N_{max} the number of collections of a level containing the greatest quantity of collections (N_{max} can be said the size of this level). Analogously, we can determine the size of each level as the number of collections of this level. Let N_{sum} be the summary size of all levels. Then in the worst case we have: $N_{sum} = O(2^{|S|})$ and $N_{max} = O(2^{|S|} / \sqrt{|S|})$.

A Structure of Interconnected Lists for Implementing Background Algorithm

The inductive rules can be used not only for extending collections, but also for cutting off both the elements of S and the collections themselves containing these deleted elements. If element j enters in s_{q+1}, then it must enter in q proper subsets of s_{q+1}. If we observe that j enters in only one doublet (pair), then it cannot enter in any triplet. If we observe that j enters in only one triplet, then it cannot enter in any quadruplet and so on. If an element enters in two and only two doublets, it means that it will enter only in one triplet. If an element enters in three and only three doublets, it can enter in only one quadruplet.

These inductive reasoning are applicable to constructing triplets from doublets, quadruplets from triplets and so on. For instance, if a doublet enters in two and only two triplets, then it can enters in one quadruplet. If a triplet enters in two and only two quadruplets, then it can enter in only one collection containing five elements. The removal from the examination of a certain element (collection) draws the removal of the collections (doublets, triplets, quadruplets,...) into which it enters.

Let us name the procedure of the inductive rule application for the removal of elements and their collections the procedure of "winnowing". It is convenient to realize this procedure with the use of a Matrix of Correspondences between indices of the set NT and the collections of indices $s \in S$. The columns of this matrix will be associated with elements of NT, the rows of it will be associated with collections of

Table 25. The matrix of correspondences for the set S(test-2) of 2-component collections

Number of collection	Collection	9	5	6	14	10	1	11	8	12	3	7	4	2
1	(9,11)	1						1						
2	(1,5)		1				1							
3	(5,12)		1							1				
4	(4,6)			1									1	
5	(6,8)			1					1					
6	(6,11)			1				1						
7	(1,14)				1		1							
8	(2,14)				1									1
9	(12,14)				1					1				
10	(2,10)					1								1
11	(3,10)					1					1			
12	(8,10)					1			1					
13	(1,2)						1							1
14	(1,4)						1						1	
15	(1,7)						1					1		
16	(1,12)						1			1				
17	(3,11)							1			1			
18	(4,11)							1					1	
19	(7,11)							1				1		
20	(8,11)							1	1					
21	(2,8)								1					1
22	(3,8)								1		1			
23	(4,8)								1				1	
24	(7,8)								1			1		
25	(2,12)									1				1
26	(3,12)									1	1			
27	(4,12)									1			1	
28	(7,12)									1		1		
29	(2,3)										1			1
30	(3,4)										1		1	
31	(3,7)										1	1		
32	(2,7)											1		1
33	(4,7)											1	1	
34	(2,4)												1	1

elements *S*. An entrance {*i*, *j*} in this matrix is equal 1, if index associated with column *j* is enters in a collection *s* associated with row *i*.

Returning to our Main Current Example, consider the Matrix of Correspondences for the set *S*(*test*-2) of 2-component collections (Table 25). In this matrix, the columns are ordered by increasing the number of collections associated with the columns.

Index 9 enters in one and only one doublet, hence (9,11) cannot be included in any triplet. We can delete the corresponding column and row. We conclude also that collection of indices (9,11) corresponds to a maximally redundant good test.

Index 5 enters in two and only two doublets, hence it is included in only one triplet (1,5,12). This triplet corresponds to a maximally redundant good test because index 5 cannot be included in any quadruplet. We can delete the corresponding column and rows 2, 3.

Index 6 enters in three and only three doublets, hence it is included in only one quadruplet (4,6,8,11). This collection corresponds to a maximally redundant good test, because this extension with index 6 cannot be included in any collection consisting of five indices. We can delete the corresponding column and rows 4, 5, 6.

By analogous reason, we conclude that collection (1,2,12,14) corresponds to a maximally redundant good test and that we can delete the corresponding column and rows 7, 8, 9.

In order to find the maximal set of indices in which an index *j* is included the following operation is performed: maxcollection(j) = {{∪ row$_i$}, *j* appears in row$_i$, *i* = 1,, *Nr*} where *Nr* is the number of rows in the Matrix of Correspondences.

Index 10 enters in three and only three doublets hence it is included in only one quadruplet (2,3,8,10). This collection does not correspond to a test. In this case, we have to construct all the triplets with index 10. These triplets (2 8 10), (2 3 10), (3 8 10) do not correspond to tests, it means that collections (2,10), (3,10), (8,10) correspond to the maximally redundant good tests. Index 10 can be deleted together with rows 10, 11, 12. Currently, we have generated the following 7 collections: (1,5,12), (4,6,8,11), (1,2,12,14), (2,3,8,10), (2,3,10), (2,8,10), (3,8,10). Table 26 shows the reduced Matrix of Correspondences.

Index 1 enters in 4 doublets. In this case, we construct the following triplets including index 1: (1,2,4), (1,2,7), (1,2,12), (1,4,7), (1,4,12), (1,7,12). Only two triplets correspond to the tests: (1,4,7) and (1, 2, 12). We conclude that index 1 cannot be included in any quadruplet; hence this index can be deleted from consideration with rows 13, 14, 15, 16.

We also can conclude that collection (1,4,7) is unique and it corresponds to a maximally redundant good test, but collection (1, 2, 12) can be deleted because it is not a good test.

Analogously, the consideration of index 11 leads to constructing the following collections: (3,4,11), (3,7,11), (3,8,11), (4,7,11), (4,8,11), (7,8,11) from which only two collections (7, 8,11) and (4,8,11) correspond to the maximally redundant tests.

We conclude that index 11 cannot be included in any quadruplet; hence this index can be deleted from consideration with rows 17, 18, 19, 20.

We also conclude that collection (7,8,11) is unique and it corresponds to a maximally redundant good test, but collection (4, 8, 11) can be deleted because it is not a good test.

Currently, we have constructed 7 + 12 = 19 collections. Table 27 shows the reduced Matrix of Correspondences.

With **index 8**, the following collection can be constructed: (2,3,8), (2,4,8), (2,7,8), (3,4,8), (3,7,8), (4,7,8). But only collection (2,7,8) corresponds to a test. We conclude that this collection corresponds to the maximally redundant good test. Index 8 can be deleted together with rows 21, 22, 23, 24.

Table 26. The reduced matrix of correspondences (step 1)

Number of collection	Collection	1	11	8	12	3	7	4	2
13	(1,2)	1							1
14	(1,4)	1						1	
15	(1,7)	1					1		
16	(1,12)	1			1				
17	(3,11)		1			1			
18	(4,11)		1					1	
19	(7,11)		1				1		
20	(8,11)		1	1					
21	(2,8)			1					1
22	(3,8)			1		1			
23	(4,8)			1				1	
24	(7,8)			1			1		
25	(2,12)				1				1
26	(3,12)				1	1			
27	(4,12)				1			1	
28	(7,12)				1		1		
29	(2,3)					1			1
30	(3,4)					1		1	
31	(3,7)					1	1		
32	(2,7)						1		1
33	(4,7)						1	1	
34	(2,4)							1	1

For **index 12**, the following collections can be constructed: (2,3,12), (2,4,12), (2,7,12), (3,4,12), (3,7,12), (4,7,12). Only two collection (3,7,12), (4,7,12) correspond to the tests. Because index 12 is included only in two triplets and cannot be included in any quadruplet we conclude that collections (3,7,12), (4,7,12) correspond to the maximally redundant tests. Index 12 can be deleted together with rows 25, 26, 27, 28.

Currently, we have constructed 19 + 12 = 31 collections. Table 28 shows the reduced correspondent matrix.

Now collection (2,3,4,7), the union of all remaining collections, corresponds to a maximally redundant test, hence the process of creating triplets is over. We have not any variant for constructing collections containing 4 indices, so the process of finding tests is over.

Currently, we have constructed 31 + 1 = 32 collections. Without the procedure of winnowing, it was necessary in Background Algorithm to form 91 + 38 + 3= 91 +41 = 132 collections, where 91 collections of two indices, 38 collections of three indices, and 3 collections – of four indices. The application of winnowing reduced the total quantity of the considered collections to 123: 91 + 32 = 123.

Table 27. The reduced matrix of correspondences (step 2)

Number of collection	Collection	8	12	3	7	4	2
21	(2,8)	1					1
22	(3,8)	1		1			
23	(4,8)	1				1	
24	(7,8)	1			1		
25	(2,12)		1				1
26	(3,12)		1	1			
27	(4,12)		1			1	
28	(7,12)		1		1		
29	(2,3)			1			1
30	(3,4)			1		1	
31	(3,7)			1	1		
32	(2,7)				1		1
33	(4,7)				1	1	
34	(2,4)					1	1

A Special Kind of Network Structure for Implementing Background Algorithm

The idea of the following algorithm is based on the functioning of a combinatory network structure, whose elements correspond to the subsets of the finite set S of indices generated in the algorithm. The elements are located in the network along the layers, so that each q - layer consists of the elements corresponding to the subsets of the cardinality equal to q. All the elements of q–layer have the same number q of inputs or connections with the elements of previous $(q - 1)$–level. Each element "is excited" only when all the connected with it elements of previous layer are active The weight of connection going from the excited element is taken as equal to 1, the weight of connection going from the unexcited element is taken as equal to 0. An element of q–layer is activated if and only if the sum of weights of its inputs is equal to q. The possible number N_q of elements (nodes) at each layer is known in advance as the number of combinations of S on q. In the process of the functioning of the network the number of its nodes can only diminish.

Table 28. The reduced matrix of correspondences (step 3)

Number of collection	Collection	3	7	4	2
29	(2,3)	1			1
30	(3,4)	1		1	
31	(3,7)	1	1		
32	(2,7)		1		1
33	(4,7)		1	1	
34	(2,4)			1	1

The advantage of this network consists in the fact that the functioning of it does not, in the first place, require the complex algorithms of changing the weights of connections and, in the second place, this network allows solving problems different, in their content, only by the interpretation of elements of network.

Let S be the set of indices of examples of the set T. A classification is given on T into two classes: the set test-1(T,K) of tests and the set $T\backslash$ test-1(T,K) of anti-tests. This classification induces the partition of S into two sets: $S(K) = \{i: i \in S, t_i \in$ test-1$(T,K)\}$ and $S\backslash S(K)$. Any collection of indices (any node of network) $s = \{i_1, i_2, \ldots i_s\}$ is associated with one and only one set $t(s)$ of attributes as follows: $t(s) = \{$the intersection of all $t_i, t_i \in$ test-1$(T,K), i \in s, s \subseteq S\}$. Any collection t of attributes is associated with one and only one collection $s(t)$ of indices of examples the intersection of which generates t: $s(t) = \{i: i \in S, t \subseteq t_i, t_i \in T\}$. For the active node s of network, the property "to be test for a given classification" for $t(s)$ is checked by the use of the following function: to_be_test$(s(t(s))) ::= (s(t(s)) \subseteq S(K))$ then *true* else *false*.

If a node does not possess the assigned property, then it is excluded from the network by setting to 0 all connections going from it to the nodes of above and below lying layers.

Sequence of the mappings $s \rightarrow t(\mathrm{s}) \rightarrow s(t(s))$ results in $s(t(s)) \supseteq s$. This sequence of mappings corresponds to the operation of generalization in the network with the use of which the set of all given examples possessing the feature $t(s)$ is determined. The generalization leads to detecting the active nodes of higher layers than some current layer in the network. Then the weights of all connections going from the node excited via generalization to the nodes of previous layer are set equal to 1, and the latter ones are excited too, if they thus far were not active. The involvement of units via the generalization is some sort of "reverse" wave of activity.

The work of this combinatorial network consists of the following steps:

Step 1. The setting of the first layer nodes of network to active state, the weights of connections leading to the second layer nodes are set equal to 1;

For each level beginning with the second one:

Step 2. The excitation of nodes, if they were not active and all their incoming traffic (links) have the weight equal to 1; checking the assigned property for the activated nodes of this layer;

Step 3. If the assigned property of node is not satisfied, then installation into 0 of all incoming and outgoing connections of this node (removal of unit is produced);

Step 4. If the assigned property of node is satisfied, then outgoing connections of this node are set to be equal to 1; if, as a result of generalization, the node of a higher layer is activated, then its incoming connections are set to be equal to 1 (the involvement of the node), and further, with the aid of "reverse" wave, the nodes of lower layers are activated;

Step 5. The propagation of "excitation" to the nodes of the following higher layer (with respect to the current one) and the passage to analyzing the following layer;

Step 6. If there are no excited nodes in the current level, then the propagation of excitation ceases;

Step 7. "The readout" of the nodes in each layer not having any connection with above lying active nodes. Such nodes correspond to the tests for the given classification of examples.

All inductive rules of expanding and winnowing the elements of network are carried out naturally due to the organization of network connections.

To illustrate the functioning of combinatorial network we consider the small current example presented in Table 9. In this example, we have:

T= {**test(T,K), anti-tests**} = {{BG, DG, AE, $ABDE$, $AEFG$}, {AD, EG, $BCDEF$}};

S = {$S(K)$, S(anti-test)} = {{1, 2, 3, 4, 5}, {6, 7, 8}};

t({1,2} = G, $s(G)$ = {1, 2, 5, 7}; this node does not correspond to a test;

t({1,3} = $\varnothing$;

t({1,4} = B, $s(B)$ = {1, 4, 8}; this node does not correspond to a test;

t({1,5} = G, $s(G)$ = {1, 2, 5, 7}; this node does not correspond to a test;

t({2,3} = $\varnothing$;

t({2,4} = D, $s(D)$ = {2, 4, 6, 8}; this node does not correspond to a test;

t({2,5} = G, $s(G)$ = {1, 2, 5, 7}; this node does not correspond to a test;

t({3,4} = AE, $s(AE)$ = {3, 4, 5}; this node corresponds to a test; in this case we immediately conclude that the node of network {3, 4, 5} will be active, and it means that all connections going to it from the elements of network {3, 5} and {4,5} can be set equal to 1.

In Figure 4 the process of exciting the elements of network for the example in question is shown. The connections of black color have the weight equal to 0, the connections of dark-blue color have the weight equal to 1.The final configuration of network is shown in Figure 5.

Figure 4. The propagation of the excitation in the network

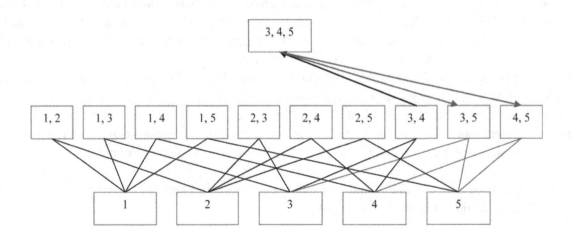

Figure 5. The result of the functioning of network

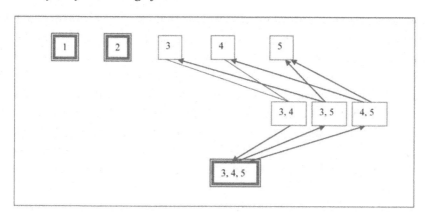

RELATED WORKS

Mining association rules from databases has attracted great interest because of its potentially very useful application. Mining association rules first was introduced by Agrawal, Imielinski, and Swami (1993). Their algorithm is called **AIS** (for Agrawal, Imielinski, and Swami). Another algorithm, called **SETM** (for Set Oriented Mining), has been introduced in (Hootsma and Swami, 1993). This algorithm uses relational operations in a relational database environment.

The next step in solving the problem of inferring association rules has been done in (Agrawal, & Sricant, 1994). The new algorithms the **Apriori**, **AprioriTid**, and **AprioriHybrid** were presented in this work. These algorithms are fundamentally different from AIS and SETM ones. They use an effective inductive method of constructing $q+1$-collections of transactions from all their q-sub-collections. The other studies in the field of mining association rules are described in (Savasere, et al., 1995) and (Toivonen, 1996).

The combinatorial explosion is a natural result of these algorithms, because they mine exhaustively all the rules satisfying the minimum support constraint as specified by the analyst. This characteristic may lead to obtaining the excessive number of rules such that the end user will have to determine which rules are worthwhile. The size of the database also plays a vital role in data mining (Toivonen, 1996). Large databases are desired for obtaining accurate results, but the efficiency of algorithms depends heavily on the size of databases. Therefore, it is highly desirable to develop an algorithm that has polynomial complexity and still being able of inferring a few rules of good quality.

The polynomial algorithms for mining association rules based on the OCAT approach and RA1 heuristic have been advanced in (Triantaphyllou, 2006). This heuristic infers set of clauses in the form of a Boolean function in CNF or DNF from two mutually exclusive collections of binary examples. In terms of association rules, each clause in the Boolean expression can be thought of as a set of frequent item sets. In (Triantaphyllou, in press), a new approach, called ARA1, for inferring association rules from databases is given. The OCAT approach is also embedded in it. This approach produces a small set of association rules in polynomial time. These rules are of high quality with 100% support level.

An efficient new approach for discovering both functional and approximate dependencies on a set of attributes has been described in (Huhtala et al., 1999). The idea of this approach has been implemented in the TANE algorithm. The major innovation is a way of determining whether a dependency is hold or not. This way is based on representing attribute sets by equivalence class partitions of the set of tuples (examples). TANE uses also an improved method for searching the space of functional dependencies.

The partition P(*A*) for each *A* belonging to a relation is computed directly from the database. Partition P(*X*), where the cardinality of *X* greater than 2, is computed as product of partitions with respect to two subsets of *X*. Two different subsets of size ‖*X*‖ - 1 will be used for obtaining P(*X*) due to the level-wise mode of generating functional dependencies when only partitions from the previous level are needed.

A functional dependency $X \rightarrow A$ holds if and only if P(*X*) = P(*A*) *(P(*X*) (P(*X*) refines P(*A*)), it means that $X \rightarrow A$ holds if and only if P(*X*) = P(*X* ∪ *A*). It implies that for checking the existence of a functional dependency it is sufficient to compare the number of classes in two partitions. The partition P(*X* ∪ *A*) is computed as the product P(*X*) and P(*A*) and the computation (as we have shown in this chapter) requires only linear time.

The worst case time complexity of the TANE is exponential with respect to the number of attributes. It is inevitable since the number of dependencies can be exponential in the number of attributes. But the time complexity of this algorithm with respect to the number of tuples is only linear.

The discovery of functional dependencies from databases has recently received a significant progress. In the paper (Yao et al., 2002), a new algorithm, called FD-Mine, has been proposed. This algorithm takes advantage of the theory of functional dependencies (FD) to reduce both the size of dataset and the number of FDs to be checked by using discovered equivalences. The pruning of the search space does not lead to lost of information.

Mannila et al. (Mannil,a & Räihä, 1994; Mannila, & Toivonen, 1997) introduced the concept of a partition in which the tuples (examples) having the same value of an attribute are placed into the same group. The problem of determining whether or not a FD holds on a given set of data can be solved by comparing the number of groups among the partitions for various attributes. The information obtained from discovered FDs is used to prune more candidates than previous approach to inferring FDs. This pruning improves the overall efficiency of the algorithm for search for FDs.

The FD-Mine algorithm uses a level-wise search where results of level *k* are used to generate level *k*+1. First, at level 1, FDs $X \rightarrow Y$ are found and stored in FD-Set F_1 where *X* and *Y* are single attributes. The set of candidates that are considered at this level is denoted by L_1. F_1 and L_1 are used to obtain candidates X_i, X_j of L_2 and all FDs of the form $X_iX_j \rightarrow Y$ are found and stored in FD-SET F_2. Next F_2, F_1, L_1, L_2 are used to obtain the candidates of L_3, and so on, until no candidates remain. It is noted in (Yao et al., 2002) that this algorithm checks fewer FDs than the TANE algorithm by using the equivalence between FDs of a current level and FDs discovered at previous levels.

CONCLUSION

In this chapter, the definition of good diagnostic test and the characterization of good tests are advanced. The concepts of good maximally redundant and good irredundant tests are introduced. The definition of the good test is based on the partition model of classifications. Some characteristic of good tests allow proposing a strategy for inferring all kinds of good diagnostic tests. We describe an algorithm called Background Algorithm based on the method of mathematical induction. This algorithm is applicable to inferring all kinds of good classification tests and, consequently, for inferring functional, implicative, and association rules from a given data set. We discuss also the possible ways of constructing an efficient algorithm for inferring good tests of any kind.

REFERENCES

Agraval, R., Mannila, H., Srikant, R., Toivonen, H., & Verkamo, A. I. (1996). Fast discovery of association rules. In U. M. Fayyard, G. Piatetsky-Shapiro, P. Smyth, & R. Utchurusamy (Eds.), *Advances in knowledge discovery and data mining* (pp. 307-328). Menlo Park, CA: AAAI Press.

Agrawal, R., Imielinski, T., & Swami, A. (1993). Mining association rules between sets of items in large databases. In P. Buneman, & S. Jajodia (Eds.), *Proceedings of the ACM SIGMOD Conference on Management of Data* (pp. 207-216). ACM Press.

Agrawal, R., & Srikant, R. (1994). Fast algorithms for mining association rules. In J. B. Bocca, M. Jarco, & C. Zaniolo (Eds.), *Proceedings of the 20th VLDB Conference.* (pp. 487-489). Morgan Kaufman.

Aho, A. V., Hopcraft, J. E., & Ullman, J. D. (1979). *The design and analysis of computer algorithms.* Moscow, USSR: Mir.

Huhtala, Y., Kärkkäinen, J., Porkka, P., & Toivonen, H. (1999). TANE: An efficient algorithm for discovering functional and approximate dependencies. *The Computer Journal, 42*(2), 100–111. doi:10.1093/comjnl/42.2.100

Mannila, H., & Raiha, K. (1994). Algorithms for inferring functional dependencies from relations. *Data & Knowledge Engineering, 12*(1), 83–99. doi:10.1016/0169-023X(94)90023-X

Mannila, H., & Toivonen, H. (1997). Level-wise search and borders of theories. *Knowledge Discovery, 1*(3), 251–258.

Megretskaya, I. A. (1988). Construction of natural classification tests for knowledge base generation. In Y. Pecherskij (Ed), *The problem of the expert system application in the national economy: Reports of the Republican workshop* (pp. 89-93). Kishinev, Moldava: Mathematical Institute with Computer Centre of Moldova Academy of Sciences.

Naidenova, X. A. (1999). The data-knowledge transformation. In V. Soloviev (Ed.), *Text processing and cognitive technologies, Issue 3* (pp. 130-151). Pushchino, Russia.

Naidenova, X. A., & Polegaeva, J. G. (1986). An algorithm of finding the best diagnostic tests. In G. E. Mintz, & P. P. Lorents (Eds.), *The application of mathematical logic methods* (pp. 63-67). Tallinn, Estonia: Institute of Cybernetics, National Acad. of Sciences of Estonia.

Naidenova, X. A., Polegaeva, J. G., & Iserlis, J. E. (1995a). The system of knowledge acquisition based on constructing the best diagnostic classification tests. In J. Valkman (Ed.), *"Knowledge-Dialog-Solution", Proceedings of International Conference in two volumes* (Vol. 1, pp. 85-95). Jalta, Ukraine: Kiev Institute of Applied Informatics.

Naidenova, X. K. (1977). Questions of the computer analysis of experimental data with the automatic classification. *Transactions of Leningrad Electro-Technical Institute, 217*, 65–70.

Naidenova, X. K. (2005). DIAGARA: An incremental algorithm for inferring implicative rules from examples. *International Journal " . Information Theories & Applications, 12*(2), 171–186.

Savasere, A., Omiecinski, E., & Navathe, S. (1995). *An Efficient algorithm for mining association rules in large databases*. Data Mining Group, Tandem Computers, Inc., Austin, TX.

Skornjakov, L. A. (1982). *The elements of the theory of structures*. Moscow: Nauka.

Sperner, E. (1928). Ein satz uber Untermengen einer Endlichen Menge. *Mathematische Zeitschrift*, *27*(11), 544–548. doi:10.1007/BF01171114

Toivonen, H. (1996). Sampling large databases for association rules. In T.M. Vijayaraman, A.P. Buchman, C. Mohan, & N.L. Sarda (Eds.), *Proceedings of the 22nd VLDB Conference* (pp. 134-145). Morgan Kaufmann.

Triantaphyllou, E. (2006). The one clause at a time (OCAT) approach to data mining and knowledge discovery. In E. Triantaphyllou, & Felici, G. (Eds.), *Data mining and knowledge discovery approaches based on rule induction techniques* (pp. 45-88). New York: Springer.

Triantaphyllou, E. (in press) *Data mining and knowledge discovery via novel logic-based approach*. Springer.

Chapter 8
The Duality of Good Diagnostic Tests

ABSTRACT

The concept of good classification test is redefined in this chapter as a dual element of interconnected algebraic lattices. The operations of lattice generation take their interpretations in human mental acts. Inferring the chains of dual lattice elements ordered by the inclusion relation lies in the foundation of generating good classification tests. The concept of an inductive transition from one element of a chain to its nearest element in the lattice is determined. The special reasoning rules for realizing inductive transitions are formed. The concepts of admissible and essential values (objects) are introduced. Searching for admissible or essential values (objects) as a part of reasoning is based on the inductive diagnostic rules. In this chapter, we also propose a non-incremental learning algorithm NIAGaRa based on a reasoning process realizing one of the ways of lattice generation. Next, we discuss the relations between the good test construction and the Formal Concept Analysis (FCA).

INTRODUCTION

We redefine the concept of the good classification test as a dual element of interconnected algebraic lattices. The process of lattice construction is considered as a knowledge elicitation or commonsense reasoning process. The operations of lattice generation take their interpretations in human mental acts. Inferring the chains of dual lattice elements ordered by the inclusion relation lies in the foundation of generating all the kinds of good classification tests. We introduce the concept of an inductive transition from one element of a chain to its nearest element in the lattice. Four possible variants of induction

DOI: 10.4018/978-1-60566-810-9.ch008

transitions are considered. The special reasoning rules realizing the inductive transitions are introduced: the rules of generalization and specification and their dual variants.

Note that reasoning begins with using a mechanism for restricting the space of searching for tests: 1) for each collection of attributes' values (objects), to avoid constructing all its subsets, 2) for each step of reasoning, to choose a collection of attributes' values (objects) without which good tests can not be constructed. For this goal, admissible values (objects) and essential values (objects) are determined. Searching for admissible or essential values (objects) is based on inductive diagnostic rules. These rules, on the one hand, realize the inductive Method of Difference (Mill, 1872); on the other hand, they give rise to diagnostic assertions involved immediately in the processes of good tests construction.

Under lattice construction, the deductive rules of the first type, namely, implications, interdictions, rules of compatibility (approximate implications), and diagnostic assertions are generated and used immediately. Hence the deductive reasoning rules (rules of the second type) are naturally drawn into inductive reasoning for pruning the search space. The detailed analysis of algorithms of searching for all GDTs in terms of constructing the algebraic lattice allowed us not only to determine the structure of inferences but also to decompose algorithms into sub-problems and operations that represent known deductive and inductive modes (modus operandi) of commonsense reasoning. Thus the class of symbolic machine learning algorithms can be transformed into the process of integral reasoning, where different rules (deductive, inductive, abductive, traductive, etc.) alternate and support each other. These are mental acts that can be found in any reasoning: stating new propositions, choosing the relevant part of knowledge and/or data for further steps of reasoning, involving a new rule of reasoning (deductive, abductive, inductive, traductive, etc.).

In this chapter, we also propose a non-incremental learning algorithm NIAGaRa based on one of the possible variants of generalization inductive reasoning rule. This algorithm generates all the GMRTs for a given sets of positive and negative examples. Next we discuss some of current works related to concept lattice construction.

CORRESPONDENCE OF GALOIS FOR GOOD CLASSIFICATION TEST DEFINITION

Let $S = \{1, 2, ..., N\}$ be the set of objects' indices (objects, for short) and $T = \{A_1, A_2, ..., A_j, ...A_m\}$ be the set of attributes' values (values, for short). Each object is described by a collection of values from T.

The definition of good tests is based on correspondences of Galois G on $S \times T$ and two relations $S \rightarrow T$, $T \rightarrow S$ (Ore, 1944; Riguet, 1948; Everett, 1944). Let $s \subseteq S$, $t \subseteq T$. Denote by t_i, $t_i \subseteq T$, $i = 1, ..., N$ the description of object with index i. We define the relations $S \rightarrow T$, $T \rightarrow S$ as follows:

$S \rightarrow T$: $t = \text{val}(s) = \{$intersection of all t_i: $t_i \subseteq T$, $i \in$ s$\}$ and

$T \rightarrow S$: $s = \text{obj}(t) = \{i: i \in S, t \subseteq t_i\}$.

Of course, we have $\text{obj}(t) = \{$intersection of all $s(A)$: $s(A) \subseteq S$, $A \in t\}$. Operations $\text{val}(s)$, $\text{obj}(t)$ are reasoning operations related to discovering the general feature of objects the indices of which belong to s and to discovering the indices of all objects possessing the feature t.

These operations possess the following properties (Birkhoff, 1954):

(i) $s_1 \subseteq s_2 \Rightarrow \mathrm{val}(s_2) \subseteq \mathrm{val}(s_1)$ for all $s_1, s_2 \subseteq S$;

(ii) $t_1 \subseteq t_2 \Rightarrow \mathrm{obj}(t_2) \subseteq \mathrm{obj}(t_1)$ for all $t_1, t_2 \subseteq T$;

(iii) $s \subseteq \mathrm{obj}(\mathrm{val}(s))$ & $\mathrm{val}(s) = \mathrm{val}(\mathrm{obj}(\mathrm{val}(s)))$ for all $s \subseteq S$;

(iv) $t \subseteq \mathrm{val}(\mathrm{obj}(t))$ & $\mathrm{obj}(t) = \mathrm{obj}(\mathrm{val}(\mathrm{obj}(t)))$ for all $t \subseteq T$;

(v) $\mathrm{val}(\cup s_j) = \cap \mathrm{val}(s_j)$ for all $s_j \subseteq S$; $\mathrm{obj}(\cup t_j) = \cap \mathrm{obj}(t_j)$ for all $t_j \subseteq T$.

The properties (i), (ii) relate to extending collections s, t as reasoning operations. Extending s by an index j^* of some new object leads to receiving a more general feature of objects:

$(s \cup j^*) \supseteq s$ implies $\mathrm{val}(s \cup j^*) \subseteq \mathrm{val}(s)$.

Extending s by an index j^* of some new object is an elementary step of generalization.

Extending t by a new value A leads to decreasing the number of objects possessing the general feature 'tA' in comparison with the number of objects possessing the general feature 't':

$(t \cup A) \supseteq t$ implies $\mathrm{obj}(t \cup A) \subseteq \mathrm{obj}(t)$.

Extending t by a new value A is an elementary step of specialization.

Extending t or s is effectively used for finding classification tests, so the property (v) is very important to control the domain of searching for tests. In order to choose a new collection $(s_i \cup j)$ such that $\mathrm{val}(s_i \cup j) \neq \emptyset$ it is necessary to choose $j, j \notin s_i$ such that the condition $(\mathrm{val}(s_i) \cap t_j) \neq \emptyset$ is satisfied. Analogously, in order to choose a new collection $(t_i \cup A)$ such that $obj(t_i \cup A) \neq \emptyset$ it is necessary to choose $A, A \notin t_i$ such that the condition $(obj(t_i) \cap obj(A)) \neq \emptyset$ is satisfied.

The properties (iii), (iv) relate to the following generalization operations (functions):

$\mathrm{generalization\_of}(t) = t' = \mathrm{val}(\mathrm{obj}(t))$; $\mathrm{generalization\_of}(s) = s' = \mathrm{obj}(\mathrm{val}(s))$.

The sequence of operations $t \rightarrow \mathrm{obj}(t) \rightarrow \mathrm{val}(\mathrm{obj}(t))$ gives that $\mathrm{val}(\mathrm{obj}(t)) \supseteq t$. This generalization operation gives the maximal general feature for objects the indices of which are in $\mathrm{obj}(t)$.

The sequence of operations $s \rightarrow \mathrm{val}(s) \rightarrow \mathrm{obj}(\mathrm{val}(s))$ gives that $\mathrm{obj}(\mathrm{val}(s)) \supseteq s$. This generalization operation gives the maximal set of objects possessing the feature $\mathrm{val}(s)$.

The generalization operations are actually closure operators (Ore, 1980). A set s is closed if $s = \mathrm{obj}(\mathrm{val}(s))$. A set t is closed if $t = \mathrm{val}(\mathrm{obj}(t))$.

These generalization operations are not artificially constructed operations. One can perform, mentally, a lot of such operations during a short period of time. We give an example of these operations. Suppose that somebody has seen two films (s) with the participation of Gerard Depardieu ($\mathrm{val}(s)$). After that he tries to know all the films with his participation ($\mathrm{obj}(\mathrm{val}(s))$). One can know that Gerard Depardieu acts with Pierre Richard (t) in several films ($\mathrm{obj}(t)$). After that he can discover that these films are the films of the same producer Francis Veber ($\mathrm{val}(\mathrm{obj}(t))$).

Namely these generalization operations are used for searching for good diagnostic tests.

Notice that these generalization operations are also used in FCA for concepts' definition (Wille, 1992; Stumme et al., 1998): a pair $C = (s, t)$, $s \subseteq S$, $t \subseteq T$, is called a concept if $s = \mathrm{obj}(t)$ and simultaneously

$t = \mathrm{val}(s)$, i. e. for a concept $C = (s, t)$ both s and t are closed. Usually, the set s is called **the extent** of C (in our notation, it is the set of indices of objects possessing the feature t) and the set of values t is called **the intent** of C.

REDEFINITION OF CLASSIFICATION TESTS AS DUAL ELEMENTS OF INTERCONNECTED LATTICES

Let $S(+)$ and $S(-) = S \setminus S(+)$ be the sets of positive and negative objects respectively.

A diagnostic test for $S(+)$ is a pair (s, t) such that $t \subseteq T$ $(s = \mathrm{obj}(t) \neq \varnothing)$, $s \subseteq S(+)$ and $t \not\subseteq t'$, $\forall t'$, $t' \in S(-)$.

Let $R = R(+) \cup R(-)$ be the set of object descriptions t_i, $i \in S$ and $S(+)$ and $S(-) = S \setminus S(+)$ be the sets of indices of positive and negative objects respectively (or simply objects, for short).

In general case, a set t is not closed for diagnostic test (s, t), i. e. the condition $\mathrm{val}(\mathrm{obj}(t)) = t$ is not always satisfied, consequently, a diagnostic test is not obligatory a concept of FCA. This condition is true only for GMRTs.

Definition 8.1. A diagnostic test (s, t), $t \subseteq T$ $(s = \mathrm{obj}(t) \neq \varnothing)$ is good for $S(+)$ if and only if any extension $s' = s \cup i$, $i \notin s$, $i \in S(+)$ implies that $(s', \mathrm{val}(s'))$ is not a test for $S(+)$.

Definition 8.2. A good test (s, t), $t \subseteq T$ $(s = \mathrm{obj}(t) \neq \varnothing)$ for $S(+)$ is **irredundant** (GIRT) if any narrowing $t' = t \setminus A$, $A \in t$ implies that $(\mathrm{obj}(t'), t'))$ is not a test for $S(+)$.

Definition 8.3. A good test for $S(+)$ is **maximally redundant** (GMRT) if any extension of $t' = t \cup A$, $A \notin t$, $A \in T$ implies that $(\mathrm{obj}(t \cup A), t'))$ is not a good test for $S(+)$.

Generating all types of tests is based on inferring the chains of pairs (s, t) ordered by the inclusion relation.

GENERATING GOOD DIAGNOSTIC TESTS AS DUAL ELEMENTS OF INTERCONNECTED LATTICES

Inferring the Chains of Dual Elements Ordered by the Inclusion Relation

We shall consider two interconnected lattices $\mathrm{OBJ} = (2^S, \cup, \cap) = (2^S, \subseteq)$ and $\mathrm{VAL} = (2^T, \cup, \cap) = (2^T, \subseteq)$, where 2^S, 2^T designate the set of all subsets of objects and the set of all subsets of values, respectively.

Inferring the chains of lattice elements ordered by the inclusion relation lies in the foundation of generating all diagnostic tests:

(1) $s_0 \subseteq \ldots \subseteq s_i \subseteq s_{i+1} \subseteq \ldots \subseteq s_m$ $(\mathrm{val}(s_0) \supseteq \mathrm{val}(s_1) \supseteq \ldots \supseteq \mathrm{val}(s_i) \supseteq \mathrm{val}(s_{i+1}) \supseteq \ldots \supseteq \mathrm{val}(s_m))$,

(2) $t_0 \subseteq \ldots \subseteq t_i \subseteq t_{i+1} \subseteq \ldots \subseteq t_m$ $(\mathrm{obj}(t_0) \supseteq \mathrm{obj}(t_1) \supseteq \ldots \supseteq \mathrm{obj}(t_i) \supseteq \mathrm{obj}(t_{i+1}) \supseteq \ldots \supseteq \mathrm{obj}(t_m))$.

The process of generating chains of form (1) is defined as an ascending process of generating lattice elements. The process of generating chains of form (2) is defined as a descending process of generating lattice elements. The process of generating lattice elements can be two-directional when chains (1) and (2) alternate.

The dual ascending and descending processes of lattice generating are determined as follows:

(3) $t_0 \supseteq t_1 \supseteq \dots \supseteq t_i \supseteq t_i+1 \supseteq \dots \supseteq t_m$ (obj$(t_0) \subseteq$ obj$(t_1) \subseteq \dots \subseteq$ obj$(t_i) \subseteq$ obj$(t_i+1) \subseteq \dots \subseteq$ obj(t_m)),

(4) $s_0 \supseteq s_1 \supseteq \dots \supseteq s_i \supseteq s_{i+1} \supseteq \dots \supseteq s_m$ (val$(s_0) \subseteq$ val$(s_1) \subseteq \dots \subseteq$ val$(s_i) \subseteq$ val$(s_{i+1}) \subseteq \dots \subseteq$ val(s_m)).

Let us remember the definitions of filter, ideal, principal filter, and principal ideal in lattices (Rasiowa, 1974) that have been given in Chapter 6 (Definition 6.3).

In our ascending and descending processes, every chain $t_0 \supseteq t_1 \supseteq \dots \supseteq t_i \supseteq t_{i+1} \supseteq \dots \supseteq t_m$ or $t_0 \subseteq t_1 \subseteq \dots \subseteq t_i \subseteq t_{i+1} \subseteq \dots \subseteq t_m$ defines the proper chain of the embedded principal ideals (filters) of the lattice VAL $= (2^T, \subseteq)$. Analogously, every chain $s_0 \supseteq s_1 \supseteq \dots \supseteq s_i \supseteq s_{i+1} \supseteq \dots \supseteq s_m$ or $s_0 \subseteq s_1 \subseteq \dots \subseteq s_i \subseteq s_{i+1} \subseteq \dots \subseteq s_m$) defines the proper chain of the embedded principal ideals (filters) of the lattice OBJ $= (2^S, \subseteq)$.

Deleting an element s or t from the consideration in a process of good test generation implies deleting the elements of its principal filters in the lattices OBJ$= (2^S, \subseteq)$ and VAL $= (2^T, \subseteq)$, respectively. Admitting an element s or t implies admitting the elements of its principal ideals in the lattices OBJ$= (2^S, \subseteq)$ and VAL $= (2^T, \subseteq)$, respectively.

Constructing lattices can be described in terms of constructing the chains of principal ideals (filters) of lattice.

Let VAL $= (2^T, \subseteq) = (2^T, \cup, \cap)$ be a lattice, α and ω be the zero element and the unit element of the lattice, respectively. The semantics of α is 'not object at all' the semantics of ω is 'not feature at all'. Denote the set 2^T by I.

Construct a chain of principal ideals in VAL beginning with the zero ideal and terminating with some maximal principal ideal:

(5) $\Delta_0 \subseteq \Delta_1(t_1) \subseteq \Delta_2(t_2) \subseteq \subseteq \Delta_i(t_i) \subseteq \subseteq \Delta_n(t_n)$.

Let $\leq$ be the relation on I defined as follows: for any $t, t' \in$ I, $t \leq t'$ if and only if $t \supseteq t'$, where $t \leq t'$ is read as "t has t' as a feature" or "t is less than t'". Then the chain (5) is engendered by the a chain

(6) $\alpha \leq t_1 \leq t_2 \leq \leq t_i \leq \leq t_n$,

where $t_i < t_{i+1}$ and there does not exist j such that $t_i < t_j < t_{i+1}$ (a chain of principal filters is defined dually).

Suppose that for an element t of I we have constructed $\Delta(t_i)$ and the non-empty set $A(t_i) = \{$I $\setminus \Delta(t_i)\}$. We note that $A(t_i)$ is empty only when $t_i = \omega$. Let $Q_\nabla(t_i)$ be a subset of all elements of A(t_i) belonging to the principal filter $\nabla(t_i)$ of t_i, i.e. $Q_\nabla(t_i) = \{q: q = x \cap t_i, x \in A(t_i)\}$.

If $Q_\nabla(t_i)$ contains only one element ω, then $\Delta(t_i)$ is maximal principal ideal and t_i is "general" feature.

$Q_\nabla(t_i)$ is a partially ordered set by the relation $\leq$ defined above. Let MinQ(t_i) be the set of minimal elements of partially ordered set $Q_\nabla(t_i)$. The elements of MinQ(t_i) are the nearest ones to t_i in I and they are just what we want for extending t_i. So, we need a method to find the set MinQ(t_i).

The following Propositions show that the task of finding the set MinQ(t_i) can be solved without generating the set $Q_\nabla(t_i)$ (Naidenova, 1979).

Proposition 8.1. Suppose that, for some $t \in$ I, we have obtained $\Delta(t)$ and $A(t) = \{$I $\setminus \Delta(t)\}$. If x is a minimal element of $A(t)$, then the element $t' = x \cap t$ of $Q_\nabla(t)$ is a minimal one in this set.

Proof of Proposition 8.1. Suppose that t' is not a minimal element of $Q_\nabla(t)$. Then there exists an element z in $Q_\nabla(t)$ such that $z \leq t'$. But then there is x' in $A(t)$ such that $x' \cap t = z$. The fact $(x' \cap t) \leq (x \cap t)$ implies $x' \leq x$. This contradiction concludes the proof.

Proposition 8.2. Suppose that, for some $t \in$ I, we have obtained $\Delta(t)$ and $Q_\nabla(t)$. If b is a minimal element of $Q_\nabla(t)$, then there is a minimal element x in $A(t) = \{I \setminus \Delta(t)\}$ such that $x \cap t = b$.

Proof of Proposition 8.2. Suppose that x is not a minimal element of $A(t)$. Then there exists x' in $A(t)$ such that $x' \leq x$. Consider the element $z = t \cap x'$. The fact $x' \leq x$ implies that $z \leq b$. This contradiction concludes the proof.

We associated the relation $\leq$ with the relation $\supseteq$ on I. But this relation can be generalized to any order relation.

A classification algorithm based on constructing the chains of objects' features ordered by $\leq$ relation and the corresponding chains of their principal ideals has been applied for analyzing two kinds of experimental data: indicatrissa of light diffusion (scattering) in atmosphere layer nearest to the Earth's surface and spectra of brightness of low layer clouds (Naidenova & Chapursky, 1978). The goal of this analysis was the finding of hypotheses suitable for generalizing the experimental data and its partitioning into natural disjoint classes.

As far as human commonsense reasoning, the inclusion relation plays the most important psychological role, that's why we choose the method "Extending s (or t) by One Element" for constructing algorithms to build algebraic lattices in the tasks of inferring good classification tests.

INDUCTIVE RULES FOR CONSTRUCTING GOOD CLASSIFICATION TESTS

The Definition of Inductive Transitions from One Element of a Chain to Its Nearest Element in the Lattice

When generating all types of classification tests we use four possible variants of inductive transition from one element of a chain to its nearest element in the lattice:

(i) from $s_q = (i_1, i_2, ..., i_q)$ to $s_{q+1} = (i_1, i_2, ..., i_{q+1})$;
(ii) from $t_q = (A_1, A_2, ..., A_q)$ to $t_{q+1} = (A_1, A_2, ..., A_{q+1})$;
(iii) from $s_q = (i_1, i_2, ..., i_q)$ to $s_{q-1} = (i_1, i_2, ..., i_{q-1})$;
(iv) from $t_q = (A_1, A_2, ..., A_q)$ to $t_{q-1} = (A_1, A_2, ..., A_{q-1})$.

Thus inductive transitions are the processes of extending or narrowing collections of values (objects). Inductive transitions can be smooth or boundary. Under smooth transition, the extending (narrowing) of collections of values (objects) is going with preserving a given property of them. These properties are, for example, "to be a test for a given class of examples", "to be an irredundant collection of values", "not to be a test for a given class of examples", "to be a good test for a given class of examples" and some others. A transition is said to be boundary if it changes a given property of collections of values (objects) into the opposite one.

We need the special rules for realizing these inductive transitions.

Note that reasoning begins with using a mechanism for restricting the space of searching for tests: (i) for each collection of values (objects), to avoid constructing all its subsets and (ii) to restrict the space of searching only to the subspaces deliberately containing the desired GMRTs or GIRTs. For this goal, admissible and essential values (objects) are used.

During the lattice construction, the deductive rules of the first type, namely, implications, interdictions, rules of compatibility (approximate implications), and diagnostic rules are generated and used immediately. The knowledge acquired during the process of generalization (specialization) is used for pruning the search space.

The Generalization Rule

The generalization rule is used to get all the collections of objects $s_{q+1} = \{i_1, i_2, \ldots i_q, i_{q+1}\}$ from a collection $s_q = \{i_1, i_2, \ldots i_q\}$ such that $(s_q, \mathrm{val}(s_q))$ and $(s_{q+1}, \mathrm{val}(s_{q+1}))$ are tests for a given class of objects.

The termination condition for constructing a chain of generalizations is: for all the extension s_{q+1} of s_q, $(s_{q+1}, \mathrm{val}(s_{q+1}))$ is not a test for a given class of positive examples.

The generalization rule uses, as a leading process, an ascending chain $(s_0 \subseteq \ldots \subseteq s_i \subseteq s_{i+1} \subseteq \ldots \subseteq s_m)$. The application of this rule for inferring GMRTs requires using the generalization operation generalization_of$(s) = s' = \mathrm{obj}(\mathrm{val}(s))$ for each obtained collection of objects.

The rule of generalization is an inductive extension rule meaning the choice of admissible objects for extending s_q. This rule realizes the Joint Method Agreement and Difference (Mill, 1872).

The extending of s results in obtaining the subsets of objects of more and more power with more and more generalized features (set of values). This operation is analogous to the generalization rule applied for star generation under conceptual clustering (Michalski, 1983).

The Specification Rule

The specification rule is used to get all the collections of values $t_{q+1} = \{A_1, A_2, \ldots, A_{q+1}\}$ from a collection $t_q = \{A_1, A_2, \ldots, A_q\}$ such that t_q and t_{q+1} are irredundant collections of values and $(\mathrm{obj}(t_q), t_q)$ and $(\mathrm{obj}(t_{q+1}), t_{q+1})$ are not tests for a given class of objects.

The termination condition for constructing a chain of specifications is: for all the extensions t_{q+1} of t_q, t_{q+1} is either a redundant collection of values or a test for a given class of objects.

This rule has been used for inferring GIRTs (Megretskaya, 1988).

The specification rule uses, as a leading process, a descending chain $(t_0 \subseteq \ldots \subseteq t_i \subseteq t_{i+1} \subseteq \ldots \subseteq t_m)$. The application of this rule for inferring GIRTs does not require using the generalization operation generalization_of$(t) = t' = \mathrm{val}(\mathrm{obj}(t))$ for each obtained collection of values.

The rule of specification is an inductive extension rule meaning the choice of admissible values for extending a given collection of values. This rule realizes the Joint Method of Agreement and Difference (Mill, 1872).

In general case, the extending of t results in obtaining the subsets of objects of less and less power with more and more specified features (set of values).

The dual generalization (specification) rules relate to narrowing collections of values (objects).

The dual generalization rule can be used to get all the collections of values $t_{q-1} = (A_1, A_2, \ldots, A_{q-1})$ from a collection $t_q = (A_1, A_2, \ldots, A_q)$ such that $(\mathrm{obj}(t_q), t_q)$ and $(\mathrm{obj}(t_{q-1}), t_{q-1})$ are tests for a given class of objects.

The dual specification rule can be used to get all the collections of objects $s_{q-1} = (i_1, i_2, \ldots, i_{q-1})$ from a collection $s_q = (i_1, i_2, \ldots, i_q)$ such that $(s_{q-1}, \mathrm{val}(s_{q-1}))$ and $(s_q, \mathrm{val}(s_q))$ are tests for a given set of positive examples.

All inductive transitions take their interpretations in human mental acts. The extending of a set of objects with checking the satisfaction of a given assertion is a typical method of inductive reasoning. For example, Claude-Gaspar Bashet de Méziriak, a French mathematician (1581 – 1638) has discovered (without proving it) that apparently every positive number can be expressed as a sum of at most four squares; for example, $5 = 2^2 + 1^2$, $6 = 2^2 + 1^2 + 1^2$, $7 = 2^2 + 1^2 + 1^2 + 1^2$, $8 = 2^2 + 2^2$, $9 = 3^2$. Bashet has checked this for more than 300 numbers. It wasn't until the late 18th century that Joseph Lagrange gave a complete proof.

In pattern recognition, the process of inferring hypotheses about the unknown values of some attributes is reduced to the maximal expansion of a collection of the known values of some others attributes in such a way that none of the forbidden pairs of values would belong to this expansion.

The contraction of a collection of values is used, for instance, in order to delete from it redundant or non-informative values.

The contraction of a collection of objects is used, for instance, in order to isolate a certain cluster in a class of objects. Thus, we distinguish lemons in the citrus fruits.

THE BOUNDARY INDUCTIVE TRANSITIONS

The boundary inductive transitions are used to get:

(1)   all the collections t_q from a collection t_{q-1} such that $(obj(t_{q-1}), t_{q-1})$ is not a test but $(obj(t_q), t_q)$ is a test, for a given set of objects;

(2)   all the collections t_{q-1} from a collection t_q such that $(obj(t_q), t_q)$ is a test, but $(obj(t_{q-1}), t_{q-1})$ is not a test for a given set of objects;

(3)   all the collections s_{q-1} from a collection s_q such that $(s_q, val(s_q))$ is not a test, but $(s_{q-1}, val(s_{q-1}))$ is a test for a given set of objects;

(4)   all the collections of s_q from a collection s_{q-1} such that $(s_{q-1}, val(s_{q-1}))$ is a test, but $(s_q, val(s_q))$ is not a test for a given set of objects.

All the boundary transitions are interpreted as human reasoning operations. Transition (1) is used for distinguishing two diseases with similar symptoms. Transition (2) can be interpreted as including a certain class of objects into a more general one. For instance, squares can be named parallelograms, all whose sides are equal. In some intellectual psychological texts, a task is given to remove the "superfluous" (inappropriate) object from a certain group of objects (rose, butterfly, phlox, and dahlia) (transition (3)). Transition (4) can be interpreted as the search for a refuting example.

The boundary inductive transitions realize the methods of difference and concomitant changes (Mill, 1872).

For their implementation, boundary transitions need special inductive reasoning rules, namely, inductive diagnostic ones.

Note that reasoning begins with using a mechanism for restricting the space of the search for tests: 1) for each collection of values (objects), to avoid constructing all its subsets, 2) for each step of reasoning, to choose a collection of values (objects) without which good tests can not be constructed. For this goal, admissible and essential values (objects) are determined. The search for the admissible or essential values (objects) uses inductive diagnostic rules.

Table 1. Example 1 of data (this example is adopted from (Ganascia, 1989)

Index of example	Height	Color of hair	Color of eyes	Class
1	Low	Blond	Bleu	1
2	Low	Brown	Bleu	2
3	Tall	Brown	Embrown	2
4	Tall	Blond	Embrown	2
5	Tall	Brown	Bleu	2
6	Low	Blond	Embrown	2
7	Tall	Red	Bleu	1
8	Tall	Blond	Bleu	1

The Inductive Diagnostic Rule. The Concept of Essential Value

First, consider the boundary transition (1): getting all the collections t_q from a collection t_{q-1} such that $(\mathrm{obj}(t_{q-1}), t_{q-1})$ is not a test but $(\mathrm{obj}(t_q), t_q)$ is a test, for a given set of objects.

The concept of an essential value is determined as follows.

Definition 8.4. Let t be a collection of values such that $(\mathrm{obj}(t), t)$ is a test for a given set of objects. We say that the value A is essential in t if $(\mathrm{obj}(t \backslash A), (t \backslash A))$ is not a test for a given set of object.

Generally, we are interested in finding the maximal subset $\mathrm{sbmax}(t) \subset t$ such that $(\mathrm{obj}(t), t)$ is a test but $(\mathrm{obj}(\mathrm{sbmax}(t)), \mathrm{sbmax}(t))$ is not a test for a given set of positive objects. Then $\mathrm{sbmin}(t) = t \backslash \mathrm{sbmax}(t)$ is the minimal set of essential values in t.

We extend t_{q-1} by choosing values that appear simultaneously with it in the objects of a given set $R(+)$ and do not appear in any object of a set $R(-)$. These values are to be said essential ones.

Let us examine an example of searching for essential values (see, please, Table 1).

Let s be equal to $\{1,2,5,7,8\}$, then $\mathrm{val}(s) = $ '*Bleu*', where $(s, \mathrm{val}(s))$ is not a test for both classes 1 and 2. We can extend $\mathrm{val}(s)$ by choosing values which appear simultaneously with it in the objects of the first class and do not appear in any object of the second class and vice versa.

Objects 1, 7, 8 of Class 1 contain value '*Bleu*' with values '*Low*', '*Blond*', '*Tall*', and '*Red*'. Objects 2, 5 of Class 2 contain value '*Bleu*' with values '*Brown*', '*Low*', and '*Tall*'. The set of essential values for Class 1 is {*Blond, Red*}, the set of essential values for Class 2 is {*Brown*}. We have the following tests containing value '*Bleu*': for Class 1 - '*Bleu Red*' (good but redundant one) and '*Bleu Blond*' (good and irredundant one), and only test (although not a good one) for Class 2 – '*Bleu Brown*'. The inductive diagnostic rule is a reasoning rule of the second type with the help of which the diagnostic assertions (rules of the firs type) are inferred. In our example, the following diagnostic assertion has been inferred: "if '*Bleu*' is true, then the diagnostic rules are *Brown* → Class 2, *Blond* → Class 1, and *Red* → Class 1. This assertion can also be transformed into several interdictions: *Bleu Brown* → not Class 1, *Bleu Blond* → not Class 2, and *Bleu Red* → not Class 2. Figure 1 illustrates the inductive diagnostic rule described above.

In general case, the extended set of attributes is not a GIT or GRMT, so we use the ascending (descending) process for inferring good tests contained in it.

The inductive diagnostic rule is based on the induction Method of Difference (Mill, 1872).

Figure 1. The result of inductive diagnostic rule for searching for essential values

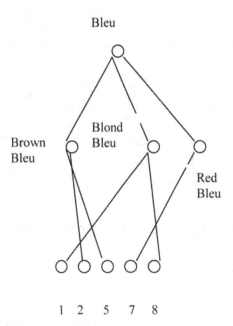

The diagnostic rule for extending a collection of values is analogous to the specialization rule defined in (Michalski, 1983), and (Ganascia, 1989). If a newly presented training example contradicts with an already constructed concept description, the specialization rule is applied to generate a new consistent concept description. A specialization method has been given in (Michalski and Larson, 1978).

The Dual Inductive Diagnostic Rule. The Concept of Essential Object

Consider the boundary inductive transition (3): getting all the collections s_{q-1} from a collection s_q such that $(s_q, \text{val}(s_q))$ is not a test, but $(s_{q-1}, \text{val}(s_{q-1}))$ is a test for a given set of objects.

For realizing this transition, we use a method for choosing objects for deleting from s_q. By analogy with an essential value, we define an essential example.

Definition 8.5. Let s be a subset of objects belonging to a given positive class of objects; assume also that $(s, \text{val}(s))$ is not a test. The object $t_j, j \in s$ is to be said an essential in s if $(s\backslash j, \text{val}(s\backslash j))$ proves to be a test for a given set of positive objects.

Generally, we are interested in finding the maximal subset $\text{sbmax}(s) \subset s$ such that $(s, \text{val}(s))$ is not a test but $(\text{sbmax}(s), \text{val}(\text{sbmax}(s)))$ is a test for a given set of positive objects. Then $\text{sbmin}(s) = s\backslash\text{sbmax}(s)$ is the minimal set of essential objects in s.

The dual inductive diagnostic rule can be used for inferring compatibility rules of the first type. The number of objects in $\text{sbmax}(s)$ can be understood as a measure of "carrying-out" for an acquired rule related to $\text{sbmax}(s)$, namely, $\text{val}(\text{sbmax}(s)) \rightarrow k(R(+))$ frequently, where $k(R(+))$ is the name of the set $R(+)$.

Next we describe the procedure with the use of which a quasi-maximal subset s of s^* is obtained such that $(s, \text{val}(s))$ is a test for given set of objects.

Table 2. Deductive rules of the first type obtained with the use of inductive rules for inferring diagnostic tests

Inductive rules	Action	Inferring deductive rules of the first type
Generalization rule	Extending s (narrowing t)	Implications
Specification rule	Extending t (narrowing s)	Implications
Inductive diagnostic rule	Searching for essential values	Diagnostic rules
Dual inductive diagnostic rule	Searching for essential objects	Compatibility rules (approximate implications)

We begin with the first object i_1 of s^*, then we take the next object i_2 of s^* and evaluate the function to_be_test $(\{i_1, i_2\}, \mathrm{val}(\{i_1, i_2\}))$. If the value of this function is "true", then we take the next object i_3 of s^* and evaluate the function to_be_test $(\{i_1, i_2, i_3\}, \mathrm{val}(\{i_1, i_2, i_3\}))$. If the value of the function to_be_test $(\{i_1, i_2\}, \mathrm{val}(\{i_1, i_2\}))$ is "false", then the object i_2 of s^* is skipped and the function to_be_test $(\{i_1, i_3\}, \mathrm{val}(\{i_1, i_3\}))$ is evaluated. We continue this process until we achieve the last object of s^*.

For instance, consider $s = \{1,7,8\}$ in Table 1. We have, after applying the procedure, described above, that $(\{1,7\}, \mathrm{val}(\{1,7\}))$ is not a test for Class 1 because of $\mathrm{val}(\{1,7\}) = Bleu$, but $(\{1,8\}, \mathrm{val}(\{1,8\}))$ is a test for Class 1 because $\mathrm{val}(\{1,8\}) = Blond\ Bleu$. The object 7 is an essential one in $\{1, 7, 8\}$.

The dual inductive diagnostic rule is based on the inductive Method of Difference (Mill, 1872).

The inductive rules of searching for diagnostic tests generate logical rules of the first type, as shown in Table 2.

In the sequel, we shall see that the deductive rules of the first type, obtained by means of inductive reasoning rules of the second type are used immediately in the process of good tests construction.

Searching for tests by means of generalization and specification rules must be organized such that the number of lattice elements to be constructed would be optimum or reasonably limited. Each collection of values (objects) must be generated only once. It is important, for any set s or t, to avoid generating all its subsets. With this goal, searching for tests is transformed naturally in a process of inductive-deductive commonsense reasoning. Implications (rules of the first type) obtained during the construction of tests are drawn immediately in this reasoning process for pruning the search space. Hence the reasoning is governed by knowledge obtained in the course of this process.

REDUCING THE RULES OF INDUCTIVE TRANSITIONS TO THE DEDUCTIVE AND INDUCTIVE COMMONSENSE REASONING RULES OF THE SECOND TYPE

Realization of the Generalization Rule for Inferring GMRTs

Any realization of this rule must allow for each element s the following actions:

-To avoid constructing the set of all its subsets,
-To avoid the repetitive generation of it.

Let S(test) be the partially ordered set of elements $s = \{i_1, i_2, \dots i_q\}$, $q = 1, 2, \dots, nt - 1$ obtained as a result of generalizations and satisfying the following condition: $(s, \mathrm{val}(s))$ is a test for a given class

$R(+)$ of positive objects. Here nt denotes the number of positive objects. Let *STGOOD* be the partially ordered set of elements s satisfying the following condition: $(s, \text{val}(s))$ is a GMRT for $R(+)$.

Consider some methods for choosing objects admissible for extending s.

Method 1. Suppose that $S(\text{test})$ and *STGOOD* are not empty and $s \in S(\text{test})$. Construct the set V:

$$V = \{\cup\, s', s \subseteq s', s' \in \{S(\text{test}) \cup STGOOD\}\}.$$

The set V is the union of all the collections of objects in $S(\text{test})$ and *STGOOD* containing s, hence, s is in the intersection of these collections. If we want an extension of s not to be included in any element of $\{S(\text{test}) \cup STGOOD\}$, we must use, for extending s, the objects not appearing simultaneously with s in the set V. The set of objects, candidates for extending s, is equal to:

$$\text{CAND}(s) = nts \backslash V, \text{ where } nts = \{\cup\, s, s \in S(\text{test})\}.$$

An object $j^* \in \text{CAND}(s)$ is not admissible for extending s if at least for one object $i \in s$ the pair $\{i, j^*\}$ either does not correspond to a test or it corresponds to a good test (it belongs to *STGOOD*).

Let Q be the set of forbidden pairs of objects for extending s: $Q = \{\{i, j\} \subseteq S(+): (\{i, j\}, \text{val}(\{i, j\}))$ is not a test for $R(+)\}$. Then the set of admissible objects is

$$select(s) = \{i, i \in \text{CAND}(s): (\forall j)\, (j \in s), \{i, j\} \notin \{STGOOD \text{ or } Q\}\}.$$

The set Q can be generated in the beginning of searching for all GMRTs for $R(+)$.

Return to our current example (Table 1). Suppose that the set *STGOOD* contains an element $\{2,3,5\}$, for which $(\{2,3,5\}, \text{val}(\{2,3,5\}))$ is a test for Class 2. Suppose that $S(\text{test}) = \{\{2,3\}, \{2,5\}, \{3,4\}, \{3,5\}, \{3,6\}, \{4,6\}\}$ and $Q = \{\{2,4\}, \{2,6\}, \{4,5\}, \{5,6\}\}$. We try to extend $s = \{3, 4\}$. Then $\text{CAND}(\{3,4\}) = \{2, 5, 6\}$ and $select(\{3, 4\}) = \{6\}$. The collection $\{3, 4, 6\}$ is not extended and it corresponds to a good test $- (\{3, 4, 6\}, Embrown)$.

Method 2. The set $\text{CAND}(s)$ is determined as described above. Index $j^* \in \text{CAND}(s)$ can be used for extending s, if for any i from s the pair $\{i, j^*\}$ corresponds a test. But then s must be in the union of all the collections containing j^*, with the exception of only the pairs which are in the set *STGOOD* (these pairs have no enlarging). Hence the following condition must be satisfied for j^*:

$$\{L(j^*) \text{ contains } s\}, \text{ where } L(j^*) = \{\cup s': j^* \in s', s' \in \{S(\text{test}) \cup STGOOD \backslash \{j^*, g\}\}\}.$$

Method 3. In this method, the set $\text{CAND}(s)$ is determined as follows. Let $s^* = \{s \cup j\}$ be an extension of s, where $j \notin s$. Then $\text{val}(s^*) \subseteq \text{val}(s)$. Hence the intersection of $\text{val}(s)$ and $\text{val}(j)$ must be not empty. The set $\text{CAND}(s) = \{j: j \in nts \backslash s, \text{val}(j) \cap \text{val}(s) \neq \emptyset\}$.

For the previous example (Table 2) we have $\text{val}(\{2\}) \cap \text{val}(\{3,4\}) = \emptyset$, $\text{val}(\{5\}) \cap \text{val}(\{3,4\}) \neq \emptyset$, and $\text{val}(\{6\}) \cap \text{val}(\{3,4\}) \neq \emptyset$. Hence we have that $\text{CAND}(\{3, 4\}) = \{5, 6\}$.

The set $ext(s)$ contains all the possible extensions of s in the form $snew = (s \cup j)$, $j \in select(s)$ and $snew$ corresponds to a test for $R(+)$. This procedure of forming $ext(s)$ executes the function generalization_of($snew$) for each element $snew \in ext(s)$.

The generalization rule is a complex process in which both deductive and inductive reasoning rules of the second type are performed (please, see Table 3).

The knowledge acquired during the process of generalization (the sets Q, L, CAND(s), S(test), *STGOOD*) is used for pruning the search in the domain space.

The generalization rule with searching for only admissible variants of generalization is not an artificially constructed operation. A lot of examples of using this rule in human thinking can be given. For example, if your child were allergic to oranges, then you would not buy not only these fruits but also orange juice and also products that contain orange extracts. A good gardener knows the plants that cannot be adjacent in a garden. A lot of problems related to placing personnel, appointing somebody to the post, finding lodging for somebody deal with partitioning a set of objects or persons into groups by taking into account forbidden pairs of objects or persons.

Realization of the Specification Rule for Inferring GIRTs

Let *TGOOD* be the partially ordered set of elements t satisfying the following condition: (obj(t), t) is a good irredundant test for $R(+)$. We denote by SAFE the set of elements t such that t is an irredundant collection of values but (obj(t), t) is not a test for R(+).

Let us recall that we find all GIRTs contained in a given GMRT already obtained for $R(+)$.

Method 1. We use an inductive rule for extending elements of SAFE and constructing $t_{q+1} = \{A_1, A_2, ..., A_{q+1}\}$ from $t_q = (A_1, A_2, ..., A_q)$ $q = 1, 2, .., na - 1$, where na is the number of values in the set T. This rule relies on the following consideration: if the collection of values $\{A_1, A_2, ..., A_{q+1}\}$ is an irredundant one, then all its proper subsets must be irredundant collections of values too and, consequently, they must be in *SAFE*.

Having constructed a set $t_{q+1} = \{A_1, A_2, ..., A_{q+1}\}$, we determine whether it is the irredundant collection of values or not. If t_{q+1} is redundant, then it is deleted from consideration. If it is a test for R(+), then it is transferred to *TGOOD*. If t_{q+1} is irredundant but not a test for $R(+)$, then it is a candidate for extension and it is memorized in *SAFE*.

We use the function to_be_irredundant(t) = if ($\forall A$) ($A \in t$) obj(t) $\neq$ obj($t \setminus A$) then true else false.

Method 2. This method is based on using the inductive diagnostic rule for directly searching for essential values of which consist GIRTs.

We begin with the collection of values $Z = \{A_4, A_{12}, A_{14}, A_{15}, A_{24}, A_{26}\}$, for which obj($\{A_4, A_{12}, A_{14}, A_{15}, A_{24}, A_{26}\}$) = {2, 3, 4, 7} and in our main current example ($s(Z)$, Z) is a GMRT for the set of positive objects (see, please, previous Chapter 7).

We need the set of negative objects in which at least one value of $\{A_4, A_{12}, A_{14}, A_{15}, A_{24}, A_{26}\}$ appears.

Table 3. Using deductive and inductive rules of the second type

Inductive rules	Process	Deductive and inductive rules of the second type
Generalization rule		
	Forming Q	Generating forbidden rules
	Forming CAND(s)	The joint method of Agreement and Difference
	Forming *select*(s)	Using forbidden rules
	Forming *ext*(s)	The method of Agreement
	Function_to_be test(t)	Using implication
	Generlization_of(*snew*)	Closing operation

Table 4. Initial set of negative examples

Index of object	R(−)
17	$A_{24}A_{26}$
23	$A_{14}A_{15}$
38	A_4A_{12}
30 48	$A_{12}A_{14}A_{15}$
31	$A_{14}\,A_{15}\,A_{26}$
42	$A_4A_{12}A_{26}$
47	$A_4A_{12}A_{14}$
37 40 41 43 44 45	$A_4A_{12}A_{14}A_{15}$
39	$A_4A_{14}A_{15}A_{26}$
46	$A_4A_{12}A_{14}A_{15}A_{24}$

We may take the projection of Z on these negative objects (see, please, Table 4).

We find by means of the inductive diagnostic rule that the value A_{26} is the only essential value in Z. Hence this value must belong to any GIRT. Next, select all the negative objects containing A_{26} (Table 5).

Now we must find the maximal subset of Z containing A_{26} and not corresponding to a test for positive objects. This subset is $\{A_4, A_{14}, A_{15}, A_{26}\}$. Hence value A_{24} or A_{12} must belong to GIRTs containing A_{26} because they are essential values in Z with respect to the subset $\{A_4, A_{14}, A_{15}, A_{26}\}$.

Next, we form the collections $\{A_{24}, A_{26}\}$ and $\{A_{12}, A_{26}\}$. But they do not correspond to tests.

Now select the set of negative objects containing $\{A_{24}, A_{26}\}$ and the set of negative objects containing $\{A_{12}, A_{26}\}$. The result is in (Table 6). These sets are used for searching essential values to extend collections $\{A_{24}, A_{26}\}$ and $\{A_{12}, A_{26}\}$.

Now we must find the maximal subset of Z containing the collections $\{A_{24}, A_{26}\}$ and the maximal subset of Z containing $\{A_{12}, A_{26}\}$ such that they do not correspond to tests for positive objects. These collections are $\{A_{24}, A_{26}\}$ and $\{A_4, A_{12}, A_{26}\}$, respectively.

In the first case, we have the set $\{A_4, A_{12}, A_{14}, A_{15}\}$ as the set of essential values in Z. Hence we form the collections $\{A_4, A_{24}, A_{26}\}$, $\{A_{12}, A_{24}, A_{26}\}$, $\{A_{14}, A_{24}, A_{26}\}$, and $\{A_{15}, A_{24}, A_{26}\}$. All these collections correspond to GIRTs for positive objects.

Table 5. Current set of negative examples containing A_{26}

Index of object	R(−)
17	$A_{24}A_{26}$
31	$A_{14}A_{15}A_{26}$
42	$A_4A_{12}A_{26}$
39	$A_4A_{14}A_{15}A_{26}$

Table 6. Current set of negative examples containing $\{A_{24}, A_{26}\}$ and $\{A_{12}, A_{26}\}$

Index of object	R(−)		Index of object	R(−)
17	$A_{24}A_{26}$		42	$A_4A_{12}A_2$

In the second case, we have the set $\{A_{14}, A_{15}, A_{24}\}$ as the set of essential values in Z. Hence we form the collections $\{A_{12}, A_{15}, A_{26}\}$, $\{A_{12}, A_{14}, A_{26}\}$. These collections correspond to GIRTs for positive examples. The essential value A_{24} is not admissible for extending $\{A_{12}, A_{26}\}$ because the collection $\{A_{12}, A_{24}, A_{26}\}$ is included in the union of all GIRTs already obtained and containing the collection $\{A_{12}, A_{26}\}$.

The algorithm builds a decision tree of tests (Table 7) and, in parallel, constructs also the appropriate tree of the subsets of negative objects used for searching essential values.

The generalization operation generalization_of(t) = val(obj(t)) is not used with the search for irredundant tests. The algorithm uses the function to_be_test(t) = if $t \not\subset t'$ for $\forall t'$, $t' \in R(-)$. The reader will find an example of the procedure of tests' tree construction in Chapter 10 of this book.

NIAGARA: NON-INCREMENTAL ALGORITHM OF ALL GMRTS GENERATION BASED ON THE GENERALIZATION RULE

An algorithm NIAGaRa based on the generalization rule is described also in (Naidenova, 2006). It is one of the possible non-incremental algorithms for inferring all GMRTs for a given set of positive examples.

The ascending process $s_0 \subseteq \ldots \subseteq s_i \subseteq s_{i+1} \subseteq \ldots \subseteq s_m$ (val(s_0) $\supseteq \ldots \supseteq$ val(s_i) $\supseteq$ val(s_{i+1}) $\supseteq \ldots \supseteq$ val(s_m)) is used in this algorithm. This process is a sequence of applications of the generalization rule for generating dual elements (s_i, val(s_i)), beginning with two initial sets $R(+) = \{t_1, t_2, \ldots, t_i, \ldots, t_{nt}\}$ and $S(+) = \{\{1\}, \{2\}, \ldots, \{i\}, \ldots, \{nt\}\}$, where nt is the number of positive examples (objects).

The procedure DEBUT (see, please, Figure 2) produces the extensions of elements of the initial set $S(+) = \{\{1\}, \{2\}, \ldots, \{i\}, \{j\}, \ldots, \{nt\}\}$ and, as result, constructs the set $\{s_{12}, s_{13}, \ldots, s_{ij}, \ldots, \}$, where $s_{ij} = \{i, j\}$, $1 < i < j < nt$.

Every element $s_{ij} = \{i, j\}$, such that (s_{ij}, val(s_{ij})) is not a test for a given set of positive examples, is recorded in the set Q of forbidden pairs of objects.

Every element $s_{ij} = \{i, j\}$, such that (s_{ij}, val(s_{ij})) is a test for a given set of positive examples, is generalized by the use of the function generalization_of (s_{ij}) and after that the result s = generalization_of(s_{ij}) is inserted in the set S(test).

Table 7. Decision tree of tests

Level 1	Level 2	Level 3
		A_4
		A_{12}
	A_{24}	
		A_{14}
A_{26}		
		A_{15}
		A_{15}
	A_{12}	
		A_{14}

Figure 2. The beginning of the procedure of inferring GMRTs

```
                         The procedure DEBUT.

Input: R(+), R(−), nt, S(+) = {{1},......,{nt}}.
Output: S(test) -  the set of collections of objects to be extended,
         Q - the set of forbidden pairs of objects, STGOOD.

Begin
STGOOD  ← ∅;  Q  ← ∅;  S(test)  ← ∅;
for i = 1,  , nt: sum(i)  ← 0;
begin do
i = S[1],..., S[nt]
j = S[i+1], ..., S[nt]
if to_be_test (val({i,j})) = false then  Q  ← Q ∪ {i,j};
    else s'  ← generalization_of({i,j});
    (∀i), i ∈ s': sum(i)  ← sum(i) + 1;
    insert s' into S(test) under lexicographically order;
end j
end i
end
begin do
(∀i) (i = 1, nt) if sum(i) = 1 then find s, i ∈ s, s ∈ S(test);
insert s into STGOOD under lexicographically order; /* s is a GMRT */
Delete s from S(test);
end
nts  ←(∪ s, s ∈ S(test));
end
```

When DEBUT terminates, it is necessary to check whether an element s of S(test) corresponds to a GMRT for a given set of positive examples or not. For this goal, we use the following rule: if some object j, for $j = 1, ..., nt$, belongs to one and only one element s of S(test), then s can not be extended and, consequently, s corresponds to a GMRT and it is deleted from S(test) and it is inserted into *STGOOD*.

S(test) is the partially ordered set containing all $s = \{i_1, i_2, ..., i_q\}$, $q = 1, 2, ..., nt$, satisfying the condition that $(s, val(s))$ is a maximally redundant test for a given set of positive examples but not a good one.

STGOOD is the partially ordered set containing all $s = \{i_1, i_2, ..., i_q\}$, $q = 1, 2, ..., nt$, satisfying the condition that $(s, val(s))$ is a GMRT for a given set of positive examples.

In its main part, the algorithm NIAGaRa infers, for every s in S(test), the set $ext(s)$ of all possible extensions of s which correspond to tests for a given set of positive examples. The algorithm realizes a directional choice of objects for extending s with the use of the generalization rule.

The procedure SELECT(s) (see also Figure 3) serves for this goal. It returns the set $select(s)$ of objects that are admissible to produce extensions of s corresponding to tests. The following sets are used in this procedure: s, $not(s)$, V, CAND(s), Q, S(test), and *STGOOD*.

Let nts be the union of all s in S(test). Under lexicographically ordering the elements of S(test), the restricted range of searching is the set $not(s) = \{i: i \in nts, i >$ "the last object of the collection s"$\}$.

The set V is determined as the set of objects which must be deleted from nts in order not to repeat the generation of the same tests.

The set of objects CAND(s) of candidates for extending s is equal to $not(s) \backslash V$. If V is empty, then CAND(s) is equal to $not(s)$. Finally, we have that $select(s) = \{i, i \in$ CAND(s): $(\forall j)(j \in s)$, $\{i, j\} \notin \{STGOOD$ or $Q\}\}$.

Figure 3. The procedure for determining the set of indices for extending s

```
                    The procedure SELECT(s).

Input: s, nts, Q, S(test), STGOOD.
Output: the set select(s) of objects for possible extensions.


not(s) = {i: i ∈ nts, i > "the last object of the collection s"}
Begin do
if not(s) = ∅ then select(s)  ← ∅;
else
   V = {∪ s', s ⊆ s', s' ∈ {S(test) ∪ STGOOD}};
   if V = ∅ then CAND(s)  ← not(s);
   else
   CAND(s)  ← not(s) \V;
     if CAND(s) = ∅ then select(s) ← ∅
     else
      select(s) = {i, i ∈ CAND(s): (∀j)(j ∈ s),
      {i,j} ∉ {STGOOD or Q}},
        where Q = {{i, j}: to_ be_ test (val({i,j})) = false};
end
```

The procedure EXTENSION(s) (see also Figure 4) takes *select(s)* and returns the set *ext(s)* of all possible extensions of *s* in the form (s ∪ j) for all j, j ∈ *select(s)*. This procedure executes the function generalization_of(s).

The procedure ANALYSIS_OF_EXTENTIONS(s) (see also Figure5) checks the set *ext(s)*. If *ext(s)* is empty and *V* is empty, then *s* corresponds to a GMRT and *s* is transferred from *S*(test) to *STGOOD*. If *ext(s)* contains one and only one element *snew*, then *snew* corresponds to a GMRT, *snew* is inserted into *STGOOD* and *s* is deleted from *S*(test). In all other cases, the set *ext(s)* substitutes *s* in *S*(test).

The set *nts* is modified during the process of inferring GMRTs and it may happen that the function to_be_test(t(nts)) = *true*. This condition indicates that the process of inferring GMRTs is over. The task also stops when *S*(test) is empty.

Table 8. The result of the procedure DEBUT for the examples of class 2 (see alsoTable 1)

S	val(s)	Test?	Generalization_of(s)	Q	S(test)
{2,3}	Brown	Yes	{2,3,5}		{2,3,5}
{2,4}	∅	No		{2,4}	
{2,5}	Brown Bleu	Yes	{2,5}		{2,5}
{2,6}	Low	No		{2,6}	
{3,4}	Tall Embrown	Yes	{3,4}		{3,4}
{3,5}	Tall Brown	Yes	{3,5}		{3,5}
{3,6}	Embrown	Yes	{3,4,6}		{3,4,6}
{4,5}	Tall	No		{4,5}	
{4,6}	Blond Embrown	Yes	{4,6}		{4,6}
{5,6}	∅	No		{5,6}	

Figure 4. The procedure for generating all possible extensions of s

```
                    The procedure EXTENSION(s).

Input: s, select(s), S(test), STGOOD.
Output: ext(s) – the set of all extensions s' of s such that
val(s') is a test and || s'|| = ||s|| + 1.
snew – a current extension of s.

  Begin
  ext(s) = ∅;
  while select(s) ≠ ∅
  snew ← s ∪ j, j ∈ select(s);
  if to_be_test(val(snew)) = false then eliminate snew; else

   Begin do
   snew ← generalization_of(snew);
   insert snew into ext(s) under lexicographically order;
   end
  end while

  end
```

Finally, the set *TGOOD* of all GMRTs for a given set of positive examples is formed as follows:

$$TGOOD = \{val(s): s \in STGOOD\}.$$

The procedure NIAGaRa (Figure 6) uses the procedures DEBUT, SELECT(s), ESTENSION(s), and ANALYSIS_ OF_ EXTENSION(s).

Figure 5. The procedure for analyzing the set of extensions of s

```
          The procedure ANALYSIS_OF_EXTENSION (s).
  Input:        ext(s), S(test), STGOOD.
  Output:       the modified sets S(test) and STGOOD.

   Begin
   if ext(s) = ∅ and V = ∅ then
    Begin    /* s corresponds to a GMRT */;
    do
     insert s into STGOOD under lexicographically order;
    end
   if ||ext(s)|| = 1 then
     Begin do /* snew corresponds to a GMRT */;
     insert snew into STGOOD under lexicographically
   order;
     end
   Begin do
   (∀ snew) (snew ∈ ext(s))
   insert snew into S(test) under lexicographically order;
   end
   S(test) ←S(test)\s;
   end
```

Table 9. The result of inferring GMRTs for the examples of class 2 (see also Table 1)

s	not(s)	V	CAND(s)	select(s)	ext(s)	Results
{2,3,5}	{6}	∅	{6}	∅	∅	{2,3,5} → *STGOOD*
{2,5}	{6}	{2,3,5}	{6}	∅	∅	{2,5} → delete
{3,4}	{5,6}	{3,4,6}	{5}	∅	∅	{3,4} → delete
{3,4,6}	∅	∅	∅	∅	∅	{3,4,6} →*STGOOD*
{3,5}	{6}	{2,3,5}	{6}	∅	∅	{3,5} → delete
{4,6}	∅	{3,4,6}	∅	∅	∅	{4,6} → delete

The following Table 8 and Table 9 illustrate the work of the procedure NIAGaRa for inferring all the GMRTs for the objects of Class 2 (Table 1). In this example, the set *STGOOD* is empty after the procedure DEBUT is over.

The other example of how the algorithm NIAGaRa works is given in the Appendix of this Chapter.

We now turn to consider the computational complexity of the algorithm and procedures described.

The problem of generating all GMRTs for a given set of positive examples is NP-complete because the number of GMRTs may be exponentially large. In the worst case, the number of GMRTs is $O(2^{|T|}/|T|^{1/2})$.

The algorithm NIAGaRa is optimal in the sense that it generates each element *s* only once.

In essence, the number of elements of the set Q determines "virtually" the computational complexity of the algorithm. The increase of this number is equivalent to the decrease of the number of positive examples. Since class 2 contains 5 positive examples (lines 2, 3, 4, 5, and 6 in Table 1), it is possible to generate 10 pairs of examples of this class. But 4 of these pairs are forbidden ones (Q has 4 elements). Therefore only 6 pairs of positive examples determine the number of dual lattice elements to be generated by the algorithm. Thus, we have a "virtual" set of positive examples with 4 elements (6 pairs can

Figure 6. The main procedure NIAGaRa for inferring GMRTs

> **The procedure NIAGaRa.**
>
> **Input:** $R(+)$, $R(-)$, *nt*, $S(+) = \{\{1\},......,\{nt\}\}$.
> **Output**: the set *TGOOD* of all GMRTs
> for positive examples.
>
> DEBUT;
> **Begin do**
> **while** $S(\text{test}) \neq \varnothing$ or to_be_test($val(nts)$) = false **do**
>
> SELECT(*s*);
> EXTENSION(*s*);
> ANALYSIS_OF_EXTENSION(*s*);
>
> $nts ::= (\cup\ s, s \in S(\text{test}));$
>
> **end while**
> construct *TGOOD* from *STGOOD*;
> **end**

Table 10. The number of combinations C_N^2, C_N^3, C_N^4 as a function of N

N	4	5	6	7	8	9	10	11	12	13	14
C_N^2	6	10	15	21	28	36	45	55	66	78	91
C_N^3	4	10	20	35	56	84	120	165	220	286	364
C_N^4	1	5	15	35	70	126	210	330	495	715	1001

be generated by four elements). As $C_4^3 = 4$, it is possible to construct only 4 triples from the set of four elements.

This estimation is very rough because we deal with the sets S(test) and Q which are not compact. Actually, only two triples have been constructed in the illustrative example (Table 9).

In our illustrative example in the Appendix, the initial set S(test) contains 25 elements (admissible pairs of positive examples). It roughly corresponds to decreasing the number of positive examples from 14 to 8.

If we know the number of pairs of elements of some set with N elements, then we can compute the number of subsets of this set with 3, 4, …, N-1 elements as follows: $C_N^3 = C_N^2 (N-2)/3$; $C_N^4 = C_N^2 [(N-3)/4][(N-2)/3]$; …… and, generally, we have:

$$! \, _N^k = C_N^2 \frac{(N-2)!}{(N-k)! \, k!}$$

Table 10 shows the number of combinations C_N^2, C_N^3, C_N^4 as a function of N. For the set of N elements when $N = 14$ the number of pairs of its elements is equal to 91, the number of triples of its elements is equal to 364 and the number of its subsets containing 4 elements is equal to 1001. Decreasing the number of pairs by 2 times (which is equivalent to decreasing N from 14 to 10) implies decreasing the number of triples by 3 times and the number of subsets containing 4 elements – by 5 times.

The computational complexity of the procedures DEBUTE, SELECT(s), ESTENSION(s) and ANALYSIS_OF_EXTENSION(s) depends on the computational complexity of the functions general-ization_of(s), to_be_test(val(s)) and the operation which inserts an element s into one of the sets ext(s), S(test) or *STGOOD*.

The function generalization_of(s) is of time complexity of order O(nt), where nt is the number of posi-tive examples. The function to_be_test(val(s)) can be reduced to checking whether obj(val(s)) contains at least one of negative examples or not. It can be implemented by the use of radix sorting which sorts n integers in time O(n) (Aho et al., 1979). Therefore the function to_be_test(val(s)) is of time complexity of order O($nt + nf$), where nt and nf the number of positive and negative examples, respectively.

The operation of inserting an element s into the sets ext(s), S(test) or *STGOOD* under lexicographi-cally ordering of these sets is reduced to lexicographically sorting a sequence of k-element collections of integers (element s is a collection of integers). A sequence of n collections, the components of which are represented by integers from 1 to m, is sorted in time of O($m + L$), where L is the sum of lengths of all the collections of this sequence (Aho et al., 1979). Consequently, if *Lext*, *Lstest*, *Lgtest* are the sums of lengths of all the collections s of ext(s), S(test) and *STGOOD*, respectively, then the time complexity of inserting an element s into ext(s) is of order O($|T| + Lext$), the time complexity of inserting an element

s into S(test) is of order $O(|T| + Lstest)$, and the time complexity of inserting an element s into *STGOOD* is of order $O(|T| + Lgtest)$.

The procedure DEBUT has a polynomial time complexity of order $O(nt^2(nt + nf) + nt^3) + O(nt^2 (|T| + Lstest)) + O(nt (|T| + Lgtest))$. The procedure SELECT($s$) has a polynomial time complexity of order $O((mt+mg) + nt^2)$, where mt – the number of elements of S(test), mg – the number of elements of *STGOOD*.

The procedure EXTENSION(s) has a polynomial time complexity of order $O(nt (nf + nt)) + O(nt^2) + O(nt (|T| + Lext))$. The procedure ANALYSIS_OF_EXTENSION(s) has a polynomial time complexity of order $O(nt (|T| + Lstest + Lgtest))$.

The algorithm NIAGaRa finds all the GMRTs for a given set of positive examples but the number of these GMRTs can be exponentially large. In this case, this algorithm will be not realistic. In the next chapter, we consider some decompositions of the problem that provide the possibility to restrict the domain of the search, to predict, in some degree, the number of tests, and to choose tests with the use of essential values and/or examples.

RELATED WORKS

By the method of construction, GMRT coincides with the concept of FCA. Really, for a GMRT (s, t), we have that s is the result of generalization operation: $s = obj(val(s'))$, where $val(s') = t = \{$intersection of all $t_i: t_i \subseteq T, i \in s'\}$. The problem of generating the set of all concepts of a formal context is extensively studied in the literature (Bordat, 1986), (Chein, 1969), (Dowling, 1993), (Ganter, 1984), (Ganter & Reuter 1991), (Kuznetsov, 1993), (Kuznetsov & Ob'edkov, 2000), (Nguifo & Njiwoua, 1998), (Norrice, 1978), (Nourine & Raynaud, 1999), and (Stumme et al., 2000).

The computational complexity analysis of these main algorithms and experimental comparisons of them can be found in (Kuznetsov & Ob'edkov, 2002) and (Fu & Nguifo, 2004b). In the work (Kuznetsov, 2004), some of these algorithms are described and their performance is compared. Other comparative studies are presented in (Godin & Chau, 2000), (Guénoche, 1998), and (Fu & Mephu, 2004a).

It is known that the number of concepts can be exponential in the size of the input context and the task of generating all the concepts of context is #P-complete (Kuznetsov, 2004). An algorithm generating all concepts can be considered optimal (with respect to the worst-case complexity) if it generates the lattice with polynomial time delay and space linear in the number of all concepts; a representation of a concept lattice can be considered reasonable if its size can not be exponentially compressed w.r.t. to the input and allows the search for a particular concept in time polynomial in the input (Kuznetsov & Ob'edkov, 2002).

It is customary to divide all the algorithms into two categories: incremental algorithms in which the concept set is modified with adding a new object (or attribute) of the context, and batch ones, which construct the concept set for the whole context from scratch. We focus in this chapter only on these latter algorithms putting off the consideration of the former ones for the next chapter.

There are two strategies to generate concepts with batch algorithms: descending or top-down and ascending or bottom-up. However, it is important whether the leading process consists directly in generating all subsets of objects (extents of objects) or all subsets of attributes (intents of concepts).

Bordat's (1986) algorithm builds not all concepts but also the concept lattices (Haase diagram). It uses a top-down strategy for inferring concepts in "breadth first" manner. The leading process of this algorithm is generating the subsets of objects of a given context with diminishing more and more their power.

Chein's (1969) algorithm uses a bottom-up strategy. It begins with considering each object g_i and its attributes for constructing the concepts of first layer L_1. Level L_{k+1} is constructed from level L_k. as follows: for every two elements $(ext_i, int(ext_i))$ and $(ext_j, int(ext_j))$ of L_k, if $(int(ext_i) \cap (int(ext_j)) \notin L_{k+1}$, then $(ext_i \cup ext_j, int(ext_i) \cap int(ext_j))$ is an element of L_{k+1}. Otherwise, merge all pairs that have the same $int(ext_i) \cap int(ext_j)$ as an element of L_{k+1}.

In Ganter's (1984) NextClosure algorithm, the leading process is the building of lexically ordered attribute subsets.

In Kuznetsov's (1993) CloseByOne algorithm, the leading process is the building of lexically ordered object subsets.

Our prime interest is of the methods by means of which the main problem of algorithms is solved: how to avoid repetitive generation of the same concept or how to test of uniqueness of generated concept. With respect to this problem, the following methods are summarized in (Kuznetsov & Ob'edkov, 2002): (1) using the lexicographical order; (2) dividing the set of concepts into several parts; (3) using hash function; (4) using an auxiliary tree structure; and (5) using attribute cache.

On account of the duality of descending and ascending strategies, an algorithm can focus on objects (extents) or attributes (intents), and every lattice algorithm has its corresponding dual one. In (Fu, & Nguifo, 2004b), all the considered algorithms are tested with their dual variants. The experimental results show that the performances of two dual algorithms are very different. The most certain results have been obtained with respect to Ganter's algorithm. This algorithm runs faster than others and it has the best performance when it focuses on the smallest number of objects or attributes of the initial context.

The previous main algorithms have serious drawbacks in the following aspects:

- They are applied only to binary data;
- They are limited by only small collections of data, in practice, a hundred objects and a few dozens of attributes (or properties).

Improvements of concepts lattice algorithms are performed in several directions:

- Data context generalization to symbolic data context (Generalized Galois Lattice (G^2L)); this generalization of Bordat (1986), Ganter (1984), and (Godin et al., 1995) algorithms was advanced in (Diday & Emilion, 1997) and (Emilion et al., 2001). Also the Galois Lattice (GL) formalism was extended to symbolic data by (Brito, 1991), (Brito, 1994) and further developed in (Polaillon, 1998a), (Polaillon, 1998b), and (Pollaillon & Diday, 1999).
- Localization of the search space by means of using some properties of concepts of Galois Lattice.
- Lexicographical order in generating the closed sets of objects or attributes;
- Partition of the set of objects (attributes) of a context into disjoint groups for creating scalable distributed calculus algorithms constructing a G^2L over a large collection of data (Fu &Nguifo, 2004b), (Baklouti et al., 2005), and (Lévy & Baklouti, 2005).

We consider in short some methods for improving concepts lattice algorithms.

The generalized context C. Let $F = F_1 \times \ldots \times F_j \times \ldots \times F_n$, be the Cartesian product of F_j, where F_j is a totally ordered finite set represented, without loss of generality, as a set of integers, say:

$$F_j = \{0, 1, \ldots, b_j\}, 0 < 1 < \ldots < b_j.$$

A function $d(i)$ associates with an object i of S, its description $d(i) = (d_1(i), d_2(i), \ldots, d_j(i), \ldots, d_n(i)) \in F = F_1 \times \ldots \times F_j \times \ldots \times F_n$, according to the attributes or properties $j \in J = \{1, \ldots, n\}$, where J is the set of all the attributes (properties), $i = \{1, \ldots, m\}$. So, in the general case, context C is an m x n array of elements $d_j(i)$ of F, and for each object i and each property j, $d_j(i)$ takes its value in the set $F_j = \{0, 1, \ldots, b_j\}, 0 < 1 < \ldots < b_j$.

Naturally, F is the Cartesian product of several lattices $F_j = <F_j, \leq_j, \vee_j, \wedge_j, O_{Fj}, 1_{Fj}>$, for $\in j \in J = \{1, \ldots, n\}$.

The relation $\leq$ on F is defined by $z = (z_1, \ldots, z_j, \ldots, z_n) \leq t = (t_1, \ldots, t_j, \ldots, t_n)$ iff $z_j \leq_j t_j$ for each j of J. We have $z \vee t = (\ldots, z_j \vee_j t_j, \ldots)$, $z \wedge t = (\ldots, z_j \wedge_j t_j, \ldots)$, $O_F = (\ldots, O_{Fj}, \ldots)$, $1_F = (\ldots, 1_{Fj}, \ldots)$, where operations $\vee_j$, $\wedge_j$ are defined as follows: $z_j \vee_j t_j = \sup (z_j, t_j) = \max(z_j, t_j)$ and $z_j \wedge_j t_j = \inf(z_j, t_j) = \min(z_j, t_j)$.

Galois connection for generalized context C is defined in (Baklouti & Lévy (2005). Let C = <S, F, d> be a context. Let E = 2^S. The mapping f: E $\rightarrow$ F is defined as follows: for each subset X of S, $f(X) = \wedge d(i): i \in X\}$ if $X \neq \emptyset$, and $f(\emptyset) = 1_F$. So, $f(X)$ is the intent of X.

The mapping g: F $\rightarrow$ E is defined as follows: $g(z) = \{i \in S: z \leq d(i)\}$, for each z of F}. So, $g(z)$ is the extent of z. The ordered pair (g, f) is called a Galois connection. The closure operations are defined as follows: h = E $\rightarrow$ E: h = g °f, and k = F $\rightarrow$ F: k = f °g. So, for each subset X of S, we have $h(X) = g(f(X)) = \{i \in S: f(X) \leq d(i)\}$, and for each z of F, we have $k(z) = f(g(z)) = \wedge\{d(i): i \in g(z)\}$.

Any subset X of S such that $X = h(X)$ is called a S-closed set, and each z of F such that $z = k(z)$ is called F-closed set. A pair (X, z) such that $f(X) = z$, and $g(z) = X$, is called a concept. The set of all such concepts constitutes the Galois lattice GL(C) associated with this context C (the order relation on GL(C) is defined by $(X, z) \leq (X', z')$ iff $X \subseteq X'$ and $z' \leq z$.).

The idea of the search space localization when listing all the closed subsets of S is proposed and realized in the algorithm ELL (Emillion, et al., 1997) which has subsequently been improved in (Baklouti et al., 2005). Let X_0 and K be two disjoint subsets of S. ELL(X_0, K) denotes a procedure which lists all the closed extensions of X_0 which contain X_0 and are contained in $X_0 \cup K$. The following proposition underpins this procedure.

Proposition 8.3 (Baklouti et al., 2005): Let X_0 and $K \neq \emptyset$ be two disjoint subsets of S. Let $i_0 \in K$. We have: $h(X_0 \cup \{i_0\}) = X_0 \cup A$, where $A = \{i \in S\backslash X_0: f(X_0) \wedge f(i_0) \leq f(i)\}$. The proof of this proposition is in (Emillion et al., 1997).

If a closed set contains X_0 and i_0, then it also contains A. Hence, if $A \subseteq K$, then $X_0 \cup A$ is the smallest closed set containing X_0 and i_0 and contained in $X_0 \cup K$. If a closed set contains X_0 and does not contain i_0, then it also does not contain any element of the set: $R = \{i \in K: f(X_0) \wedge f(i) \leq f(i_0)\}$.

The following pseudo-code is a recursive version of the algorithm (Baklouti & Lévy, 2005).

```
Procedure ELL (X₀, K)
GL = Ø /* GL is a list of concepts*/
Var i₀: element of S; z, z₀: elements of F; X, A, R: subsets of S;
Begin
```

```
z₀ = f(X₀);
if K ≠ ∅ then
begin
Choose an element i₀ of K;
z = z₀∧ f(i₀); A = {i ∈ S\ X₀: z ≤ f(i)};
ifA ⊆ Kthen
begin
X = X₀ ∪ A; insert node (X, z) in GL;
ELL (X, K\A);
end;
R = {I ∈ K: z₀ ∧ f(i) ≤ f(i₀)}; ELL (X₀, K\R);
end
end
```

In (Baklouti et al., 2005), an iterative version of this algorithm is proposed in order to speed up the search what is very important for very large datasets. The iteration version requests to choose an element i_0 of K. If i_0 is chosen at every iteration as the smallest element of K with respect to its ordering, then the concepts are generated in lexicographic order.

Scalable Distributed G²L calculus. Parallel algorithms for General Galois lattice building have been proposed in (Baklouti & Lévy, 2003). A new improved solution to parallelize the computation with large contexts is based on a new algorithm SD-ELL.

SD-ELL algorithm (Baklouti & Lévy, 2005) is composed of two procedures. The first one computes the sets of objects K_i ($i = \{1, ..., n\}$, n is the number of the computed sets K_i) and the second one is duplicated on different machines to compute independently all the closed sets corresponding to each K_i. The second procedure of SD-ELL is the iterative version of ELL.

A major problem of SD-ELL is the storage of the collection of the closed concepts produced, presumably very large and of unknown size. This problem is solved by a Scalable Distributed Data Structure (SDDS). The storage of the great number of closed sets is based on scaling dynamically the number of server nodes with the growth of the closed concepts.

Product order and lexicographic order. Two order relations $\leq$ and $\preccurlyeq$ are usually defined on F. Let $y = (y_1, ..., y_n)$, $z = (z_1, ..., z_n) \in$ F. Then the product order $\leq$ is defined as follows: $y \leq z$ iff $\forall j = 1, ..., n$: $y_j \leq z_j$. The lexicographic order (LO.) $\preccurlyeq$ (or prefix order) is defined as follows: $y \preccurlyeq z$ iff $(y = z)$ or $(\exists j \in \{1, ..., n\}: y_j < z_j$ and $(y_k = z_k \ \forall \ k < j))$.

As usual, $y < z$ (vs. $y \prec z$) means that $y \leq z$ (vs. $y \preccurlyeq z$) and $y \neq z$. It is easy to verify that F is partially ordered for $\leq$ and totally ordered for $\preccurlyeq$. The greatest element of F for $\preccurlyeq$ is: $b = (b_1, ..., b_n) = 1_F$.

The function **inflex** (X_n, Y_n) takes the value '*true*' iff X_n precedes Y_n in L.O.

The next in lexicographical order of X_n. For this goal (to define the next of a given X_n in LO.), each element of F receives its transition subscript i as follows: if $X_n = (x_1, x_2, ..., x_{i-1}, x_i, b_{i+1}, b_{i+2}, ..., b_n)$ and $x_i < b_i$, then its transition subscript is i.

This subscript is designated by $i^+(X_n)$. Of course, $i^+(X_n) = 0$ iff $X_n = 1_F$. Knowing the transition subscript of X_n, we can determine the next element of X_n in LO., what does the following function **next**(X, i, Y, $i^+(X)$) (Lévy & Baklouti, 2005).

This procedure determines $Y = X+$, the next element of X_n in LO.

For every $X = (x_1, x_2, \ldots, x_{i-1}, x_i, b_{i+1}, b_{i+2}, \ldots, b_n)$, other than 1_F, we define the element X^* of F as follows: $X^* = (x_1, x_2, \ldots, x_{i-1}, b_i, b_{i+1}, b_{i+2}, \ldots, b_n)$, if $i^+(X) = i$. Consequently, $X \preccurlyeq X+ \preccurlyeq X^*$ for every X of F, other than 1_F.

There are several relationships between product-order and LO. on F (Lévy & Baklouti, 2005).

Proposition 8.4: $\forall X$ and Y of F, if $X \leq Y$, then $X \preccurlyeq Y$.

Proposition 8.5: Whatever are X and Y of F, if X is different of 1_F, then: $X+ \leq Y \leq X^*$ iff $X+ \preccurlyeq Y \preccurlyeq X^*$.

Next closed itemset according to lexicographical order. Let C = (S, F, d) be a context and a be an element of F. We search for the first element y of F which is a closed itemset of the lattice TG(C) and such as a is strictly less than y in LO. The following proposition is analogous proposition 8.2.

Proposition 8.6: Let a^+ be the following of a in LO. We pose $X = g(a^+) \subseteq S$, and $y = k(a^+) = f(X) \in$ F.

If $a^+ \leq y \leq a^*$, then y is the first closed itemset of TG(C) following a in LO. Otherwise, there is no closed item z of TG(C) between a^+ and a^*, and the following closed itemset of a in LO is to be searched from the next of a^*. The properties established previously lead to the second version of **the Ganter algorithm,** namely, **Procedure GANTER2(C: context)** (Lévy & Baklouti, 2005) for context C = <S, F, d > such as F provided with the product-order.

```
Procedure GANTER2 (C: context)
Var a, a⁺, a*: elements of F; X element of E; i, i⁺, nf: integer; {nf
= number of closed itemsets of the lattice}
Begin
nf = 0; a =0_F; i = n; X = g(a); y = f(X);
If (y = a) thenbeginnf = 1 + nf; show (X, y); end;
While (i > 0) then
Begin
next (a, i, a⁺, i⁺); a = a⁺; i = i⁺; X = g(a); y = f (X);
If (for every j < i we have y_j = a_j) thenbeginnf = 1 + nf; show (X,
y); a = y; i = n; end;elsei = i - 1;
end
end
```

Distributed construction of TG(C). Distributed (or parallelized) version of the algorithm GANTER2 is based on a decomposition of the construction of TG(C) into many parts by the partition of F into intervals each of which generates some fragment of TG(C) with the use of different processor. We note TG(C, u, v) the set of closed itemset (X, y) of TG(C) such as $u \preccurlyeq y \prec v$, and the interval of TG(C) is denoted by [u, v[. The main problem of the work distribution between various processors is to generate partition which is as adequate as possible with respect to the capacity of the various available processors. In paper (Lévy & Baklouti, 2005), some mathematical tools are presented that help to build a balanced partition.

The authors consider the method of balanced partition construction to be more efficient than the context-based approaches proposed in (Baklouti & Lévy, 2003) and (Valtchev et al., 2002) which need to compute the Cartesian product of two Galois lattices.

A parallel algorithm for lattice construction in Formal Concept Analysis is constructed by Kengue1 et al. (2005). They propose a novel divide-and-conquer (D&C) approach that operates by data slicing.

In this paper, the authors present a new parallel algorithm, called DAC-ParaLaX, which borrows its main operating primitives from an existing sequential procedure and integrates them into a multi-process architecture. The algorithm has been implemented using a parallel dialect of the C ++ language and its practical performances have been compared to those of a homologue sequential algorithm.

Recently, rather new direction in concept lattice construction began to be developed. It deals with the realization of closure operator by means of a special kind of three-layered neural network. Rudolph (2007) introduces the basic notions of closure operator and implication and shows their correspondence. Then he defines a 3-layered feed-forward network and provides two ways of encoding a formal context's closure operator into this neural network.

Recently, a novel neural network approach CLANN based on concept lattices was proposed with the advantage to be suitable for finding the architecture of the neural network when the apriori knowledge is not available. However CLANN is limited to application with only two-class of data, which is not often the case in practice. Nguifo et al. (2008) propose a novel approach M-CLANN in order to treat multi-class data. Carried out experiments showed the soundness and efficiency of this approach on different datasets compared to standard machine learning systems. It also comes out that M-CLANN model considerably improved CLANN model when dealing with two-class data.

CONCLUSION

The methodology presented in this chapter provides a framework for solving diverse and very important problems of constructing machine learning algorithms based on an unified logical model in which it is possible to interpret any elementary step of logical inferring as a human mental operation. This methodology is more general than the FCA because it deals with object classifications that are not formal concepts in terms of the FCA (good irredundant tests contained in a good maximally redundant test).

The lattice theory is used as a mathematical language for constructing and using good classification tests. The definition of good tests is based on correspondences of Galois G on $S \times T$, where S is a given set of objects and T is a set of attributes' values (values, for short). Any classification test is a dual element of the Galois Lattice generated over a given context (S, T). We redefine, in this chapter, the concepts of a good maximally redundant test (GMRT) and a good irredundant test (GIRT) for a given classification of objects as dual objects of Galois lattice.

Inferring the chains of dual lattice elements ordered by the inclusion relation lies in the foundation of generating all types of diagnostic tests. The following inductive transitions from one element of a chain to its nearest element in the lattice are used: (i) from s_q to s_{q+1}, (ii) from t_q to t_{q+1}, (iii) from s_q to s_{q-1}, (iv) from t_q to t_{q-1}, where q, $q+1$, $q-1$ are the cardinalities of enumerated subsets of objects and values.

The following special rules are introduced for realizing the inductive transitions: generalization rule, specification rule, dual generalization rule, dual specification rules. These rules relate to extending or narrowing collections of objects (values).

Note that reasoning begins with using a mechanism for restricting the space of searching for tests: for each collection of values (objects), to avoid constructing all its subsets. For this goal, admissible values (objects) for extending $t_q (s_q)$ and essential values (objects) for narrowing $t_q (s_q)$ are determined.

Searching for admissible or essential values (indices) is based on inductive diagnostic rules. During the lattice construction, the implicative assertions are generated and used immediately. The knowledge acquired during the process of generalization (specialization) is used for pruning the search in the domain space.

We consider algebraic description of algorithms for finding classification tests to be very important because the following considerations:

- Algorithms constructed are independent on concrete implementation methods of lattice operations. It permits to make them reusable by different conceptual interpretations of lattice operations and different representation forms of objects;
- Algebraic model for constructing algorithms is theoretically interesting because it permits to solve the problem of proving the correctness of algorithms, to evaluate their effectiveness, and to investigate their comparative characteristics in a unified manner.

The lattice structure is a structure of knowledge and the processes of lattice construction become a knowledge manipulation or commonsense reasoning processes. All the operations of lattice construction take their interpretations in human mental acts. Our next step towards the developing commonsense reasoning model is to transform good diagnostic tests inferring into an incremental process. This step will be done in the next chapter.

REFERENCES

Aho, A. V., Hopcraft, J. E., & Ullman, J. D. (1979). *The design and analysis of computer algorithms*. Moscow, USSR: Mir.

Baklouti, F., & Lévy, G. (2003). *Parallel algorithms for general galois lattices building*. Paper presented at the 5th Workshop on Distributed Data and Structures (WDAS'03), Thessaloniki, Greece.

Baklouti, F., & Lévy, G. (2005). Distributed and general galois lattice for large data bases. In R. Bělohlávek & V. Snášel (Eds.), *Proceedings of International Workshop on Concept Lattice and their Application (CLA)*, (pp. 197-206). Ostrava, Czech Republic: Amphora Research group.

Baklouti, F., & Lévy, G., & Emillion. (2005). A fast and general algorithm for galois lattices building. *The Electronic Journal of Symbolic Data Analysis*, *2*(1), 19–31.

Birkhoff, G. (1954). *Lattice theory*. Moscow, USSR: Foreign Literature.

Bordat, J.-P. (1986). Calcul Pratique du Treillis de Galois d'une Correspondence. *Mathématique . Informatique et Sciences Humaines*, *24*(94), 31–47.

Brito, P. (1991) *Analyse de données symboliques. Pyramides d'Héritage*. Unpublished doctoral dissertation, University Paris IX Dauphine.

Brito, P. (1994). Order structure of symbolic assertion objects. *IEEE Transactions on Knowledge and Data Engineering*, *6*(5), 830–835. doi:10.1109/69.317710

Chein, M. (1969). Algorithme de Recherche des Sous-Matrices Premières d'une Matrice. *Bull. Math. Soc. Sci. Math. R.S. Roumanie*, *13*, 21–25.

Diday, E., & Emilion, R. (1997). Treillis de Galois Maximaux et Capacités de Choquet. *Cahier de Recherche de l'Acadèmie des Sciences*. Paris, t. 325 . *Série, I*, 261–266.

Dowling, C. E. (1993). On the irredundant generation of knowledge spaces. *Journal of Mathematical Psychology, 37*(1), 49–62. doi:10.1006/jmps.1993.1003

Emilion, R., Lambert, G., & Lévy, G. (1997). *Algorithms pour les Treillis de Galois*. Paper presented at the meeting of Indo-French Workshop, University Paris IX – Dauphine.

Emilion, R., Lambert, G., & Lévy, G. (2001). *Algorithms for general galois lattice building*. Technical report. CERIA. France: University PARIS IX Dauphine.

Everett, J. (1944). Closure operators and Galois theory in lattices. *Transactions of the American Mathematical Society, 55*(1), 514–525. doi:10.2307/1990306

Fu, H. Nguifo, E. M. (2004a). Etude et Conception d'Algorithmes de Génération de Concepts Formels. In J.-F. Boulicault, & B. Crémilleux (Eds.), *Revue d'Ingénierie des Systèmes d'Information (ISI)*. *9*(3-4), 109-132.

Fu, Huaiguo, & Nguifo, E. M. (2004b). A parallel algorithm to generate formal concepts for large data. In P. Eklund (Ed.), *Concept lattices, Proceedings of the second International Conference on FCA (ICFCA'04)* (LNCS 2961, pp. 394-411). Springer.

Ganascia, J. - Gabriel. (1989). EKAW - 89 tutorial notes: Machine learning. In J. Boose, B. Gaines, J.G. Ganascia (Eds.), *EKAW'89: Third European Workshop on Knowledge Acquisition for Knowledge-Based Systems* (pp. 287-296). Paris, France.

Ganter, B. (1984). Two basic algorithms in concepts analysis. *FB4-Preprint, No. 831*. Technische Hochschule Darmstadt.

Ganter, B., & Reuter, K. (1991). Finding all closed sets: A general approach. *Order, 8*, 283–290. doi:10.1007/BF00383449

Godin, R., & Chau, T. T. (2000). Comparaison d'Algorithmes de Construction de Hiérarchies de Classes. *L'Object, 5*(3), 321–338.

Godin, R., Missaoui, R., & Alaoui, H. (1995). Incremental concept formation algorithms based on galois lattices. *Computational Intelligence, 11*(2), 246–267. doi:10.1111/j.1467-8640.1995.tb00031.x

Guénoche, A. (1990). Construction du Treillis de Galois d'une Relation Binaire. *Math. Inf. Si. Hum, 28*(109), 41–53.

Kengue1, J. F. D., Valtchev, P., & Djamegni, C. T. (2005). A parallel algorithm for lattice construction in formal concept analysis. In R. Godin & B. Ganter (Eds.), *Formal concept analysis* (LNAI 3403, pp. 249-264). Berlin/Heidelberg: Springer.

Kuznetsov, S. O. (1993). A fast algorithm for computing all intersections of objects in a finite semi-lattice. *Automatic Documentation and Mathematical Linguistics, 27*(5), 11–21.

Kuznetsov, S. O. (2004). Complexity of learning in context lattices from positive and negative examples. *Discrete Applied Mathematics, 142*, 111–125. doi:10.1016/j.dam.2003.11.002

Kuznetsov, S. O., & Ob'edkov, S. A. (2000). Algorithm for the construction of the set of all concepts and their line diagram. *Preprint, MATH-Al-05*. The Technische Universität Dresden.

Kuznetsov, S. O., & Ob'edkov, S. A. (2002). Comparing the performance of algorithms for generating concept lattices. *Journal of Experimental & Theoretical Artificial Intelligence, 14*(2-3), 189–216. doi:10.1080/09528130210164170

Lévy, G., & Baklouti, F. (2005). A distributed version of the ganter algorithm for general Galois lattices. In R. Bělohlávek & V. Snášel (Eds.), *Proceedings of International Workshop on Concept Lattice and their Application (CLA)* (pp. 207-221). Ostrava, Czech Republic: Amphora Research Group.

Megretskaya, I. A. (1988). Construction of natural classification tests for knowledge base generation. In Y. Pecherskij (Ed.), *The problem of the expert system application in the national economy: Reports of the Republican Workshop* (pp. 89-93). Kishinev, Moldava: Mathematical Institute with Computer Centre of Moldova Academy of Sciences.

Michalski, R. S. (1983). A theory and methodology of inductive learning. *Artificial Intelligence, 20*, 111–161. doi:10.1016/0004-3702(83)90016-4

Michalski, R. S., & Larsen, I. B. (1978). Selection of most representative training examples and incremental generation of VL1 hypotheses: The underlying methodology and the description of programs ESEL and AQII. *Report No. 78-867*. Dep. of Comp. Science, Univ. of Illinois at Urbana-Champaign, IL.

Mill, J. S. (1872). *The system of logic ratiocinative and inductive being a connected view of the principles of evidence, and the methods of scientific investigation* (Vol.1). London, West Strand.

Naidenova, X. A. (1979). *Automation of experimental data classification processes based on the algebraic lattice theory*. Unpublished doctoral dissertation, Saint-Petersburg Electro – Technical University.

Naidenova, X. A. (2006). An incremental learning algorithm for inferring logical rules from examples in the framework of the common reasoning process. In E. Triantaphyllou, & G. Felici (Eds.), *Data mining and knowledge discovery approaches based on rule induction techniques* (pp. 89-146), New York: Springer.

Naidenova, X. A., & Chapursky, L. I. (1978). Application of algebraic approach in automatic classification of natural objects. In K. Condratiev (Ed.), *The problems of atmosphere's physics* (pp. 84-98). Leningrad, USSR: Publishing House of Leningrad University.

Nguifo, E. M., Tsopzé, N., & Tindo, G. (2008). M – CLANN: Multi-class concept lattice-based artificial network for supervised classification. In *Artificial Neural Networks ICANN* (LNCS 5164, pp. 812-821). Berlin – Heidelberg, Germany: Springer.

Nguifo, M. E., & Njiwoua, P. (1998). Using lattice based framework as a tool for feature extraction. In H. Lui, & H. Motoda (Eds.), *Feature extraction, construction, and selection: A data mining perspective*. Kluwer.

Norris, E. M. (1978). An algorithm for computing the maximal rectangles in a binary relation. *Revue Roumaine de Mathématiques Pures et Appliquées, 23*(2), 243–250.

Nourine, L., & Raynaud, O. (1999). A fast algorithm for building lattices. *Information Processing Letters*, *71*, 199–204. doi:10.1016/S0020-0190(99)00108-8

Ore, O. (1944). Galois connexions. *Transactions of the American Mathematical Society*, *55*(1), 493–513. doi:10.2307/1990305

Ore, O. (1980). *Theory of graph.* Moscow, USSR: Nauka.

Polaillon, G. (1998a). *Organisation et Interprétation par les Treillis de Galois de Données de Type Multivalué, Intervalle ou Histogramme.* Unpublished doctoral dissertation, Université Paris IX Dauphine.

Polaillon, G. (1998b). Interpretation and reduction of Galois lattices of complex data. In A. Rizzi, M. Vichi, & H.-H. Bock (Eds.), *Advances in data science and classification* (pp. 433-440). Springer-Verlag.

Polaillon, G., & Diday, E. (1999). Reduction of symbolic Galois lattices via hierarchies. In *Proceedings of the Conference on Knowledge Extraction and Symbolic Data Analysis* (KESDA'98) (pp. 137-143). Luxembourg: Office for Official Publications of the European Communities.

Rasiova, H. (1974). *An algebraic approach to non-classical logic* (Studies in Logic, Vol. 78). Amsterdam-London: North-Holland Publishing Company.

Riguet, J. (1948). Relations binaires, fermetures, correspondences de Galois. *Bulletin des Sciences Mathématiques*, *76*(3), 114–155.

Rudolph, S. (2007). Encoding closure operators into neural networks. In A. S. d'Avila Garcez, P. Hitzler, & G. Tamburrini (Eds.), *Proceedings of the Third International Workshop on Neural Symbolic Learning and Reasoning (IJCAI'07), CEUR Workshop Proc.* (Vol. 230).

Stumme, G., Taouil, R., Bastide, Y., Pasquier, N., & Lakhal, L. (2000). Fast computation of concept lattices using data mining techniques. In M. Bouzeghoub, M. Klusch, W. Nutt, & U. Sattler (Eds.), *Proceedings of the 7th International Workshop on Knowledge Representation Meets Databases* (KRDB 2000) (Vol. 29, pp. 129-139). Berlin, Germany: CEUR-WS.org.

Stumme, G., Wille, R., & Wille, U. (1998). Conceptual knowledge discovery in databases using formal concept analysis methods. In *Principles of Data Mining and Knowledge Discovery* (LNCS 1510, pp. 450-458). Berlin, Heidelberg: Springer.

Valtchev, P., Missaoui, R., & Lebrun, P. (2002). A partition based approach toward construction Galois (concept) lattices. *Discrete Mathematics*, *256*, 801–829. doi:10.1016/S0012-365X(02)00349-7

Wille, R. (1992). Concept lattices and conceptual knowledge system. *Computers & Mathematics with Applications (Oxford, England)*, *23*(6-9), 493–515. doi:10.1016/0898-1221(92)90120-7

APPENDIX

The data to be processed are in Table 11 (the set of positive examples) and in Table 12 (the set of negative examples) (see, please, Main Current Example, Chapter 7). Table 13, Table 14, and Table 15 contain the results of the procedure DEBUT, i.e. the sets Q, S(test), and *STGOOD*, respectively. Table 16 presents the extensions of the elements of S(test). Table 17 contains the results of the procedure NIAGaRa, i.e. the sets *STGOOD* and *TGOOD*.

Table 11. The set of positive examples R(+)

index of example	R(+)
1	$A_1 A_2 A_5 A_6 A_{21} A_{23} A_{24} A_{26}$
2	$A_4 A_7 A_8 A_9 A_{12} A_{14} A_{15} A_{22} A_{23} A_{24} A_{26}$
3	$A_3 A_4 A_7 A_{12} A_{13} A_{14} A_{15} A_{18} A_{19} A_{24} A_{26}$
4	$A_1 A_4 A_5 A_6 A_7 A_{12} A_{14} A_{15} A_{16} A_{20} A_{21} A_{24} A_{26}$
5	$A_2 A_6 A_{23} A_{24}$
6	$A_7 A_{20} A_{21} A_{26}$
7	$A_3 A_4 A_5 A_6 A_{12} A_{14} A_{15} A_{20} A_{22} A_{24} A_{26}$
8	$A_3 A_6 A_7 A_8 A_9 A_{13} A_{14} A_{15} A_{19} A_{20} A_{21} A_{22}$
9	$A_{16} A_{18} A_{19} A_{20} A_{21} A_{22} A_{26}$
10	$A_2 A_3 A_4 A_5 A_6 A_8 A_9 A_{13} A_{18} A_{20} A_{21} A_{26}$
11	$A_1 A_2 A_3 A_7 A_{19} A_{20} A_{21} A_{22} A_{26}$
12	$A_2 A_3 A_{16} A_{20} A_{21} A_{23} A_{24} A_{26}$
13	$A_1 A_4 A_{18} A_{19} A_{23} A_{26}$
14	$A_{23} A_{24} A_{26}$

Table 12. The set of negative examples R(−)

index of example	R(−)	index of example	R(−)
15	$A_3A_8A_{16}A_{23}A_{24}$	32	$A_1A_2A_3A_7A_9A_{10}A_{11}A_{13}A_{18}$
16	$A_7A_8A_9A_{16}A_{18}$	33	$A_1A_5A_6A_8A_9A_{10}A_{19}A_{20}A_{22}$
17	$A_1A_{21}A_{22}A_{24}A_{26}$	34	$A_2A_8A_9A_{18}A_{20}A_{21}A_{22}A_{23}A_{26}$
18	$A_1A_7A_8A_9A_{13}A_{16}$	35	$A_1A_2A_4A_5A_6A_7A_9A_{13}A_{16}$
19	$A_2A_6A_7A_9A_{21}A_{23}$	36	$A_1A_2A_6A_7A_8A_{10}A_{11}A_{13}A_{16}A_{18}$
20	$A_{10}A_{19}A_{20}A_{21}A_{22}A_{24}$	37	$A_1A_2A_3A_4A_5A_6A_7A_{12}A_{14}A_{15}A_{16}$
21	$A_1A_{10}A_{20}A_{21}A_{22}A_{23}A_{24}$	38	$A_1A_2A_3A_4A_5A_6A_9A_{11}A_{12}A_{13}A_{16}$
22	$A_1A_3A_6A_7A_9A_{10}A_{16}$	39	$A_1A_2A_3A_4A_5A_6A_{14}A_{15}A_{19}A_{20}A_{23}A_{26}$
23	$A_2A_6A_8A_9A_{14}A_{15}A_{16}$	40	$A_2A_3A_4A_5A_6A_7A_{11}A_{12}A_{13}A_{14}A_{15}A_{16}$
24	$A_1A_4A_5A_6A_7A_8A_{11}A_{16}$	41	$A_2A_4A_5A_6A_7A_9A_{10}A_{11}A_{12}A_{13}A_{14}A_{15}A_{19}$
25	$A_7A_{10}A_{11}A_{13}A_{19}A_{20}A_{22}A_{26}$	42	$A_1A_2A_3A_4A_5A_6A_{12}A_{16}A_{18}A_{19}A_{20}A_{21}A_{26}$
26	$A_1A_2A_3A_5A_6A_7A_{10}A_{16}$	43	$A_4A_5A_6A_7A_8A_9A_{10}A_{11}A_{12}A_{13}A_{14}A_{15}A_{16}$
27	$A_1A_2A_3A_5A_6A_{10}A_{13}A_{16}$	44	$A_3A_4A_5A_6A_8A_9A_{10}A_{11}A_{12}A_{13}A_{14}A_{15}A_{18}A_{19}$
28	$A_1A_3A_7A_{10}A_{11}A_{13}A_{19}A_{21}$	45	$A_1A_2A_3A_4A_5A_6A_7A_8A_9A_{10}A_{11}A_{12}A_{13}A_{14}A_{15}$
29	$A_1A_4A_5A_6A_7A_8A_{13}A_{16}$	46	$A_1A_3A_4A_5A_6A_7A_{10}A_{11}A_{12}A_{13}A_{14}A_{15}A_{16}A_{23}A_{24}$
30	$A_1A_2A_3A_6A_{11}A_{12}A_{14}A_{15}A_{16}$	47	$A_1A_2A_3A_4A_5A_6A_8A_9A_{10}A_{11}A_{12}A_{14}A_{16}A_{18}A_{22}$
31	$A_1A_2A_5A_6A_{11}A_{14}A_{15}A_{16}A_{26}$	48	$A_2A_8A_9A_{10}A_{11}A_{12}A_{14}A_{15}A_{16}$

Now we give the results of applying the algorithm NIAGaRa on the training set of examples (Tables 11 and 12).

Input: $S = \{\{1\}, \{2\}, \ldots, \{14\}\}$; $T = \{A_1,\ldots, A_{26}\}$; $STGOOD = \varnothing$; $S(\text{test}) = \varnothing$; $Q = \varnothing$.

Output: After implementation of the procedure DEBUT we have the following sets $S(\text{test})$, $STGOOD$, and Q, respectively (Tables 13, 14, 15).

Table 13. The content of the S(test) after the DEBUT of the algorithm NIAGaRa

1,4	1,4,7	1,5	1,5,12	1,12	2,3,4	2,7	2,8	2,10
3,7	3,7,12	3,8	3,10	3,11	4,6,8,11	4,6,11	4,6,11	4,7
4,8	4,11	4,12	7,8	7,11	7,12	8,10	8,11	

Table 14. The content of the set STGOOD after the DEBUT of the ALGORITHM NIAGaRa

1,2,12,14	9,11	13

Table 15. The set Q after the DEBUT of the algorithm NIAGaRa

1,3	1,6	1,8	1,9	1,10	1,11	1,13	2,5	2,6
2,9	2,11	2,13	3,5	3,6	3,9	3,13	3,14	4,5
4,9	4,10	4,13	4,14	5,6	5,7	5,8	5,9	5,10
5,11	5,13	5,14	6,7	6,9	6,10	6,12	6,13	6,14
7,9	7,10	7,13	7,14	8,9	8,12	8,13	8,14	9,10
9,13	9,14	10,11	10,12	10,13	10,14	11,12	11,13	11,14
12,1	12,14	13,14						

Table 16. The extensions of the elements of S(test)

S	not(s)	V	CAND(s)	select(s)	Result
1,4,	5,6,7,8,10, 11,12	1,4,7	5,6,8,10, 11,12	12	Delete s
1,4,7	8,10,11,12	$\varnothing$	8,10,11,12	12	s - GMRT
1,5	6,7,8,10,11,12	1,5,12	6,7,8,10,11	$\varnothing$	Delete s
1,5,12	$\varnothing$	$\varnothing$	$\varnothing$	$\varnothing$	s - GMRT
1,12	$\varnothing$	$\varnothing$	$\varnothing$	$\varnothing$	Delete s
2,3,4	6,7,8,10,11,12	$\varnothing$	6,7,8,10, 11,12	7,8,12	{2,3,4,7} - GMRT
2,7	8,10,11,1	2,3,4,7	8,10,11, 12	8,12	{2,7,8} - GMRT
2,8	10,11,12	2,7,8	10,11,12	10	Delete s
2,10	11,12	$\varnothing$	11,12	$\varnothing$	s - GMRT
3,7	8,10,11,12	2,3,4,7,12	8,10,11	8,11	Delete s
3,7,12	$\varnothing$	$\varnothing$	$\varnothing$	$\varnothing$	s - GMRT
3,8	10,11,12	$\varnothing$	10,11,12	10,11	s - GMRT
3,10	11,12	$\varnothing$	11,12	$\varnothing$	s - GMRT
3,11	12	$\varnothing$	12	$\varnothing$	s - GMRT
4,6,8,11	12	$\varnothing$	12	$\varnothing$	s - GMRT
4,6,11	12	4,6,8,1	12	$\varnothing$	Delete s
4,7	8,10,11,12	2,3,4,7	8,10,11, 12	8,11,12	{4,7,12} - GMRT
4,8	10,11,12	4,6,8,11	10,12	$\varnothing$	Delete s
4,11	12	4,6,8,11	12	$\varnothing$	Delete s
4,12	$\varnothing$	4,7,12	$\varnothing$	$\varnothing$	Delete s
7,8	10,11,12	2,7,8	10,11,12	11	{7,8,11} - GMRT
7,11	12	7,8,11	12	$\varnothing$	Delete s
7,12	$\varnothing$	3,4,7,12	$\varnothing$	$\varnothing$	Delete s
8,10	11,12	$\varnothing$	11,12	$\varnothing$	s - GMRT
8,11	12	4,6,7,8,11	12	$\varnothing$	Delete s

In the following Tables, A_+ denotes the collection of values A_{14}, A_{15} and A_* denotes the collection of values A_8, A_9.

Table 17. The sets STGOOD and TGOOD for the examples of tables 11 and 12

№	STGOOD	TGOOD	№	STGOOD	TGOOD
1	13	$A_1 A_4 A_{18} A_{19} A_{23} A_{26}$	9	2,7,8	$A_4 A_{22}$
2	2,10	$A_4 A_* A_{26}$	10	1,5,12	$A_2 A_{23} A_{24}$
3	3,10	$A_3 A_4 A_{13} A_{18} A_{26}$	11	4,7,12	$A_{20} A_{24} A_{26}$
4	8,10	$A_3 A_6 A_4 A_{13} A_{20} A_{21}$	12	3,7,12	$A_3 A_{24} A_{26}$
5	9,11	$A_{19} A_{20} A_{21} A_{22} A_{26}$	13	7,8,11	$A_3 A_{20} A_{22}$
6	3,11	$A_3 A_7 A_{19} A_{26}$	14	2,3,4,7	$A_4 A_{12} A_* A_{24} A_{26}$
7	3,8	$A_3 A_7 A_{13} A_4 A_{19}$	15	4,6,8,11	$A_7 A_{20} A_{21}$
8	1,4,7	$A_5 A_6 A_{24} A_{26}$	16	1,2,12,14	$A_{23} A_{24} A_{26}$

Chapter 9
Towards an Integrative Model of Deductive–Inductive Commonsense Reasoning

ABSTRACT

The most important steps in the direction to an integrative model of deductive-inductive commonsense reasoning are made in this chapter. The decomposition of inferring good classification tests is advanced into two kinds of subtasks that are in accordance with human mental acts. This decomposition allows modeling incremental inductive-deductive inferences. We give two basic recursive procedures based on two kinds of subtasks for inferring all good maximally redundant classification tests (GMRTs): ASTRA and DIAGaRa. An incremental algorithm INGOMAR for inferring all GMRTs is presented too. The problems of creating an integrative inductive-deductive model of commonsense reasoning are discussed in the last section of this chapter.

INTRODUCTION

The incremental approach to developing machine learning algorithms is one of the most promising directions in creating intelligent computer systems. Two main considerations determine the interest of researchers to the incrementality as an instrument for solving learning problems. The first consideration is related to the nature of tasks to be solved. In a wide range of problems, a computer system must be able to learn incrementally for adapting to changes of the environment or user's behavior. An example of incremental learning can be found in (Maloof, & Michalski, 1995), where a dynamic knowledge-based system for computer intrusion detection is described. Incremental clustering for mining in a data-warehousing environment is another interesting example of incremental learning (Ester, et al., 1998).

DOI: 10.4018/978-1-60566-810-9.ch009

The second consideration is related to the intention of researchers to create more effective and efficient data mining algorithms in comparison with non-incremental ones. This goal implies the necessity to answer the following questions: how to select the next training example in order to minimize the number of steps in the learning process? How to select the relevant part of hypotheses already induced in order to bring them in agreement with a certain training example? The problem of how to best modify an induced Boolean function when the classification of a new example reveals that this function is inaccurate is considered in (Nieto et al., 2002). In this paper, the problem is solved by minimizing the number of clauses that must be repaired in order to correctly classify all available training examples. An efficient algorithm for discovering frequent sets in incremental databases is given in (Feldman et al., 1997).

The distinction between an incremental learning task and an incremental learning algorithm is clarified in (Giraud-Carries, 2000). A learning task is incremental if the training examples used to solve it become available over time, usually one at a time. A learning algorithm is incremental if for given training examples $e_1, e_2, \ldots, e_i, e_{i+1}, \ldots, e_n$ it produces a sequence of hypotheses $h_1, h_2, \ldots, h_i, h_{i+1}, \ldots, h_n$, such that h_{i+1} depends only on h_i and current example e_i. As it has been shown in (Giraud-Carries, 2000), it is possible to use an incremental algorithm for both non-incremental and incremental tasks.

The analysis of existing learning algorithms shows that non-incremental data processing can be a part of an incremental algorithm (see the example in (Nieto, et al., 2002)) while incremental data processing can be embodied in a non-incremental algorithm. From the more general point of view, the incrementality is a mode of inductive reasoning for creating learning algorithms.

Induction allows extending the solution of a sub-problem with lesser dimension to the solution of the same problem but with greater dimension (forward induction) and vice versa (backward induction). There does not exist only one way of applying induction to the same problem, but many different ways that lead to different methods of constructing algorithms.

Traditionally, the inductive hypothesis in machine learning problems is described as follows: we know how to solve a learning problem for the training set of n-1 examples, thus we know how to solve the same problem for the training set of n examples. But another induction hypothesis might be the following: we know how to solve a learning problem with n/k training examples where k is the number of subsets into which the set of training examples is partitioned. Therefore, we can solve the same task with n training examples. Namely this inductive hypothesis is used in (Wu, & Lo, 1998) for a multi-layer induction algorithm. The initial data set in this algorithm is divided into a number of subsets of equal size. In the first step, a set of rules is learned from the first subset of examples by the help of a generalization operation. The rules thus obtained (which might be redundant) are refined with the use of the other subsets of data. Successive application of the generalization and reduction operations allows for more accurate and more complex rules to be constructed.

In the present chapter, the following inductive hypothesis (backward induction) is used: we know how to solve a learning problem for the training set of n examples, thus we know how to solve the same problem for the training set of n-1 examples. We introduce the subtasks decreasing the size of a main problem by finding good tests contained in only one positive example or good tests containing only a given subset of values (attributes). These subtasks involve into the process of tests inferring only restricted context (subcontext of initial main problem). Solving these subtasks requires to produce some incremental strategies allowing to generate in each subtask only new tests.

THE DECOMPOSITION OF INFERRING GOOD DIAGNOSTIC TESTS INTO SUBTASKS

To transform good diagnostic tests inferring into an incremental process, we introduce two kinds of subtasks:

For a given set of positive examples:

1. Given a positive example t, find all GMRTs contained in t, more exactly, all $t' \subset t$, $(obj(t'), t')$ is a GMRT;
2. Given a non-empty collection of values X (maybe only one value) such that it is not a test, find all GMRTs containing X. more exactly, all Y, $X \subset Y$, $(obj(Y), Y)$ is a GMRT.

Each example contains only some subset of values from T; hence each subtask of the first kind is simpler than the initial one. Each subset X of T appears only in a part of all examples; hence each subtask of the second kind is simpler than the initial one.

There are the analogies of these subtasks in natural human reasoning. Describing a situation, one can conclude from different subsets of the features associated with this situation. Usually, if somebody tells a story from his life, then somebody else recalls a similar story possessing several equivalent features. We give, as an example, a fragment of the reasoning of Dersu Usala, the trapper, the hero of the famous book of Arseniev, V. K; (1950), (translated from the Russian (Arseniev, 1941)). He divided the situation into the fragments in accordance with separate evidences (facts) and then he concluded from each evidence independently.

On the shore there was the trace of bonfire. First of all, Dersu noted that the fire ignited at one and the same place many times. It means that here was a constant ford across the river. Then he said that three days ago a man passed the night near the bonfire. It was an old man, the Chinese, a trapper. He did not sleep during entire night, and in the morning he did not begin to cross the river and he left. The fact that one person was here was possible to conclude on the only track on the sand. Dersu was derived the conclusion that this person was the trapper, on the wooden rod, which one uses for the device of trap for small animals. That this was the Chinese Dersu learned on the manner to arrange bivouac and on the deserted old foot-wear. That this was the old man, Dersu understood after inspecting the deserted foot-wear: young person first tramples nose edge of foot-wear, but old man will trample heel.

The Subtask of the First Kind

We introduce the concept of an object's (example's) projection $proj(R)[t]$ of a given positive object t on a given set $R(+)$ of positive examples. The $proj(R)[t]$ is the set $Z = \{z: (z$ is non empty intersection of t and $t') \& (t' \in R(+)) \& ((obj(z), z)$ is a test for a given class of positive objects$)\}$.

If the $proj(R)[t]$ is not empty and contains more than one element, then it is a subtask for inferring all GMRTs that are in t. If the projection contains one and only one element t, then $(obj(t), t)$ is a GMRT.

To make the operation of forming a projection perfectly clear we construct the projection of $t_2 = $ '*Low Brown Bleu*' on the objects of the second class (see, please, Chapter 8, Table 1). This projection includes t_2 and the intersections of t_2 with the examples t_3, t_4, t_5, t_6 (Table 1).

For checking whether an element of the projection is a test or not we use the function to_be_test(t) in the following form: to_be_test(t) = if $obj(t) \subseteq s(+)$, then *true* else *false*, where $s(+)$ is the set of positive

Table 1. The intersections of t_2 with the objects of class 2

Index of example	Height	Color of hair	Color of eyes	Test?
2	Low	Brown	Bleu	Yes
3		Brown		Yes
4				-
5		Brown	Bleu	Yes
6	Low			No

objects, $obj(t)$ is the set of all positive and negative objects the descriptions of which contain t. If $s(-)$ is the set of negative objects, then $S = s(+) \cup s(-)$ and $obj(t) = \{i: t \subseteq t_i, i \in S\}$.

The intersection $t_2 \cap t_4$ is the empty set. The intersection $t_2 \cap t_6$ does not correspond to a test for Class 2 because $obj(Low) = \{1,2,6\} \not\subseteq s(+)$, where $s(+)$ is equal to $\{2,3,4,5,6\}$. Finally, we have the projection of t_2 on the objects of Class 2 in Table 2.

The subtask turns out to be very simple because the intersection of all the rows of the projection corresponds to a test for Class 2: $val(\{2,3,5\}) = $ '*Brown*', $obj(Brown) = \{2,3,5\}, \subseteq s(+)$.

The Subtask of the Second Kind

We introduce the concept of an attributive projection $proj(R)[A]$ of a given value A on a given set $R(+)$ of positive examples. The projection $proj(R)[A] = \{t: (t \in R(+)) \& (A$ appears in $t)\}$. Another way to define this projection is: $proj(R)[A] = \{t_i: i \in (obj(A) \cap s(+))\}$. If the attributive projection is not empty and contains more than one element, then it is a subtask of inferring all GMRTs containing a given value A. If A appears in one and only one object X, then A does not belong to any GMRT different from X. Forming the projection of A makes sense if A is not a test and the intersection of all positive objects in which A appears is not a test too, i.e. $obj(A) \not\subseteq s(+)$ and $t' = t(obj(A) \cap s(+))$ does not correspond to a test for $R(+)$.

Denote the set $\{obj(A) \cap s(+)\}$ by $splus(A)$. In Table 1 (Chapter 8), we have:

$obj(+) = \{2,3,4,5,6\}$, $splus(Low) \rightarrow \{2,6\}$, $splus(Brown) \rightarrow \{2,3,5\}$, $splus(Bleu) \rightarrow \{2,5\}$, $splus(Tall)$ $\rightarrow \{3,4,5\}$, $splus(Embrown) \rightarrow \{3,4,6\}$, and $splus(Blond) \rightarrow \{4,6\}$.

For the value '*Brown*' we have:

$obj(Brown) = \{2,3,5\}$ and $obj(Brown) = splus(Brown)$, i.e. $obj(Brown) \subseteq s(+)$.

Table 2. The projection of t_2 on the objects of class 2

Index of example	Height	Color of hair	Color of eyes	Test?
2	Low	Brown	Bleu	Yes
3		Brown		Yes
5		Brown	Bleu	Yes

Table 3. The result of reducing the projection after deleting the values 'brown' and 'embrown'

Index of example	Height	Color of hair	Color of eyes	Test?
2	Low		Bleu	No
3	Tall			No
4	Tall	Blond		No
5	Tall		Bleu	No
6	Low	Blond		No

Analogously for the value *'Embrown'* we have: obj(*Embrown*) = {3,4,6} and obj(*Embrown*) ⊆ $s(+)$.

These values are irredundant and simultaneously maximally redundant tests because $val(\{2,3,5\})$ = *'Brown'* and $val(\{3,4,6\})$ = *'Embrown'*. It is clear that these values cannot belong to any test different from the tests obtained. We delete *'Brown'* and *'Embrown'* from further consideration with the result shown in Table 3. Now none of the remaining rows of Class 2 corresponds to a test because obj(*Low, Bleu*) = {1,2}, obj(*Tall*) = {3,4,5,7,8}, obj(*Tall, Blond*) = {4,8}, obj(*Tall, Bleu*) ={5,7,8}, *obj(Low, Blond*) = {1,6} ⊄ $s(+)$.

The subtasks of the first and second kind form some **subcontexts** of an initial context. Choosing values or examples for subtasks manages the process of inferring good tests.

Multiplication Operation for the Projections

We define the multiplication operation of a value A on an object t as the operation of forming subtasks for finding all GMRTs that contain A and, simultaneously, are contained in t:

1. Choose all the objects containing A (in their descriptions),
2. In each obtained objects t', choose only the values which appear in t, i.e., construct the intersection $z = t' \cap t$,
3. Take z for the projection if it corresponds to a test for the given set of positive objects.

For illustration of this operation, we shall construct the subtask based on the product $A_{13} \times t_8$ in our Main Current Example (see, please, also Tables 25, 26 in APPENDIX of this Chapter):

1. The objects containing A_{13} are t_8, t_3, t_{10},
2. t_8 contains the following values: A_3, A_6, A_7, $A*$, A_{13}, $A+$, A_{19}, A_{20}, $A_{21} A_{22}$,
3. The result is in Table 4.

In this projection we have,

$obj(A_7)$ = {3,8} ⊆ $s(+)$, $val(\{3,8\})$ = $\{A_3 A_7 A_{13} A_+ A_{19}\}$, and $(obj(\{3,8\})$, $val(\{3,8\})$ is the GMGT;

$obj(A_{20})$ = {8,10} ⊆ $s(+)$, $val(\{8,10\})$ = $\{A_3 A_6 A_* A_{13} A_{20} A_{21}\}$, and $(obj(\{8,10\})$, $val(\{8,10\})$ is the GMGT.

Multiplication of an example t by a value A performed as follows:

1. Choose all t' for which the intersection $z = t' \cap t$ is not empty and correspond to a test for a given set of positive objects,
2. Take in the projection all z containing A.

The result of multiplication can be empty projection.

It is clear that the multiplication operation is commutative.

The arguments of multiplication can be subsets of values (objects). If an argument is a subset of objects, then we have to build the union of all values contained in these objects. If an argument of multiplication is a subset of values, then we have to build the union of all objects containing at least one of these values. For instance, under multiplying $A+$, A_{13}, $A*$ by t_8 (Main Current Example) we have the following projection (Table 5):

In this projection,

$$val(obj(A_{19})) = \{A_3, A_7, A_{13}, A_+, A_{19}\} \text{ and } val(obj(A_{22})) = \{A_+, A_{22}\}; (obj(\{A_{19}\}), val(obj(A_{19}))) \text{ and}$$
$$(obj(\{A_{22}\}), val(obj(A_{22}))) \text{ are the GMRTs for the positive objects in Main Current Example.}$$

Building a projection (forming a subtask) permits increasing the possibility of finding all tests contained in this projection by using only one examination of it. Restricting the search for tests to a sub-context of the given context favors separation tests, i.e. increases the possibility to find values each of which will belong only to one GMRT in this sub-context.

Any family of GMRTs $(obj(t_1), t_1), (obj(t_2), t_2), \ldots, (obj(t_i), t_i), (obj(t_j), t_j), (obj(t_k), t_k)$ is the completely separating systems (Dickson, 1969). It means that for any pair (t_i, t_j) there is a pair of values (A_q, A_f), such that A_q appears in t_i and does not appear in t_j, and A_f appears in t_j and does not appear in t_i. Analogously, for any pair $obj(t_i)$, $obj(t_j)$, there is a pair of objects q, h such that q appears in $obj(t_i)$ and does not appear in $obj(t_j)$, h appears in $obj(t_j)$ and does not appear in $obj(t_i)$. For instance, in our Main Current Example, we have five GMRTs contained in the object t_8 (Table 6). It is easy to see that the property of completely separation is satisfied for these GMRTs.

Consider the projection obtained as the result of $t_8 \times A_{20}$ (Table 7).

In this projection, we have

$obj(A_7) = splus(A_7) = \{4,6,8,11\}$, and $val(\{4,6,8,11\}) = \{A_7A_{20}A_{21}\}$ correspond to the GMRT;

$obj(A_{22}) = splus(A_{22}) = \{7,8,11\}$, and $val(\{7,8,11\}) = \{A_3A_{20}A_{22}\}$ correspond to the GMRT;

Table 4. The result of the product $A_{13} \times t_8$

$t \backslash A$	A_3	A_6	A_7	A_*	A_{13}	A_+	A_{19}	A_{20}	A_{21}	A_{22}
t_8	3	6	7	*	13	+	19	20	21	22
t_3	3		7		13	+	19			
t_{10}	3	6		*	13			20	21	

Table 5. The result of the product $(A_+, A_{13}, A_*) \times t_8$

$t \backslash A$	A_3	A_6	A_7	A_*	A_{13}	A_+	A_{19}	A_{20}	A_{21}	A_{22}
t_8	3	6	7	*	13	+	19	20	21	22
t_2			7	*		+				22
t_3	3		7		13	+	19			
t_4		6	7			+		20	21	
t_7	3	6				+		20		22
t_{10}	3	6		*	13			20	21	

Table 6. The illustration of the completely separation property for GMRTs

N	STGOOD	TGOOD	N	STGOOD	TGOOD
1	{8,10}	$A_3A_6A_*A_{13}A_{20}A_{21}$	4	{2,7,8}	A_+A_{22}
2	{3,8}	$A_3A_7A_{13}A_+A_{19}$	5	{7,8,11}	$A_3A_{20}A_{22}$
3	{4,6,8,11}	$A_7A_{20}A_{21}$			

$\mathrm{obj}(A_{13}) = \mathrm{obj}(A_*) = splus(A_{13}) = splus(A_*) = \{8,10\}$, and $\mathrm{val}(\{8,10\}) = \{A_3A_6A_*A_{13}A_{20}A_{21}\}$ correspond to the GMRT.

All the GMRTs contained in t_8 are obtained for one examination of this projection.

SPECIAL OPERATIONS FOR FORMING SUBTASKS

The decomposition of good classification tests inferring into subtasks of the first and second kinds implies introducing a set of special rules to realize the following operations: choosing an object (value) for a subtask, forming a subtask, reducing a subtask and some other rules controlling the process of inferring good tests.

Reducing Subtasks. The Foundation for Reducing Subtasks of the First and Second Kinds

The following theorem gives the foundation for reducing projections both of the first and the second kind.

THEOREM 9.1.

Let A be a value from T, $(\mathrm{obj}(X), X)$ be a maximally redundant test for a given set $R(+)$ of positive objects and $\mathrm{obj}(A) \subseteq \mathrm{obj}(X)$. Then A does not belong to any GMRT for $R(+)$ different from $(\mathrm{obj}(X), X)$.

Table 7. The result of the product $t_8 \times A_{20}$

$\wedge A$	A_3	A_6	A_7	A_*	A_{13}	A_+	A_{19}	A_{20}	A_{21}	A_{22}
t_8	A_3	A_6	A_7	A_*	A_{13}	A_+	A_{19}	A_{20}	A_{21}	A_{22}
t_6			A_7					A_{20}	A_{21}	
t_4		A_6	A_7			A_+		A_{20}	A_{21}	
t_7	A_3	A_6				A_+		A_{20}		A_{22}
t_{11}	A_3		A_7				A_{19}	A_{20}	A_{21}	A_{22}
t_{10}	A_3	A_6		A_*	A_{13}			A_{20}	A_{21}	

Proof of Theorem 1

Case 1. Suppose that A appears in Y and (obj(Y), Y) is a GMRT for $R(+)$ different from (obj(X), X). Then obj(Y) is a proper subset of obj(A). However we have that obj(A) ⊆ obj(X) and hence obj(Y) is a proper subset of obj(X). However it is impossible because the set of GMRTs is a Sperner system and hence obj(Y) and obj(X) does not contain each other (Sperner, 1928).

Case 2. Let (obj(X), X) be the maximally redundant test for $R(+)$ but not a good one. Suppose that there exists a GMRT (obj(Y), Y) such that A appears in Y. Next observe that obj(Y) is a proper subset of obj(A) and obj(Y) is a proper subset of obj(X). Then $X \subset Y$ and X is not a maximally redundant test. We have a contradiction. End of Proof.♠

This theorem has been demonstrated in (Naidenova et al, 1995b).

To illustrate the way of reducing projections, we consider another partition of the rows of Table 1 (Chapter 8) into the sets of positive and negative examples as shown in Table 8.

Let $s(+)$ be equal to {4,5,6,7,8}. The value *'Red'* corresponds to a test for positive examples because obj(*Red*) = *splus*(*Red*) = {7}. Delete *'Red'* from the projection. The value *'Tall'* does not correspond to a test because obj(*Tall*) = {3,4,5,7,8} and it is not equal to *splus*(*Tall*) = {4,5,7,8}. The attributive projection of the value *'Tall'* on the set of positive examples is in Table 9.

In this projection, *splus*(*Bleu*) = {5,7,8}, val(*splus*(*Bleu*)) = *'Tall Bleu'*, obj(*Tall Bleu*) = {5,7,8} = *splus*(*Tall Bleu*), hence *'Tall Bleu'* correspond to a test for Class 2. We have also that *splus*(*Brown*) = {5}, but {5} ⊆ {5,7,8} and, consequently, there does not exist any good test containing simultaneously the values *'Tall'* and *'Brown'*. We delete *'Bleu'* and *'Brown'* from the projection as shown in Table 10.

However, now rows 5 and 7 do not correspond to tests for Class 2 and they can be deleted as shown in Table 11. The intersection of the remaining rows of the projection is *'Tall Blond'*. We have that obj(*Tall Blond*) = {4,8} ⊆ $s(+)$ and (obj(*Tall Blond*), *Tall Blond*) is the test for Class 2.

As we have found all the tests for Class 2 containing *'Tall'* we delete *'Tall'* from the examples of this class as shown in Table 12

Next we can delete rows 5, 7, and 8 because they do not correspond to tests for Class 2. The result is in Table 13.

The intersection of the remaining examples of Class 2 gives a test (obj(*Blond Embrown*), *Blond Embrown*) because obj(*Blond Embrown*) = *splus*(*Blond Embrown*) = {4,6} ⊆ $s(+)$.

The choice of values or objects for forming projections requires special consideration.

In contrast to incremental learning, where the problem is considered of how to choose relevant knowledge to be best modified, here we come across the opposite goal to eliminate irrelevant knowledge not to be processed.

Table 8. Example 2 of a data classification

Index of example	Height	Color of hair	Color of eyes	Class
1	Low	Blond	Bleu	1
2	Low	Brown	Bleu	1
3	Tall	Brown	Embrown	1
4	Tall	Blond	Embrown	2
5	Tall	Brown	Bleu	2
6	Low	Blond	Embrown	2
7	Tall	Red	Bleu	2
8	Tall	Blond	Bleu	2

Table 9. The reduced projection of the value 'tall' on the set R(+)

Index of example	Height	Color of hair	Color of eyes	Class
4	Tall	Blond	Embrown	2
5	Tall	Brown	Bleu	2
7	Tall		Bleu	2
8	Tall	Blond	Bleu	2

Choosing Objects and Values for Forming Subtasks

It is convenient to choose essential values in an object and essential object in a projection for the decomposition of the main problem of inferring GMRTs into the subtasks of the first or second kind.

We give a small example of inferring all the GMRTs for the instances of Class 1 presented in Table 8.

Here we have: $S(+) = \{1,2,3\}$, obj(Low) → $\{1,2,6\}$, obj($Brown$) → $\{2,3,5\}$, obj($Bleu$) → $\{1,2,5,7,8\}$, obj($Tall$) → $\{3,4,5,7,8\}$, obj($Embrown$) → $\{3,4,6\}$, and obj($Blond$) →$\{1,4,6,8\}$.

We discover that the value 'Low' is essential in lines 1 and 2. Then it is convenient to form the subtask of the second kind for this value as shown in Table 14.

In Table 14, $S(+) = \{1,2\}$, splus(Low) → $\{1,2\}$, splus($Brown$) → $\{2\}$, splus($Bleu$) → $\{1,2\}$, and splus($Blond$) →$\{1\}$.

We have that val(splus($Bleu$)) = '$Low\ Bleu$' corresponds to a test for class 1. Analogously, for the value '$Brown$', we have that val(splus($Brown$)) = '$Low\ Brown\ Bleu$' corresponds to a test for Class 1 but not a good one because of splus($Brown$) ⊆ $splus(Bleu)$.

It is clear that these values cannot belong to any test different from the tests already obtained. We delete the values '$Brown$' and '$Bleu$' from further consideration in this subtask.

But after deleting these values, lines 1, 2 do not correspond to tests for Class 1. Hence the subtask is over.

Return to the main problem. Now we can delete the value 'Low' from further consideration because we have got all good tests containing this value for Class 1. But we know that the value 'Low' is essential in lines 1 and 2, this fact means that these lines do not correspond to tests for Class 1 after deleting this value. The following step may be the inference of all irredundant tests contained in line 3 (covering

Table 10. The projection of the value 'tall' on R(+) without the values 'bleu' and 'brown'

Index of example	Height	Color of hair	Color of eyes	Class
4	Tall	Blond	Embrown	2
5	Tall			2
7	Tall			2
8	Tall	Blond		2

Table 11. the projection of the value 'tall' on R(+) without lines 5 and 7

Index of example	Height	Color of hair	Color of eyes	Class
4	Tall	Blond	Embrown	2
8	Tall	Blond		2

only one line 3) for Class 1. In our case, the collection of values '*Brown Embrown*' corresponds to a GIRT contained in line 3.

An Approach for Searching for Essential Values

Of course, searching for essential values is performed with the use of inductive diagnostic rule (see, please, Chapter 8).

Let $(obj(t), t)$ be a test for positive examples. Construct the set of intersections $\{t \cap t': t' \in R(-)\}$. It is clear that these intersections do not correspond to tests for positive examples. Take one of the intersections with the maximal number of values in it. The values complementing this maximal intersection in t is the minimal set of essential values in t.

Return to Table 8. Exclude the value '*Red*' (we know that '*Red*' corresponds to a test for Class 2) and find the essential values for the examples t_4, t_5, t_6, t_7, and t_8. The result is in Table 15.

Consider the value '*Embrown*' in t_6: $splus(Embrown) = \{4,6\}$, $val(\{4,6\}) = $ '*Blond Embrown*' and $(obj(Blond\ Embrown), Blond\ Embrown)$ is a test for Class 2.

Table 12. The result of deleting the value 'tall' from the set R(+)

Index of example	Height	Color of hair	Color of eyes	Class
1	Low	Blond	Bleu	1
2	Low	Brown	Bleu	1
3	Tall	Brown	Embrown	1
4		Blond	Embrown	2
5		Brown	Bleu	2
6	Low	Blond	Embrown	2
7			Bleu	2
8		Blond	Bleu	2

Table 13. The result of deleting 5, 7, and 8 from the Set R(+)

Index of example	Height	Color of hair	Color of eyes	Class
1	Low	Blond	Bleu	1
2	Low	Brown	Bleu	1
3	Tall	Brown	Embrown	1
4		Blond	Embrown	2
6	Low	Blond	Embrown	2

The value '*Embrown*' can be deleted. But this value is only one essential value in t_6 and, therefore, t_6 can be deleted too. After that *splus*(*Blond*) is modified to the set {4,8}.

We observe that val({4,8}) = '*Tall Blond*' and (obj(*Tall Blond*), *Tall Blond*) is a test for Class 2. Hence the value '*Blond*' can be deleted from further consideration together with the row t_4.

Now the intersection of the rows t_5, t_7, and t_8 produces the test (obj(*Tall Bleu*), *Tall Bleu*) for Class 2.

An Approach for Searching for Essential Objects

An approach for searching for essential objects is suported by the dual inductive diagnostic rule.

Generally, we need the set *STGOOD* to find essential objects in some subset $s*$ for which $(s*, \text{val}(s*))$ is not a test. Let $s* = \{i_1, i_2, ..., i_q\}$. Construct the set of intersections $\{s* \cap s': s' \in STGOOD\}$. Any obtained intersection $s* \cap s'$ corresponds to a test for positive examples. Take one of the intersections with the maximal number of indices. The subset of $s*$ complementing in $s*$ the maximal intersection

Table 14. The subtask for the value 'low'

Index of example	Height	Color of hair	Color of eyes	Class
1	Low	Blond	Bleu	1
2	Low	Brown	Bleu	1

Table 15. The essential values for the examples t_4, t_5, t_6, t_7, and t_8

Index of example	Height	Color of hair	Color of eyes	Essential values	Class
1	Low	Blond	Bleu		1
2	Low	Brown	Bleu		1
3	Tall	Brown	Embrown		1
4	Tall	Blond	Embrown	Blond	2
5	Tall	Brown	Bleu	Bleu, Tall	2
6	Low	Blond	Embrown	Embrown	2
7	Tall		Bleu	Tall, Bleu	2
8	Tall	Blond	Bleu	Tall	2

is the minimal set of essential objects in s^*. For instance, $s^* = \{2,3,4,7,8\}$, $(s^*, \text{val}(s^*))$ is not a test for positive objects, $s' = \{2,3,4,7\}$, $s' \in STGOOD$, hence t_8 is the essential object with respect to s^*.

In the beginning of inferring GMRTs, the set *STGOOD* is empty. In the previous chapter (Chapter 8), the procedure with the use of which a quasi-maximal subset s of s^* is obtained such that $(s, \text{val}(s))$ is a test for given set of positive objects. This procedure can be used for generating an initial content of the set STGOOD. For this goal, it is a sufficient act to find for each splus(A), $A \in T$ a subset sbmax(splus(A)) $\subseteq$ splus(A) such that (sbmax(splus(A)), val(sbmax(splus(A))) is a test for a given set of positive objects.

Now we demonstrate the process of generating an initial content of STGOOD and finding all GMRTs for Class 2 with the use of the data presented in Table 16. This table is adopted from (Quinlan, & Rivest, 1989). Here $T = \{Sunny, Overcast, Rain, Hot, Mild, Cool, High, Normal, No, Yes\}$.

For Class 2, we have

SPLUS = {splus(A), for all $A \in T$ } = {splus(*No*) → {3,4,5,9,10,13}, splus(*Normal*) → {5,7,9,10,11,13}, splus(*Overcast*) → {3,7,12,13}, splus(*Mild*) → {4,10,11,12}, splus(*Rain*) → {4,5,10}, splus(*Cool*) → {5,7,9}, splus(*High*) → {3,4,12}, splus(*Yes*) → {7,11,12}, splus(*Sunny*) → {9,11}, splus(*Hot*) → {3,13}}.

We observe that some splus(A) correspond to the tests which can serve for initial content of the set STGOOD: val(splus(*Sunny*)) = {*Sunny, Normal*}, val(splus(*Overcast*)) = {*Overcast*}, val(splus(*Rain*)) = {*Rainy, No*}, val(splus(*Hot*)) = {*Mild, Hot, No*}. The last test ({splus(*Hot*), {*Overcast, Hot, No*}) is a test for Class 2 but not a good one. The other tests are inserted in *STGOOD*. Values *Sunny, Overcast, Rain, Hot* can be deleted from consideration. After that objects 3, 4, 7, 12 can be deleted too.

The set SPLUS is modified with the following result:

Table 16. The data for generating an initial content of STGOOD

Index of example	Outlook	Temperature	Humidity	WindY	Class
1	Sunny	Hot	High	No	1
2	Sunny	Hot	High	Yes	1
3	Overcast	Hot	High	No	2
4	Rain	Mild	High	No	2
5	Rain	Cool	Normal	No	2
6	Rain	Cool	Normal	Yes	1
7	Overcast	Cool	Normal	Yes	2
8	Sunny	Mild	High	No	1
9	Sunny	Cool	Normal	No	2
10	Rain	Mild	Normal	No	2
11	Sunny	Mild	Normal	Yes	2
12	Overcast	Mild	High	Yes	2
13	Overcast	Hot	Normal	No	2
14	Rain	Mild	High	Yes	1

SPLUS = {splus(A), for all $A \in$ T\{*Sunny, Overcast, Rain, Hot*}} = {splus(*No*) → {5,9,10,13}, splus(*Normal*) → {5,9,10,11,13}, splus(*Mild*) → {10,11}, splus(*Cool*) → {5,9}, splus(*High*) → {12}, splus(*Yes*) → {11}}.

We observe that some splus(A) correspond to the good tests: val(splus(*No*)) = {*No, Normal*}, val(splus(*Mild*)) = {*Mild, Normal*}. At the same time splus(*Cool*), splus(*High*), and splus(*Yes*) correspond to the tests but not good ones because splus(*Cool*) ⊆ splus(*No*), splus(*High*) ⊆ splus(*Overcast*), and splus(*Yes*) ⊆ splus(*Mild*).

The values «*Mild*», «*No*», «*Cool*», «*Yes*» can be deleted from the consideration and after that the task of inferring all GMRTs for the class 2 is over.

An Approach for the Choice of Subtasks

Let us remark that if we have the initial content of the set of *STGOOD*, we can search for essential objects in order to choose a subtask for inferring tests based on the multiplication operation.

Consider our Main Current Example to illustrate one of the possible methods of finding essential objects different from the dual induction diagnostic rule defined in Chapter 8.

For searching for essential objects, we use the set SPLUS of all splus(A), $A \in T$ and the initial set *STGOOD*. The initial set *STGOOD* for Main Current Example is the following:

STGOOD = {{2,8}, {3,8}, {3,10}, {4,12}, {1,4,7}, {1,5,12}, {2,7,8}, {3,7,12}, {1,2,12,14}, {2,3,4,7}, {4,6,8,11}}.

SPLUS for Main Current Example is given in Table 17.

Suppose that we can find all z such that $z \in STGOOD$, $z \subseteq$ splus(A). Clearly that objects of the set splus(A)\{∪ z} are essential with respect to splus(A).

Table 18 contains, for each splus(A), $A \in T$, the set {∪ z}, z, $z \in STGOOD$, $z \subseteq$ splus(A) and the set splus(A)\ {∪ z} of essential objects with respect to splus(A) and, consequently, with respect to A.

Choosing an essential object for a subtask, we can choose simultaneously an essential value in the description of this object. The list of essential values for some objects in Main Current Examples is represented in Table 19.

Table 17. The set SPLUS for main current example

SPLUS = {splus(A): s(A) ∩ s(+), A ∈ T}:	
splus(A_8) → {2,8,10}	Splus(A_{22}) → {2,7,8,9,11}
splus(A_{13}) → {3,8,10}	splus(A_{23}) → {1,2,5,12,13,14}
splus(A_{16}) → {4,9,12}	splus(A_3) → {3,7,8,10,11,12}
splus(A_1) → {1,4,11,13}	splus(A_4) → {2,3,4,7,10,13}
splus(A_5) → {1,4,7,10}	splus(A_6) → {1,4,5,7,8,10}
splus(A_{12}) → {2,3,4,7}	splus(A_7) → {2,3,4,6,8,11}
splus(A_{18}) → {3,9,10,13}	splus(A_{24}) → {1,2,3,4,5,7,12,14}
splus(A_2) → {1,5,10,11,12}	splus(A_{20}) → {4,6,7,8,9,10,11,12}
splus(A_9) → {2,3,4,7,8}	splus(A_{21}) → {1,4,6,8,9,10,11,12}
splus(A_{19}) → {3,8,9,11,13}	splus(A_{26}) → {1,2,3,4,6,7,9,10,11,12,13,14}

Table 18. Forming essential objects

splus(A)	{∪ z}, $z \in STGOOD$, $z \subseteq$ splus(A)}	Essential objects in splus(A)
splus (A_*)	2,8	10 (t_{10})
splus(A_{13})	3,8,10	
Splus(A_{16})	4,12	9 (t_9)
splus (A_1)	1,4,11, 13	
splus (A_5)	1,4,7	10 (t_{10})
Splus(A_{18})	3,10	9,13 (t_9, t_{13})
splus (A_2)	1,5,12	10,11 (t_{10}, t_{11})
splus (A_*)	2,3,4,7,8	
splus(A_{19})	3,8	9,11,13 (t_9, t_{11}, t_{13})
splus (A_{22})	2,7,8	9,11 (t_9, t_{11})
splus (A_{23})	1,2,5,12,14	13 (t_{13})
splus (A_3)	3,7,8,12	10,11 (t_{10}, t_{11})
splus (A_4)	2,3,4,7,10	13 (t_{13})
splus (A_6)	1,4,7	5,8,10 (t_5, t_8, t_{10})
splus (A_7)	4,6,8,11	2,3 (t_3, t_2)
splus (A_{24})	1,2,3,4,7,12,14,5	
splus (A_{20})	4,6,8,11	7,9,10, 12 (t_7, t_9, t_{10}, t_{12})
splus (A_{21})	4,6,8,11	1,10,12 (t_1, t_{10}, t_{12})
splus (A_{26})	1,2,3,4,7,10,12,14	6,9,11,13 (t_6, t_9, t_{11}, t_{13})

We observe that A_{22} is only essential value in object t_9 and, at the same time, t_9 is essential with respect to A_{22}. It means that if we find all the tests contained in t_9 and containing A_{22}, it will be possible to delete from consideration object t_9 and also value A_{16} because splus(A_{16}) will correspond to the test already existing in *STGOOD*.

After solving a subtask, it is necessary to correct the lists of essential objects with respect to all current sets splus(A), $A \in T$, and the list of essential values with respect to the remained objects.

Table 20 contains the list of the subtasks that have been solved for inferring all GMRTs in Main Current Example. It turned out to be sufficient to solve only 9 subtasks.

DIAGaRa: an Algorithm for Inferring GMRTs with the Use of the Subtasks of the First Kind

The decomposition of inferring GMRTs into subtasks of the first or second kind gives the possibility to construct incremental algorithms. The simplest way to do it consists of the following steps (Figure 1): choose object (value), form subtask, solve subtask, delete object (value) after the subtask is over, reduce $R(+)$ and T and check the condition of ending the main task. This process involves deductive reasoning as its inherent part: one must choose object or value for a subproblem by using different criteria or considerations.

In the sequel, we give two algorithms for inferring GMRTs:

1) ASTRA the core of which is the decomposition of the main problem into the subtasks of the second kind combined with searching essential values. This algorithm is described in APPENDIX 1 to this Chapter;

2) DIAGaRa the core of which is the decomposition of the main problem into the subtasks of the first kind combined with searching essential objects.

The DIAGaRa is based on using The Basic Recursive Algorithm for solving a subtask of the first kind (Figure 2). The initial information for finding all the GMRTs contained in a positive example (object) is the projection of this example (object) on the current set $R(+)$. Essentially the projection is simply a subset of examples (objects) defined on a certain restricted subset t^* of values. Let s^* be the subset of objects from $R(+)$ which have produced the projection.

It is useful to introduce the characteristic $W(t)$ of any collection t of values named by the weight of t in the projection: $W(t) = \|obj(t) \cap s^*\|$ is the number of positive objects of the projection containing t. Let WMIN be the minimal permissible value of weight.

Let *STGOOD* be the partially ordered set of elements s satisfying the condition that $(s, val(s))$ is a good test for $R(+)$.

The basic algorithm consists of applying the sequence of the following steps:

Step 1. Check whether the intersection of all the elements of projection corresponds to a test and if so, then s^* is stored in *STGOOD* if s^* corresponds to a good test at the current step; in this case, the subtask is over. Otherwise the next step is performed (we use the function to_be_test(t): if obj(t) $\cap S(+) = $ obj(t) (obj$(t) \subseteq S(+)$) then *true* else *false*).

Table 19. Essential values in essential objects

Essential object	Essential values	Essential object	Essential values
t_9	A_{22}	t_{11}	A_7A_{22}
t_{13}	A_{18}	t_{12}	$A_{23}A_{24}$
t_5	A_2	t_7	$A_{22}A_{24}$
t_6	A_{21}	t_2	$A_*A_{22}A_{26}$
t_1	$A_{21}A_{24}$	t_3	$A_{18}A_{19}A_{26}$
t_{10}	A_*A_{13}	t_8	$A_7A_{20}A_{21}A_{22}$

Table 20. The list of subtasks for main current example

Subtasks	Elements memorized in STGOOD	Deleted objects	Deleted values
$t_9 \times A_{22}, t_{13} \times A_{18}$	{9,11}), ({13}	t_9, t_{13}	A_{16}, A_{18}
$t_{11} \times A_{22}$	{7,8,11}		
$t_{10} \times A_*, ..t_{10} \times A_{13}$	{8,10}	t_{10}	$A_*, A_{13}, A_4, A_5,$
$t_6 \times A_{21}$		t_6	
$t_{11} \times A_7$	{3,11}	t_{14}, t_{11}, t_5	$A_1, A_2, A_{19}, A_{22}, A_{23}$
$t_{12} \times A_{24}$	{4,7,12}	t_{12}	
$t_1 \times A_{24}$		t_1, t_2, t_3, t_7	A_{26}, A_{21}, A_{24}

Figure 1. The steps of test inferring with the decomposition into the subtasks of first or second kind

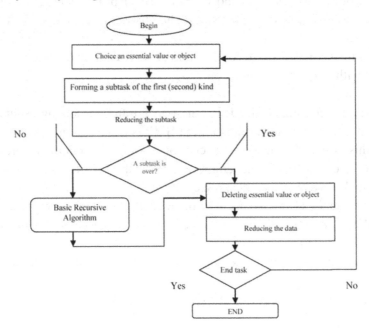

Step 2. For each value A in the projection, the set splus(A) = {s^* ∩ obj(A)} and the weight $W(A)$ = ‖*splus*(A)‖ are determined and if the weight is less than the minimum permissible weight WMIN, then the value A is deleted from the projection. We can also delete the value A if $W(A)$ is equal to WMIN and (splus (A), val(splus(A)) is not a test – in this case A will not appear in a maximally redundant test t with $W(t)$ equal to or greater than WMIN.

Step 3. The generalization operation is performed as follows: t' = val(splus(A)), $A \in t^*$; if t' corresponds to a test, then the value A is deleted from the projection and splus(A) is stored in *STGOOD* if splus(A) corresponds to a good test at the current step.

Step 4. The value A can be deleted from the projection if splus(A) ⊆ s' for some $s' \in STGOOD$.

Step 5. If at least one value has been deleted from the projection, then the reduction of the projection is necessary. The reduction consists in deleting the elements of projection that do not correspond to tests (as a result of previous eliminating values). If, under reduction, at least one element has been deleted from the projection, then Step 2, Step 3, Step 4, and Step 5 are repeated.

Step 6. Check whether the subtask is over or not. The subtask is over when either the projection is empty or the intersection of all elements of the projection corresponds to a test (see, please, Step

Figure 2. The main block of DIAGaRa

$$s^* \leftarrow s(+) = \{1, \quad, nt\};$$
$$t^* \leftarrow T;$$
Do
Begin
1. to find all the GMRTs for a given set of positive examples with the use of the basic algorithm of solving subtask of the first kind;
End

1). If the subtask is not over, then the choice of an essential object in this projection is performed and the new subtask is formed with the use of this essential object. The new subsets s^* and t^* are constructed and the basic algorithm runs recursively. We give in the Appendix 2 to this Chapter an example of the work of the algorithm DIAGaRa.

An Approach for Forming the Set *STGOOD*. The important part of the basic algorithm is how to form the set *STGOOD*. Let $L(S)$ be the set of all subsets of the set S. $L(S)$ is the set lattice (Rasiova, 1974). The ordering determined in the set lattice coincides with the set-theoretical inclusion. It will be said that subset s_1 is absorbed by subset s_2, that is $s_1 \leq s_2$, if and only if the inclusion relation is hold between them, that is $s_1 \subseteq s_2$. Under formation of *STGOOD*, a collection s of object is stored in *STGOOD* if and only if it is not absorbed by any element of this set. It is necessary also to delete from *STGOOD* all the elements that are absorbed by s if s is stored in *STGOOD*. Thus, when the algorithm is over, the set *STGOOD* contains all the collections of objects that correspond to GMRTs and only such collections. Essentially the process of forming *STGOOD* is an incremental procedure of finding all maximal elements of a partially ordered set. The set *TGOOD* of all the GMRTs is obtained as follows: *TGOOD* $= \{(s, \text{val}(s)), (\forall s) (s \in STGOOD)\}$.

CASCADE: A Variant of Inferring GMRTs Based on the Procedure DIAGaRa

The algorithm CASCADE serves for inferring all the GMRTs of maximal weight. At the beginning of the algorithm, the values are arranged in decreasing order of weight such that $W(A_1) \geq W(A_2) \geq \dots \geq W(A_m)$, where $A_1, A_2, \dots, A_m$ is a permutation of values. The shortest sequence of values $A_1, A_2, A_j, j \leq m$ is defined such that it correspons to a test for positive objects and *WMIN* is made equal to $W(A_j)$. The procedure DIAGaRa tries to infer all the GMRTs with weight equal to *WMIN*. If such tests are obtained, then the algorithm stops. If such tests are not found, then *WMIN* is decreased, and the procedure DIAGaRa runs again.

The Estimation of the Number of Subtasks to Be Solved

The number of subtasks at each level of recursion is determined by the number of essential objects in the projection associated with this level. The depth of recursion for any subtask is determined by the greatest cardinality (call it '*CAR*') of set-theoretical intersections of elements $s \in STGOOD$ corresponding to GMRTs: $CAR = \max (\|s_i \cap s_j\|, \forall(s_i, s_j) s_i, s_j \in STGOOD)$. In the worst case, the number of subtasks to be solved is of order $O(2^{CAR})$.

An Approach to Incremental Inferring Good Diagnostic Tests

Three Mental Acts of Incremental Commonsense Reasoning

Incremental supervised learning is necessary when a new portion of observations or objects (examples) becomes available over time. Suppose that each new object comes with the indication of its class membership. The following actions are necessary with the arrival of a new object:

- Checking whether it is possible to perform generalization of some existing GMRTs for the class to which the new object belongs (a class of positive objects, for certainty), that is, whether it is possible to extend the set of objects covered by some existing GMRTs or not;
- Inferring all the GMRTs contained in the new object description;
- Checking the validity of the existing GMRTs for negative objects, and if it is necessary:
- Modifying the tests that are not valid (test for negative objects is not valid if it is included in a positive object description, that is, in other words, it accepts an object of positive class).

Thus the following mental acts are performed:

- Pattern recognition and generalization of knowledge (increasing the power of already existing inductive knowledge);
- Increasing knowledge (inferring new knowledge);
- Correcting knowledge (diagnostic reasoning + knowledge modification).

Thus the process of inferring all the GMRTs is divided into the subtasks that conform to three acts of reasoning:

- Pattern recognition or using already known rules (tests) for determining the class membership of a new positive object and generalization of the rules that recognize it correctly (deductive reasoning and increasing the power of already existing inductive knowledge);
- Inferring new rules (tests) that are generated by a new positive object (inductive reasoning a new knowledge);
- Correcting rules (tests) of alternative (negative) classes that accept a new positive object (these rules do not permit to distinguish a new positive object from some negative objects) (deductive and inductive diagnostic reasoning to modify knowledge).

The first act reveals the known rules satisfied with a new object, the induction base of these rules can be enlarged. The second act can be reduced to the subtask of the first kind. The third act can be reduced either to the inductive diagnostic rule followed by the subtasks of the first kind or only to the subtask of the second kind. One of the possible ways of using incremental commonsense reasoning for GMRTs generation is implemented in algorithm INGOMAR.

INGOMAR: An Incremental Algorithm for Inferring All GMRTs

Thus, the process of inferring all the GMRTs is divided into three acts. The first act is performed by the procedure GENERALIZATION ($STGOOD$, $j*$) (Figure 3).

The second act is reduced to the subtask of the first kind. The procedure FORMSUBTASK($j*$) is intended for preparing initial data for inferring all the GMRTs contained in the object with the index $j*$: the set S(test)(+) is the set of collections of objects to be extended and the set Q(+) is the set of forbidden pairs of objects. This procedure is presented in Figure 4. The procedure NIAGaRa can be used for inferring all the GMRTs contained in the description of object with index $j*$.

The third act of incremental learning is reduced either to the inductive diagnostic rule described in Chapter 8 together with the subtask of the first kind or only to the subtask of the second kind. We may

Figure 3. The procedure for generalizing the existing GMRTs

> **The procedure**
> **GENERALIZATION (*STGOOD*(+), *j**).**
>
> **Input:** *j**, the set *STGOOD*(+) of known
> GMRTs for the class of positive examples,
> the set *R*(-) of negative examples.
> **Output:** *STGOOD*(+)
> modified by the generalization.
>
> **Begin**
> ($\forall s$) ($s \in STGOOD$(+))
>   if to_be_test(val($s \cup j^*$)) = true **then**
> $s \leftarrow$ generalization ($s \cup j^*$);
> **end**

use the algorithm NIAGaRa or the algorithm DIAGaRa (like any non-incremental algorithm) for solving subtasks of both the first and the second kind. Next we use the procedure NIAGaRa.

Let *t* be an invalid test for some negative object. Correcting *t* consists of two steps:

- Applying the diagnostic rule in order to find the set of essential values with the use of which *t* can be extended and constructing the extensions *tnew* of *t*;
- Forming a subtask of· the first kind for each extension *tnew* of *t* in order to find all the GMRTs for the negative objects contained in *tnew* and solving the subtask with the use of the procedure NIAGaRa.

Figure 4. The procedure for preparing data for inferring the GMRTs contained in a new example

> **The procedure FORMSUBTASK(*j**).**
>
> **Input:** *j**, *R*(+), *R*(−), *s*(+), *STGOOD*(+).
> **Output:** *S*(test)(+) - the set of collections of objects
> to be extended;
>   *Q*(+) - the set of forbidden pairs of objects.
>
> **Begin**
> *S*(test)(+) $\leftarrow$ {*j**}; *Q*(+) $\leftarrow \varnothing$; *nts* $\leftarrow$ *s*(+);
> ($\forall i$) $i \in nts, i \neq j^*$
>   if to_be_test(val({*j**, *i*})) = true **then do**
>
>   **Begin**
>   *s* = generalization_of({*j**, *i*});
>   insert *s* into *S*(test)(+) under lexicographically
> order;
>   **end**
>   **else** *Q*(+) $\leftarrow$ *Q*(+) $\cup$ {*j**, *i*};
>   **end**

Let CORRECT(t) be the procedure for correcting the invalid test t and finding new tests for negative objects. We must consider four possible situations that can take place when a new object comes to the learning system:

- The knowledge base is empty and does not contain any object of the class to which a new object belongs and any alternative object;
- The knowledge base contains only objects of the positive class to which a new object belongs;
- The knowledge base contains only objects of the negative class;
- The knowledge base contains objects of both the positive and the negative classes.

The second situation conforms to the generalization process taking into account only the similarity relation between examples of the same class. This problem is known in the literature as inductive inference of generalization hypotheses or unsupervised generalization. An algorithm for solving this problem in the framework of a mathematical model based on Galois's connections can be found in (Kuznetzov, 1993).

Let CONCEPTGENERALIZATION [j*](S(+), $STGOOD$(+)) be the procedure of generalization of positive examples in the absence of negative examples. The procedure INGOMAR (for INcremental inferring GOod MAximally Redundant tests) is presented in Figure 5. We give an example of the work of the procedure INGOMAR. The data in Table 16 are intended for processing by this incremental learning procedure.

Figure 5. The incremental procedure INGOMAR

```
The  procedure  INGOMAR.

Input : j*, R, S, STGOOD, Q. Output: R, S, STGOOD, Q.
begin
k ← class(j*); S(+)  ←  S(k);  R(+)  ← R(k); R(-)  ← R/R(+);
N  ← N + 1;  j*  ← N, where N is the number of objects;
S(+)  ← j* ∪ S(+);   R(+)  ← t_j* ∪ R(+);
STGOOD(+)  ←  STGOOD(k);
STGOOD(-)  ← ∪ STGOOD(kl), ∀kl, kl ≠ k;
if  N = 1 then  STGOOD(+) ← {j*} ∪ STGOOD(+);  else
if  N ≠ 1 and ‖S(+)‖ = 1 then

begin
STGOOD(+)  ←  {j*} ∪ STGOOD(+);
if (∃s), s ∈ STGOOD(-), val(s) ⊆ t_j*
then CORRECT(val(s)); end
else
if  N ≠ 1 and S(-) = ∅ then

CONCEPTGENERALIZATION [j*](S(+), STGOOD(+));
else   /* N ≠ 1 and ‖S(+)‖ ≠ 1 and S(-) ≠ ∅ */
begin
if STGOOD(+) ≠ ∅ then
GENERALIZATION(STGOOD(+), j*); end
FORMSUBTASK (j*);
NIAGaRa [j* | (S(test)(+), R, S, STGOOD (+), Q (+));
if (∃ s), s ∈ STGOOD (-), val(s) ⊆ t_j*
then CORRECT (val(s));
end
```

In Table 21 and Table 22, $Q(1)$ and $Q(2)$ are the sets of forbidden pairs of objects of Class 1 and Class 2, respectively.

The sets $STGOOD(1)$ and $STGOOD(2)$ in these tables accumulate the collections of objects that correspond to the GMRTs for Class 1 and Class 2, respectively, at each step of the algorithm.

Table 23 contains the results of working the procedure INGOMAR.

The Integrative Inductive-Deductive Model of Commonsense Reasoning

Up to this moment we considered only supervised learning, but integrative inductive-deductive reasoning must also encompass unsupervised learning. This mode of learning is involved in reasoning when a new portion of observations or objects (examples) becomes available over time but without the indication of their class membership. Then the following actions are necessary with the arrival of a new object:

- Pattern recognition and generalization of knowledge (increasing the power of already existing inductive knowledge);
- Inferring new knowledge.

In this case, a teacher is absent. Only knowledge is available. A new object description can currently be complete or incomplete, i.e. some attribute values can be unknown or not observable.

If we deal with completely described object, then the following results of reasoning are possible:

- Class of the new object is determined clearly;
- There are determined several classes to which the new object can belong to;
- An object is absolutely unknown, i.e. there is some new values of attributes in its description.

In the situations of uncertainty, there are the following ways of reasoning with the use of training examples (it is the reasoning based on the past experience):

- To infer the hypotheses about unknown values of attributes;
- To define the training examples that are similar to the newly coming example in most degree and to infer new rule for describing this group of similar examples.

Table 21. The records of step-by-step results of the incremental procedure INGOMAR

j*	Class(J*)	Q(1), Q(2)	STGOOD(1), STGOOD(2)
{1};	1	$Q(1)$ =Empty	$STGOOD(1)$: {1}
{2}	1	$Q(1)$ =Empty	$STGOOD(1)$:{1,2};
{3}	2	$Q(2)$ =Empty	$STGOOD(2)$:{3}
{4}	2	$Q(2) \cup \{\{3,4\}\}$	$STGOOD(2)$:{3}, {4}
{5},	2	$Q(2) \cup \{\{3,4\}, \{3,5\}\}$	$STGOOD(2)$:{3}, {4,5};
{6}	1	$Q(1) \cup \{\{1,6\}, \{2,6\}\}$	$STGOOD(1)$:{1,2}, {6}
{7}	2	$Q(2) \cup \{\{4,7\},\{5,7\}\}$	$STGOOD(2)$:{3,7},{4,5}
{8}	1	$Q(1) \cup \{\{6,8\}\}$	$STGOOD(1)$:{1,2,8}, {6}
{9}	2	$Q(2) \cup \{\{3,9\}, \{4,9\}, \{7,9\}\}$	$STGOOD(2)$:{3,7},{4,5},{5,9}

Table 22. The records of step-by-step results of the incremental procedure INGOMAR

J*	Class(J*)	Q(1), Q(2)	STGOOD(1), STGOOD(2)
{10}	2	$Q(2) \cup \{\{3,10\},\{7,10\}\}$	$STGOOD(2):\{3,7\},\{4,5,10\},\{5,9,10\}$
{11}	2	$Q(2) \cup \{\{3,11\},$ $\{4,11\}, \{5,11\},\{7,11\}\}$	$STGOOD(2):\{3,7\},\{4,5,10\},\{5,9,10\},$ $\{10,11\},\{9,11\}$
{12}	2	$Q(2) \cup \{ (4,12),$ $(5,12), (9,12), (10,12)\}$	$STGOOD(2): \{3,7,12\},\{4,5,10\},$ $\{5,9,10\},\{10,11\},\{9,11\},\{11,12\};$
{13}	2	$Q(2) \cup \{\{4,13\},$ $\{11,13\}\}$	$STGOOD(2): \{3,7,12,13\},\{4,5,10\},$ $\{5,9,10,13\},\{10,11\},\{9,11\},\{11,12\}$
{14}	1	$Q(1) \cup \{\{1,14\},$ $\{2,14\}, \{8,14\}\}$	$STGOOD(1):\{1,2,8\}, \{6,14\}$
		{11,12} is invalid for Class 2	$STGOOD(2):\{3,7,12,13\},\{4,5,10\},$ $\{5,9,10,13\},\{10,11\},\{9,11\},$

Table 23. The sets TGOOD(1) and TGOOD(2) produced by the procedure INGOMAR

TGOOD(1)	TGOOD(2)
({1,2,8}, Sunny High)	({4,5,10}, Rain No)
({6,14), Rain Yes)	({5,9,10,13}, Normal No)
-	({10,11}, Mild Normal)
-	({9,11}, Sunny Normal)
-	({3,7,12,13}, Overcast)

Consider some instances of pattern recognition reasoning by using the rules obtained by the procedure INGOMAR.

Example 1.

The new weather descriptions are complete, for example,

<Overcast, Cool, High, No>; *<Sunny, Cool, Normal, Yes>*; *<Sunny, Mild, High, Yes>*.

In all these situations, we find the rules, which allow us to recognize the weather class.

Example 2.

If the weather descriptions are incomplete, then it is possible, that none of the rules is applicable. But we can use the training set of examples to infer possible or most probable variants of the weather class.

Assume that the weather description is: *<Rain, Mild, High>*

We construct the decision tree as follows:

Rain: Class 2 (Observations 4, 5, 10); Class 1 (Observations 6, 14) → **Mild**: Class 2 (Observation 4, 10); Class 1 (Observation 14) → **High**: Class 2 (Observation 4); Class 1 (Observation 14).

It is a situation of uncertainty. Consequently, a step of conditional or diagnostic reasoning is necessary. We can consider hypothetically the possible values of attribute **Windy**; then we comclude that

If **Windy** = *No*, then Class 2;

If **Windy** = *Yes*, then Class   1.

Really we have obtained the following diagnostic rule:

"If we observe that (**Outlook** = *Rain*) & (**Temperature** = *Mild*) & (**Humidity** = *High*), then if **Windy** = *No*, then Class 2; else Class   1.

Note that, during deductive or pattern recognition reasoning, we address really our past expierence and advance hypotheses in the form of new diagnostic rules of the first type; it is the inductive step of reasoning.

Example 3.

The weather description is: *<Hot, Yes>*.
    The reasoning tree is:

Hot: Class 1 (Observations 1, 2); Class 2 (Observations 3, 13) → **Yes**: Class 1 (Observations 2); Class 2 (Observations -).

Now we can formulate hypothetically a new forbidden rule: "*Hot, Yes* → Class 2 *false*" or, in another form, "If we observe that (**Temperature** = *Hot*) & (**Windy** = *Yes*), then it is never observed Class 2". The training set contains few examples of Class 1, it explains that we could not infer this rule as a good test, but it can exist as an assumption.

Example 4.

The weather description is: *<Sunny, Mild, Low, No>*.
    Here we meet the new value of Humidity – "*Low*". Assume that the sets of values of Humidity and Temperature are ordered and *Low < Normal < High* and *Mild < Cool < Could*. Assume that the functions of distance on the attribute domains are also defined. Then the computer system realizing the pattern recognition process can induce that *<Sunny, Mild, Low, No>* is nearer to the example of Class 2 *<Sunny, Cool, Normal, No>* than to the example of Class 1 *<Sunny, Mild, High, No>*. A new feature for Class 2 can be formed, namely, *<Sunny, Low >*.
    One of the important problems of integrating deductive and inductive reasoning is connected with the realization of on-line interactive method for creating and modifying the context of reasoning. Failures in reasoning or appearance of new data can require to add new attributes to the context.
    The task of incremental generating a logical context for email messages classification is considered in (Ferré, & Redoux, 2002). This paper is based on two hypotheses: (1) for each new piece of data that arrives, an object is created, and added to the context; (2) the world outside an application is in constant

Table 25. The set of negative examples R(-)

Index of example	R(-)	Index of example	R(-)
15	$A_5A_8A_{16}A_{23}A_{24}$	32	$A_1A_2A_3A_7A_9A_{13}A_{18}$
16	$A_7A_8A_9A_{16}A_{18}$	33	$A_1A_5A_6A_8A_9A_{19}A_{20}A_{22}$
17	$A_1A_{21}A_{22}A_{24}A_{26}$	34	$A_2A_8A_9A_{18}A_{20}A_{21}A_{22}A_{23}A_{26}$
18	$A_1A_7A_8A_9A_{13}A_{16}$	35	$A_1A_2A_4A_5A_6A_7A_9A_{13}A_{16}$
19	$A_2A_6A_7A_9A_{21}A_{23}$	36	$A_1A_2A_6A_7A_8A_{13}A_{16}A_{18}$
20	$A_{10}A_{19}A_{20}A_{21}A_{22}A_{24}$	37	$A_1A_2A_3A_4A_5A_6A_7A_{12}A_{14}A_{15}A_{16}$
21	$A_1A_{20}A_{21}A_{22}A_{23}A_{24}$	38	$A_1A_2A_3A_4A_5A_6A_9A_{12}A_{13}A_{16}$
22	$A_1A_3A_6A_7A_9A_{16}$	39	$A_1A_2A_3A_4A_5A_6A_{14}A_{15}A_{19}A_{20}A_{23}A_{26}$
23	$A_2A_6A_8A_9A_{14}A_{15}A_{16}$	40	$A_2A_3A_4A_5A_6A_7A_{12}A_{13}A_{14}A_{15}A_{16}$
24	$A_1A_4A_5A_6A_7A_8A_{16}$	41	$A_2A_3A_4A_5A_6A_7A_9A_{12}A_{13}A_{14}A_{15}A_{19}$
25	$A_7A_{13}A_{19}A_{20}A_{22}A_{26}$	42	$A_1A_2A_3A_4A_5A_6A_{12}A_{16}A_{18}A_{19}A_{20}A_{21}A_{26}$
26	$A_1A_2A_3A_6A_7A_{16}$	43	$A_4A_5A_6A_7A_8A_9A_{12}A_{13}A_{14}A_{15}A_{16}$
27	$A_1A_2A_5A_6A_{13}A_{16}$	44	$A_3A_4A_5A_6A_8A_9A_{12}A_{13}A_{14}A_{15}A_{18}A_{19}$
28	$A_1A_3A_7A_{13}A_{19}A_{21}$	45	$A_1A_2A_3A_4A_5A_6A_7A_8A_9A_{12}A_{13}A_{14}A_{15}$
29	$A_1A_4A_5A_6A_7A_8A_{13}A_{16}$	46	$A_1A_3A_4A_5A_6A_7A_{12}A_{13}A_{14}A_{15}A_{16}A_{23}A_{24}$
30	$A_1A_2A_3A_6A_{12}A_{14}A_{15}A_{16}$	47	$A_1A_2A_3A_4A_5A_6A_8A_9A_{12}A_{14}A_{16}A_{18}A_{22}$
31	$A_1A_2A_5A_6A_{14}A_{15}A_{16}A_{26}$	48	$A_2A_8A_9A_{12}A_{14}A_{15}A_{16}$

Table 26. The set SPLUS of the collection splus(A) for all A in Table 24

$SPLUS = \{splus(A_i): s(A_i) \cap s(+), A_i \in T\}$:	
$splus(A_*) \rightarrow \{2,8,10\}$	$Splus(A_{22}) \rightarrow \{2,7,8,9,11\}$
$splus(A_{13}) \rightarrow \{3,8,10\}$	$splus(A_{23}) \rightarrow \{1,2,5,12,13,14\}$
$splus(A_{16}) \rightarrow \{4,9,12\}$	$splus(A_3) \rightarrow \{3,7,8,10,11,12\}$
$splus(A_1) \rightarrow \{1,4,11,13\}$	$splus(A_4) \rightarrow \{2,3,4,7,10,13\}$
$splus(A_5) \rightarrow \{1,4,7,10\}$	$splus(A_6) \rightarrow \{1,4,5,7,8,10\}$
$splus(A_{12}) \rightarrow \{2,3,4,7\}$	$splus(A_7) \rightarrow \{2,3,4,6,8,11\}$
$splus(A_{18}) \rightarrow \{3,9,10,13\}$	$splus(A_{24}) \rightarrow \{1,2,3,4,5,7,12,14\}$
$splus(A_2) \rightarrow \{1,5,10,11,12\}$	$splus(A_{20}) \rightarrow \{4,6,7,8,9,10,11,12\}$
$splus(A_*) \rightarrow \{2,3,4,7,8\}$	$splus(A_{21}) \rightarrow \{1,4,6,8,9,10,11,12\}$
$splus(A_{19}) \rightarrow \{3,8,9,11,13\}$	$splus(A_{26}) \rightarrow \{1,2,3,4,6,7,9,10,11,12,13,14\}$

evolution. The article presents a method for incremental constructing a logical context by the assignment of new attributes to object descriptions. The existing context plays the role of a dynamic schema to help users to keep consistency in their object descriptions. This method can be compared to the context-based query refinement that has been advanced in (Ferré, & Ridoux, 2001).

RELATED WORKS

This chapter is devoted to elaborating the efficient and incremental algorithms for constructing concepts in a commonsense reasoning manner. The problems of generating the set of all concepts together with their lattice order (the diagram graph) has been well studied in FCA.

The family of faster algorithms for constructing a Concept (Galois) Lattice has been advanced by Vicky Choi (2006). His algorithms compute all concepts and identify all successors of each concept. The main idea of the algorithms consists in reducing efficiently adjacency list of each object. The method used for this goal is very similar to using and reducing attributive projections in our algorithms ASTRA and DIAGaRa.

With the use of our terminology, we shall shortly describe the basic algorithm of V. Choi as follows. The only difference in terminology concerns the following replacements: the denotation val() is substituted by attr() and T will be the set of attributes. Also the attributes are considered to be binary features.

For each subset $X \subseteq T$, consider the set res $(X) = \{A \in T \backslash X: \mathrm{obj}(X) \cap \mathrm{obj}(A) \neq \varnothing\}$. The set res($X$) is the set of attributes and only those attributes that can be used for extending X. An equivalence relation $\approx$ is defined on res(X) as follows. $A \approx B \Leftrightarrow \mathrm{obj}(X) \cap \mathrm{obj}(A) = \mathrm{obj}(X) \cap \mathrm{obj}(B)$, for $A \neq B \in \mathrm{res}(X)$.

Let $S_1, S_2, \ldots, S_t$ be the equivalence classes induced by $\approx$ on res(X), i.e. res(X) = $S_1 \cup \ldots \cup S_t$. The set $\{S_1, S_2, \ldots, S_t\}$ is called AttrChild(X).

For convenience, we shall write $X \cup S_i$ as XS_i and use the notation $X \cup$ AttrChild(X) = $\{XS: S \in \mathrm{AttrChild}(X)\}$. Note that, by definition, $\mathrm{obj}(XS_k) = \mathrm{obj}(X) \cap \mathrm{obj}(S_k) = \mathrm{obj}(X) \cap \mathrm{obj}(A)$ for some $A \in S_k$.

Constructing a concept lattice requires generating all concepts and identifying each concept's successors.

Recall that (obj(Y), Y) is a successor of obj(X), X) in the lattice GL = $<L, \subseteq>$, where L is the set of all concepts, if and only if Y is a successor of X in the lattice $<2^T, \subseteq>$.

Let Succ(X) denote all the successors of X, then Succ(X) $\subseteq X \cup$ AttrChild(X). However, not every child of X is a successor of X. Similarly, if P is predecessor of X, then P is parent of X but it is not necessary that every parent of X is a predecessor of X. The following proposition gives the condition for $XS \in$ Succ(X) to be closed: for $S \in$ AttrChild(X), if $XS \in$ Succ(X), then XS is closed. The converse is also true. Consequently, we have that Succ(X) = $\{XS: XS$ is closed, $S \in$ AttrChild(X)$\}$.

The algorithm of Vicky Choi for concept lattice construction starts with the top concept (O, attr(O)), where O is the set of all considered objects. It processes the consept by computing all its succesors, and then recursively processes each successor by either the Depth First Search (DFS) order or Breadth First Search (BFS) order.

Let $C = (\mathrm{obj}(X), X)$ be a concept. First, all the children Child(C) = $\{(\mathrm{obj}(XS), XS): S \in \mathrm{Attr}(\mathrm{Child}(X)\}$ are computed. Then for each $S \in \mathrm{Attr}(\mathrm{Child}(X)$, it is tested if XS is closed. If XS is closed, then (obj(XS), XS) is a successor of C. Since a concept can have several predecessor, it can be generated several times. It must be checked that each concept is processed once and only once. The pseudo-code of the algorithm based on BFS is given in (Choi, 2006).

The efficiency of the algorithm depends on the efficient implementation of three procedures: (1) computing Child(C); (2) testing if an attribute set is closed; (3) testing if a concept already exists.

The analysis of the computation complexity for these procedures can be found in (Choi, 2006). It has been demonstrated in this chapter that the running time of the basic algorithm is

$$O(\Sigma_{a \in \mathrm{ext}(C)} \mid \mathrm{nbr}(a) \mid),$$

for each concept C, where $|nbr(a)|$ is the number of attributes adjacent to the object a. It is as fast as the current best algorithms for the problem as Choi (2006) informs. However, the modification of the basic algorithm with dynamically updating adjacency lists has the running time equal to polynomial delay for each concept C:

$$O(\Sigma_{a \in ext(C)} \mid cnbr(a) \mid),$$

where $cnbr(a)$ is the reduced adjacency list of a. Note that an algorithm runs in polynomial delay time if the generation of each output is only polynomial in the size of input (Johnson et al., 1988).

It is faster than the best known algorithms for constructing Galois Lattice. Updating adjacency lists is performed with the use of the equivalence relation defined on $res(X)$ and described above. Note that, a tree structure is used in algorithms of Choi (2006) to memorize the object sets, so it takes linear time to search and insert (if not exists) an object set in the tree.

An incremental concept lattice construction algorithm, called AddIntent, is proposed in (Merwe et al., 2004). As it is informed, this algorithm outperformed some published algorithms for most types of contexts and was close to the most efficient algorithm. The current best estimate for the algorothm's upper bound complexity is $O(|L| |G|^2 \max(|g'|))$, where L is a Concept Lattice, G is a set of objects, each object g of which possesses at most $\max(|g'|)$ attributes ($g' = atr(g)$).

The algorithm AddIntent is the improved version of an earlier algorithm AddAtom (Merwe, & Kourie, 2002). AddIntent is an incremental algorithm, i.e. it takes as input the lattice L_i produced by the first i objects of the context and inserts the next object g to compute a new lattice L_{i+1}. Lattice construction is described in terms of four sets of concepts: modified concepts, generator concepts, new concepts, and old concepts.

The key problem of the algorithm is how to identify all modified concepts in order to add g to their extents and how to generate every new concept exactly once. AddIntent solves these problems more efective than the algorithms of Norris (1978) and of Godin et al. (1995). AddIntent constructs the diagram graph which orders concepts from most to least general ones; the traversing of the diagram graph in a bottom-up fashion is performed for exluding some concepts from further consideration.

The algorithm (designated "Algorithm 5") proposed by Valtchev et al. (2002; 2003) uses a similar methodology for constructing lattice, but direct comparison of this algorithm and AddIntent has not yet been conducted and it is a topic of further research (Merwe et al., 2004).

CONCLUSION

In this chapter, the decomposition of inferring good classification tests into subtasks of the first and second kinds is introduced. This decomposition involves searching essential values and objects, eliminating values, cutting off objects, choosing values or objects for subtasks, extending or narrowing collections of values, extending or narrowing collections of objects, using forbidden rules, forming subtasks and some others actions. This decomposition allows, in principle, to transform the process of inferring good tests into a "step by step" reasoning process.

We have described some inductive algorithms for inferring good maximally redundant tests. These algorithms are: ASTRA, DIAGaRa, and INGOMAR. We did not focus on the efficiency of our algorithms, although we understand that the questions of computational complexity of reasoning are very important. We intend to give more attention to the complexity problems in future contributions.

The development of full on-line integrated deductive and inductive reasoning is of great interest but it requires the cooperative efforts of many researchers. The main problem in this direction is the choice of data structure underlying the algorithms of inferring good diagnostic tests and the development of an on-line interactive model to support users in constructing and modifying the context of deductive-inductive reasoning.

REFERENCES

Arseniev, V. K. (1941). *Dersu, the trapper: Exploring, trapping, hunting in Ussuria* (1st ed.). New York: E. P. Dulton.

Arseniev, V. K. (1950). *In the thickets of Ussuria land*. Moscow, USSR: The State Publishing House of Geographical Literature.

Choi, V. (2006). *Faster algorithms for constructing a concept (Galois) lattice*. Paper presented at SIAM Conference on Discrete Mathematics (arXiv: DM/0602069). Univ. of Victoria, Canada.

Dickson, T. J. (1969). On a problem concerning separating systems of a finite set. *J. of Comb. Theory*, 7, 191–196. doi:10.1016/S0021-9800(69)80011-6

Ester, M. Kriegel, H. P., Sander, J., Wimmer, M., & Xu, X. (1998). Incremental clustering for mining in a data warehousing environment. In A. Gupta, O. Shmueli, & J. Widom (Eds.), *Proceedings of the 24th VLDB Conference* (pp. 323-333). New York: Morgan Kaufman

Feldman, R., Aumann, Y., Amir, A., & Mannila, H. (1997). Efficient algorithms for discovering frequent sets in incremental databases. In J. Peckham (Ed.), *Proceedings of ACM SIGMOD Workshop on Research Issue on Data Mining and Knowledge Discovery* (pp. 59-66). Tucson, AZ: ACM Press.

Ferré, S. (2001). Complete and incomplete knowledge in logical information systems. In S. Benferhat, & P. Besnard (Eds.). *Symbolic and quantitative approaches to reasoning with uncertainty, Proceedings of 6th European Conference* (ECSQARU'01) (LNCS 2143, pp. 782-791). Berlin/Heidelberg: Springer.

Ferré, S., & Ridoux, O. (2002). The use of associative concepts in the incremental building of a logical context. In *Conceptual Structures: Integration and Interfaces, Proceedings of the 10th International Conference on Conceptual Structures* (ICCS'02) (LNCS 2393, pp. 299-313). Berlin/Heidelberg: Springer.

Giraud-Carrier, C. (2000). A note on the utility on incremental learning. *AI Communications*, 13(4), 215–223.

Godin, R., Missaoui, R., & Alaoui, H. (1995). Incremental concept formation algorithms based on Galois lattices. *Computational Intelligence*, 11(2), 246–267. doi:10.1111/j.1467-8640.1995.tb00031.x

Johnson, D. S., Yannakakis, M., & Papadimitrou, C. H. (1988). On generating all maximal independent sets. *Information Processing Letters*, 27, 119–123. doi:10.1016/0020-0190(88)90065-8

Maloof, M. A., & Michalski, R. S. (1995). A method for partial memory incremental learning and its application to computer intrusion detection. In *Proceedings of the 7th IEEE International Conference on Tools with Artificial Intelligence* (pp. 392-397). Los Alamitos, CA: IEEE Press.

Merwe, D., & Kourie, D. (2002). Compressed pseudo-lattices. *Journal of Experimental & Theoretical Artificial Intelligence*, *14*, 229–254. doi:10.1080/09528130210164215

Merwe, D., Obiedkov, S., & Kourie, D. (2004). AddIntent: A new incremental algorithm for constructing concept lattices. In P. W. Eklund (Ed.), *Concept Lattices, Proceedings of the second International Conference on FCA, (ICFCA'04)* (LNCS 2961, pp. 372-385). Berlin/Heidelberg: Springer.

Naidenova, X. A., Plaksin, M. V., & Shagalov, V. L. (1995b). Inductive inferring all good classification tests. In J. Valkman (Ed.), *Knowledge-Dialog-Solution, Proceedings of International Conference in two volumes* (Vol. 1, pp. 79-84). Jalta, Ukraine: Kiev Institute of Applied Informatics.

Naidenova, X. A., Polegaeva, J. G., & Iserlis, J. E. (1995a). The system of knowledge acquisition based on constructing the best diagnostic classification tests. In J. Valkman (Ed.), *Knowledge-Dialog-Solution, Proceedings of International Conference in two volumes* (Vol. 1, pp. 85-95). Jalta, Ukraine: Kicv Institute of Applied Informatics.

Nieto, S., Triantaphyllou, E., Chen, J., & Liao, T. W. (2002). An incremental learning algorithm for constructing Boolean function from positive and negative examples. *Computers & Operations Research*, *29*(12), 1677–1700. doi:10.1016/S0305-0548(01)00050-8

Norris, E. M. (1978). An algorithm for computing the maximal rectangles in a binary relation. *Revue Roumaine de Mathématiques Pures et Appliquées*, *23*(2), 243–250.

Quinlan, J. R., & Rivest, R. L. (1989). Inferring decision trees using the minimum description length principle. *Information and Computation*, *80*(3), 227–248. doi:10.1016/0890-5401(89)90010-2

Rasiova, H. (1974). *An algebraic approach to non-classical logic* (Studies in Logic, Vol. 78). Amsterdam-London: North-Holland Publishing Company.

Sperner, E. (1928). Ein satz uber Untermengen einer Endlichen Menge. *Mathematische Zeitschrift*, *27*(11), 544–548. doi:10.1007/BF01171114

Valtchev, P., & Duquenne, V. (2003). Toward scalable divide and conquer method for computing concepts and implications. In E. SanJuan, A. Berry, A. Sigayret, & A. Napoli (Eds.), *Knowledge Discovery and Discrete Mathematics, Proceedings of the 4th Intl. Conference Journées de l'Informatique Messine* (JIM'03) (pp. 3-15). INRIA.

Valtchev, P., Missaoui, R., Godin, R., & Meridji, M. (2002). Generating frequent itemsets incrementally: two novel approaches based on Galois lattice theory. *Journal of Experimental & Theoretical Artificial Intelligence*, *14*, 115–142. doi:10.1080/09528130210164198

Valtchev, P., Rouane, M. N., Huchard, M., & Roume, C. (2003). Extracting formal concepts out of relational data. In E. SanJuan, A. Berry, A. Sigayret, & A. Napoli (Eds.), *Knowledge Discovery and Discrete Mathematics, Proceedings of the 4th Intl. Conference Journées de l'Informatique Messine* (JIM'03) (pp. 37-49). INRIA.

Wu, X., & Lo, W. (1998). Multi-layer incremental induction. In H.-Y. Lee, & H. Motoda (Eds.), *Topics in artificial intelligence, Proceedings of the 5-th Pacific Rim International Conference on Artificial Intelligence* (pp. 24-32). Springer-Verlag.

APPENDIX 1

ASTRA: An Algorithm for Inferring GMRTs with the Use of Subtasks of the Second Kind

A recursive procedure for using attributive subtasks for inferring GMRTs has been advanced in (Naidenova et al., 1995b). It has been implemented in the system of knowledge acquisition SISIF (Naidenova et al., 1995a).

Let Test-1 and FM be the sets of positive and negative examples (objects), respectively. Let also U = $\{A_1, ..., A_n\}$ be the set of attributes' values appearing in object descriptions. Let N = $\{1, ...i, ...j,..., m\}$ be the set of indices of positive objects. As earlier, t_i, $i \in N$ denotes i-th object.

The relation of absorption is defined as follows: object i is absorbed by object j if and only if $t_i \subseteq t_j$.

Let v be an object and M be the set of objects. The function inc(v, M) is defined as follows:

```
inc(v,M) ::=
if v is absorbed by at least one of elements of Mthentrueelse-
false.
```

Let $s \subseteq$ NT, and $t(s)$ – the intersection of all object's descriptions from Test-1 the indices of which are in s. The function kt(s) is defined as follows:

```
kt(s) ::=
if inc(t(s), FM) = falsethentrueelsefalse.
```

kt(s) is equal to *true* if $(s, t(s))$ is a test for positive objects.
The following denotations are used too:

```
| |      - the modulus of a number,
|| ||    - the power of a set,
U[i]     - i-th element of the set U,
s(A)     - indices of elements of the set Test-1 containing value
A,
SNT      - the set of all subsets of NT,
S(test) = {snt: (snt ∈ SNT) & kt(snt)}.
```

The following operators are used in the algorithm:
$(kt(s(U[i]) \cap NT)$ & inc(s(U[i]), S(test))) – the condition of modifying S(test);
$U ::= U \setminus \{U[i]\}$ – deleting i-th attribute;
$NT ::= NT \setminus \{NT[i]\}$ – deleting i-th object;
(inc(U, FM) or inc(NT, S(test))) – the condition of going out of recursion (return of recursion).
The following procedures are used in the algorithm: DELATR (for searching for GMRTs and deleting attributes from current subtask), DELSTR (for deleting objects from current subtask), NUMATRSUBTASK (for choosing an attribute for forming subtask), FORMSUBTASK (for forming subtask), GE-

NALLMAXGOODTESTS (the maim procedure of test generation).

```
DELATR
    (
    input: U, NT;
    output: U, flag
    )
    begin
    i ::= 1;
    flag ::= 0;
    while i ≤ || U ||
        beginif inc(s(U[i]) ∩ NT, S(test))
        thenbegin
            U::= U\{U[i]};
            flag::= 1;
            endelseif kt(s(U[i]) ∩ NT)
        thenbegin
            j ::=1
            while j ≤ || S(test) ||
                beginif S(test)[j] is absorbed by s(U[i]) ∩ NT
                        begin
                        S(test)::= S(test)\{S(test)[ j ]}
                        endend
                S(test)::= S(test) ∪ (s(U[i]) ∩ NT);
                end
            U::= U\{U[i]};
            flag::= 1;
            endend
    going out of procedure;
    end
```

The procedure of deleting objects from current subtask

```
DELSTR
    (
    input: U, NT;
    output: NT, flag
    )
    begin
    i ::= 1;
    flag ::= 0;
    while i ≤ || NT ||
        beginif inc(Test-1[NT[i]] ∩ U,FM)
        thenbegin
```

```
                          NT ::= NT\{NT[i]};
                          flag ::= 1;
                          endend
          going out of procedure;
          end
```

The procedure of determining the number of attribute for forming a new subtask (the choice of subtask)

```
NUMATRSUBTASK
     (
     input: U, NT;
     output: na
     )
     begin
     i ::= 1;
     max ::= 0;
     min ::= || NT ||;
     while i ≤ || U ||
          beginif max < || s(U[i]) ||
          thenbegin
               max ::= || s(U[i]) ||;
               endif min > || s(U[i]) ||
          thenbegin
               min ::= || s(U[i]) ||;
               endend
     med ::= ( min + max ) / 2;
     dif ::= || NT ||
     while i ≤ || U ||
          beginif ( dif > | med - || s(U[i]) || | )
          thenbegin
               na ::= i;
               dif ::= | med - || s(U[i]) || |;
               endend
     going out of procedure;
     end
```

The Procedure of forming subtask

```
FORMSUBTASK
     (
     input: na,U, NT;
     output: SUBU, SUBNT
     )
```

```
begin
i ::= 1;
SUBNT ::= s(U[na]) ∩ NT;
while i ≤ || SUBNT ||
    begin
    SUBU ::= SUBU U ( test-1[SUBNT[i]] ∩ U );
    end
going out of procedure;
end
```

The main procedure of GMRTs generation

```
GENALLMAXGOODTESTS
    (
    input: U, NT;
    )
    begin
    flag ::= 1;
    whiletruebeginwhile flag=1
            begin
            DELATR(U, NT, U, flag);
            if flag = 1
            thenbegin
                DELSTR(U, NT, NT, flag);
                endendif (inc(U, FM) or inc(NT, S(test)))
        thenbegin
            going out of procedure;
            end
        SUBU ::= empty;
        SUBNT ::= empty;
        NUMATRSUBTASK(U, NT, na);
        FORMSUBTASK(na,U, NT, SUBU, SUBNT);
        GENALLMAXGOODTESTS(SUBU, SUBNT);
        U ::= U\{U[na]};
        DELSTR(U, NT, NT, flag);
        endend
```

Note that Test-1, S(test), FM is available for all procedures of the algorithm: they are global sets. As the result of algorithm, S(test) contains all s for which $(s, t(s))$ is a GMRT for positive objects and only these tests.

APPENDIX 2

Example of the Work of Algorithm DIAGaRa

The data to be processed are in Table 24 and Table 25 (the set of positive and negative examples, respectively).

Table 24. The set of positive examples R(+)

Index of example	R(+)
1	$A_1A_2A_5A_6A_{21}A_{23}A_{24}A_{26}$
2	$A_4A_7A_8A_9A_{12}A_{14}A_{15}A_{22}A_{23}A_{24}A_{26}$
3	$A_3A_4A_7A_{12}A_{13}A_{14}A_{15}A_{18}A_{19}A_{24}A_{26}$
4	$A_1A_4A_5A_6A_7A_{12}A_{14}A_{15}A_{16}A_{20}A_{21}A_{24}A_{26}$
5	$A_2A_6A_{23}A_{24}$
6	$A_7A_{20}A_{21}A_{26}$
7	$A_3A_4A_5A_6A_{12}A_{14}A_{15}A_{20}A_{22}A_{24}A_{26}$
8	$A_3A_6A_7A_8A_9A_{13}A_{14}A_{15}A_{19}A_{20}A_{21}A_{22}$
9	$A_{16}A_{18}A_{19}A_{20}A_{21}A_{22}A_{26}$
10	$A_2A_3A_4A_5A_6A_8A_9A_{13}A_{18}A_{20}A_{21}A_{26}$
11	$A_1A_2A_3A_7A_{19}A_{20}A_{21}A_{22}A_{26}$
12	$A_2A_3A_{16}A_{20}A_{21}A_{23}A_{24}A_{26}$
13	$A_1A_4A_{18}A_{19}A_{23}A_{26}$
14	$A_{23}A_{24}A_{26}$

We begin with $s^* = S(+) = \{\{1\}, \{2\}, ..., \{14\}\}$, $t^* = T = \{A_1, A_2, ..., A_{26}\}$, $SPLUS = \{splus(A_i): A_i \in t^*\}$ (see, please, *SPLUS* in Table 26). In Tables 26, 27, A_* denotes the collection of values $\{A_8, A_9\}$ and A_+ denotes the collection of values $\{A_{14}, A_{15}\}$ because $splus(A_8) = splus(A_9)$ and $splus(A_{14}) = splus(A_{15})$.

Table 27. The sets STGOOD and TGOOD for the examples of Table 24

№	STGOOD	TGOOD
1	{2,3,4,7}	$A_4A_{12}A_+A_{24}A_{26}$
2	{1,2,12,14}	$A_{23}A_{24}A_{26}$
3	{4,6,8,11}	$A_7A_{20}A_{21}$

We use the algorithm DIAGaRa for inferring all the GMRTs having a weight equal to or greater than WMIN = 4 for the training set of the positive and negative examples represented in Tables 23 and 24.

Please observe that $splus(A_{12}) = \{2,3,4,7\}$ and $t(\{2,3,4,7\})$ corresponds a test, therefore, A_{12} is deleted from t^* and $splus(A_{12})$ is inserted into *STGOOD*. Then $W(A_*)$, $W(A_{13})$, and $W(A_{16})$ are less than WMIN, hence we can delete A_*, A_{13}, and A_{16} from t^*. Now t_{10} is not a test and can be deleted.

After modifying $splus(A)$ for A_5, A_{18}, A_2, A_3, A_4, A_6, A_{20}, A_{21}, and A_{26} we find that $W(A_5) = 3$, therefore, A_5 is deleted from t^*. Then $W(A_{18})$ turns out to be less than WMIN and we delete A_{18}, this implies deleting t_{13}. Next we modify $splus(A)$ for A_1, A_{19}, A_{23}, A_4, A_{26} and find that $splus(A_4) = \{2,3,4,7\}$. A_4 is deleted from t^*. Finally, $W(A_1)$ turns out to be less than WMIN and we delete A_1.

We can delete also the values A_2, A_{19} because $W(A_2)$, $W(A_{19}) = 4$, $t(splus(A_2))$, $t(splus(A_{19}))$ do not correspond to tests and, therefore, these values will not appear in a maximally redundant test t with $W(t)$ equal to or greater than 4. After deleting these values we can delete the examples t_9, t_5 because A_{19} is essential in t_9, and A_2 is essential in t_5. Next we can observe that $splus(A_{23}) = \{1,2,12,14\}$ and $t(\{1,2,12,14\})$ corresponds to a test; thus A_{23} is deleted from t^* and $splus(A_{23})$ is inserted into *STGOOD*. We can delete the values A_{22} and A_6 because $W(A_{22})$ and $W(A_6)$ are now equal to 4, $t(splus(A_{22}))$ and $t(splus(A_6))$ do not correspond to tests, and these values will not appear in a maximally redundant test with weight equal to or greater than 4. Now t_{14} and t_1 are not tests and can be deleted.

Choose t_{12} as a subtask because now this example is essential in $splus(A_{21})$ and in $splus(A_{24})$. By resolving this subtask, we find that t_{12} does not produce a new test. We delete it. Then $splus(A_{21})$ is equal to $\{4,6,8,11\}$, $t(\{4,6,8,11\})$ corresponds to a test, thus A_{21} is deleted from t^* and $splus(A_{21})$ is inserted into *STGOOD*. We can also delete the value A_{24} because $t(splus(A_{24}))$ corresponds to the GMRTs already obtained.

We can delete the value A_3 because $W(A_3)$ is now equal to 4, $t(splus(A_3))$ does not correspond to a test and this value will not appear in a maximally redundant test with weight equal to or greater than 4. We can delete t_6 because now this example is not a test. Then we can delete the value A_{20} because $t(splus(A_{20}))$ corresponds to the GMRTs already obtained. These deletions imply that all of the remaining rows t_2, t_3, t_4, t_7, t_8, and t_{11} are not tests. The list of the GMRTs with the weight equal to or greater than WMIN = 4 is given in Table 27.

Chapter 10
Towards a Model of Fuzzy Commonsense Reasoning

ABSTRACT

This chapter summarizes some methods of inferring approximate diagnostic tests. Considering the sets of approximately minimal diagnostic tests as "characteristic portraits" of object classes we have developed a model of commonsense reasoning by analogy. The system DEFINE of analogical inference with some results of its application is described. Mining approximate functional, implicative dependencies and association rules is based on the same criteria and on applying the same algorithm realized in the Diagnostic Test Machine described shortly in this chapter. Some results of inferring "crisp" and approximate tests with the use of Diagnostic Test Machine are give in Appendix to this chapter.

INTRODUCTION

Real-world problems require very often the necessity of approximate reasoning. Several theories have been advanced to model human rough reasoning and to deal with the uncertainty and imprecision of data. The most known among them are the fuzzy set theory (Zade, 1965), the probability theory (Pearl, 1988), and the rough set theory (Pawlak, 1982). The fuzzy set theory is used more than the others. It serves as a "transformer" of numerical scales into symbolic scales the values of which are usually linguistic terms or concepts. Note that the interpretation (meaning) of linguistic terms depends on the context of reasoning. Linguistic terms are relativistic: a man of average height will be high in a "Lilliputians" country and low in a country of giants. The fuzzy approach serves as an "interface between numerical and conceptual scales" (Dubois et al., 2006). So, if we obtained a fuzzy rules or scales as a result of learning, then we have to use them for pattern recognition or decision making in the same context. By this reason, diagnostic psychological tests are reconstructed in time.

DOI: 10.4018/978-1-60566-810-9.ch010

Machine learning is inherently inductive process and, naturally, even "crisp" rules have a certain degree of confidence. We shall distinguish some kinds of uncertainty:

- Rule (dependency) is not satisfied in a given dataset, but it could be satisfied if to eliminate some examples from this dataset. It is said that this rule has the degree of confidence and support calculated with respect to the dataset;
- Rule (dependency) is satisfied in a given dataset, but the dataset imperfect or insufficient for reliable conclusions. In this case, the calculation of statistical significance for the rule and its confidence limits has to be estimated (if the dataset has probabilistic nature). If it is not the case, then it is necessary to check the steadiness of the rule under changing the conditions of observations or under appearing new examples;
- The task "to find all the rules satisfying a given restriction" is replaced by the task "to find only a part of rules satisfying a given restriction";
- The request "to find minimal (maximal) or optimal rule with respect to a given criterion" is replaced by the request "to find quasi–minimal (maximal) or quasi – optimal rule, i.e. rule approximating a given criterion.

In this chapter, we concentrate on some fast heuristics for inferring approximately minimal diagnostic tests and their application in the tasks of forest aerial image interpretation (Naidenova, 1981; Naidenova, & Polegaeva, 1983; 1985).

SOME FAST HEURISTICS FOR INFERRING APPROXIMATELY MINIMAL DIAGNOSTIC TESTS (AMDTS)

We begin with the definitions and terminology.

Let $\{A_1, \ldots A_n\}$ be a set of multi-valued attributes. Combinations of attributes' values are object descriptions. A set of object descriptions (objects, for short) is denoted by Q. Let $P(Q) = \{Q_1, Q_k\}$ be a partition of the set Q unto k disjoint classes.

The problem is to construct for all pairs of sets $Q_i, Q_j \in P(Q)$, $i, j = 1, \ldots., k$, a collection (of hopefully small size) of diagnostic tests T_{ij} distinguishing the examples of Q_i (viewed as the set of positive examples) from the examples of Q_j (viewed as the set of negative examples) (i.e., these tests correctly classify all the examples Q_i and reject all the examples of Q_j).

Note that we search for quasi minimal tests, i.e. the number of attributes in each test must be as small as possible. This problem is solved by the incremental Algorithm UPRAV.

Algorithm UPRAV

The core of the algorithm is a program module for distinguishing a positive example from all the negative examples. We explain the work of algorithm as follows.

If the list of texts for distinguishing Q_i from Q_j is empty, then an example e_i+ is taken from Q_i and quasi-minimal test is constructed (with the use of procedure POISK) to distinguish this example from all the negative examples of Q_j. The first result is obtained and memorized. For each following positive example, it is checked whether at least one of the tests already obtained accepts it (the procedure

RROV is used for this goal). If there is a test accepting e_i+, then 1) the pair "index of test, index of e_i+" is memorized, 2) the next positive example is selected from Q_i. If there is not a test accepting e_i+, then the procedure POISK searches for quasi-minimal test to distinguish it from all the examples of Q_j. This process continues until a set of tests is constructed for all positive examples. The result of the algorithm encompasses:

- The list of tests T_{ij};
- The list of indices of positive examples in accordance with indices of tests accepting these examples;
- The list of the discriminatory indices of tests (The discriminatory index of test is the number of examples' pairs (one example from Q_i, one example from Q_j) distinguished by test). The discriminatory index of test is a measure of information quantity contained in this test.

The iterative procedure UPRAV is described as follows:

```
i = 0; T = Ø; (initialization); Q_i, Q_j;
FOR each example e+ of Q_i mt = POISK(e+, Q_j);
   if mt ∉ T then T = T ∪ mt;
   discriminatory index(mt) = 1;
   else discriminatory index(mt) = discriminatory index(mt) + 1;
END FOR
End
```

Each quasi-minimal test is constructed in a manner such that it accepts as many positive examples as possible and, simultaneously, rejects all negative examples. For forming quasi-minimal tests, heuristic procedure POISK is used. The procedure POISK is described as follows:

```
Input: e+ - a positive example;
Q_j - a set of negative examples.
Output: a quasi minimal test distinguishing e+ from all examples of
Q_j.
Step 1: For the pair (e+, e-), computing kw(e-), e- ∈ Q_j, kw(e-) =
{the number of attributes distinguishing e+ from e- by their val-
ues};
Step 2: Computing for each attribute A, discriminatory index mw(A),
where mw(A) = {the number of negative examples different from e+ by
value of A;
test::= Ø
DO WHILE (Q_j ≠ Ø)
1. Choose a negative example with minimal value of kw;
2. Among attributes distinguishing this example from e+, choose an
attribute L with maximal value of mw;
3. test = test ∪ L;
4. for each e- distinguished by L from e+
```

```
for each attribute A distinguishing e- from e+
    mw(A) = mw(A) - 1;
    delete e- from Q_j;
REPEAT
```

The advantages of the algorithm POISK are 1) the search for tests is fast and 2) the memory space is small (it is linear with respect to the number of examples and attributes).

The drawback of this algorithm is its dependence on the ordering of examples.

A MODEL OF COMMONSENSE REASONING BY ANALOGY BASED ON THE SETS OF AMDTS

Approximately minimal or quasi minimal test distinguishing an example e from examples of class Q_x is a collection of attributes $\{A_1, A_2,, A_k\}$ such that e differs from any example of Q_x by value of at least one attribute of this collection.

There are a plethora of algorithms for searching for tests, however if a certain algorithm is chosen then it is possible to consider it as a function $\varphi(e, Q_x) = \{A_1, A_2,, A_k\}$.

This function possesses the property that for familiar examples it will return the familiar or the same tests.

Let T_{ij} be the set of tests such that any example $e \in Q_i$ is different from all examples of Q_j by at least one test of T_{ij} and for every test $t \in T_{ij}$ there is an example e' such that it different from all examples of Q_j only by this test. In other words, T_{ij} is the necessary and sufficient set of tests for distinguishing Q_i and Q_j.

The set T_{ij} is also a function $f(Q_i, Q_j)$ determined by a certain test construction algorithm.

The set T_{ij} is considered to be stable or changeable insignificantly with respect to different collections of examples from the same class Q_i.

Let T_{ij} be the set of tests distinguishing the sets Q_i, Q_j of examples. Let T_{ij}^* be the set of tests distinguishing the sets Q_x, Q_j of examples, where Q_x, Q_i are taken from the same sampling (class) of examples. We assume that for T_{ij} and T_{xj}:

- The number of tests completely coinciding in these sets must be rather great;
- The number of tests in these sets must differ insignificantly;
- The number of tests in the intersection of these sets must be rather great;
- For equal tests of these sets, their discriminatory abilities must differ insignificantly.

Analogical reasoning is defined as follows (Naidenova, 1982).

Assume that the sets T_{ij} for all training sets Q_i, Q_j of examples, $i, j \in \{1, 2, ..., nk\}$, where nk is the number of classes, have been obtained. Let Q_x be a subset of examples belonging to one and the same but unknown class $x \in \{1, 2, .., nk\}$. Construct nk sets T_{xj} of tests, $T_{xj} = f(Q_x, Q_j), j \in \{1, 2, ..., nk\}$. If examples of Q_x belong to class $k \in \{1, 2, ..., nk\}$, then, in accordance with our assumption, the set of tests T_{xj} must be more similar to $T_{kj}, j \in \{1, 2, ..., nk\}$ than to T_{ij} for all $i \neq k, i \in \{1, 2, ..., nk\}$.

This method can be considered as "inference by analogy" because we use the assumption of analogical properties of tests for similar examples constructed with the use one and the same functional transformation (algorithm).

The main problem of this method for identifying unknown class of examples is related to the choice of the criterion or the measure of similarity between sets of tests. It is more reliable to use several criteria and to make decision based on the rule of "voting" between these criteria.

Example of Inference by Analogy

Here Q is a set of training examples partitioned into 5 disjoint classes. The examples are described by 9 attributes (see, please, Table 1).

Table 2 contains a list of quasi-minimal tests for all pairs Q_i, Q_j, $i,j \in \{1, 2, 3, 4, 5\}$ of classes.

Let two examples be represented for recognizing class to which they belong to:

$$Q_x = \{<3\ 4\ 3\ 5\ 3\ 4\ 2\ 1\ 1>, <4\ 4\ 3\ 3\ 2\ 4\ 2\ 3\ 5>\}.$$

Table 3 contains quasi-minimal tests distinguishing collection of examples Q_x from the sets of examples Q_1, Q_2, Q_3, Q_4, Q_5. These tests were obtained by means of the same algorithm that has been used for searching for tests represented in Table 2.

Compare the sets of tests for every pair $(Q_x - Q_j)$, $j \in \{1, 2, 3, 4, 5\}$ with the sets of tests for corresponding pair $(Q_y - Q_j)$, $j \in \{1, 2, 3, 4, 5\}$, where Q_y is taken from $\{Q_1, Q_2, Q_3, Q_4, Q_5\}$.

One of the possible decision rules says that if Q_x and Q_y are taken from the same class of examples, then the intersection of corresponding sets of tests $\{Q_x - Q_j, Q_y - Q_j\}$, $j \in \{1, 2, 3, 4, 5\}$ must be greater than for $Q_x - Q_z$, for all $z \neq y$.

The intersection of two sets of tests is referred to as the subset of coincident tests in these sets.

The illustration of this decision rule is given in Table 4.

Using this decision rule, we can conclude that Q_x and Q_5 were taken from the same class.

Table 1. The set of training examples

Q\Attributes:	1	2	3	4	5	6	7	8	9	Class
Index of example										
1	1	1	1	1	1					1
2		1			1			1		1
3			2			1			4	1
4			2	4	1	1	3	2	4	Q_1
5	1	2	1	1	2	1	1	2	1	Q_2
6		2								2
7		1			2			2		2
8										3
9										3
10	3	4			3			3		4
11	4									4
12	3		5			1			5	4
13	3		3	5	4	4	2	4	1	Q_5
14		2	3		2	4	2	2	1	Q_5

Table 2. The sets of tests for given classes of objects

Pairs of classes	Tests T_{ij} (collections of attributes)	The number of tests
$Q_1 - Q_1$	{4,7}	1
$Q_1 - Q_2$	{2}	1
$Q_1 - Q_3$	{3}, {9}	2
$Q_1 - Q_4$	{1}, {2}, {3}, {5}	4
$Q_1 - Q_5$	{1}, {2}, {3}, {4}, {5}, {6}	6
$Q_2 - Q_1$	{2}	1
$Q_2 - Q_2$	{4}, {7}	2
$Q_2 - Q_3$	{2}, {3}, {4}	3
$Q_2 - Q_4$	{1}, {2}, {3}	3
$Q_2 - Q_5$	{1}, {6}, {7}	3
$Q - Q_1$	{3}, {9}	2
$Q_3 - Q_2$	{2}, {3}, {4}	3
$Q_3 - Q_3$	{2}, {7}, {9}	3
$Q_3 - Q_4$	{1}, {2}, {3}, {4},{5}, {9}	6
$Q_3 - Q_5$	{1}, {2}, {3}, {4},{5}, {6}, {7}, {9}	8
$Q_4 - Q_1$	{1}, {2}, {3}, {5}	4
$Q_4 - Q_2$	{1}, {2}, {3}	3
$Q_4 - Q_3$	{1}, {2}, {3}, {4},{5}, {9}	6
$Q_4 - Q_4$	{4}, {6}, {7}, {9}	4
$Q_4 - Q_5$	{6}, {7}	2
$Q_5 - Q_1$	{1}, {2}, {3}, {4}, {5}, {6}	6
$Q_5 - Q_2$	{1}, {6}, {7}	3
$Q_5 - Q_3$	{1}, {2}, {3}, {4},{5}, {6}, {7} {9}	8
$Q_5 - Q_4$	{6}, {7}	2
$Q_5 - Q_5$	{8}	1

Table 3. The sets of tests for examples of unknown class

Pairs of classes	Tests T_{xj} (collections of attributes)	The number of tests
$Q_x - Q_1$	{1}, {2}, {3}, {4}, {5}, {6}	6
$Q_x - Q_2$	{1}, {2}, {3}, {6}, {7}	5
$Q_x - Q_3$	{1}, {2}, {3}, {4}, {5}, {6},{7}, {8},{9}	9
$Q_x - Q_4$	{6},{7}	2
$Q_x - Q_5$	{8},{9}	2

Table 4. The application of decision rule to the set Qx

Number of coincident tests	$Q_1 - Q_1$	$Q_2 - Q_1$	$Q_3 - Q_1$	$Q_4 - Q_1$	$Q_5 - Q_1$
$Q_x - Q_1$	0	1	1	4	6
	$Q - Q_2$	$Q_2 - Q_2$	$Q_3 - Q_2$	$Q_4 - Q_2$	$Q_5 - Q_2$
$Q_x - Q_2$	1	1	2	3	3
	$Q_1 - Q_3$	$Q_2 - Q_3$	$Q_3 - Q_3$	$Q_4 - Q_3$	$Q_5 - Q_3$
$Q_x - Q_3$	2	3	3	6	8
	$Q_1 - Q_4$	$Q_2 - Q_4$	$Q_3 - Q_4$	$Q_4 - Q_4$	$Q_5 - Q_4$
$Q_x - Q_4$	0	0	0	2	2
	$Q_1 - Q_5$	$Q_2 - Q_5$	$Q_3 - Q_5$	$Q_4 - Q_5$	$Q_5 - Q_5$
$Q_x - Q_5$	0	0	1	0	1
Sum of coincidences	3	4	7	15	20

Let us remark that this example is taken from the real task, and the set Q_x of objects is recognized correctly.

DEFINE: the System for Analogical Reasoning

The system DEFINE (Gnedash, et al., 1983), (Naidenova, 1983), (Naidenova, & Polegaeva, 1989) is based on the pattern recognition method described above. Principal structure of DEFINE is shown in Figure 1.

Describe the role of each program of the system. Three programs RDING are intended for inputting initial data and its transformation into attribute-value representation. In particular, if features of objects are continuous, then their discretization is required. In the case of using images of objects, the special complex of programs is used for calculating the values of some characteristics of images, extracting objects, calculating features of objects, and transforming them into attribute-value representation.

Program SLOT forms the training and controlling sets of objects based on a given rule or a random choice. The programs UPRAVL, PROV1, POISK and MINOR serve for constructing the sets of tests T_{ij} distinguishing the sets Q_i, Q_j of object examples.

Program TREE serves for compact representation of the set T_{ij} in the form of special structure – "vector-tree". This structure allows quickly checking whether a test t is contained in T_{ij}. Tests in the form of trees require less volume of memory space.

Block "Learning" constructs the set of tests $T = \{ T_{ji} \}$ and transforms them into the form of trees.

Block "Deciphering" constructs the set $T = \{ T_{xi} \}$ for unknown or control collection of examples.

Program REPLY realizes several decision rules for estimating the degree of similarity between the sets T_{xi}, T_{ji}, $j \in \{1, 2,, nk\}$, $i = \{1, 2,, nk\}$.

Program JUDGE performs the final decision.

Block "Analysis" investigates initial data and gives the information about the degree of similarity and distinction between given classes of objects and some others informative characteristics.

Figure 1. The structure of the system DEFINE

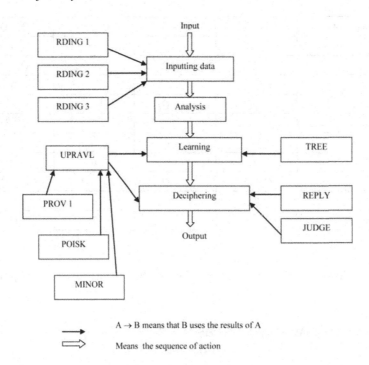

Program TREE

Algorithm TREE serves for transforming the test matrix into the structure of vector-tree or Decision Tree Matrix. Tests are lexicographically ordered and they are represented as the branches of an ordered decision tree, an example of which is given in Table 5.

The structure of tree is represented in the form of vector, the example of which, for the tree of Table 5, is given in Table 6.

Generally, the structure of tree is determined as follows:

If i-th component of vector-tree contains the value of a node, then $(i+1)$-th component:

a)   contains the index of component containing the value of next node of the same level of tree if such a node exists;

b)   is equal to 0 if such a node is absent;

$(i + 2)$-th component of vector-tree contains:

a)   the value of next node of the same branch if such an element exists;

b)   0, if the next node of the same branch is absent and there is not an offshoot of the considered node;

c)   -1 if the next node of the same branch is absent but the offshoots of considered node are present.

Table 5. Decision tree matrix

List of decisions	Ordered list of decisions	Decision tree
2, 8	1, 3, 2	1 ---3 ---2
1, 3, 2	2, 8	2 ---8---
2, 8, 15	2, 8, 15	|
7, 5	3, 4, 5	15
7, 2, 1	7, 2, 1	3 ---4 ---5
3, 4, 5	7, 5	7 ----2 ---1
		|
		---5

If j-th component of vector-tree is equal -1, then the value of the next node of offshoot is contained in $(j+1)$-th component of vector-tree.

The first element of vector-tree contains the value of the first node of decision tree at the first level.

The first version of DEFINE has been implemented in FORTRAN for running on EC. The second version of DEFINE has been realized in Turbo C 2.0 DOS 3.0 on computers PC AT/XT and compatible ones with Video adapter CGA or emulating regime CGA. The module Define.exe has been 52 kb executable module.

The Results of DEFINE's Application

The system DEFINE has been used for deciphering the predominant species of trees based on aero photographs with the scale 1: 3000 (Naidenova, 1983), (Gnedash et al. 1983). The forest parts have been picked out in the Chagodotchenskij forestry of Vologda region. The following types of trees have been chosen: pine-tree, aspen, birch, and fir-tree.

The class of pine-trees has been partitioned into two subclasses: pine-tree 1 – the trees of 70 years old, and pine-tree 2 – the trees of 115 years old.

For training and controlling sets of samples, the trees that are well recognized through stereoscope have been picked out with space distribution approximately equal to 15 -20 trees par 4-5 hectares.

Images of trees have been analyzed by using the stereoscope. An operator has estimated visually the following set of photometrical and texture properties of trees:

Table 6. The vector-tree representation for the tree of table 5

Component of vector	1	2	3	4	5	6	7	8	9	10	11	12	13	14	15	16	17	18	19
Component value	1	8	3	0	2	0	0	2	16	8	0	-1	15	0	0	3	23	4	0
Component of vector	20	21	22	23	24	25	26	27	28	29	30	31	32						
Component value		0	0	7	0	2	30	1		0	5		0						

1.   Color of the illuminated part of crown;
2.   Color of the shaded part of crown;
3.   Form of the projection of crown;
4.   Form of the edge of the projection;
5.   Form of the illuminated part of crown;
6.   Form of the shaded part of crown;
7.   Structure of crown;
8.   Texture of crown;
9.   Passage from the illuminated to the shaded part crown;
10. Density of crown;
11. Closeness of crown;
12. Form of branches;
13. Size of branches;
14. Form of apex;
15. Convexity of crown;

For evaluating the color, the scale of color standards has been used. For coding the other properties, the semantic scales have been developed. The number of gradations of properties on the semantic scales was within the limits from 3 to 12. 500 images of trees, 100 trees for each species have been analyzed. The analysis has been produced independently by two operators. The training set of samples has contained according to 60 descriptions for each species of trees, the set of control samples has contained according to 40 descriptions for each species of trees.

Two methods have been used for deciphering. The first method (Method 1) deals with recognizing the species to which belongs a subset of control trees taken from an unknown class. The decision rule is based on recognizing the number of completely coincident tests in the conformable matrixes of tests T_{xi}, T_{ji}, $j \in$ {birch, pine-tree 1, pine-tree 2, aspen, fir-tree}, $i \in$ {birch, pine-tree 1, pine-tree 2, aspen, fir-tree}. The totalities of control examples are considered belonging to the species of trees for which the sum of agreements is the greatest, i.e. the result is i-th species for which sum$\{\|T_{xj} \cap T_{ij}\|, j \in$ {birch, pine-tree 1, pine-tree 2, aspen, fir-tree} is maximal among all $i \in$ {birch, pine-tree 1, pine-tree 2, aspen, fir-tree}.

In the Table 7, the percentage of the correct answers obtained with the use of Method 1 is given.

The second method (Method 2) has been implemented for recognizing the species to which belongs a single sample of tree not belonging to training sets of trees. For this goal, we restructure the sets of

Table 7. Deciphering the species of trees (Method 1)

The type of tree (control samples)	Results of Deciphering				
	Birch	Pine-tree1	Pine-tree 2	Aspen	Fir-tree
Birch	100%	-	-	-	-
Pine-tree1		100%			
Pine-tree2			10%		
Aspen				100%	
Fi-re					100%

tests obtained for the training sets of trees. Consider the result of learning for the species y, i. e. the corresponding sets of tests T_{yj}, $j \in$ {birch, pine-tree 1, pine-tree 2, aspen, and fir-tree}. We associate each test into the set $T[y] = \{\cup T_{yj}\}$, $j \in$ {birch, pine-tree 1, pine-tree 2, aspen, and fir-tree}} with the list of all species, from which this test distinguishes the totality of trees y.

As a result, we have the following table of tests (Table 8), where y, $y \in$ {birch, pine-tree 1, pine-tree 2, aspen, fir-tree} correspond to the rows of table and in each row $j \in$ {birch, pine-tree 1, pine-tree 2, aspen, and fir-tree}.

For example, the following collection of the tests has been obtained for a single tree to be identified (Table 9).

Let us compare the tests for this single tree with the tests in the appropriate row of table 8.

If test coincides with a certain test in the row, then let us note the list of species associated with this test. We have the following result:

For $T[$birch$]$: {},
For $T[$pine-tree 1$]$: {aspen, birch, fir-tree},

Table 8. The tests for recognizing a single tree

Group of Tests	Species $j \in$ {birch, pine-tree 1, pine-tree 2, aspen, and fir-tree}.
$T[$birch$]$	{2}: {pine-tree 1, pine-tree 2, fir-tree}; {7}: {aspen}; {12}: {aspen};{1}: {birch}; {5}:{fir-tree};
$T[$pine-tree 1$]$	{2}: {aspen, birch, fir-tree}; {4, 6}: {pine-tree 2}; {7}: {pine-tree 2} {11}: {pine-tree 2}; {2, 4, 5}: {pine-tree 2}; {3, 7}: {pine-tree 2} {1, 2, 5}: {pine-tree 2}; {8}: {pine-tree 2};{2, 10, 11}: {fir-tree} {4, 9}: {pine-tree 2};{2, 4, 7}: {pine-tree 2}; {1, 5, 6}: {pine-tree 2}; {5}: {fir-tree}; {1}: {fir-tree}; {4}: {fir-tree}; {1, 7}: {fir-tree}; {3, 5}: {fir-tree}; {4, 14}: {fir-tree}; {2, 5}: {fir-tree}; {2, 7}: {fir-tree};
$T[$pine-tree 2$]$	{2}:{aspen, birch, fir-tree}; {4, 6}: {pine-tree 1}; {7}:{pine-tree 1}; {11}: {pine-tree 1}; {2, 4, 5}: {pine-tree 1}; {3, 7}: {pine-tree 1} {1, 2, 5}: {pine-tree 1}; {8}: {pine-tree 1};{2, 10, 11}: {fir-tree} {4, 9}: {pine-tree 1}; {2, 4, 7}: {pine-tree 1}; {1, 5, 6}: {pine-tree 1}; {1}: {aspen}; {5}: {fir-tree}; {4}: {fir-tree}; {5, 14}: {fir-tree}; {12}:{fir-tree}; {1, 7}: {fir-tree}; {6}: {fir-tree}; {1, 2, 7}: {fir-tree};
T[aspen]	{7}: {birch}; {1}: {pine-tree 1, pine-tree 2, fir-tree}; {2}: {pine-tree 1, pine-tree 2, fir-tree}; {12}: {birch, fir-tree} {2, 3}: {fir-tree}; {14}: {fir-tree};
T[fir-tree]	{1}: {birch, aspen, pine-tree 1}; {2}: {birch, aspen, pine-tree 1, pine-tree 2}; {5}: {birch, pine-tree 1, pine-tree 2}; {4}: {pine-tree 1, pine-tree 2} {1, 7}: {pine-tree 1}; {3, 5}: {pine-tree 1}; {4, 14}: {pine-tree 1}; {2, 5}: {pine-tree 1}; {2, 7}: {pine-tree 1}; {12}: {pine-tree 2, aspen}; {2, 4}: {pine-tree 2}; {1, 7, 13}: {pine-tree 2}; {6}: {pine-tree 2}; {1, 2, 7}: {pine-tree 2}; {2, 3}: {aspen}; {14}: {pine –tree 2, aspen}

Table 9. Test description of a single tree of unknown class

Species of tree	Birch	Pine-tree 1	Pine-tree 2	Aspen	Fir-tree
?	-	{2}	{2}	{7}	{1}

For T[pine-tree 2]: {aspen, birch, fir-tree},

For T[aspen]: {birch},

For T[fir-tree]: {birch, aspen, pine-tree 1, pine-tree 2}.

It is easy to observe that the intersection of all not empty sets $T[y]$, $y \in$ {pine-tree 1, pine-tree 2, aspen, fir-tree} contains only one species – "birch".

Each test with respect to each species rejected by it has the corresponding number of positive examples covered by it (the weight of test, or the number of positive examples accepted by this test). The weights can be used as the additional factors for decision making, especially in the cases when we obtain several hypotheses about the membership of an example. For tests in Table 9, we have the following associated lists of weights (expressed in%) presented in Table 10:

The sum of weights for 'birch' is maximal in this case.

In the Table 11 the percentage of the correct answers obtained with the use of Method 2 is given.

In this case, the part of 22% of the pine trees of 70 years old has been recognized not correctly.

The analysis of the stability of tests has been also carried out. Tables 12 and 13 contain the results of experiments according to the data of one of the operators and Table 14 contains the results of experiments based on the data of both operators together.

If the data of only one operator is used, then we observe the disappearance of some tests with decreasing the volume of training set of examples. The number of unique tests proves to be not great.

Results demonstrate, perhaps, the possibility to decrease the volume of training set in subsequent experiments.

The frequency of occurring attributes in tests shows the usefulness or their informative power. Attributes 10 and 15 did not enter any test, so they are least informative. Attribute 2 possesses the greatest informative power. To the informative attributes belong also attributes 1, 3, 4, 5, 6, 7, 12, and 14.

Table 10. Deciphering the species of trees (Method 2)

	Test 1 = {2}	Test 2 = {2}	Test 3 = {7}	Test 4{ = 1}
Species rejected	{aspen, birch, fir-tree}	{aspen, birch, fir-tree}	{birch}	{birch, aspen, pine-tree 1}
Weights	{96, 100, 20}	{97, 100, 20}	{35}	{66, 26, 45}

Table 11. Deciphering the species of trees (Method 2)

	Results of Deciphering				
The type of tree (control samples)	Birch	Pine-tree1	Pine-tree 2	Aspen	Fir-tree
Birch	100%	-	-	-	-
Pine-tree1		100%			
Pine-tree2		22%	78%		
Aspen				100%	
Fir-tree					100%

Table 12. Estimation of test stability (the scale 1: 3000, Operator 1)

The volume of training set	100%	60%		40%	
The number of tests	Repeated	Repeated	Unique	Repeated	Unique
The pair of type trees to be deciphered					
Brch- Pine-tree 1	4	3	-	2	-
Birch- Pine-tree 2	3	3	-	1	-
Birch-aspen	12	10	-	10	1
Birch – fir-tree	2	1	-	2	-
Pine-tree 1- Pine-tree 2	11	8	1	8	-
Pine-tree 1 – aspen	3	3	-	2	-
Pine-tree 1 – fir-tree	5	5	-	3	-
Pine-tree 2 – aspen	7	6	-	4	-
Pine-tree 2 –fir-tree	4	4	2	2	-
Aspen – fir-tree	2	2	-	2	-

Table 13. Estimation of test stability (the scale 1: 3000, Operator 2)

The volume of training set	100%	60%		40%	
The number of tests	Repeated	Repeated	Unique	Repeated	Unique
The pair of type trees to be deciphered					
Brch- Pine-tree 1	1	1	-	1	-
Birch- Pine-tree 2	1	1	-	1	-
Birch-aspen	2	2	-	2	-
Birch – fir-tree	3	3	-	2	-
Pine-tree 1- Pine-tree 2	12	6	4	8	-
Pine-tree 1 -aspen	2	2	-	2	-
Pine-tree 1 – fir-tree	6	5	4	5	2
Pine-tree 2 - aspen	2	2	-	2	-
Pine-tree 2 –fir-tree	11	8	1	6	2
Aspen – fir-tree	5		-	3	-

Generally, the results of experiments testify about the fitness of the method of reasoning by analogy based on AMDTs for the task of deciphering the type of predominant species of trees with the use of the semantically scaled features extracted by operators from aero photographs.

The system DEFINE has been applied very successfully for processing multi-spectral information (Naidenova, & Polegaeva, 1983).

Table 14. Estimation of test stability (the scale 1: 3000, Operator 1 and Operator 2)

The volume of training set	100%	60%		40%	
The number of tests	Repeated	Repeated	Unique	Repeated	Unique
The pair of type trees to be deciphered					
Birch- Pine-tree 1	2	2	-	2	-
Birch- Pine-tree 2	3	3	-	3	-
Birch-aspen	10	10	-	10	-
Birch – fir-tree	3	3	-	3	-
Pine-tree 1- aspen	4	4	-	4	-
Pine-tree 1 – fir-tree	8	8	-	8	-
Pine tree 2 aspen	8	8	-	8	-
Pine-tree 2 – fir-tree	11	11	-	11	-
Aspen – fir-tree	6	6	-	6	-

DISCOVERING APPROXIMATE LOGICAL RULES

Mining Functional and Implicative Dependencies with Uncertainty

An approximate functional dependency (Kivinen, & Mannila, 1995) is a functional dependency that almost holds. Such dependencies arise in many databases when there is a natural dependency between attributes, but some rows contain errors or represent exceptions to the rule. The necessity in inferring approximate dependencies can be implied by the impossibility to collect the data the quality and quantity of which satisfy completely the given requests. The discovery of unexpected but meaningful approximate dependencies seems to be an interesting and desired goal in many data mining applications.

There are many possible ways of defining the approximation of functional dependency. In terms of relations of databases, a *functional dependency* over a relation schema R is an expression $X \rightarrow A$, where $X \subseteq R, A \in R, A \notin X$. The dependency *holds* in a given relation r over R if and only if for all pairs of rows $t, u \in r$ we have: if $t[B] = u[B]$ for all $B \in X$, then $t[A] = u[A]$ (we also say that t and u *agree* on X and A). A functional dependency $X \rightarrow A$ is *minimal* (in r) if A is not functionally dependent on any proper subset of X. The dependency $X \rightarrow A$ is *trivial* if $A \in X$.

The definition of approximate functional dependency is based on the minimum number of rows that need to be removed from the relation r for $X \rightarrow A$ to hold in r. The error $e(X \rightarrow A)$ is determined in (Huhtala et al, 1999) as follows:

$$e(X \rightarrow A) = \min\{\|s\|, s \subseteq r \text{ and } X \rightarrow A \text{ holds in } r \backslash s) / |r|.$$

This measure is interpreted as the fraction of rows with exceptions or errors affecting the dependency. Given an error threshold ε, $0 \le \varepsilon \le 1$, it is said that $X \rightarrow A$ is an *approximate dependency* if and only if $e(X \rightarrow A)$ is at most ε.

In (Huhtala et al, 1999), the following inference task is solved with the use of the algorithm TANE: given a relation r and a threshold ε, find all minimal non-trivial approximate dependencies in r.

The approximate implicative dependencies are mined analogously (the same algorithm works). Approximate implication is a compatibility rule, in our terminology. The rule of compatibility presents the most frequently observed combination of attribute values that is different from a law (an implication) with only several exceptions the admissible number of which (in %) is given by the user.

It is possible to define the approximate dependency (implicative or functional) by giving the number (in %) of negative examples accepted by this quasi dependency.

Generally, we can formulate the following task of inferring approximate dependencies. Let Q be a collection of examples given by the values of a set T of attributes. Let $P(Q)$ be a partition of Q into positive and negative examples. The problem is formulated as follows: find a collection $X \subseteq T$, with $\|X\| = M$ such that it distinguishes the number ep of pairs (h_i, h_j) of examples, h_i, h_j belong to different classes in $P(Q)$, $M \leq M$max, and ep $\geq EP$min, where Mmax, EPmin are the given restrictions expressed in %.

If T is a set of attribute values, then the previous problem is transformed in inferring approximate implications. Let examples(+) and examples(-) be the numbers of positive and negative examples, respectively, covered by a rule $x \rightarrow k$ generated on attributes' values T. Then the power $p(x \rightarrow k)$ of rule $x \rightarrow k$ is determined as follows:

$$p(x \rightarrow k) = (\text{examples}(+) / (\text{examples}(+) + \text{examples}(-)) \times 100.$$

If $p(x \rightarrow k) = 1$, then strict implicative dependencies are constructed.

If $p(x \rightarrow k) \neq 1$, then association dependencies are constructed.

Mining Association Rules with Uncertainty

Most of the researchers concentrate on inferring fuzzy association rules with categorical attributes. However, quantitative attributes are more typical in real-world applications. An algorithm for inferring association rules with quantitative values of attributes have been proposed in (Srikant, & Agrawal, 1996).

Association rules are patterns that offer useful information on dependencies that exist between the sets of items. Current association rule mining techniques such as the Apriori algorithm extract often exponentially large number of rules. To give a meaning to these rules one needs to order or group the rules in some fashion such that the useful patterns are highlighted. Various measures of the usefulness of rules have been proposed but, unfortunately, it is very difficult to compare these measures because of, as Koh et al., (2008) show, different metrics capture different dependencies among variables.

Usefulness measures are divided into two types: objective and subjective measures. Objective measures are based on probability, statistics, or information theory. These measures are domain independent and require minimal user participation. Some objective measures are symmetric with respect to the permutation of items, while others are not. Currently there are more than 50 objective measures proposed (this data extracted from (Koh et al., (2008).

Subjective measures take into account both the data and the user's requirements. Hence, subjective measures need expert domain knowledge. These measures determine whether a rule is novel, actionable, and surprising. Some reviews of the "interestingness" of measures for association rules can be found in (Geng & Hamilton, 2006; McGarry, 2005; Tan & Kumar, 2000). The analysis in (Koh et al., (2008) is limited to the objective measures discussed in literature (Huynh et al., 2006; Lenca et al., 2004; Tan et al., 2004; Vaillant et al, 2004).

Lenca et al. (2004) propose 20 objective measures evaluated with the use of 8 different evaluation criteria. In this approach, weights are assigned to each property that the user considers to be important.

Huynh et al. (2006) introduced a new tool ARQUAT to study the specific behavior of 34 objective measures using a specific dataset. The problems solved by ARQUAT are divided into five task-oriented groups: rule analysis, correlation analysis, clustering analysis, sensitivity analysis, and comparative analysis. Despite the fact that there have been many exploratory analyses carried out on these measures, a way to compare the behavior of the objective measures effectively has still not been found.

Generally, evaluating an objective measure, say M, is based on calculating 2×2 contingency tables. Table 15 is the contingency table for a rule $A \rightarrow B$ held in dataset D.

Here $n(AB)$ denotes the number of transactions containing both A and B in dataset D. N denotes the total number of transactions or $\|D\|$. $Pr(A) = n(A)/N$ is used to denote the probability of A. $Pr(B|A)$ is the conditional probability of B given A and $n(A)/n(AB)$.

In (Koh et al., (2008), the authors advanced a new visualization technology to help users in selecting an appropriate objective measure. In general, the relationships between two binary variables A and B in $A \rightarrow B$ dependency can be expressed in terms of the range of $Pr(A)$, $Pr(B)$, and $Pr(AB)$ from 0 to 1. Then a three-dimensional plot of the results is constructed. The x-axis contains values of T, y-axis contains values of R, and z-axis contains values of L, where $T = Pr(AB)$, $L = Pr(A \neg B)$, $R = Pr(\neg AB)$, and $N = Pr(\neg A \neg B)$.

Obviously, the main unsolved problem of mining association rules is the problem of meaningful managing the search for these rules in the reasonably restricted practical context.

Mining fuzzy association rules is often based on the Apriori algorithm (Kuok et al., 2001). But many new algorithms appear at present. A simple example of mining fuzzy association rules is given in (Olson, & Delen, 2008). This example is based on 10 data points of applicants for appliance loans, whose attributes are *Age, Income, Assets, Debts, Credit* (with *Red* for bad credit, *Amber* for some credit problems, and *Green* for clean credit record), *Want* (the amount requested in the appliance loan application) and *Result* {it is equal to 1 if all payments were received on time and 0 if not (late or default)}. A new attribute *Risk* is generated by using the formula *Risk = Assets - Debts - Want*.

The attributes *Income* and *Risk* have three fuzzy regions; *Credit* and *Result* have two fuzzy regions. Weights for each attribute could be based both on some multiple criteria method and on direct expert opinion. The weights of attributes in this algorithm are the following *Credit* (0.8) ≥ *Risk* (0.7) ≥ *Income* (0.55) ≥ *Age* (0.45). Next, consider the work of the algorithm.

Step 1. Transform quantitative or categorical values into fuzzy values. Category intervals would need to be established based on past experience or some calculations such as dividing the data into equal sized groups:

Table 15. The contingency table for rule $A \rightarrow B$ in dataset D

Item	A	¬A	Total
B	$n(AB)$	$n(\neg AB)$	$n(B)$
¬B	$n(A \neg B)$	$n(\neg A \neg B)$	$n(\neg B)$
Total	$n(A)$	$n(\neg A)$	N

Attribute *Age* is transformed into *Young* (R_{11}), *Middle* (R_{12}), and *Old* (R_{13}) fuzzy categories;
Attribute *Income* is transformed into *High* (R_{21}), *Middle* (R_{22}), and *Low* (R_{23}) fuzzy categories;
Attribute *Risk* is transformed into *High* (R_{31}), *Middle* (R_{32}), and *Low* (R_{33}) fuzzy categories;
Attribute *Credit* is transformed into *Good* (R_{41}) and *Bad* (R_{42}) fuzzy categories; and
Attribute *Result* is transformed into *On Time* (R_{51}) and *Default* (R_{52}) fuzzy categories.

Step 2. Calculate weighted support Sup(R_{jk}). *Sup* (R_{jk}) is the proportion of cases with the given condition, multiplied by the weight for the attribute in question. Results are given in Table 16.

The complete list of categories is: C_1 = {(R_{11}), (R_{12}), (R_{13}), (R_{21}), (R_{22}), (R_{23}), (R_{31}), (R_{32}), (R_{33}), (R_{41}), (R_{51}), (R_{52})}.

Step 3: Let *minsup* = 0.25. If for *jk Sup* (R_{jk}) ≥ *minsup*, then put R_{jk} in the set of large 1-itemsets (L_1). Here L_1 = {(R_{11}), (R_{22}), (R_{31}), (R_{41}), (R_{51})}.

Step 4: If L_1 is null, stop.

Step 5: Join itemsets in L_1 to generate the candidate set C_2 of category pairs.

C_2 = {(R_{11}, R_{22}), (R_{11}, R_{31}), (R_{11}, R_{41}), (R_{11}, R_{51}), (R_{22}, R_{31}), (R_{22}, R_{41}), (R_{22}, R_{51}), (R_{31}, R_{41}), (R_{31}, R_{51}), (R_{41}, R_{51})}.

Note that itemsets such as (R_{11}, R_{12}) having categorical classes of the same attribute would not be retained in C_2.

Step 6: Perform the following actions for each newly formed candidate 2-itemset in C_2:

(a) Calculate the membership value of each transaction datum. Take (R_{11}, R_{22}) as an example. The derived membership value is calculated taking into account that the membership function value for R_{11} is equal to 1 and the membership function value for R_{22} is also equal to 1. Thus the membership value of (R_{11}, R_{22}) is: min(0.45 × 1, 0.55 × 1) = 0.45;

(b) Calculate the support value of each candidate 2-itemset in C_2.

Sup((R_{11}, R_{22})) = 0.235. The results for other 2-itemsets are given in Table 17.

Table 16. Support values by category

Category	Weight	Sup(R_{jk})
Age Young R_{11}	0.45	0.261
Age Middle R_{12}	0.45	0.135
Age Old R_{13}	0.45	0.059
Income High R_{21}	0.55	0.000
Income Middle R_{22}	0.55	0.490
Income Low R_{23}	0.55	0.060
Risk High R_{31}	0.70	0.320
Risk Middle R_{32}	0.70	0.146
Risk Low R_{33}	0.70	0.233
Credit Good R_{41}	0.80	0.576
Credit Bad R_{42}	0.80	0.224

Table 17. Support values for 2-itemsets

2-itemset	Support	2-itemset	Support
(R_{11}, R_{22})	0.235	(R_{22}, R_{41})	0.419
(R_{11}, R_{31})	0.207	(R_{22}, R_{51})	0.449
(R_{11}, R_{41})	0.212	(R_{31}, R_{41})	0.266
(R_{11}, R_{51})	0.230	(R_{31}, R_{51})	0.264
(R_{22}, R_{31})	0.237	(R_{41}, R_{51})	0.560

(c) Check if the support value of each candidate 2-itemset is larger than or equal to minsup, then put it in L_2. Here L_2 = {(R_{22}, R_{41}), (R_{22}, R_{51}), (R_{31}, R_{41}), (R_{31}, R_{51}), (R_{41}, R_{51})}.

Step 7: Since L_2 is not null, repeat Steps 5–6 to find L_3 and C_3 of 3-itemsets. The four support values for 3-itemsets are 0.417 for (R_{22}, R_{41}, R_{51}), 0.198 for (R_{22}, R_{31}, R_{41}), 0.196 for (R_{22}, R_{31}, R_{51}), and 0.264 for (R_{31}, R_{41}, R_{51}). Thus L_3 = {(R_{22}, R_{41}, R_{51}), (R_{31}, R_{41}, R_{51})}. The next step is for C_4, with C_4 = {$(R_{22}, R_{31}, R_{41}, R_{51})$} but its support value – 0.1957 < minsup, so L_4 is null. Then go to Step 8.

Step 8: Collect the large itemsets together. Here only L_1, L_2, and L_3 exist.

Step 9:

(a) Construct association rules for each large 2-itemset and 3-itemset;

(b) Calculate the confidence value for each association rule. Table 18 gives the results.

Step 10: Assume minconf = 0.90. Output the relative and interesting association rules with Conf ≥ minconf. The following rules are output to users, the number in parentheses is confidence value:

If Income is middle, then payment will be received on time $R_{22} \rightarrow R_{51}$; (91.6%)

If Credit is good, then payment will be received on time $R_{41} \rightarrow R_{51}$; (97.2%)

If Income is middle and Credit is good, then payment will be received on time $R_{41}, R_{22} \rightarrow R_{51}$; (99.5%)

If Risk is high and Credit is good, then payment will be received on time $R_{31}, R_{41} \rightarrow R_{51}$; (99.25%).

Table 18. Confidence scores

L_2 conf	conf	L_3 conf	Conf
$R_{22} \rightarrow R_{41}$	0.855	$R_{41}, R_{22} \rightarrow R_{51}$	0.995
$R_{41} \rightarrow R_{22}$	0.727	$R_{41}, R_{51} \rightarrow R_{22}$	0.744
$R_{22} \rightarrow R_{51}$	0.916	$R_{22}, R_{51} \rightarrow R_{41}$	0.928
$R_{51} \rightarrow R_{22}$	0.697	$R_{31}, R_{41} \rightarrow R_{51}$	0.993
$R_{31} \rightarrow R_{41}$	0.831	$R_{31}, R_{51} \rightarrow R_{41}$	1.000
$R_{41} \rightarrow R_{31}$	0.462	$R_{51}, R_{41} \rightarrow R_{31}$	0.472
$R_{31} \rightarrow R_{51}$	0.825		
$R_{51} \rightarrow R_{31}$	0.410		
$R_{41} \rightarrow R_{51}$	0.972		
$R_{51} \rightarrow R_1$	0.870		

THE DIAGNOSTIC TEST MACHINE

Diagnostic Test machine (DTM) is a software program for knowledge acquisition from raw data, classification and reasoning support. DTM implements supervised leaning based on notion of good diagnostic test. The system allows extracting of all implications, interdictions and associations from teaching samples and predicts according with acquired knowledge. The Programmer is Victor Shagalov.

The system consists of:

- Data Base (DB), domain's specifications and learning samples;
- Machine learning algorithms;
- Knowledge base (KB) of "if-then" rules;
- Forecast subsystem;
- Reasoning support subsystem.

The system features are:

- Training set and its description can be imported in the system from flat- or XML-file or via build-in DB-browser;
- The system can work with continuous and nominal data types;
- Unknown values are supported;
- It's possible to select multiple goal attributes;
- Automatic attribute discretization is performed. Some variants of discretization continuous attributes are available;
- The system extracts all implications, interdictions and associations, with optional search limitations (rule's power, accuracy, length, and depth of search);
- Prediction of goal value(s);
- Explanation of predictions;
- The system maintains multiple domains and experiments on them;
- Friendly user interface.

Underlying storage:

- Domains DB and KB are stored "unprocessed" Oracle Berkeley DB JE. It provides high performance, great capacity and recoverability.
- Test space: is of 100 000 lines; attribute space is of 300. Archive without restriction.

System requirements:

- J2SE 6 or higher;
- Java drivers for used DBs.

DTM was implemented as pure Java application. The following open source framework was used: ASM, bean-binding, log4j Copyright: Sun, Oracle.

For describing the system, we use the following terminology.

Row data – initial data;

Test space is the working space of the system, including current set of attributes (attributes selected by the user), domains of attributes (after categorization), training set of examples, goal attribute (value), result dependencies. Test space is conserved in db system, it is the persistent object.

Sampler is a block included in Test space. It constructs randomly training set and testing set (control) of examples for each experiment.

Shuffler is included in Sampler.

Domain of attributes: Quality, Quantity, Integer.

Export and Import of data are realized by Block 1.

Block 1 constructs the linkage with any data base (Java drivers) and realizes import data. It realizes viewing data from concrete table memorized in db system; it is a row data set with a name and structure.

The point of menu *Prepare row data* allows realizing the preprocessing of row data.

Block 2 inputs row data and forms a context for experiments.

The AutoCat button 'Give Goals' allows inputting a collection of goal attributes or a collection of goal values with viewing the results. This block performs the categorization of attributes (the button 'Change of Attribute Type): the results are in domains of two types – quality and numeric (quantity). Binarization and discretization of attributes is performed in this block.

Together with categorization, it is computed STATISTICS, i. e. the information quantity and significance indices are calculated for attributes. Non informative attributes are excluded.

Control parameters for the search for tests are: Minimum Rule Power in % (the size of the covering of rule) and Degree of Belief (DBf) of rule calculated by the formula:

$$DBf(rule) = (examples(+)/ (examples(+) + examples(-)) \times 100,$$

where examples(+) is the number of covered positive examples, examples(-) is the number of covered negative examples). If DBf = 1, then strict rules are constructed.

The point of Menu 'Option TASK' allows the user to select one of the possibilities for inferring:

- Strict Rules;
- Fuzzy Rules;
- Strict Functional Dependencies;
- Fuzzy functional dependencies.

All these tasks are different by the form of representation of the inclusion relations extracted from data and they are solved by the use of the same algorithm tuned (adjusted) by the user for inferring a certain type of dependencies.

An example of Diagnostic Test Machine application is given in Appendix to this chapter.

The training set of mushroom records has been drawn from The Audubon Society Field Guide to North American Mushrooms (Lincoff, 1981). This data set includes descriptions of hypothetical samples corresponding to 23 species of gilled mushrooms in the Agaricus and Lepiota Family (Lincoff, 1981; pp. 500-525). Each species is identified as definitely edible, definitely poisonous, or of unknown edibility and not recommended. This latter class was combined with the poisonous one. The Audubon Society

Field Guide clearly states that there is no simple rule for determining the edibility of a mushroom.

In Appendix we give the attribute description and the results of one of experiments conducted with the training set of 8124 instances of mushrooms. The number of attributes is equal to 22 (all nominally valued).

For evaluating of pattern recognition capability of rules, we conducted a series of 10 controlling experiments for which the training and controlling sets of samples were randomly selected. In each experiment, the number of training samples was equal to 974 and the number of control samples was equal to 7150. The table 19 shows the results of pattern recognition in all 10 experiments.

These result turned out to be better with respect to classification accuracy than the results informed in (Schlimmer, 1987) (95%) for the same set of data.

RELATED WORKS

We can pay the reader's attention to several works of review character: an article of Zhai et al. (2006) on knowledge acquisition and uncertainty in fault diagnosis, an article of Chen et al (2006) on fuzzy logic in discovering association rules, and an overview of Liao (2006) on fuzzy modeling methods.

An excellent work of Nicos Pelekis et all (2005) is devoted to the Fuzzy Miner system. It is a tool for classification of numerical data. This approach does not need a defuzzification process. The system can be considered as a system for function approximation and it, with slight changes, can work as a predictor rather than as a classifier. The system is very flexible in that its components are adapted to various classification objectives. Linguistic representation of the produced fuzzy rules allows naïve user interpreting easily these rules. Fuzzy Miner was evaluated with the use of the Athens Stock Exchange (ASE, 2004) data set. The result of evaluation turned out to be successful.

A decision tree software See5 is considered in (Shi et al., 2005). It allows users to select options to soften thresholds through selecting a fuzzy option. This option would insert a buffer at boundaries. The buffer is determined based on analysis of sensitivity of classification to small changes in the threshold.

Table 19. The evaluation of the recognition quality of rules inferred by diagnostic test machine

N	Good Prediction	Bad Prediction	Non Prediction
1	7026	124	0
2	7003	147	0
3	6995	155	0
4	6871	279	0
5	7000	150	0
6	6982	168	0
7	6921	229	0
8	6944	206	0
9	6953	197	0
10	7037	113	0
Total	69732	1768	0
Total, %	97.5	2.5	0

It is a model with adjusted set boundaries.

See5 was used in an experiment on a real set of credit card data (Shi et al., 2005). The data set had 6000 observations of 64 variables. The output or goal variable was for indicating if bankruptcy is present or absent. Among variable, 9 were binary and 3 categorical. The goal variable had two values "GOOD" and "BAD" with respect to financial success. The training set contained 960 bankrupt outcomes and 5040 without bankrupt ones. Minimum support was varied over the setting of 10, 20, and 30 cases. Pruning confidence factor were also varied from 10% (greater pruning), 20%, 30%, and 40%.

The very extensive investigations are directed to the fuzzification of formal concept. There are many different ideas how to enlarge crisp concept to fuzzy concept but all these ideas come mostly from several considerations:

- Definition of fuzzy implication or inclusion relation;
- Definition of fuzzy ordering relation between fuzzy sets;
- Definition of fuzzy ordering relation between fuzzy intervals;
- Definition of fuzzy relation or link between object and its attribute values.

These definitions are introduced by various mathematical techniques. The main idea is to identify fuzzy sets with their membership functions taking their values in the complete lattice L. Thus it is defined fuzzy lattice or L-fuzzy lattice valued by crisp lattice L.

Arturo A. L. Sangalli (1996) has given a common view on constructing lattices of fuzzy objects. The collection of fuzzy subsets of a set X forms a complete lattice that extends the complete lattice $P(X)$ of crisp subsets of X. In this paper, the author interprets this extension as a special case of the "fuzzification" of an arbitrary complete lattice A and shows how to construct a complete fuzzy lattice $F(A, L)$, where L is the valuation lattice that extends A while preserving all supreme and infinume relations in A. Some familiar fuzzifications (fuzzy subgroups, fuzzy subalgebras, fuzzy topologies, etc.) are considered as special cases of the construction proposed.

Trajkovski (1998) has advanced the idea of fuzzification of the ordering of a crisp lattice to obtain a weakly reflexive lattice valued ordering relation. The paper deals with one possible approach to the definition of lattice valued fuzzy lattice (L-fuzzy lattice).This article concerns a connection of fuzzy logic and lattice theory. Namely, the fuzzy sets form a Heyting lattice with union and intersection of fuzzy sets as meet and join operations.

Ath. Kehagias, At., and Konstantinidou, M. (2003) introduce L-Fuzzy Valued **Inclusion** Measure, L-Fuzzy Similarity and L-Fuzzy Distance. A measure of inclusion is a relation between fuzzy sets A and B, which indicates the degree to which A is contained in (is a subset of) B. A novel L-fuzzy valued measure of inclusion introduced by the authors is a fuzzy order. Furthermore, this measure can be used in order to define a L-fuzzy similarity and a L-fuzzy distance between fuzzy sets. L-fuzzy inclusion measure can be viewed as an L-fuzzy valued implication operators. The different approaches to fuzzification of inclusion relation are also discussed in this work.

Bandler and Kohout (1980) obtain several inclusion measures from fuzzy implication operators. A related approach is that of (Willmott, 1986; 1980), (Kundu, 2000), where the transitivity of inclusion measure is also studied. Bustince (2000) introduces an inclusion measure which takes values in the partially ordered set of interval valued fuzzy sets.

In the paper (Liu, 2008), the author studies the generalization of rough sets over fuzzy lattices through both the constructive and axiomatic approaches. In the constructive approach, the basic properties of generalized rough sets over fuzzy lattices are obtained. In the axiomatic approach, a set of axioms is constructed to characterize the approximation of generalized rough sets over fuzzy lattices.

In the paper (Trajkovski, & Čukić), two types of fuzzy lattices valued by lattices are introduced. The peculiarity of this work is that instead of fuzzyfying the membership of the elements in the carrier of a lattice, L-valuating lattices are obtained by fuzzification of the ordering relation of the carrier. This work is inspired by the investigation of partially ordering in the papers of Šešelia and Tepavčević, A. (1993; 1994; 1995).

Kehagias, Ath. (2002) defines a fuzzy interval to be a fuzzy set such that its cuts are closed intervals of a reference (valued) lattice $(X, \sqsubseteq)$. Given a fuzzy set $M: X \to L$, the p-cut of M is denoted by Mp and defined as follows $Mp = \{x: M(x) \geq p\}$. A fuzzy lattice is a fuzzy set such that its cuts are sub-lattices of a "reference" (valued) lattice $(X, \sqsubseteq)$.

Lattice-valued (L-fuzzy) covering or fuzzy neighboring relation arising from a given lattice-valued order is investigated in (Šešelia, 2007). *L-fuzzy Lattices* are extensively studied by Tepavcevic, A. and Trajkovski, G. (2001).

The greatest attention is paid however fuzzyfying the formal concept analysis.

Radim Bělohlávek and Vilém Vychodil (2005) analyze what is fuzzy concept lattice. The paper is an overview of several approaches to the notion of concept lattice from the point of view of fuzzy logic. The main aim of the authors is to clarify relationships between the various approaches to this notion. A natural idea, developed in fuzzy logic, is to assign to an object a truth degree to which the object has a (fuzzy) attribute. Degrees are taken from an appropriate scale L of truth degrees (Ganter, & Wille, 1999). The authors propose another way based on considering the data table entries as truth degrees in fuzzy logic and proceed analogously as it is done in the FCA, just "replacing classical (bivalent) logic with fuzzy logic". Recently, the second way gained a considerable interest. The structures which result this way are called fuzzy concept lattices, fuzzy Galois connections, etc.

A common point of the considered approaches is the notion of a fuzzy context, i.e. the input data. Let L be a scale of truth degrees. Then, a fuzzy context (L-context, or L-context) is a triplet $<X, Y, I>$ where X and Y are sets of objects and attributes, respectively, and $I: X \times Y \to L$ is a fuzzy relation (L-relation) between X and Y. A degree $I(x, y) \in L$ is interpreted as a degree to which object x has attribute y. The authors give the detail comparative analysis of existing approach to defining fuzzy concept lattices.

Burusco and Fuentes-Gonsáles (1994)) have given the definition of fuzzy concepts on the basis of the classical inclusion relation between fuzzy concepts. But it turned out that these fuzzy concepts do not satisfy some useful properties which hold in the classical case, namely $A \subseteq A{\uparrow}{\downarrow}$ and $B \subseteq B{\downarrow}{\uparrow}$, where $A{\uparrow}{\downarrow}$ and $B{\downarrow}{\uparrow}$ denote the closures of set A and B, respectively. The generalized approach to defining fuzzy concepts has been later advanced to include so-called implication operators (Burusco, & Fuentes-Gonzáles, 2000).

The approach of Bělohlávek (1998) is considered to be a feasible way to develop FCA and related structures in a fuzzy setting. This approach is developed in many aspects: (Bělohlávek, 2004) deals with a fuzzy order on formal concepts; Galois connections and closure operators are studied in (Bělohlávek, 1999; 2001; 2002a). An algorithm for generating all formal concepts based on Ganter's algorithm (Ganter B., & Wille R.1999) is presented in (Bělohlávek, 2002b). Several issues related to many-valued contexts, approximate reasoning, attribute implications are studied in (Pollandt, 1997). Attribute implications are studied also in (Bělohlávek, & Vychodil, 2005a; 2005b).

The approach proposed by Yahia and Jaova (2001) and, independently, by Krajči (2003) is called "one-sided fuzzy approach". It is interesting that the extents of concepts in this approach are crisp sets while the intents are fuzzy sets, but one can have fuzzy extents and crisp intents too.

Another approach is presented in (Snášel et al., 2002). The basic idea is to consider, for a given L-context $<X, Y, I>$, formal contexts $<X, Y, {}^aI>$ for $a \in K$, $K \subseteq L$. That is, one takes a-cuts ${}^aI = \{<x, y> \mid I(x, y) \geq a\}$ of the original fuzzy relation I for each $a \in K$. K contains truth degrees which are considered important, relevant, sufficiently covering L, etc. Since ${}^aI$ is an ordinary relation, $<X, Y, {}^aI>$ is an ordinary formal context. Therefore, one can apply (ordinary) formal concept analysis to each $<X, Y, {}^aI>$.

Krajči (2005) studies a so-called generalized concept lattice. In the previous approaches to concept lattices, formal concepts are defined as certain pairs $<A, B>$ where for A and B we can have the following possibilities: both A and B are crisp sets, both A and B are fuzzy sets, A is crisp and B is fuzzy, A is fuzzy and B is crisp. Krajči suggests to consider three sets of truth degrees, namely, a set L_X (for objects), L_Y (for attributes), and L (for degrees to which objects have attributes, i.e. table entries).

Given sets X and Y of objects and attributes, one can consider a fuzzy context as a triplet $<X, Y, I>$, where I is an L-relation between X and Y, i.e. $I \in L^{X \times Y}$. Furthermore, one can consider L_X-sets A of objects and L_Y-sets B of attributes, i.e. $A \in L_X{}^X$ and $B \in L_Y{}^Y$. Furthermore, Krajči asserts that L_X and L_Y are complete lattices and L is a partially ordered set.

Denote all the partial orders on L_X, L_Y, and L by $\leq$.. Likewise, infima and suprema in both $<L_X, \leq>$ and $<L_Y, \leq>$ will be denoted by $\wedge$ and $\vee$ respectively.

Krajči introduces the operation $\otimes: L_X \times L_Y \to L$ satisfying the following relations:

for each index set J and all $a, a_j \in L_X$, $b, b_j \in L_Y$, and $c \in L$

$a_1 \leq a_2$ implies $a_1 \otimes b \leq a_2 \otimes b$,

$b_1 \leq b_2$ implies $a \otimes b_1 \leq a \otimes b_2$,

if $a_j \otimes b \leq c$ for each $j \in J$, then $(\vee_{j \in J} a_j) \otimes b \leq c$,

if $a \otimes b_j \leq c$ for each $j \in J$, then $a \otimes ((\vee_{j \in J} b_j) \leq c$.

That is, we have a three-sorted structure $<L_1, L_2, L, \otimes, \leq, \ldots>$ of truth degrees.

In order to define fuzzy formal concept Krajči introduces two mapping: M1: $L_X{}^X \to L_Y{}^Y$ and M2: $L_X{}^X \to L_Y{}^Y$. Then a formal concept in $<X, Y, I>$ is defined as a pair $<A, B> \in L_X{}^X \times L_Y{}^Y$ such as M1(A) = B and M2(B) = A.

In the paper (Xie et al., 2007), a fast and automatic algorithm is proposed, called FCLB algorithm, for generating fuzzy concepts from a given fuzzy formal context and a set of fuzzy sets. This algorithm builds a fuzzy concept lattice and represents it graphically. This work has been applied successfully to the social navigation system helping users in finding information more effectively. The algorithm uses a new fuzzy concept lattice (FCL) model proposed in (Liu et al. 2007). This model deals with the continuous membership degree in fuzzy formal context. The fuzzy concepts are defined via the order relation as follows:

A triple $(G, A, \tilde{I})$ is called a fuzzy formal context. Where $G = \{x_1, x_2, \cdot, x_n\}$ is a set of objects, and $A = \{a_1, a_2, \cdot, a_m\}$ is a set of attributes, $\tilde{I}$ is a fuzzy relation mapping from $G \times A$ to interval $[0, 1]$, i.e. $\tilde{I}: G \times A \to [0, 1]$. If $\tilde{I}(x, a) = \alpha$, then the object x has the attribute a with the degree α.

Let (G, A, ˜I) be a fuzzy formal context, "→" is an implicative operator, for all ˜X: G→[0, 1], ˜B: A→[0, 1]. The mapping operators are defined as follows (Zhang, &. Qiu, 2005):

$$\tilde{X}^*(a) = \wedge_{x \in G}(\tilde{X}(x) \to I(x, a)),$$

$$\tilde{B}^*(x) = \wedge_{a \in A}(\tilde{B}(a) \to I(x, a)).$$

A pair (˜X, ˜B) is called a fuzzy concept if and only if ˜X*= ˜B, ˜B*= ˜X. ˜X is called its extent, and ˜B is called its intent. The subset $L(G,A,\tilde{I})=\{(\tilde{X}, \tilde{B})|\tilde{X}^*= \tilde{B}, \tilde{B}^*= \tilde{X}\}$ with the order relation ≤, i.e. the lattice $L((G,A,\tilde{I}), \leq)$ is called a complete fuzzy concept lattice.

The FCLB algorithm generates all the fuzzy concepts from a given fuzzy formal context (G, A, ˜I) and a set of fuzzy sets $\tilde{L} = \{\tilde{X}(x)|x \in G\}$. The following problems are resolved in the algorithm: (1) How to generate fuzzy concepts; (2) How to prune redundant fuzzy concepts; (3) How to seek out all the partial ordered sets; (4) How to locate fuzzy concepts.

The social navigation system model based on FCL obtains a fuzzy formal context by formalizing users' traces, and then obtains fuzzy sets based on the query words people left. The fuzzy formal concepts are generated by the fuzzy sets and the fuzzy formal context and the FCL is constructed.

The fuzzy lattice reasoning (FLR) classifier is presented in (Kaburlasos et al., 20070 for inducing descriptive, decision-making knowledge (rules) in the continuous and integer data domains structured as an algebraic lattice. Tunable generalization is possible based on non-linear (sigmoid) positive valuation functions. The FLR classifier can work with missing data. Learning is carried out both incrementally and fast by computing disjunctions of join-lattice interval conjunctions. The application of FLR deals with the problem of estimating ambient ozone concentration from both meteorological and air-pollutant measurements. The results compare favorably with the results obtained by C4.5 decision trees and back-propagation neural networks.

CONCLUSION

We have considered, in this chapter, some fast heuristics for inferring approximately minimal diagnostic tests based on which a model of commonsense reasoning by analogy is constructed. This model has been implemented in the system called DEFINE. The results of this system's application for recognizing the type of tree species with the use of aerial photographs have been described. We discussed the different approach to mining approximate rules. Then we have presented the system called 'Diagnostic Test Machine' destined for inferring the broad class of logical dependencies from raw data: functional dependencies (strict and fuzzy (approximate)), implicative dependencies (strict and fuzzy (approximate)), decision trees based on obtained dependencies, logical rules based on obtained dependencies (implicative ones), association rules. Our future work is directed to the development of Diagnostic Test Machine as a tool for commonsense reasoning in real applications.

REFERENCES

ASE. (2004). *The Athens stock exchange closing prices*. Retrieval March 26, 2004 from httt://www.ase. gr/content/en/MarcetData/Stocks/Prices/default.asp

Bandler, W., & Kohout, L. (1980). Fuzzy power sets and fuzzy implication operators. *Fuzzy Sets and Systems, 4*, 13–30. doi:10.1016/0165-0114(80)90060-3

Bělohlávek, R. (1999). Fuzzy Galois connections. *Math. Logic Quarterly, 45*(4), 497–504.

Bělohlávek, R. (2001). Fuzzy closure operators. *Journal of Mathematical Analysis and Applications, 262*, 473–489. doi:10.1006/jmaa.2000.7456

Belohlavek, R. (2002). *Fuzzy relational systems: Foundations and principles*. IFSR International Series on System Sciences and Engineering, Vol. 20. Springer.

Bělohlávek, R. (2002a). Fuzzy Closure Operators II. *Soft Computing, 7*(1), 53–64. doi:10.1007/s00500-002-0165-y

Bělohlávek, R. (2002b). Algorithms for fuzzy concept lattices. In *Proc. of the Fourth Int. Conf. on Recent Advances in Soft Computing* (pp.67-68). RASC Nottingham, United Kingdom.

Bělohlávek, R. (2004). Concept lattices and order in fuzzy logic. *Annals of Pure and Applied Logic, 128*, 277–298. doi:10.1016/j.apal.2003.01.001

Bělohlávek, R., & Vychodil, V. (2005). What is a fuzzy concept lattice? In R. Bělohlávek & V. Snášel (Eds.), *Proceedings of the 3rd International Conference on Concept Lattice and Their Applications (CLA'05), Olomouc, Czech Republic* (pp. 34-45). Retrieved from http://ceur-ws.org/Vol-162/

Bělohlávek, R., & Vychodil, V. (2005a). Implications from data with fuzzy attributes vs. scaled binary attributes. In R. Krishnapuram (Ed.), *Proceedings of the IEEE International Conference on Fuzzy Systems*, (pp. 1050–1055). Reno, NV: Publisher FUZZ-IEEE.

Bělohlávek, R., & Vychodil, V. (2005b). Fuzzy attribute logic: Attribute implications, their validity, entailment, and non-redundant basis. In Y. Liu, G. Chen, & M. Ying (Eds.), *Fuzzy Logic, Soft Computing & Computational Intelligence, Proceedings of the Eleventh International Fuzzy Systems Association World Congress* (Vol. 1, pp. 622–627). Tsinghua University Press and Springer.

Burusco, A., & Fuentes-Gonzáles, R. (1994). The study of the L-fuzzy concept lattice. *Mathware & . Soft Computing, 3*, 209–218.

Burusco, A., & Fuentes-Gonzáles, R. (2000). Concept lattice defined from implication operators. *Fuzzy Sets and Systems, 114*(3), 431–436. doi:10.1016/S0165-0114(98)00182-1

Bustince, H. (2000). Indicator of inclusion grade for interval-valued fuzzy sets. Application to Approximate Reasoning Based on Interval-Val ued Fuzzy Sets. *International Journal of Approximate Reasoning, 23*, 137–209. doi:10.1016/S0888-613X(99)00045-6

Chen, G., Wei, Q., & Kerre, E. E. (2006). Fuzzy logic in discovering association rules: An overview. In E. Triantaphyllou, & G. Felici (Eds.), *Data mining and knowledge discovery approaches based on rule induction techniques* (pp. 459-493). New York: Springer.

Dubois, D., Hullermeier, E., & Prade, H. (2006). A systematic approach to the assessment of fuzzy association rules. *Data Mining and Knowledge Discovery, 13*(2), 1–26. doi:10.1007/s10618-005-0032-4

Ganter, B., & Wille, R. (1999). *Formal concept analysis. Mathematical foundations*. Springer-Verlag, Berlin.

Geng, L., & Hamilton, H. J. (2006). Interestingness measures for data mining: A survey. *ACM Computer Surveys, 38*(3), 9(1-32).

Gnedach, I., & Danulis, E. Krilova, J., & Naidenova, X. (1983). Deciphering objects on the basis of similarity-difference relations in multi-valued feature space. In D. I. Orekhov. (Ed.), *Application of remote sensing data and computers for the investigation of natural resource of the earth* (pp. 26-47). Leningrad, USSR: Leningrad Institute for Informatics and Automation of the USSR Academy of Sciences (LIIAN).

Huhltala, Y., Kärkkäinen, J., Porkka, P., & Toivonen, H. (1999). TANE: An efficient algorithm for discovering functional and approximate dependencies. *The Computer Journal, 42*(2), 100–111. doi:10.1093/comjnl/42.2.100

Huynh, X. H., Guillet, F., & Briand, H. (2006). Evaluating interestingness measures with linear correlation graph. In *Advances in Applied Artificial Intelligence* (LNCS 4031, pp. 312-321). Berlin/Heidelberg: Springer.

Iba, W., Wogulis, J., & Langley, P. (1988). Trading off simplicity and coverage in incremental concept learning. In J. E. Larid (Ed.), *Proceedings of the 5th International Conference on Machine Learning* (pp. 73-79). Ann Arbor, Michigan: Morgan Kaufmann.

Kaburlasos, V. G., Athanasiadis, I. N., & Mitkas, P. A. (2007). Fuzzy lattice reasoning (FLR) classifier and its application for ambient ozone estimation. *International Journal of Approximate Reasoning archive, 45*(1), 152-188.

Kehagias, A. (2002). *The lattice of fuzzy intervals and sufficient conditions for its distributivity*. The Computing Research Repository. Retrieved from http://arxiv.org/abs/cs.OH/0206025 (CS Arxiv TR cs.OH/0206025, 2002).

Kehagias, A., & Konstantinidou, M. (2003). L-Fuzzy valued inclusion measure, L-Fuzzy similarity and L-Fuzzy distance. *Fuzzy Sets and Systems, 136*, 313–332. doi:10.1016/S0165-0114(02)00407-4

Kivinen, J., & Mannila, H. (1995). Approximate dependency inference from relations. *Theoretical Computer Science, 149*(1), 129–149. doi:10.1016/0304-3975(95)00028-U

Koh, Y. S. O'Keefe, R., & Rountree, N. (2008). Current interestingness measures for association rules: What do they really measure? In D. Tan (Ed.), *Data mining and knowledge discovery technologies* (pp. 36-58). New York: Springer.

Krajči, S. (2003). Cluster based efficient generation of fuzzy concepts. *Neural Network World, 5,* 521–530.

Krajči, S. (2005). A generalized concept lattice. *Logic Journal of IGPL, 13*(5), 543–550. doi:10.1093/jigpal/jzi045

Kundu, S. (2000). A representation theorem for min-transitive fuzzy relations. *Fuzzy Sets and Systems, 109,* 453–457. doi:10.1016/S0165-0114(97)00373-4

Kuok, C., Fu, A., & Wong, H. (1998). Mining fuzzy association rules in databases. *SIGMOD Record, 27,* 41–46. doi:10.1145/273244.273257

Lenca, P., Meyer, P., Vaillant, B., & Lallich, S. (2004). *Multi-criteria decision aid for interestingness measure selection* (Tech. Rep. No. LUSSI-TR- 2004-01-EN). LUSSI Department, GET / ENST Bretagne.

Liao, T. W. (2006). Mining human interpretable knowledge with fuzzy modeling methods: An overview. In E. Triantaphyllou, & G. Felici (Eds.), *Data mining and knowledge discovery approaches based on rule induction techniques* (pp. 495-549). New York: Springer.

Lincoff, G. H. (1981). *Mushroom records drawn from the Audubon society field guide to North American mushrooms.* New York: Alfred A. Knopf.

Liu, G. (2008). Generalized rough sets over fuzzy lattices. *Information Sciences: An International Journal archive, 178*(6), 1651-1662.

Liu, Z. T., Qiang, Y., & Zhou, W. (2007). A fuzzy concept lattice model and its incremental construction algorithm. *Chinese Journal of Computers, 30*(2), 184–188.

McGarry, K. (2005). A survey of interestingness measures for knowledge discovery. *The Knowledge Engineering Review, 20*(1), 39–61. doi:10.1017/S0269888905000408

Mitsuishi, T., & Bancerek, G. (2003). Lattice of FuzzySets1. *Formalized Mathematics, 11*(4), 393–398.

Naidenova, X.A. (1981). The automation of forest-planting's natural compositions identification methods with the use of instrument features extracted from aero-photographs of forests (Scales 1: 2000 – 1: 5000) by the Operators. *Technical Report V.I, stage V.I.I.2,* vol. 1. Leningrad, USSR: North Western Forest-Management Enterprise «Lesproject».

Naidenova, X. A. (1981). Segmentation and analysis of forest's aerial photographs. In V. M. Ovseevich (Ed.), *Automated systems of image processing, Theses of reports of the First All Union Conference on Automated Image Processing Systems* (pp. 208-209) Moscow, USSR: Nauka.

Naidenova, X.A. (1982). Relational model for analyzing experimental data. *The transaction of Acad. Sci. of USSR, series «Technical cybernetics»,* 4, 103-119.

Naidenova, X. A. (1983). Developing a method of computer-based identification of forest-planting's natural compositions with the use of aero-photographs of forest. *Technical Report H7a.* Leningrad, USSR: North Western Forest-Management Enterprise «Lesproject».

Naidenova, X. A., & Polegaeva, J. G. (1984). Application of similarity-distinction relations for processing multi-spectral information. In V.P. Pyatkin (Ed.), *Image processing and remote investigations. Theses of reports of the All Union Conference, part 3* (pp. 67-68). Novosibirsk, USSR: Academy of Science, the Siberian branch.

Naidenova, X. A., & Polegaeva, J. G. (1985). Model of human reasoning for deciphering forest's images and its implementation on computer. In A. I. Michaylov (Ed.), *Semiotic aspects of the intellectual activity formalization*, Theses of reports of School-Seminar "Kutaisi-85" (pp.49-52). Moscow, USSR: VINITI.

Naidenova, X. A., & Polegaeva, J. G. (1989). DEFINE - The system for generating hypotheses and reasoning by analogy on the basis of inferring functional dependencies. In V.M. Ponomarev (Ed.), *The Problem of Expert System Creation*. Preprint of the Leningrad Institute for Informatics and Automation of the USSR Academy of Sciences (LIIAN), issue 111 (pp. 20-21). Leningrad, USSR: LIIAN.

Olson, D., & Delen, D. (2008). *Advanced data mining techniques*. Berlin Heidelberg: Springer-Verlag.

Pawlak, Z. (1982). Rough sets. *International Journal of Computer and Information Sciences, 11*, 341–356. doi:10.1007/BF01001956

Pearl, J. (1988). *Probabilistic reasoning in intelligence systems. Networks of plausible inference*. San Mateo, CA: Morgan Kaufmann.

Pelekis, N., Theodoulidis, B., Kopanakis, I., & Theodoridis, Y. (2005). Fuzzy miner: Extracting fuzzy rules from numerical patterns. In G. Felici & C. Vercellis (Eds.), *Mathematical methods for knowledge discovery and data mining* (pp. 299-321). New York: Springer.

Pollandt, S. (1997). *Fuzzy Begriffe*. Berlin/Heidelberg: Springer-Verlag.

Sangalli, A. A. L. (1996). Lattice of fuzzy objects. *International Journal of Mathematics and Mathematical Sciences, 19*(4), 759–766. doi:10.1155/S0161171296001056

Schlimmer, J. S. (1987). *Concept acquisition through representational adjustment*. Unpublished doctoral dissertation (Technical Report 87-19). Department of Information and Computer Science, University of California, Irvine.

Šešelia, B. (2007). L-fuzzy covering relation. *Fuzzy Sets and Systems, 158*(22), 2456–2465. doi:10.1016/j.fss.2007.05.019

Šešelia, B., & Tepavčević, A. (1993). Partially ordered and relational valued algebras and congruencies. *Review of Research* of Faculty *of Sciences, Univ. of Novi Sad . Math. Ser., 23*(1), 273–287.

Šešelia, B., & Tepavčević, A. (1994). Partially ordered and relational valued fuzzy relations II. *Review of Research* of Faculty *of Sciences, Univ. of Novi Sad . Math. Ser., 24*(1), 245–260.

Šešelia, B., & Tepavčević, A. (1995). Partially ordered and relational valued fuzzy relations I. *Fuzzy Sets and Systems, 72*, 205–213. doi:10.1016/0165-0114(94)00352-8

Shi, Y., Peng, Y., Kou, G., & Chen, Z. (2005). Classifying credit card accounts for business intelligence and decision making: A multi-criteria quadratic programming approach. *International Journal of Information Technology & Decision Making*, *4*(4), 581–599. doi:10.1142/S0219622005001775

Snášel, V., Duráková, D., Vojtáš, P., & Krajči, S. (2002). Fuzzy concept order. In V. Duquenne, B. Ganter, M. Liquiere, M. Nguifo, & G. Stumme (Eds.), *Advances in Formal Concept Analysis for Knowledge Discovery in Databases, Proceedings of the Workshop FCAKDD of the 15ᵗʰ European Conference on Artificial Intelligence (ECAI'02)* (pp. 94-98). Lyon, France: Univ. of Lyon.

Srikant, R., & Agrawal, R. (1996). Mining quantitative association rules in large relational tables. In H. V. Jagadish & I. S. Munick (Eds.), *Proceedings of the ACM SIGMOD International Conference on Management of Data* (pp. 1-12). Montreal, Canada: ACM Press.

Tan, P. N., & Kumar, V. (2000). *Interestingness measures for association patterns: A perspective* (Tech. Rep. No. TR 00-036). Department of Computer Science and Engineering, University of Minnesota.

Tan, P. N., Kumar, V., & Srivastava, J. (2004). Selecting the right objective measure for association analysis. *Information Systems*, *29*(4), 293–313. doi:10.1016/S0306-4379(03)00072-3

Tepavcevic, A., & Trajkovski, G. (2001). L-fuzzy Lattices: An introduction. *Fuzzy Sets and Systems*, *123*, 209–216. doi:10.1016/S0165-0114(00)00065-8

Trajkovski, G. (1998). An approach toward defining L-fuzzy lattices. In J. Bezdeck & L.O. Hall (Eds.), *Proceedings of the North American Fuzzy Information Processing Society (NAFIPS) Conference* (pp. 221 – 225). New York: Institute of Electrical and Electronics Engineers.

Trajkovski, G., & Čukić, B. (1999). On two types of L^M fuzzy lattices. In B. Reusch (Ed.), *Computational Intelligence, Theory and Applications, Proceedings of 6ᵗʰ Fuzzy Days International Conference* (LNCS 1625, pp. 272-281). Dortmund, Germany: Springer-Verlag.

Vaillant, B., Lenca, P., & Lallich, S. (2004). A clustering of interestingness measures. In E. Suzuki, & S. Arikawa (Eds.), *Discovery Science, Proceedings of 7ᵗʰ International Conference* (LNCS 3245, pp. 290-297). Springer-Verlag.

Willmott, R. (1980). Two fuzzier implication operators in the theory of fuzzy power sets. *Fuzzy Sets and Systems*, *4*, 31–36. doi:10.1016/0165-0114(80)90061-5

Willmott, R. (1986). On the transitivity of containment and equivalence in fuzzy power set theory. *Journal of Mathematical Analysis and Applications*, *120*, 384–396. doi:10.1016/0022-247X(86)90224-6

Xie, Ch., Yi, L., & Du, Y. (2007, October). *An algorithm for fuzzy concept lattices building with application to social navigation*. Paper presented at International Conference on Intelligent Systems and Knowledge Engineering (ISKE'2007), Chengdu, China. Retrieved from http://www.atlantis-press.com/php/download_paper.php?id=1417

Yahia, S., & Jaoua, A. (2001). Discovering knowledge from fuzzy concept lattice. In A. Kandel, M. Last, & H. Bunke (Eds.), *Data mining and computational intelligence, studies in fuzziness and soft computing* (Vol. 68, pp. 167-190). Physica-Verlag.

Zade, L. A. (1965). Fuzzy sets. *Information and Control, 8,* 338–356. doi:10.1016/S0019-9958(65)90241-X

Zhai, L.-Y., Khoo, L.-P., & Fok, S.-C. (2006). Knowledge acquisition and uncertainty in fault diagnosis: A rough sets perspective. In E. Triantaphyllou & G. Felici (Eds.), *Data mining and knowledge discovery approaches based on rule induction techniques* (pp. 359-394). New York: Springer.

Zhang, W. X., & Qiu, G. F. (2005). *Uncertain decision making based on rough sets.* Tsinghua University Press, Beijing.

APPENDIX: AN EXAMPLE OF DIAGNOSTIC TEST MACHINE APPLICATION

Data Description:

1. Title: **Mushroom Database**
2. Sources:
    Mushroom records drawn from the Audubon Society Field Guide to North American Mushrooms (Lincoff, 1981).
3. Past Usage:
    The Mushroom Database has been used in (Schlimmer, 1987). In this work, a staging result is reported: asymptotically to 95% classification accuracy after reviewing 1000 instances. This database has also been used in (Iba et al., 1988) practically with the same results.
4. Relevant Information:
    This data set includes descriptions of hypothetical samples corresponding to 23 species of gilled mushrooms in the Agaricus and Lepiota Family (Lincoff, 1981, pp. 500-525). Each species is identified as definitely edible, definitely poisonous, or of unknown edibility and not recommended. This latter class was combined with the poisonous one.
5. **Number of Instances**: 8124.
6. **Number of Attributes**: 22 (all nominally valued). Table 20 contains the information of attribute domains.
7. Missing attribute values: 2480; all of them (denoted by "*") for attribute #11.
8. Classes to be distinguished: edible mushrooms = e, poisonous mushrooms = p:
9. Class distribution: the number of edible mushrooms is 4208 (51.8%); the number of poisonous mushrooms is 3916 (48.2%); the total number of mushrooms is 8124 instances (http://www.ailab.si/orange/datasets).

Table 20. The attribute domains

N	Atribute	Attribute Domain
1	cap-shape	bell=**b**, conical=**c**, convex=**x**, flat=**f**, knobbed=**k**, sunken=**s**
2	cap-surface	fibrous=**f**, grooves=**g**, scaly=**y**, smooth=**s**
3	cap-color	brown=**n**, buff=**b**, cinnamon=**c**, gray=**g**, green=**r**, pink=**p**, purple=**u**, red=**e**, white=**w**, yellow=**y**
4	bruises?	bruises=**t**, no=**f**
5	odor	almond=**a**, anise=**l**, creosote=**c**, fishy=**y**, foul=**f**, musty=**m**, none=**n**, pungent=**p**, spicy=**s**
6	gill-attachment	attached=**a**, descending=**d**, free=**f**, notched=**n**
7	gill-spacing	close=**c**, crowded=**w**, distant=**d**
8	gill-size	broad=**b**, narrow=**n**
9	gill-color	black=**k**, brown=**n**, buff=**b**, chocolate=**h**, gray=**g**, green=**r**, orange=*o*, pink=**p**, purple=**u**, red=**e**, white=**w**, yellow=**y**
10	stalk-shape	enlarging=**e**, tapering=**t**
11	stalk-root	bulbous=**b**, club=**c**, cup=**u**, equal=**e**, rhizomorphs=z, rooted=**r**, missing=**?**
12	stalk-surface-above-ring	ibrous=**f**, scaly=**y**, silky=**k**, smooth=**s**
13	stalk-surface-below-ring	ibrous=**f**, scaly=**y**, silky=**k**, smooth=**s**

14	stalk-color-above-ring	brown=**n**, buff=**b**, cinnamon=**c**, gray=**g**, orange=**o**, pink=**p**, red=**e**, white=**w**, yellow=**y**
15	stalk-color-below-ring	brown=**n**, buff=**b**, cinnamon=**c**, gray=**g**, orange=**o**, pink=**p**, red=**e**, white=**w**, yellow=**y**
16	veil-type	partial=**p**, universal=**u**
17	veil-color	brown=**n**, orange=**o**, white=**w**, yellow=**y**
18	ring-number	none=**n**, one=**o**, two=**t**
19	ring-type	cobwebby=**c**, evanescent=**e**, flaring=**f**, large=**l**, none=**n**, pendant=**p**, sheathing=**s**, zone=**z**
20	spore-print-color	black=**k**, brown=**n**, buff=**b**, chocolate=**h**, green=**r**, orange=**o**, purple=**u**, white=**w**, yellow=**y**
21	population	abundant=**a**, clustered=**c**, numerous=**n**, scattered=**s**, several=**v**, solitary=**y**
22	habitat	grasses=**g**, leaves=**l**, meadows=**m**, paths=**p**, urban=**u**, waste=**w**, woods=**d**

Table 21 contains the values of information quantity and significance indices

Table 21. The indices of attributive information quantity and significance

N	Attribute name	Information quantity	Significance	Attribute Domain
1	cap-shape	0.11812	15.06584	x, b, s, f, k, c
2	cap-surface	0.17665	17.87402	s, y, f, g
3	cap-color	0.12830	12.29980	n, y, w, g, e, p, b, u, c, r
4	bruises	0.49465	47.85781	t, f
5	odor	0.96936	85.00059	p, a, l, n, f, c, y, s, m
6	gill-attachment	0.04103	13.27837	f, a
7	gill-spacing	0.25657	35.43617	c, w
8	gill-size	0.49949	53.04002	n, b
9	gill-color	0.44739	65.44208	k, n, g, p, w, h, u, e, b, r, y, o
10	stalk-shape	0.10116	9.20766	e, t
11	stalk-root	0.31039	25.74046	e, c, b, r
12	stalk-surface-above-ring	0.53473	60.21576	s, f, k, y
13	stalk-surface-below-ring	0.51736	58.64006	s, f, y, k
14	stalk-color-above-ring	0.41091	19.77351	w, g, p, n, b, e, o, c, y
15	stalk-color-below-ring	0.26669	19.44034	w, p, g, b, n, e, y, o, c
16	veil-type	0.0,	0.0	p
17	veil-color	0.04563	15.31730	w, n, o, y
18	ring-number	0.10709	20.36332	o, t, n
19	ring-type	0.54289	51.52860	p, e, l, f, n
20	spore-print-color	0.73731	52.45023	k, n, u, h,w, r, o, y, b
21	population	0.44400	41.44308	s, n, a, v, y, c
22	habitat	0.32024	31.64784	u, g, m, d, p, w, l
23	**class**	1.0,	141.48947	p, e

The next tables present the results of Diagnostic Test Machine performance.

The Table 22 contains the **fuzzy rules for Class p** with the value of minimal Rule Power index equal to 25% and Degree of Belief index equal to 0.7.

Table 22. Fuzzy rules for Class p

N	Power	Accuracy	GMRT
0	3248	0.77	bruises = f & gill-attachment = f & veil-type = p & veil-color = w & ring-number = o
1	3152	0.96	bruises = f & gill-attachment = f & gill-spacing = c & veil-type = p & veil-color = w & ring-number = o
2	2848	0.72	gill-attachment = f & veil-type = p & veil-color = w & population = v
3	2504	0.95	bruises = f & gill-attachment = f & veil-type = p & veil-color = w & ring-number = o & population = v
4	2228	1.00	bruises = f & gill-spacing = c & stalk-surface-above-ring = k & veil-type = p & veil-color = w
5	2224	0.89	gill-attachment = f & gill-size = n & veil-type = p & ring-number = o
6	2160	1.00	odor = f & gill-attachment = f & gill-spacing = c & veil-type = p & veil-color = w & ring-number = o
7	2160	1.00	bruises = f & gill-attachment = f & gill-spacing = c & stalk-surface-below-ring = k & veil-type = p & veil-color = w & ring-number = o
8	1952	0.91	bruises = f & gill-attachment = f & gill-size = n & veil-type = p & veil-color = w & ring-number = o
9	1812	0.76	veil-type = p & spore-print-color = w
10	1768	0.97	bruises = f & gill-attachment = f & gill-size = n & veil-type = p & ring-number = o & ring-type = e & spore-print-color = w
11	1768	0.97	gill-attachment = f & gill-size = n & veil-type = p & veil-color = w & ring-number = o & spore-print-color = w
12	1760	1.00	bruises = f & gill-attachment = f & gill-spacing = c & gill-size = n & veil-type = p & veil-color = w & ring-number = o & ring-type = e & spore-print-color = w & population = v
13	1528	0.97	cap-surface = y & bruises = f & gill-attachment = f & gill-spacing = c & veil-type = p & veil-color = w & ring-number = o
14	1520	0.89	bruises = f & gill-attachment = f & stalk-shape = e & veil-type = p & veil-color = w & ring-number = o
15	1496	0.97	gill-attachment = f & stalk-shape = e & stalk-root = b & veil-type = p & veil-color = w & ring-number = o
16	1392	1.00	bruises = f & gill-attachment = f & gill-spacing = c & stalk-shape = e & stalk-root = b & veil-type = p & veil-color = w & ring-number = o
17	1328	0.84	cap-surface = s & gill-attachment = f & gill-spacing = c & veil-type = p & veil-color = w & ring-number = o
18	1296	1.00	bruises = f & gill-attachment = f & gill-spacing = c & stalk-color-above-ring = p & veil-type = p & veil-color = w & ring-number = o
19	1296	1.00	bruises = f & gill-attachment = f & gill-spacing = c & stalk-color-below-ring = p & veil-type = p & veil-color = w & ring-number = o
20	1268	0.96	bruises = f & veil-type = p & veil-color = w & habitat = d
21	1232	0.96	bruises = f & gill-attachment = f & veil-type = p & veil-color = w & ring-number = o & habitat = d
22	1232	0.96	cap-shape = f & bruises = f & gill-attachment = f & gill-spacing = c & veil-type = p & veil-color = w & ring-number = o
23	1152	1.00	cap-surface = s & gill-attachment = f & gill-spacing = c & stalk-shape = t & veil-type = p & veil-color = w & ring-number = o
24	1120	0.96	cap-surface = s & gill-attachment = f & veil-type = p & veil-color = w & ring-number = o & population = v
25	1096	1.00	cap-surface = s & gill-attachment = f & gill-spacing = c & veil-type = p & veil-color = w & ring-number = o & population = v
26	1088	0.96	cap-surface = s & gill-attachment = f & gill-size = n & veil-type = p & veil-color = w & ring-number = o
27	1088	0.92	gill-attachment = f & gill-spacing = c & gill-size = n & stalk-surface-below-ring = s & veil-type = p & veil-color = w & ring-number = o
28	1040	1.00	cap-surface = s & gill-attachment = f & gill-spacing = c & gill-size = n & veil-type = p & veil-color = w & ring-number = o
29	1008	1.00	bruises = f & gill-attachment = f & gill-spacing = c & veil-type = p & veil-color = w & ring-number = o & habitat = p
30	1008	0.95	C ap-color = n & gill-attachment = f & gill-spacing = c & gill-size = n & veil-type = p & veil-color = w & ring-number = o

The Table 23 contains the **fuzzy rules for Class e** with the value of minimal Rule Power index equal to 25% and Degree of Belief index equal to 0.7.

Table 23. Fuzzy rules for Class e

N	Power	Accuracy	GMRT
31	3640	0.70	stalk-surface-above-ring = s & veil-type = p
32	3408	0.97	odor = n & veil-type = p
33	3152	0.79	veil-type = p & ring-type = p
34	2874	0.98	odor = n & gill-size = b & veil-type = p
35	2832	0.98	odor = n & veil-type = p & ring-number = o
36	2752	0.85	bruises = t & gill-attachment = f & stalk-surface-above-ring = s & veil-type = p & veil-color = w
37	2688	1.00	odor = n & gill-size = b & veil-type = p & ring-number = o
38	2640	0.99	odor = n & gill-attachment = f & veil-type = p & veil-color = w & ring-number = o
39	2448	1.00	odor = n & stalk-surface-above-ring = s & veil-type = p & ring-number = o
40	2400	1.00	odor = n & stalk-surface-below-ring = s & veil-type = p & ring-number = o
41	2064	1.00	odor = n & gill-spacing = c & stalk-surface-above-ring = s & veil-type = p & ring-number = o
42	1872	0.80	gill-attachment = f & stalk-surface-above-ring = s & veil-type = p & veil-color = w & ring-number = o & habitat = d
43	1832	0.91	gill-attachment = f & stalk-root = b & veil-type = p & veil-color = w & ring-type = p & habitat = d
44	1824	1.00	bruises = t & gill-attachment = f & stalk-shape = t & stalk-root = b & stalk-surface-above-ring = s & stalk-surface-below-ring = s & veil-type = p & veil-color = w & ring-number = o & ring-type = p & habitat = d
45	1784	0.98	odor = n & gill-attachment = f & gill-spacing = c & veil-type = p & veil-color = w & habitat = d
46	1744	0.89	veil-type = p & ring-number = o & spore-print-color = n
47	1736	1.00	odor = n & gill-attachment = f & gill-spacing = c & gill-size = b & stalk-root = b & veil-type = p & veil-color = w & ring-type = p & habitat = d
48	1648	0.88	gill-attachment = f & veil-type = p & veil-color = w & ring-number = o & spore-print-color = k
49	1648	1.00	gill-size = b & veil-type = p & ring-number = o & spore-print-color = n
50	1600	1.00	gill-attachment = f & gill-size = b & veil-type = p & veil-color = w & ring-number = o & spore-print-color = k
51	1548	0.99	cap-shape = x & odor = n & veil-type = p
52	1512	0.99	cap-surface = f & odor = n & gill-attachment = f & veil-type = p & veil-color = w
53	1488	0.99	odor = n & gill-attachment = f & stalk-color-below-ring = w & veil-type = p & veil-color = w & ring-number = o
54	1476	1.00	cap-shape = x & odor = n & gill-size = b & veil-type = p
55	1456	0.97	bruises = f & odor = n & veil-type = p
56	1433	0.70	cap-surface = y & gill-attachment = f & stalk-surface-above-ring = s & veil-type = p & veil-color = w
57	1408	0.89	gill-attachment = f & gill-size = b & stalk-color-above-ring = w & stalk-color-below-ring = w & veil-type = p & veil-color = w & habitat = g
58	1398	0.97	cap-shape = f & odor = n & veil-type = p
59	1392	1.00	cap-surface = f & odor = n & gill-attachment = f & gill-size = b & veil-type = p & veil-color = w
60	1373	0.97	cap-surface = y & bruises = t & gill-attachment = f & gill-spacing = c & gill-size = b & stalk-surface-above-ring = s & veil-type = p & veil-color = w
61	1344	1.00	odor = n & veil-type = p & ring-number = o & spore-print-color = n
62	1338	0.72	cap-shape = f & stalk-surface-above-ring = s & veil-type = p

63	1333	0.97	cap-surface = y & gill-attachment = f & gill-spacing = c & gill-size = b & veil-type = p & veil-color = w & ring-type = p
64	1330	0.72	stalk-shape = e & stalk-surface-above-ring = s & veil-type = p
65	1312	1.00	cap-surface = y & bruises = t & gill-attachment = f & gill-spacing = c & gill-size = b & stalk-surface-above-ring = s & veil-type = p & veil-color = w & ring-number = o & ring-type = p
66	1296	1.00	cap-surface = f & gill-attachment = f & stalk-shape = t & veil-type = p & veil-color = w & ring-number = o
67	1296	1.00	odor = n & gill-attachment = f & veil-type = p & veil-color = w & ring-number = o & spore-print-color = k
68	1296	1.00	gill-attachment = f & stalk-shape = t & veil-type = p & veil-color = w & ring-number = o & spore-print-color = n
69	1296	1.00	cap-shape = x & odor = n & stalk-surface-above-ring = s & veil-type = p
70	1284	0.93	cap-surface = f & gill-attachment = f & stalk-surface-above-ring = s & veil-type = p & veil-color = w
71	1284	0.93	cap-surface = f & gill-attachment = f & stalk-surface-below-ring = s & veil-type = p & veil-color = w
72	1272	1.00	cap-shape = x & odor = n & stalk-surface-below-ring = s & veil-type = p
73	1264	0.98	bruises = f & odor = n & gill-attachment = f & veil-type = p & veil-color = w
74	1264	1.00	bruises = f & odor = n & gill-size = b & veil-type = p
75	1264	0.91	bruises = t & gill-attachment = f & stalk-surface-above-ring = s & veil-type = p & veil-color = w & ring-number = o & ring-type = p & spore-print-color = n
76	1236	1.00	cap-surface = f & odor = n & gill-attachment = f & stalk-surface-above-ring = s & veil-type = p & veil-color = w
77	1236	1.00	cap-surface = f & odor = n & gill-attachment = f & stalk-surface-below-ring = s & veil-type = p & veil-color = w
78	1200	0.92	gill-attachment = f & gill-spacing = w & stalk-color-above-ring = w & veil-type = p & veil-color = w
79	1200	1.00	bruises = f & odor = n & gill-attachment = f & stalk-color-above-ring = w & stalk-color-below-ring = w & veil-type = p & veil-color = w
80	1192	0.99	cap-color = n & gill-size = b & veil-type = p
81	1187	0.76	cap-surface = y & gill-attachment = f & stalk-surface-above-ring = s & stalk-surface-below-ring = s & veil-type = p & veil-color = w
82	1168	0.99	cap-color = n & odor = n & veil-type = p
83	1152	0.92	cap-surface = f & gill-attachment = f & veil-type = p & veil-color = w & ring-type = p
84	1126	0.76	cap-surface = y & gill-attachment = f & stalk-surface-above-ring = s & stalk-surface-below-ring = s & veil-type = p & veil-color = w & ring-number = o
85	1120	1.00	cap-color = n & gill-size = b & veil-type = p & ring-number = o
86	1104	1.00	cap-surface = f & odor = n & gill-attachment = f & veil-type = p & veil-color = w & ring-type = p
87	1104	1.00	bruises = f & odor = n & gill-attachment = f & gill-spacing = w & stalk-color-above-ring = w & veil-type = p & veil-color = w
88	1096	1.00	cap-color = n & odor = n & gill-size = b & veil-type = p
89	1080	0.97	odor = n & veil-type = p & ring-number = o & population = v
90	1060	1.00	cap-shape = x & odor = n & veil-type = p & ring-type = p
91	1056	1.00	odor = n & stalk-surface-above-ring = s & veil-type = p & ring-number = o & population = v

The Table 24 contains the **strict rules for Class p** with the value of minimal Rule Power index equal to 10%.

Table 24. Strict rules for Class p

N	Power	Accuracy	GMRT
0	2228	1.00	bruises = f & gill-spacing = c & stalk-surface-above-ring = k & veil-type = p & veil-color = w
1	2160	1.00	odor = f & gill-attachment = f & gill-spacing = c & veil-type = p & veil-color = w & ring-number = o
2	2160	1.00	bruises = f & gill-attachment = f & gill-spacing = c & stalk-surface-below-ring = k & veil-type = p & veil-color = w & ring-number = o
3	1760	1.00	bruises = f & gill-attachment = f & gill-spacing = c & gill-size = n & veil-type = p & veil-color = w & ring-number = o & ring-type = e & spore-print-color = w & population = v
4	1392	1.00	bruises = f & gill-attachment = f & gill-spacing = c & stalk-shape = e & stalk-root = b & veil-type = p & veil-color = w & ring-number = o
5	1296	1.00	bruises = f & gill-attachment = f & gill-spacing = c & stalk-color-above-ring = p & veil-type = p & veil-color = w & ring-number = o
6	1296	1.00	bruises = f & gill-attachment = f & gill-spacing = c & stalk-color-below-ring = p & veil-type = p & veil-color = w & ring-number = o
7	1152	1.00	cap-surface = s & gill-attachment = f & gill-spacing = c & stalk-shape = t & veil-type = p & veil-color = w & ring-number = o
8	1096		cap-surface = s & gill-attachment = f & gill-spacing = c & veil-type = p & veil-color = w & ring-number = o & population = v
9	1040	1.00	cap-surface = s & gill-attachment = f & gill-spacing = c & gill-size = n & veil-type = p & veil-color = w & ring-number = o
10	1008	1.00	bruises = f & gill-attachment = f & gill-spacing = c & veil-type = p & veil-color = w & ring-number = o & habitat = p
11	960	1.00	cap-surface = s & bruises = f & gill-attachment = f & gill-size = n & veil-type = p & veil-color = w & ring-number = o
12	876	1.00	cap-color = e & bruises = f & gill-spacing = c & veil-type = p & veil-color = w & spore-print-color = w
13	872	1.00	gill-attachment = f & gill-size = n & stalk-color-below-ring = w & veil-type = p & veil-color = w & ring-number = o & spore-print-color = w
14	712	1.00	cap-color = g & bruises = f & gill-attachment = f & stalk-shape = e & stalk-root = b & veil-type = p & veil-color = w & ring-number = o
15	672	1.00	cap-color = y & bruises = f & gill-attachment = f & stalk-shape = e & veil-type = p & ring-number = o
16	624	1.00	bruises = f & gill-attachment = f & stalk-shape = e & stalk-root = b & veil-type = p & veil-color = w & ring-number = o & habitat = d
17	612	1.00	gill-attachment = f & gill-spacing = c & gill-size = b & stalk-root = b & veil-type = p & veil-color = w & habitat = g
18	560	1.00	cap-surface = y & gill-attachment = f & gill-spacing = c & gill-size = n & stalk-surface-below-ring = s & veil-type = p & veil-color = w & ring-number = o
19	504	1.00	gill-attachment = f & gill-color = g & stalk-shape = e & stalk-root = b & veil-type = p & veil-color = w
20	504	1.00	cap-surface = y & cap-color = n & gill-attachment = f & gill-spacing = c & gill-size = n & veil-type = p & veil-color = w & ring-number = o
21	496	1.00	cap-shape = f & cap-surface = s & gill-attachment = f & gill-spacing = c & veil-type = p & veil-color = w & ring-number = o
22	480	1.00	bruises = f & gill-attachment = f & gill-size = n & stalk-surface-below-ring = s & veil-type = p & veil-color = w & ring-number = o & habitat = d
23	480	1.00	bruises = f & gill-attachment = f & gill-color = p & stalk-shape = e & stalk-root = b & veil-type = p & veil-color = w & ring-number = o

The Table 25 contains the **strict rules for Class e** with the value of minimal Rule Power index equal to 10%.

Table 25. Strict rules for Class e

N	Power	Accuracy	GMRT
24	2688	1.00	odor = n & gill-size = b & veil-type = p & ring-number = o
25	2064	1.00	odor = n & gill-spacing = c & stalk-surface-above-ring = s & veil-type = p & ring-number = o
26	1824	1.00	bruises = t & gill-attachment = f & stalk-shape = t & stalk-root = b & stalk-surface-above-ring = s & stalk-surface-below-ring = s & veil-type = p & veil-color = w & ring-number = o & ring-type = p & habitat = d
27	1736	1.00	odor = n & gill-attachment = f & gill-spacing = c & gill-size = b & stalk-root = b & veil-type = p & veil-color = w & ring-type = p & habitat = d
28	1648	1.00	gill-size = b & veil-type = p & ring-number = o & spore-print-color = n
29	1600	1.00	gill-attachment = f & gill-size = b & veil-type = p & veil-color = w & ring-number = o & spore-print-color = k
30	1476	1.00	cap-shape = x & odor = n & gill-size = b & veil-type = p
31	1392	1.00	cap-surface = f & odor = n & gill-attachment = f & gill-size = b & veil-type = p & veil-color = w
32	1344	1.00	odor = n & veil-type = p & ring-number = o & spore-print-color = n
33	1312	1.00	cap-surface = y & bruises = t & gill-attachment = f & gill-spacing = c & gill-size = b & stalk-surface-above-ring = s & veil-type = p & veil-color = w & ring-number = o & ring-type = p
34	1296	1.00	gill-attachment = f & stalk-shape = t & veil-type = p & veil-color = w & ring-number = o & spore-print-color = n
35	1296	1.00	cap-shape = x & odor = n & stalk-surface-above-ring = s & veil-type = p
36	1296	1.00	odor = n & gill-attachment = f & veil-type = p & veil-color = w & ring-number = o & spore-print-color = k
37	1296	1.00	cap-surface = f & gill-attachment = f & stalk-shape = t & veil-type = p & veil-color = w & ring-number = o
38	1272	1.00	cap-shape = x & odor = n & stalk-surface-below-ring = s & veil-type = p
39	1264	1.00	bruises = f & odor = n & gill-size = b & veil-type = p
40	1236	1.00	cap-surface = f & odor = n & gill-attachment = f & stalk-surface-above-ring = s & veil-type = p & veil-color = w
41	1236	1.00	cap-surface = f & odor = n & gill-attachment = f & stalk-surface-below-ring = s & veil-type = p & veil-color = w
42	1200	1.00	bruises = f & odor = n & gill-attachment = f & stalk-color-above-ring = w & stalk-color-below-ring = w & veil-type = p & veil-color = w
43	1120	1.00	cap-color = n & gill-size = b & veil-type = p & ring-number = o
44	1104	1.00	cap-surface = f & odor = n & gill-attachment = f & veil-type = p & veil-color = w & ring-type = p
45	1104	1.00	bruises = f & odor = n & gill-attachment = f & gill-spacing = w & stalk-color-above-ring = w & veil-type = p & veil-color = w
46	1096	1.00	cap-color = n & odor = n & gill-size = b & veil-type = p
47	1060	1.00	cap-shape = x & odor = n & veil-type = p & ring-type = p
48	1056	1.00	odor = n & stalk-surface-above-ring = s & veil-type = p & ring-number = o & population = v
49	1048	1.00	cap-color = n & gill-size = b & stalk-surface-above-ring = s & veil-type = p
50	1048	1.00	gill-attachment = f & gill-spacing = c & stalk-surface-above-ring = s & veil-type = p & veil-color = w & population = y
51	1040	1.00	gill-attachment = f & gill-spacing = c & veil-type = p & veil-color = w & ring-type = p & population = y
52	1032	1.00	cap-color = g & odor = n & gill-attachment = f & veil-type = p & veil-color = w
53	1032	1.00	odor = n & stalk-surface-below-ring = s & veil-type = p & ring-number = o & population = v
54	1012	1.00	cap-color = n & odor = n & stalk-surface-below-ring = s & veil-type = p

55	1012	1.00	cap-color = n & odor = n & stalk-surface-above-ring = s & veil-type = p
56	968	1.00	odor = n & gill-attachment = f & gill-spacing = c & veil-type = p & veil-color = w & population = y
57	960	1.00	odor = n & gill-attachment = f & gill-size = b & veil-type = p & veil-color = w & ring-type = e
58	914	1.00	cap-shape = f & gill-attachment = f & stalk-root = b & veil-type = p & veil-color = w & ring-type = p & habitat = d
59	912	1.00	odor = n & gill-attachment = f & stalk-root = b & veil-type = p & veil-color = w & ring-number = o & population = v
60	912	1.00	cap-surface = f & odor = n & gill-attachment = f & stalk-color-below-ring = w & veil-type = p & veil-color = w
61	900	1.00	cap-shape = x & odor = n & gill-attachment = f & stalk-root = b & veil-type = p & veil-color = w
62	896	1.00	gill-spacing = c & gill-size = b & stalk-shape = e & stalk-surface-above-ring = s & veil-type = p & ring-number = o & ring-type = p
63	888	1.00	cap-surface = f & odor = n & gill-attachment = f & stalk-root = b & veil-type = p & veil-color = w & ring-number = o
64	888	1.00	bruises = f & odor = n & stalk-surface-above-ring = s & veil-type = p
65	888	1.00	cap-color = n & gill-spacing = c & gill-size = b & veil-type = p & ring-type = p
66	880	1.00	gill-size = b & gill-color = n & veil-type = p & ring-number = o
67	872	1.00	cap-shape = x & odor = n & gill-attachment = f & stalk-color-below-ring = w & veil-type = p & veil-color = w
68	864	1.00	gill-attachment = f & gill-spacing = w & stalk-shape = t & stalk-color-above-ring = w & stalk-color-below-ring = w & veil-type = p & veil-color = w & ring-number = o
69	840	1.00	bruises = f & odor = n & stalk-surface-below-ring = s & veil-type = p
70	840	1.00	cap-color = n & odor = n & gill-spacing = c & veil-type = p & ring-type = p
71	756	1.00	odor = n & gill-attachment = f & gill-color = p & veil-type = p & veil-color = w
72	712	1.00	odor = n & gill-color = n & veil-type = p & ring-number = o
73	696	1.00	cap-shape = x & cap-surface = y & bruises = t & gill-attachment = f & gill-spacing = c & gill-size = b & stalk-surface-above-ring = s & veil-type = p & veil-color = w
74	666	1.00	cap-shape = x & cap-surface = y & gill-attachment = f & gill-spacing = c & gill-size = b & veil-type = p & veil-color = w & ring-type = p
75	656	1.00	gill-attachment = f & gill-color = n & stalk-shape = t & veil-type = p & veil-color = w & ring-number = o
76	624	1.00	cap-color = e & bruises = t & odor = n & gill-attachment = f & gill-spacing = c & gill-size = b & stalk-surface-above-ring = s & stalk-surface-below-ring = s & veil-type = p & veil-color = w
77	624	1.00	cap-color = n & odor = n & gill-attachment = f & stalk-root = b & veil-type = p & veil-color = w
78	600	1.00	odor = n & gill-attachment = f & stalk-surface-above-ring = s & veil-type = p & veil-color = w & ring-type = e
79	600	1.00	odor = n & gill-attachment = f & stalk-surface-below-ring = s & veil-type = p & veil-color = w & ring-type = e
80	592	1.00	bruises = f & odor = n & stalk-shape = e & veil-type = p & ring-type = p
81	588	1.00	cap-shape = f & cap-surface = f & gill-attachment = f & stalk-surface-above-ring = s & veil-type = p & veil-color = w & ring-number = o
82	588	1.00	cap-shape = f & cap-surface = f & gill-attachment = f & stalk-surface-below-ring = s & veil-type = p & veil-color = w & ring-number = o
83	576	1.00	cap-color = n & gill-attachment = f & gill-size = b & stalk-color-below-ring = w & veil-type = p & veil-color = w
84	576	1.00	cap-color = n & gill-attachment = f & gill-size = b & stalk-color-above-ring = w & veil-type = p & veil-color = w
85	528	1.00	odor = n & gill-attachment = f & gill-size = b & stalk-shape = e & veil-type = p & veil-color = w & ring-number = t & spore-print-color = w

86	528	1.00	cap-shape = x & gill-size = b & stalk-shape = e & stalk-surface-above-ring = s & veil-type = p
87	528	1.00	cap-color = n & odor = n & gill-attachment = f & stalk-color-below-ring = w & veil-type = p & veil-color = w
88	516	1.00	cap-shape = x & gill-size = b & stalk-shape = e & veil-type = p & ring-type = p
89	496	1.00	cap-shape = x & gill-attachment = f & gill-size = b & stalk-shape = e & stalk-color-above-ring = w & veil-type = p & veil-color = w
90	496	1.00	cap-shape = x & gill-attachment = f & gill-size = b & stalk-shape = e & stalk-color-below-ring = w & veil-type = p & veil-color = w
91	496	1.00	gill-attachment = f & gill-size = b & stalk-shape = e & stalk-color-above-ring = w & stalk-color-below-ring = w & veil-type = p & veil-color = w & ring-type = p & population = s
92	476	1.00	gill-attachment = f & gill-color = w & stalk-surface-above-ring = s & veil-type = p & veil-color = w & ring-number = o & habitat = d
93	472	1.00	gill-attachment = f & gill-color = w & stalk-root = b & veil-type = p & veil-color = w & ring-type = p & habitat = d
94	456	1.00	bruises = f & odor = n & gill-attachment = f & stalk-surface-below-ring = f & stalk-color-above-ring = w & veil-type = p & veil-color = w & ring-number = o
95	432	1.00	cap-shape = x & gill-size = b & stalk-shape = e & stalk-surface-below-ring = s & veil-type = p

Chapter 11
Object–Oriented Technology for Expert System Generation

ABSTRACT

A technology for rapid prototyping expert systems or intelligent systems as a whole is proposed. The main constituents of the technology are the object-oriented model of data and knowledge representation and the mechanism for data-knowledge transformation on the basis of an effective algorithm of inferring all good classification tests. An approach to expert system development by means of this technology is analyzed. The toolkits for expert system generation are described and the application of these tools to the development of a small geological expert system is demonstrated.

INTRODUCTION

The epoch of certain skepticism with respect to expert systems came after the period of the bloom of their development and application in the 80s-90s of past century. This is explained by several reasons:

- Extremely complex proved to be the problem of obtaining knowledge directly from the experts;
- The knowledge packed into knowledge bases is actually static and isolated from its bearers – the experts;
- The mechanisms of machine learning on which creating new knowledge is based, prove frequently to be labor-consuming and do not cover all problems of data mining. In reality, any applied problem requires the full-scale application of entire arsenal of data mining methods including statistical methods, preliminary data analysis, formation and interpretation of knowledge.

DOI: 10.4018/978-1-60566-810-9.ch011

However, the loss of interest in expert system development is not entirely justified. This activity is an excellent research field allowing finding some new solutions for the problems of dynamic interaction of data and knowledge in computers.

In this chapter, the experience of creating a small and rather simple expert system is described in which the problem of data-knowledge interaction has been solved on the basis of integrating deductive and inductive inferences.

The following programs have been created for maintaining the process of automated development of expert system: the Former of Problem Domain (or Problem Domain Generator), the Interface Generator (or Object-Oriented Window's Editor), and the Editor of Knowledge and Data. The program of Knowledge Interpreter performs the deductive inference in expert system. The program BESTTEST realizes the inductive inference of logical rules of the first type from expert examples. The expert system has been applied to selecting the necessary and sufficient collections of aircraft and satellite surveys of earth's surface with the goal of automated geological mapping.

AN OBJECT-ORIENTED MODEL FOR DATA AND KNOWLEDGE REPRESENTATION

The main requirements to the knowledge bases of expert systems can be formulated as follows:

- The naturalness of knowledge representation with the point of view of experts;
- The possibility of direct completion of knowledge base by experts;
- The natural interaction between the data and knowledge bases.

The object - oriented model of knowledge representation meets these requirements most adequately.

An object-oriented model of data and knowledge representation is based on the following basic elements: CLASS OF OBJECT (OBJECT, as a particular case of CLASS), ATTRIBUTE, VALUE of ATTRIBUTE and LINK. The creation of domain models is directed by a domain expert. This model is used for generating the schemes of database and the interface to the data and knowledge bases of expert system, simultaneously. Therefore the model of database is also object-oriented (OODM). The object-oriented knowledge model (OOKM) is an extension of the OODM and the rules contained in knowledge base are viewed as the links between the conceptual unites of database (attributes, values of attributes).

Our approach to developing expert systems supports the following technology:

- Analysis of problem domain;
- Creating the object - oriented model of problem domain;
- Creating the interface to data and knowledge bases;
- Entering and editing data and knowledge via the interface obtained;
- Developing the mechanism of logical inference for a particular application;
- Evolution of expert system with the use of machine learning mechanisms.

The main advantages of the technology proposed are:

- The simplicity of data-knowledge integration;
- The possibility of creating a diversity of independent models of problem domain;
- The simplicity of data-knowledge updating;
- The possibility to transform the development of expert systems in the natural evolution of their knowledge.

Attribute. Value of Attribute

An elementary unit of knowledge is an attribute with its unambiguous range of values and domain of definition. The domain of definition is the set of objects possessing the property associated with this attribute. Thus the attribute is the function assigned on a set of objects. The range of attribute values has the name coincident with the name of attribute.

The isolation of a sub-range of attribute's values is an elementary step of classification. Attributes are similar to classifications. For example, using, function COLOR with a certain set of objects as its domain, we can form the assertions of such a type as 'THE COLOR OF SNOW IS WHITE' or 'SNOW WHITE', if we omit the name of attribute.

Complex functions are built from the elementary ones as follows: $A(B(x))$, where the domain of function A is the range of function B, for example, 'THE FATHER OF MY FATHER'. New attributes can be created with the aid of different operations - logical, arithmetical, taxonomic, classification - on the set of elementary attributes.

In our expert system, we are limited, for this goal, to inferring functional relations between attributes, implications between values of attributes, and isolating sub-ranges of the attribute ranges.

Object. Class of Objects

We assume object to be any concept, real thing or abstraction used by the specialists. The object is described by a set of attributes which are necessary and sufficient for identifying all exemplars of this object. We assume class of objects to be any collection of objects having the same values of a set of attributes and possessing the name and the meaning. Object is a special kind of class.

In our expert system, we use the following objects: one target object 'SURVEY', and the objects 'TASK', GEOLOGICAL CONDITION', and 'LANDSCAPE' determining the target object.

Links

The knowledge of specialists in the task under discussion consists of three components:

- Knowledge of the geological tasks and the conditions for their conducting - geological conditions, landscape conditions, etc;
- Knowledge of the types of remote surveys;
- Knowledge of the regular connections between the conditions of surveying and the types of surveys.

The knowledge of the first two categories represents a relatively conservative component of knowledge. This knowledge is frequently expressed in the form of hierarchical classifications of concepts (ontology) produced in the domain of application. For example, the landscapes are divided into the types and the subtypes, the geological time is divided into the geological epochs, and the geological conditions are divided into the classes in accordance with the geological periods of their formation and so on.

The hierarchical classifications can be represented by the use of functional dependencies. In our case, THE TYPE OF LANDSCAPE can be considered as the attribute of object or class LANDSCAPE, and THE SUBTYPE OF LANDSCAPE - as the attribute with respect to THE TYPE OF LANDSCAPE. As a result, we have a class LANDSCAPE with two attributes, connected functionally:

SUBTYPE OF LANDSCAPE $\rightarrow$ THE TYPE OF LANDSCAPE $\rightarrow$ LANDSCAPE;

(tundra, desert,....) $\rightarrow$ THE TYPE OF LANDSCAPE;

(lake - glacial plains,...) $\rightarrow$ THE SUBTYPE OF LANDSCAPE.

The functional connections between attributes can be reduced to the implicative connections between the values of attributes entering the functional dependencies. For example, we have that

THE SUBTYPE OF LANDSCAPE = lake - glacial plains $\rightarrow$ THE TYPE OF LANDSCAPE = tundra.

There are also many-valued dependencies between objects and/or between attributes of one and the same object as well as between attributes of different objects. For example, concept GEOLOGICAL TASK is determined with the aid of two attributes THE TYPE OF TASK and THE SCALE OF TASK. One scale can be related to the tasks of several types and one task can be connected with the different scales. The connections between values of attributes can also be syntactic. These connections are expressed with the aid of special procedures.

AN APPROACH TO EXPERT SYSTEM DEVELOPMENT

Analysis of Problem Domain

Our technology and tools OODM and OOKM have been used for developing a geological expert system to assist the users in choosing the necessary and sufficient aerial and satellite surveys under solving the tasks of geo-mineral-genetic mapping.

The analysis of problem domain consists in revealing the main components of knowledge necessary and sufficient for solving the given task. For our geological task, the following objects have been defined: TASK, LANDSCAPE, GEOLOGICAL CONDITION, and SURVEY. The target object SURVEY has three attributes: ROLE OF SURVEY, THE KIND OF SURVEY, and THE TYPE OF SURVEY. This object is functionally defined by the other objects, i.e. we have the following dependency:

TASK, LANDSCAPE, GEOLOGICAL CONDITION $\rightarrow$ SURVEY.

This functional dependency allows defining the values of all attributes of SURVEY via the values of attributes of objects TASK, LANDSCAPE, and GEOLOGICAL CONDITION. The values of TASK, LANDSCAPE, and GEOLOGICAL CONDITION are given by the users. The classifications of objects and the dependencies revealed in the problem domain are used for constructing the OODM and OOKM of expert system.

Creating the Object-Oriented Models of Data and Knowledge

The object-oriented model is used for the representation of both data and knowledge. An object description corresponds to a scheme of relation and a collection of object instances associated with the scheme corresponds to a relation of database. The links between objects in the form of dependencies constitute the content of the system knowledge base. The results of problem domain analysis are encoded by the use of the Former of Problem Domain (or Problem Domain Generator). This program incarnates the ontology of problem domain.

Creating the Interface to Data and Knowledge Bases

Each object is associated with a set of interconnected windows for inputting and outputting of attribute values of this object. For example, object TASK has two associated with it windows THE TYPE OF TASK and THE SCALE OF TASK (Figure 1). These windows are connected in the correspondence with a many-valued dependence assigned by the expert.

If the user selects Task 1, then Windows 1 will be displayed for choosing the scale of the task, if Task 2 is selected, then Windows 2 will be displayed for the same goal. If the user selects Scale 1: 50000, then 'Task of Types 1' and 'Task of Type 2' will be displayed.

In the following example (Table 1), the types of geological conditions are considered. Selecting the conditions are limited by the forbidden rule: the pairs of conditions (1, 2), (3, 4), and (5, 6) is impossible.

Entering and Editing Data and Knowledge

The program EDITOR OF KNOWLEDGE AND DATA provides the users with the possibilities to enter and edit knowledge and data. The dependencies between objects and attribute values are expressed in the form of "if – then" rules and, in parallel, in a limited natural language.

Table 1. The list of options for geological condition

The Type of Geological Conditions
1. Quaternary, sedimentary
2. Quaternary, volcanic
3. Napped, sedimentary
4. Napped, volcanic
5. Folded, metamorphic
6. Folded, sedimentary-volcanic

Figure 1. Link between windows of an object

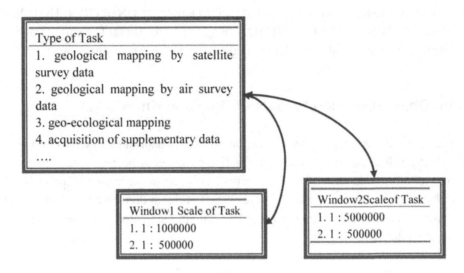

The content of the system database is formed by entering facts or examples of surveys' selections in real situations of geological mapping. Each fact joins the concrete descriptions of all objects TASK, LANDSCAPE, GEOLOGICAL CONDITION, and SURVEY associated with a real work of surveying for some already implemented task of geological mapping.

The representation of data and knowledge by the use of single formalism allows to combine data and knowledge from the very first days of the existence of an expert system and to provide the natural way for the machine learning application for data-knowledge transformation and verification.

Creating the Mechanism of Logical Inference

The logical inference in our expert system is maximally reflects the mode of experts' reasoning in the tasks of selecting the types of surveys. It realizes the model of deductive reasoning described in Chapter 5. The interpreter of rules determines all the possible combinations of surveys induced from the given geological task of mapping and the conditions in which this task will be carried on.

Expert System Realization and Evolution

The first version of the expert system has been implemented on C++ for IBM PC and compatible computers. The evolution of this system bases on inputting new facts in the data base and new rules in the knowledge base. The new rules can be directly included in the knowledge base by the experts or inferred from facts by the use of machine learning algorithm BESTTEST described in (Naidenova et al., 1995a; 1995b). Inputting facts and rules by the experts is supported by the program EDITOR OF KNOWLEDGE AND DATA. This program is tuned to the domain-dependent object-oriented model of data and knowledge. The program BESTTEST infers functional and implicative dependencies from facts and extracts new classes of objects with their collections of assigned attributes.

THE TOOL-KITS FOR EXPERT SYSTEM GENERATION

The object-oriented model is used for both data and knowledge representation. Using one and the same model for data and knowledge provides the following possibilities:

- to integrate data and knowledge in the beginning of an expert system generation;
- to construct an object-oriented interface to the expert system;
- to facilitate updating data and knowledge because of modifying each object is performed independently.

Naturally, updating the database is accompanied by updating the knowledge by inferring new rules from facts, and updating the knowledge base from the side of expert can evoke inputting new facts into the database.

The Former (Generator) of Problem Domain

The Former of Problem Domain (or Problem Domain Generator) is an interactive program encoding the results of problem domain analysis. This program allows entering, editing, browsing objects, attributes and their values with the use of menu and functional keys.

The Interface Generator (the Object-Oriented Window's Editor)

The Interface Generator creates a set of windows and the links between them. This program is practically an object - oriented windows editor.

Each object is represented by a group of windows, each of which is associated with one attribute of this object and permits to enter the attribute values. The knowledge engineer in collaboration with the domain expert gives the links between attributes based on the acquired relations in the problem domain.

The Interface Generator supports the following user actions:

- Creation, deletion, modification and location of windows;
- Fulfillment of windows;
- Creation the fields for entering knowledge/data;
- Creating the helps associated with windows;
- Editing the links between windows.

The Link Editor allows to the user:

- Establishing the links between objects and windows
- Linking windows in accordance with a given order taking into account known dependencies between attributes.

The Links between windows determine the order of querying the users in the process of logical inference.

It is possible, in principle, to use machine learning for inferring the links between windows based on the windows generated by the domain expert and a given set of training object examples.

The results of working the Interface Generator are used by the programs Editor of Knowledge and Data and Logical Inference.

The interface generated not only reflects the ontology of problem domain but produces a certain part of logical inference with the rules working "inside" the objects.

The Editor of Knowledge and Data

This program provides the users with the traditional possibilities to edit knowledge and data. There are the following possibilities:

- Choice of the knowledge base;
- Creating a new rule;
- Editing rules;
- Viewing rules in the text form;
- Deleting rules.

The maximal size of knowledge base is equal to 65535.

Logical Reasoning

The Reasoning Rules

In our model of logical inference, the following two kinds of reasoning rules are used:

- Rules creating an exemplar of object of a given type and establishing the values of its attributes;
- Rules extending object descriptions.

The reasoning rule of the first type creates the initial descriptions of objects. The initial description of an object exampler has the value of one of attributes of this object in its right part and its left part is either empty or contains the value of at least one attribute of this object different from the attribute of its right part. Thus, with the use of this reasoning rule, the Interpreter initiates the exemplars of object with the partial descriptions.

The rule of the second kind infers the unknown values of attributes in the object descriptions. This reasoning rule performs the extention of initiated examplars of object based on the content of knowledge base.

The program of logical inference (the Interpreter) maximally extends the descriptions of all initiated exemplars of the target object. It determines a minimal combination of the target object exemplars the descriptions of which do not include one another and do not contradict the knowledge and the conditions given by the user.

The work of this program includes the following operations:

- Loading the knowledge base;
- Querying the user;
- Running the Interpreter of Reasoning Rules
- Output the results;
- Explanation the results.

Loading the knowledge base is performed both automatically and by the user request. Then the querying of user is performed. The user may skip some questions.

The Interpreter of Reasoning Rules

The Interpreter of Reasoning Rules analyzes the examplars of already initiated objects and the following acts are performed:

1. If there exist the equal (non distinguished) examplars of the same object, then only one examplar is retained;
2. If two examplars of the same object are compartible, then they are joined.

Descriptions are compartible if they do not contain different values of one and the same attribute and in the same time their joint description does not contains any forbidden combination of attribute values.

Result of the Interpreteter's work is the minimal set of distinct and maximally extended target object's examplers. The descriptions of obtained exemplars of the target object are demonstrated to the user in terms of his application domain. The text on the monitor can be viewed by the use of scrolling.

The result of inference is memorized in the database of the system.

EXAMPLES OF USING THE EXPERT SYSTEM TO ASSIST IN CHOOSING THE TYPES OF ARIEL AND SATELLITE SURVEYS FOR GEO-MINERALOGICAL MAPPING

Consider several examples of logical inference.

Example 1. The situation given by the user is presented in Table 2.
The rules performed by Interpreter

Table 2 The query of the user for example 1

Object	Attribute	Value
Task	Type of Task	Geo-minerogenetic mapping
	Scale of Task	1:200000
Landscape	Type of Landscape	Tundra
Geological Region	Type of Region	Cover – Volcanic

1. If Task, Type of Task = Geo mineral-genetic mapping
    Then Survey, Role of Survey = General & Type of Survey = Photo.
2. If Survey, Role of Survey = General & Task, Scale of Task = 1:
200000,
      Then Survey, Scale of Survey = 1:200000.
3. If Survey, Role of Survey = General & Scale of Survey = 1:100000
or 1: 50000 or 1: 200000
      Then Survey, Kind of Survey = Cosmic.
4. If Task, Type of Task = Geo mineral-genetic mapping
    Then Survey, Role of Survey = Additional &
              Survey, Type of Survey = Photo &
              Survey, Kind of Survey = Cosmic &
                  If Task, Scale of Task = 1:200000
                  Then Survey, Scale of Survey = 1:500000.
5. If Landscape = Tundra or
                          Forest-Tundra (boreal-subtropical) or
                          Taiga (boreal) or
                          Broad-leaved (sub-boreal, humid) or
                          Forest-steppe (semi-humid) or
                          Desert (extra-arid) or
                          Subtropical
    Then Survey, Role of Survey = Additional &
            Survey, the Type of Survey = Multi-zonal &
            Survey, the Kind of Survey = Cosmic &
                If Task, Scale of Task = 1:200000
                Then Survey, Scale of Survey = 1:500000.

Table 3. The results of interpreter's work for example 1

Object	Attribute	Value
Survey 1	Role of Survey	Principle
	Type of Survey	Photo
	Scale of Survey	1:200000
	Kind of Survey	Cosmic
Survey 2	Role of Survey	Additional
	Type of Survey	Photo
	Kind of Survey	Cosmic
	Scale of Survey	1:500000
Survey 3	Role of Survey	Additional
	Type f Survey	Multi-zonal
	Kind of Survey	Csmic
	Scale of Survey	1:500000

The answer of the Interpreter is presented in Table 3.

Example 2. The situation given by the user is presented in Table 4.
The answer of the Interpreter is presented in Table 5.

RELATED WORKS

The object oriented paradigm has become the dominant force in creating computer systems. Two reasons seem to promote this phenomenon:

- Object orientation enables specialists to think about application development the same way they think about the world around them - in terms of "things" rather than "processes". Hence, object-oriented programming (OOP) is more "intuitive" than other programming paradigms;
- Object orientation supports creating reusable software structures and leads to accelerating the design and implementation of computer systems.

But the first thesis is discussed. While most people say that OOP "is more natural and intuitive than non-OOP, they also say that OOP demands a lot of time and attention. With the point of view of cognitive psychologist, Joseph Schmuller (1996), it's a question of individual differences: perhaps some people think primarily in terms of objects, others in terms of processes.

In the work (Lin et al., 2003), a new object-oriented rule model (NORM) is proposed based on the concepts of learning and thinking behavior of human. It provides high maintainability and reusability through the object-oriented approach. There are considered four basic relations between knowledge concepts defined in NORM: Reference, Extension-of, Trigger and Acquire. These relations are helpful in describing the cooperation of the different knowledge concepts. In addition, it is described how to construct and maintain a knowledge base under this model. The rule base system platform DRAMA is also introduced in this paper. The system DRAMA is used in a learning management system to infer the knowledge for selecting appropriate learning content for different students.

In the article, "Objects in Business," Jerry Huchzermeier (1996) explains how object orientation will ultimately revolutionize business applications and catalyze Business Process Reengineering. Object orientation helps to build today's most important corporate applications. The thought process behind object orientation (viewing the real world in terms of its "players" rather than its "actions") leads to systems that model businesses in contrast to the systems that only support businesses.

A new methodology for integrated object-oriented expert systems development in business forecast-

Table 4. The query of the user for example 2

Object	Attribute	Value
Task	Type of Task	Geo-mineralogical mapping
	Scale of Task	1:100000
Landscape	Type of Landscape	Desert (extra arid)
Geological Region	Type of Region	Cover – sedimentary

Table 5. The results of interpreter's work for example 2

Object	Attribute	Value
Survey 1	Role of Survey	Principle
	Tpe of Survey	Photo
	Scale of Survey	1:100000
	Kind of Survey	Aero
Survey 2	Role of Survey	Additional
	Type of Survey	Photo
	Kind of Survey	Cosmic
	Scale of Survey	1:500000
Survey 3	Role of Survey	Additional
	Type of Survey	Radiolocation
	Scale of Survey	1:100000
Survey 4	Role of Survey	Additional
	Type of Survey	Photo
	Kind of Survey	Aero
	Scale of Survey	1:50000
Survey 5	Role of Survey	Additional
	Type of Survey	Infra red
	Scale of Survey	1:100000
	Kind ofSurvey	Aero
Survey 6	Role of Survey	Additional
	Type of Survey	Multi-zonal
	Kind o Survey	Cosmic
	Scale of Survey	1:20000

ing is advanced by Ng. Freeman S. (1997). This research is an attempt to tackle some of the existing problems of using expert systems in business forecasting. Creating effective business forecasting expert systems requires the smooth integration of statistical data and forecasting heuristics capable of obtaining accurate and acceptable forecasting results. The literature survey reveals that the existent formal expert systems development methodology is insufficient for business forecasting purposes. Various enhancements to business forecasting expert systems have been considered including the integration of statistical techniques, decision support systems, neural networks, and the object-oriented approach. None except the object-oriented approach can satisfy the criteria of consistent representation of quantitative data, heuristics knowledge and full development life cycle coverage. A new methodology, "Methodology for Integrated Object-Oriented Expert Systems Development (MIOOESD)", has been developed. MIOOESD covers the full development cycle systematically in procedures, techniques, and documentation. A business forecasting expert system (called "Intelligent Forecaster", IF) has been successfully developed and implemented using MIOOESD. As the author states, the experience gained from implementing this system leads to a better understanding of the object-oriented expert systems approach in business forecasting.

Effective programming is very necessary to support object-oriented modeling data and knowledge. With this point of view, it is interesting the work on elaborating R++ programming language (Weiss, & Pos, 1998). R++ rules share the object-oriented properties of C++ member functions: inheritance, polymorphism, and dynamic binding. R++ is an extension to the C++ language that adds support for object-oriented rules. This language allows modeling rule-based inferring on the basis of constructing links between objects, classes and values of attributes. Rules can be seen as a communication mechanism rather than as a way of declaratively encoding knowledge, even though rules are used in both ways. Integrating R++ with C++ gives the possibility to effectively code declarative and procedural knowledge. The use of R++'s object-oriented rules significantly aided the design and implementation of ANSWER, the operation support system responsible for monitoring and maintaining the AT&T.

The issue 2 of PC/AI March-April 2001, vol. 15 outlines a number of technologies with a focus on Intelligent Web Applications and Object Oriented Development (OOD). One of the articles (Wegener, 2001) discusses the use of an object-oriented technology based on the more traditional AI and OOD languages. Although some of these languages have been applied for a long time (Lisp - 1958, Prolog - 1972, Smalltalk - 1972, and Dylan - 1992), they compare very favorably with their more modern counterparts. These languages have many improvements currently and the explosion in the platform capabilities. Wegener, H. takes a detailed look at the Dylan programming language and some of its semantic constructs.

The paper (Dlodlo et al., 2007) describes the design of an expert system integrating both object-oriented and rule-based reasoning approaches. The system is based on the premise that the design of a component should be separated from the implementation details. Separation of object definitions from rules that manipulate them in the knowledge base, and separation of the object-based knowledge base from the object-based inference engine, means that any changes made to any one of these components do not necessarily require the changes of the other components. Dependencies between components of an object, the inheritance properties, and the extendibility and reusability of objects are just some of the advantages of object-oriented approach in this application.

The authors (Ramamoorthy & Sheu, 1988) address the impact of object-oriented models on programming environments, expert systems and databases. The authors also discuss related problems and highlight important research directions.

Researchers and software designers come to a conclusion that identifying objects is an ill-defined task and there is no unified methodology for object-oriented software design. In (Wahono & Far, 1999), the authors suggest an approach to solve the difficulties of object-oriented design by developing a distributed expert system that contains design patterns and rules that aims at automating object-oriented design process in an interactive way. A novel point is the using of an interactive user interface to enable software designer and the system communicate with each other in order to determine the best design, without disturbing the creativity of the designer.

For Krause et al. (1993), a product model must contain information including data, their structure and algorithms. The algorithms correspond to the bridge between the user, the data and the structure.

According to Szykman et al. (2000), it is of very importance the implementing of interfaces for creating, editing and browsing the design information that are easy and effective to use.

Juri, Saia and De Pennington (1990) proposed and implemented a product model in which two levels of abstraction are defined: the level of the part, and the level of the features.

In the paper (Maziero et al., 2000b), an Expert System for CAD to model and support product design is presented. The product is represented through a hierarchical structure that allows the user to navigate across the product's components. A graphical interface was also developed, which shows visually to the user the contents of the product structure. Features are used as building blocks for the parts that compose the product. The object-oriented methodology was used as a means to implement the product structure.

Maziero et al., (2000a) consider the classifications of features as they have been proposed by different researchers. A feature is a set of information adequately grouped in order to represent a product. Features are classified by their functions with respect to the product. Features can also be static and dynamic. The static features are primarily structural in their function, whereas the dynamic features perform the transfer of movement or energy to fulfill their function. There are the classifications of features into primary and secondary, and also into external and internal. Xue, Yadev and Norrie (1999) introduced the concept of an "aspect feature", which is a group of descriptions in a model for a particular product development purpose, such as design, manufacture and assembly.

The expert system must be adapted to certain variations that may occur when implementing a new application. The proposed modeling system (Maziero et al., 2000b) performs the following functions:

(a) The sub-module "Product Navigator" is used to navigate across the Product Data Structure. The navigator is tuned with the graphical interface, so that the user visualizes graphically the portion that corresponds to any location in the product structure. (b) The sub-module "Feature Manipulator" is responsible for feature instantiation, which consists of the following steps: the user chooses a feature in the Feature Library, and then he/she inputs its attributes. Some of the functions performed by the feature manipulator are: insert, modify and delete operations. In order to execute those functions, the feature manipulator communicates with the Expert System in order to verify the consistency of the operations. (c) The sub-module Auxiliary Functions contains some supporting functions, such as the one that performs mapping of the product structure into the graphical structure of the commercial CAD system. (d) The sub-module Information Assignment is responsible for fitting parts for each other. This function is performed through queries to the Manufacturing and Assembly Database, from which the requested information is obtained. The Communication Interface is responsible for the communication between the modeling and analytical modules and the inference engine, which is linked with the knowledge base. This interface converts data from the product data structure to the format of the expert system and vice-versa.

Wannarumon et al. (2007) proposes a new concept in developing collaborative design system. Simulation of Supply Chain Management (SCM) is added to collaborative design called 'SCM–Based Design Tool'. Designers and customers can collaborate by the system. JAG (Jewelry Art Generator), the system based on artificial intelligence techniques is integrated into the system. The proposed system can be used as a decision tool too. The system is developed on Web–assisted product development environment. The SCM-based design tool is integrated with an intelligent design system using in jewelry design and manufacturing.

The SCM is an effective methodology for various industries and businesses. Itt combines many processes in product life cycle from the use of raw materials to the stage that consumer purchases product. Therefore, the goal of this research is to analyze and identify objects that are necessary for modeling supply chain framework used in collaborative design and manufacturing.

SCM is the network of facilities and distribution options to support an association of vendors, suppliers, manufacturers, distributors, retailers, and other trading partners. Effective management of supply chain systems can be achieved by identifying customer service requirements, determining inventory placement and levels, and creating effective policies and procedures for the coordination of supply chain activities.

Rezayat (2000) propose the Enterprise-Web portal for life-cycle support. He suggests Web-based electronic access to design and manufacturing information within the extended enterprise based on a universal interface, open standards, ease of use, and ubiquity. He recommends combining the distributed object standards with the Web standards and protocols to create the Object Web.

Rossetti and Chan (2003) define the primary objects required for supply chain simulations and the relations of these objects. Xiang et al., (2005) present a collaborative design networks to represent collaborative design knowledge as multi-agent graphical models. They propose a set of algorithms that allow agents to produce an overall optimal design by autonomous evaluation of local designs.

The web-based part library used in collaborative design, concurrent engineering, virtual enterprise and SCM is developed in (Li,Y. et al., 2006).

The approach to construct the collaborative design and manufacturing network is based on Object-Oriented Modeling (OOM). The Unified Modeling Language (UML) is a set of OOM notations standardized by the Object Management Group (France et al., 1997). UML enables to depict the supply chain system like as a particular domain in OOM.

The system is created based on Web platform to support communications, collaborations and sharing data/information among users in the supply chain. The activities within the framework are viewed as dynamic actions that make up as a dynamic system. It is considered 24 systemic object classes. There exist 7 classes that represent the facilities within the supply chain simulation framework: CADSystem, DesignSystem, InspectionUnit, ManufacturingUnit, Model-MakingUnit, PackagingUnit, and WarehouseCenter. The major roles of facilities are supporting services, manufacturing products, distributing and delivering products/services to customers.

Relationship Network is designed as a complex system that represents the interconnected network nodes. Such nodes exchange and share data and information. A Relationship connects a pair of nodes and specifies the flow of information between them. A Node represents a facility in the supply chain framework. Customer, Designer, Model-Maker, and Supplier are viewed as actors in the supply chain framework. The UML sequence diagram illustrates the flow of data, information, materials along the entire framework.

Bentley (1999) considers the major elements of evolutionary algorithms in art and design such as genotype, phenotype, genetic operator, fitness function and selection.

Some expert systems developed comparatively recently indicate that the design expert system continues to be interesting for the specialists.

López-Moralis et al., (2008) describes Automated Hydroponics Greenhouses representing novel food production systems including modules for supervising the cultivated soil, as well as prevention, diagnosis and control of pests and diseases. In this setting, the design and implementation of an Integral Intelligent System called JAPIEST, is proposed which is focused on the prevention, diagnosis and control of diseases that affect tomatoes.

Mike Cresswick's focuses on an object-based expert system that helps with the cleanup of hazardous waste sites. This task involves a tortuous maze of complex regulations. Regional Project Manager in the Superfund Branch of Delaware's Department of Natural Resources and Environmental Control use an object oriented expert system to identify the regulations that govern cleanup activities at specific sites.

Leung (2007) deals with modeling inexact rule-base reasoning. The introduction of fuzzy concepts into object-oriented knowledge representation (OOKR) as a structural knowledge representation scheme is presented. Some new fuzzy concepts and operations are introduced in order to handle inheritance mechanisms and to model the relations among classes, instances, and attributes. A framework for handling all the possible fuzzy concepts in OOKR at both the dynamic and static level is proposed. A prototype of the expert system shell, the system EX-1, has been developed too.

In the questionnaire analysis (Chu et al., 2009), the task how to find a statistically significant difference between two or more groups of samples in a continuous measure is one of the major problems to research. The process of finding the statistically significant differences is highly dependent on researchers' intuition and experience, and the original questionnaire data may not be good enough for this goal. In this paper, a data warehouse and a forward-chaining rule-base expert system is built with three kinds of indicators - Increase, Step-Down, and Dice, for drilling down the data warehouse to assist researchers in exploring the data and to select appropriate statistics methods for finding possible significant differences. The prototype of this expert system has been implemented, and the results of experiments showed that finding the significant difference becomes easier, and the users were interested in the idea of this system.

CONCLUSION

We described the object-oriented model for knowledge and data representation, tool, and technology to facilitate rapid prototyping and, in the sequel, evolving of expert systems. Our approach has been inspired by the comprehension of the following integrity principles of intelligence: a unified language for data-knowledge representation, a unified learning approach, and a mechanism of supporting commonsense reasoning. The object-oriented model of problem domain is created by an expert with the use of the program Former of Problem Domain. In this program, it is used well known ideas of object-oriented programming expanded by a concept of link between attributes, values of attributes, objects and classes of objects. The advanced approach allows creating databases and knowledge bases in the framework of one and the same data and knowledge representation formalism. The object-oriented model of problem domain supports both rule-based inference for solving user's tasks and machine learning for the new knowledge elicitation from experts' examples.

REFERENCES

Bentley, P. (1999). *Evolutionary design by computers*. San Francisco: Morgan Kaufmann Publishers.

Chu, Y.-S., Tseng, S.-S., Tsai, Y.-J., & Luo, R.-J. (2009). An intelligent questionnaire analysis expert system. *Expert Systems with Applications*, *36*(2), 2699–2710. doi:10.1016/j.eswa.2008.01.076

Creswick, M. (1996). Objects and the environment - Site remediation. *PC/AI, 10*(2).

Dlodlo, N., Cyprian, L. H., Metelerkamp, C. R., & Botha, A. F. (2007). Integrating an object-oriented approach and rule-based reasoning иn the design of a fabric fault advisory expert system. *Fibre & . Textile in Eastern Europe, 15*(3), 68–71.

France, R., Evans, A., & Lano, K. (1997). The UML as a formal modeling notation. In H. Kilov, B. Rumpe, & I. Simmonds (Eds.), *Proc. OOPSLA'97 Workshop on Object-Oriented Behavioral Semantics, Atlanta, October 6th 1997* (pp. 75-81). Munich University of Technology, Tum-19737.

Huchzermeier J. (1996). Objects in business - Thinking in objects. *PC/AI, 10*(2).

Juri, A. H., Saia, A., & De Pennington, A. (1990). Reasoning about machining operations using feature-based models. *International Journal of Production Research, 28*(1), 153–171. doi:10.1080/00207549008942690

Krause, F.-L., Kimura, F., Kjellberg, T., & Lu, S. C.-Y. (1993). Product modeling. *Annals of the CIRP, 42*(2), 695–706. doi:10.1016/S0007-8506(07)62532-3

Leung, K. S., & Wong, M. N. (2007). Fuzzy concepts in an object-oriented expert system shell. *International Journal of Intelligent Systems, 7*(2), 171–192. doi:10.1002/int.4550070206

Li, Y., Lu, Y., Liao, W., & Lin, Z. (2006). Representation and share of part feature information in Web-based parts library. *Expert Systems with Applications, 31*(4), 697–704. doi:10.1016/j.eswa.2006.01.009

Lin, Y. T., Tseng, S. S., & Tsai, C.-F. (2003). Design and implementation of new object-oriented rule base management system. *Expert Systems with Applications, 25*(3), 369–385. doi:10.1016/S0957-4174(03)00064-2

López-Morales, O. López-Ortega, Ramos-Fernández, J., & Muñoz, L.B. (2008). JAPIEST: An integral intelligent system for the diagnosis and control of tomatoes diseases and pests in hydroponics greenhouses. *Expert Systems with Applications, 35*(4), 1506–1512. doi:10.1016/j.eswa.2007.08.098

Maziero, N. L., Espíndola, J. C., Ferreira, J. C. E., Pacheco, F. S., & Prim, M. F. (2000b). A feature-based object-oriented expert system to model and support product design. *Journal of the Brazilian Society of Mechanical Sciences, 22*(4), 524–543. doi:10.1590/S0100-73862000000400003

Maziero, N. L., Ferreira, J. C. E., & Pacheco, F. S. (2000a). An expert and procedural system for automatic identification of assembled parts. In J. M. Usher & H. Parsaei (Eds.), *Computer-aided process and assembly planning: Methods, tools and technologies*. The Netherlands: Gordon & Breach.

Naidenova, X. A., Chagalov, V. L., & Gladkov, D. V. (1993). Object-oriented technology for expert system generation. In P. Brezillon & V. Stefanuk (Eds.), *From theory to practice, Proceedings of the East-West Conference on Artificial Intelligence (EWAIC'93)* (pp. 223-226). Moscow, Russia: International Centre for Scientific and Technical Information (ICSTI).

Naidenova, X. A., Chagalov, V. L., Gladkov, D. V., & Kildushevskaja, Z. V. (1993). An object-oriented expert system generation. *International Journal " . Information Theory and Applications, 1*(5), 3–17.

Naidenova, X. A., Plaksin, M. V., & Shagalov, V. L. (1995b). Inductive inferring all good classification tests. In J. Valkman (Ed), *Knowledge-Dialog-Solution, Proceedings of International Conference in two volumes (KDS'95)* (Vol. 1, pp. 79-84). Kiev, Ukraine: Kiev Institute of Applied Informatics

Naidenova, X. A., Polegaeva, J. G., & Iserlis, J. E. (1995a). The system of knowledge acquisition based on constructing the best diagnostic classification tests. In J. Valkman (Ed.), *Knowledge-Dialog-Solution, Proceedings of International Conference in two volumes (KDS'95)* (Vol. 1, pp. 85-95). Kiev, Ukraine: Kiev Institute of Applied Informatics.

Ng, F. S. W. (1997). *A new methodology for integrated object-oriented expert systems development in business forecasting.* Unpublished MPhil Thesis in Information Systems. Hong Kong: Dept. of Information Systems, City University of Hong Kong.

Ramamoorthy, C. V., & Sheu, P. C. (1988). Object-oriented systems. *IEEE Expert: Intelligent Systems and Their Applications, 3*(3), 9–15.

Rezayat, M. (2000). Enterprise-Web portal for life cycle. *Computer Aided Design, 32*(2), 85–96. doi:10.1016/S0010-4485(99)00092-5

Rossetti, D., & Chan, H.-T. (2003). Supply chain management simulation: A prototype object-oriented supply chain simulation framework. In S. Chick, P. J. Sánchez, D. Ferrin, & D. J. Morrice (Eds.), *Driving Innovation, Proceedings of the 35th Winter Simulation Conference (WSC'03), New Orleans, Lousiana USA, December 7-10* (pp. 1612-1620). ACM Press.

Schmuller, J. (1996). Editorial: Object and intuitions. *PC/AI, 10*(2).

Szykman, S., Bochenek, C., Racz, J. W., Senfaute, J., & Sriram, R. D. (2000). Design repositories: Engineering design's new knowledge base. *IEEE Intelligent Systems, 15*(3), 48–55. doi:10.1109/5254.846285

Wahono, R. S., & Far, B. H. (1999). OOExpert: Distributed expert system for automatic object-oriented software design. *Proceedings of the Annual Conference of JSAI, 13,* 671–672.

Wannarumon, S., Ritvirool, A., & Boonrit, T. (2007). Collaborative design system based on object-oriented modeling of supply chain simulation: A case study of Thai jewelry industry. *International Journal of Computer, Information, and Systems Science, and Engineering, 1*(2), 128–135.

Wegener, H. (2001). What's behind the Dyland language? A brief overview. *PC/AI, 15*(2).

Weiss, G. M., & Ros, J. P. (1998). Implementing design patterns with object-oriented rules. [SIGS Publication Inc.]. *Journal of Object-Oriented Programming, 11*(7), 25–35.

Xiang, Y., Chen, J., & Havens, W. S. (2005). Optimal design in collaborative design network. In *Proceedings of the 4th International Conference on Autonomous Agents and Multi-agent Systems (AAMAS'05)* (pp. 241-248). New York: ACM.

Xue, D., Yadev, S., & Norrie, D. H. (1999). Knowledge base and database representation for intelligent concurrent design. *Computer Aided Design, 31*(2), 131–145. doi:10.1016/S0010-4485(99)00021-4

Chapter 12
Case Technology for Psycho-Diagnostic System Generation

ABSTRACT

The automated workstation (AWS) for psychologists and physiologists must be an instrument that allows adaptive programming applied psycho-diagnostic expert systems (APDS). For this goal, the AWS must contain toolkits for 1) the automated specification of adaptive psycho-diagnostic systems (APDS) directed by an expert; 2) the adaptation of these systems to changeable conditions of their functioning. We propose an automated technology for creating APDS, the main peculiarity of which consists in using machine learning methods to choose, validate, define and redefine the main constructive elements of psycho-diagnostic testing and decision making procedures utilized in the developed psycho-diagnostic systems.

INTRODUCTION

Machine learning and knowledge acquisition from experts have distinct capabilities that appear to complement one another. The integration of these approaches can both improve the accuracy of system's knowledge and reduce the time of APDS development. The expert systems created by means of the integrated approach possess higher accuracy than those created only by knowledge elicitation from experts without using machine learning methods.

We describe a software, called GENINTES (GENERATOR + INTERPRETER of EXPERT SYSTEMS), realizing an integrated CASE – technology (Naidenova et al., 1996a; Naidenova et al., 1996b) for expert system rapidly prototyping, creating and evolution.

DOI: 10.4018/978-1-60566-810-9.ch012

We consider both the statistical and logical (symbolic) methods of machine learning, so our approach encompasses the automated knowledge acquisition methods for a wide range of knowledge types.

The GENINTES is oriented to creating psycho-diagnostic systems. But it can be applied for creating diagnostic systems in medicine too. The GENINTES (the first version) has been realized in Visual Basic 6.0 on PC for XP operation system.

A TECHNOLOGY FOR FAST PROTOTYPING COMPLETELY DEFINED PSYCHO-DIAGNOSTIC EXPERT SYSTEMS

The development of psycho-diagnostic expert systems (PDSs) is a very complicated and time consuming process, as these systems include not only the diagnostic testing procedures but the knowledge required to interpret the results of testing.

In this chapter, a CASE - technology is proposed for constructing and developing computer PDS that allows automating two tightly interrelated processes:

- Knowledge acquisition;
- Design of PDS.

The psycho-diagnostic is based on the methods of psychometric psychology. This science treats mental states as concepts which, on the one hand, determine the different aspects of human behavior and reasoning and, on the other hand, they are determined themselves through independent personal characteristics. For example, the quality of scholar children works depends on their intelligence measured by the diagnostic test consisted of different tasks requiring intellectual capability and including specially constructed questions. The investigations have shown that such important features of personality as introversion - extraversion, agreeableness, conscientiousness, quality of intellect and emotional stability are main factors reflected in performance on tests of personality (Kimble, 1994).

The traditional technique of creating PDS assumes that a new PDS is elaborated for every special application of psycho-diagnostic testing. This approach has the following disadvantages:

- An expert provides every new PDS with both specific and well known domain knowledge;
- Knowledge used in an isolate PDS is fragmented, partial; it is difficult to compare it with knowledge contained in the other PDSs. For this reason, common practice of PDS's application does not influence essentially on the theoretical models in psycho-diagnostic;
- As a rule, different PDSs use different models of knowledge and different programming environments;
- The development of PDSs is rather expensive and time-consuming.

The CASE-technology assumes that the accent of designing PDS is moved from the narrow goal of programming a final product to the goal of analyzing psychological test as a structural unit of knowledge. At the first plan the following questions are advanced:

- What knowledge in principle allows constructing psycho-diagnostic test (DT)? How this knowledge is generated and what is its syntactic structure?

- What is a structure of the process of constructing DT?
- What are the rules of integration of separate DT in a whole system?

DT as a structural unit of knowledge goes through several transformations in its development:

- Informal definition of a psychological concept;
- The birth of the name of a psychological characteristic (PCh), corresponding to the concept formatted;
- Definition and choice personal characteristics closely connected or determining desirable PCh and such that they can be measurable (MChs);
- Elaboration of a questionnaire to measure MChs and formation of a hypothesis of functional relationship MChs → PCh;
- Experimental checking of the hypothesis MChs → PCh (*);
- Correction of the hypothesis and repetition of the previous phases if the hypothesis is refused or adoption of it;
- Formation of a functional operation (FO): MChs → PCh (*);
- Programming the functional operation and the test questionnaire (*).

The stages marked by * in principle can be automated. The stages of experimental checking hypotheses, creating diagnostic models and programming the final PDT are greatly supplied with the mathematical methods and algorithms (Duck, 1994).

The most difficult problems are those of formation and standardization of the functional operation (FO), realizing the mapping MChs → PCh. In psycho-diagnostics, the linear diagnostic rules dominate; the tradition experiment is limited by an elementary scheme of the addition of values of PChs in spite of knowing that the fitness of linear models for many tasks rests problematic (Duck, 1994). In our opinion, it can be explained by the fact that the methods of machine learning for extracting functional operations from experimental data are insufficiently elaborated. Many attempts of using the pattern recognition methods for this goal have not a remarkable success since the application of these methods requires a lot of heuristics.

One more key problem of the CASE - technology concerns the integration of a variety of DTs in a whole PDS. The integration requires the available mechanisms of accumulating knowledge of the relationships between PChs and, simultaneously, of the relationships between PChs and corresponding goal concepts or goal characteristics (GChs). Some examples of goal characteristic are "the successfulness of studies in high school", "belonging to a type of personality or a certain group of people", "the readiness for a certain action", "the fitness for a certain profession" (for example, for military service), and many others.

It is important not only to fix the relationships known to psychologists but to discover new ones automatically via the analysis of experimental materials. The validation of knowledge discovered and the clearance its role in the formation of a model of personality is a natural task in psychometrics.

Acquiring knowledge about the character and structure of Pchs → GCh relations is the bottleneck in elaborating PDS. Two ways are possible to copy with these difficulties:

- Using the methods analogous those that are used for constructing Mchs → PCh relations;
- Using the methods of knowledge discovery or data mining based on the experience borrowed from the others areas of expert systems application.

Expert's Knowledge Acquisition and Specification of PDSs as Interrelated Processes

The model of domain knowledge underlying the CASE-technology proposed is a result of generalization of the long-term experience acquired by the specialists engaged in the process of creating and using the diagnostic psychological and psycho-physiological tests and, simultaneously, it is the result of the analysis of contemporary trends in developing computer systems based on knowledge and oriented to fast prototyping the applied program systems.

The CASE-technology is based on two models of knowledge: the model of knowledge embodied in PDS (M1) and the model of knowledge of the designing of PDS (M2). Both models are object - oriented.

M1 is a meta-structure describing the concepts, connections between them and processes of knowledge and data transformation used in any PDS. M1 includes the following main concepts: characteristic (Ch) (measured and inferred), computational scheme (CS), computational expression (CE), operation (Op), and scale (Sc), logical rule (of the first type) (LR), inference model (IM), conclusion (C), and diagnosis (D). Models M1 and M2 are operational: the relationships between concepts can be viewed as both the schemes of inference and the procedures of concepts transformation when the operations are added to the schemes of relationships.

The process of constructing PDS is a sequence of transforming incomplete specification of a projected PDS from one state to another till its final state will be obtained under which the union of the specification with the program of an interpreter gives the ready PDS.

Knowledge Modeling. Syntax of Knowledge

Psychological Characteristics (Measured and Inferred)

Characteristic is a directly measured or inferred variable associated with a psychological or physiological property. Each characteristic has the name and the domain of values.

The domains of characteristic values are given by the scales of different types: symbol or nominal, Boolean, interval, numeric. The symbolic or nominal scales are not ordered. The natural order 'greater – smaller' of numeric scales can be interpreted, for example, as the relations 'better – worse', 'frequently – rarely', 'weakly – strongly'. Values of nominal scales are incomparable.

A subset of characteristics is marked out. This is the subset of directly measured characteristics or determined with the use of questionnaires, tests, tasks and other procedures of direct testing. A single question or a task of test can, strictly speaking, also considered as an elementary characteristic with its domain of values. All remaining characteristics are inferred ones.

Each PCh can have several scales of the different types; also the same scale can be associated with several characteristics. Scale is considered as a special attribute the values of which are computed during the functioning of the ready PDS. One and the same characteristic can have several values computed with the use of different scales.

The following constructive links are realized in PDS: 1) MChs → PCh; 2) MChs, PChs → PCh; 3) PChs → PCh; 4) PCh → Scales; 5) PChs → Operations; 6) PChs → Classes of PCHs; 7) PCh → DTs; 8) PCh → Attributes of PCh; 9) Scale → Attributes of Scale, and some others.

Figure 1. The structure of the questionnaire "Adaptability"

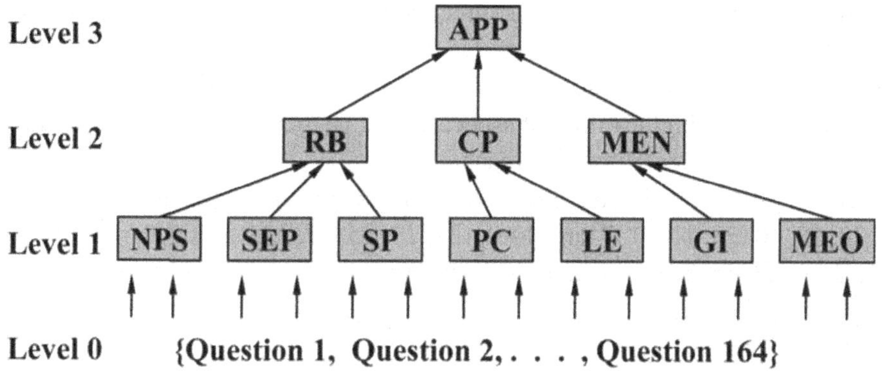

Here: MEO - moral and ethical orientation; GI - group identification; LE - learning experience; PC - principle of contact; SP - sociality; SEP - self estimation of personality; NPS - nervous - psychological stability; RB - regularity of behavior; CP - communicative potentiality; MEN - moral and ethic norms; APP - adaptive potentiality of personality.

Conclusions and Diagnoses

Conclusions are the concepts described with the use of GChs. Conclusions are expressed frequently in the form of text in natural language. In many clinical decisions, PDSs include not only laboratory tests but other sources of information for diagnosis such as disease history and physical examination of patients. This information must be taken into account when conclusions are formulated.

Computational Schemes (CSs) (the Relations of Computability)

Hierarchical structure where each Ch is represented as a node connected, by arrows, with characteristics necessary for producing its value is called computational scheme.

To each inferred characteristic, a level is attached in the hierarchical structure of computational scheme as follows: the level of characteristic is greater by 1 than maximal level of the characteristics directly participating in forming its value. For example, consider the structure of testing method "Adaptability" (Maklalov, 1995) (Figure 1).

One and the same characteristic can have several computational schemes. In this case, this characteristic must have several different proper names considered as synonyms and its computational schemes will be equivalent. Equivalent schemes are interchangeable.

However from the point of a psychologist's view, the equivalence can be considered to be rather strong assumption. Instead of equivalences, correlation dependencies between characteristics are taken into account. If the correlation link between two characteristics is sufficiently high, then they can be considered as interchangeable in some situations. Correlation dependencies between psychological characteristics (factors) are widely investigated in literature on psycho-diagnostics. As an example, we may refer to the article (Hugan et al., 1994) in which the data is given about the correlation between five factors of American Personality Test and the descriptive scales entering the other tests of personality. In this work, the estimation of the correlation between personality factors and the criterion of effective leadership is given. Knowledge of correlations between characteristics is very important for constructing computational schemes.

As a rule, the direct constituents of a Ch form a set of correlated Chs or a set of mutually independent Chs. It is true also for any set of questions as direct constituents of characteristics of higher levels in computational scheme.

In the previous example (see, please Figure 1), RB, CP, and MEN are the independent direct constituents of APP connected with the different aspects of human behavior but they are equally important for evaluating the adaptive potentiality of personality.

For characteristic SEP of level 1, the direct constituents are the following questions of test "Adaptability" {(29, 30, 39, 70, 73, 118, 137, and 146), (31, 23, 25, 87, 132, and 140). The questions of these two groups are discerned by their psychological content:

Question 30: "I am not sure of myself".

Question 23: "the state of my health is not worse than the state of health of the majority of my closed friends".

Real calculations of characteristics' values depend greatly on the degree of independency (dependency) between their direct constituents (components).

If several tests measuring independent characteristics are used together for predicting a single criterion, then such a collection of tests is called 'test battery'. The main problem arising with using test batteries concerns the method of integrating (unifying) results of separate tests for computing the value of the integral criterion.

For this goal, two types of procedures are used: equations of multiple regression (Howell, 1997) and profile analysis (McDermott et al., 1989).

Functional Operations. Scales. Computational Expressions (CEs)

Computational scheme (CS) defines only the relationships of computability of Ch but not a method of computing its values. CS are transformed into computational expression (CE) if for each node of CS the operations (Op) will be defined to compute the value of Ch associated with this node based on the values of its direct constituents.

The following ways are used to determine Op: formula, a table giving the values of a Ch for all the combinations of values of its direct constituents (this table determines a functional relationship or dependency), a set of logical rules based on dependencies of different types.

The two first forms of operations are most typical in psycho-diagnostics; they make up a class of functional relationships between values of characteristics. Constructing functional relations is not a simple problem. We shall consider some examples of constructing functional relations assuming that the domains of characteristics' values are finite sets of integers. This assumption is in accordance with the main scales used in psycho-diagnostics:: scale of "raw" balls (Anastasi, & Urbana, 1988), T- scale of McCall (McCall, 1922), standard IQ scale (Glutting, & Kaplan, 1990), standard nine valued scale of stanines (Bartlett, & Edgerton, 1966), standard ten–valued scale of stens (Canfield, 1951), C – scale (Guilford, & Fruchter, 1978) and some others.

Scale is a special type of attribute. Several different scales can be associated with one characteristic; one and the same scale can be associated with several different characteristics. Hence characteristic can have several values in different scales.

Table 1. The accordance between "raw" balls and stens for APP and its direct constituents

Values in stens	Direct constituents: in "raw"balls			Sum APP: in "raw" balls
	RB	CP	MEN	
1	46 and >	27-31	18 and >	62 and >
2	38-45	22-26	15-17	51-61
3	30-37	17-21	12-14	40-50
4	22-29	13-16	10-11	33-39
5	16-21	10-12	7-9	28-32
6	13-15	7-9	5-6	22-27
7	9-12	5-6	3-4	16-21
8	6-8	3-4	2	11-15
9	4-5	1-2	1	6-10
10	0-3	0	0	1-5

The scales used in computational expressions are main or principal ones. As a rule, for all characteristics, only one principal scale of "raw" balls is used.

The principal scale of a characteristic and its direct constituents depends on the type of operations used for calculating this characteristic. Hence the choice of scales is connected with the process of giving concrete operations in the nodes of CS.

Besides the principal scale, some additional scales can be given for each characteristic. Hence the rules of transitions must be given from the principal scale to all the additional scales. These rules are also in the class of functional relations.

For example, characteristic APP and its direct constituents (Figure 1) are associated with the scale of "raw" balls as their principal scale and with the scale of stens as their additional scale. Consequently, it is necessary to give the functional relations for recalculating the values of these characteristics in "raw" balls to the values in stens. There exist special procedures for constructing these functional relations (Anastasi, 1988). These procedures are based on statistical methods. The example of functional relations between "raw" balls and stens for characteristics APP, RB, CP, and MEN of the Adaptability method is given in Table 1 (Maklakov, 1995).

Constructing operations implies involving the following triple of relationship: Operations ↔ Characteristics ↔ Scales of Characteristics (Figure 2).

Figure 2. Three components of operation's construction

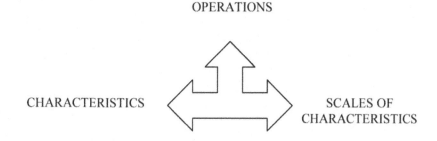

OPERATIONS

CHARACTERISTICS

SCALES OF
CHARACTERISTICS

For example, consider the computational scheme containing a node associated with the FO $X_1, X_2,...,$ $X_{k-1} \rightarrow X_k$. We assume that this FO is realized with the use of "+" operation. Then in order to specify the calculation we have to define the following knowledge:

- The main (principal) scale *MS* for calculating $X_1, X_2,..., X_k$;
- The additional scale AS_k for recalculating the values of X_k;
- The functional relation FO: $MS \rightarrow AS_k$;
- The computational expression for defining the sum:

$s(X_k) = s(X_1 + X_2 + ... + X_{k-1}) = s(X_1) + s(X_2) + ... + s(X_{k-1})$, where $s(X_i) \in \text{dom}(X_i)$, $i = 1, 2, ..., k$ and the limits of $\text{dom}(X_k)$ are determined as follows:

$s_{min}(X_k) = \min\{s_{min}(X_1), s_{min}(X_2),, s_{min}(X_{k-1})\},$

$s_{max}(X_k) = s_{max}(X_1) + s_{max}(X_2) + ... + s_{max}(X_{k-1}).$

Consider the direct product $D = \text{dom}(X_1) \times \text{dom}(X_2) \times ... \times \text{dom}(X_{k-1})$. Each element of D corresponds with one and only one value of X_k. It is not difficult to reveal that addition operation generates the partition of D into disjoint blocks each of which contains corteges of D correlated with one and the same value of X_k.

For example, let $A = B + C$, $\text{dom}(B) = \text{dom}(C) = \{1, 2, 3\}$. $D = \text{dom}(B) \times \text{dom}(C) = \{(1,1), (1,2), (2,1), (1, 3), (2, 2), (3, 1), (2, 3), (3, 2), (3, 3)\}$. Dom $(A) = \{2, 3, 4, 5, 6\}$. Figure 3 shows the ordered set D and its partition into the levels (ordinal classes) of corteges with equal values of A.

Let $U = \{A_1, A_2,.., A_n\}$ be a set of characteristics (say, attributes) with the domains of values $\text{dom}(A_i)$, $i = 1,..., n$, where $\text{dom}(A_i)$ - a finite set of integers. Assume that it is necessary to construct FO $A_1 A_2 ... A_n \rightarrow A_g$ (A_g is said to be an external criterion). Hence it is necessary to associate one and only one value of A_g with each combination of values of $A_1, A_2,.., A_n$. The number of values of A_g can not great (as a rule, it is the number of the types or classes of individuals related to a certain activity).

Figure 3. The ordinal classes of addition operations

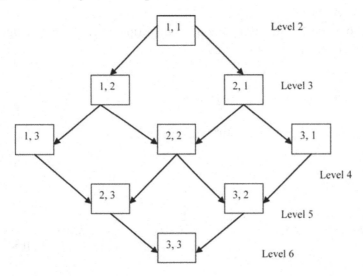

Table 2. Type groups of RB, CP, and MEN

Stens	Values in the scale of "raw balls"			The typical group
	RB	CP	MEN	
1	46 и >	27-31	18	3
2	38-45	22-26	15-17	3
3	30-37	17-21	12-14	3
4	22-29	13-16	10-11	3
5	16-21	10-12	7-9	2
6	13-15	7-9	5-6	2
7	9-12	5-6	3-4	2
8	6-8	3-4	2	1
9	4-5	1-2	1	1
10	0-3	0	0	1

The difficulty occurs when FO can not be defined analytically and it is defined by a table the rows of which correspond to the elements of Cartesian product $D = \text{dom}(A_1) \times ... \times \text{dom}(A_n)$, and the columns of which correspond to characteristics $A_1,..., A_n$. An additional column A_g must be formed in the process of constructing FO. It is not difficult to do if the number of elements of D not great and the number of values of A_g is known in advance. But if the number of elements of D is great, then this task become very difficult to do manually. It is more difficult, if the number of values of A_g is unknown and must be chosen by the psychologist in the process of constructing FO. As an example, we consider how the typical groups of individuals dependent on characteristic APP have been obtained (Figure 1).

The direct constituents of APP in the method "Adaptability" are RB, CP, and MEN. These characteristics are independent within the measurable limits. Consequently, the psychologist tries to evaluate all possible combinations of values of these characteristics. Since the number of these combinations is rather great even with using the scale of stens (10 x 10 x 10 = 1000) the psychologist tries to decrease it by introducing some groups or types of individuals with respect to each constituent RB, CP, and MEN. The domains of values of these characteristics were partitioned into 3 disjoint groups associated with the concepts (see, please Table 2) "rather low result (3)", "good result (2)", "very good result (1)".

Now the number of typical groups for each characteristic is equal to 3 and the number of all combinations of these types is equal to 3 x 3 x 3 = 27. These combinations were called "statistical types of Adaptability" (Maklakov, 1995).

However 27 types of Adaptability are yet rather great. How the psychologist can decrease the number of types of APP? Two principal ways are possible:

1. The psychologist observes the certain types of adaptive personal behavior in real life independently of measurable characteristics RB, CP, and MEN. He describes these types of behavior. Then it is necessary to examine whether exists or not a functional dependency between characteristics RB, CP, and MEN and the observed types of adaptive behavior. It is made by means of experimental exploration of a representative set of individuals.
2. The psychologist analyzes the ordering on Cartesian product of measurable characteristics and builds an equivalence relation on it taking into account this ordering.

In our case, the ordering on $D = \text{dom}(RB), \times \text{dom}(CP) \times \text{dom}(MEN)$ is defined as follows: cortege $<x,$ $y, z>$ is greater than cortege $<x', y', z'>$ if and only if each component x, y, z of it is equal to or greater than x', y', z', respectively. This natural ordering assumes that characteristics RB, CP, and MEN are of equal meaningfulness (worth) with respect to APP. The natural ordinal classes or levels are generated in D as the collections of incomparable corteges of D belonging to the same level of the ordering in D. However the ordinal classes or the typical groups of APP determined by the psychologist do not coincide with the natural ordinal classes in D, as it can be seen in Table 3. It is explained as follows. The psychologist considers the typical groups of CP, RB, and MEN to contribute differently in forming the typical groups of APP. Consequently, they have the different weights when the typical groups of APP are determined: changing the typical group of RB by 1 is equivalent approximately to changing the typical group of CP or MEN by 2. The weight of typical groups of CP is more than the weight of typical groups of MEN. Hence cortege $<3\ 3\ 1>$ is not equivalent to cortege $<3\ 1\ 3>$ (Table 3).

The psychologist considers corteges $<1\ 1\ 3>$ and $<1\ 3\ 1>$ to be better than cortege $<1\ 2\ 2>$ (although these corteges belong to the same ordinal class in natural ordering on D).

It is possible to describe the typical groups of APP determined by the psychologist by means of the following new characteristics (attributes) $A, B, C,$ and D:

Table 3. The type groups of adaptability (APP)

Statistical types of APP	Groups			Type groups of APP	Interpretation
	RB	CP	MEN		
1	1	1	1	1	Optimal adaptability, conserving normal functional state, capacity for work and hard work
2	1	1	2		
3	1	2	1		
4	1	1	3	2	Stable adaptability, quick and without difficulties
5	1	3	1		
6	2	1	1		
7	2	1	2		
8	2	2	1		
9	1	2	2	3	Unstable adaptability; but it can become stable with the aid of strong personal protective and compensatory psychological mechanisms
10	1	2	3		
11	1	3	2		
12	1	3	3		
13	2	1	3		
14	2	2	2		
15	2	3	1		
16	3	1	1		
17	2	3	2	4	Insufficient adaptability; success is determined by environmental conditions; constant control is indispensable
18	2	3	3		
19	2	2	3		
20	3	1	2		
21	3	1	3		
22	3	2	1		
23	3	2	2		
24	3	2	3	5	Low adaptability; success of adaptability is mainly determined by environmental conditions
25	3	3	1		
26	3	3	2		
27	3	3	3		

Table 4. The statistical types of APP described by the new attributes

Statistical types	A	B	C	D	The type groups of APP
1	0	0	0	0	1
2, 3	0	1	1	1 or 1.5	
4, 5	0	2	1	2 or 3	2
6	1	0	0	2	
7, 8	1	1	1	3 or 3.5	
9	0	2	2	2.5	3
10, 11	0	3	2	3.5 or 4	
12	0	4	2	5	
13, 15	1	2	1	4 or 5	
14	1	2	2	4.5	
16	2	0	0	4	
17, 19	1	3	2	5.5 or 6	4
18	1	4	2	7	
20, 22	2	1	1	5 or 5.5	
23	2	2	2	6.5	
21	2	2	1	6	
25	2	2	1	7	5
24,26	2	3	2	7.5 or 8	
27	2	4	2	9	

```
A: x(RB) - 1.
B: (y(CP) - 1) + (z(MEN) - 1).
C = {
        0, if the values of CP and MEN = 1;
        1, if the value of only one of characteristics CP, MEN ≠ 1;
        2, if the values of both characteristics CP and MEN ≠ 1}.
D: 2*(x(RB) -1) + 1.5*(y(CP) - 1) + 1*(z(MEN) - 1).
```

Table 4 represents the typical groups of APP via the values of the new attributes.

Table 5 contains the rules describing the type groups of APP via the values of the new attributes.

The rules or FO approximating a typological classification given by the domain expert can be called Logical Test (LT) in contrast to traditional DT based on measurement. Logical Tests can be constructed by the domain experts or by inferring logical rules from the experimental data with the use of machine learning methods.

Consider the characteristic "Group of professional fitness" (GPF) for which the following FO is given: PP, NP, GIC, GAC → GPF, where PP - positive social psychological properties, NP - negative social psychological properties, GIC - general intellectual capabilities, GAC - general adaptive capabilities. Each characteristic reflects the set of some behavioral, intellectual, psychological or moral properties.

Table 5. The rules describing the type groups of APP by the new attributes

Rules for description of the type groups of APP
1. If x[D] ≤ 1.5, then the type group of APP = 1;
2. If x[D] ≥ 7.5, then the type group of APP = 5;
3. If x[A] = 0 & y[B] = 2 & z[C] = 1, then the type group of APP = 2;
4. If x[A] = 0 & y[B] = 2 & z[C] = 2, then the type group of APP = 3;
5. If x[A] = 1 & y[B] < 2, then the type group of APP = 2;
6. If x[A] = 0 & y[B] > 2, then the type group of APP = 3;
7. If x[A] = 1 & y[B] = 2, then the type group of APP = 3;
8. If x[D] = 4, then the type group of APP = 3;
9. If x[A] = 1 & y[B] ≥ 3, then the type group of APP = 4;
10. If x[A] = 2 & y[B] = 1, then the type group of APP = 4;
11. If x[A] = 2 & y[D] = 6 or 6.5, then the type group of APP = 4;
12. If x[A] = 2 & y[D] = 7.0, then the type group of APP = 5.

Let the characteristics have the following ranges of values:

GPF: {1, 2, 3, 4} for four groups of fitness;

PP, NP: {expressed surely, exist (there exist some of positive (negative) properties), absent (no positive (negative) properties)};

GIC, GAC take their values in the following intervals: {[1-2], [3-4], [5-10]}.

The relation defining completely FO contains 81 corteges of values of characteristics PP, NP, GIC, and GAC. However this relation can be approximated only by 13 rules produced by the procedure of inductive inferring rules from examples implemented in the system of knowledge acquisition SIZIF (Naidenova et al.1995a), (Naidenova, & Polegaeva, 1992). These rules are given in Table 6.

Introducing FO in the computational model permits to extend naturally this model and to provide the expert with the possibility of describing not only analytical dependencies but the functions defined with the use of logical rules, for example, the functional relations between the scales of PChs represented in the form of decision tables, the procedures for identifying (recognizing) objects (individuals, characteristics, tasks). Functional relations are considered as constituent elements of knowledge and they can be used to simulate the conceptual reasoning and decision making used by the experts.

The considered computational model allows specifying and creating the questionnaires as well as the processes of interpreting the results of testing (decision making processes) imitating the expert's behavior. An item of test (question or task) is considered as an atomic test. Hence a test or test battery is a computational structure defined on the set of atomic and non atomic tests by means of the same formalism used to specify problem-solving methods. We use the same syntax for describing both arithmetical calculations and logical reasoning as well as controlling processes.

The possibilities of the computational model are also enlarged in order to include the means for the specification of interactive procedures of entering the responses of the tests takers, the data of measurements, and the other observations.

Table 6. The rules for characteristic GPF

Rules	GPF
If s(NP) = absent & s(GIC), s(GAC) $\in$ [5-10]	1
If s(NP) = exist & s(GIC), s(GAC) $\in$ [5-10]	1
If s(NP) = absent & s(GIC) $\in$ [5-10] & s(GAC) $\in$ [3-4]	2
If s(NP) exist & s(GIC) $\in$ [5-10] & s(GAC) $\in$ [3-4]	2
If s(NP) = absent & s(GIC) $\in$ [3-4] & s(GAC) $\in$ [5-10]	2
If s(NP) = exist & s(GIC) $\in$ [3-4] & s(GAC) $\in$ [5-10]	2
If s(NP) absent & s(GIC), s(GAC) $\in$ [3-4]	3
If s(NP) = exist & s(GIC), s(GAC) $\in$ [3-4]	3
If s(PP) = exist & s(GIC), s(GAC) $\in$ [3-4]	3
If s(PP) = absent & s(GIC), s(GAC) $\in$ [3-4]	3
If s(GIC) $\in$ [1-2]	4
If s(GAC) $\in$ [1-2]	4
If s(PP), s(NP) = expressed surely	4

One of the peculiarities of our computation model is also its operational capability. The process of conceptual knowledge acquisition (concepts + operational schemes) is not separated from the acquisition of problem solving operations, and, as a result, the knowledge base produced is directly executable.

Dependencies

Dependency is one of the most important constituents of knowledge that serves as a source of inference rule. Dependencies determine connections between psychological concepts (characteristics). Semantic of dependencies and their properties influence on the way of their utilization. We consider the following dependencies: "class – subclass", "object – feature", correlation, equivalence, ordering, weights, implications, functional dependencies, associations, and some others. Constraints are also dependencies of the special kind: forbidden combinations of attribute (characteristic) values, thresholds, coefficients of confidence, intervals of values and so on.

Inference Rules

Inference rules are rules or mechanisms of using known dependencies. They can be used by means of different methods of reasoning. For example, correlations between characteristics can determine the interchangeability relations between computational schemes or tests applying to evaluating these characteristics. Functional relations connecting the values of some characteristics with those of their direct constituents can be given in the form of table or decision tree.

Inference rules can be divided into universal or commonsense reasoning rules and special rules or experts' rules reflecting the peculiarities of application domain.

Commonsense reasoning rules have been described in Chapter 4 of this book.

Consider some examples of special reasoning rules.

Example 1. Resolving contradictions

Let OC1 and OC2 be the characteristics evaluating organizational capability with the use of two different methods: the diagnostic test (OC1) and the biographic data (OC2). It is possible that values of OC1 and OC2 turn out not consistent. Assume that the possible values' combinations of these characteristics are determined by the following Table 7:

The expert must give a rule identifying the conflict between OC1 and OC2 and a way of decision making in this situation.

Example 2

Operation (!*) of "generalization to the better" defines the values of characteristic GPE (General Positive Estimation) based on two characteristics PP (Positive social psychological properties) and GPS (General Physical State) in such a way that they can not be worse than the values of characteristic PP. Table 8 shows the values of GPE obtained by the operation of "generalization to the better".

In some cases, the reply on one question of DT can improve the value of a characteristic obtained by the use of independent testing. For example, if a respondent participated in the battle actions, then the value of PCh "Military Training" can be generalized to the better.

Analogously, the operation of "generalization to the worse" is constructed.

Models of Logical Inference

Inference rules are aggregated in the model of logical inference to obtain the values of goal characteristics. The inference model is determined by the form of representation and content of the dependencies between characteristics. In our system, the model of rule-based forward logical inference is used. We also assimilate the ideas lying in the foundation of some knowledge acquisition tools: PROTEGE, AIDE, KADS (Ericson, & Musen, 1992), (Gappa, & Poeck, 1992), and (Greboval, & Kassel, 1992).

Table 7. The possible values' combinations of characteristics OC1 and OC2

OC1	OC2
High	High
High	Low
Low	High
Low	Low

Table 8. Example of the operation of generalization to the better

!*	Estimation of PP:	Estimation of General Physical State:				
		Very Low	Low	Average	High	Very High
	Absent (A)	A	A	E	E	E
	Exist (E)	E	E	E	ES	ES
	Expressed Surely (ES)	ES	ES	ES	ES	ES

Specification of Conceptual Knowledge as Inference Process Directed by an Expert

The process of prototyping of PDS is a sequential and well structured process which can be briefly described by the following way (Naidenova et al., 1997).

Specification of Concepts (Process 1)

The basic sets of concepts are specified. The main concepts of expert system are the following:

- Characteristics;
- Scales;
- Diagnostic tasks;
- Diagnostic tests;
- Diagnostic test takers or patients;
- Computational schemes and expressions;
- Control procedures;
- Logical rules;
- Functional relations;
- Graphical objects;
- Diagnosis;
- Questionnaires;
- Text objects (for example, the description of the expert system).

Each concept is specified by means of its attributes and classes. The values of attributes can be given directly by the experts or by means of specifying computational expressions.

Specification of Computational Schemes (Process 2)

The computational schemes are given as the relations on the set of concepts. The computational schemes can aggregate (connect) the concepts of one type (for example, scales or psychological characteristics) or the concepts of different types (for example, symptoms and diseases, diagnostic tests and diagnostic tasks, or diagnostic tasks and psychological characteristics). Computational schemes have linear or treelike structure. The succession of computations is realized by means of special rules of conditional (unconditional) transitions.

The formation of computational schemes is performed as follows:

- The choice of a node of computational scheme;
- The giving of computed characteristic;
- The giving of constituents of computed characteristic. It is possible to give the existed and available diagnostic test with the use of which the value of characteristic can be computed or entered;
- The giving of principal and additional scales for computed characteristic;
- The giving of unconditional or conditional transition to the next node.

Specification of Computational Expressions (Process 3)

In accordance with the computational scheme, the operations and procedures are defined for the necessary calculations. So the computational schemes are transformed into computational expressions (CEs) or specifications of computational processes. The set of CEs can include logical expressions, for example, rules for recognition of concepts classes with the use of the values of appropriate attributes.

The CEs are divided into the following groups:

- Arithmetical and logical expressions;
- Functional relations;
- The system of logical rules of the first type defined in Chapter 4: (implications, interdictions, rules of compatibility and so on);

The CEs are also divided into two groups depending on the possibility of using inductive inference for their formation:

- CEs are determined only by means of expert's specification;
- CEs can be inferred automatically from training samples.

For interpreting of CEs, the different procedures are used. Some of these procedures are reduced to performing calculations in consecutive order, but the others require the realization of rule-based logical inference.

The control mechanism determining the conditional or unconditional transitions (branching) of calculations is realized by the logical rules giving the order of switching the operations in the process of real calculations. These logical rules include special variables the values of which depend on the results of calculations.

The process 3 is analogous to the process of specifying computations with the use of any programming language. The peculiarity of our programming language consists in the fact that the forward deductive and inductive engines are incorporated in it.

Figure 4 demonstrates the levels of knowledge specification of PDS.

Figure 4. The levels of knowledge specification process

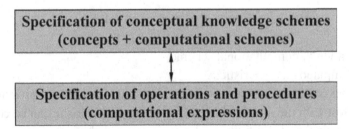

Transformation of Computational Schemes into an Object-Oriented Database

The processes 1 and 2 correspond to specifying the conceptual knowledge of problem domain. The model of conceptual knowledge that includes the basic sets of concepts and the computational schemes determines the appropriate scheme of the database system which is constructed in parallel the formation of conceptual knowledge.

The database of PDS includes the following object-oriented relations:

- Diagnostic Tasks;
- Diagnostic Tests;
- Psychological Characteristics;
- Scales;
- Diagnostic Test Takers;
- Psychological Characteristics – Scales – Diagnostic Tasks (Diagnostic Tests);
- Diagnostic Test Takers – Diagnostic tests;
- Psychological Characteristics – Computational Procedures;
- Scales – Diagnostic Tasks;
- Diagnostic Tasks – Diagnostic Tests;
- Diagnostic Tasks – Psychological Characteristics – Graphical Procedures;
- Diagnostic Tasks – The Order of Calculations;
- Diagnostic Tasks – Computational Schemes;
- Psychological Characteristics – The level of Computational Hierarchy.

The Figure 5 demonstrates the process of creating PDSs. The expert (the psychologist) gives concepts, attributes, computational schemes and other relations, scales, operations, rules, the type of procedures and their parameters and so on. In fact, he gives the knowledge used for forming automatically the database of the future PDS.

Figure 5. The knowledge-data generation

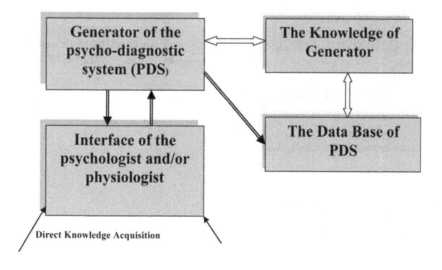

The Interpreter of Specifications as a Mechanism of Functioning PDSs

CEs specify the knowledge needed to produce calculations but the real functioning of PDS is realized by the program of an interpreter. Hence the PDS ready to functioning contains the database and the program of interpreter which will produce calculations in accordance with the sequences of computational expressions beginning with testing an individual and terminating with generating final decisions and recommendations. The program of interpreter rests the same for all PDSs. It requires a modification when new relations are introduced. This event implies introducing some new types of computations.

The database (DB) with the interpreter makes up the ready PDS, as shown in Figure 6.

The interpreter realizes functioning PDS, i.e. determines the values (initial, intermediate, final) of all concepts and puts them into DB.

The interpreter performs all necessary calculations including deductive and inductive logical inferences, dialog with the user and outputting the results obtained.

The interpreter gives the user the possibility to viewing all intermediate results of calculations or inferences. The interpreter has a good resource of data visualization procedures.

The interpreter works autonomously, it does not require the functioning of the generator, realizing the specification of knowledge.

The CASE-technology described has been implemented and used for creating a series of applied PDSs, for example, the expert system for diagnosing of acid-base disorders in human organism. A distinction was considered between the primary processes generating an acid-base disorder and the body's compensatory responses. There are the four types of acid-base disorders: respiratory acidosis, metabolic acidosis, respiratory alkalosis, and metabolic alkalosis; each of these disorders is covered in a systematic way: definition, causes, maintenance, metabolic effects, compensation, correction, assessment, prevention.

Figure 6. The ready-to-work PDS

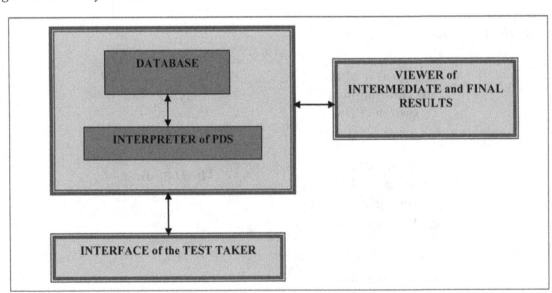

A TECHNOLOGY OF ADAPTIVE PROGRAMMING PDSS

A technology of programming Adaptive Psycho-Diagnostic Systems (APDS) is based on automatically extracting some constructive parts of psycho-diagnostic systems from experimental data. The process of APDS's generation is divided into two stages: the first stage is to form the conceptual level of domain knowledge (concepts and operational schemes); at the second stage, the problem is solved to adapt the incompletely defined PDS to the real conditions of its functioning. The main peculiarity of this technology consists in effectively using data mining and, particularly, machine learning procedures for the final specification of APDS.

The problems of diagnostics of psychological and psycho-physiological health states of human population, the prognosis of dynamic change of health under the influence of different natural factors such as ecological ones, professional conditions and so on, the early detection of health parameters' deflection from their normal values form a base of planning the preventive activities in medicine.

The important condition for perfecting the procedures of early and reliable diagnosis, treatment and continuous observation and control of human health consists in creating computerized methods of diagnostics and other instruments adaptable by their parameters to the different changeable conditions of human life and professional activity in the environment.

There are the different kinds of adaptation used for creating adaptive psycho-diagnostic testing methods:

- The adaptation to the peculiarities of diagnostic task by means of choice of an appropriate set of testing methods or batteries of tests, the choice of the collection of psychological characteristics to be tested and so on;
- The adaptation of psychological tests to an individual. The goal of adaptive testing is to present to the test taker only those items that will yield useful information; this goal is reached by adjusting item coverage to the response characteristics of individual test takers (Anastasi, 1988). The term "adaptive" means that the instrument is capable to determine when enough information has been collected from an individual to predict the final score with accuracy. Adaptive testing permits to identify an individual in the space of some psychological and psycho-physiological characteristics without exposing to a test taker numerous items that are too easy or too difficult, and too mild or too intense in order to define the individual's level (Laatsch, & Choca, 1994).
- The adaptation of test parameters to the changeable condition of testing, for example, social-psychological peculiarities of the population of individuals, some ecological factors and so on.
- The adaptation of processing the results of testing and decision making to the changeable condition of testing.

We consider two last kinds of adaptation.

Incomplete Specification of PDS by an Expert

The CASE-technology described can be used to support a way for creating the adaptive PDSs (APDSs) (Naidenova et al., 1997).

It has been already noted that many elements of domain knowledge are defined on the basis of the previous analysis of training sets composed of collected examples that have been observed.

At the first stage, the generator PDS is used to form the conceptual level of domain knowledge - the specialist introduces the basic sets of concepts, relational schemes, classifications and all the elements of necessary computations that do not require any additional definition. At this stage, the data - knowledge bases are constructed. The result of this stage is an incompletely defined APDS.

Next problem is to adapt the incomplete knowledge and computational processes to the real conditions of functioning APDS. For this goal, the procedures of inductive inference of knowledge from data must be used. We consider the following procedures as the most important for psycho-diagnostic systems: regression and correlation analysis, inferring implicative dependencies and decision rules from examples, inferring functional dependencies, extracting concepts and attributes from observations, inferring descriptions of classes. Hence the machine learning mechanism becomes the central part of our CASE-technology.

Of course, the process of inferring knowledge from data can not be completely automated and must be controlled by the experts.

Figure 7 represents the modified process of generating incompletely defined knowledge base. Figure 8 represents the structure of the CASE-technology for PDS generation with knowledge acquisition based on machine learning methods.

Inductive Inferring Some Constituent Elements of Knowledge from Examples

The expert's knowledge is always a result of inductive inference (statistical or logical) during the analysis of the training set of examples.

The main constructive elements of PDS that obtained as a result of inferring knowledge from data are the following ones:

- Scales of PChs;
- Functional relations between Scales;

Figure 7. The modified scheme of generating incompletely defined APDS

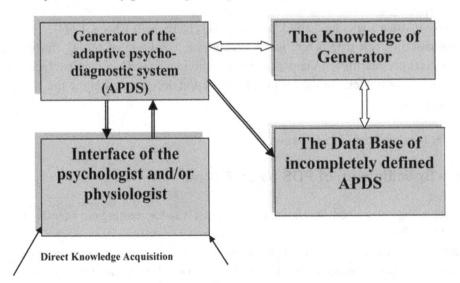

Figure 8. The tool of development of APDS

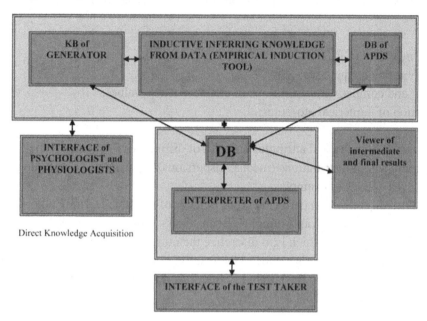

- Diagnostic decision tree;
- Regression equations;
- Logical rules;
- Correlative links;
- Weight coefficients;
- Intervals of values on continuous scales; and some others.

Statistical Inductive Inference

The subjects of statistical inductive inference can be scales, intervals of attribute values, coefficients of regression equations, generalized factors, coefficients of correlation between the PChs and so on.

Table 9 demonstrates the main statistical inductive methods used for knowledge acquisition from the experimental facts or examples given by the expert.

Table 9. Statistical inductive inference

Statistical Inductive Inference
Constructing scales to measure psycho-diagnostic characteristics
Factor analysis
Correlation analysis
Constructing regression equations; approximation of empirical curves
Extracting generalized experts estimates of facts
Bayesian regression models
Plausible reasoning
Estimation and prediction based on statistical inference
Estimation and comparison of distributions
Statistical methods of discretization

The first version of GENINTES supports the following applications of statistical inductive inference:

- Constructing scales of PCh;
- Inferring regression equations;
- Estimating and comparing distributions of characteristics' values;
- Discretization of numerical attributes.

The discretization of numerical attributes has a lot of difficulties in practice, especially in case when the standard parameters of distributions (means, dispersions) of attribute's values do not differ significantly for two given classes of examples.

Unlike "on-line" discretization performed by a number of machine learning algorithms for inferring decision trees or decision rules from examples (Bruha et al., 2000), (Fayyad & Irani, 1993), we use an "off-line" algorithm the idea of which is to discretize the numerical attribute in such a way that the frequencies of occurrence of attribute's values in the resulting intervals should differ as much as possible for samplings of two goal classes. The number of intervals is defined to be not more than three (Gubler, 1977), (Runyon,1982), and(Runyon, & Haber, 1991).

Logical Inductive Inference

Generally, inductive logical inference is intended for constructing Logical Diagnostic Tests. The subjects of logical inductive inference can be classes or types of PChs, classes of the test takers, attributes for describing classes, causal or functional dependencies between PChs or between PChs and a goal factors (external criteria). Table 10 demonstrates the main inductive logical methods used for knowledge acquisition from the experimental facts or examples given by the experts. The first version of GENINTES supports the first five problems from Table 10.

The Process of PDS Evolution

The evolution of PDS is performed as a result of its functioning: during the use of a PDS, the accumulation of the good, erroneous, and difficult diagnostic decisions are performed. Then, if it is necessary, the PDS is modified and improved by the use of GENERATOR creating a new version of it (see, please Figure 9). If we change and modify GENERATOR, then INTERPRETER can also require a modifica-

Table 10. Logical inductive inference

Logical Inductive Inference
Partitioning the domains of attribute values into intervals (discretization)
Extracting informative attributes and values
Inferring causal and functional dependencies from data
Inferring decision tree from examples
Formation classes of objects, concepts, hierarchical classification
Cluster-branching methodology for adaptive test construction
Learning control strategies and heuristics through experimentation
Evaluation of the degree of dependence (independence) between characteristics or factors

Figure 9.The scheme of PDS evolution

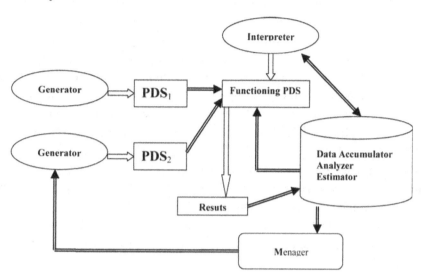

tion, but it is not necessary in general case when existing computation schemes are improved without programming principal new models of inferring PGhs.

RELATED WORKS

The literature contains a number of studies demonstrating successful applications of techniques for integrating machine learning with knowledge acquisition from experts. Buntine and Stirling (1991) describe the development of an expert system for routing in the manufacture of coated steel products. Although they do not use software that directly integrates machine learning with knowledge acquisition from experts, they describe a process that tightly couples the two.

The knowledge acquisition tool MOBAL (Morik et al., 1993) and its forerunner BLIP (Morik, 1987), has been applied to a wide variety of knowledge acquisition tasks. These systems use first-order representations and they provide tools for specifying ontology, learning rules from examples, revising rules, and learning new predicates from examples. The user and learning systems collaborate to construct an expert system.

Morik et al. (1993) present a case study in which MOBAL was used to acquire knowledge of basic German traffic laws. Another case study examined the use of MOBAL for creating a prototype of expert system for diagnosis of infantile jaundice (Morik et al., 1993).

The Telecommunications Security Domain (Sommer et al., 1994; Morik et al., 1993) is presented as a further study of knowledge acquisition using MOBAL. It covers the specification, validation and application of a security policy for communications network access control.

In (Webb et al., 1999), the authors compare the integrated use of machine learning during knowledge acquisition with each constituent approach in isolation. This research was the part of a project that developed the Knowledge Factory system. A brief description of this system is presented in this paper and more details about the system are available in (Webb, 1992; 1996; Webb & Wells, 1995).

The Knowledge Factory employs simple knowledge representation schemes because, as the authors note, many users have great difficulty with the first-order representations commonly used by knowledge acquisition environments (Kodratoff & Vrain, 1998). So the knowledge representation scheme is restricted to flat attribute-value classification rules and the knowledge base is restricted to a set of production rules. Moreover, the antecedent of a rule consists of tests on attribute values and the consequent is a simple classification statement. All rules directly relate input attributes to an output class. This simple attribute-value representation contrasts with the first-order representations usually used by the majority of integrated systems (De Raedt, 1992; Morik et al., 1993; Nedellec & Causse, 1992; Schmalhofer & Tschaitschian, 1995; Tecuci & Kodratoff, 1990; Tecuci, G. (1995); Wilkins, 1988).

The machine learning facilities support induction of new rules and inductive refinement of existing rules. The machine learning algorithm, DLGref2 (Webb, 1993), adds rule refinement capabilities to DLG (Webb & Agar, 1992), which is in turn a variant of Michalski's (1983) AQ.

In the paper (Koono et al., 2001), various relationships between knowledge and software engineering are analyzed. Moreover, some details of human design knowledge are revealed and humanistic aspects of design are discussed.

As Wahono and Far (2002) have pointed, many projects focusing on computer aided software engineering (CASE) tools for object-oriented analysis and design concentrate on object-oriented notation and forward/reverse engineering, but the methodology for object identification and refinement is not developed well. This paper presents an approach to the methodology of object identification and refinement from software requirements, based on object-based formal specification (OBFS). An example of a software project using this methodology for an air traffic control system is given.

In the paper (Wahono, & Far, 1999) an approach to solve the difficulties of object-oriented design by developing a distributed expert system that contains formulated design patterns and rules that aims at automating object-oriented design process in an interactive way is advanced. In the framework of this research, a new interactive user interface to enable software designer and the system communicate with each other in order to determine the best design has been elaborated. In this paper, the authors present the system architecture and the research outlines.

It is interesting that Far and Halim (2005) study the concept of Functional Reasoning (FR) that enables people to derive and explain function of artifacts in a goal-oriented manner. FR has been independently employed in various disciplines, including philosophy, biology, sociology, and engineering design, and enhanced by the techniques borrowed from computer science and artificial intelligence. A typical FR system in engineering design usually incorporates representational mechanisms of function concept together with description mechanisms of state, structure, or behavior, and explanations and reasoning mechanisms to derive and explain functions. Understanding the underlying assumptions, logical formulation, and limitations of FR theories help developers assessing their systems correctly. This paper gives a review of various FR theories and their underlying assumptions and limitations.

An approach towards developing a Knowledge Based Software Engineering (KBSE) tool by merging a conventional CASE tool with the expert system technology has been advanced and developed by B. H. Far in collaboration with H. Chen, Z. Koono, T. Takizawa and the other researchers in the 1992-1999 years. Experimental expert systems CREATOR2 and CREATOR3 have been implemented and applied to design of switching software. The CREATOR2 has the following features: 1) representing software design knowledge, composed of design product knowledge and design process knowledge, 2) using frame technology; and 3) integrating knowledge based reasoning techniques with a SDL CASE tool (Far, Takizawa, & Koono, 1993). CREATOR3 is an extension of the CREATOR2 system. These systems have supported a uniform modeling and advanced reasoning environment for software design.

Software design involves two knowledge categories, namely, design product knowledge and design process knowledge. The representation of software design knowledge in reusable form, in a structure that integrates these two knowledge categories is a key feature of software design.

The design product knowledge includes domain-specific concepts and constraints. The SDL language was used for representing the design product knowledge. In SDL a system is viewed as a collection of 'blocks' embodying concurrent 'processes'. A process is represented by an Extended Finite State Machines (EFSM) that communicates with other processes through discrete signals. SDL has both graphic (SDL/GR) and text-based (SDL/PR) versions. A designer has to prepare an initial design sketch using graphic symbols of the SDL CASE tool. In CREATOR2/3, this design sketch is transformed to a structure of class and instance frames automatically. Each SDL/GR symbol is associated with a frame that embodies all the information related to that symbol, such as its class, function, name, connections, etc.

Design process is viewed as a progression towards a goal by applying detailing patterns. The design process knowledge involves design rules acquired from human design, and tacit knowledge to make such patterns operational.

The main idea of this design technology is to follow design steps of human designers, extract their knowledge in an actual design case and reuse this knowledge in similar cases. This process requires proper documentation of the design steps. SDL can generate design documents. In CREATOR2, the design rules are classified in 4 groups defined by TASK-RULE, DECISION-RULE, OUTPUT-RULE, and INPUT-RULE.

In the CREATOR3, a collection of 'design schemas' that embody the tacit knowledge has been incorporated. Each design schema is a coded form of a human design activity. Those schemas are collected and applied in three successive phases.

The LEARN unit keeps records of the design rules that are already used. This is necessary for saving time in similar design cases and when a design rule is applied repetitively. The knowledge acquisition through documentation shows learning effect, therefore after accumulating enough rules, the implemented system can perform the job almost automatically.

In fact, CREATOR-SYSTEMS give a unified framework for representing both the design process and the design product knowledge.

Far (2002) began to develop a new approach to software engineering dealing with the development of multi-agent systems (MAS). In this paper the author presents a framework for agent-based software development called Agent-SE. The methods for generating organizational information for cooperative and coordinative agents have been advanced in this work too.

A large number of Agent-Oriented Software Engineering (AOSE) methodologies have been evolved in order to assist in building intelligent software. This emerging technology results in some difficulties for a developer when deciding which methodology can best fit a prospective application. In this paper, Hafez and Far (2008) present a reliable framework based on adopting state-of-the-art statistical procedures to evaluate AOSE methodologies and propose a set of metrics that can help in selecting the most appropriate methodology, or assembling more than one, to accommodate the anticipated features.

CONCLUSION

In this chapter, the problems of creating the CASE - technology are considered for elaborating psycho-diagnostic expert system. The main peculiarities of this technology are analyzed and the models of knowledge are proposed allowing describing concepts and inference mechanisms embodied in PDS and the processes of constructing PDS. The knowledge and data models are object-oriented and operational. The functional operator is viewed as a key component of knowledge representation. An approach is given to solve the problem of helping the users in forming functional mappings.

The tool for PDS construction integrates the direct knowledge acquisition from experts and the methods of machine learning (statistical and logical) for automated knowledge acquisition from the sets of data given by the experts. The CASE – Technology proposed permits integrating and coordinating knowledge of independent experts; it gives the possibility for collecting difficult and erroneous diagnostic cases in the database of PDS and using this information for improving the functioning of PDSs.

REFERENCES

Anastasi, A. (1988). *Psychological testing*. New York: Macmillan.

Anastasi, A., & Urbina, S. (1997). *Psychological testing* (7th ed.). New York: Prentice Hall.

Bartlett, C. J., & Edgerton, H. A. (1966). Stanine values for ranks for different numbers of things ranked. *Educational and Psychological Measurement, 26*, 287–289. doi:10.1177/001316446602600203

Bruha, I., Kralik, P., & Berka, P. (2000). Genetic learner: Discretization and fuzzification of numerical attributes. *Intelligent Data Analysis archive, 4*(5), 445-460.

Buntine, W., & Stirling, D. (1991). Interactive induction. In J. E. Hayes, D. Michie, & я E. Tyugu (Eds.), *Machine Intelligence, 12*.

Canfield, A. A. (1951). The "sten" scale – A modified C – scale. *Educational and Psychological Measurement, 11*, 295–297. doi:10.1177/001316445101100213

De Raedt, L. (1992). *Interactive theory revision*. Academic Press: London.

Duck, V. A. (1994). *Computer psycho-diagnostics*. St.-Petersburg: Bratstvo.

Ericson, H., & Musen, M. A. (1992). Conceptual models for automatic generation of knowledge acquisition tools. In T. Wetter, K.-D. Althoff, J. H. Boose, B. R. Gaines, & M. Linster (Eds.), *Current Developments in Knowledge Acquisition - EKAW'92, 6th European Knowledge Acquisition Workshop*, (LNCS 599, pp. 14-36). Heidelberg and Kaiserslautern, Germany: Springer.

Far, B. H. (2002). A framework for agent-based software development. In H. Shafazand (Ed.), *Information and communication technology, EurAsia-ICT'02, Proceedings of the First EurAsian conference* (LNCS 2510, pp.990-997). Berlin: Springer

Far, B. H., & Halim, E. A. (2005). Functional reasoning theories: Problems and perspectives. *Artificial Intelligence for Engineering Design, Analysis and Manufacturing, 19*(2), 75–88. doi:10.1017/S0890060405050080

Far, B. H., Takizawa, T., & Koono, Z. (1993). Software creation: An SDL-based expert system for automatic software design. In O. Faergemand & A. Sarma (Eds.), *SDL '93: Using Objects* (pp. 399-410). North-Holland: Elsevier Publishing Co.

Fayyad, U. M., & Irani, K. B. (1993). Multy-interval discretization of continuous-values attributes for classification learning. In R. Bajcsy (Ed.), *Proceedings of the 13th International Joint Conference on Artificial Intelligence, Chambéry, France, August 28 -September 3. IJCAI'93* (pp. 1022-1029). Morgan Kaufmann.

Gappa, U., & Poeck, K. (1992). Common ground and differences of the KADS and strong problem solving shell approach. In T. Wetter, K.-D. Althoff, J. H. Boose, B. R. Gaines, & M. Linster (Eds.), *Current Developments in Knowledge Acquisition - EKAW'92, 6th European Knowledge Acquisition Workshop* (LNCS 599, pp. 75-94). Heidelberg and Kaiserslautern, Germany: Springer.

Glutting, J. J., & Kaplan, D. (1990). Stanford – Binet intelligence scale: Fourth Edition: Making the case for reasonable interpretation. In C. R. Reynolds, & R.W. Kamphaus (Eds.), *Handbook of psychological and educational assessment of children: Intelligence and achievement* (pp. 277-295). New York: Guilford Press.

Greboval, G., & Kassel, G. (1992). An approach to operational conceptual models: The shell AIDE. In T. Wetter, K.-D. Althoff, J. H. Boose, B. R. Gaines, & M. Linster (Eds.), *Current Developments in Knowledge Acquisition - EKAW'92, 6th European Knowledge Acquisition Workshop* (LNCS 599, pp. 37 54). Heidelberg and Kaiserslautern, Germany: Springer.

Gubler, E. V. (1977). The divergence of distributions as a measure of difference between two populations and of the information index of features. In *Medical – social investigations* (pp. 83 –90). Riga.

Guilford, J. P., & Fruchter, B. (1978). *Fundamental statistics in psychology and education* (6th ed.) (pp. 484-487). New York: McGraw-Hill.

Hafez, E. A., & Far, B. (2008). On the evaluation of agent-oriented software engineering methodologies: A statistical approach. In M. Kolp (Ed.), *Agent-oriented information systems IV, the 8th international bi-conference workshop, AOIS'06* (LNCS 4898, pp. 105-122). Berlin: Springer.

Howell, D. C. (1997). *Statistical methods for psychology* (4th ed.). Belmont, CA: Duxbury Press.

Hugan, R., Curphy, G. J., & Hogan, J. (1994). What we know about leadership, effectiveness and personality. *The American Psychologist, 49*(6), 493–504. doi:10.1037/0003-066X.49.6.493

Kimble, G. A. (1994). A frame of reference for psychology. *The American Psychologist, 49*(6), 510–519. doi:10.1037/0003-066X.49.6.510

Kodratoff, Y., & Vrain, C. (1998). Acquiring first order knowledge about air traffic control. In R. Michalski, I. Bratco, & M. Kubat (Eds.), Methods and applications of machine learning, data mining and knowledge discovery (pp. 353-386). John Wiley and Sons.

Koono, Z., Chen, H., Abolhassani, H., & Far, B. H. (2001). Design knowledge and software engineering. *Journal of Natural Sciences, 6*(1-2), 46–58.

Laatsch, L., & Choca, J. (1994). Cluster-branching methodology for adaptive testing and the development of the adaptive category test. *Psychological Assessment, 6*(4), 345–351. doi:10.1037/1040-3590.6.4.345

Maklakov, A. (1995). Technique of estimating the level of the development of personal adaptive attributes. In *Psychological Security of the Battle Activity of Military Units and Subdivisions* (pp. 19-35). The Main Military Medical Administration.

McCall, W. A. (1922). *How to measure in education*. New York: Macmillan.

McDermott, P. A., Glutting, J. J., Jones, J. N., & Noonan, J. V. (1989). Typology and prevailing composition of core profiles in the WAIS–R standardization sample. *Psychological Assessment*, *1*, 118–125. doi:10.1037/1040-3590.1.2.118

Michalski, R. S. (1983). A theory and methodology of inductive learning. In R. S. Michalski, J. G. Carbonell, & T. M. Mitchell (Eds.), *Machine learning: An artificial intelligence approach* (pp.83-129). Palo Alto, CA: Tioga Publishing.

Morik, K. (1987). Acquiring domain models. *International Journal of Man-Machine Studies*, *26*, 93–104. doi:10.1016/S0020-7373(87)80038-X

Morik, K., Wrobel, S., Kietz, J.-U., & Emde, W. (1993). *Knowledge acquisition and machine learning: Theory, methods, and applications*. Academic Press: London.

Naidenova, X. Ermakov, A. & Levitch, S. (1997). Generating psychodiagnostic expert system. In A. Zakrevskij, P. Bibilo, L. Zolotorevitch, & Y. Pottosin (Eds.), *Computer-Aided Design of Discrete Devices (CAD DD'97), Materials of Second International Conference, 12-14 November, Minsk* (Vol. 2, pp. 214-221). Minsk, Byelorussia: Institute of Technical Cybernetics of National Academy of Science.

Naidenova, X., Ermakov, A., & Maklakov, A. (1996a). CASE-technology for psychodiagnostics. *International Journal Information Theories & Applications*, *4*(6), 33–40.

Naidenova, X., Ermakov, A., & Maklakov, A. (1996b). A new technology of creating automated systems for psychological and physiological diagnostic. [in Russian]. *Naval Medical Journal*, *3*(5), 18–23.

Naidenova, X. A., & Polegaeva, J. G. (1992). *SIZIF – The system of knowledge acquisition from experimental facts*. In J.L. Alty, & L.I. Mikulish (Eds.), *Industrial Applications of Artificial Intelligence, Proceedings of the IFIP TC5/WG5.3 International Vonference on Artificial Intelligence in CIM, Leningrad, USSR, 16-18 April* (pp. 87-92). Amsterdam, The Netherlands: Elsevier.

Naidenova, X. A., Polegaeva, J. G., & Iserlis, J. E. (1995a). The system of knowledge acquisition based on constructing the best diagnostic classification tests. In J. Valkman (Ed.), *Knowledge-Dialog-Solution, Proceedings of International Conference in two volumes (KDS'95)* (Vol. 1, pp. 85-95). Kiev, Ukraine: Kiev Institute of Applied Informatics.

Nedellec, C., & Causse, K. (1992). Knowledge refinement using knowledge acquisition and machine learning methods. In T. Wetter, K.D. Althoff, J. Boose, B.R. Gaines, M. Linster, & F. Schmalhofer (Eds.), *Proceedings of the 6th European Knowledge Acquisition Workshop on Current Developments in Knowledge Acquisition* (pp. 171-190). Heidelberg and Kaiserslautern, Germany: Springer.

Runyon, R. (1982). *The handbook on nonparametric statistics* (Translated in Russian). Moscow: Mir.

Runyon, R. T., & Haber, A. (1991). *Fundamentals of behavioral statistics* (7th ed.). New York: McGraw-Hill.

Schmalhofer, F., & Tschaitschian, B. (1995). Cooperative knowledge evolution for complex domains. In G.Tecuci & Y. Kodratoff (Eds.), *Machine learning and knowledge acquisition: Integrated approaches* (pp. 145-166). London: Academic Press.

Sommer, E., & Morik, K., Andrre, J.-M., & Uszynski, M. (1994). What online machine learning can do for knowledge acquisition: A case study. *Knowledge Acquisition, 6*, 435–460. doi:10.1006/knac.1994.1020

Tecuci, G. (1995). Building knowledge bases through multi-strategy learning and knowledge acquisition. In G. Tecuci & Y. Kodratoff (Eds.), *Machine learning and knowledge acquisition: Integrated approaches* (pp. 13-50). London: Academic Press.

Tecuci, G., & Kodratoff, Y. (1990). Apprenticeship learning in imperfect domain theories. In Y. Kodratoff & R. Michalski (Eds.), *Machine learning: An artificial intelligence approach* (pp. 514-551). San Mateo, CA: Morgan Kaufmann.

Wahono, R. S., & Far, B. H. (1999). Automatic object-oriented software design. *Proceedings of the Annual Conference of JSAN, 13*, 671–672.

Wahono, R. S., & Far, B. H. (2002). A framework for object identification and refinement process in object-oriented analysis and design. In *Cognitive Informatics, Proceedings of the First IEEE International Conference* (pp. 351-360).

Webb, G. I. (1992). Man-machine collaboration for knowledge acquisition. In L. Sterling (Ed.), *Proceedings of the Fifth Australian Joint Conference on Artificial Intelligence* (AI'92) (pp. 329-334). Singapore: World Scientific.

Webb, G. I. (1993). DLGref2: Techniques for inductive knowledge refinement. In *Proceedings of the IJCAI Workshop on Machine Learning and Knowledge Acquisition: Common Issues, Contrasting Methods, and Integrated Approaches* (pp. 236-252). Chambery, France.

Webb, G. I. (1996). Integrating machine learning with knowledge acquisition through direct interaction with domain experts. *Knowledge-Based Systems, 9*, 253–266. doi:10.1016/0950-7051(96)01033-7

Webb, G. I., & Agar, J. W. M. (1992). Inducing diagnostic rules for glomerular disease with the DLG machine learning algorithm. *Artificial Intelligence in Medicine, 4*, 3–14. doi:10.1016/0933-3657(92)90010-M

Webb, G. I., & Wells, J. (1995). Recent progress in machine-expert collaboration for knowledge acquisition. In X. Yao (Ed.), *Proceedings of the Eighth Australian Joint Conference on Artificial Intelligence* (AI'95) (pp. 291-298). Singapore: World Scientific.

Webb, G. I., Wells, J., & Zheng, Z. (1999). Experimental evaluation of integrating machine learning with knowledge acquisition. *Machine Learning, 35*, 5–23. doi:10.1023/A:1007504102006

Wilkins, D. C. (1988). Knowledge base refinement using apprenticeship learning techniques. In *Proceedings of the Seventh National Conference on Artificial Intelligence* (AAAI'88) (pp. 646-651). St. Paul, MN: The AAAI Press / The MIT Press.

Chapter 13
Commonsense Reasoning in Intelligent Computer Systems

ABSTRACT

This chapter deals with the description of possible mechanisms for data-knowledge organization and management in intelligent computer systems. Challenges and future trends will be discussed in the last section of this chapter, followed by the concluding remarks.

INTRODUCTION

We shall consider the intelligent computer system as a system capable to commonsense reasoning. The database system is intelligent if it communicates with the users by means of commonsense reasoning on conceptual knowledge rather than by means of special formal query languages. In this chapter, we attempt to formulate the main principles which could be posed in the foundation of constructing intelligent computer database systems first of all.

Furthermore, we shall examine the basic difficulties of commonsense reasoning realization in computers both from the side of the organization of data-knowledge interaction and from the side of the realization of machine learning.

These difficulties are connected with the solution of the following four problems:

- Data-knowledge interaction;
- Representation or structural organization of data and knowledge;

DOI: 10.4018/978-1-60566-810-9.ch013

- Integration of conceptual clustering and supervised conceptual machine learning, in which, for interpreting objects' classifications, it is drawn the knowledge of intelligent system instead of the knowledge of a supervisor;
- Procedural analysis and synthesis (genesis) of objects from elementary components.

Certainly, we cannot give the comprehensive solution of these problems. Our modest task is intended for formulating the main directions of future studies for their solution.

INTEGRATION OF DATA AND KNOWLEDGE

The integration of data and knowledge is an important constituent of the integration of all type of reasoning in intelligent computer systems. Probably the solution of one of these problems draws the solution of another. We consider some ideas of interaction between data and knowledge.

Data as a Source of Conceptual Knowledge

Knowledge engineering has arisen from a paradigm in which knowledge is considered as something to be separated from data and functioning autonomously with the problem solving application. But the functioning of intelligence results in cognitive structures through an organization of successive and constant actions performed on data. It implies the impossibility of considering knowledge out of data, data out of knowledge, and the mechanisms of commonsense reasoning out of data and knowledge. We believe that:

1. The same object-oriented model must be used for the representation of both data and knowledge;
2. The same algorithms of machine learning (commonsense reasoning) must be used for:
    ◦ Transformation of data to knowledge,
    ◦ Data-knowledge communication,
    ◦ User-knowledge communication,
    ◦ Modification of data and knowledge models.

Really, transformation of data to knowledge implies data-knowledge communication as well as modification of data and knowledge models implies this communication too; user-knowledge communication also implies data-knowledge communication. Thus only one process is required for realizing all kinds processes listed above.

We introduce the following necessary terminology.

- **PATTERNS** are directly observed and registered entities of real situations. The world perceived by man (and by computer) must be divided into separate phenomena referred to as objects.
- **OBJECT** is a set of patterns obeying some constant relationships or regularities. We can extract objects starting with the elementary functions or attributes. The application of an elementary function is an elementary classification. It is necessary to note that the functional dependencies link objects with their attributes. Extracting objects is performed under the control of knowledge.

- **ATTRIBUTE** is a function with the domain of its definition and the domain of its values (the range of function). For example, the function COLOUR_OF() has images as the domain of its definition and it has the set {red, blue, ..} as its range, where 'red, bleu,..' are symbols designating the phenomena of color. We also form complex functions as follows: $A(B(X))$, where the domain of function A includes the range of function B. Extracting sub-domains is also an elementary classifying action and "class" is the synonym of 'domain'.
- **KNOWLEDGE** is defined as a totality of relationships or regularities connecting patterns with patterns, patterns with attributes, attributes with objects, attributes with attributes, and objects with objects and classes. We also consider the classes of regularities, for example, space and time regularities, structure regularities, logical regularities and so on.
- **DATA** are the patterns directly perceived by a system and having a lowest degree of generalization. Naturally, the data are the source of knowledge. Can the data be separated from the knowledge? Studies of real thinking show that this separation is impossible in principle. Any perception of external world by man assumes the transformation of input information into a certain organizational structure. The introduction of data assumes performing simultaneously multiple operations for data analyzing and memorizing the results of analyzing in a certain generalized structure of knowledge. In this sense, the relational database is, in reality, a base of knowledge, since the scheme of database rigidly determines what data is generally possible to be introduced and in what form they will exist in computer. Obtaining new knowledge from the databases requires the extraction of initial records and their "release" from the schemes. This "release" function in OLAP and OLAM technologies is performed by the Data Cubes.

If we turn ourselves to the analysis of thinking from the point of view of knowledge formation, then, as the studies of psycho-physiologists show, there is a certain initial cognitive organization, which controls perception. This cognitive organization assumes that in processing input information the objects and properties, the three-dimensional space and temporary relations between objects, and the cause-effect relations are extracted, i.e. the relations of the types "to depend on", "to influence", "to undergo action", "to experience influence", "to act on". The cognitive structure is oriented to the construction of objects, properties, and the interdependencies between them that reflect the possible conversions of objects, their modification and development. In the cognitive structure, the possibility of mapping events and facts into the form of trinomial proposal (connection) is potentially placed. The mechanism working with the perception performs both the generalization, abstraction, splitting into parts or elements, and combining elements into new structures.

The properties of cognitive processes can be summarized as follows:

- Input information is converted with the perception into the structure of knowledge (the principle of indivisibility of data and knowledge); there does not exist, apparently, not systematized data;
- The process of data transformation into knowledge is multilevel;
- The process of data transformation into knowledge is multi-systemic.

Probably, introducing the data into a database must be accompanied by the simultaneous creation of some system of knowledge over the data. Each unit of data can be accompanied, at least, by some keywords reflecting the associations of this unit with the elements of knowledge - objects, actions, properties, etc. Then it is possible to construct a conceptual lattice on these keywords, to classify data, and input them into a system of knowledge.

For example, the relation "Student, Course, Discipline, Teacher, Audience" can be associated with the following knowledge:

"Student (the educational institution: institute, university, college) (to learn, to pass exams, to listen to the lectures); Course (the year of studies, the time of studies); Discipline (the subject of studies: biology, chemistry, physics,..); The lecture (it is read by a teacher, it is created by a teacher, it is studied by students, …)".

Then the fact that "Ivanov learns in the college" gives the possibility to infer that "Ivanov is a student, studies disciplines, listens to lectures and passes exams". The fact that "Ivanov is a biologist" will cause a question, "what is biologist?"

We have found in (Huchard, M. et al., 2007) an example of enhancing the classical (object × attribute) data representations with a new dimension that is made out of inter-object links in databases. Consequently, the discovered concepts can be linked by associations in conceptual data models. The borders for the application of the relational mining task are provided by a relational context family, a set of binary data tables representing individuals of various sorts (e.g., human beings, companies, vehicles, etc.) related by additional binary relations. No restrictions are imposed on the relations in the dataset. But a major challenge is the processing relational loops among data items. However a method for constructing concepts based on an iterative approximation of the final solution is proposed in this work and illustrated through its application to the restructuring of class hierarchies in object-oriented software engineering, which are described in UML.

The idea of Data Bases annotations goes back to the suggestion of Tim Berners-Lee (1998) to use ontology for making explicit semantic annotations on Web resources. By analogy, Conceptual Graphs (CGs) have been applied for representing ontology and semantic annotation of a structured documents database. This project is resulted in CGKAT, the system integrated a CG-represented ontology extending WordNet and enabled to associate a base of CGs to a structured document. The user could ask queries about either the base of CGs or the document contents and CGKAT could retrieve relevant document elements via a projection of the user's query on the CG base associated to the documents (Martin, 1997).

This system used two languages for representing ontology: RDF - Resource Description Framework (Lassila, & Swick, 1999) and CGs. As inference mechanism, the search engine CORESE based on CGs has been implemented. This approach evolved towards so-called "Corporate Semantic Web" approach (Dieng-Kuntz, & Corby, 2005).

A semantic search engine CORESE or an ontology search engine for the semantic Web enables to retrieve Web resources annotated in RDF. This search engine uses the correspondence between CG and RDF(S) languages, where RDF(S) is a version of RDF. The CORESE ontology representation language enables to represent ontology by a class hierarchy and a property hierarchy separately. It uses links between concepts and between relations when it needs to match a query with annotation. In the knowledge model of CORESE, ontological knowledge and assertion knowledge (logical rules of "if – then" type) are distinguished. The assertion knowledge is positive, conjunctive and existential and it is represented by directed labeled graphs. An RDF graph representing an annotation or query is translated into a CG. The class (property) hierarchy in an RDF SCHEMA is translated into a concept (resp. relation) type hierarchy in a CG support. But this approach is contrary to object-oriented formalism where properties must be defined as attributes inside classes. The projection operation is the basis of reasoning in the CG model. A query is processed in the CORESE engine by projecting the corresponding CG into the CGs obtained by translation of the RDF annotations. Thus a projection of the query graph is transformed into their annotation graph.

However RDF schema does not offer the possibility to deduce new knowledge from existing one. This possibility has been developed in an extension of RDF (Corby, & Faron, 2002). As a result, CORESE integrates an inference engine based on forward chaining. The rules are applied once the annotations are loaded in CORESE and before the query processing. Hence the annotation graphs are augmented by rule inferences before the query graph is projected on them.

Summing up the aforesaid, we come to the conclusion that data must interact with knowledge. This means that the construction of databases must begin with modeling knowledge and clearing up the orientation of potential knowledge development. We believe that

DATABASE ≠ SIMPLE REPOSITORY OF FACTS

The modern languages for ontology representation allow users, with different technical backgrounds, to collaborate in the construction of distributed knowledge bases. For example, COE (Collaborative Ontology Environment) is a prototype of such a tool combining an intuitive graphical user interface based on concept maps that facilitate ontology construction and understanding with sophisticated cluster concept analysis to aid the search for relevant concepts (Coffey, et al., 2004).

Many research groups carry on the works for defining standards and technologies for the purpose of data on the Web will be organized and linked in a way that it can be used for more effective discovery, automation, integration, and reuse across different applications. Conceptual Graphs for Semantic Web Application is one of these technologies. The advantages of Conceptual Graph formalism have been demonstrated via several real-world applications in the framework of Corporate Semantic Web (Dieng, & Hug, 1998), (Dieng-Kuntz et al., 2004).

Knowledge is a Means of Data Organization and Management

The inseparability of data from knowledge with respect to their interacting is manifested in the fact that knowledge (it exists from the very beginning of database construction) governs the process of inputting data in databases. First, there is a mechanism (or it must exist) of recognizing the fact that a thing was already earlier perceived or already known. Then there is the possibility of revealing a new thing not having appeared earlier or not corresponding to what earlier was known. For example, if it was known that birds have wings and fly, but information appears, that X is a bird, has wings, but it does not fly, then "knowing system" must ask "why it does not fly?". The formation of knowledge cannot occur without this ability to ask. The perception of new things is combined in reality with questions "what is this?", "for what goal is this?" Probably, the computer knowledge base must know how to pose these questions and to obtain the answers on them.

The mechanism of control from the side of knowledge is connected directly with the mechanism of recognition, with the revealing of similar and new data, with the discovering of contradictions with already known facts. In the process of analyzing new data, the necessity also occurs to change the context of reasoning, i.e. to select the appropriate knowledge and data connected with this knowledge. We believe that entering data must be governed by knowledge and data must aim at developing knowledge:

KNOWLEDGE SERVES FOR MANAGING THE PROCESSES OF DATA ENTERING AND ORGANIZING

Deductive and Inductive Query Answering

The queries to intelligent computer systems can be of the following types:

- The factorial queries when the answers can be obtained directly from the data;
- The conceptual queries when the answers can be obtained via the knowledge.

Consequently, the intelligent system must be capable to recognize the type of query.

The conceptual queries must be interpreted (understood) via the knowledge. Furthermore, the answers to these questions require the use of data and knowledge by means of commonsense reasoning.

The process of commonsense reasoning can require inputting new data and/or knowledge. This process is performed incrementally via the dialog with the user. The intelligent system works like thinking individual as follows:

- PERCEPTION PHASE or ENTERING THE QUERY;
- COMPREHENSION or UNDERSTANDING THE QUERY (pattern recognition phase);
- FULFILLMENT OF ANSWER TO THE QUERY (commonsense reasoning phase);
- QUERYING THE USER if it is necessary and RETURNING to the phase of PERSEPTION.

Entering data/knowledge can have the different goals:

- "IT IS NECESSARY TO KNOW"- a simple message of the user;
- ENTERING NEW DATA WITH ASSIMILITION OF THEM BY the INTELLIGENT SYSTEM"; it implies the implementation of dialog and supervised or unsupervised learning process; the result of this process is the renovated knowledge.

The process of learning is an interactive and step-by-step procedure in realization of which the program of inductive inference, on the one hand, receives the control from the user, on the other hand it can perform refining the query, selecting the necessary context of reasoning, and inferring new knowledge for replying the query.

The context of query answering is considered in the framework of Reiter's default logic. As an example, the paper T. Linke T. Schaub can serve (1998). A proof-oriented approach has been developed for deciding whether a default theory has an extension containing a given query. The actual query-answering phase follows after a compilation phase in which the examination of the entire set of default rules is done only once. It allows inspecting only the necessary part of default rules in the actual query-answering part.

This work uses the result of the paper (Schaub, 1994) in which a methodology for query answering in default logics via structure-oriented theorem proving has been introduced.

The logic-based integration of query processing and knowledge discovery in the framework of combined inference databases (CID) construction is proposed in (Aragao, & Fernandes, 2004). The authors noted that classical query languages cannot satisfy the currently needs for extracting knowledge from large databases. This paper aims to give a unified semantics for both deductive or query answering and inductive tasks (classification, clustering, association, etc). The logic used in this approach is *p*-Datalog extending the proof and model theories of classical Datalog.

The integration and possible structural organization of data and knowledge are considered in next Section of this Chapter.

STRUCTURAL ORGANIZATION OF DATA AND KNOWLEDGE

Conceptual Model of Data and Knowledge

We are interested in analyzing the cognitive structures of knowledge that are reflected, for example, in the terms of problem domains and in the rules forming these terms. We give some example of forming geological terms about the earth's surface relief with respect to some geological processes.

The terms are divided into the following classes:

- *Natural objects*: relief, landscape, elements of relief, elements of landscape, deposit, sagging, minerals, rocks, classes of rocks and minerals, geo-morphological structure and so on;
- *Processes* forming relief, landscape, rocks, geo-morphological structures and other natural formations;
- *Temporary periods* of the action of processes or/and their eventual results (the existence of objects in the time);
- Forms of objects;
- Space locations of objects;
  Properties of objects and the degree of their manifestation.

In Table 1, Table 2, Table 3, Table 4, and Table 5, some fragments of the dictionary of terms with the indication of their content are given.

One and the same term (word) can have different contents. For example, the term designating a process can also designate the visible result of this process, for example, "lowering" means both a process of lowering place, and the very place of the lowering in comparison with the surrounding landscape.

The terms designating the elements of relief, are word-forming for the terms designating the forms of relief. The same forming role with respect to the forms of relief is performed by the terms designating processes. For example: if the process of melting of glacier previously occurred, then the relief is "water-glacial"; if ridges and hills predominate in the relief, then it is "hilly- ridge". Here we have already complex terms, formed of two and more components; the different, by their content, relations are implemented between the components of these complex terms: relation "part-whole" (relief, which consists of the hills and the ridges), relation "to be formed with the aid of a process", "to be the result of a process" (relief, formed by a glacier). The complex terms give the possibility to assume that the specialists implicitly use the reasoning rules of "if - then" form. For example, knowledge, that a certain

Table 1. The terms designating processes

TERM	SEMANTICS OF TERM
Accumulation	Process forming or having an effect on the formation of relief as a whole or a certain element of relief; Process facilitates the appearance of some specific geo-morphological structure
Ventilation	
Equalization	
Denudation	
Ice formation	
Lowering	
Sedimentary accumulation	
Raising	
Settling	
Saggig	
Smoothing	
Melting	
Transgression	
Erosion	

process generates a specific result, gives the possibility to make an immediate conclusion in the form of production rule: "if an ice formation relates to the quaternary period, then it is continental - coved".

Processes can be combined or coexist with each other, they can go one after another, alternating and partially overlapping. Therefore for describing the form of relief it is frequently necessary to operate

Table 2. the terms designating the elements of relief

TERM	SEMANTICS OF TERM
Swamp	The elements of relief
Elevation	
Hills	
Ridge	
Dune	
Hillock, prominence	
Hollow	
Glacier	
Moraine	
Ravine	
Lake	
Plateaus	
Plain	
Slope	
Terrace	
Space between rivers	
Hill	

Table 3. The terms designating the forms of relief

TERM	SEMANTICS OF TERM
Accumulative	Forms of relief
Ridgy-Hilly	
Hilly	
Water-glacial	
Ridgy	
Denudational	
Glacial	
Frozen	
Monotinic	
Sea accumulative	
Flat	
Flat-wavy	
Flat-hilly	
Hilly-morainal (hilly-morainic)	
Ravined	
Dismembered	
Eolian	

Table 4. The terms designating the temporary periods

TERM	SEMANTICS OF TERM
Preglacial	Temporary periods are associated with the processes and with the results of the processes occurred in the specific period of time. The results of processes are, for examples, deposits, elements of relief, geo-morphological structures
Cainozoik	
Glacial	
Interglacial	
Mesozoic	
Mesozoic-Cainozoic	
Cretaceous	
Lower Quaternary	
Permian	
Pleistocene	
Late Quaternary	
Post-glacial	
Tertiary	
Quaternary	

Table 5. The terms designating the character of sediments

TERM	SEMANTICS OF TERM
Alluvial	Nature of deposits or sediments reflecting their composition and the processes of their formation
Boulder - pebbly	
Clay	
Glacial	
Morainal	
Sandy	
Fluvioglacial	

with the complex terms consisting of two or more attributive components.

The timing of objects or processes is achieved by two methods:

- Directly, with the aid of geological scales,
- It is defined by correlation with any process, place or object, for which the timing is known.

These two methods of timing are frequently used simultaneously, for example, "preglacial quaternary". Here time indexing is achieved by two methods - with the aid of the geological time scale and with the aid of the correlation with the process of ice formation.

Prefixes "pre", "post" (with respect to the process), "later", " earlier", "lower", "upper" refine the time interval of a process or geological object: "Late Quaternary deposits", "Tertiary species", "Late Quaternary ice formation". The terms designating geological species, elements of relief and accumulative processes are word-forming for constructing the terms reflecting the character of geological deposits.

There exist the terms expressing the relation of co-existence of two and more objects in the time and the space (Table 6). As such terms, the verbs are used most frequently. These relations are frequently accompanied by the estimation of the degree of manifestation (good, vividly, clearly, most, predominantly).

There exist the terms expressing the naming relation, the relation "object - property", the relation of comparison, the degree of property's manifestation, and the degree of confidence (typically, frequently,

Table 6. The terms designating co-existence in time and space

TERM	SEMANTICS OF TERM
To be expressed	Relation of co-existence in the time and (or) the space of several objects. It is accompanied by the estimation of the degree of its manifestation
To be observed	
To be timed to	
To be developrd	
To be diffused	
To be attended	
Typical	
To be characterized	

rarely, always, never). It is very often that, for different relations, one and the same form of natural language expressions, namely the attributive form is used. Attributes can be formed from the different terms indicating processes, the periods of time, elements of relief, sediments, locations in the space, qualities. Object can have several attributes, for example, "prolonged denudation leveling off", "selective denudation", and "significant newest raisings".

The attributes of quantitative and qualitative assessments are universal; they can be combined with any terms: long, short, steep, main thing, selective. One part of them can be expressed with the aid of a quantitative measure, the other part - only with the aid of linearly or partially ordered scales of estimations. Some attributes are combined only with the specific terms: they form the steady word combinations: "calm flow", "calm tectonics", and "steep slope". The attributive relations can be expressed not only by adjectives, but also by nouns with the preposition or without it: "the height of slope", "the slope with the height of", and "the fluctuation of height".

The analysis of terms and methods of forming the complex terms shows that their semantic (meaningful) structure corresponds to the relations between the natural phenomena (processes, objects), how specialists understand them. The semantic basis of terms is the non-linguistic reality.

The concept of geological process is the basic structural component of knowledge. The process occurs in the time and the space; it produces the specific result such as a visible picture of natural landscape, the parts of which are the different elements having diverse forms and distributions in the space. Since geological processes cover not only surface, but the entire earth's crust they determine also the deep structure of the earth's crust, the form of layers and folds, the composition and properties of geological species and so on. Specifically, the knowledge about geological processes permits the implementation of "transferring" of the time of processes and some of their properties to the objects formed by these processes. It is also possible "transferring" the properties of elements of relief to the relief as a whole.

The model of problem domain knowledge is object-oriented. In Figure 1, a fragment of geological knowledge is given. This fragment reflects the relationships between processes, forms of relief and geomorphological structures. The relations "part-whole", "object-property" can be defined recursively.

Each object can be represented by its specific object-oriented scheme. For example, the sediments

Figure 1. The fragment of the structure of problem domain knowledge

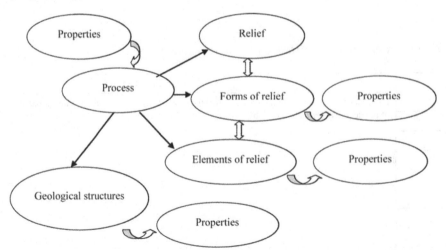

are described by their composition, the nature of bedding, the thickness of deposits, and the temporary range of their formation. The relief is described through its elements; it is characterized by the degree of its dismemberment, by its morphological signs. But in the system of knowledge there is nothing isolated. The knowledge of specialists contains the interrelations between the objects, between the properties of one and the same object, and between the properties of different objects.

These connections make it possible to derive (infer) the necessary consequences of well-known facts or to exclude the objects or properties incompatible with the knowledge of specialists. For example, the plain is defined as the unity of relief and sedimentary deposits. The unity of relief and deposits in nature is reached via the processes forming them. The discrepancy of the descriptions of some parts of a common geo-morphological picture is revealed by checking the combinability of different consequences of known processes and their coordination with each other.

We can see that

THE SCHEMAS OF SPECIALISTS' KNOWLEDGE NOT ONLY OBJECT-ORIENTED BUT THEY ARE INFERENCE-ORIENTED TOO

One of the approaches to conceptual modeling knowledge and data is to unify two concepts: the data schema and the model of object. This can be done by combining the relational and object-oriented database models with receiving the Relational Object-Oriented Database Model (ROODM). This idea has been advanced in (Naidenova, 1979).

Relations in the ROODM will correspond with object models. The properties and classes of objects are defined by the use of attributes. The links between objects determine the different relations between them, mainly the "if - then" relation, for example: "if the landscape properties are known, then the predominant species of trees can be determined". The associative links between objects are also very important. They determine the combinability of objects (multi-valued links).

Generally, the links between objects are functional. The functions can be either finite or infinite. A function f: $U \rightarrow V$ is called finite if it is defined only on a finite set of points in U. If the function is finite, then we may store it explicitly as the functional relation. If the function is infinite, then we can store its definition via formulas or procedures that compute argument-value pairs of this function.

Attribute is an atomic type in our model and object is a set of atomic types and a set of functional dependencies between them. For example, *Ore deposit $\rightarrow$ Type of rock, Line $\rightarrow$ Direction of Line* are the functions, and *Line, Ore deposit, Type of rock,* and *Direction of Line* are the atomic types.

The links between the object and its attributes are functional. The functional relation is represented as a set of causal dependencies or implicative rules.

Consider some examples of objects and links between them. The examples of objects are:

ORE DEPOSIT $\rightarrow$ (NAME, TYPE OF ROCK, ENVIRONMENT, FRACTURE);

LINE $\rightarrow$ (LENGTH, DIRECTION, LOCATION);

FRACTURE $\rightarrow$ TYPE OF FRACTURE.

The relationship '$\rightarrow$' is an inference relationship from objects to their properties or from objects to objects. For example, the following relationships between objects have been inferred:

Figure 2. The example of object classification

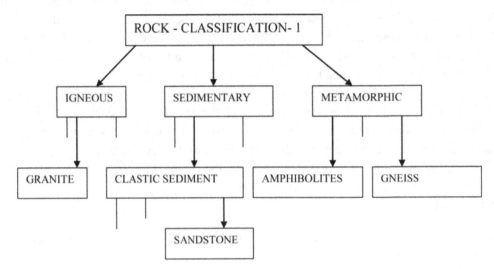

LINE → TYPE_OF_FRACTURE;

FRACTURE → TYPE_OF_ORE_DEPOSIT.

These new functions allow concluding from the properties of one object to another property of the same object or to the properties of some other object.

We introduce a new complex construction called 'CLASSIFICATION' or 'STRUCTURE'. In general, we deal with algebraic lattices given on the set of objects with 'is - a' relation. An example of Classification is given in Figure 2. The atomic set ROCK which is defined as a population of rocks (a set of exemplars of rocks) is linked with the classification ROCK - CLASSIFICATION - 1 by means of functional relationships:

ROCK → ROCK - CLASSIFICATION-1.

For the same object we can define a number of classifications independently. For example, rocks may be classified according to their commercial potentiality, their genesis or any alternative aspect that may be useful. The set of exemplars (population) of object can be empty, but the functional links between object and its classifications must be kept as knowledge about this object.

PROPERTY can be viewed as a classification too. For example, for rocks, we can consider their physical and chemical properties. The properties are the classifications observed or tested by means of some physical processes out of computer. We often define the classifications via a combination of properties of object.

There exist many approaches to modeling knowledge by the use of the formalism of conceptual data schemes. Representing knowledge for the purpose of solving some problem is strongly affected by the nature of this problem and inference strategy to be applied to solving it. This characteristic is the reason of disparity between ontology and conceptual data schemes (e.g. EER, ORM, UML, etc).

Jarrar (2005) considers that unlike a conceptual schema or classical knowledge base that captures semantics for a given application, the main advantage of ontology is that it captures domain knowledge highly independently of any particular application. Ontology constitutes a formal conceptualization of a particular domain of interest that is shared by a group of people. Jarrar investigates three foundational challenges in ontology engineering: reusability, application independence, and evolution. Based on these challenges, he derives the ontology-engineering methodological principles.

The main principle is the double articulation of ontology suggesting that ontology is built as separate domain axiomatizations and application axiomatizations. While a domain axiomatization focuses on the characterization of the intended models of a domain vocabulary; the application axiomatization mainly focus is on the usability of this vocabulary according to certain application/usability perspectives. The more an axiomatization is independent of application perspectives, the less usable it is. In contrast, the closer an axiomatization is to application perspective, the less reusable it will be.

Hovy (2005) investigates the methodology of ontology construction. He noted that "it has not been able to build large, widely used, general-purpose semantic theories or semantic resources required for practical use at the scale of natural language processing and similar applications; such semantic data and theories as do exist are almost always limited to small-scale (or toy) application. Knowledge representation work has been excellent in developing formalisms for representation, and for investigating the properties and requirements of various classes of deductive systems. But for practical applications such formalisms need content; the deduction systems need to work on something" (Hovy, 2005; p. 92). Furthermore, he notes that there is still not a systematic and the theoretically motivated methodology in ontology construction. He has identified five types of practically used motivations for ontology construction: the philosophers, the cognitive scientists, the linguists, the Artificial Intelligence specialists, and the domain specialists.

The difficult problems of data-knowledge bases design are 1) how to integrate ontology and conceptual knowledge modeling in problem domains; 2) how to integrate already existing relational data models and conceptual data models of problem domains. One of the solutions of the second problem is proposed by Sitompul, & Noah (2006). They advanced a design methodology for conceptual data warehouse development called the transformation-oriented methodology. This methodology translates an Entity-Relationship (ER) model into a specification language model and then transforms it into an initial problem domain model. A set of synthesis and diagnosis rules gradually transform the problem domain model into the multidimensional model. A prototype knowledge base tool called the DWDesigner has been developed for realizing this methodology. The multidimensional model produced by the DWDesigner is presented in a graphical form for its visualization. The studies of this methodology have been conducted in a number of design problems, such as university, business and hospital domains.

The most important phase of this technology, namely, the specification language formulation stage is unfortunately produced manually. This phase translates the input represented in the form of ER model into a specification where each entity in the ER model is configured as a class structure with the name of the entity as the class name and its properties as the class properties. The entity properties specified in the class structure consist of attribute, identifier, subclass, aggregation and relationship. The translation of the ER model into the specification language model is guided by a set of syntax rules and the result becomes the initial representation of the application domain (the problem domain model). In the third stage, the inference of new facts is performed. This stage may cause the appearance of redundancies and inconsistencies within the database. Consequently, some diagnostic tasks are necessary to be solved to prevent the database from such discrepancies.

Conceptual Lattice as a Structure Combining Data and Knowledge

The role of conceptual lattice is very essential because the lattices not only underlie the functioning of data-knowledge system on the basis of commonsense reasoning operations but also realize combining data and knowledge in a whole formation. Lattice is an ideal language for representing data-knowledge and realizing procedures of data-knowledge transformation.

The main problem in realizing lattice structure for conceptual knowledge manipulation consists in combining physical level of objects examples and conceptual level of objects themselves. This problem has been solved in the Concept-oriented Model (CoM) advanced in (Savinov, 2009).

The main characteristic of these approaches to conceptual modeling consists in the fact that the CoM is based on the theory of ordered sets. The author writes that "Particularly, one source of inspiration when developing CoM was FCA and Lattice Theory" (Savinov, 2009, p. 171).

The cognitive ordered structure determines semantic properties of each element of CoM depending on its relative position among other elements, while the element itself is referred to as an identifier.

The important property of CoM is its duality: CoM combines two structures called the physical and the logical. Physical structure can be relational hierarchical database where each element has one permanent position and one permanent physical context.

Logical structure has a multidimensional hierarchical form where each element has its logical context that can change in the course of time. The operations within physical structure mean creating or deleting elements while the operations with elements within logical structure result in only a change of their properties. Entering or deleting data can directly imply some correspondent changes in logical structure implemented via a mechanism of commonsense reasoning or knowledge construction.

The logical ordering of elements plays the very important role in CoM. Logical links can be interpreted in terms of object-oriented model of data (knowledge) as links 'object – attribute – value'. Namely if one element is positional above another element, then it is interpreted as a value, while the second element is interpreted as an object possessing this value. So, an element plays the role of a value with respect to lower level elements (sub-elements) connected with it and it plays the role of an object with respect to higher level elements (super-elements) connected with it.

Formally the CoM is defined as follows. The main constituent element, called a concept, consists of two classes: a reference class and an object class. This duality is used to distinguish identity modeling responsible for how elements are represented and accessed from entity modeling responsible for how elements are characterized by other elements. The consequence of such separation is that two types of element composition are used: collection and combination. Thus an element is $E = \{a, b, \ldots\} <c, d, ..>$, where $\{\ \}$ and $<\ >$ denote a collection and a combination, respectively. A collection can be considered as a set of elements connected via logical links and identified by means of references. A combination is analogous to fields of an object or columns of tables identified by positions and connected via logical links.

Physical structure can be easily produced by removing all properties (fields, columns) from elements.

If $g = \{\} <a, b, c>$, then g is characterized by values a, b, and c. Properties of an object indicate groups which it belongs to and, simultaneously, an object is a group for all other objects for which it serves as the value of some attribute. If $g = \{\} < a, b, c>$, then g belongs to three groups: a, b, and c.

A physical collection of N concepts is denoted by $R = \{C_1, C_2, \ldots C_N\}$. For each concept $C = \{i_1, i_2, \ldots$

i_M} <$C_1, C_2, \ldots C_K$>, the set {$i_1, i_2, \ldots i_M$} is a physical collection of data items or concept instances, and the set <$C_1, C_2, \ldots C_K$> is a collection of its super-concepts.

Each data item has the empty physical collection and a combination of other data items of the model called super-items (while this item is called a sub-item), i.e. $i = \{\ \} \{i_1, i_2, \ldots i_M\} \in C$.

A named link from sub-concept to super-concept is referred to as a dimension. A dimension can be considered as a unique position of a super-concept in the definition of sub-concept.

In an expression <$x_1: C_1, x_2: C_2, \ldots x_k: C_k$>, super-concepts <$C_1, C_2, \ldots C_k$> are called domains of dimensions $x_1, x_2, \ldots x_k$. Each dimension is represented by one path in the concept structure; the number of edges in the path is the dimension rank.

The concept of dimension allows constructing the dimensionality views of concept level of OLAP technology; consequently, the CoM belongs to a class of multidimensional models of OLAP technologies.

One more important operational possibility of CoM is the possibility to easily perform an operation of projection: given an item, or set of items, it is possible to get related items by specifying some path in the concept structure. Moving up along a dimension to super-items can be considered as the construction of a projection.

Logical navigation must be based on ordering the elements of CoM. Currently a derived property of a concept has been defined in the CoM as a named definition of a query returning one or more items for each item from this concept.

The CoM is very promising with respect to realizing the integration data and knowledge. Currently the development of a concept-oriented query language is an important future trend for the CoM. But if we take into account that the concept structure is undoubtedly the concept lattice, and then it becomes clear that this CoM is ideally compatible with the model of commonsense reasoning proposed in this book on the basis of lattice as its working space. For example, based on combining hierarchical knowledge with classical rule-based formalisms, Hitzler, & Krötzsch (2006) have introduced an expressive commonsense query language for formal contexts. Although this approach is conceptually based on order-theoretic paradigms, it can be implemented on top of standard answer-query programming systems. Advanced features, such as default negation and disjunctive rules, thus become practically available for processing contextual data.

DIFFICULTIES OF MACHINE LEARNING

Data-Knowledge Transformation with the Use of Supervised Machine Learning

We understand under the natural human commonsense reasoning a reasoning with the aid of which conceptual knowledge is built. As our investigation have shown, commonsense reasoning is equivalent to learning with the aid of which the gradual creation, accumulation, application, and modification of knowledge is performed. This reasoning is applicable to data of any nature, of any level of generalization or specialization.

The process of knowledge extraction from data can be represented as a multistage process, at each step of which occurs the conversion of concepts of lower levels to concepts of higher levels; this conversion is based on the basis of one and the same principle independent on the level of generalization and the nature of data. The concepts or patterns of a lower level with their extracted properties serve as the initial data for constructing the concepts of higher levels.

In technical systems, there are principally two ways of constructing concepts of higher level of generalization: 1) the use of program modules based on known mathematical methods and knowledge of specialists about the invariant properties of concepts, and 2) the use of inductive inference of concepts from examples. The methods of learning, realized as reasoning, are applicable when the concepts of lower level can be described with the aid of attributes. But also the inductive inference of concepts from examples requires the huge efforts of a supervisor. The activity of supervisor includes: 1) forming the examples of concepts, 2) giving the classification of examples, 3) analyzing the results of learning, 4) entering new attributes or classifications, 5) generalizing the results, 6) clustering objects, and so on. To illustrate the process of concept construction, we describe the formation of concept "rectangular object" with the analysis of lines extracted in the image.

EXAMPLE 1: *Extraction of Rectangles from Schemes of Lineaments*

We start with a list of lines (Table 7) and their directions (the angles between lines with respect to a given coordinate axis). This list is the result of the lineament analysis of image.

Then we partition lines into the equivalent classes with respect to their directions (Table 8): each class consists of lines having the same direction (of course, we means that it is given the precision needed for determination of the equality of lines directions).

Then we determine for each pair of classes the difference between the directions of lines of these

Table 7. Directions of line

Line	Direction of line
A	d_a
B	d_b
...	....
V	d_v

Table 8. Partition of lines by their directions

Line	Class of direction	Direction of lines
A	1	d_1
C		
....		
B	2	d_2
W		
.....		
.....		
V	K	d_k
....		

Figure 3. Pairs of classes i, j with difference(d_i, d_j) = 90°

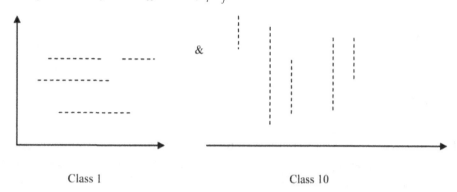

Class 1   Class 10

classes. Then we select all pairs of classes the difference of directions for which is equal 90° (Table 9- and Table 10).

For the pair of classes *i, j* with Difference(d_i, d_j) = 90°, we determine for each line of Class *i* all the lines of Class *j* which intersect it (Table 11 and Figure 3).

The role of supervisor consists in isolating examples of rectangles in Table 11. Role of the program of machine learning consists in building the rules of the formation of rectangles on the basis of selected examples.

The Rule extracted by a machine learning program is:

"*a, b* are lines of the same direction z_1

Table 9. The pairs of classes with the difference between line directions for these classes

Pair of Classes i, j	Difference (d_i, d_j)
1, 6	20°
1, 10	90°
....	....

Table 10. Pairs of classes with perpendicular lines

Pairs of Classes i, j with Difference(d_i, d_j) = 90°
1, 10
2, 5
....

Table 11. The perpendicular and being intersected lines

Line of Class 1	Lines of Class 10 intersecting line of Class 1
A	*c*
B	*d, c*
Q	*v, l, p*
....	....

& a is intersected by lines d, c;

& d, c are lines of the same direction z_2;

& difference $z_1 - z_2 = 90°$;

& b is intersected by d, c ".

For constructing the procedure for searching for rectangles in images, the following operations have been used: classifying the lines by the property "all lines with equal direction"; selecting the pairs of classes of perpendicular lines; for each line y of a given class, selecting the set INTERSECT(y) of all perpendicular lines belonging to another class and intersecting y; selecting the pairs of parallel lines a, b of the same class for which the intersection of sets INTERSECT(a), INTERSECT(b) is not empty. The result is the description of goal concept and the procedure of its extraction from images. The activity of supervisor includes:

- Selecting the features of lines;
- Giving the classifications of lines.

However the data pre-processing (the lineament analysis of images) including the definition of lines via a system of given features precedes machine learning the concept of rectangle.

Our next example shows that the tasks of machine learning require not only the giving of a set of training examples but the giving of original models of inductive inference.

EXAMPLE 2: *Image Understanding for Geology - Analysis and Identification of Geo-Morphological Structures.*

Objects to be identified are:

- Ring Structure (or Ring Fracture) (RS);
- Group of Ring Structures (GRS);
- Complex Ring Structure (CRS);

Figure 4. Examples of ring structures' configurations

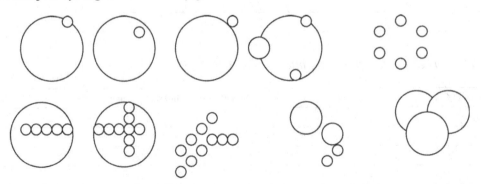

- Fracture (FR);
- FRacture Strip (or Conjugated Fractures) FRS;
- RAdial Structures (RAS);
- Partial Radial Structure (PRAS);
- Displacement (DI);
- FOld (FO).

The examples of Ring Structures are given in Figure 4.

The primitive structures under consideration are:

- Straight line (L);
- Arc(A);
- Oval(O;)
- Wave (wave fracture) (W).

Process of identification has the two parts: analysis and synthesis (Table 12).

During the phase of image understanding, a transformation of image is accomplished from the iconic form to a relational structure: the raw data acquired by the sensors are represented as an iconic image, and the objects acquired by the process of object identification are represented by a relational structure.

We start with a contour binary image obtained after the image preprocessing and image segmentation stages (Denisov, & Plaksin, 1991).

In order to identify the segments of contour binary image as the primitive structures it is necessary to determine the values of their features. The special procedures perform the association of each seg-

Table 12. The processes of analysis and synthesis

Analysis	Synthesis:
Image preprocessing	Merging primitives
Image segmentation	Feature calculation
Feature calculation	Identification of structures (objects)
Identification of primitive structures	

Table 13. Rules identifying primitive structures

Primitive	Identifying rules
Line	Coincidence of the ideal line calculated based on the initial and terminal points with the real points of the chain; max divergence $\leq$ a given constant;
Arc	(x is not line) & (x is not wave) & $\cos(x) \geq$ a given constant, where x is a segment determined by the initial, terminal and middle points;
Oval	d - distance between the initial and terminal points of segment, l - length of segment x; the rule: ($d \leq k * l$) & ($s_1/s_2 \leq$ a given constant), where s_1, s_2 - the biggest and the smallest side of rectangle, respectively, k is a given constant;
Wave	Presence of bending points; l- length of segment x, h - divergence from line between two bending points, R - image resolution; the rule: ("presence of bending points" is true) & (condition that $d \geq k_1*R$, $h \geq k_2*d$, $k_1 = 2.5$, $k_2 = 0.5$ is true for not less then two periods between two bending points).

ment with its features and with its label corresponding to one of the primitive structures - 'Line', 'Oval', 'Arc', or 'Wave'. One of the possible collections of primitive structures' features given in (Denisov, & Plaksin, 1991) is the following:

- Length of segment;
- Coordinates of the initial and terminal points of segment;
- Coordinates of the rectangle circumambulating segment;
- Directions of segment determined by its initial and terminal points;
- Average direction of segment;
- Chain code of segment;
- The curvature values in each point of the chain code of segment;
- Coordinates of the bending points of segment.

It is necessary to note that the features of segments are defined to satisfy the invariant conditions with respect to scale changing, displacements and turning. It is given an admissible degree of the uncertainty to compare segments with the use of tuned thresholds.

Several ways for constructing the rules identifying the primitive structures are possible: 1) to use the special procedures developed in advance or 2) to use the machine learning inference system for deducing rules automatically based on the examples of the primitive structures already selected on a image by the supervisor). The training set of primitive structures can also be constructed automatically by partitioning these structures into clusters on the basis of analyzing their features.

In (Denisov, & Plaksin, 1991), the following expert's rules for identifying the primitive structures are used (Table 13).

The rules of primitive structures' identification allow extracting the smallest elements or atoms that called atomic ovals, lines, arcs and waves. The real lines, arcs, ovals, waves include atomic primitives as their parts, so the complex primitives L, A, O, W are formed from atomic ones by successive sticking them. The relationships PART-WHOLE between atomic and complex primitives are used. The structure of primitives is recursive. The rules of inferring complex primitive are defined as follow.

The first group of rules:

$l \rightarrow L$;

$l, L \rightarrow L$;

$a \rightarrow A$;

$a, A \rightarrow A$

$w \rightarrow W$

$w, W \rightarrow W$;

$o \rightarrow O$;

The second group of rules:

A, L→ A;

L, L → A;

A, W → W;

O, A → O;

O, L → O;

A, A → O.

The rules of the first group are considered as rules of extending primitive structures. These rules are performed under the following restrictions: 1) the number of complex structures must be as small as possible; 2) for each complex structure, an invariant property is preserved; 3) a complex structure is finally constructed if adding to it any atomic primitive structure not belonging to it implies changing its type.

The rules of the second group are considered as rules of compatibility for some pairs of intermediate structures. The following task must be solved to construct the complex structures: 'to merge intermediate structures so that 1) the number of structures obtained would be as small as possible; 2) for any pair p_i, p_j of complex structures p_i does not include p_j and p_j does not include p_i.

This process includes the two main operations: merging (extending) and refining structures.

The rules of ring structures' generation are the following:

O → RS;

RS, A → RS;

RS, RS → RS;

RS, RS → GRS;

GRS, RS → GRS;

GRS, RS → CRS;

CRS, RS → CRS;

A, A → DI ∨ FO;

DI, A → DI;

FO, A → FO;

FO, FO → FO;

W, A →FO W;

W → FO ∨ PRAS;

L, L → FR ∨ PRAS;

FR, L → FR;

FR, FR → FRS;

FRS, FR → FRS;

L, W → PRAS;

L, PRAS → PRAS ∨ FR;

W, PRAS → PRAS ∨ FR.

The refinement operation is needed to reduce the number of intermediate structures constructed during the object formation process. As a whole, inferring geo-morphological structures is a mode of inductive-deductive commonsense reasoning with the using of generalizing and specializing object descriptions.

We can see that the key problem of machine learning is the problem of analyzing initial patterns and decomposing them into elementary objects in accordance with a system of some features, as a rule, known in advance.

Our next example shows the possibility to charge the computer with the task of analyzing initial patterns and decomposing them into their constituent elements.

EXAMPLE 3: *Catching the Rules of Forming the Adverbs from the Adjectives in French Language*

We shall proceed from the assumption that all elements of natural languages are constructive objects (CO). Thus, words are constructed from letters of an alphabet; proposal consists of words, text from proposals.

Furthermore, each CO is compound: words have, in their composition, stems, prefixes, suffixes, and ending. Words are divided into syllables. Compound proposal is constructed of simple proposals.

The mechanism "of perceiving" and analyzing COs must allow the recognition of any structural part of these objects.

The mechanisms of machine learning must allow:

a) Extracting concepts as groups of objects and giving the names to them if they have the sense in some context;

b) Forming the characteristic features of concepts making it possible to distinguish them from each other;

c) Forming the classifications of concepts on the basis of the connections between them - associative, implicative, functional, and structural, etc.

Naming objects is one of the very important operations of learning. If a group of objects can be named it means that this group makes sense as a concept.

The teacher can give examples or counterexamples of concepts and thus accelerate the process of learning.

Determining COs is based on a constructive process generating them.

Let A be an alphabet. Words in the alphabet A are obtained as the result of a constructive process based on the following rules (Markov, 1984):

1) Empty word is a word in A;

2) If P is a word in A, then Pξ is a CO, where ξ is any letter of A.

The rules of generating COs are also the rules of recognizing these objects.

Figure 5 illustrates the main phases of learning the rules of recognizing COs.

The automated extraction of conceptual knowledge is based on realizing two universal mechanisms: 1) the extraction of structural elements all COs and 2) the formation of concepts and the structures of concepts. As the first mechanism for our goal, we shall use the Normal Algorithm of Markov (Markov, 1984). The second mechanism is the inductive inference of regularities from the data. The author does not know the projects in which would adapt consecutively both these mechanisms for automated extraction of knowledge in natural language processing.

We give an example of catching the rules of forming the adverbs from the adjectives in French language.

Figure 5. The phases of learning rules for recognizing constructive objects

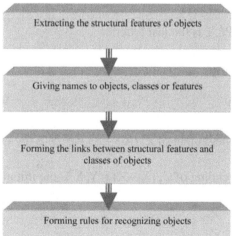

The Normal Algorithm of Markov is an ideal instrument for analyzing such COs' as words. With its aid, it is possible to separate all the beginnings and ending of words, to determine the end addition of word to its beginning, to determine the beginning of word supplementing its ending, and to determine the entry of one word into another together with the structure of this entry.

Let us give principal notations and operations of Markov's algorithm. By P, Q, R, S, we denote words and, by ξ, ψ, ζ, we denote letters.

Alphabet::= the letters;

Word::= a set of letters;

Empty word = empty set of letters::= Λ;

Word::= P|Pξ, where P is a word, ξ is letter; $\Lambda\xi=\xi$.

Graphical equality of words is =;

Graphical inequality of words is $\neq$;

Concatenation of words: [P,Q]; [P, empty]::= P; [P,Qξ]::=[P,Q]ξ .

Inverse operation is defined as follows:

[Λ! = Λ;

[Pξ ! = ξ[P;

[ξ! = ξ ;

[PQ!= [Q![P!;

[[P!!=P;

Q = ξP, ξ is the first letter, Q = Pξ, ξ is the last letter;

Q = PX, P is the beginning of word;

Q = XP, P is the ending of word;

XY = Z, consequently, X is the beginning of Z, (X $\leftarrow$ Z) = Y, Y is the end addition of X in Z;

YX = Z, consequently, X is the ending of Z, (X$\rightarrow$Z) = Y, Y is the initial addition of X in Z;

[Xd is the length of X;

[P(A) is the projection of word P on alphabet A.

Examining the lists of the beginnings of pair of words enables to reveal whether these words have non-empty common beginnings. It is possible to determine the greatest common beginning (GCB) or the greatest common ending (GCE) of pair of words. Also it is possible to determine the entry of one word into another and the structure of this entry, if it occurs. The following determinations are necessary for this. It will be said that words P, Q are mutually simple to the left, if there does not exist the non-empty beginning of both P and Q.

Whatever words P and Q, words R, S and T can be built such, that (1) P =RS, (2) Q = RT and that S is mutually simple to the left with T.

Whatever words P and Q, there is an only triplet of words R, S and T satisfying conditions (1) and (2) and such, that S mutually simple to the left with T. Word R in the only triplet of words R, S, T satisfying conditions (1) and (2) and such, that S mutually simple to the left with T is called the greatest common beginning (GCB) of words P and Q. Whatever word P and Q, GCB of these words is unique.

Any common beginning of words P and Q is the beginning of their GCB. Any beginning of GCB of two words is their common beginning.

The greatest common ending (GCE) of two words is determined analogously.

Any non-empty word P allows the unique representation in the form Pξ and the unique representation in the form ξP. The letter ξ in the unique representation of non-empty word in the form Pξ is called the last letter of word. The letter of ξ in the unique representation of the non-empty word in the form ξP is called the first letter of word.

P enters in Q (Q contains P) if there is a pair of words R, S, such that Q = RPS.

If there is a pair of words R, S, such that Q = RPS, then there is U such, that P is the beginning of U and U is the ending of Q.

Whatever U, if P is the beginning of U, and U is the ending of Q, then P enters in Q.

If there is a pair of words R, S such that Q = RPS, then there is T such, that P is the ending of T and T is the beginning of Q.

Whatever T, if P is the ending of T, and T is the beginning of Q, then P enters in Q.

On the basis of these assertions we can compose the list of all words, entering a given word Q. For this goal, we compose the list of all endings of Q and for each ending of Q we compose the list of all its beginnings. The union of all last lists gives the desired list of all words, entering Q.

The entry of word P into word Q is determined as follows: Q = R*P*S, where R is the left wing, P is the basis, and S is the right wing of this entry.

We shall call entry with the empty left wing 'initial entry' and we shall call entry with the empty right wing end entry.

Initial entry is: *P* (P ← Q). End entry is: (P → Q) *P*.

For our example of Markov's Normal Algorithm application, we have chosen some adverbs of manner with the suffix "*ment*" and formed from the feminine or masculine adjectives in French.

The initial data for reconstructing the rules of forming the adverbs from the adjectives were the following:

• The fixed alphabet and the partition of alphabet into the vowel and consonants letters;
• Three non-empty sets of the words: the set of the adverbs (ADV) of manner, the sets of the masculine (MADJ) and feminine (FADJ) adjectives from which the given adverbs are formed in French.

The training data are given in Table 14.

We compare words inside of the sets of adverbs and adjectives and the words from the pairs of sets: MADJ - FADJ, MADJ - ADV, FADJ - ADV. The following structures of words were revealed:

The greatest common part of a pair of words (let us name its basis) is their GCB:

Case A. Word 1 = basis + ending 1; Word 2 = basis + ending   2.

Case B. Word 1 = basis; Word 2 = basis + ending   2.

Case C. Word 1 = basis; Word 2 = basis; Word 1 = Word   2.

The greatest common part of a pair of words (let us name its end) is their GCE:

Case D. Word 1 = beginning 1 + end 1; Word 2 = beginning 2 + end   2.

Case E. Word 1 = end; Word 2 = beginning 2 + end.

Case F. Word 1 = end; Word 2 = end; Word 1 = Word   2.

The classification of the adverbs with respect to their GCEs is given in Figure 6. The GCEs of adverbs are considered as the features of their classes. One of the sub-sets of adverbs has several GCEs: "*ment*", "*ent*", "*nt*", and "*t*". However we are interested in choosing the feature of maximal length. In addition, the expert has interpreted the feature "*ment*" as the suffix of adverbs.

The structure analysis of MADJs has produced the following sets of their GCEs with the groups of

Figure 6. The structure of obtained GOE of adverbs

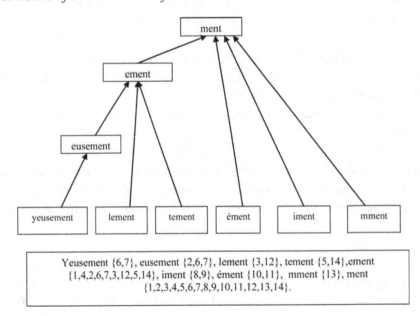

Yeusement {6,7}, eusement {2,6,7}, lement {3,12}, tement {5,14}, ement {1,4,2,6,7,3,12,5,14}, iment {8,9}, ément {10,11}, mment {13}, ment {1,2,3,4,5,6,7,8,9,10,11,12,13,14}.

Table 14. The initial data for reconstruction of the adverbs

	MADJ	**FADJ**	**Adverb (ADVs)**
1	Vif	Vive	Vivement (vividly)
2	Heureux	Heureuse	Heureusement (happyly)
3	Général	Générale	Généralement (generally)
4	Large	Large	Largement (largely)
5	Correct	Correcte	Correctement (correctly)
6	Joyeux	Joieuse	Joyeusement (joyfully)
7	Ennuyeux	Ennuyeuse	Ennuyeusement (tediously)
8	Joli	Joli	Joliment (beautifully)
9	Vrai	Vraie	Vraiment (truly)
10	Aisé	Aisée	Aisement (comfortably)
11	Obstiné	Obstinée	Obstinement (obstinately)
12	Fou	Folle	Follement (stupidly)
13	Pénétrant	Pénétrante	Pénétramment (acutely)
14	Lent	Lente	Lentement (slowly)

words corresponding with these GCEs: "*t*"for {5,13,14}, "*nt*" for {13,14}, "*i*" for {8,9}, "*é*" for {10,11}, "*eux*" for {2,6,7}, "*yeux*" for {6,7}, "*vif*" for (1), "*fou*" for {12}, "*large*" for {4}, and "*général*" for {3}, where the numbers are the indices of corresponding words (see, please Table 14).

The last letters of MADJs have been found too:

Table 15. The structure of initial entries of MADJs into ADVs

	MADJ	**ADV**	**Initial entry of MADJ in ADV**	**End addition ofInitial entry of MADJ in ADV**
1	Vif	Vivement	No	
2	Heureux	Heureusement	No	
3	Général	Généralement	Yes	Ement
4	Large	Largement	Yes	Ment
5	Correct	Correctement	Yes	Ement
6	Joyeux	Joyeusement	No	
7	Ennuyeux	Ennuyeusement	No	
8	Joli	Joliment	Yes	Ment
9	Vrai	Vraiment	Yes	Ment
10	Aisé	Aisément	Yes	Ment
11	Obstiné	Obstinément	Yes	Ment
12	Fou	Follement	No	
13	Pénétrant	Pénétramment	No	
14	Lent	Lentement	Yes	Ement

Figure 7.

Table 16. The GCBs of MADJ and ADVs

	GCB of MADJ and ADV	End addition of GCB in MADJ	End addition of GCB in ADV
1	Vi	F	Vement
2	Heureu	X	Sement
3	Général	Empty	Ement
4	Large	Empty	Ment
5	Correct	Empty	Ement
6	Joyeu	X	Sement
7	Ennuyeu	X	Sement
8	Joli	Empty	Ment
9	Vrai	Empty	Ment
10	Aisé	Empty	Ment
11	Obstiné	Empty	Ment
12	Fo	U	Llement
13	Pénétra	Nt	Mment
14	Lent	Empty	Ement

Table 17. The structure of initial entries of FADJs into ADVs

	FADJ	ADV	Initial entry of FADJ in ADV	End addition of Initial entry of FADJ in ADV
1	Vive	Vivement	Yes	Ment
2	Heureuse	Heureusement	Yes	Ment
3	Générale	Généralement	Yes	Ment
4	Large	Largement	Yes	Ment
5	Correcte	Correctement	Yes	Ment
6	Joyeuse	Joyeusement	Yes	Ment
7	Ennuyeuse	Ennuyeusement	Yes	Ment
8	Joli	Joliment	Yes	Ment
9	Vraie	Vraiment	No	
10	Aisйe	Aisément	No	
11	Obstinée	Obstinément	No	
12	Folle	Follement	Yes	Ment
13	Pénétrante	Pénétramment	No	
14	Lente	Lentement	Yes	

Table 18. The GCBs of FADJ and ADVs

	GCB of FADJ and ADV	End addition of FADJ	End addition of ADV
1	Vive	Empty	Ment
2	Heureuse	Empty	Ment
3	Générale	Empty	Ment
4	Large	Empty	Ment
5	Correcte	Empty	Ment
6	Joyeuse	Empty	Ment
7	Ennuyeuse	Empty	Ment
8	Joli	Empty	Ment
9	Vrai	E	Ment
10	Aisé	E	Ment
11	Obstiné	E	Ment
12	Folle	Empty	Ment
13	Pénétra	Nte	Mment
14	Lente	Empty	Ment

(t, l, x, f) for the words with the indices in the set (1,2,3,5,6,7,13,14);

$(i, é, u, e,)$ for the words with the indices in the set (4,8,9,10,11,12).

Table 15, Table 16, Table 17, Table 18, Table 19, and Table 20 represent the results of determining GCBs for the words of the following pairs of classes: MADJs - ADVs, FADJs - ADVs, MADJs - FADJs.

Table 19. The GCBs of MADJs and FADJs

	MADJ	FADJ	GCB	End addition of MADJ	End addition of FADJ
1	Vif	Vive	Vi	F	Ve
2	Heureux	Heureuse	Heureu	X	Se
3	Général	Générale	Général	-	E
4	Large	Large	Large	-	-
5	Correct	Correcte	Correct	-	E
6	Joyeux	Joyeuse	Joyeu	X	Se
7	Ennuyeux	Ennuyeuse	Ennuyeu	X	E
8	Joli	Joli	Joli	-	-
9	Vrai	Vraie	Vrai	-	E
10	Aisй	Aisée	Aisé	-	E
11	Obstiné	Obstinée	Obstiné	-	E
12	Fou	Folle	Fo	U	Lle
13	Pénétrant	Pénétrante	Pénétrant	-	E
14	Lent	Lente	lent	-	E

Table 20. The structure of initial entries MADJs into FADJs

	MADJ	FADJ	Initial entry of MADJ in FADJ	End addition of initial entry of MADJ in FADJ
1	Vif	Vive	No	
2	Heureux	Heureuse	No	
3	Général	Générale	Yes	E
4	Large	Large	Yes	-
5	Correct	Correcte	Yes	E
6	Joyeux	Joyeuse	No	X
7	Ennuyeux	Ennuyeuse	No	X
8	Joli	Joli	Yes	-
9	Vrai	Vraie	Yes	E
10	Aisé	Aisée	Yes	E
11	Obstiné	Obstinée	Yes	E
12	Fou	Folle	No	-
13	Pénétrant	Pénétrante	Yes	E
14	Lent	Lente	Yes	E

When the classes of words and their structural features are obtained it is possible to search for the rules describing the classes of adverbs through the features of adjectives. Searching for the rules has produced the following results. The greatest quantity of the initial entries into the adverbs is produced by the feminine adjectives; in this case, the structure of adverbs takes the form (Figure 7):

This structure corresponds to the following rules of the formation of adverbs:

1) From the adjective having the identical phonetic and orthographical masculine and feminine forms with the ending equal to the mute "e": large - large - largement (widely), intense - intense - intensément (intensively); commode - commode - commodément (conveniently);

2) From the FADJs having the form of MADJ ending with consonant letter (pronounced or mute); in this case, the form of FADJ ends with a pronounced consonant letter and the mute "e": heureux - heureuse - heureusement (happily); général - générale - généralement (generally), précis - présise - précisément (precisely/accurately);

Figure 8.

MADJ + ment

Figure 9.

MADJ - nt+ mment

The following class of adverbs is revealed (Figure 8):

3)   From the MADJs ending with vowel letter; the form of FADJ, in this case, ends with the mute "e": vrai – vraie - vraiment (really/actually); aisé - aisée - aisément (comfortably); obstiné - obstinée - obstinément (obstinately); this group also includes gaiement (gaily), assidu - assidue - assidùment (assiduously).

The following class of adverbs is also revealed (Figure 9):

4)   from the MADJs ending with "ent" and "ant": courant - courante - couramment (fluently); prudent - prudente - prudemment (carefully)

The reconstruction obtained of the rules of forming adverbs from adjectives is not unique but it is good with respect to the minimizing of possible number of such rules. In this example, the task of supervisor consisted in selecting the useful and making sense (interpreted) features. Specifically, this selection determines what classes of objects (concepts) will be built.

The search for sense or the interpretation of classes of objects exists also in the task of conceptual clustering: the clusters in this task are characterized only from the point of view of the degree of similarity of objects inside them and, simultaneously, with the point of view of the degree of difference between them.

The search for the descriptions of clusters or their interpretations in terms of some useful features is the task of supervised machine learning. However it is desirable to interpret classes of objects or clusters on the basis of knowledge related to it. For this goal, it is necessary to draw into the task of interpreting classes or clusters all possible knowledge related to this task perhaps with the use of ontology. It will expand the field of computer's reasoning. If we wait for the new and unexpected discoveries from the intellectual systems, then we must teach them to search for the sense of classifications independently of man.

FUTURE TRENDS OR KEY AREAS OF POTENTIAL FUTURE RESEARCH ON MACHINE LEARNING AS COMMONSENSE REASONING

The incorporation of commonsense reasoning mechanism into data-knowledge processing is becoming an urgent task in intelligent computer system and conceptual data-knowledge design. There is not a methodology supporting the solution of this task. We try briefly to describe the problems waiting for their solution. We come from the consideration that data-knowledge communication at all stages of functioning intelligent computer systems is central for realizing commonsense reasoning. Note that we believe that a new methodology for data-knowledge communication has to be created by the use of a systemic approach to modeling cognitive activity.

We take into account that data are the source of conceptual knowledge and that knowledge is the means of data organization and management. The following processes are based on commonsense reasoning.

1.   Entering and eliminating data:

a) Entering data: by the user or by querying from the side of system (knowledge);

b) Eliminating data: by the user or from the side of system (for example, "freezing" data-knowledge).

Entering data by the user implies solving a pattern recognition task of whether data already exist (or can be inferred) or they are unknown. If the data are unknown, then inferring the consequences from these data is necessary, namely, correcting knowledge and inferring new knowledge (dependencies, tests, statements) from the data. With this point of view, knowledge is active (Pospelov, 1992). These inference processes have been considered in Chapter 9 when incremental commonsense reasoning was discussed. In fact, entering data means enlarging and correcting knowledge in order it would be consistent with current situation (data).

Eliminating data implies eliminating knowledge inferable from this data. This is the deductive phase of commonsense reasoning.

2. Deductive and inductive query answering requires commonsense reasoning in the form of dialog user - intelligent system or/and intelligent system – ontology. This reasoning includes:

a) Pattern recognition of the meaning of query (what is required: fact, example, sets of examples, concept, dependency, or classification?);

b) Forming the context of query (domain of reasoning);

c) Pattern recognition of conceptual level of query:
   - Factorial level;
   - Conceptual level with a certain degree of generalization.

There can be the following variants of reasoning results

- Reply is in the context of reasoning;
- Reply is inferred from the context of reasoning;
- Reply requires entering or inferring new knowledge.

This reasoning is connected with extending data about situation (query) consistent with the system's knowledge.

The last variant of results of reasoning requires to perform enlarging the context of reasoning and involving inductive steps of inferring (machine learning) new knowledge. This mode of reasoning was described in Chapter 4, 5.

3. Knowledge optimization is the work for intelligent system itself, consequently, it requires unsupervised conceptual learning (self-learning) based on unsupervised conceptual clustering (or object generalization) and interpreting results of clustering (or generalization) via the system's or ontological knowledge.

4. Automated development of intelligent systems with the incorporated commonsense reasoning mechanisms is currently not supported by any programming language or programming technology. This technology must include:
   - The possibility to specify concepts (objects) with their properties and inferential links between them;

Figure 10. The architecture of intelligent computer system based on commonsense reasoning

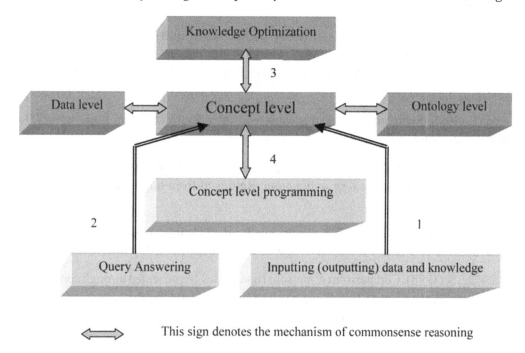

This sign denotes the mechanism of commonsense reasoning

- ◦ The possibility to induce some constituent elements of intelligent system's knowledge from data by the use of learning mechanisms;
- ◦ The possibility to incorporate the mechanisms of commonsense reasoning in developed systems.

The mechanisms of commonsense reasoning must be an integral part of programming language. Figure 10 shows the architecture of intelligent system in which above listed processes 1, 2, 3, 4 are realized with the use of one and the same mechanism of commonsense reasoning. The other problems are creating a new generation of concept-oriented query languages and intelligent interfaces for the computers of new generations.

CONCLUSION

In this chapter, we considered only the principal ideas of data-knowledge organization and using in the intelligent data-knowledge based system. The term "intelligence system" means that the system is capable to perform commonsense reasoning operations at any stage of its functioning, i. e. under performing query answering and updating data and knowledge. More exactly, the functioning of intelligent system as a whole is a commonsense reasoning process.

REFERENCES

Aragão, M. A. T., & Fernandes, A. A. A. (2004). Logic-based integration of query answering and knowledge discovery. In H. Christiansen, M.-S. Hacid, T. Andreasen, & H.L. Larsen (Eds.), *Proc. 6th International Conference on Flexible Query Answering Systems, 24-26 June 2004, Lyon, France* (LNCS 3055, pp. 68-83). Springer-Verlag.

Berners-Lee, T. (1998, September). Semantic Web road map. Retrieved from http://www.w3.org/DesignIssues/Semantic.html

Corby, O., & Faron, C. (2002). CORESE: A corporate Semantic Web engine. *WWW'2002 Workshop on Real World RDF and Semantic Web Application*. Retrieved from http://paul.rutgers.edu/~kashyap/workshop.html

Denisov, D. A., & Plaksin, M. V. (1991). Object synthesis in remote sensing imagery understanding. *International Journal of Systems and Technology, 3*, 249–256. doi:10.1002/ima.1850030310

Dieng, R., & Hug, S. (1998). Comparison of "personal ontologies" represented through conceptual graphs. In H. Prade (Ed.), *Proceedings of 13th European Conference on Artificial Intelligence* (ECAI'98) (pp. 341-345). Chichester, UK: John Wiley & Sons.

Dieng-Kuntz, R. Minier, D., Corby, F. Ruzicka, M., Corby, O., Alamarguy, L., & Luong, P.-H. (2004). Medical ontology and virtual staff for health network. In E. Motta, N. Shadbolt, A. Stutt, & N. Gibbins (Eds.), *Engineering knowledge in the age of the Semantic Web, Proceedings of 14th International Conference (EKAW '04)* (LNCS 3257, pp. 187-202). Springer. Coffey, J.W., Eskridge, T.C., & Sanchez, D.P. (2004). A case study in knowledge elicitation for institutional memory preservation using concept maps. In A. J. Cañas, J. D. Novak, F.M. González, (Eds.), *Concept maps: Theory, Methodology, Technology, Proceedings of the First International Concept Mapping Conference (CCM'04)* (Vol. 1, pp. 151-157). University of Navarra, Spain: Palmona.

Dieng-Kuntz, R., & Corby, O. (2005). Conceptual graph for Semantic Web applications. In F. Dau, M.-L. Mugnier, & G. Stumme (Eds.), *Conceptual structures: Common semantics for sharing knowledge* (ICCS'05) (LNAI 3596, pp. 19-50). Springer.

Hitzler, P., & Krötzsch, M. (2006). Querying formal contexts with answer set programs. In H. Schärfe, P. Hitzler, & P. Ohrstrom (Eds.), *Conceptual Inspiration and Application, Proceedings of the 14th International Conference on Conceptual Structures (ICCS'06)* (LNAI 4068, pp. 413-426). Springer.

Hovy, E. (2005). Methodologies for the reliable construction of ontological knowledge. In F. Dau, M.-L. Mugnier, & G. Stumme (Eds.), *Conceptual structures: Common semantics for sharing knowledge* (ICCS'05) (LNAI 3596, pp. 91-106). Springer.

Huchard, M., Rouane Hacene, M., Roume, C., & Valtchev, P. (2007). Relational concept discovery in structured datasets. *Annals of Mathematics and Artificial Intelligence archive, 49*(1-4), 39-76.

Jarrar, M. (2005). *Towards methodological principles for ontology engineering*. Unpublished doctoral dissertation, Free University of Brussels.

Lassila, O., & Swick, R. R. (1999). *Resource description framework (RDF) model and syntax specification. W3C Recommendations.* Retrieved February 22, 1999 from http://beta.w3.org/TR/REC-rdf-syntax

Linke, T., & Schaub, T. (1998). An approach to query-answering in Reter's default logic and underlying existence of extensions problem. In J. Dix, L. Fariñas del Cerro, & U. Furbch (Eds.), *Logics in Artificial Intelligence, Proceedings of the Sixth European Conference on Logics in Artificial Intelligence* (LNCS 1489, pp. 233-237). Springer-Verlag.

Markov, A. A., & Nagornij, N. M. (1984). *The theory of algorithms.* Moscow: Nauka.

Martin, P. (1997). CGKAT: A knowledge acquisition and retrieval tool using structured documents and ontologies. In D. Lukose, H. Delugach, M. Keeler, L. Searle, & J. F. Sowa (Eds.), *Conceptual structures: Fulfilling Peirce's dream. Proceedings of the 5th International Conference on Conceptual Structures (ICCS'97)* (LNAI 1257, pp. 581-584). Berlin, Germany: Springer.

Naidenova, X. A. (1979). *Automation of experimental data classification processes based on the algebraic lattice theory.* Unpublished doctoral dissertation, Leningrad Electro – Technical Institute.

Pospelov, D. A. (1992). Knowledge in intelligent systems. [in Russian]. *Program Products and Systems, 3,* 68–85.

Savinov, A. (2005). Concept as a generalization of class and principles of the concept-oriented programming. *Computer Science Journal of Moldova, 13*(3), 292–335.

Savinov, A. (2009). Concept-oriented model. In V. E. Ferraggine, J. H. Doorn, & L. C. Rivero (Eds.), *handbook of research on innovations in database technologies and applications: Current & future trends* (pp. 171-180). Hershey, PA: Information Science Reference

Schaub, T. (1994). A new methodology for query-answering in default logics via structure-oriented theorem proving. *Journal of Automated Reasoning, 15*(1), 95–165. doi:10.1007/BF00881832

Sitompul, O. S., & Noah, S. A. (2006). A transformation-oriented methodology to knowledge-based conceptual data warehouse design. *Journal of Computer Science, 2*(5), 460–465.

Conclusion

This book is dedicated mainly to investigating classification as an integral part of commonsense reasoning and revealing the unique connection between commonsense reasoning and machine learning. A model of classification reasoning on the basis of the algebraic lattice theory has been proposed.

As a mathematical structure, the algebraic lattice makes it possible to give various interpretations to the lattice ordering. As a process, classification has dual nature. It is the partition of objects into classes and at the same time it is connected with expressions, in terms of a problem domain, describing objects and classes of objects in this classification.

Using the partition lattice as the foundation of algebra of classifications has a high methodological value, since any lattice of object descriptions can be connected with an appropriate partition lattice in which attributes, values of attributes, and object descriptions take their interpretations.

We have shown that the processes of classification are reduced to commonsense reasoning meaningfully connected with extracting and using knowledge in the form of implicative, functional and associative logical dependences between objects, classes and their properties.

The following step in our consideration was one of reducing the problems of symbolic supervised machine learning to approximating the classifications given on the sets of objects considered in different applications, such as natural language processing, image understanding, speech recognition, automated extraction of ontology, conceptual knowledge modeling, and so on.

We succeeded in decomposing the algorithms of lattice construction into separate operations and subtasks interpreted as the mental human acts in which the deductive and inductive steps of reasoning are not isolated from each other, moreover, they are interconnected and inductive inference draws the deductive rules of reasoning, and deductive inference draws the inductive rules of reasoning.

The model of commonsense reasoning proposed in this book is illustrated by some examples of the experts' reasoning in the tasks of pattern recognition of natural objects in some natural-science investigations.

We hope that reducing some machine learning problems to commonsense reasoning will contribute to developing new technologies for data-knowledge integration.

Of course, revealing the connection between machine learning and commonsense reasoning is only the first and, perhaps, timid step in the direction of modeling natural human reasoning in computers. Many methodological questions of this modeling arise. All these questions can be united into the following basic categories:

1. Organization of the interaction between data and knowledge on a new basis. The data must not simply be accumulated without the interference of knowledge in the process of data assimilation. The data must be introduced into an intelligent system under control of knowledge of this system and they must contribute to immediate revision of system knowledge.
2. The form of data-knowledge representation must provide the dynamic formation of commonsense reasoning contexts and the possibility of effective application of algebraic lattice (Galois's lattice) structures for realizing this reasoning.
3. It is necessary to solve the methodological problems of integrating the technologies of data and knowledge bases modeling with the contemporary technologies of developing ontology.
4. It is necessary to develop the machine learning methods in the direction of their larger automation. Currently, the semantic interpretation of object classes generated in computers is determined by attributes given by a supervisor in advance.
    It is desirable that a computer would possess larger freedom in using ontology knowledge for interpreting the results of commonsense reasoning.
5. The realization of commonsense reasoning requires developing sophisticated systems for pre-processing diverse external information such as speech, image, and texts etc. The pre-processing must includes the automated analysis of external stimuli, the extraction of their structural elements and their features. Currently, all programs of processing input information are built on experts' knowledge personified in algorithms and rules of pattern recognition, but not on the systems of knowledge about objects produced in a computer itself.

There is no doubt that the solution of these crucial problems requires efforts and cooperation of the specialists of different fields: mathematics, logic, artificial intelligence, psycholinguistics, the theory of programming, machine learning, knowledge engineering, neurophysiology, biology, and many others.

We hope that the book will contribute to the union of the different fields' specialists in their efforts to model commonsense reasoning in computers.

About the Author

Xenia Naidenova is a senior researcher of the Group of Psycho Diagnostic Systems' Automation at the Military Medical Academy (St. Petersburg, Russia). She is currently the head of Project DIALOG: Methods of Data Mining in Psychological and Physiological Diagnostics. Dr. Naidenova received a diploma of engineering with a specialty in computer engineering (1963) and a PhD in technical sciences (1979), both from the Lenin Electro-Technical Institute of Leningrad. In 1999 she received a senior researcher diploma from the Military Medical Academy (St. Petersburg, Russia). She has guided the development of several program systems on knowledge acquisition and machine learning including DEFINE, SIZIF, CLAST, LAD, and diagnostic test machines and has published over 150 papers. Dr. Naidenova is a member of the Russian Association for Artificial Intelligence and is on the Program Committee for the KDS.

Index

Symbols

(OLAP) 50

A

abduction 35, 46, 47
accommodation 16, 17, 20, 23
adaptive psycho-diagnostic systems (APDS) 337, 355
algebraic lattice 126, 127, 136, 139, 162
algorithmic (deductive) inference 34
algorithmic inference 34
anticipation mechanisms 19
APDS 337, 355, 356, 357
approximate reasoning 13
Apriori algorithm 293, 294
apriorism 15
Aristotle 5, 6, 7, 12, 29
ARQUAT 294
artifacts 17
artificial intelligence 1, 3, 4, 9, 15, 19, 23, 28, 29, 31
AsB 107, 108, 109
Assertion Base (AsB) 107
assimilation 16, 17, 23
association rule mining techniques 293
association rules 279, 293, 294, 296, 299, 3 03, 305, 306, 308
ASTRA 245, 259, 269, 270, 273
Attribute Base (AtB) 107
automated workstation (AWS) 337
AWS 337

B

Bacon 3, 9, 10, 11, 29, 30, 32, 33
Bayesian approach 42

Bayesian networks 42, 64, 68
best diagnostic test 166, 188
Best Irredundant Tests 170
Best Maximally Redundant Test 170
BESTTEST 320, 324
BIR 170
BIRTs 188, 190, 191, 192
BMR 170
Boolean 43, 50, 58, 59, 60, 62, 75
Boolean or multi-valued attributes 58
boundary transitions 218
boundary values 89
branching 352, 363, 364

C

CG 369, 370
CID 54, 63, 372
CLANN 236, 239
classes of objects 76, 77, 81, 82, 86
classification 6, 10, 12, 14, 21, 22, 23, 122, 123, 124, 126, 127, 129, 130, 137, 138, 141, 142, 143, 144, 145, 146, 155, 159, 160, 161, 162
class of objects 77, 83, 321
closure operator 236
clustering analysis 294
COE 370
cognitive conflict 16
cognitive mechanisms 1
cognitive organization 368
cognitive processes 3, 4, 12, 14
Collaborative Ontology Environment 370
CoM 380, 381
combined inference databases 372
Combined Inference Databases (CID) 54